Contemporary Economics

An Applications Approach

4e

ROBERT J. CARBAUGH

Professor of Economics

Central Washington University

THOMSON

—————— ™

SOUTH-WESTERN

Australia · Brazil · Canada · Mexico · Singapore · Spain · United Kingdom · United States

THOMSON

SOUTH-WESTERN

Contemporary Economics: An Applications Approach, 4th Edition
Robert J. Carbaugh

VP/Editorial Director:
Jack W. Calhoun

Editor-in-Chief:
Alex von Rosenburg

Publisher:
Steve Momper

Developmental Editor:
Katie Yanos

Marketing Manager:
Brian Joyner

Production Project Manager:
Kelly N. Hoard

Manager of Technology, Editorial:
Vicky True

Technology Project Editor:
Pam Wallace

Web Coordinator:
Karen Schaffer

Manufacturing Coordinator:
Sandee Milewski

Production House:
LEAP Publishing Services, Inc.

Compositor:
International Typesetting
and Composition

Printer:
Transcontinental
Louiseville, QC

Art Director:
Michelle Kunkler

Cover and Internal Designer:
Chris Miller

Cover Images:
© Getty Images, Inc.

Library of Congress Control
Number: 2005934283

For more information about our
products, contact us at:
Thomson Learning Academic
Resource Center
1-800-423-0563

Thomson Higher Education
5191 Natorp Boulevard
Mason, OH 45040
USA

Contents in Brief

Contents

PART 2   The Microeconomy 29

CHAPTER 6

Imperfect Competition 131

CHAPTER 7

Labor Market Issues 155

CHAPTER 8

Government and Markets 179

PART 3

The Macroeconomy 203

CHAPTER 9

The Mixed Economy of the United States 204

CHAPTER 10

Gross Domestic Product and Economic Growth 231

CHAPTER 11

The Business Cycle, Unemployment, and Inflation 257

CHAPTER 12

Macroeconomic Instability: Aggregate Demand and Aggregate Supply 285

CHAPTER 13

Fiscal Policy and the Federal Budget 309

CHAPTER 14

Money and the Banking System 333

CHAPTER 15

The Federal Reserve and Monetary Policy 357

PART 4

The International Economy 379

CHAPTER 16

The United States and the Global Economy 380

Preface

As a university instructor, I have enthusiastically taught the one-term survey of economics course for more than 25 years to undergraduate students majoring in business, economics, and other disciplines. Most of the students who take my course are still in their teens and have modest awareness of economics. They are interested in learning but want to know how economics relates to their daily lives. Learning economic theory, by itself, means little to most students. I sometimes hear students ask, "What good is theory if it doesn't help me get a job or increase my income?"

To make my survey of economics course come alive for these students, I combine a clear and concise presentation of microeconomic and macroeconomic theory with an abundance of contemporary applications. For each economic principle, I relate real-world examples taken from current newspapers, magazines, government reports, and economic journals. Also, I show videos to my students that deal with issues such as reforming the Social Security system, the flat-rate tax proposal, and the European Monetary Union. To help my students become informed consumers, I discuss topics such as obtaining mortgages with fixed or variable interest rates and the cost of driving an automobile.

Indeed, combining real-world applications with an exciting and sometimes humorous presentation of economic theory is the main focus of my course. The positive feedback that I have received indicates that I have developed an approach to teaching that makes economics come alive to students.

This pedagogical approach is integrated into my textbook *Contemporary Economics: An Applications Approach*, 4e. The strong sales of the first three editions of this text have convinced me that my approach is meeting the needs of a considerable number of students and faculty. It is with pleasure that I have prepared a fourth edition of this textbook.

MEETING STUDENTS' NEEDS

A challenge faced by instructors of a survey of economics course is that many of their students go on to take courses in *Principles of Microeconomics* and *Principles of Macroeconomics*. To be meaningful for these students, a survey of economics course must provide an introduction to microeconomics and macroeconomics without duplicating the principles courses.

A strength of *Contemporary Economics* is that it addresses such a need. By combining a relatively small number of theoretical tools with an abundance of contemporary applications, my textbook is not an abbreviation of a principles textbook. Rather, it is a distinct survey of economics for economics majors who wish to take an introductory course prior to taking more rigorous courses in the principles of microeconomics and macroeconomics and for non-majors who wish to take only one course in this field.

Contemporary Economics is mainly written for students at four-year colleges and universities and also for junior and community colleges. However, this textbook is highly attractive for high schools that offer an introductory course in economics.

DISTINGUISHING FEATURES

The distinguishing features of my textbook include clear and concise presentation of economic theory, global coverage in every chapter, integration of contemporary issues throughout theoretical presentations, and the inclusion of consumer economics topics.

Presentation of Theory

Presenting economic theory in a clear and easy-to-understand manner is the foundation of this textbook. Students can easily relate to the economic theories because they are presented in terms of realistic examples that should appeal to students of all backgrounds and abilities. For example, supply and demand analysis is presented in terms of the market for compact discs (CDs), the costs of production in terms of computer printers, perfect competition in terms of the Puget Sound Fishing Company, monopoly in terms of De Beers (the diamond monopoly), and oligopoly in terms of Boeing and Airbus. These contemporary examples are reinforced by additional real-world examples that come from publications such as *The Wall Street Journal, Business Week,* and *The New York Times.*

For example, Chapter 5, *Competition and Monopoly: Virtues and Vices,* discusses why cable television rates are so high. The discussion combines theoretical topics such as barriers to entry, natural monopoly, and potential competition with the pricing of cable television. Being familiar with cable television, students can easily identify with its pricing implications.

Students who have read my textbook have commented that not only is the presentation clear and easy to understand but that they could remember the specific examples that illustrated the theories throughout the textbook. Moreover, all diagrams throughout my textbook use numbers (for example, 10 CDs at a price of $10) on their axes to make the examples familiar and obvious to the student. Many other textbooks use letters on their axes (for example, OA units of product X at a price of OY), which students tend to find remote from their daily lives. Finally, my textbook emphasizes only the economic models that are essential to an introductory understanding of economics: production possibilities analysis, supply and demand for particular markets, production and the costs of production, perfect competition and monopoly, and aggregate supply and demand.

Global Content

No survey of economics textbook can ignore discussion of the global economy. *Contemporary Economics* addresses this issue with a two-pronged approach. First, I globalize each chapter so that students will not think of the U.S. economy in isolated terms as they read this textbook.

For example, Chapter 7, *Labor Market Issues,* discusses whether jobs outsourcing by U.S. companies is a threat or opportunity for American workers. This topic is continually publicized by the news media and is familiar to students. They learn how the U.S. labor market is linked to labor markets in other countries such as India and China.

I have also introduced a global component by including separate chapters on international trade, finance, and development. Chapter 16, *The United States and the Global Economy,* discusses the principle of comparative advantage and the effects of free trade and protectionism. Chapter 17, *International Finance,* provides an introduction to the U.S. balance of payments, the foreign exchange market, and the factors that cause fluctuations in the dollar's exchange value. Chapter 18, *Economic Systems and the Developing Countries,* discusses alternative economic systems and the role of developing countries in the global economy.

Real World Applications

Contemporary Economics: An Applications Approach lives up to its name by emphasizing applications and policy questions as often as possible. I have written this textbook for the student who is taking economics for the first time, and I stress the material that students should and do find interesting about the study of our economy. Therefore, I have devoted much attention to applications and policy questions that students hear about in the news and bring from their own lives.

For example, Chapter 9, *The Mixed Economy of the United States,* discusses the future of the U.S. social security system. Students learn how its pay-as-you-go system of social security can be threatened when the number of workers paying taxes to support the system falls relative to the number of beneficiaries. Of particular interest is whether Americans should be allowed to place a portion of their payroll taxes in personal retirement accounts.

Not only are my applications current, but they also show a concern for the diversity among students. As often as possible, I have used examples that are familiar to students: I-Pod, Microsoft, Northwest Airlines, Wendy's, Ticketmaster, and the like.

Consumer Economics Applications

To help students become informed consumers, *Contemporary Economics* includes applications in consumer economics. Examples include shopping for a mortgage loan, compound interest, electronic codes on a personal check, and shopping for a credit card. I have incorporated these topics into my survey of economics class, and my students have found them to be interesting and beneficial to their lives.

For example, Chapter 4, *Production and the Costs of Production,* discusses the costs of driving an automobile. Students learn about the fixed costs and variable costs of driving and how to calculate the cost of driving on a per-mile basis. These concepts provide a nice transition to the costs of production that are discussed later in the chapter.

SUPPLEMENTARY MATERIALS

To help students master the tools of economic analysis, Koushik Ghosh of Central Washington University has prepared an excellent *Study Guide* (ISBN-0-324-31460-4). Each chapter provides a summary of important points and learning objectives, matching review questions, multiple-choice questions, true-false questions, and application exercises.

To assist instructors in the teaching of this textbook, Margaret Landman of Bridgewater State College has written an *Instructor's Manual* with test bank (ISBN-0-324-31458-2). Part I contains learning objectives, lecture hints and ideas, discussion starters, and brief answers to end-of-chapter study questions and problems. Part II contains a comprehensive test bank with multiple-choice, true-false, and essay questions. An electronic test bank (ISBN-0-324-31481-7) is also available to instructors.

In this age of computing, no textbook package would be complete without Web-based resources. Visit **http://carbaugh.swlearning.com,** where you will find many useful pedagogical enrichment features, including NetLink Exercises, which draw upon the expanded Netlinks feature at the end of each chapter. While the Netlinks direct the student to an appropriate economics Web site to gather data and other relevant information, the NetLink Exercises allow students to access these Web sites to answer pertinent and practical questions that relate to economics. The Web site also contains a small set of quiz questions for each chapter. In addition, students and instructors alike can address questions and provide commentary directly to the author with the *Talk to the Author* feature. Return often to **http://carbaugh.swlearning.com** to access pertinent updates by the author, reflecting developments in the economy as situations emerge. For other high-tech study tools, visit the South-Western Economic Resource Center at **http://economics.swlearning.com**.

Also available on the Web site are PowerPoint slides created by Steve Norton of Okno Consulting Group, Ann Arbor, Michigan. These slides can be easily downloaded. The slides offer instructors flexibility in enhancing classroom lectures. Slides may be edited to meet individual needs. They also serve as a study tool for students.

In addition to the book's regular Web site, we can also bundle CarbaughXtra! (**http://carbaughxtra.swlearning.com**) with new copies of the text. This password-protected site offers a robust set of multimedia learning tools, including:

- The Graphing Workshop. This is a one-stop learning resource for help in mastering graphs, with tutorials, interactive graphing tools, and exercises organized by chapter.

- CNN Online Video Clips. CNN video segments bring the real world to students. The accompanying exercises help illustrate how economics is important to their daily lives.

- "Ask the Instructor" video clips. Via streaming video, difficult concepts are explained and illustrated. This is an especially helpful review tool for visual learners.

- Xtra quizzing. Students can create and take randomly generated quizzes on whichever chapters they wish to test themselves, offering them extra practice for exams.

- Economic Applications (e-con apps). A suite of highly acclaimed and content-rich dynamic Web features has been developed specifically for economics students. *EconDebate,* written by John Kane from SUNY Oswego, provides the most current economic policy debates. The site also provides *EconNews,* a news summary service of important news-breaking reports, *EconData,* and *EconLinks.*

ACKNOWLEDGMENTS

This textbook could not have been written and published without the assistance of many individuals. I am pleased to acknowledge those who provided helpful suggestions and often detailed reviews:

- John Olienyk, Colorado State University

- Koushik Ghosh, Central Washington University

- John Adams, Texas A&M International University

- Bruce Pietrykowski, University of Michigan—Dearborn

- Tesa Stegner, Idaho State University

- Clifford Hawley, West Virginia University

- Rolando Santos, Lakeland Community College

- Karin Steffens, Northern Michigan University

- Pam Whalley, Western Washington University

- Margaret Landman, Bridgewater State College

- Barry Kotlove, Edmonds Community College

- R. Edward Chatterton, Lock Haven University

- Z. Edward O'Relley, North Dakota State University

- Laurence Malone, Hartwick College

- Vicki Rostedt, University of Akron

- Kishore Kulkami, Metropolitan State College

- David Hammes, University of Hawaii, Hilo

- Gary Galles, Pepperdine University

- Bruce Billings, University of Arizona

- Barry Goodwin, North Carolina State University

- Wike Walden, North Carolina State University

- Joseph Samprone, Georgia College and State University

- Robert Grafstein, University of Georgia

- Mark Healy, William Rainey Harper College

- Vani Kotcherlakota, University of Nebraska

- Donald A. Coffin, Indiana University, Northwest

- Naga Pulikonda, Indiana University, Kokomo

- F. P. Biggs, Principia College

- Ken Harrison, The Richard Stockton College of New Jersey

- Donald Bumpass, Sam Houston State College

- Sandra Peart, Baldwin-Wallace College

- Michael Rosen, Milwaukee Area Technical College

- Nicholas Karatjas, Indiana University of Pennsylvania

- Ernest Diedrich, St. John's University

- Arthur Janssen, Emporia State University

- Ralph Gray, De Pauw University

- Maria V. Gamba-Riedel, The University of Findlay

- Anthony Patrick O'Brien, Lehigh University

- Charles W. Smith, Lincoln Land Community College

- Paul Comoli, University of Kansas

- Walton Padelford, Union University

- David Gillette, Truman State University

I would also like to thank my colleagues at Central Washington University—Tim Dittmer, David Hedrick, Richard Mack, Peter Saunders, and Chad Wassell—for their advice and help while I was preparing the manuscript.

It has been a pleasure to work with my editors, Katie Yanos and Steve Momper. In particular, Katie provided many valuable suggestions and assistance in seeing this edition to its completion. Special thanks is given to Kelly Hoard, who orchestrated the production of this book. Also, Brian Joyner did a wonderful job in advertising and marketing this textbook, and to the staff of LEAP Publishing Services, Inc. who did an excellent job in carrying out production. Finally, I am grateful to my students, who commented on the manuscript.

I would appreciate any comments, corrections, or suggestions that faculty or students wish to make, so that I can continue to improve this textbook in the years ahead. Please contact me! Thank you for permitting this text to evolve to the fourth edition.

Bob Carbaugh
Department of Economics
Central Washington University
Ellensburg, Washington 98926
Phone: (509) 963-3443
Fax: (509) 963-1992
E-mail: carbaugh@cwu.edu

About the Author

ROBERT J. CARBAUGH

Known for his excellence in teaching, Robert J. Carbaugh is Professor of Economics at Central Washington University. He has been lauded with top teaching awards that include the 1984 Excellence in Teaching Award at University of Wisconsin, Eau Claire; and the Distinguished Professor of the University award at Central Washington University in 1993. In 1996, Professor Carbaugh was named the Scholar of the Year by the Phi Kappa Phi Honorary Society at Central Washington University. In 2001, he received the Distinguished Professor of the University award for Research at Central Washington University. In 2004, Professor Carbaugh was invited by the Directors of the Oxford Round Table to present a lecture, "Trade and Environmental Frictions in the Global Steel Industry." The lecture was presented at Oxford University in England.

With a Ph.D. in economics from Colorado State University, Professor Carbaugh specializes in economic theory and international economics. For over 25 years, Professor Carbaugh has taught these subjects, as well as managerial economics, money and banking, and both introductory and intermediate levels of microeconomics and macroeconomics. His cogent and lively teaching style makes his courses highly popular at Central Washington University.

Professor Carbaugh has authored and co-authored numerous articles for publications such as *International Review of Economics and Business, Challenge, World Competition: Law and Economic Review, International Trade Journal, Quarterly Journal of Economics and Business*, and *Journal of Asian Economics*. He has presented papers at professional meetings, including the Eastern Economics Association, Midwestern Economics Association, and the Western Economics Association. Professor Carbaugh is also well known for his distinguished textbook, *International Economics* (South-Western/Thomson Learning), now in its 10th edition. Professor Carbaugh resides in Ellensburg, Washington.

Contemporary Economics

An Applications Approach

4e

ROBERT J. CARBAUGH

Professor of Economics

Central Washington University

PART

1

Introduction

CHAPTER 1

Scarcity and Choice

Chapter objectives

After reading this chapter, you should be able to:

1. Discuss the nature of economics and the economic way of thinking.

2. Explain how the concept of scarcity relates to the concept of opportunity cost.

3. Identify the causes of economic growth and decline.

4. Identify the opportunity cost of national security.

5. Describe the purpose and effects of economic sanctions.

economics IN CONTEXT

In the years following World War II, the United States sacrificed in order to equip itself with a national defense that could meet the threat posed by the Soviet Union. Trillions of dollars were spent to produce jet aircraft, tanks, missiles, submarines, and other defense goods. Indeed, the resources of the United States were scarce. Producing more defense goods resulted in fewer libraries, schools, golf courses, and other civilian goods. Put simply, the United States sacrificed civilian goods to produce more military goods.

Each time the United States developed a new military system, the former Soviet Union developed a more costly system of its own. Were it not for scarce resources, the Soviets could have produced more civilian goods and more military goods. Because of scarcity, however, the Soviet economy produced fewer civilian goods to fulfill the everyday needs of its people. Moreover, the Soviet Union was less efficient at producing goods than were the United States and other countries. Civilian goods were thus in short supply and of poor quality in the Soviet Union, which led to bitter complaints by its people. In 1992, the Soviet Union collapsed under the pressure of its disenchanted citizens. Suddenly, the world appeared to be a calmer and more secure place to live.

That tranquility dramatically ended, however, when terrorists attacked the United States on September 11, 2001. To improve national security, the United States once again increased its expenditures on military goods. However, producing more military goods meant that less resources would be available for the production of civilian goods such as police and fire protection, hospitals, and highways.

The question of how an economy should use its scarce resources is a main focus of public debate for all societies. In this chapter, we will examine the economic choices that must be made in every society because of scarcity.

WHAT IS ECONOMICS?

Economics means different things to different people. To some it means making money in stocks, bonds, and real estate. To others, it means understanding how to own and operate a business. To the president of the United States, it may mean developing a new federal budget or formulating plans to reform the welfare system. Although these issues are part of economics, the subject has broader dimensions. **Economics** is first and foremost the study of *choice* under conditions of *scarcity*. Both individually and as a society, we attempt to choose wisely. We are forced to do so because human and property resources are limited, and it takes resources to produce cellular phones, computers, autos, CD players, and other goods and services that we desire. *to whom?*

Obtaining the greatest value from resources is the goal of economic choice. At a personal level, we have limited income to spend on the many items we want. For example, we might forgo purchasing a Jeep Grand Cherokee in order to have funds to pay tuition at Northwestern University. Businesses also face alternatives. Should a company use its scarce funds to replace its photocopiers instead of buying new computers? Moreover, government has to make choices. Should tax dollars be used to purchase additional tanks and missiles, or should these dollars be used to finance the construction of a new highway system?

The field of economics is quite broad. Its reach extends from personal issues—why does a pound of butter cost more than a pound of margarine?—to issues of national and global importance—will an economic slump in Asia cause the U.S. economy to decline? The field of economics is generally divided into two categories—microeconomics and macroeconomics.

Microeconomics

Microeconomics is the branch of economics that focuses on the choices made by households and firms and the effects those choices have on particular markets. We can use microeconomics to understand how markets work, to make personal or managerial decisions, and to analyze the impact of government policies. Consider these microeconomic issues:

- How would a higher tax on cigarettes affect consumption by teenagers?
- Why do convenience stores often disappear after several years?
- How would a ban on immigrant workers from Mexico affect U.S. apple growers?
- Should I stockpile coffee today if I expect poor future growing conditions in Brazil?
- Should I put my savings in a bank account or invest them in the stock market?
- If Sears decreases its appliance prices, how will Wal-Mart respond?
- Will an increase in the federal minimum wage help the working poor?
- Should Social Security payments be linked to the rate of inflation?

Macroeconomics

The other branch of economics is macroeconomics. **Macroeconomics** is concerned with the overall performance of the economy. Macroeconomics does not focus on the activities of individual households, firms, or markets; instead, it focuses on the behavior of the economy itself. It deals especially with the determination of total output, the level of employment, and the price level.

We study macroeconomics to learn how the entire economy works and about the controversies concerning economic policies. Among the macroeconomic topics that we will examine are the following:

- Why do some economies grow more rapidly than others?
- What causes unemployment?
- Why do economies experience inflation?
- Is a strong currency always good and a weak currency always bad?
- Should the government adopt policies to increase savings and investment and to reduce consumption?
- Should the government pass a constitutional amendment to eliminate federal budget deficits?
- Who controls the money supply?
- How does a decrease in interest rates affect the economy?

The two branches—microeconomics and macroeconomics—converge to form modern economics.

THE ECONOMIC WAY OF THINKING

The practice of economics often calls for an analysis of complex problems. Although economists may differ in their ideological views, they have developed an "economic way of thinking." This methodology uses several principles.

Every Choice Has a Cost

Because human and property resources are scarce, individuals and society must choose how to best use them. Making prudent choices requires trading off one thing for another. At the core of economics is the notion that "there is no free lunch." A friend may buy your lunch, making it "free" to you, but there is still a cost to someone and, ultimately, to society. This notion expresses the fundamental issue of economics—that every choice involves a cost. *"opportunity cost"*

The cost of any choice is the value of the best opportunity forgone in making it. For example, you can choose to remain in college or quit college. If you quit, you may find a job at Burger King and earn enough money to buy some Levi's jeans, rent some videos, go golfing and skiing, and hang out with your friends. If you remain in college, you will not currently be able to afford all of these things. However, your education will enable you to find a better job later, and then you will be able to afford these and many other items.

People Make Better Choices by Thinking at the Margin

Economists maintain that people make better choices by thinking "at the margin." Making a choice at the margin implies deciding to do a little more or a little less of an activity. As a student, you can allocate the next hour to sleeping or studying. In making this decision, you compare the benefit of extra study time to the cost of forgone sleep.

As an example of thinking at the margin, consider United Airlines' decision of how much to charge passengers who fly standby. Assume that flying a 300-seat jetliner from Seattle to New York costs the airline $90,000. Therefore, the average cost (per seat) is $300 ($90,000/300 = $300). You might conclude that United Airlines should always charge at least $300 per ticket. However, the airline can increase its profits by thinking at the margin. Suppose that a jetliner is going to take off with one empty seat. A standby passenger is waiting at the gate and is willing to pay $200 to fly from Seattle to New York. Should United Airlines sell him a ticket at this price? Yes, because the cost of flying one more passenger is negligible. Although the *average* cost of flying a passenger is $300, the *marginal* (extra) cost is only the cost of a can of Sprite, a bag of pretzels, and a chicken sandwich. As long as United Airlines earns revenues that are more than the marginal cost, adding an extra passenger is profitable.

Rational Self-Interest

WE ASSUME: Economics is founded on the assumption of rational self-interest. This means that people act as if they are motivated by self-interest and respond predictably to opportunities for gain. In other words, people try to make the best of any situation. Often, making the best of a situation involves maximizing the value of some quantity. As a student, getting high grades may be your incentive to study hard because they may help you obtain a job interview with a particular employer or get accepted into a prestigious graduate school.

Throughout this text, we will assume that economic incentives underlie the rational decisions of people. We will assume that a firm's owners want to maximize profit so they improve their well-being. Also, we will assume that households seek to maximize satisfaction from consuming goods and services. Because income is limited and goods have prices, we cannot buy all the things we would like to have. Therefore, we should choose an attainable combination of goods that will maximize our satisfaction. Of course, self-interest does not always imply increasing one's wealth as measured in dollars and cents or one's satisfaction from goods consumed. In addition to economic motivations, people also have goals pertaining to friendship, love, helping others, creating works of art, and the like.

Economic Models

Like other sciences, economics uses models. In chemistry, you may have seen a model of an atom—a device with blue, green, and red balls that represent neutrons, electrons, and protons. Architects construct cardboard models of skyscrapers before they are built. Economic models are not built with plastic or cardboard, but rather from words, diagrams, and mathematical equations.

Economic models, or theories, are simplified representations of the real world that we use to help us understand, explain, and predict economic phenomena in the real world. Economic models explain inflation, unemployment, wage rates, exchange rates, and more. For example, an economic model might tell us the effects on the quantity of compact discs (CDs) that consumers will purchase if the sellers raise the price. Other models explain how changes in interest rates in the economy affect investment spending by business. Throughout this textbook, we will use economic models to help us understand contemporary economic issues.

Positive versus Normative Economics

It is important to realize that economics is not always free of value judgments. In thinking about economic questions, we must distinguish questions of fact from questions of fairness.

Positive economics describes the facts of the economy—it deals with the way in which the economy works. Among the questions that positive economics considers are: Why do computer scientists earn more than janitors? What is the economic effect of reducing taxes? Does free trade result in job losses for less-skilled workers? Although these questions are difficult to answer, they can be addressed by economic analysis and empirical evidence.

Normative economics involves value judgments that cannot be empirically tested. Ethical standards and norms of fairness underlie normative economics. For example, should the United States penalize India for violating U.S. patent and copyright laws? Should welfare payments be reduced in order to encourage the unemployed to find income-producing jobs? Should all Americans have equal access to health care? Indeed, because these questions involve value judgments instead of facts, there are no right or wrong answers. Both positive and normative economics are important and will be considered throughout this textbook.

Why do economists often appear to give conflicting advice to policymakers? Because economists do not fully understand how the economy operates, they often disagree about actual cause-and-effect relationships. Moreover, economists may have different value judgments, and thus different normative views, about what policies should attempt to accomplish.

The first part of this chapter has given us an overview of economics and the economic way of thinking. We will now examine the economic problem of scarcity.

SCARCITY

Whether you are taking just one economics course or majoring in economics, the most important topic you will address is scarcity. Scarcity means that there are not enough, nor can there ever be enough, goods and services to satisfy the wants and needs of everyone. Consider your own situation. Can you afford the school that you would most prefer to

economics
IN ACTION

Frederick Smith: Entrepreneur

Frederick Smith, founder of FedEx, is one of America's successful entrepreneurs. He comes from a family tradition based on transportation. His grandfather was a steamboat captain, and his father established a regional bus company that turned into a cornerstone of the Greyhound Bus system. Learning to fly as a teenager, Smith worked weekends as a charter pilot while working on an economics degree at Yale University in the 1960s.

While flying faculty and other passengers around, Smith had an idea that resulted in a radical change in the transportation business. He realized that besides flying people, he often delivered spare parts for firms that could not wait for United Airlines and others to ship essential components to customers. In 1965, Smith formalized his notion of an express delivery service in a term paper written in an economics course. Although lore has it that Smith received a modest grade of "C" for his efforts, he recalls doing better.

After serving a tour of duty with the Marines in Vietnam, Smith began to pursue his ambition. With $4 million backing from his family and $80 million from other investors, he built from scratch the Federal Express

Corporation (FedEx) in 1971. Its vow: guaranteed 1-day delivery of packages between two points in the United States.

However, FedEx was no overnight success. The firm drummed up only seven packages for its first day's run. Therefore, Smith hired additional sales staff to boost sales. Yet deficient volume wasn't the only problem. Until the late 1970s, the U.S. Postal Service was able to use its monopoly power to prevent FedEx from delivering documents. Also, strict airline regulations initially limited FedEx to flying small aircraft instead of more efficient larger ones. Smith was in such dire need of funds that he traveled to Las Vegas to play the blackjack tables. He sent the $27,000 he won back to FedEx.

Smith's perseverance yielded success. By 1980, Americans came to rely on FedEx's promise to deliver packages by the next day. Although FedEx's success has led to many competitors, it is still the dominant firm, with a 44-percent share of the express delivery market. Its fleet of 650 aircraft and 71,000 trucks transport some 5.5 million packages each day. And all because a college economics major could visualize an opportunity that others couldn't.

Source: "Frederic Smith: Father of the Overnight Delivery Service," Academy of Achievement, Washington, D.C., February 2005; Dean Foust, "No Overnight Success," *Business Week,* September 20, 2004, p. 18; and "Welcome to Federal Express," available at http://www.fedex.com.

---

attend or the car that you would most like to own? Do you have sufficient financial resources for all the clothes, computers, concerts, and sporting events that you want? Societies also encounter the scarcity problem. Money devoted to national defense is not available for education or food stamps.

The source of the scarcity problem is that people have *limited resources* to satisfy their *unlimited material wants*. Resources, or **factors of production**, are inputs used in the production of goods and services that we want, such as CD players and textbooks. The total quantity of resources that an economy has at any one time determines how much output the economy can produce. The factors of production are classified as follows:

1. **Land.** Land refers to all natural resources—such as raw materials, land, minerals, forests, water, and climate—used in the productive process.

2. **Labor.** This resource includes all physical and mental efforts that people make available for production. Services of professional baseball players, accountants, teachers, and autoworkers all fall under the heading of labor.

ENTREPRENEURSHIP

CAPITAL

3. **Capital.** Capital, or investment goods, refers to goods used to produce other goods and services. It includes such things as machinery, tools, computers, computer software, buildings, and roads. Notice that economists do not consider money to be capital because it is not directly used in production.

4. **Entrepreneurship.** This factor of production is a special type of labor. An entrepreneur is a person who organizes, manages, and assembles the other factors of production to produce goods and services. Entrepreneurs seek profits by undertaking such risky activities as starting a new business, creating new products, or inventing new ways of accomplishing things. Bill Gates (founder of Microsoft Corp.), Levi Strauss (founder of Levi Strauss Co.), and Henry Ford (founder of Ford Motor Co.) are examples of highly successful entrepreneurs.

These factors of production have a common characteristic: They are in limited supply. Quantities of mineral deposits, capital equipment, arable land, and labor (time) are available only in finite amounts. Due to the scarcity of resources and the limitation this scarcity imposes on productive activity, output will thus be limited.

Limited resources conflict with unlimited wants. Human wants are said to be unlimited because no matter how much people have, they always want more of something. Because not all wants can be fulfilled, individuals must choose which ones to fulfill with limited available resources. In a world of scarcity, every want that ends up being fulfilled results in one or more other wants remaining unfulfilled.

SCARCITY AND OPPORTUNITY COST

The reality of scarcity forces us to make choices that involve giving up another opportunity to do or use something else. For example, the cost of going to a Chicago Bulls' basketball game includes the value of what is sacrificed to attend. Economists use the term opportunity cost to denote the value of the best alternative sacrificed. Part of the cost of attending a Bulls' game is the price of the ticket. This price represents the other goods and services you could have purchased with that money instead. In addition, there is the most valuable alternative use of the time devoted to watching the game. Perhaps you could have used this time to study for an upcoming economics exam. The opportunity cost of attending the game thus equals the ticket price plus the difference in your test score that the additional study time would have yielded. Let us consider several applications of opportunity cost.

The Opportunity Cost of Attending College

Another example is the opportunity cost of attending college. It is not simply the dollar amount listed in your college catalog. Money spent on tuition, fees, textbooks, and supplies is only part of the opportunity cost; the income that you could have earned during the years that you are spending in classes is also part of the opportunity cost.

Table 1.1 shows the estimated out-of-pocket costs of a year of college for the average student in 2004–2005. For example, the third column of the table shows the cost for an average in-state resident at four-year state colleges to be $15,214. Of this amount, the student pays $5,132 in tuition and fees, $853 in books and supplies, $6,177 for room and board, $1,109 for transportation, and $1,943 in other expenses.

Is the student's opportunity cost for a year of state college $15,214? No. Some of this cost occurs whether or not the student attends college. For example, you would have to assume room and board expenses, say, by living in an apartment, even if you did not attend college. This cost is not eliminated even if you lived at home because your family might have been able to rent your room to someone else. The same applies to transportation and other expenses, at least the portion that you would have assumed if you were not in college. Suppose that these expenses are the same whether or not you attend college.

Table 1.1	Average Cost of a Year of College, 2004–2005		
Type of Institution	Two-Year Public (commuter)	Four-Year Public (resident)	Four-Year Private (resident)
Tuition and fees	$ 2,076	$ 5,132	$20,082
Books and supplies	773	853	870
Room and board	5,747	6,177	6,617
Transportation	1,146	1,109	1,031
Other costs	1,608	1,943	1,524
Total costs	$11,350	$15,214	$30,124

Source: From *Trends in College Pricing: 2004–2005*, The College Board at http://www.collegeboard.com. Based on the College Board's *Annual Survey of Colleges.*

The opportunity cost of attending college thus consists of tuition and fees ($5,132) and books and supplies ($853), which total $5,985.

In addition, the opportunity cost of a year of college includes the amount of forgone income. Assuming that you earn $10 an hour and reduce your work hours by 30 hours a week during the 32 weeks a year you are in college, the forgone earnings represent a cost of $9,600 ($10 × 30 hours × 32 weeks) a year. It should be noted that most students will use their education to generate future earnings that will more than offset this sum. Nevertheless, the $9,600 also represents an opportunity cost of attending college.

The opportunity cost of a year of college thus includes the payments for tuition and fees ($5,132), payments for books and supplies ($853), plus the $9,600 of forgone income. This sum totals $15,585. Notice that this amount is greater than the estimated $15,214 of out-of-pocket costs shown in Table 1.1.

Some students find the opportunity cost of attending college to be even higher. Suppose you are a talented baseball player or tennis player who could play professionally after graduating from high school. The opportunity cost of a year at college could easily exceed $100,000. Tiger Woods, a professional golfer, faced this dilemma after attending Stanford University for two years. Upon winning his third straight U.S. Amateur golf title, he chose to turn pro rather than continue his studies at Stanford. Immediately, he became a multimillionaire with contracts—worth more than $40 million—from Nike and Titleist in hand. It is no wonder that talented athletes often consider the opportunity cost of their college education to be too high and thus drop out of school in pursuit of professional sports.

Opportunity Costs and Choices

Suppose that your student club conducts a fund raiser, and each club member agrees to spend eight hours working at a Saturday car wash. A local service station donates its parking area and water, while your club supplies washcloths and detergent. Club members wave their signs at passing motorists in an attempt to lure business.

After washing several vehicles, the members determine that they can wash 10 compacts or five minivans in one hour's time. In an 8-hour day, 80 compacts (8 × 10 = 80) or 40 minivans (8 × 5 = 40) could therefore be washed.

Figure 1.1 illustrates the combinations of compacts and minivans that could be washed in an 8-hour day. Devoting the entire day to washing compacts results in 80 washed cars,

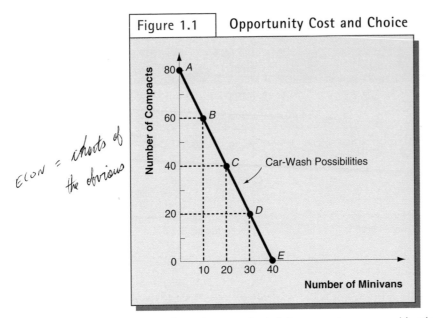

Figure 1.1   Opportunity Cost and Choice

ECON = charts of the obvious

In an 8-hour day, a student club can wash many combinations of minivans and compacts. Line *AE* illustrates these combinations given the assumption that the entire day is devoted to washing the two types of vehicles. The line is downward sloping, suggesting that there is a trade-off between the number of compacts and the number of minivans that can be washed. Along line *AE*, the opportunity cost of each additional washed minivan is two compacts that are not washed.

shown by point *A* in the figure. Conversely, devoting the entire day to washing minivans results in 40 washed minivans, shown by point *E*. Let us connect these two combinations with line *AE*. Other combinations (*B*, *C*, *D*) are attainable on this line. Line *AE* thus shows all possible combinations of compacts and minivans that could be washed in a day.

Sliding down line *AE*, we see that there is an opportunity cost for washing minivans. For every 10 minivans that our club washes, it must sacrifice the washing of 20 compacts. This implies that the opportunity cost for each additional washed minivan equals two compacts ($20 \div 10 = 2$) that are not washed. Why does this trade-off occur? Given an 8-hour day, as more hours are devoted to the washing of minivans, fewer hours can be devoted to washing compacts. The 8-hour limitation of our Saturday car wash thus forces our club to make choices concerning how much effort should be devoted to washing compacts or minivans. Tabular and graphical relationships are further discussed in "Exploring Further 1.1" at the end of this chapter.

CHECK POINT

1. What is economics?

2. Differentiate between microeconomics and macroeconomics.

3. Identify the major principles of the economic way of thinking.

4. How does scarcity force an individual to incur opportunity costs?

5. What opportunity cost do you face in attending college?

THE PRODUCTION POSSIBILITIES CURVE AND OPPORTUNITY COST

Just as scarcity affects the car-wash choices of a student club, it also influences the production choices of a nation. The relationship between the ideas of scarcity and choice that an entire nation faces can be illustrated by a **production possibilities curve**. A production possibilities curve illustrates graphically the maximum combinations of two goods that an economy can produce, given its available resources and technology. Several assumptions underlie an economy's production possibilities curve:

1. **Fixed resources.** The quantities of all resources, or factors of production, are held constant. This means that there are no changes in the economy's labor, machinery, and the like. Existing resources can only be transferred from the production of one good to the production of another good.

2. **Fully employed resources.** Everyone who wants a job has one, and all other resources are being used. All resources are producing the maximum output possible.

3. **Technology unchanged.** The existing technology is held fixed with no new innovations or inventions taking place.

Note that the assumptions of fixed resources and fixed technology imply that we are looking at our economy at a specific point in time, or over a very short period. Over a relatively long period, it is possible for resources to change and technological advances to occur.

Figure 1.2 illustrates a hypothetical economy that has the capacity to produce various combinations of VCRs and computers. If all resources are devoted to computer production, 6 million computers per year can be produced, denoted by point *A* in the figure. If all resources are devoted to VCR production, 3 million VCRs per year can be produced, denoted by point *D*. Between the extremes of points *A* and *D* are other possible combinations of the two goods, denoted by points *B* and *C*. Connecting these points with a curve results in the economy's production possibilities curve.

The production possibilities curve in Figure 1.2(a) is downward-sloping due to the problem of scarcity. Resources of land, labor, capital, and entrepreneurship are limited to particular amounts at any one point in time. In a fully employed economy, more resources going into the production of VCRs leads to fewer resources being left for the production of computers. To produce more VCRs, the cost will be a lower output of computers. The figure thus illustrates a basic truth of economics: All choices have opportunity costs.

Economic Inefficiency

Because all points along a production possibilities curve depict maximum output with given resources and technology, an economy realizes economic efficiency when operating along the curve. What if the economy does not employ all of its resources at their maximum capacity? For example, during economic downturns some workers probably cannot find work, and some plants and equipment may become underutilized. In this situation, an economy fails to realize the output potential of its production possibilities curve, and economic inefficiency occurs.

In Figure 1.2(b), point *E* shows an inefficient output combination for an economy that realizes unemployed labor or other underutilized resources; only 1 million VCRs and 1 million computers are produced. With full employment, the economy could produce a larger output combination, say 2 million VCRs and 3 million computers, shown by point

Figure 1.2 | Production Possibilities Curve

A production possibilities curve shows graphically the various combinations of two goods that an economy can produce with full employment, fixed resources, and fixed technology. Points inside the production possibilities curve are economically inefficient, while points outside the curve are unattainable given an economy's existing resources and technology.

C in the figure. Comparing these two points, we see that unemployment results in forgone output equal to 2 million computers and 1 million VCRs. Generalizing, the effect of unemployment is illustrated graphically by a point *beneath* the production possibilities curve. This point is attainable but usually not desirable.

Even if an economy can fully employ all of its resources at their maximum capacity, certain output combinations cannot be realized. In Figure 1.2(b), any point outside the economy's production possibilities curve, say point *F*, is *unattainable* because it lies beyond the economy's current production capabilities. The economy cannot achieve this output combination with its existing resources and technology. Scarcity restricts an economy to operating at points along or beneath its production possibilities curve.

Do economies actually operate along their production possibilities curves? Strictly speaking, no. Economies always experience some degrees of unemployment and underproduction that cause them to operate beneath their production possibilities curves. A production possibilities curve can thus be viewed as a yardstick against which an economy's production performance can be measured.

To what extent has the United States been able to utilize its industrial capacity? A measure of such utilization is the **capacity utilization rate**, which is the ratio of an industry's production to its capacity. According to this measure, an industry operating at full capacity would operate at 100-percent capacity utilization; a rate less than 100 percent implies at least some idle plants and equipment.

Table 1.2 illustrates capacity utilization rates for major U.S. industries. We see that in January 2005 all U.S. industries combined operated at 79-percent capacity utilization. The capacity utilization rates for the economy's manufacturing, mining, and utilities sectors in January 2005 equaled 78.0 percent, 86.6 percent, and 83.5 percent, respectively. The table also shows capacity utilization rates for particular U.S. manufacturing industries.

Table 1.2	Capacity Utilization Rates for Major U.S. Industries		
		1972–2004 Average	January 2005
Total industry		81.0%	79.0%
Manufacturing:		79.8	78.0
Wood products		80.0	81.5
Iron and steel		80.5	81.4
Machinery		78.8	79.5
Aerospace and transportation equipment		72.4	65.8
Paper		88.1	88.2
Chemicals		78.4	76.8
Petroleum		86.1	91.9
Mining		87.1	86.6
Utilities		86.8	83.5

Source: From Federal Reserve Statistical Release, *Industrial Production and Capacity Utilization*, available at http://www.federalreserve.gov/releases/.

Law of Increasing Opportunity Cost

Figure 1.3 illustrates the production possibilities curve of our hypothetical economy as previously discussed. Notice that the production possibilities curve is bowed outward, or concave. This is because the opportunity cost of VCRs increases as more VCRs are produced. Moving from point *A* to point *B* along the curve, the opportunity cost of one

Figure 1.3	The Law of Increasing Opportunity Cost

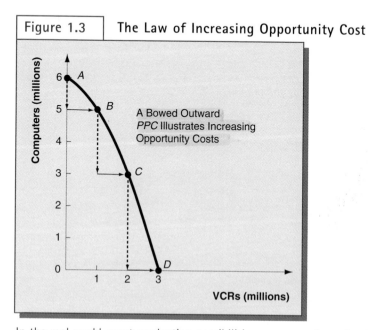

In the real world, most production possibilities curves are bowed outward (concave). This means that, for most goods, the opportunity cost increases as we produce more of them. Increasing opportunity costs occur when resources are not completely adaptable to alternative uses.

VCR is one computer; between points *B* and *C*, the opportunity cost is two computers; and between points *C* and *D*, the opportunity cost is three computers. These opportunity costs represent what occurs in the real world for most goods: Opportunity costs increase as we produce more of a good. This relationship is known as the law of increasing opportunity cost.

But *why* do opportunity costs generally increase as we produce more of a good? The answer is because *resources are not completely adaptable to alternative uses*. For example, some workers have skills that are more useful for producing VCRs than other workers have. When a company first starts producing VCRs, it employs workers who are most skilled at VCR production. The most skilled workers are those who can produce VCRs at lower opportunity costs than others. Yet, as the company produces more VCRs, it finds that it has already employed the most skilled workers; thus, it must employ workers who are less skilled in VCR production. These workers produce VCRs at higher opportunity costs. Where two skilled workers could produce a VCR in a day, it may take as many as five unskilled workers to produce it in the same amount of time. As more VCRs are produced, the opportunity cost of producing VCRs thus increases.

ECONOMIC GROWTH

At any particular point in time, an economy cannot be outside its production possibilities curve. Over time, however, expanding output potential is possible for an economy. This occurs through economic growth, which refers to increased productive capabilities of an economy made possible by either an increasing resource base or technological advances.

Economic growth entails an outward shift in an economy's production possibilities curve so that more of all goods can be produced. Figure 1.4 illustrates the significance of an

| Figure 1.4 | The Effect of Economic Growth on the Production Possibilities Curve |

Economic growth shifts a production possibilities curve outward and makes it possible to produce more of all goods. Prior to growth in productive capacity, point *C* was on *PPC₀* and points *E, F,* and *G* were unattainable. After growth, shown by *PPC₁*, points *E, F,* and *G* (and many other previously unattainable combinations) are attainable.

outward shift in a production possibilities curve. Before the occurrence of economic growth, suppose an economy can produce 2 million VCRs and 3 million computers, shown by point C along PPC_0. Due to growth in the economy's resource base or technological advances, the production possibilities curve shifts outward to a higher level, PPC_1. Economic growth permits the economy to produce more computers (a movement to point E), more VCRs (a movement to point G), or more of both goods (a movement to point F). Many other previously unattainable combinations also become attainable with economic growth. In short, economic growth allows the economy to produce more of everything! However, growth does not guarantee that the economy will operate at a point along the higher production possibilities curve. The economy might fail to fulfill its expanded possibilities.

One way to increase an economy's production capacity is to gain additional resources. More (or better trained) workers or more (or improved) plants and equipment increase a nation's output potential. Worker productivity is also facilitated by investment in infrastructures such as roads, bridges, airports, and utilities. Another way to achieve economic growth is through research and development of new technologies. Technological development allows increased output to be produced with the same quantity of resources. A faster photocopier, a more smoothly operating assembly line, or a new-generation computer system are examples of technological advances.

Throughout the twentieth century, agriculture was a highly productive sector of the U.S. economy. In 1910, the United States had roughly 32 million farmers, which constituted 35 percent of the U.S. population; in 2005, there were about 5 million farmers constituting less than 2 percent of the U.S. population. During this period, total farm output greatly expanded. How could a declining number of farmers produce greater output? The answer is improved technology. Where farmers once farmed with negligible capital equipment, today they use modern tractors, computers, pesticides, cellular phones, and the like. As a result, more food has been produced by fewer farmers. As farmers left farms, they entered manufacturing and service industries such as computers, automobiles, aircraft, accounting services, and engineering. Technological advances in farming thus made it possible to produce additional goods in other sectors of the economy. The result was an outward shift in the U.S. production possibilities curve.

ECONOMIC DECLINE

Just as an expanding resource base causes an economy's production possibilities to increase, decreasing resources can likewise reduce an economy's output potential. During World War II, the production possibilities of Europe and Japan decreased. The war disrupted people's lives, and many people did not survive the war. Entire factories, roads, bridges, railway networks, electrical utilities, and other types of capital goods were reduced to rubble. Destructive effects of the war caused the production possibilities curves of Europe and Japan to shift inward.

The physical devastation of Europe and Japan caused by World War II yielded some paradoxical effects for these war-devastated economies. Because a large share of their stock of capital goods was destroyed by the war, these nations had to rebuild their industries from scratch. They did so with the most up-to-date factories and equipment. The result was a substantial increase in labor productivity, which allowed these economies to realize production possibilities exceeding those that existed before the war. Conversely, nations that had been spared the devastation of the war had their prewar technologies in place and grew slower than those whose stock of capital goods was destroyed and replaced with more modern technology.

For example, the United States was the most powerful steel-producing nation in the world immediately following World War II. The U.S. steel industry came out of the war intact, accounting for nearly half of the world's steel output. Moreover, U.S. firms produced more steel than all of Europe combined and almost 20 times as much as Japan! During the 1950s and 1960s, however, the absence of foreign competition resulted in U.S. steel companies' becoming lethargic. Instead of investing in new plants, they manufactured steel in outmoded plants using obsolete technologies and paid wages almost twice the average of all other U.S. manufacturing sectors. In contrast, Japan and Europe replaced the steel factories that were devastated by the war with modern plants that used the most efficient equipment. By the 1970s, productivity of Japanese and European steel companies was increasing relative to the productivity of U.S. companies, and the competitiveness of U.S. companies dwindled. The threat of foreign competition forced U.S. steel companies to shut down many obsolete factories in the 1980s and replace them with modern plants and equipment.

Natural disasters can also reduce an economy's output potential. For example, in 1995, a major earthquake occurred in Kobe (Japan), a city of 1.5 million people. The city accounted for almost 5 percent of Japan's industrial output, while the port, the nation's second busiest, handled about 10 percent of foreign trade. In addition to the tragic loss of more than 5,000 lives, estimates on total material damage were nearly $60 billion, equivalent to 1.25 percent of Japan's national output. The reduction in Japan's stock of capital goods was about 0.5 percent due to the earthquake. Overall, the earthquake led to Japan's potential output falling by at least 0.3 percent in the first two years following the earthquake.[1]

ECONOMIC GROWTH: TRADE-OFFS BETWEEN CURRENT AND FUTURE CONSUMPTION

The production possibilities curve and economic growth can be used to investigate the trade-off between current and future consumption. This trade-off can be illustrated for nations producing consumer goods and capital goods.

Consumer goods are goods such as food, electricity, and clothing that are available for immediate use by households. They do not contribute to future production in the economy. Capital goods, such as factories and machines, are used for producing other goods and services in the future. Instead of being consumed today, capital goods are a source of an economy's economic growth potential.

A nation that sacrifices current consumption to invest in capital goods is forward looking. Rather than getting instant satisfaction from the production of capital goods, the nation increases its capacity to produce consumer goods in the future. This is similar to students attending college. Students devote time to study that could have been spent working, earning income, and therefore engaging in a higher level of consumption. Most students decide to postpone consumption because they expect education to increase their productivity and income, allowing greater consumption in the future.

Figure 1.5 illustrates the production possibilities curves for the United States and Japan. The two axes of each production possibilities curve are designated as consumer goods (current goods) and capital goods (goods for the future). Assume that the two nations are identical in every respect except that the U.S. choice along its production possibilities curve strongly favors consumer goods as opposed to capital goods; let this be designated by point A in Figure 1.5(a). Conversely, Japan's choice along its production possibilities curve strongly favors capital goods and is denoted by point A' in Figure 1.5(b).

So our tax laws should encourage this

---

[1] "Macroeconomic Impact of the Japanese Earthquake," *World Economic Outlook* (International Monetary Fund), May 1995, p. 16.

| Figure 1.5 | Economic Growth in the United States and Japan |

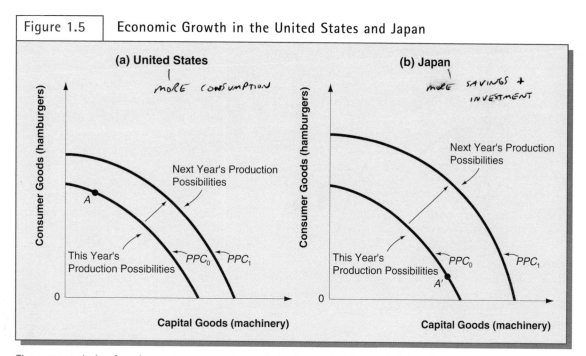

The current choice favoring consumer goods, made by the United States in (a), will cause a modest outward shift in the U.S. production possibilities curve. A current choice favoring capital goods, as made by Japan in (b), will lead to a greater outward shift in the Japanese production possibilities curve. The extra goods, made possible by economic growth, thus result in a greater improvement in the living standard of Japan.

The relatively large accumulation of capital goods allows the Japanese economy to grow faster than the U.S. economy. In Figure 1.5, this is illustrated by the production possibilities curve of Japan shifting farther to the right than the U.S. curve. Over time, Japan's faster growth rate allows it to produce more consumer goods than the United States. This increase in production, however, requires Japanese households to sacrifice current consumption in exchange for future consumption.

PRODUCTION POSSIBILITIES APPLICATIONS

The production possibilities concept can be applied to issues pertaining to national security. Let us consider the application of the production possibilities concept to the terrorist attacks of September 11, 2001, on the United States and the economic sanctions levied by the United States against Iraq in 1990.

Opportunity Cost of National Security

The terrorist attacks of September 11, 2001, on the United States resulted in a tragic loss of life for thousands of innocent Americans. It also jolted America's golden age of prosperity and the promise it held for global growth that existed throughout the 1990s. Because of the threat of terrorism, Americans became increasingly concerned about their safety.

Immediately following the terrorist attacks, businesses and government made greater efforts to improve their security. For example, Quality Carriers Inc., the country's biggest chemical trucker, rehired the $5,000-a-month night-shift security guard it had previously

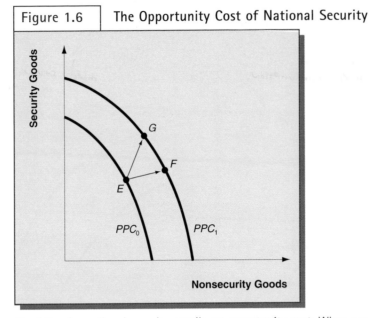

Figure 1.6 | **The Opportunity Cost of National Security**

Providing for national security entails an opportunity cost. When we use land, labor, and capital to produce security goods, we sacrifice other things we could have produced with them.

only because no

goals are produced

let go at its tanker-truck terminal in Newark, New Jersey. The company also paid two drivers a total of $1,200 to re-park any vehicles loaded with chemicals in plain view and under security lights. For Quality Carriers, achieving extra security required the firm to use more of its resources to protect the company from terrorists, resulting in fewer resources being available for transporting chemicals for its customers. In like manner, security procedures were beefed up at power plants, communication companies, airports, and government buildings following the September 11 attacks.

Simply put, providing for national security entails an opportunity cost. When we employ labor, capital, and land for security, we sacrifice other things we could have produced with them. To demonstrate this point, consider Figure 1.6, which depicts hypothetical production possibilities curves for the United States. The vertical axis denotes the annual production of security goods (for example, metal detectors and X-ray monitors), and the horizontal axis denotes the annual production of goods other than security (for example, televisions and autos), which contribute directly to our standard of living. Because of technological progress and the growth in the nation's stock of plant and equipment, the nation's production possibilities curve shifts outward, as shown by the movement from curve PPC_0 to curve PPC_1.

Assume that prior to September 11, the United States was located at point E along curve PPC_0. Also assume that in a normal year, economic growth would result in the United States moving from point E on curve PPC_0 to point F on curve PPC_1. This means that we would realize a modest increase in production of security goods, but most of our growth would have been used to produce additional quantities of autos, televisions, and other things we enjoy. Because of the terrorist attacks of September 11, however, we move from point E to point G. Notice that although we produce additional quantities of nonsecurity goods, we do not produce *as much more* of those goods as we would have. This limits our economic well-being as measured by the quantity of nonsecurity goods available for our consumption. Therefore, providing national security results in an opportunity cost in terms of other goods that we enjoy.

Table 1.3	Selected Economic Sanctions of the United States	

Year Initiated	Country	Target Objective
1999	Serbia	Improve human rights
1998	Pakistan	Discourage nuclear proliferation
1998	India	Discourage nuclear proliferation
1992	Serbia	Terminate civil war in Bosnia-Herzegovina
1990	Iraq	Terminate Iraq's military takeover of Kuwait
1985	South Africa	Improve human rights
1983	Soviet Union	Retaliate for downing of Korean airliner
1979	Iran	Release U.S. hostages

Economic Sanctions and Economic Decline

In our world, nations often disagree with each other's policies. In the 1980s, for example, the United States disputed South Africa's discriminatory laws against blacks (apartheid). Human rights abuses in China have also met strong criticism in the United States in the 1990s.

Besides the threat of war, are there other ways to convince a foreign government to modify its domestic policies? An alternative is economic sanctions, which are government-imposed limitations, or complete bans, placed on customary trade or financial relations among nations. Economic sanctions have been used to preserve national security, protect human rights, combat international terrorism, and reduce nuclear proliferation. The nation initiating the sanctions, the *imposing nation*, hopes to impair the economic capabilities of the recipient *target nation*. The goal of economic sanctions is to inspire the people of the target nation to force their government to alter its policies. Table 1.3 provides examples of economic sanctions imposed by the United States for foreign policy objectives. Let us consider the sanctions imposed by the United States on Iraq in 1990.

In August 1990, the Iraqi military crossed into Kuwait and within six hours occupied the entire nation. Iraqi President Saddam Hussein maintained that his forces had been invited into Kuwait by a revolutionary government that had overthrown the Kuwaiti emir and his government. In response to Iraq's aggression, a United Nations resolution called for economic sanctions to be levied against Iraq. Trade and financial boycotts were imposed by virtually all members of the UN, with only a few hard-line Iraqi allies refusing to cooperate. Under the sanctions program, imposing nations banned exports to Iraq, terminated purchases of Iraqi oil, and suspended investment in, and loans to, Iraq. If Saddam Hussein could not be convinced to leave Kuwait, it was hoped the sanctions would pressure the Iraqi people or military into removing him from office.

Figure 1.7 can be used to illustrate the goal of the UN sanctions levied against Iraq. The figure shows the hypothetical production possibilities curve of Iraq for machines and oil. Prior to the imposition of sanctions, suppose that Iraq is able to operate at maximum efficiency, as shown by point A along production possibilities curve PPC_0. Under the sanctions program, a refusal of the imposing nations to purchase Iraqi oil leads to idle wells, refineries, and workers in Iraq. Unused production capacity thus forces Iraq to move inside PPC_0. If imposing nations also target productive inputs, and thus curtail equipment sales to Iraq, the output potential of Iraq would decrease. This is shown by an inward shift of Iraq's production possibilities curve to PPC_1. Economic inefficiencies and

Figure 1.7	Effects of Economic Sanctions

Trade and financial bans placed against a target nation have the effect of forcing the nation to operate inside its production possibilities curve. Economic sanctions can also result in a leftward (inward) shift in the target nation's production possibilities curve.

reduced production possibilities, caused by economic sanctions, are thus intended to inflict hardship on the people and government of Iraq.

Although the sanctions imposed hardship on the people of Iraq, Saddam Hussein's grip on power was so strong in the early 1990s that he could not be removed from office or be forced to modify his expansionist policies, even though a majority of Iraqi citizens suffered great economic hardship. This led to President George Bush's conclusions that sanctions would not succeed and that military intervention (Operation Desert Storm) was necessary to force Iraq out of Kuwait.

Following the ouster of the Iraqi army from Kuwait in 1991, the United Nations continued to impose sanctions against Iraq. The sanctions were to be kept in place until Iraq agreed to scrap its nuclear and biological weapons programs. However, Saddam Hussein dug his heels in and refused to make concessions. Therefore, the sanctions program continued until 2003, when they were lifted following the U.S. and UK war with Iraq.

Sanctions were devastating for Iraq. Analysts estimate that Iraq's economy shrunk more than two-thirds because of the sanctions. Moreover, that figure understates the extent of contraction. Every sector of the Iraqi economy depended to some degree on imports. The simplest textile mills could not operate without foreign-made parts; farmers needed imported pumps to run their irrigation systems; and the government could not repair war-damaged telephone, electricity, water, road, and sewage networks without material from abroad. As a result, factories and businesses shut down, forcing people out of work. Government employees remained on the job, but inflation reduced the purchasing power of their salaries to a pittance. Scientists, engineers, and academics abandoned their professions to drive taxis, sell liquor and cigarettes, and fish for a living. Crime and prostitution flourished. Moreover, the people of Iraq suffered from lack of food and medicine. Indeed, sanctions affected the lives of all Iraqis every moment of the day.

In this chapter, we examined the economic choices that must be made in every society because of scarcity. The next chapter considers the role of demand and supply in analyzing market transactions.

CHECK POINT

1. How can we use a production possibilities curve to illustrate opportunity cost for a nation?

2. Concerning economic growth, does it make any difference whether an economy devotes more resources to the production of capital goods as opposed to the production of consumer goods?

3. Identify the opportunity cost of national security.

4. When economic sanctions are placed on a country, how can they affect its production possibilities?

Chapter Summary

1. The source of an economy's scarcity problem is that people have limited resources to satisfy their unlimited material wants.

2. Resources, or factors of production, are inputs used in the production of goods and services. They include land, labor, capital, and entrepreneurship.

3. The reality of scarcity forces us to make choices that involve giving up another opportunity to do or use something else. Economists use the term opportunity cost to denote the value of the best alternative sacrificed.

4. A production possibilities curve illustrates graphically the maximum combinations of two goods that an economy can produce, given its available resources and technology. An economy located along its production possibilities curve operates at maximum efficiency.

5. As we move along an outward-bowed production possibilities curve, opportunity costs increase as more of a good is produced. Increasing opportunity costs occur because resources are not completely adaptable to alternative uses.

6. Economic growth entails an outward shift in an economy's production possibilities curve so that more of all goods can be produced. It is made possible by an increase in an economy's resource base or technological advances.

7. The terrorist attacks of September 11, 2001, on the United States forced the nation to beef up its national security. However, devoting additional resources for national security entails an opportunity cost in terms of other goods that Americans could consume.

8. Economic sanctions are government-imposed limitations placed on trade and financial relations among nations. The nation initiating the sanctions, the imposing nation, hopes that economic hardship caused by sanctions will inspire the target nation to alter its political or military policies. Economic sanctions can force a target nation to locate beneath its production possibilities curve and can even cause the target nation's production possibilities curve to shift inward.

Key Terms and Concepts

economics (3)

microeconomics (4)

macroeconomics (4)

models (6)

theories (6)

positive economics (6)

normative economics (6)

scarcity (6)

factors of production (7)

opportunity cost (8)

production possibilities curve (11)

efficiency (11)

inefficiency (11)

capacity utilization rate (12)

law of increasing opportunity cost (14)

economic growth (14)

consumer goods (16)

capital goods (16)

economic sanctions (19)

independent variable (25)

dependent variable (26)

direct relationship (26)

inverse relationship (26)

slope (26)

Self-Test: Multiple-Choice Questions

1. A bowed-outward production possibilities curve illustrates

   a. increasing opportunity costs.
   b. constant opportunity costs.
   c. decreasing opportunity costs.
   d. zero opportunity costs.

2. The U.S. production possibilities curve will shift outward if

   a. resources are used less efficiently.
   b. unemployment and underproduction are eliminated.
   c. additional resources are discovered in the United States.
   d. Americans' tastes for all goods and services become stronger.

3. Economic sanctions levied against a target country are intended to cause the

   a. country to slide downward along its production possibilities curve.
   b. country to produce under conditions of increasing opportunity cost.
   c. country to move to a point inside its production possibilities curve.
   d. country's production possibilities curve to shift outward.

4. As a subject matter, economics is most concerned with

   a. making money in stocks, bonds, and real estate.
   b. understanding how to own and operate a business.
   c. the study of choice under conditions of scarcity.
   d. the allocation of unlimited resources among limited human wants.

5. The subject of macroeconomics would be most concerned with how

   a. a tax on cigarettes would affect consumption by teenagers.
   b. a ban on immigrant workers from Mexico would affect U.S. apple growers.

    c. poor growing conditions in Canada would affect the price of wheat.
    d. national output and employment respond to changes in government spending.

6. *Positive economics* is concerned with all of the following questions *except*

    a. Why do engineers earn more than librarians?
    b. Do import tariffs protect the jobs of domestic workers?
    c. Will reducing income taxes cause households to work additional hours?
    d. Should welfare payments be increased to help the poor?

7. The factors of production include all of the following *except*

    a. money.
    b. entrepreneurship.
    c. capital.
    d. labor and land.

8. The United States would move from a point on its production possibilities curve to a point inside the curve if there was a(n)

    a. increase in the unemployment rate.
    b. rise in the level of price inflation.
    c. fall in the productivity of labor.
    d. decline in the birth rate.

9. If the slope of a straight line is –2, then the two variables in the graph are

    a. directly related.
    b. inversely related.
    c. cross related.
    d. not related.

10. In a graph between study time and grades in an economics course,

    a. study time and grades are generally considered to be inversely related.
    b. study time is the independent variable and grades are the dependent variable.
    c. the slope of the graph is generally considered to be negative.
    d. the graph generally appears as a downward-sloping straight line.

Answers to Multiple-Choice Questions

1. a   2. c   3. c   4. c   5. d   6. d.   7. a   8. a   9. b   10. b

Study Questions and Problems

1. Suppose you receive a weekly income of $100, which you spend entirely on pizza and deluxe hamburgers. The price of a pizza is $10, and the price of a hamburger is $5. On a diagram, draw a line that shows your consumption possibilities. What is the opportunity cost of a hamburger? Would the opportunity cost of a hamburger change if the prices of pizza and hamburgers were cut in half? Calculate the opportunity cost of pizzas and hamburgers for each of the following changes.

    a. An increase in the price of pizzas to $20.
    b. An increase in the price of hamburgers to $10.
    c. A decline in weekly income to $80.
    d. A rise in weekly income to $120.

Table 1.4	Production Possibilities Table					
		Production Alternatives				
Product	A	B	C	D	E	F
Steel (tons)	0	1	2	3	4	5
Aluminum (tons)	20	18	15	11	6	0

2. Table 1.4 shows a production possibilities table for steel and aluminum.

   a. Plot these production possibilities data on a diagram. Upon what assumptions is your production possibilities curve drawn?
   b. What is the opportunity cost of the first ton of steel? Between which points is the opportunity cost of a ton of steel the greatest?
   c. Explain how this curve reflects the law of increasing opportunity cost.
   d. Label a point G inside the curve. Why is this point inefficient? Label a point H outside the curve. Why is this point unattainable?
   e. Why might the production possibilities curve shift inward? Why might it shift outward?

3. How does each of the following affect the location of an economy's production possibilities curve?

   a. A war leads to casualties for civilian workers.
   b. A new technology permits more oil to be extracted from a well.
   c. The economy's unemployment rate rises from 4 percent to 6 percent of the labor force.
   d. The economy decides to produce more CD players and fewer radios.

4. In the 1990s, civil war erupted in Bosnia. The war led to the destruction of natural resources and capital and caused casualties that decreased the supply of labor for the production of consumer goods and capital goods. Illustrate the impact of the war on Bosnia's production possibilities curve for consumer goods and capital goods.

5. Draw an economy's production possibilities curve for automobiles and airplanes. Assume a technological breakthrough occurs that allows greater productivity for autoworkers but not airplane workers. Draw a new production possibilities curve. Suppose instead that the technological breakthrough allowed greater productivity for airplane workers but not autoworkers. Draw a new production possibilities curve.

6. In response to Iraq's invasion of Kuwait in 1990, the United States and its allies imposed trade and financial sanctions on Iraq. Imports of Iraqi oil were terminated as were exports of machinery, parts, and the like, to Iraq. Bank loans to Iraq and business investment in Iraq were also curtailed. Illustrate the effects of the economic sanctions on Iraq's production possibilities curve for textiles and oil. Under what conditions would the sanctions most likely have caused Iraq to withdraw from Kuwait?

EXPLORING FURTHER 1.1: A PRIMER ON TABLES AND GRAPHS

As you glance at this text, you will notice many tables and graphs. They are included to help you visualize and understand economic relationships. To understand how tables and graphs are constructed, let us consider an example that is familiar to you: The relation between study time and grades in a college course.

Table 1.5	Studying Pays Off in an Economics Issues Class		
	Course Grade	Course Grade Point Average	Hours of Study per Week
	F	0.0	0
	D	1.0	2
	C	2.0	4
	B	3.0	6
	A	4.0	8

Suppose that we conduct a survey of all students who recently completed an economics issues course, asking the number of hours they devoted to study each week and their course grade. The resulting information is shown in Table 1.5. According to the table, students who did not study at all received an *F* in the course. Students studying four hours per week, on average, received a grade of *C* (2.0), and those who studied eight hours per week received a grade of *A* (4.0). In the table, other grades are associated with other amounts of study time.

Let us now use the data in the table to construct Figure 1.8. We will want to show visually how course grades change as study time changes. Study time is the determining factor, the **independent variable,** and it is placed on the horizontal axis of the figure.

Figure 1.8	Study Time–Grade Relationship in an Economics Issues Class

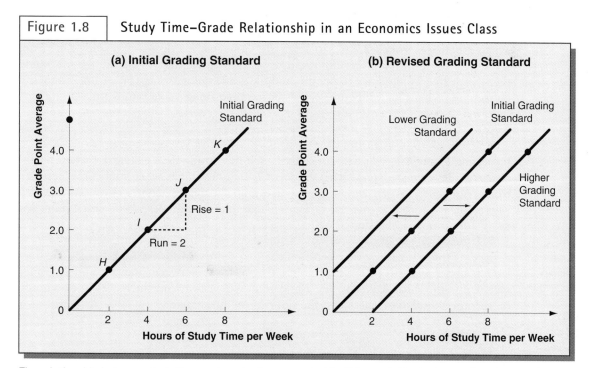

The relationship between study time and grades is represented by this graph. Study time and grades are directly related because their values change in the same direction, resulting in an upward-sloping line. The slope of this straight line is the ratio of the vertical change to the horizontal change between any two points. When factors other than study time are allowed to change, the graph of the relationship between study time and grades will shift to a new location.

The course grade is the **dependent variable**; it depends on study time and is located on the vertical axis.

To plot pairs of study time and grades on a graph, start at the origin, where the axes meet. Count rightward two units on the horizontal axis, then count upward one unit parallel to the vertical axis, and then mark the spot. We've arrived at the point marked *H*, where two hours of study time yield a grade of 1.0 (*D*). To plot the next pair, we go two units rightward from point *H* and then upward one unit, arriving at point *I*, where four hours of study yield a grade of 2.0 (*C*). In similar manner, we can plot all remaining pairs in Table 1.5, as the points *J* and *K*. Once we have plotted the various points describing the relationship between grades and study time, we can connect them with a line (or curve). This line shows how grades are related to the time spent studying. Because the graph is a straight line, we can say that the relationship between study time and grades is *linear*.

The study time–grade line in Figure 1.8(a) slopes *upward* to the right, illustrating a direct (positive) **relationship** between study time and grades. That is, more hours of study time yield higher grades and fewer hours of study time yield lower grades. Alternatively, if higher grades were associated with less study time, the line in the figure would slope *downward* to the right. Here we have an inverse (negative) **relationship** because grades and study time would change in opposite directions.

Movements along Study Time–Grade Line

Referring to Figure 1.8(a), what causes movements from one point to another along the fixed study time–grade line? Such movements are caused by a change in the amount of time devoted to studying economics. Increases in study time result in an upward movement along this line, and decreases in study time result in a downward movement.

To illustrate such movements, as study time increases from four hours to six hours, we slide upward along the study time–grade line from point *I* to point *J*, and the grade point average increases from a 2.0 (*C*) to a 3.0 (*B*). Conversely, a decrease in study time from six hours to four hours would result in a downward movement along the study time–grade line from point *J* to point *I*, and the grade point average falls from 3.0 to 2.0. Put simply, a change in study time causes us to move along a fixed study time–grade line.

Slope of the Study Time–Grade Line

Inspecting Figure 1.8, you will notice that each time study time increases by two hours, course grades increase by one letter grade, or 1.0. For example, when study time increases from two hours to four hours, the course grade increases from 1.0 (*D*) to 2.0 (*C*). Therefore, we conclude that the rate of change in course grades is one grade point for every 2-hour increase in study time.

The **slope** of our study time–grade line between any two points, say *I* and *J*, is defined as the vertical distance between the two points (the "rise") divided by the horizontal distance between the two points (the "run"). Between points *I* and *J*, grades increase on the vertical axis by one grade point when study time increases by two hours on the horizontal axis. Therefore, the slope of the line equals:

$$\text{Slope} = \frac{\text{Vertical change}}{\text{Horizontal change}} = \frac{1}{2} = 0.5$$

Notice that the slope of 0.5 is positive because grades and study time change in the same direction; that is, grades and study time are directly or positively related. The slope of 0.5 indicates that there will be a one grade point increase for every 2-hour increase in study time.

Similarly, it tells us that for every 2-hour decrease in study time there will be a decrease of one grade point. Because each two hours of additional study results in an improvement of one grade point, our graph is a straight line. Put simply, the slope of any straight line remains constant between all points along the line.

Alternatively, if higher grades were associated with less study time, the study time–grade line would slope downward to the right. Therefore, the slope of the line would have a negative value.

Shifts in the Study Time–Grade Line

So far, we have focused on relationships where grades in an economics issues course depend on one other variable, study time. However, we recognize that grades are affected by more factors than just study time, such as the grading standard of the instructor, the academic abilities of students, and the availability of tutors for the course. When grades are affected by both study time and some other variable, changes in that other variable generally induce a *shift* in the study time–grade line. This is because whenever we draw the line between study time and grades, we are holding constant every other variable that might possibly affect grades.

Suppose that the instructor in the economics issues course decided to raise her grading standard, making it more difficult to achieve every other grade than an *F*. To achieve a grade of 2.0 (*C*), a student would now have to study six hours per week instead of only four hours, as shown in Figure 1.8(a). Whereas students could previously receive a grade of 3.0 (*B*) by studying six hours a week, they now must study eight hours to get that grade.

Figure 1.8(b) illustrates the effect of the higher grade standard. In the figure, we have redrawn the study time–grade line from Figure 1.8(a), this time labeling the line *Higher Grading Standard*. Notice that the new line lies to the *right* of the initial line. This means that the underlying relationship between study time and grades has changed: Students now must study a greater amount of time to achieve each grade other than *F*. Alternatively, if the instructor lowered her grading standard, making it easier to achieve course grades, the study time–grade line would shift to the *left*, as shown by the line labeled *Lower Grading Standard*.

Recall that our study time–grade line may shift in response to factors other than changes in grading standards. For example, if academic abilities of students increase, they could grasp economic principles in a shorter period of time, and the line would shift to the left. Similarly, greater availability of qualified tutors would cause the line to shift leftward.

This section used the example of study time and grades in an economics issues class to illustrate several concepts:

- Independent and dependent variables

- Direct and inverse relationships

- Movement along a line

- Slope of a line

- Shifts in a line

Notice that these concepts also apply to economic relationships, such as supply and demand, investment, and consumption, which you will learn about as you read this text. Familiarize yourself with these concepts and be able to apply them to graphs contained in subsequent chapters.

the
Microeconomy

Market Transactions: Demand and Supply Analysis

Chapter objectives

After reading this chapter, you should be able to:

1. Identify the major factors affecting demand.

2. Identify the major factors affecting supply.

3. Explain how prices and quantities are determined in competitive markets.

4. Explain why prices sometimes decrease and sometimes increase.

5. Predict how prices and quantities will respond to changes in demand or supply.

economics IN CONTEXT

For five seasons, baseball superstar Alex Rodriguez was a dynamic player for the Seattle Mariners. Nicknamed A-Rod, he displayed dazzling defense and potent offense. The slugging shortstop, considered by some to be the best player in baseball, was also very gracious to the fans. A-Rod talked to them, autographed their baseball programs, and threw baseballs to them during batting practice. A-Rod even threw a ball to this author, who caught it bare-handed in the upper deck of Safeco Field (not bad, huh?).

Despite A-Rod's overwhelming popularity in Seattle, 2000 was the last year of his contract with the Mariners. Rather than re-signing with the Mariners, A-Rod became a free agent, which meant that he could sell his services to the highest bidder. In 2001, the 25-year-old superstar signed a 10-year megacontract with the Texas Rangers for $252 million. Columnists, gasping at the size of the contract, criticized the Rangers for breaking baseball's bank and setting a course for sports ruin. Officials in the Major League Baseball commissioner's office said that they were stupefied and the sport was in a crisis situation. In 2004, Rodriguez was traded to the New York Yankees.

Why do athletes, such as Alex Rodriguez and Tiger Woods, earn more than the local telephone operator? Demand and supply. Why does a typical medical doctor earn $150,000 or more per year while a primary schoolteacher earns only $30,000? Demand and supply. Why do fresh watermelons cost 20 cents a pound in July and 50 cents a pound in April? You guessed it: Demand and supply. Why did the price of CD players fall from around $800, when they were first introduced in 1983, to less than $200 today? You're right again: Demand and supply. The workings of demand and supply explain many economic questions. Indeed, demand and supply are the most basic and powerful of all the economic tools that you will study in this text.

This chapter introduces demand and supply analysis of market transactions, which shows how prices are determined by the competition among buyers for goods and services offered by competing sellers. Markets play a key role in dealing with the problem of scarcity because they ration the available quantities of goods and services to buyers.

MARKETS

A **market** is a mechanism through which buyers (demanders) and sellers (suppliers) communicate to trade goods and services. Markets exist in many forms. The local farmers' market, espresso stand, grocery store, and barbershop are all familiar markets. Pike Place Market in Seattle, Washington, is famous for its fresh fish, fruits, and vegetables. The New York Stock Exchange is a national market in which buyers and sellers of stocks and bonds communicate with each other. At the international level, major banks such as Chase Manhattan Bank and Fuji Bank trade currencies in the foreign currency market. These markets link potential buyers to potential sellers.

This chapter concerns competitive markets in which many sellers compete for sales to many buyers who are competing with one another for available products. Therefore, each seller has negligible effect on market price because other sellers are supplying similar goods. A seller has no motivation to cut price below the going price, and if she charges a higher price, buyers will purchase products from other suppliers. Similarly, no single buyer can affect the price because each buyer purchases a negligible quantity. To understand how markets operate, we must first understand the principles of demand and supply.

marketing ____,

DEMAND

How many Rolls-Royce automobiles will be bought this year? In explaining buyer behavior, economists emphasize the demand for goods and services. Demand is a schedule that shows various amounts of a good or service a buyer is *willing and able* to purchase at each possible price during a particular period. Just because an individual desires a Rolls-Royce does not necessarily mean that she has a *demand* for it. She also has to be able to pay the $250,000 price for a Rolls-Royce and be willing to purchase it instead of another vehicle such as a Mercedes Benz or BMW.

The amount of a product demanded depends on many factors such as the following:

- Price of the product
- Prices of related products
- Consumer income
- Expectations of future price changes
- Tastes
- Number of consumers

In analyzing the behavior of buyers, we will pay special attention to the relationship between the quantity demanded and the price of a good. To study this relationship, we hold constant all other factors that affect buyer behavior.

It is helpful to distinguish between *individual demand*, which is the demand of a particular buyer, and *market demand*, which is the sum of individual demands of all buyers in the market. In most markets, there are many buyers, sometimes thousands or millions. Unless otherwise noted, when we talk about demand, we will be referring to market demand.

The Demand Curve and the Law of Demand

Figure 2.1(a) shows the market demand schedule for CDs. The first column of the figure shows possible prices for CDs. The second column shows the quantities of CDs demanded per week at different prices, assuming that other determinants that affect buyer behavior remain constant. The data in the demand schedule show that when the price of CDs is $25, consumers demand 1,000 CDs per week. At a price of $20, 2,000 CDs per week are demanded, and so forth.

A market demand curve is a graphical portrayal of the data comprised by a market demand schedule. Figure 2.1(b) shows the weekly demand curve for CDs by plotting the data from the table. Points on the vertical axis represent price, and points on the horizontal axis represent quantity demanded.

Notice that the market demand curve slopes downward, reflecting the **law of demand:** Price and quantity demanded are *inversely* or negatively related, assuming that other factors affecting the quantity demanded remain the same. A higher price results in a decrease in quantity demanded; a lower price results in an increase in quantity demanded. We call the law of demand a "law" because it has widespread application to buyer behavior. When Ford finds itself overstocked with automobiles that it wants to get rid of, what does it do? It typically announces a sale in anticipation that a lower price will encourage buyers to purchase additional Ford automobiles.

The pricing of candy provides an example of the law of demand. Mars, Inc. once conducted a pricing experiment for its M&Ms. Over a 1-year period, the price of a bag of M&Ms was held constant in 150 stores throughout the United States while the content

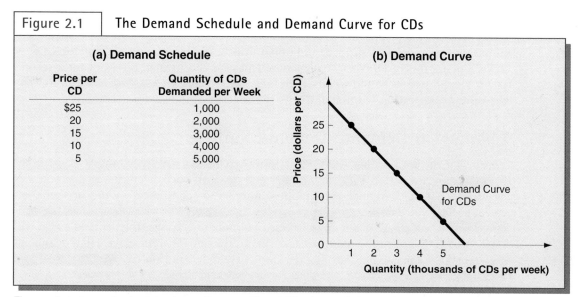

| Figure 2.1 | The Demand Schedule and Demand Curve for CDs |

(a) Demand Schedule

Price per CD	Quantity of CDs Demanded per Week
$25	1,000
20	2,000
15	3,000
10	4,000
5	5,000

(b) Demand Curve

The market demand schedule shows the quantity of CDs demanded at various prices by all consumers. The market demand curve is a graphical portrayal of the data comprised by the market demand schedule. The market demand curve slopes downward, indicating that as price decreases, the quantity demanded increases. This inverse relationship between the change in the price of a good and the change in quantity demanded is known as the law of demand.

weight of the bag was increased. With price kept constant and content weight increased, the price per ounce decreased. In the stores where the price declined, sales soon increased by 20 to 30 percent. As the law of demand predicts, a decrease in the price of M&Ms results in an increase in the quantity demanded.

For a particular demand curve, a change in price results in a movement along the demand curve. In Figure 2.1(b), if the price of CDs falls from $15 to $10, consumption increases from 3,000 to 4,000 CDs per week. We call the movement along the demand curve, which results from a change in price, a **change in quantity demanded**. Notice that a change in quantity demanded is a movement along a particular demand curve rather than a shift in the demand curve.

What Explains the Law of Demand?

For most products, consumers are willing to buy more units at a lower price than at a higher price. This notion of the law of demand appears to be an accurate description of consumer behavior. Economists explain this law in terms of the substitution effect, the income effect, and the law of diminishing marginal utility.

According to the **substitution effect**, when the price of a CD falls, other determinants of demand remaining the same, its price falls relative to the prices of all other like goods, such as audio cassette tapes. Consumers have an incentive to substitute the cheaper good, CDs, for audiocassettes tapes, which are now relatively more expensive. The lower price of CDs thus results in an increase in the quantity demanded.

The **income effect** also explains the law of demand. According to this principle, a decrease in the price of a CD creates an increase in the purchasing power of consumers' money incomes. As a result, consumers can purchase a greater quantity of CDs with a given amount of money income. Generally speaking, the rise in purchasing power provides consumers with the incentive to purchase more of the product. In this manner, a lower price of CDs results in an increase in the quantity demanded.

Finally, there is the principle of **diminishing marginal utility** (satisfaction). According to this principle, as a person consumes additional units of a particular good, each additional unit provides less and less additional utility. We can readily see this for CDs. A buyer's desire for a CD, when she has none, may be very strong; the want for a second CD is less pronounced, and so on. Therefore, additional CDs are "not worth it" unless the price decreases. This notion underlies the concept of the law of demand.

Changes in Demand: Demand Shifters

Recall that the relationship between the price of a good and the quantity of the good demanded over a period depends on other determinants such as consumer tastes, prices of related goods, consumer expectations, number of consumers in the market, and consumer income. For a particular demand curve, we assume that these other determinants remain constant. When any of these determinants change, the demand curve will *shift* either outward to the right or backward to the left. Therefore, we call a change in a variable that can cause a shift in a demand curve a demand shifter. We call a shift in a demand curve, caused by a demand shifter, a change in demand. *as opposed to a qty demanded*

Figure 2.2 shows a change in the demand for CDs. Because of changing determinants of demand, if consumers become willing and able to purchase additional CDs at each possible price, the result will be an *increase* in demand. This is seen in the figure by a *rightward* shift in the demand curve, from *old demand curve* to *new demand curve*. Conversely, if the determinants of demand change to cause consumers to be less willing and able to purchase CDs at each possible price, a *decrease* in demand will occur—the demand curve will shift *leftward*. Let us examine how each demand shifter affects the location of the demand curve.

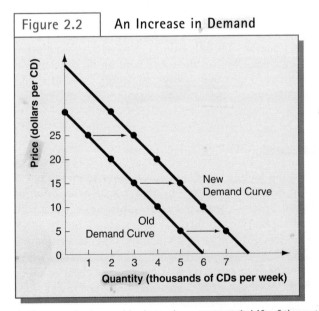

| Figure 2.2 | An Increase in Demand |

An increase in demand is shown by an outward shift of the entire demand curve, indicating that more of the product is demanded at each price. An increase in demand for a product can be caused by:

- A favorable change in consumer tastes
- A rise in incomes if the product is a normal good; a fall in incomes if the product is an inferior good
- An increase in the price of a substitute good; a decrease in the price of a complementary good
- Consumer expectations of higher future prices
- A rise in the number of buyers served by the market

1. **Consumer tastes.** Changing consumer tastes can have important effects on demand. A change in consumer tastes that makes a product more popular will shift the demand curve to the right. For example, as the popularity of country music singer Faith Hill increases, consumers tend to demand more of her CDs. Conversely, if the New York Yankees have a losing season and become less popular with their fans, demand for tickets for their baseball games will shift leftward.

   Improving student tastes energized enrollment at Gonzaga University in the fall semester of 1999. During the National Collegiate Athletic Association's (NCAA) basketball tournament the previous spring, the men's basketball team of Gonzaga received notoriety when it defeated University of Minnesota, Stanford University, and University of Florida; the team ultimately was defeated by the University of Connecticut, which won the NCAA tournament. The national television exposure given to Gonzaga opened the eyes of prospective students from Florida, Maine, Texas, and other distant locations. When they looked at Gonzaga, they saw a high-quality university in the pleasant surroundings of Spokane, Washington. This resulted in a 37-percent increase in applications to Gonzaga. In the fall semester of 1999, freshman enrollment reached a record 703, more than 50 better than any previous year. By 2004, freshman enrollment stood at 907 students. Indeed, the notoriety of the basketball team's on-court success contributed to an increase in the demand for education at Gonzaga.

2. **Number of buyers.** Recall that the market demand is the sum of the individual demands of all consumers in the market. If the number of consumers in the market increases, market demand will shift to the right; a decrease in the number of consumers results in a leftward shift in market demand. In Eugene, Oregon, for example, local merchants are pleased to see student consumers attending the University of Oregon in September; this causes an increase in the demand for their products. When many students return to their homes in other cities over the December holidays, the demand for these products in Eugene decreases.

3. **Consumer income.** College students are well aware that changes in income affect demand. We classify products into two broad categories, depending on how demand for the product responds to changes in income. The demand for **normal goods** *increases* as income *rises* and *falls* as income *decreases.* Most goods, such as ski trips or new cars, are normal goods. People like these goods and will buy more of them as their income rises. In contrast, inferior goods are goods such as public transportation, low-quality clothing, secondhand appliances, less expensive cuts of meat, and low-quality peanut butter. The demand for inferior goods actually *falls* as income *increases;* households will switch away from consuming these inferior goods to consuming normal goods such as new cars and sirloin steak. Conversely, *decreases* in income cause the demand for inferior goods to *increase.*

4. **Prices of related goods.** Changes in the prices of related goods can also affect the demand curve for a particular product. When we draw the demand curve for, say, Pepsi-Cola, we assume that the prices of Coca-Cola and other colas remain constant. Suppose we relaxed this assumption and allowed the price of Coca-Cola to change. If the price of Coca-Cola were to fall suddenly from $5 to $4 per case, there would be an incentive for consumers to switch from Pepsi-Cola to Coca-Cola. After all, Pepsi-Cola and Coca-Cola are substitute goods. For substitute goods, a *reduction* in the price of one good will *decrease* the demand for the other good; conversely, an *increase* in the price of one good will *increase* the demand for the other good.

   A second type of related good is a complementary good. Complementary goods "go together" in that they are used in conjunction with each other. Some examples of complementary goods are CD players and CDs, peanut butter and jelly, hamburgers and french fries, cookies and milk, and spaghetti and meat sauce. If the price of CD players falls, we will buy more CD players and, therefore, we will buy more CDs—so the demand for CDs increases. Conversely, an increase in the price of peanut butter results in a decrease in the quantity of peanut butter demanded and thus a decline in the demand for jelly. For complementary goods, a *decrease* in the price of one good will *increase* the demand for the other good; conversely, an *increase* in the price of one good will *decrease* the demand for the other good.

5. Expected future prices. The demand for gasoline may change merely because people change their expectations about tomorrow's price of gasoline. When Saddam Hussein ordered his Iraqi army to invade Kuwait in 1990, many people expected that oil supplies would be disrupted because of war. The anticipated shortage of gasoline, and the resulting price increase, prompted many people to fill their tanks at each opportunity, thus increasing the demand for gasoline. In this manner, changes in consumer expectations can cause the demand curve for a product to change.

Another example of consumer reaction to expected future prices occurred in 2002 when Oregon smokers purchased cartons of cigarettes by the armload before a 60-cents-per-pack increase in the state tax on cigarettes. The state tax went from 68 cents to $1.28 after voters approved the tax hike by a two-to-one margin. Following the tax hike, a pack-a-day smoker pays $219 more a year, or $467.20, in taxes, for the habit.

CHECK POINT

1. Describe the law of demand and the explanations for the law of demand.

2. Differentiate between a change in quantity demanded and a change in demand, identifying the reason(s) for each. How is each change represented graphically?

3. What factors cause a demand curve to shift? What happens to a demand curve when each of these factors changes?

SUPPLY

The other side of our market model involves quantities of goods and services that sellers would like to offer to the market. Supply is a schedule showing the amounts of a good or service that a firm or household is willing and able to sell at each possible price during a specified period. Supply in economics could refer to the number of ice cream bars a grocery store wants to sell or the number of hours a worker is willing to work.

The quantity of a particular good or service that suppliers plan to sell depends on many factors:

- Price of the good

- Price of resources

- Technology

- Prices of other goods produced

- Expected future prices

- Taxes and subsidies

- Number of suppliers

In analyzing the behavior of suppliers, we will emphasize the relationship between the quantity supplied and the price of a good. Therefore, we will hold constant all other determinants that affect supplier behavior.

It is helpful to distinguish between *individual supply*, which is the supply of a particular seller, and *market supply*, which is the sum of individual supplies of all sellers in the market. Unless otherwise noted, when we talk about supply, we will be referring to market supply.

The Supply Curve and the Law of Supply

Supply shows us the quantity that will be offered for sale at various prices. Supply refers to the schedule that relates price and quantity and thus is called a supply schedule or a supply curve.

Figure 2.3(a) shows a market supply schedule for CDs. The first column of the figure shows possible prices for CDs. The second column shows the quantities of CDs supplied per week at different prices, assuming that other determinants of supply are unchanged. We call this amount the **quantity supplied.** Notice that the quantity supplied refers to a single point on a supply schedule: As price changes, quantity supplied changes, but not the entire supply schedule. The data in our supply schedule show that when the price of CDs is $5, producers supply 1,000 CDs per week. At a price of $10, 2,000 CDs are supplied per week, and so forth.

A market **supply curve** is a graphical portrayal of the data comprised by a market supply schedule. Figure 2.3(b) shows the weekly supply curve for CDs plotted from the data from the table. Points on the vertical axis show price, and points on the horizontal axis show quantity supplied. Notice that the data indicate an *upward-sloping* supply curve that shows a positive or *direct* relationship between price and quantity supplied. As the price of CDs increases, the quantity supplied increases; as price decreases, quantity supplied decreases. We know this relationship as the law of supply. The law of supply states that, in general, sellers are willing and able to make available more of their product at a higher price than a lower price, other determinants of supply being constant.

The tendency for the cost of additional output to increase explains the law of supply—that is, it costs more to produce the second unit of output than the first, more to produce

total cost not unit cost

Figure 2.3	The Supply Schedule and Supply Curve of CDs

(a) Supply Schedule

Price per CD	Quantity of CDs Supplied per Week
$25	5,000
20	4,000
15	3,000
10	2,000
5	1,000

(b) Supply Curve

The market supply schedule shows the quantity of CDs supplied, at various prices, by all sellers. The market supply curve is a graphical portrayal of the data comprised by the market supply schedule. The market supply curve is upward sloping, showing that as price increases, the quantity supplied increases. The direct relationship between the change in the price of a product and the change in the quantity supplied is known as the law of supply.

the third than the second, and so on. To produce more CDs, suppose manufacturers have to hire more labor and purchase additional raw materials. If these resources are in relatively short supply, CD manufacturers may have to pay higher prices to obtain them, which results in higher and higher costs. Other things constant, the only way that CD manufacturers would be induced to produce additional CDs would be when the price of CDs rises. As a result, a higher price calls forth a greater level of output supplied to the market.

Oil Firms Squeeze More Crude from Wells

Does the law of supply pertain to oil production? Yes! Major oil firms, such as Shell and ExxonMobil, realize that, as existing oil wells dry up, producing more oil requires deeper drilling and exploration for new oil fields. Because these activities add to a producer's costs, they require a higher market price. Unless price rises, a firm cannot realize a net gain (profit) from producing more oil. Consider the following example.

From Alaska's North Slope to the Gulf of Mexico, oil producers have invested billions of dollars in *improved oil recovery*—unconventional technology designed to extract additional crude oil from existing wells. Conventional drilling methods tap only about 15 percent of a typical well's potential, leaving 85 percent of the oil still locked in the earth.

Oil firms have long realized that, by introducing substances deep into underground formations, they can wring more crude oil from existing wells. For example, water forced into crevices in subterranean rocks can flush oil out and, because the oil is lighter, push it up a nearby well. Also, steam injected underground helps thin and loosen trapped oil. Moreover, carbon dioxide and natural gas can be used to flush out stubborn oil. Even gravel and walnut shells are blasted into wells, the idea being to create cracks in adjacent rock and draw more oil into wells. Overall, these improved oil recovery techniques can squeeze up to 15 to 26 percent additional oil from a well as compared to what could be extracted by using conventional drilling methods.

Although improved oil recovery techniques can increase the productivity of a well, they are expensive to implement. The cost of enhanced recovery methods varies widely, though most common methods range between $5 and $10 a barrel. In the 1990s, industry analysts estimated that if the market price of oil were $20 a barrel, improved oil recovery would generate an additional 3.3 billion barrels of crude oil. A market price of $28 a barrel would justify more expensive technologies that could result in up to 7.7 billion additional barrels being harvested from wells; at a market price of $32 a barrel, about 10.6 billion more barrels would be available.

By 2005, crude oil was selling at a high enough price (more than $60 a barrel) and did so long enough for oil firms to justify the additional costs of improved oil recovery techniques to extract every barrel possible. The high price of oil especially spurred oil exploration and production in the Gulf of Mexico. Thus, Shell and ExxonMobil announced plans to make additional investments in deep-water projects. ExxonMobil expected that by 2010, deep-water production would account for about 20 percent of its oil output.

Changes in Supply: Supply Shifters

price doesn't move a supply or demand curve

Recall that a supply curve refers to the entire relationship between the quantity supplied of a product and its price, other determinants of supply remaining unchanged. When these other determinants change, the supply curve will *shift* either outward to the right or backward to the left. Therefore, we call a change in a variable that can shift the supply curve a **supply shifter**. A shift in a supply curve, induced by a supply shifter, is called a **change in supply**.

Figure 2.4 shows a change in the supply of CDs. Because of changing determinants of supply, if producers become willing and able to supply additional CDs at each possible

Figure 2.4 | An Increase in Supply

An increase in supply is shown by a rightward shift of the entire supply curve, showing that more CDs are supplied at each price. An increase in supply of a good can be caused by:

- A decrease in the price of resources used to produce a good
- New technologies that reduce the cost of producing a good
- Expectations of future falling prices of a good may cause sellers to increase their current supply to the market
- A decrease in an excise tax on the sale of a good
- An increase in subsidies to producers of a good

price, the result will be an *increase* in supply. This is seen in the figure by a *rightward* shift in the supply curve, from *old supply curve* to *new supply curve*. However, if the determinants of supply change to cause suppliers to be less willing and able to supply CDs at each possible price, a *decrease* in supply will occur—the supply curve will shift to the *left*. Let us examine how each supply shifter affects the location of the supply curve.

1. **Resource prices.** The possible profit at a particular price depends on the prices a supplier must pay for resources to produce a good or service. For example, a *decrease* in the prices of labor and materials used to produce CDs decreases the cost of producing CDs, resulting in a greater profit for selling a particular quantity. This *increases* the supply of CDs. Conversely, increases in resource prices result in falling profitability and a decrease in supply.

2. **Technology.** *Improvements* in technology tend to reduce the amount of resources needed to produce a given level of output, resulting in lower costs of production and increased supply. For example, the development of a new technology by Texas Instruments has reduced the cost of producing calculators and increased their supply.

3. **Prices of other goods.** If a DaimlerChrysler[1] assembly line can manufacture minivans or pickup trucks, the quantity of minivans manufactured depends on the price of trucks, and the quantity of trucks manufactured depends on the price of minivans. Given the price of minivans, a decline

---

[1] In 1999, Chrysler Corporation of the United States and Daimler-Benz of Germany merged and became DaimlerChrysler. Throughout this text, we will refer to Chrysler Corporation as DaimlerChrysler.

in the price of trucks signals to DaimlerChrysler that switching to minivans with a higher relative price yields higher profit. The result is an increase in the supply of minivans.

4. **Expected future prices.** Expectations affect the current output of producers. For example, the 1990 invasion of Iraq into Kuwait resulted in oil companies anticipating that oil prices would increase significantly. Their initial response was to withhold part of their oil from the market so that they could realize larger profits later when oil prices increased. Such a response shifted the supply curve for oil to the left.

5. **Taxes and subsidies.** Certain taxes, like excise taxes, have the same impact on supply as an increase in the price of resources. The effect of an excise tax placed on the sale of gasoline imposes an additional cost on gas stations, and the supply curve shifts to the left. Conversely, subsidies are the opposite of taxes. When the state of Washington financed most of the construction cost of a new stadium for the Seattle Seahawks football team, it, in effect, lowered the cost of Seahawk football games and increased their supply.

6. **Number of suppliers.** Because market supply is the sum of the amounts supplied by all sellers, it depends on the number of sellers in the market. If the number of sellers increases, supply will shift to the right. For example, in 2000, the National Hockey League expanded its membership to include Minneapolis/St. Paul, thus shifting the market supply curve outward to the right.

CHECK POINT

1. Describe the law of supply and what causes the supply curve to normally slope upward.

2. Distinguish between a change in quantity supplied and a change in supply, identifying the reason(s) for each.

3. What factors cause a supply curve to shift? What happens to a supply curve when each of these factors changes?

DEMAND, SUPPLY, AND EQUILIBRIUM

Buyers and sellers have different views of product price because buyers *pay* the price and sellers *receive* it. Therefore, a higher price is favorable for a seller but is unfavorable for a buyer. As price increases, sellers increase their quantity supplied while buyers decrease their quantity demanded. Through the interaction of demand and supply, we can find a price at which the quantity buyers want to purchase equals the quantity that sellers will offer for sale.

 Market equilibrium occurs when the price of a product adjusts so that the quantity that consumers will purchase at that price is identical to the quantity that suppliers will sell. At the point of market equilibrium, the forces of demand and supply balance so that there is no tendency for the market price to change over a given period.

Figure 2.5 combines the demand and supply curves introduced in Figures 2.1 and 2.3. Referring to Figure 2.5(a), notice that the two curves intersect at a price of $15 per CD. At this price, the quantity buyers want to purchase (3,000 CDs) equals the quantity sellers wish to offer for sale (3,000 CDs). The market for CDs is therefore in equilibrium, implying that there is no tendency for price to change unless the demand or supply curves shift. The price that sets buyers' intentions equal to sellers' intentions is called the **equilibrium price**. Notice that the equilibrium price acts to ration CDs so that everyone who

Figure 2.5 | Equilibrium in the CD Market

(a) Market Equilibrium

(b) Eliminating Surpluses and Shortages

The demand and supply schedules represent the market for CDs. The intersection of the market supply curve and market demand curve indicates an equilibrium price of $15 and an equilibrium quantity of 3,000 CDs bought and sold per week. Any price above $15 will result in a weekly surplus of CDs, and pressure exists to push the price downward. Similarly, any price below $15 will result in a weekly shortage of CDs, and pressure exists to push the price upward. By influencing the quantities supplied and demanded, adjustments in price serve to promote market equilibrium.

wants to purchase the product will find it available, and everyone who wants to sell the product can do so successfully.

If the market does not initially establish the equilibrium price, competition among suppliers to sell the product and competition among buyers to purchase the product will cause price to move to the equilibrium level. Figure 2.5(b) shows the same supply and demand curves we have examined in Figure 2.5(a), but this time the initial price is $25 per CD. At this price, we refer to the supply curve and find that suppliers are willing to sell 5,000 CDs per week; referring to the demand curve, we find that buyers are willing to purchase 1,000 CDs per week. The amount by which quantity supplied exceeds quantity demanded, 4,000 CDs, is called a **surplus,** or excess supply. The surplus in the market will not be permanent. To clear the market of their unsold CDs, sellers will reduce the price. The price reduction results in a decrease in quantity supplied and an increase in quantity demanded, serving to eliminate the surplus. The weekly surplus in the CD market will be eliminated when price falls to $15, at which the supply and demand curves intersect.

Just as a price above the equilibrium price results in a surplus, a price below the equilibrium price will entail a shortage. Referring to Figure 2.5(b), suppose the initial price is $5 per CD. At this price, we refer to the supply curve and find that the quantity supplied is 1,000 CDs per week; referring to the demand curve, we find that the quantity demanded is 5,000 CDs per week. The amount by which quantity demanded exceeds quantity supplied, 4,000 CDs, is called a **shortage,** or excess demand. With the shortage, competitive bidding by buyers serves to push the price upward. A rising price causes an increase in the quantity supplied and a decrease in quantity demanded until the equilibrium price is restored at $15 per CD.

We have seen how adjustments in price coordinate the decisions of buyers and sellers. If the price is above the equilibrium level, excess supply sets in motion forces to cause price and quantity to return to their equilibrium levels. If price is below the equilibrium level, excess demand results in forces to cause price and quantity to return to their equilibrium levels. By regulating quantities supplied and demanded, adjustments in price serve to promote market equilibrium.

SHIFTS IN DEMAND AND SUPPLY

Market equilibrium is the combination of price and quantity at which the plans of sellers and buyers synchronize. Once a market attains equilibrium, that combination of price and quantity will remain unchanged unless a shifter (determinant) of supply or demand changes. A change in a determinant will cause a shift in the supply curve or demand curve; the result will be a change in the equilibrium price and quantity.

Figure 2.6 illustrates the effects of changes in the demand and supply of CDs. In the four cases illustrated, the original equilibrium occurs at the intersection of market supply curve (S_0) and market demand curve (D_0). At the equilibrium price of $15 for each CD, 3,000 units are demanded and supplied per week.

First, let us consider the effects of a change in demand, assuming that supply is constant. Referring to Figure 2.6(a), suppose that rising popularity of CDs results in an *increase* in market demand from D_0 to D_1. When demand increases, the price that makes the quantity demanded equal the quantity supplied is $20 per CD. At this price, 4,000 CDs are bought and sold each week. Therefore, an increase in demand for a product causes both its equilibrium price and equilibrium quantity to increase.

Conversely, suppose that declining popularity for CDs results in a *decrease* in market demand from D_0 to D_1 as seen in Figure 2.6(b). Because of the decrease in demand, the equilibrium price falls to $10 per CD, and the equilibrium quantity declines to 2,000 CDs per week. Therefore, a decrease in the demand for a product causes both its equilibrium price and equilibrium quantity to fall.

Let us now consider the effects of a change in supply, assuming that demand is constant. Referring to Figure 2.6(c), assume new cost-saving technologies are introduced in CD manufacturing plants, resulting in the market supply of CDs increasing from S_0 to S_1. Following the increase in supply, the new equilibrium price is $10 per CD, and the equilibrium quantity is 4,000 units. Therefore, an increase in supply causes equilibrium price to fall but equilibrium quantity to increase.

Finally, suppose that rising wages result in the market supply of CDs shifting from S_0 to S_1 in Figure 2.6(d). With the new market supply curve, the equilibrium price is $20 per CD, and the equilibrium quantity is 2,000 units. Therefore, when supply decreases, the equilibrium quantity declines, and the equilibrium price rises.

We can now make the following predictions, other factors remaining constant:

- When demand increases, both the equilibrium price and the equilibrium quantity increase.

- When demand decreases, both the equilibrium price and the equilibrium quantity decrease.

- When supply increases, the equilibrium price falls and the equilibrium quantity rises.

- When supply decreases, the equilibrium price rises and the equilibrium quantity falls.

In each of the preceding examples of how equilibrium price and quantity are affected by changes in supply or demand, only one side of the market changed while the other side remained constant. In reality, however, more complicated changes involving changes in both demand and supply might occur. For example, both the demand and supply of natural gas might decrease at the same time. Although simultaneous changes in demand and supply are not illustrated in this chapter, try applying your graphing skills to the examples in Table 2.1. See if you can verify the conclusions of each example.

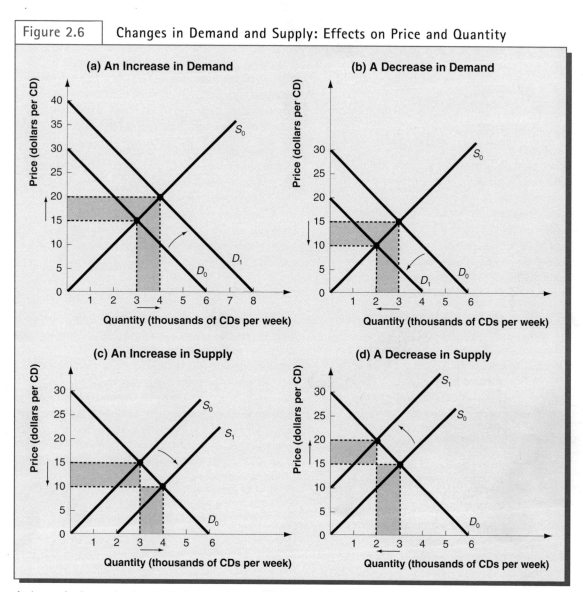

| Figure 2.6 | Changes in Demand and Supply: Effects on Price and Quantity |

A change in demand or in supply changes the equilibrium price and quantity in the market. Panels (a) and (b) show the effects of an increase and decrease in demand; panels (c) and (d) show the effects of an increase and decrease in supply.

| Table 2.1 | Impacts of Changes in Both Demand and Supply |

Change in Demand	Change in Supply	Impact on Equilibrium Price	Impact on Equilibrium Quantity
1. decrease	decrease	indeterminate*	decrease
2. increase	increase	indeterminate*	increase
3. decrease	increase	decrease	indeterminate*
4. increase	decrease	increase	indeterminate*

*Indeterminate suggests that price (quantity) might increase, decrease, or stay the same.

economics
IN ACTION

Rush-Hour Horrors: Congestion Pricing

Traffic jams. Most of us have endured them and perhaps even said a few choice words while sitting in them. Longer commutes not only cost time, but money, too. Congestion means reduced fuel efficiency and more wear and tear on vehicles and roads. We build new roads, but we often end up with congestion, as more people choose driving over other modes of transportation. We could build new mass transit systems, but getting people to use existing ones is tough enough. What else is there to do?

Economists realize that this dilemma is typical of most economic problems—like determining how much an acre of land is worth—and thus has a similar solution, namely, market forces. Like acres of land, roads are a scarce resource, which our market system effectively divvies up through prices. And prices act to clear away market imbalances between supply and demand.

Congestion occurs when too many drivers want to use the roads, which have fixed capacity, at the same time because their price is too low. Raising the price, which is now essentially zero, would reduce the quantity demanded and better allocate the limited space.

Governments usually provide roads through tax dollars, which are used to pay for their construction and maintenance. Thus, drivers believe they are already paying their way for road and highway usage through gas taxes and licensing fees. What drivers are actually paying for, however, is their direct use of roads. When a person chooses to drive,

that person's activity adds an additional car to the traffic flow, which slows the commute cost for all drivers. This additional cost, which occurs solely because one extra person chooses to drive, is a "social" cost of driving and is not usually paid for through taxes or fees.

Many economists argue that drivers should be assessed tolls to reduce the amount of rush-hour traffic. Under this system, a person driving during rush hour would have to pay a toll. This would force a driver to decide if she is willing to pay the price or find an alternative. Electronic metering devices, which read signals from small, prepaid transponders inside cars, are currently available. These devices not only keep traffic moving but can also automatically raise or lower tolls at different times of the day.

In response to tolls, some drivers might carpool, change their schedules, or commute via mass transit to either pay lower tolls or avoid paying them at all. These drivers, now aware of the true cost of their commutes, would alter their habits because this higher cost would be greater than the price they would be willing to pay to drive to work alone during rush hour. In time, then, the real demand for roads and highways would be revealed, promoting better infrastructure decisions and better use of pavement, time, and money.

The use of price rationing for road use has been used in Singapore, which has greatly reduced rush-hour traffic jams. In conjunction with other measures to control traffic, tolls have helped reduce traffic in central Singapore by 45 percent during peak hours. However, adverse side effects also occurred. For example, just outside the central business district, traffic jams worsened as motorists traveled on routes they could drive on without paying.

CHECK POINT

1. Explain how the forces of supply and demand push the price toward equilibrium.

2. Draw a diagram that shows how shortages cause price to rise toward equilibrium and surpluses cause price to fall toward equilibrium.

3. What happens to equilibrium price and quantity in a competitive market in each of the following cases: (a) Supply increases. (b) Supply decreases. (c) Demand increases. (d) Demand decreases.

CONTEMPORARY APPLICATIONS OF SUPPLY AND DEMAND

Now that we have learned about the effects of changes in demand and supply, let us apply our principles to some real-world situations. Consider the following applications.

U.S. Steel Makers Rebound as Economy Strengthens and Dollar Weakens

In response to pressures from surging imports, in the late 1990s, Nucor Corporation of Charlotte, North Carolina, notified customers of price cuts for its most important steel products, slashing prices to their lowest levels in six years. These reductions amounted to $20 a ton for cold-rolled, hot-rolled, and galvanized steel. For hot-rolled steel, the $20-per-ton reduction amounted to a decrease of 7 percent to $270 a ton. In 1997, a ton of hot-rolled steel had sold for $300 a ton.

In the months prior to the price cuts, steel from Russia, Japan, Brazil, and other countries arrived on the U.S. market in record amounts, and much of it was offered at prices 20 percent below the prevailing U.S. market prices. Foreign steel stacked up on U.S. docks, on ships, and in warehouses, causing U.S. steel makers to fear that they could be wiped out by foreign competition. As U.S. consumers switched to cheaper foreign steel, U.S. steel makers cut their prices in an attempt to preserve their sales.

What triggered the rush of foreign steel into the United States? One factor was declining foreign demand for steel. In 1998, for example, sluggish economies resulted in declining orders for steel in Russia and Japan. To keep their factories running, Russian and Japanese steel makers turned to a vibrant U.S. market and flooded it with cheap steel. Another factor was the decline in the exchange value of the Russian ruble and Japanese yen. As the economies of Russia and Japan weakened in 1998, the value of their currencies declined against the dollar. This meant that Russian and Japanese steel was cheaper for Americans, in terms of dollars. As a result, American consumers switched from U.S.-made steel to steel produced by the Russians and Japanese.

This bleak situation confronting U.S. steel makers changed by 2004. They realized increases in sales and earnings due to increased demand for their products and also increases in base prices. A stronger U.S. economy contributed to rising sales by U.S. steel makers. Also, a weaker dollar in terms of foreign currencies made U.S. steel cheaper abroad, while imported steel became more expensive in the United States. These factors resulted in increased sales of U.S.-made steel, allowing them to return to profitability.

Analysis   Referring to Figure 2.7, suppose that American consumers consider U.S. and Russian steel to be substitute goods. As Russian steel makers cut the price, Americans demand greater quantities of Russian steel. Therefore, the demand curve for U.S.-made steel decreases from D_0 to D_1. Given the existing U.S. supply curve of steel, this leftward shift in demand suggests that less U.S.-made steel will be purchased and that its price will also decrease. With the passage of time, market forces reverse themselves. A stronger U.S. economy and a weaker dollar cause the demand curve for U.S.-made steel to shift from D_1 toward D_0, resulting in higher prices and increased earnings for U.S. steel makers.

"That's easy," you may be saying as you read the previous example, which showed you how to apply the principles of supply and demand to a contemporary issue. Can you conduct economic analysis on your own? As you read the following applications, be sure that you can draw supply and demand graphs and use them to explain the effects of changing market conditions. Can you differentiate between the demand shifters and supply shifters in these applications?

Figure 2.7 | U.S. Steel Market

Tons of U.S.–Made Steel (thousands)

Consumers Fume as Gasoline Prices Heat Up

After years of cheap and plentiful energy, prices were jumping at the turn of the century. From 1999 to 2005, the price of oil jumped from about $15 to more than $60 a barrel, and gasoline climbed to more than $2.50 a gallon throughout much of the nation. Indeed, motorists fumed over the escalation of gasoline prices.

Much of the same situation existed in the early 1970s, when the oil-producing nations of the Middle East moved to curtail supplies and hike prices. But that decade's energy crunch led to a period in the early 1980s when Americans began to think in terms of conservation, not consumption. The change yielded phenomenal results. From 1973 to 1986, U.S. energy consumption was constant, even though national output increased 43 percent. Also, by 1988, cars were getting an average of 26 miles per gallon (mpg), versus only about 15 mpg before the crunch. Consumers benefited twice from this new policy of conservation. They didn't need to buy as much gasoline, and they paid less per gallon of gas.

But once prices tumbled, consumers stopped caring about how much energy they used. The demand for gasoline soared, there were more vehicles on the road than ever before, and people were driving them more than ever. Also, people were buying bigger, heavier cars, minivans, and sports-utility vehicles and getting commensurately lousy gas mileage. Moreover, people insisted on driving the highways at 70 to 80 mph, paying a 10-percent to 15-percent penalty in gas mileage over, say, 55 mph. Having abandoned its brief flirtation with conservation in the 1980s, the United States found itself vulnerable to energy shortfalls and escalating prices. During the 1990s, U.S. energy demand rose by 15 percent, and the result was the tripling of oil prices at the turn of the century.

Rising crude prices also pushed up the cost of gasoline in other countries. Table 2.2 shows retail prices of a gallon of unleaded premium gasoline in August 2005. Notice that the price of a gallon in The Netherlands was about two and one half times as much as in the United States, and that taxes accounted for 63 percent of the price. Compared to the United States, many other countries rely more on taxes as a way of encouraging the conservation of energy.

To offset rising oil prices, the United States would have to increase the supply and/or decrease demand one of the following ways:

- Raising the fuel economy standards mandated by the federal government. Analysts estimated that if the gas mileage of new cars had increased by only one mile per gallon each year since

Table 2.2	Retail Price of Premium Gasoline, August 2005 (U.S. dollars per gallon)			
Country	Retail Price (excluding tax)	Tax	Retail Price (including tax)	Tax as a Percent of Total Retail Price
United Kingdom	$1.97	$4.09	$6.06	67%
Germany	2.12	3.89	6.01	65
France	1.97	3.68	5.65	65
Belgium	2.10	3.79	5.89	64
The Netherlands	2.46	4.16	6.62	63
Italy	2.22	3.61	5.83	62
United States	2.17	0.39	2.56	15

Source: Energy Information Administration, available at http://www.eia.doe.gov/. Scroll to "By Geography, " to "International," to "Petroleum," to "Prices," and to "Weekly Retail Premium Gasoline Prices: Selected Countries."

1987, and the mileage of light trucks by a half-mile per gallon, the United States would be saving 1.3 million barrels of oil each day. However, increasing fuel economy standards would meet resistance from auto producers, who would see their production costs increasing because of this policy.

- Increasing the federal excise tax on gasoline from the existing 35 cents per gallon to, say, $4 per gallon. Although the resulting hike in the price of gasoline would provide an incentive for consumers to conserve, this would conflict with the preference of Americans for low-priced gasoline. Moreover, rising gasoline prices would especially harm low-income consumers with the least ability to pay.

- Allowing oil companies to drill on federal land designated as wilderness in Alaska, where there is a good chance they might find oil. Perhaps, but what happens when the wilderness is destroyed, never to return? Who pays for that?

- Pressuring the Middle East nations to increase the supply of oil. However, if boosting the supply of foreign oil is one way to ease energy shortages, it also makes the U.S. economy more vulnerable to outside politics.

Achieving these measures involves difficult choices for Americans. This is why forming an energy policy for the United States is very difficult.

Nurse Shortage: A Bitter Pill for Patients

Professional nursing was born of a shortage.[2] The lack of medical personnel on the front lines of the Crimean War in the 1850s meant that British casualties were three times as likely to have died from hospital-born diseases as from battle wounds. Through their efforts at nutrition and personalized care, Florence Nightingale and her cadre of nurses reduced the mortality rate in British military hospitals from 42 percent to just over 2 percent.

Nurses are just as critical to our health now as they were during the Crimean War, but we still don't have enough of them. In 2004, the American Hospital Association estimated that in the nation's hospitals, 126,000 registered nurse (RN) positions—11 percent of the

---

[2] Carrie Conaway, "Diagnosis: Shortage," *Regional Review*, Third Quarter, 2001, Federal Reserve Bank of Boston.

total—were vacant. Though hospitals account for 60 percent of RN employment, the lack of nurses extended to nursing homes and doctors' offices. Simply put, the number of nurses is increasing every year, but not quickly enough to keep up with the growing demand for their services. The culprits are both long-term trends, such as expanded opportunities for working women, and factors like the effects of the cost-cutting imperative of managed care.

As recently as 30 years ago, there were plenty of nurses: Women chose nursing in record numbers. Since then, falling birth rates meant that the number of people available to go into nursing each year has decreased. At the same time, the proportion of women choosing nursing as a career has also declined. The combination of declining birth rates and smaller proportions of people entering nursing careers means that each year we produce only half the number of RNs we did 30 years ago, even though the U.S. population is nearly 40 percent larger today. New RNs are not being created fast enough to replace retirees.

Cost-cutting measures by hospitals have also contributed to the nursing shortage. In the mid-1990s, hospitals were in a quandary. They needed more RNs to take care of an increasingly older and sicker patient load. But nurses were also their biggest expense. When the dust cleared, 38,000 nurses had lost their jobs.

At least part of the shortage would be eliminated if wages and working conditions for nurses were appealing enough to attract more people to the profession. However, it's not just wages and working conditions that keep people out of nursing; it's also the public image of what nurses do. Nurses complain that they are often not portrayed as bright, articulate, or innovative, or as working independently and functioning at a high level. Men in particular seem to find the nursing image unappealing.

Enticing more people into nursing will be a challenge. Nonetheless, some organizations are tackling the issue. For instance, schools, employers, and the government are working to increase the supply of RNs by offering scholarships, developing new training programs, and educating people about nursing careers. But will these efforts be enough?

In this chapter, we examined demand and supply analysis of market transactions. The next chapter broadens our understanding of demand and supply by considering contemporary applications of these principles.

Chapter Summary

1. A market is a mechanism through which buyers and sellers communicate to trade goods and services. Through the price system, markets link potential buyers to potential sellers.

2. Demand is a schedule that shows various amounts of a good or service buyers are willing and able to purchase at each possible price during a particular period. A demand curve is a graphical portrayal of the data comprised by a demand schedule. A movement along a demand curve, resulting from a change in price, is called a change in quantity demanded.

3. According to the law of demand, price and quantity demanded are inversely related, assuming the other factors affecting the quantity demanded remain the same. Economists explain the law of demand in terms of the substitution effect, the income effect, and the principle of diminishing marginal utility.

4. A demand shifter is a variable that causes a shift in a demand curve. Among the most important demand shifters are consumer tastes, number of buyers, consumer income, prices of related goods, and expected future prices. When a demand shifter causes an increase in demand, the demand curve shifts rightward; a decrease in demand is shown by a leftward shift in the demand curve.

5. Supply is a schedule or curve showing the amounts of a good or service that firms or house-holds are willing and able to sell at various prices during a specified period. The quantity supplied refers to a single point on a supply curve. Changes in quantity supplied are caused by changes in the price of the product.

6. According to the law of supply, sellers are willing and able to make available more of their product at a higher price than a lower price, other determinants of supply being constant. The tendency for the cost of additional output to increase explains the law of supply.

7. A supply shifter is a variable that causes a shift in a supply curve. Among the major supply shifters are resource prices, technology, prices of other goods, expected future prices, taxes and subsidies, and the number of suppliers. When a supply shifter results in an increase in supply, the supply curve shifts rightward; a decrease in supply is shown as a leftward shift in the supply curve.

8. In a competitive market, equilibrium occurs when the price of a product adjusts so that the quantity that consumers will purchase at that price is identical to the quantity that suppliers will sell. The price that sets buyers' intentions equal to sellers' intentions is called the equilibrium price. A surplus of a product results in price falling to its equilibrium level; a shortage of a product results in price rising to its equilibrium level.

9. Concerning shifts in the demand curve or supply curve, we can make the following predictions, other factors remaining constant:

   - When demand increases, both the equilibrium price and the equilibrium quantity increase.

   - When demand decreases, both the equilibrium price and the equilibrium quantity decrease.

   - When supply increases, equilibrium price falls and equilibrium quantity rises.

   - When supply decreases, equilibrium price rises and equilibrium quantity falls.

Key Terms and Concepts

market (31)

demand (32)

demand curve (32)

law of demand (32)

change in quantity demanded (33)

substitution effect (33)

income effect (33)

diminishing marginal utility (34)

demand shifter (34)

change in demand (34)

normal good (35)

inferior good (35)

substitute good (35)

complementary good (35)

supply (36)

quantity supplied (37)

supply curve (37)

law of supply (37)

supply shifter (38)

change in supply (38)

market equilibrium (40)

equilibrium price (40)

surplus (41)

shortage (41)

Self-Test: Multiple-Choice Questions

1. At the market equilibrium price, the quantity

   a. supplied just equals the quantity demanded.
   b. supplied exceeds the quantity demanded by the maximum amount.
   c. demanded exceeds the quantity supplied by the maximum amount.
   d. supplied and the quantity demanded equal zero.

2. If the price of automobiles increases, it is likely that fewer automobile batteries will be purchased at any given price because automobiles and batteries are

   a. inferior goods.
   b. normal goods.
   c. substitute goods.
   d. complementary goods.

3. Suppose an increase in their incomes induces consumers to purchase more oranges at any given price. Also suppose that an abundant orange harvest results in a lower price, causing consumers to purchase more oranges. These situations are respectively characterized by a(n)

   a. increase in quantity demanded—decrease in demand.
   b. decrease in quantity demanded—increase in demand.
   c. increase in demand—increase in quantity demanded.
   d. decrease in demand—increase in quantity demanded.

4. A decrease in the price of calculators accompanied by an increase in the quantity sold would result from a(n)

   a. decrease in demand.
   b. increase in demand.
   c. decrease in supply.
   d. increase in supply.

5. An increase in income will

   a. increase the demand for inferior goods and decrease the demand for normal goods.
   b. increase the demand for normal goods and decrease the demand for inferior goods.
   c. increase the demand for inferior goods and leave the demand for normal goods unchanged.
   d. increase the demand for normal goods and leave the demand for inferior goods unchanged.

6. If the market price is below the equilibrium price, the

   a. price will increase, quantity demanded will increase, and quantity supplied will decrease.
   b. price will increase, quantity demanded will decrease, and quantity supplied will increase.
   c. price will decrease, quantity demanded will increase, and quantity supplied will decrease.
   d. price will decrease, quantity demanded will decrease, and quantity supplied will increase.

7. The supply curve of gasoline will shift rightward in response to all of the following *except*

   a. an increase in the availability of crude oil used in gasoline production.
   b. seller expectations of the development of gasoline-conserving automobiles.
   c. technological improvements in the production of gasoline.
   d. lower prices of labor and capital used in gasoline production.

8. Over a period of time, suppose the quantity sold of grapefruit increases and the price also increases. This could be caused by a(n)

   a. increase in the supply of grapefruit.
   b. decrease in the supply of grapefruit.

    c. increase in the demand for grapefruit.

    d. decrease in the demand for grapefruit.

9. As the price of a good increases, consumers tend to switch their purchases toward substitutes and away from this good. This explains why the demand curve for this good

    a. is vertical.

    b. is horizontal.

    c. slopes upward to the left.

    d. slopes downward to the right.

10. A shortage of corn occurs when

    a. the quantity of corn demanded exceeds the quantity supplied.

    b. the quantity of corn supplied exceeds the quantity demanded.

    c. corn production is higher this year than last year.

    d. corn production is lower this year than last year.

Answers to Multiple-Choice Questions

1. a   2. d   3. c   4. d   5. b   6. b   7. b   8. c   9. d   10. a

Study Questions and Problems

1. When personal computers were first introduced in the 1980s, their price exceeded $5,000. Since then, the price has decreased dramatically. Use supply and demand analysis to explain the price reduction of computers. What effect did the price reduction have on the quantity of computers demanded?

2. By the 1970s, postwar baby boomers reached working age, and it became more acceptable for married women with children to work outside the home. Using supply and demand analysis, explain how the increase in female workers likely affected the equilibrium wage and employment.

3. Suppose a decrease in the demand for the Boeing 777 jetliner results in a sharp decline in the demand for Boeing engineers. Use supply and demand analysis to explain the impact on salaries paid to engineers and on the amount of their labor supplied.

4. A severe frost in 1994 destroyed about 25 percent of Brazil's coffee crop. Using supply and demand analysis, explain the impact of the frost on the price of coffee and the quantity of coffee demanded.

5. The tastes of many U.S. consumers have shifted away from beef and toward chicken. Using supply and demand analysis, explain how this change affects equilibrium price and quantity in the markets for chicken and beef.

6. Suppose that the implementation of the North American Free Trade Agreement (NAFTA) permits low-cost shirts, manufactured in Mexico, to enter the shirt market of the United States. Draw a graph showing the likely effects of their entry on the price and quantity of shirts supplied by U.S. firms.

7. Which of the following goods are likely to be classified as normal goods or services?

    a. Snow skiing

    b. Foreign travel

    c. Lima beans

    d. Computers

    e. Used cars

8. Which of the following goods are likely to be classified as substitute goods? Complementary goods?

   a. Cookies and milk
   b. Pizza Hut pizza and Domino's pizza
   c. Automobiles and batteries
   d. E-mail and first-class mail
   e. Wheaties and Cheerios

9. Assume that one of the following events occurs. How will each event affect the quantity demanded or demand curve for gasoline?

   a. The market population decreases.
   b. The price of gasoline falls.
   c. Buyers' incomes decrease.
   d. Buyers expect that the price of gasoline will fall in the future.
   e. The price of automobiles increases.
   f. The price of gasoline rises.

10. Assume that one of the following events occurs. How will each event affect the quantity supplied or supply curve of audio cassettes?

    a. The price of audio cassettes increases.
    b. The price of resources used to produce audio cassettes increases.
    c. Manufacturers expect that the price of audio cassettes will fall in the future.
    d. New cost-saving technologies are developed to manufacture audio cassettes.
    e. The number of audio cassette manufacturers increases.
    f. The price of audio cassettes decreases.

11. Construct a market demand curve and market supply curve for computers based on the data in Table 2.3.

    a. What is the equilibrium price and the equilibrium quantity of computers?
    b. Find the price at which there would be a surplus of 40 computers and plot it on your diagram. How would the forces of supply and demand push the price back to equilibrium?
    c. Find the price at which there would be a shortage of 60 computers and plot it on your diagram. How would the forces of supply and demand push the price back to equilibrium?

Table 2.3	Supply and Demand Schedules of Computers	
Price	Quantity Demanded per Week	Quantity Supplied per Week
$ 400	90	10
800	80	20
1,200	70	30
1,600	60	40
2,000	50	50
2,400	40	60
2,800	30	70
3,200	20	80

d. Suppose that new cost-saving technologies result in manufacturers supplying 20 additional computers at each price. Construct a new supply curve to show this situation. What is the new equilibrium price of computers and the new equilibrium quantity?

e. Suppose instead that rising prices of resources used to produce computers result in manufacturers supplying 20 fewer computers at each price. Construct a new supply curve to show this situation. What is the new equilibrium price of computers and the new equilibrium quantity?

f. Suppose instead that rising incomes cause buyers to demand 20 additional computers at each price. Construct a new demand curve to show this situation. What will be the new equilibrium price of computers and the new equilibrium quantity?

g. Suppose instead that worsening preferences cause buyers to demand 20 fewer computers at each price. Construct a new demand curve to show this situation. What will be the new equilibrium price of computers and the new equilibrium quantity?

Demand and Supply Applications

Chapter objectives

After reading this chapter, you should be able to:

1. Explain the relationship between the responsiveness of quantity demanded to a change in price.

2. Describe the manner in which a firm's total revenue is influenced by price changes.

3. Assess the advantages and disadvantages of governmental price ceilings and price supports on individual markets.

4. Explain why health care is so expensive for Americans.

economics IN CONTEXT

Economists have long maintained that, "there is no such thing as a free lunch." Even if the lunch is on the house, someone has to pay for the resources used to grow, prepare, and serve the food.

Although residents of the state of California are among the richest in the nation, they have demanded cheap electricity, low rents, and free college. To obtain them, they have elected government officials who ignore the laws of demand and supply and keep prices low, below market equilibrium levels. By 2001, however, Californians were paying the price for this defiance in the form of shortages of electricity, which resulted in shut-down businesses and darkened homes.

Government officials in California have traditionally attempted to ensure cheap electricity for state residents by mandating price ceilings on the retail price. Yet in 2001, a robust economy and unseasonably cold weather resulted in the demand for electricity rising faster than supply could respond. California's utility companies thus had to purchase power from out-of-state utilities at very high prices and then sell it to consumers at the low, state-controlled prices. Without the price ceiling, the shortage of electricity would have caused power prices to rise until supply and demand came into balance. Businesses and households would voluntarily respond to the higher prices by reorganizing production, turning down thermostats, and shutting off lights. With the price ceiling, however, shortages prevailed, which imposed much hardship on Californians.

The previous chapter introduced supply and demand analysis of market transactions. We learned that competitive markets can guide the allocation of resources to produce the goods and services people demand. This chapter broadens our understanding of supply and demand analysis. We will consider how sensitive buyers or sellers really are to a change in price. We will also examine whether a seller's revenue will rise or fall following a change in price. Finally, as an application of demand and supply principles, we will analyze the potential effects of governmental price ceilings and price floors on individual markets.

PRICE ELASTICITY OF DEMAND

Suppose you are the ticket manager for the Los Angeles Lakers, a professional basketball team. You are contemplating increasing the price of your tickets, and you wonder how your fans will react. According to the law of demand, an increase in price will result in a decrease in quantity demanded. But how much will the quantity demanded fall in response to the price hike? The answer to your question depends on the price elasticity of demand.

The **price elasticity of demand** measures how responsive, or sensitive, buyers are to a change in price. The price elasticity of demand looks at the percentage change in quantity demanded relative to the percentage change in price. The elasticity formula is

$$E_d = \frac{\text{Percentage change in quantity demanded}}{\text{Percentage change in price}}$$

where E_d is the elasticity coefficient.[1]

Suppose that attendance at the Lakers' games decreases by 10 percent when the price of tickets increases by 5 percent. Thus, the price elasticity of demand is 2, calculated as follows:

$$E_d = \frac{\text{10-Percent change in quantity demanded}}{\text{5-Percent change in price}}$$

$$= 2$$

The value of the elasticity coefficient, 2, suggests that game attendance changes 2 percent for each 1-percent change in the price of a ticket.

You may have noticed that instead of 2, the value of E_d should be –2. This is because price and quantity demanded are inversely related according to the law of demand. In our example, the increase in ticket prices causes the numerator in our formula to be positive (+10 percent), while the decrease in game attendance causes the denominator to be negative (–5 percent). As a result, E_d will have a negative value. By convention, economists drop the minus sign when calculating the price elasticity of demand, realizing that price and quantity demanded move in opposite directions.

reversed

Depending on the response of buyers to a change in price, demand is characterized as elastic, inelastic, or unit elastic.

- **Elastic.** Demand is elastic when the percentage change in quantity demanded is greater than the percentage change in price, meaning that E_d is greater than 1. Example: A 20-percent reduction in the price of Pepsi Cola causes a 30-percent increase in quantity demanded. Specifically, E_d is 1.5 in this case (30/20 = 1.5).

- **Inelastic.** Demand is inelastic when the percentage change in quantity demanded is less than the percentage change in price, meaning that E_d is less than 1. Example: A 30-percent increase in the price of Levi's jeans causes a 10-percent decrease in quantity demanded. Specifically, E_d is 0.33 in this case (10/30 = 0.33).

- **Unit elastic.** Demand is unit elastic when the percentage change in quantity demanded equals the percentage change in price, meaning that E_d equals 1.0. Example: An 8-percent decrease in the price of Timex watches causes an 8-percent increase in quantity demanded (8/8 = 1.0).

Table 3.1 shows estimated price elasticities of demand for selected products. When making such estimates, economists distinguish between a period during which consumers have little time to adjust (the short run) and a period during which consumers can fully adjust to a price change (the long run). From the table, we see that the short-run price elasticity of demand for medical care is 0.3, which means that the demand for medical care is inelastic. Our elasticity estimate suggests that if the price of medical care were to change by, say, 10 percent, quantity demanded would change by 3 percent. The table also shows

---

[1] Economists use the midpoint formula to calculate the elasticity between two points on a demand curve (or supply curve). This formula uses the averages of the two quantities and two prices under consideration for reference points. According to the midpoint formula, the percentage change in quantity equals the change in the quantity divided by the average of the two quantities; the percentage change in price equals the change in price divided by the average of the two prices. Therefore, the price elasticity of demand equals:

$$E_d = \frac{\text{Change in quantity}}{\text{Sum of quantities/2}} \div \frac{\text{Change in price}}{\text{Sum of prices/2}}$$

Table 3.1	Estimated Price Elasticities of Demand	

	Elasticity Coefficient	
Item	Short Run	Long Run
Airline travel	0.1	2.4
Medical care	0.3	0.9
Automobile tires	0.9	1.2
Gasoline	0.2	0.7
Housing	0.3	1.9
Automobiles	1.9	2.2
Movies	0.9	3.7
Natural gas	1.4	2.1

Sources: From Robert Archibald and Robert Gillingham, "An Analysis of the Short-Run Consumer Demand for Gasoline Using Household Survey Data," *Review of Economics and Statistics,* November 1980, pp. 622–628; and Hendrik Houthakker and Lester Taylor, *Consumer Demand in the United States* (Cambridge: Harvard University Press, 1970), pp. 56–149.

that the short-run price elasticity of demand for automobiles is 1.9, suggesting that the demand for automobiles is elastic. Our elasticity estimate implies that a 10-percent change in the price of automobiles would result in a 19-percent change in the quantity demanded.

DETERMINANTS OF PRICE ELASTICITY OF DEMAND

As seen in Table 3.1, the demand for automobiles is elastic while the demand for housing and gasoline are inelastic. What factors account for differences in the price elasticity of demand?

Availability of Substitutes

The demand for a product is more *elastic* if *many* substitutes are available for it. If there are numerous substitutes available for a product, consumers can easily switch their purchases to substitutes when there is a price hike for that product. For example, suppose that the price of Shell gasoline rises. Because there are many substitutes for Shell gasoline, such as Conoco, Arco, and Texaco, motorists will turn to the readily available substitute gasolines as the price of Shell gasoline rises. We would expect the quantity demanded of Shell gasoline to decrease significantly in response to the price hike.

If a good has *few* substitutes, its demand tends to be more *inelastic*. Medical care has no close substitutes, for example. The short-run price elasticity of demand for medical care is estimated to be about 0.3. It is very inelastic.

Many companies hire celebrities to advertise their merchandise. For example, Michael Jordan, a retired basketball star, advertises Nike shoes. What message is he trying to convey? He is suggesting that, for Michael Jordan, Nike shoes are the "only" ones worth having, and all other shoes are clearly inferior. If consumers accept Jordan's message and desire to be like him, they will also feel that there are no good substitutes for Nike shoes. As a result, the demand for Nike shoes becomes more inelastic.

Owners of professional basketball teams price their tickets with the elasticity of demand in mind. In 1997, for example, fans encouraged by the Miami Heat's victory in Game 2 of the Eastern Conference play-offs against the New York Knicks were shocked *price = what the market will bear*

when they lined up to buy tickets for the next play-off home game. The cheap seats at Miami Arena, which went for $20 in Games 1 and 2 out of the best-of-7 series, jumped unexpectedly to $50 for Game 5. Moreover, the $90 seats jumped to $130. The Heat's management defended the price hikes, arguing that winning Game 5 was a necessity for the future success of the team. The management apparently felt that because Heat fans could not get along without attending Game 5, they would tolerate a price hike. As things turned out, Miami Arena was filled to capacity in spite of the higher priced tickets.

Proportion of Income

Most consumers spend a large proportion of their income on automobiles and housing. A 10-percent rise in the prices of these goods results in price increases of perhaps $2,000 and $15,000, respectively. These price hikes are likely to substantially reduce consumers' ability to purchase these goods and to result in significant decreases in quantity demanded. The demand for goods on which a *large* proportion of personal income is spent therefore tends to be quite *elastic*.

On the other hand, a 10-percent increase in the price of a ballpoint pen means a price increase of perhaps 5 cents. This increase is an insignificant fraction of consumer income and will not likely result in significant decreases in quantity demanded. The demand for goods on which we spend a *small* fraction of our income thus tends to be more *inelastic*.

Time

Suppose that Puget Sound Energy announces an increase in the price of natural gas. How will Washington households react? The answer depends partly on how much time we allow for a response. If we consider the household reaction to the price increase by tomorrow, the response will likely be very small. Households have their existing gas-burning furnaces and stoves and cannot significantly reduce quantity demanded as the price increases.

If we give households a year to react to the price hike, however, their response will be much greater. Some households will switch from furnaces burning natural gas to oil-burning furnaces; others will switch from natural gas-burning stoves to electric stoves. In general, demand tends to be more elastic with time because consumers find more substitutes for goods over longer periods. This explains why the short-run elasticity coefficient of natural gas in Table 3.1 is less elastic at 1.4 than the long-run elasticity coefficient of 2.1. The same line of reasoning applies to other goods shown in Table 3.1.

The price elasticity of demand has many applications. One is the rising cost of health care, as discussed in "Exploring Further 3.1" at the end of this chapter.

AIRLINES FAIL TO PASS ON FULL 10-PERCENT TICKET TAX TO PASSENGERS

The concept of price elasticity of demand has many applications. For example, it can help determine how much of an excise tax is borne by the buyer in the form of a higher price. Let us consider the effects of an excise tax levied on the sale of airline tickets.

In 1997, the U.S. government levied a 10-percent excise tax on the sale of domestic airline tickets. American carriers, such as Delta and Northwest Airlines, attempted to raise ticket prices by the full amount of the tax. Because of market conditions, however, the airlines could raise fares by only 4 percent. As we will see, the price elasticity of demand helps explain this situation.

Assume the equilibrium price of airline tickets is $500, as shown at point *A* in Figure 3.1. Now assume that the government imposes a 10-percent tax on the sale of tickets, yielding

| Figure 3.1 | 10-Percent Tax Imposed on the Sale of Airline Tickets |

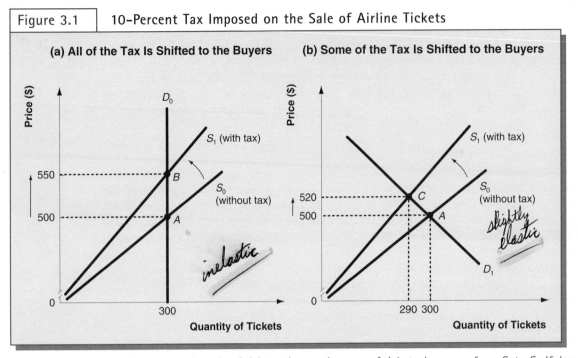

(a) All of the Tax Is Shifted to the Buyers

(b) Some of the Tax Is Shifted to the Buyers

With a 10-percent tax imposed on the sale of tickets, the supply curve of tickets decreases from S_0 to S_1. If demand is perfectly inelastic (D_0), all of the tax will be shifted to buyers. If demand is somewhat elastic (D_1), a portion of the tax will be shifted to buyers, and the remaining portion is absorbed by the seller. In general, with a given supply curve, the more elastic the demand curve for tickets, the smaller the portion of the tax shifted to buyers.

$50 of tax revenue on each ticket sold. Because the tax results in an increase in the cost of doing business for the airlines, their supply curve shifts up by 10 percent, from S_0 to S_1.

Suppose the demand curve for tickets is perfectly inelastic, denoted by D_0 in Figure 3.1(a). Given the extreme situation of perfectly inelastic demand, flying is of such importance to travelers that they will purchase a fixed quantity of tickets at any price. Because travelers are completely insensitive to price changes, airlines can increase fares from $500 to $550, a 10-percent increase. As a result, airline passengers bear all of the tax in the form of a higher price.

In practice, the quantity demanded for flying decreases as fares increase. This implies that the demand curve for tickets exhibits some price elasticity. This is shown by curve D_1 in Figure 3.1(b). As the supply curve of tickets shifts from S_0 to S_1, following the imposition of the 10-percent tax, the equilibrium price rises from $500 to $520, an amount less than the tax. Thus, the airlines absorb the remainder of the tax. In general, with a specific supply curve, the *more elastic* the demand curve for a product, the *smaller* the portion of a tax shifted to buyers.

When the U.S. government imposed a 10-percent tax on the price of airline tickets, fares fluctuated sharply as carriers tried to add as much of the tax as they could. American Airlines, Delta Air Lines, and others raised fares on most routes by 10 percent after the tax was levied. However, they retreated when Northwest Airlines refused to follow suit. Northwest boosted fares only 4 percent, an amount that most airlines matched. United Airlines and Continental Airlines went from a 10-percent increase down to a 4-percent hike as events unfolded. A few carriers, such as Southwest Airlines, did not raise fares at all and thus absorbed the 10-percent tax.

Northwest reasoned that a full 10-percent increase in fares might drive away more traffic than it was worth. A company spokesperson announced that 4 percent was appropriate to market conditions. Apparently, Northwest felt that because the demand for its tickets was quite elastic it would lose many customers if it raised fares by the full amount of the tax.

C H E C K   P O I N T

1. What is the price elasticity of demand?

2. How is the price elasticity of demand measured?

3. Concerning the price elasticity of demand, differentiate between elastic demand, unit elastic demand, and inelastic demand.

4. Why is demand more elastic for some products and more inelastic for others?

PRICE ELASTICITY OF DEMAND AND TOTAL REVENUE

The price elasticity of demand can also help the managers of a business decide whether or not to change price in order to increase sales revenues. For example, in 1991, Apple Computer, Inc., cut the prices on some models of its Macintosh computers by as much as 50 percent in an attempt to stimulate quantity demanded. The market reaction to the price reduction was extraordinary. By the end of the year, Apple announced that the sales of its Macintosh computers had increased by 85 percent and that its revenues had sky-rocketed. In 1982, Apple again slashed prices, which resulted in rising sales and increased revenues. Clearly, these price reductions benefited Apple.

Determining the impact of a change in price on a firm's total revenue is crucial to the analysis of many problems in economics. **Total revenue** (*TR*) refers to the dollars earned by sellers of a product. It is calculated by multiplying the quantity sold (*Q*) over a period by the price (*P*):

$$TR = P \times Q$$

For example, suppose that Dell Computer Corporation charges $3,000 for a computer, and 10,000 computers were sold last month. Total revenue on the sale of computers equaled $30 million ($3,000 \times 10,000 = $30 million). This amount also equals the total expenditures by consumers over this period.

Suppose that Dell reduces the price of its computers by 10 percent. Although quantity demanded will increase, will the firm's total revenue rise? The problem in determining the effect of a price change on the total revenue of computers is that a change in price and a change in quantity would move in *opposite* directions. A decrease in price results in an increase in quantity demanded, and an increase in price causes quantity demanded to decrease. However, total revenue is calculated by multiplying price times quantity. It is not clear how Dell's total revenue will react to the opposing forces of price and quantity.

To determine the impact of a price change on Dell's total revenue, we need to know the consumers' response to the change in price. This response is measured by the price elasticity of demand. Consider the following situations:

handwritten margin note: high elasticity for your product can be good because sales work

- **Elastic demand.** Suppose the elasticity of demand coefficient for Dell computers is 2. If Dell reduces computer prices by 10 percent, quantity demanded will increase by 20 percent. Because the percentage increase in quantity demanded is greater than the percentage decrease in price, the firm's total revenue will rise following the price cut. Conversely, a price increase of 10 percent would result in a 20-percent decrease in quantity demanded and thus a decline in the firm's total revenue. In general, total revenue will move in the *opposit* direction of the price change when demand is *elastic.*

- **Inelastic demand.** Suppose the elasticity of demand coefficient for Dell computers is 0.5. If Dell slashes computer prices by 10 percent, quantity demanded will rise by only 5 percent, and total revenue will decrease. Conversely, a 10-percent price hike will cause quantity demanded to fall by 5 percent, resulting in an increase in total revenue. In general, total revenue will move in the *same* direction of the price change when demand is *inelastic.*

- **Unit elastic demand.** Suppose the elasticity of demand coefficient for Dell computers is 1.0. If Dell reduces computer prices by 10 percent, quantity demanded will increase by 10 percent, and total revenue will remain unchanged. In like manner, a 10-percent increase in price will leave total revenue unchanged. In general, a change in price will *not* induce a change in total revenue when demand is *unit elastic.*

APPLICATIONS OF PRICE ELASTICITY OF DEMAND AND TOTAL REVENUE

All businesses face the question of what price to charge for their products. The answer is not always obvious. Increasing the price of something often has the effect of reducing sales as price-sensitive consumers seek alternatives or simply do without. For every product, the extent of that sensitivity is different. Indeed, pricing is a tricky business. It requires a clear understanding of the demand curve and elasticity, as seen in the following examples.

Colleges Hike Tuition to Offset Cutback in State Aid to Higher Education

From 1999 to 2004, the bill for Emily Mitchell's education at Central Washington University (CWU) increased by 44 percent. In 2002 alone, her tuition went up 14 percent, and it increased by another 9 percent in 2003 and 7 percent in 2004.

Emily Mitchell's experience was common for college students in the early 2000s. Plagued by declining appropriations of tax revenue from state legislatures, caused by a slowdown in state economies, college administrators weighed how far they could push tuition to balance their budgets without driving away students. Administrators noted that if tuition were not raised, revenue shortfalls would trigger a layoff of faculty and staff. This would result in a decline in the number of courses offered to students, which would delay their graduation from college.

Analysis Figure 3.2 illustrates the effect of a tuition increase on the total tuition revenue for CWU. Referring to Figure 3.2(a), let us consider the effect on total revenue of an increase in tuition from $4,000 to $5,000 per year when demand is inelastic. In this case, the decline in attendance caused by the tuition hike will not offset the increase in tuition revenue per student. The net result is that total tuition revenue will increase from $24 million to $28 million when tuition is raised.

| Figure 3.2 | Tuition and Total Tuition Revenue |

For Central Washington University, whether or not a tuition hike will increase total tuition revenue depends on the student elasticity of demand. If demand is inelastic, a tuition increase results in increased total revenue. But if demand is elastic, an increase in tuition results in declining total revenue.

But when tuition increases, some students may question whether attending CWU is worthwhile. Perhaps they will switch to a private university or will drop out of school to seek full-time employment. Therefore, a relatively large decrease in attendance may occur following a tuition hike, suggesting that demand is elastic. Referring to the elastic demand curve shown in Figure 3.2(b), when tuition increases from $4,000 to $5,000 the decrease in attendance more than offsets the increase in tuition per student. Thus, total revenue decreases from $24 million to $23 million. The attempt to increase total revenue by raising tuition backfires when demand is elastic.

Pittsburgh Pirates Underestimate Fan Reaction: Ticket Price Hike Was Wrong

How should a major league baseball team set a price for its home games? Consider the case of the Pittsburgh Pirates.

In 2002, Pittsburgh Pirates owner Kevin McClatchy, unhappy that the ongoing debate over an unpopular ticket price increase was drawing attention away from his improved baseball team, announced that the price hike was a mistake. In reaction to fan unrest that saw 40 percent of the team's season ticket holders cancel their seats in 2002, McClatchy said 2003 season ticket prices would not be raised. McClatchy indicated that the price hike was a decision he regretted and that is why the Pirates would not increase ticket prices for 2003.

In October 2001, only days after the Pirates ended a 62–100 season that was its worst in 16 years, team management hiked prices by $1 to $2 per game for thousands of seats in PNC Park. The public's displeasure over the price increase drew attention throughout the 2002 season and apparently caught the Pirates by surprise. Four weeks into the season, they rolled back the increase on nearly 4,000 outfield seats and refunded the difference to season ticket holders. That rollback didn't come in time to halt the mass cancellation of season tickets that saw home attendance drop about 8,000 per game, despite the Pirates' unexpected good start to the season.

Table 3.2	Price Elasticity of Demand for Mail Services of the U.S. Postal Service	

Mail Classification	Demand Elasticity
First-class letters	0.31
Priority mail	0.75
Express mail	1.49
Periodicals	0.17
Parcel post	1.19
Bound printed matter	0.23
Media mail	0.14

Source: From Postal Rate and Fee Changes, 1997. Testimony of Dr. George Tolley to the U.S. Postal Commission, July 1997, Docket No. R97-1, available at http://www.prc.gov. Select "Contents," "Docketed Cases and Matters," "Rate," and then locate the testimony of George Tolley.

Analysis   When the Pirates contemplated raising ticket prices for the 2002 season, they apparently felt that most fans would continue to attend home games, and thus demand was relatively inelastic. With inelastic demand, a price increase would generate additional revenues for the team. However, widespread outcry against the price hike suggested that demand was much more elastic than the Pirates estimated. The team's management subsequently cut prices to bolster sagging attendance and support revenues.

Rate Hikes Boost Revenues of U.S. Postal Service

In 2002, the U.S. Postal Service was in severe financial straits, facing a decline in business use of first-class letter mail. Alternatives such as e-mail, faxes, and cell phones increasingly substituted for hard-copy letters, thus reducing the amount of business mail handled by the postal service. The slowdown of the U.S. economy that began in 2001 also contributed to a decline in business mail.

In 2002, the postal service increased the price of a stamp for a first-class letter from 34 cents to 37 cents, an 8.8-percent increase. Priority mail rates increased by 10 percent, and rates on other mail services such as parcel post and periodicals were also raised. Whether the revenues of the postal service would rise or fall depended on the response of users to the rate hikes.

Consider the response of Bear Creek Corporation of Medford, Oregon.[2] Prior to the rate hike on priority mail, the firm sent some 900,000 packages of gourmet cheesecakes, pears, and other specialty items by priority mail, the postal service's economical way to mail packages for delivery in as little as two or three days. Following the rate hike on priority mail, however, households could not count on the mail carrier to bring them cinnamon swirls and chocolate truffles. Why? Bear Creek maintained that priority mail was less attractive than its more reliable private-sector competitors—FedEx and United Parcel Service (UPS). Because of the rate hike, Bear Creek expected its catalog retailers to ship 15 to 20 percent fewer priority mail packages. As the manager of Bear Creek stated, "There's a lot of alternatives out there."

Analysis   The purpose of rate hikes on mail is to increase the revenues of the postal service. If there are few substitutes available, the demand for mail tends to be relatively inelastic, and a rate hike results in rising revenues for the postal service. As seen in Table 3.2,

---

[2] "A Deal No More, Priority Mail Is Prey for Rivals," *The Wall Street Journal*, January 24, 2001, pp. B-1 and B-4.

the price elasticity of demand for first-class letters and priority mail is estimated to be 0.31 and 0.75, respectively, suggesting that the demand for these mail services is inelastic. Therefore, we would expect the revenues of the postal service on these services to increase following a rate hike.

CHECK POINT

1. What conclusions can be drawn about the price elasticity of demand when a firm's price and total revenue move in opposite directions? In the same direction? What if total revenue remains unchanged following a change in price?

2. Why did many U.S. colleges rapidly increase tuition in the early 2000s?

3. Why did the Pittsburgh Pirates roll back ticket price hikes in 2002?

4. What contributed to rising revenues for the U.S. Postal Service following rate hikes on mail in 2002?

PRICE CEILINGS AND PRICE FLOORS

Having learned about the reaction of consumers to price changes, let us next consider the issue of fairness. Occasionally, government officials feel that demand and supply result in prices that are unfairly low to sellers or unfairly high to buyers. Government may enact price controls to address these problems. When government imposes a price ceiling on a product, it establishes the maximum legal price a seller may charge for that product. Conversely, government establishes a price floor to prevent prices from falling below the legally mandated level. Let us analyze the effects of government price controls on individual markets.

how should "fairness" be decided? - and by whom?

Rent Controls Make Housing More Affordable

Rent controls have been used in more than 200 U.S. cities, including New York, Boston, San Francisco, and Washington, DC. The objective is to protect low-income households from escalating rents caused by perceived housing shortages and to make housing more affordable to the poor. By the late 1990s, however, many cities had cut back their rent controls because of the de-escalation of rent inflation and the public's receptiveness to free-market economics applied to housing.

The economic effects of rent controls are illustrated in Figure 3.3. Assume initially that the equilibrium rent for a 2-bedroom apartment in New York City equals $600 per month, shown by the intersection of the market supply curve (S_0) and market demand curve (D_0). To protect renters from the possibility of escalating rents, suppose the municipal government passes a rent-control law that freezes the monthly rent at $600. Because the ceiling rate equals the market-equilibrium rate, the ceiling does not affect the market.

Because of the rising population in New York City, suppose the market demand curve for apartments shifts to D_1. Prices try to rise to $900, the price that would occur in a free market, but are prevented from doing so by the rent ceiling. Those renters who already have apartments are protected from the government-placed lid on rent because they pay $600 rather than $900 per month.

Figure 3.3 | Rent Ceilings and Housing Shortages

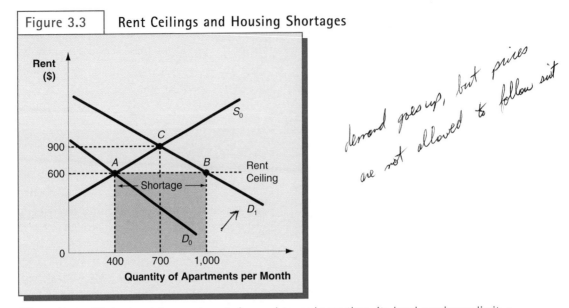

demand goes up, but prices are not allowed to follow suit

When the equilibrium rent for apartments is equal to, or lower than, its legal maximum limit, a rent ceiling has no effect on the market. This occurs when the rent ceiling is $600 and the demand and supply curves for apartments are D_0 and S_0, respectively. When the equilibrium rent is above its ceiling, the ceiling takes effect and a shortage occurs. This situation occurs when the rent ceiling is $600 and the demand and supply curves are D_1 and S_0, respectively.

Although the rent ceiling protects current renters from rising prices, it results in adverse side effects. Because the $600 ceiling is set below the equilibrium level, families would like to be able to rent 1,000 apartments. However, landlords will be willing to supply only 400 apartments at the ceiling price. Thus, when the rent ceiling is set below the free-market equilibrium price, a shortage of 600 apartments occurs. In 1978, for example, several thousand University of California students could not find housing in Berkeley, following the imposition of rent controls. Many of them slept at the university's gymnasium until suitable housing could be found.

Initially, if the ceiling on rent is not very much below the equilibrium price, the adverse effects of rent control may be hardly perceptible. As time passes, however, these effects grow and yield the following results:

- **The future supply and quality of rental apartments will diminish.** Because rent ceilings reduce the profitability of apartments for landlords, they serve as a disincentive to the construction of new rental housing. Potential investors in apartments will find it more profitable to invest in shopping malls or office buildings that are not subject to rent controls.

- **Under-the-table markets may develop.** When landlords cannot increase rent, they often adopt other means to collect income. Landlords may require a renter to make under-the-table payments just to get a key ("key money") to the apartment. Other renters may have to purchase the landlord's furniture at outrageous prices to obtain an apartment.

- **Discrimination occurs in the rationing of apartments.** Because price no longer serves its rationing role under rent ceilings, landlords may ration available apartments to families according to other criteria such as race or religion.

- **Rent controls benefit the wealthy.** Because rent controls pertain to units of apartments and are not based on the income of renters, they can benefit the rich. For example, wealthy individuals

they were intended to help the poor!

such as singer Carly Simon and Mayor Ed Koch have taken advantage of living in New York City, where rent ceilings hold down the cost of apartments.

In spite of these problems, rent controls have their proponents. They argue that eliminating controls wouldn't spur the construction of any low-income rental housing, just more luxury housing. So low-income people who benefit from current regulations, they say, would be displaced. Because current renters benefit from rent controls while landlords and future renters suffer, the political lines are clearly drawn on the rent-control debate.

Should Federal Interest-Rate Ceilings Be Imposed on MasterCard and VISA?

Do you pay too much interest on your MasterCard or VISA accounts? This has been a topic of much controversy.

During the 1960s, the VISA and MasterCard associations developed the infrastructure for a nationwide credit card payment system and convinced merchants to accept their cards. However, state laws limited the amount of interest that could be charged on credit card loans. By the 1970s, high inflation and high interest rates resulted in banks issuing credit cards to suffer losses. They maintained that interest rate ceilings set by most states were too low to make credit card lending profitable.

In 1978, the Supreme Court changed the interpretation of laws for all types of consumer loans. It ruled that federally chartered banks could charge the highest interest rate allowed in their home state to customers living anywhere in the United States, including states with restrictive ceilings on interest rates. Therefore, major credit card companies began locating to states such as Delaware with liberal or no ceilings. They made credit card loans to households in states with restrictive ceilings and charged them the higher interest rates allowed in Delaware.

To hang on to the credit card business, many other states loosened interest rate ceilings. In the 1980s, most states capped credit card interest rates between 12 and 18 percent. By the early 2000s, caps were in the 18- to 24-percent range, and many states moved in the direction of removing the caps altogether.

government hurting consumers — just like S+L scandal

Critics of banks, which issue credit cards, have complained that there is a wide gap between card rates and the interest rates that banks pay for money. They note that banks may pay, say, 2-percent interest, to attract our savings deposits and use this money to lend to credit card borrowers at, say, 16-percent interest. As a result, banks can earn large profits on their credit card operations. Such high charges on credit card balances are characterized as excessive and unfair to consumers.

However, banks issuing credit cards argue that the high interest rates reflect the realities of pricing a complex product in a competitive market. Besides interest-rate charges, other pricing decisions include the level of annual fees, the billing cycle to be used, the length of the interest-free grace period, and various service fees. Bankers note that the cost of obtaining deposits to fund credit card operations typically represents less than 40 percent of a bank's overall cost of operating a credit card plan. Other costs, which include various processing and billing expenses and fraud and credit losses, are significant and do not vary with the cost of money.

Consumer groups have called for the federal government to impose a nationwide interest-rate ceiling on credit card accounts. However, a ceiling on interest rates would encourage banks to reduce costs or increase revenues. For example, banks might tighten credit standards for borrowers so as to decrease collection costs, reduce services offered with credit cards such as discounts on transportation and lodging, curtail grace periods for making payments, and increase the annual fee charged to cardholders. Although a federal

effect = ? is there high demand for credit cards?

interest-rate ceiling on credit cards would help consumers in terms of their monthly interest bills, it could lead to other burdens imposed on users.

Agricultural Price Floors Boost Incomes of Farmers

We have previously examined the effects of governmental price ceilings imposed on the sale of a product. Let us now consider the effects of price floors.

In 1933, when farmers were suffering from low market prices during the Great Depression, the Agricultural Adjustment Act was passed. This act set *price floors* on many agricultural products, such as cotton and wheat, to increase the income of farmers. Under this program, the government guaranteed a minimum price above the equilibrium price and agreed to buy any quantity the farmers were unable to sell at the legal price.

Figure 3.4 shows how a price floor works for one farm commodity, wheat. With a free and competitive market, the intersection of the market supply curve (S_0) and market demand curve (D_0) establishes the equilibrium price at $4 per bushel. Nine million bushels of wheat are produced and sold per year at this price, yielding an income of $36 million for farmers.

To support farmers' incomes, suppose the government sets a price floor for wheat at $5 per bushel. The higher price induces wheat farmers to increase production to 11 million bushels but causes consumers to demand only 7 million bushels. As a result, there is a surplus of 4 million bushels. To prevent the surplus from causing the price of wheat to fall, the government purchases the surplus and stores it. In this manner, farmers can sell 11 million bushels of wheat at a price of $5 per bushel, thus realizing an income of $55 million. This amount exceeds the income that farmers would earn in a free market.

A result of agricultural price supports is the transfer of money from consumers and taxpayers to farmers. This transfer works in two ways. First, for each bushel of wheat that

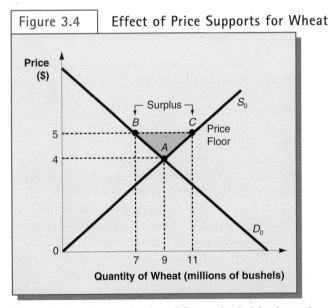

| Figure 3.4 | Effect of Price Supports for Wheat |

The agricultural support price of $5 per bushel is above the market-equilibrium price of $4 per bushel. The support price results in an increase in quantity supplied and a decrease in quantity demanded, causing a surplus of 4 million bushels per year. To prevent price from falling below the support level, the government purchases the surplus and stores it. The cost to taxpayers of purchasing the surplus is $20 million.

consumers purchase, they pay a higher price ($5) than they would have paid without a price support ($4). Second, when the government purchases the 4 million bushel surplus at a price of $5 per bushel, it comes at a cost to taxpayers of $20 million. As you can see, when price supports interfere with the operation of a free and competitive market, the result tends to be a misallocation of resources: Households pay higher prices for wheat, as well as higher taxes to subsidize farmers. Moreover, inefficient and high-cost farmers can still realize profits when subsidized by price supports. These inefficiencies have resulted in political pressure to reduce or eliminate government subsidies to farmers. ★

This chapter broadened our understanding of demand and supply by considering contemporary applications of these principles. The next chapter considers the role of productivity and costs of production in influencing business decisions.

C H E C K   P O I N T

1. Why does government sometimes impose price controls on individual markets?

2. What are the advantages and disadvantages of a legal price ceiling imposed on the sale of a product? How about a legal price floor?

3. As explained in this chapter, which of the following are price ceilings? Price floors?

   a. Rent controls
   b. Controls on credit card interest rates
   c. Agricultural price controls

Chapter Summary

1. The price elasticity of demand measures how sensitive buyers are to a change in price. Depending on the response of buyers to a change in price, demand is characterized as elastic, inelastic, or unit elastic.

2. Demand tends to be more elastic for some products and less elastic for others. Among the major determinants of the price elasticity demand are the availability of substitutes, the proportion of buyer income spent on a product, and the time period under consideration.

3. If a firm's price and total revenue move in opposite directions, demand is elastic. If the firm's price and total revenue move in the same direction, demand is inelastic. If the firm's total revenue does not respond to a change in price, demand is unit elastic.

4. Occasionally, the government will impose price controls on individual markets in which prices are considered unfairly high to buyers or unfairly low to sellers. When government imposes a price ceiling on a product, it establishes the maximum legal price a seller may charge for that product. Conversely, government establishes a price floor to prevent prices from falling below the legally mandated level.

5. Although price controls on individual markets attempt to make prices more "fair" for buyers and sellers, they interfere with the market's allocation of resources. Price ceilings that are set below the equilibrium price level result in market shortages of a product. Price floors that are set above the equilibrium level entail market surpluses.

Key Terms and Concepts

price elasticity of demand (56)

elastic demand (57)

inelastic demand (57)

unit elastic demand (57)

total revenue (61)

price ceiling (65)

price floor (65)

rent controls (65)

health maintenance organizations (HMOs) (75)

preferred provider organizations (PPOs) (76)

Self-Test: Multiple-Choice Questions

1. Price elasticity of demand will be greater the

   a. shorter the time period involved.
   b. smaller the number of substitutes for the good.
   c. more the good is considered to be a necessity than a luxury.
   d. larger the item in a consumer's budget.

2. For which of the following goods is demand likely to be most inelastic?

   a. Medical care
   b. Sony CD player
   c. Air travel on United Airlines
   d. Honda Accord automobile

3. Suppose that government officials are contemplating a gasoline tax and a tax on energy that includes gasoline, natural gas, coal, and electricity. Assuming that the objective is to maximize total tax revenue, the gasoline tax will raise

   a. more revenue because the demand for gasoline is more elastic than the demand for energy.
   b. more revenue because the demand for gasoline is less elastic than the demand for energy.
   c. less revenue because the demand for gasoline is more elastic than the demand for energy.
   d. less revenue because the demand for gasoline is less elastic than the demand for energy.

4. If the government imposes a 5-percent tax on airline tickets, and the air carriers are able to increase ticket prices by the full amount of the tax, we would expect the price elasticity of demand for airline tickets to be

   a. perfectly elastic.
   b. relatively elastic.
   c. relatively inelastic.
   d. perfectly inelastic.

5. If the government imposes a ceiling on rent charged for private apartments, and the ceiling is set below the market-equilibrium rent, we would expect

   a. a surplus of rental apartments in the immediate future.
   b. an increase in the profits of landlords.
   c. a decrease in housing discrimination against the poor.
   d. some rental apartments to be abandoned or poorly maintained by landlords.

6. If the price elasticity of demand for automobiles is 0.8, a 10-percent increase in the price of automobiles would cause the quantity demanded to decline by

   a. 2 percent.
   b. 4 percent.
   c. 8 percent.
   d. 12 percent.

7. Total revenue will increase if price

   a. decreases and the elasticity of demand equals 0.6.
   b. decreases and the elasticity of demand equals 1.0.
   c. increases and the elasticity of demand equals 0.3.
   d. increases and the elasticity of demand equals 2.0.

8. If the state of California levies a tax of 50 cents per pack on the sale of cigarettes in order to increase tax revenues, it will realize the most revenue if the demand for cigarettes is

   a. highly elastic.
   b. somewhat elastic.
   c. highly inelastic.
   d. somewhat inelastic.

9. If the federal government levies a price floor on wheat, it may also have to

   a. produce some of the wheat itself.
   b. purchase the surplus wheat.
   c. initiate programs to reduce demand in the private sector.
   d. initiate programs to increase supply in the private sector.

10. When there is a rightward shift in the supply curve of corn, total revenue will

   a. increase only if demand is relatively elastic.
   b. increase only if demand is relatively inelastic.
   c. decrease only if demand is relatively elastic.
   d. decrease only if demand is perfectly elastic.

Answers to Multiple-Choice Questions

1. d   2. a   3. c   4. d   5. d   6. c   7. c   8. c   9. b   10. a

Study Questions and Problems

1. Suppose that researchers estimate that for every 1-percent change in the price of computers, quantity demanded will change by 2.5 percent. Describe the price elasticity of demand for computers. What if researchers estimate that the quantity demanded for computers will change by 0.5 percent in response to a 1-percent change in price?

2. Economists estimate the short-run price elasticity of demand for airline travel to be 0.1, 0.3 for housing, 1.5 for glass, and 1.9 for automobiles. What is the meaning of these elasticity coefficients?

3. Why is demand relatively inelastic for medical care and gasoline but relatively elastic for movies and automobiles?

4. An advertisement once appeared in the *Seattle Times:* "Wanted, two Sonics tickets for next week's game against the Bulls. Will pay any price. Phone Joe at 271-4597." If Joe really meant what he stated in his ad, what could you infer about his price elasticity of demand for tickets?

5. How will the following changes in price affect a firm's total revenue?

   a. Price rises, and demand is inelastic.
   b. Price falls, and demand is elastic.
   c. Price rises, and demand is unit elastic.
   d. Price falls, and demand is inelastic.
   e. Price rises, and demand is elastic.
   f. Price falls, and demand is unit elastic.

6. Suppose the U.S. Postal Service announces an increase in the price of first-class mail in order to generate additional revenue. What can you infer regarding the price elasticity of demand for first-class mail?

7. Suppose the Grand Central Movie Theater reduces the price of popcorn by 20 percent, but consumers purchase only 10 percent more of the product. What does this indicate about the price elasticity of demand, and what will happen to total revenue as a result of the price reduction?

8. Assume the price elasticity of demand for corn is 0.6 and that farmers have a record harvest—corn production is higher than ever. What will happen to the total revenue received by farmers?

9. Suppose the price elasticity of demand for airline travel is 0.4 in the short run and 2.2 in the long run. If airlines raise the price of tickets, what will happen to their total revenue over these time periods?

10. Assume the price elasticity of demand for labor is 0.2. If a labor union succeeds in negotiating an 8-percent increase in hourly wages, what effect would this have on its members?

11. Table 3.3 shows the demand schedule and supply schedule for apartments.

    a. Draw the supply curve and demand curve for apartments from the data given in the table. What is the equilibrium rent and the quantity of apartments rented?
    b. Suppose the government imposes a legal rent ceiling at $400 per month. How many apartments will be demanded and supplied? What is the size of the shortage?
    c. How will landlords likely cope with the rent ceiling?

12. Table 3.4 shows the supply schedule and demand schedule for milk. Quantities are in gallons.

    a. Draw the supply curve and demand curve for milk from the data given in the table. What is the equilibrium price? How much milk will be produced and sold? How much revenue will farmers receive from the sale of milk?

Table 3.3   Market for Apartments

Rent (monthly)	Quantity Supplied	Quantity Demanded
$700	1,000	200
600	800	400
500	600	600
400	400	800
300	200	1,000

Table 3.4	Market for Milk		
	Price	Quantity Supplied (gallons)	Quantity Demanded (gallons)
	$0.50	5,000	9,000
	1.00	6,000	8,000
	1.50	7,000	7,000
	2.00	8,000	6,000
	2.50	9,000	5,000

b. Suppose the government imposes a price floor on milk equal to $2 per gallon. How much milk will be produced and purchased? What is the size of the surplus?

c. If government maintains the floor price by purchasing all the unsold milk from farmers, how much will the government pay? How much revenue will the farmers receive, from consumers and the government, from the sale of milk? What might the government do to dispose of the surplus?

EXPLORING FURTHER 3.1: WHY IS HEALTH CARE SO EXPENSIVE?

Americans are living longer, healthier lives. Since 1960, average life expectancy has increased by more than five years. American physicians have access to the best technologies in the world. At the same time, the share of the nation's income devoted to health care has been growing rapidly, and today many Americans lack health insurance. Growing concern about rising costs of health care and limited access to insurance has led to the development of a wide variety of proposals for health care reform.

In many respects, the health care industry resembles other industries such as legal services and transportation. It supplies a service—health care—in response to consumer demand. But the demand for health care is different from the demand for many other services because most people do not pay for their care directly. Instead, the government and private insurers pay most health care expenses. The supply of health care also differs from that of many other service industries. Consumers rely on providers for information about health care services, and these providers are heavily regulated, primarily by other health care providers. Finally, many people believe that health care is inherently different from other goods and services. They believe that everyone should be entitled to health care. This belief may result in people *overconsuming* health care services, in which they receive excessive care even if the extra benefit of that care is extremely low.

The increasing costs of health care services are basically the result of a relatively inelastic demand curve that increases much more rapidly than the supply curve. Figure 3.5 shows the market for health care services. Assume the equilibrium price for these services is $200, as shown at the point of intersection of supply curve (S_0) and demand curve (D_0). Suppose the supply curve of health care services increases to S_1 but the demand curve increases by a larger amount to D_1. Because the increase in demand pulls the price of health care services up by a larger amount than the increase in supply pushes price down, the price of health care services increases to $250.

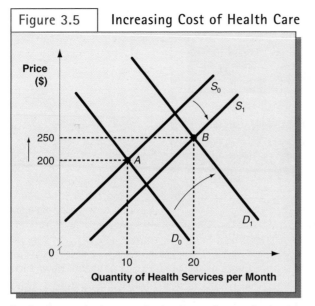

| Figure 3.5 | Increasing Cost of Health Care |

In the figure, the increase in the demand curve for health care services is larger than the increase in the supply curve. Because the increase in demand pulls the price of health care up by a larger amount than the increase in supply pushes price down, the price of health care increases.

Demand for Health Care Services

We will first examine the demand for health care services by considering the price elasticity of demand. Consumers of medical services, such as doctors' and hospitals' services, generally are not very responsive to changes in price. This is because people consider medical care to be a necessity rather than a luxury. Researchers estimate that the price elasticity of demand for medical care is about 0.2. This means that a 10-percent increase in the price of medical care would decrease quantity demanded by only 2 percent. Inelastic demand for medical care explains in part why doctors and hospitals have strong incentives to raise prices: When demand is inelastic, the seller's total revenue increases when the price of the service is increased.

Besides being inelastic, the demand curve for health care has shifted to the right over time, thus putting upward pressure on price. Let us examine some of the reasons why the demand for health care services has increased.

- **Rising incomes.** Rising incomes of households in the United States have caused the demand curve for health care services to increase. Economists estimate that per-capita spending on health care increases approximately in proportion to increases in per-capita income.

- **An aging population.** As people age, the demand curve for health care services increases because older people tend to become ill more frequently and remain ill for longer periods.

- **Health insurance.** Because people with health insurance are protected against the full cost of a serious illness or injury, they are likely to go to the doctor more often and choose more complex procedures, thus increasing the demand curve for health care services.

- **Physician incentives.** Because physicians generally know more about health care than their patients, they specify the types and amounts of medical tests and procedures to be consumed.

When physicians are paid separately for each service they render, they have the motivation to specify tests and procedures that are not essential. Moreover, because every patient represents a potential source of a malpractice suit, physicians tend to recommend more services than are justified medically in order to protect themselves against malpractice suits.

Supply of Health Care Services

Supply factors have also contributed to higher prices of medical services. For example, the supply of doctors in the United States has risen from 435,000 doctors in 1980 to more than 700,000 in 2005, an increase of about 60 percent. However, this increase in supply was more than offset by an increase in demand, and the price of services provided by doctors rose during this period.

The supply of doctors is also characterized by relatively high barriers to entry. Besides the considerable financial resources and time it takes to train doctors, barriers have existed to keep human resources out of the medical field. Critics have maintained that the American Medical Association has willingly kept admissions to medical school, and thus the supply of doctors, artificially low with the intent of increasing the ability of doctors to increase the price of their services. In recent years, however, these problems have become less serious. The number of practicing doctors has increased, and the profession's ability to limit price competition has declined.

Another cause of rising health care prices is slow productivity growth in the health care industry. Health care is a labor-intensive service, and it is usually harder to increase productivity for services than for goods. For example, how would you noticeably raise the productivity of nurses in the birthing room of a hospital?

Finally, we will consider technology. Technological advancements, such as open-heart surgery and body scanners, increase the quantity and quality of hospital services. The use of new surgical techniques has flourished in recent years. Although improved surgical techniques have lengthened the lives of many Americans, they have been costly to develop and administer, thus adding to the cost of health care.

Containing the Cost of Health Care

What, if anything, can be done to contain the growth in the cost of health care without decreasing access to health care?

Responding to increasing medical costs, insurance companies have enacted significant deductibles and co-payments on their policyholders. Rather than covering the full cost of, say, a back operation, the insurance company may require that the patient pay the first $300 of each year's medical cost (the deductible) and 20 percent of all additional costs (the co-payment). The effect of the deductible and co-payment is to discourage patients from overconsuming medical care, thus reducing the costs of the insurance company.

Traditional health care insurance does not provide doctors the incentive to control costs. Under a traditional insurance policy, insurance companies pay for most medical procedures. If hospitals and doctors are fully reimbursed for their services, they have little incentive to discourage patients from getting excessive care.

To address this situation, many employers have required their employees to join health maintenance organizations (HMOs) such as Kaiser Foundation. An HMO is an association of health care providers that has its own facilities, such as clinics and hospitals. Under this system, payments to doctors and hospitals are based on a prearranged schedule of fixed fees that has been negotiated between the insurance companies and the providers. Because doctors and hospitals are paid a fixed amount per patient, their profits rise as they cut their costs. Therefore, doctors and hospitals have the incentive to control costs.

Some insurance companies have established preferred provider organizations (PPOs), which are organizations that contract with numerous doctors and hospitals to provide health care to their subscribers. The PPO is made up of a network of recommended or preferred hospitals and doctors who have agreed to provide care based on a prearranged, discounted price schedule. Because these fees are less than those usually charged, PPOs reduce health insurance premiums and health care expenditures. The patient receives a directory of participating doctors and hospitals and is given, say, 80-percent reimbursement of health care costs when treated by doctors and hospitals that participate in the plan. Patients can obtain care from doctors and hospitals not on the PPO recommended list, but only if they are willing to pay more for the care than a preferred provider would charge.

Is There a Prescription for High-Cost Drugs?

As we have learned, the cost of going to physicians and hospitals has soared in recent years. So has the cost of prescription drugs. What can be done to hold down the cost of drugs?

Consider the case of Diane Hummel. After a heart attack scare, Ms. Hummel visited her medical clinic in Santa Clara, California, for a cholesterol check. Her readings were unfavorable and so she obtained a prescription for a type of drug called a statin. Within two months, her cholesterol had decreased to a healthy level. It's the type of outcome you would expect from Zocor or Lipitor, two heavily advertised pills that are the top-selling statins. However, Ms. Hummel purchased lovastatin, a generic substitute for Zocor and Lipitor, at a much lower cost.

The use of generic drugs is an attempt to slow the escalation of drug costs. However, making drugs affordable is difficult because every remedy threatens to disturb the historical balance the United States tries to maintain between getting the best medicine and making it affordable. The U.S. patent system provides drug manufacturers a 20-year monopoly on their products so that they have an incentive to make large expenditures on research. Drug companies note that every time inexpensive generic drugs take a dollar of sales away from their high-priced drugs, their ability to conduct research declines and, 20 years from now, some patient will suffer.

Health plans have long advocated generic-substitution strategies, and most states have laws that permit pharmacists to give patients available generics rather than brand-name pills. But these efforts have not lived up to their potential, and consumer advocates believe stronger steps are necessary.

Forced competition is another possible solution to high drug cost. For example, to hold down the costs of prescription drugs, British Columbia (Canada) makes consumers pay for premium drugs. The government health program, which provides prescription-drug coverage to the elderly and the poor without insurance, pegs its reimbursement rate to the cheapest drug in a class, assuming the drug is as effective as more expensive drugs. Patients who want more expensive drugs have to pay the difference themselves.

International comparisons of drug prices have shown that American consumers often pay a lot more for their prescriptions than do citizens in other countries. According to the General Accountability Office, the average drug that sells for $1 in the United States would sell for 71 cents in Germany, 68 cents in Sweden, 64 cents in Canada, and 51 cents in Italy. Frequently, this price disparity stems from the fact that some countries, especially those with nationalized health care systems, can negotiate lower prices due to greater buying power.

The rising cost of prescription drugs has become an ongoing issue for households, insurance providers, and government policymakers. Any single solution is unlikely. Instead, making drugs more affordable will require a number of prescriptions.

Production and the Costs of Production

Chapter objectives

After reading this chapter, you should be able to:

1. Distinguish between the short run and the long run and between a fixed input and a variable input.

2. Describe how the law of diminishing returns relates to the productivity of a variable input in the short run.

3. Identify the costs of production that a firm realizes in the short run.

4. Explain how economies of scale and diseconomies of scale affect the long-run average total cost curve of a business firm.

5. Distinguish between accounting profit and economic profit.

economics IN CONTEXT

For years, McDonald's has attempted to maximize the output of its existing resources. At every McDonald's restaurant, some workers specialize in taking orders, others prepare food, and others serve customers at the drive-through window operation. Many McDonald's restaurants have installed automated machines to prepare french fries, thus increasing labor productivity. Moreover, McDonald's sophisticated cash registers are user friendly. They merely require an employee to touch a key with a picture of, say, a Big Mac to record price rather than enter the dollar price of the hamburger on the cash register. This saves time and money for the firm.

Because McDonald's operates in thousands of locations, it can standardize operating procedures and menus, further adding to company efficiency. Moreover, McDonald's trains its managers at its Hamburger University, and the firm can spread the cost of its advertising over thousands of individual restaurants. These procedures result in cost savings for the firm.

However, some problems exist for McDonald's. Because the firm's menu is standardized throughout the nation, if customers in some parts of the nation do not like a product, it generally is not included on the menu despite its popularity elsewhere. McDonald's McRib sandwich, for example, was not popular with some consumers and was dropped from the national menu. Another problem with McDonald's geographically uniform menu is that the ingredients must be available throughout the nation and cannot be subject to shortages or sharp price fluctuations.

In today's economy, business managers face great pressure to reduce cost while maintaining or improving product quality. Competition has forced firms such as McDonald's, Boeing, Intel, and General Motors to incorporate the latest technologies to fulfill these objectives. Moreover, employees of these companies must undergo retraining programs to increase their productivity. It turns out that for most goods and services, cost and output are closely related, implying that the theory of production is intertwined with the theory of cost. In this chapter, we will learn about production and the costs of production.

SHORT RUN VERSUS LONG RUN

The time frame in which a company plans its operations influences the production techniques that it selects. In general, a company's production may take place in the short-run or the long-run period. These periods are not defined in days, weeks, or months, but rather conceptually.

The **short run** is a period in which the quantity of at least one input is fixed and the quantities of the other inputs can be varied. A **fixed input** is any resource for which the quantity cannot be varied during the period under consideration. For example, the productive capacity of large machines or the size of a factory cannot easily be changed over a short period. In agriculture and some other businesses, land may be a fixed resource. There are also **variable inputs** whose quantities can be altered in the short run. Typically, variable inputs of a firm include labor and materials. In response to a change in demand, the firm can employ more or fewer variable inputs but not alter the capacity of its factory.

The **long run** is a period in which *all* inputs are considered as *variable* in amount. There are no fixed inputs in the long run. Over the long run, firm managers may contemplate alternatives such as constructing a new factory, modifying an existing factory, installing new equipment, or selling the factory and leaving the business. How long is the long run? That depends on the industry under consideration. For Burger King or Pizza Hut, the long

Table 4.1	A Production Function for Chocolate Chip Cookies

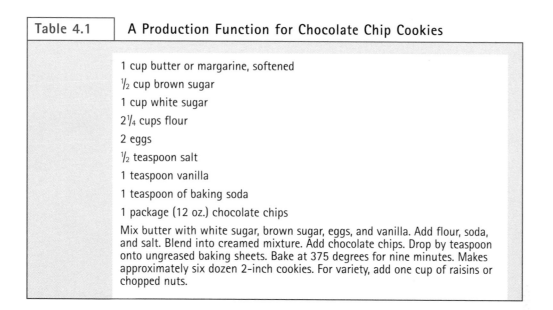

1 cup butter or margarine, softened

$\frac{1}{2}$ cup brown sugar

1 cup white sugar

$2\frac{1}{4}$ cups flour

2 eggs

$\frac{1}{2}$ teaspoon salt

1 teaspoon vanilla

1 teaspoon of baking soda

1 package (12 oz.) chocolate chips

Mix butter with white sugar, brown sugar, eggs, and vanilla. Add flour, soda, and salt. Blend into creamed mixture. Add chocolate chips. Drop by teaspoon onto ungreased baking sheets. Bake at 375 degrees for nine minutes. Makes approximately six dozen 2-inch cookies. For variety, add one cup of raisins or chopped nuts.

run may be six months, since that is the time required to add new franchises. For General Motors or Ford, several years may be required to construct a new factory.

PRODUCTION FUNCTION

The transformation of resources into output does not occur haphazardly. When Daimler-Chrysler or Toyota produces automobiles, for example, they take many resources (land, labor, capital, and entrepreneurship) and, by using a technological production process, transform them into output. Production refers to the use of resources to make outputs of goods and services (for example, steel, locomotives, and banking services) available for human wants.

The relationship between physical output and the quantity of resources used in the production process is called a **production function**. For example, a production function might tell us that with one lathe a machinist could produce a maximum of 20 axles per day. With one lathe and an assistant, a machinist could produce up to 30 axles per day. Note that the production function specifies the *maximum* amount of output that can be produced with a given amount of resources.

Next time you make chocolate chip cookies, be aware that the recipe you are using is an example of a production function. The recipe provides the types and amounts of resources and the processes required to produce a particular number of cookies. The resources include the ingredients shown in Table 4.1—brown sugar, white sugar, eggs, butter, and the like—and also kitchen equipment and the labor of the cook. The recipe also includes instructions for combining the various resources to produce cookies. Similarly, production functions in industry and agriculture specify the level of output and resources used in the production process.

SHORT-RUN PRODUCTION

To illustrate the production function, consider the simplest case—when there is one fixed resource and one variable resource. Figure 4.1 shows the short-run production function of Denver Block Company, a manufacturer of cement blocks used in the construction of buildings. Assume that the essential resources in the production of blocks are capital (a factory including a block machine, cement mixer, and forklift) and labor. Also suppose

| Figure 4.1 | Short–Run Production Function of Denver Block Company |

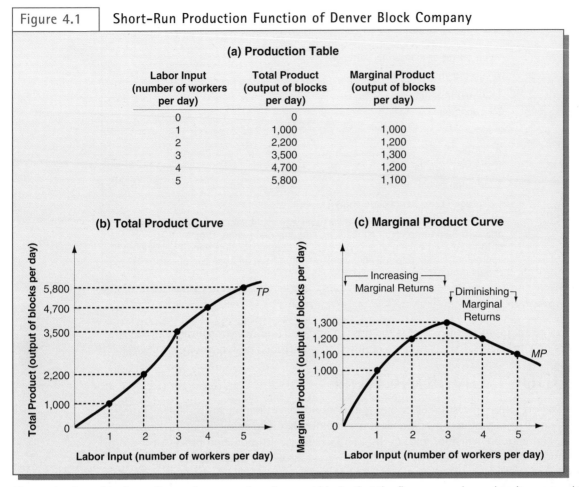

(a) Production Table

Labor Input (number of workers per day)	Total Product (output of blocks per day)	Marginal Product (output of blocks per day)
0	0	
1	1,000	1,000
2	2,200	1,200
3	3,500	1,300
4	4,700	1,200
5	5,800	1,100

(b) Total Product Curve

(c) Marginal Product Curve

The production table shows the maximum number of cement blocks that the firm can produce when it uses one block machine and different amounts of labor. The total product curve and marginal product curve are based on these data. The law of diminishing returns accounts for the shape of the firm's product curves in the short run.

that the factory is already constructed and has a fixed capacity. For simplicity, suppose that the only resource that we can vary is labor, even though in reality the production of cement blocks requires other resources such as water, cement, sand, and gravel. As expected, using more workers with the machinery generally results in more blocks being produced; using fewer workers produces fewer blocks.

The purpose of a production function is to tell us how many blocks we can manufacture with varying amounts of labor. Refer to Figure 4.1(a), which shows a production function relating the total number of blocks produced in column 2 to the amount of labor in column 1. Employing zero workers results in no blocks being produced. A single machine operator can produce 1,000 blocks a day, adding a second operator increases output to 2,200 blocks per day, and so on. Figure 4.1(b) shows this **total product** (*TP*) schedule graphically.

We are also interested in how many additional blocks are produced for each additional worker employed. The **marginal product** (*MP*) of labor is equal to the change in output that results from changing labor by one unit, holding all other inputs fixed.

$$MP = \Delta \text{ Total product}/\Delta \text{ Labor}$$

where Δ, the Greek letter *delta*, denotes the change in a variable.

why does this line curve?

The marginal product of labor is calculated in Figure 4.1(a). When Denver Block Company increases labor from zero to one worker, total output rises from zero to 1,000 blocks per day. The marginal product of the first worker is thus 1,000 blocks. Employing a second worker results in total output rising from 1,000 blocks to 2,200 blocks, and thus the marginal product of the second worker equals 1,200 blocks. Similar calculations generate the remainder of the marginal product of labor. The marginal product curve is shown graphically in Figure 4.1(c).

Inspecting the marginal product curve, we see that the marginal productivity of labor rises for a while when the amount of labor used is low. Eventually, the marginal productivity of labor decreases. The principle that explains the falling portion of the marginal product curve is the **law of diminishing marginal returns:** After some point, the marginal product diminishes as additional units of a variable resource are added to a fixed resource.

In Figure 4.1(c), the marginal product of labor increases for the first three workers hired. Beginning with the fourth worker, however, marginal product declines. Diminishing returns therefore begin with the fourth worker employed in block manufacturing.

It is easy to understand the reasons for the shape of the marginal product curve in Figure 4.1(c). If Denver Block Company employs just one worker, that person has to perform all of the aspects of block manufacturing: mixing concrete, operating the block machine, and driving the forklift. If the firm hires a second person, the two workers can specialize in different aspects of block manufacturing. Therefore, two workers can produce more than twice as much as one. The marginal product of the second worker is thus more than the marginal product of the first worker, and the firm realizes increasing marginal returns. As the firm continues to add workers to the machinery, however, some workers may be underutilized because they have little work to do while waiting in line to use the machinery. Because the addition of yet ever more workers continues to increase output, but by successfully smaller increments, the firm realizes diminishing marginal returns.

Here's a familiar example of the law of diminishing returns. Suppose that the total learning in your survey of economics course depends on the quality of this textbook, your intelligence, the effectiveness of your professor, and the time you devote to study. Assume that the first three variables are fixed, implying that they do not vary throughout the course. Now let us include hours of study time per day over the duration of the course to determine increased course learning. Will the second hour devoted to studying economics increase learning by as much as the first hour? How about the third hour, and so on? You will probably find that diminishing returns to learning will eventually occur as successively more hours are devoted to studying economics each day. In other words, the marginal product of an additional hour of study will decrease, and eventually become zero.

Technological Improvements

In discussing the general shapes of a firm's product curves, we assumed that the state of technology, quality of human resources, and the amount of capital equipment remained constant as the firm changed its use of a variable resource. But what happens when these factors change? As explained below, these factors are *shifters,* which cause entire product curves to shift upward or downward.

Recall that technology consists of society's pool of knowledge concerning production in industry and agriculture. An important aspect of technology is that it sets restrictions on the amount and types of goods that can be produced from a given amount of resources: A firm cannot produce more than is allowed by existing technology. Referring to Figure 4.1, a technological change that increases productivity *shifts* the whole total product curve and marginal product curve upward. This means that each worker can produce more output *shift of curve — as opposed to movement along it*

so that diminishing returns are delayed to a higher level of output per worker. Technological improvements can thus overcome the adverse effects of the law of diminishing returns. As long as technology improves, diminishing returns can be avoided.

In addition to technological improvements, education, training, and capital investment can also induce upward *shifts* in a firm's total product curve and marginal product curve. For example, increased education results in smarter workers, and vocational training provides specific job skills. Moreover, capital investment relieves strains on production capacity and increases output per worker. This is why economists advocate education, training, investment, and research and development as important factors that increase worker productivity and living standards.

Wendy's Beefs up Productivity at Drive-Through Window

Let us apply the principle of productivity improvements to Wendy's.[1] As you read this section, notice factors that contribute to upward shifts in the marginal product curve and total product curve, thus delaying the law of diminishing returns.

"Hi may I take your order–please" says the drive-through attendant at Wendy's Old-Fashioned Hamburgers in Darien, Illinois. This greeting takes only one second—two seconds faster than is required in Wendy's employee manual—and the speed of it was clocked by a high-tech timer costing $2,000. The timer has helped knock eight seconds off the average takeout delivery time at this restaurant. But manager Ryan Tomney wants greater efficiency. "Every second," he says, "is business lost."

At 25 fast-food restaurant chains ranked in a recent study, motorists spent an average of 204 seconds from arrival at the menu board to exit from the pickup window. At Wendy's, that time was only 150 seconds. This made Wendy's 17 seconds faster than McDonald's, 21 seconds faster than Burger King, and second to none.

Yet far from being satisfied, Wendy's is hustling to increase its drive-through speed, and for good reason. Not long ago, drive-through was a hole punched through the wall to augment dining-room sales. But today, almost two-thirds of fast-food revenue comes through that hole. Now that most of the best restaurant locations have been accounted for, drive-through may be the last battleground for fast-food market share in the United States.

Certainly, the seven drive-through employees at Mr. Tomney's restaurant show incredible precision and attention to detail. The griller keeps 25 square burgers sizzling on the grill and, within five seconds of a customer's order, puts one on a bun. Once the meat hits the bun, the griller sends it to the sandwich makers, who have no more than seven seconds to complete each customized creation. Watching the procedure, Mr. Tomney looks for ways to save time. The bun grabber retrieves buns from the warmer the instant she hears a customer order through her headset. But watching her wait for customer orders, Mr. Tomney sees a second that could be saved. She had only one hand on the bunwarmer door, rather than the required two, which cost her time.

Using product development, employee retraining, and new technology, Burger King, McDonald's, Taco Bell, Arby's, and others are all striving for the drive-through market. The latest menu addition at McDonald's is aimed specifically at the drive-through customer—salad in a container that fits in car cup holders. Burger King is implementing see-through bags that permit customers to quickly check that all items are included. Arby's is working on a new version of its special sauce that is less likely to spill.

The chain that most consistently offers the fastest service will attract more customers. Regular drive-through customers know that a 5-car line at one chain is likely to move faster than a 3-car line at another. By some estimates, increasing drive-through efficiency

---

[1] "An Efficiency Drive: Fast-Food Lanes Are Getting Even Faster," *The Wall Street Journal*, May 18, 2000, p. A-1.

consumer
ECONOMICS IN ACTION

How Much Does It Cost to Drive?

How much does it cost to drive? Let us apply the notion of economic cost to driving. Some of your driving costs depend on the number of miles driven (gasoline), while other costs (vehicle registration) are fixed.

Each year, the American Automobile Association (AAA) estimates the costs of driving. Table 4.2 shows AAA

estimates for an individual who purchased a 2004 automobile and drove 15,000 miles per year. We see that the cost of driving a Chevrolet Cavalier was estimated to be 44.8. cents per mile, while the estimated cost of driving a Ford Taurus was 58.4 cents per mile.

As you read the table, notice which costs fall under the headings *fixed costs* and *variable costs*. You should be able to apply these concepts to the production costs that are discussed in this chapter.

Table 4.2   The Cost of Driving

	2004 Chevrolet Cavalier	2004 Ford Taurus
Variable costs:	Costs per Mile (in cents)	Costs per Mile (in cents)
Gasoline and oil	5.4	6.7
Maintenance	3.5	6.5
Tires	0.5	1.0
	9.4	14.2
	15,000 miles	15,000 miles
	×9.4¢	×14.2¢
Variable costs for driving 15,000 miles a year	$1,410	$2,130
Fixed costs:	Cost per Year	Cost per Year
Insurance	$1,606	$1,397
License, registration, taxes	352	421
Depreciation	2,812	4,051
Finance charge*	542	760
	$5,312	$6,629
Total cost (yearly)	$6,722	$8,759
Cost per mile**	44.8¢	58.4¢

handwritten annotation: FC higher — but VC lower + overall lower

*10% down; loan @ 6% interest for five years.

**Total cost/15,000 miles = Cost per mile.

Source: From American Automobile Association, *Your Driving Costs*, 2004.

by 10 percent bolsters sales at the average fast-food restaurant by $54,000 per year. In 2002, the average fast-food restaurant did about $590,000 in sales.

The biggest price of speed, however, is accuracy. A customer who arrives home only to find something missing or wrong with her order is unlikely to take much comfort in how quickly she zipped through the line. Another problem is the morale of drive-through workers, who often complain that they cannot keep pace with the service goals of the restaurant. Indeed, demanding productivity increases from drive-through employees, who are paid low wages and have high turnover rates, can be tricky.

SHORT–RUN PRODUCTION COSTS

If you ask managers about the competitiveness of their firms, their answers are likely to include a discussion of their costs. Costs are an extension of the production process. To illustrate, assume that DaimlerChrysler pays its workers $40 an hour and that 30 hours of labor are required to assemble a vehicle. The cost of assembly totals $1,200 per vehicle ($40 × 30 = $1,200). Suppose that improving technology results in a 10-percent increase in labor productivity: only 27 hours of labor are now required to assemble a vehicle. Assembly costs now total $1,080 ($40 × 27 = $1,080) per vehicle. In this manner, higher worker productivity results in lower production costs and thus increased profits for DaimlerChrysler. Higher productivity would also result in increased wages for DaimlerChrysler workers if they could capture some of the productivity gains as higher wages.

Total Fixed, Total Variable, and Total Costs

Let us consider the hypothetical costs that Hewlett-Packard (HP), a manufacturer of computer printers, realizes in the short run when it employs both fixed inputs and variable inputs.

First, we will consider the fixed costs of HP. Total fixed costs are costs that do not vary with output. Managers often refer to their fixed costs as *overhead costs*. They include such things as the cost of machinery, lease payments on some equipment, rent on a building, property taxes, and interest payments on a loan. The monthly value of Hewlett-Packard's fixed inputs is its monthly fixed cost. We see in column 2 of Table 4.3 that the firm's total fixed costs are $50. In Figure 4.2(a), these total fixed costs are shown by the horizontal line at $50. Fixed costs remain constant no matter how many printers are produced.

The production of printers also results in variable costs for HP. Total variable costs are costs that change as the rate of output is changed. They include payments for most labor, materials, storage and warehousing, shipping, electricity, and fuel. As HP produces more printers, more variable inputs are employed and thus its total variable costs increase. Total variable costs are therefore dependent on weekly or monthly output. Total variable

Table 4.3	Hypothetical Cost Schedules for HP Printers in the Short Run

Quantity Produced per Day	Total Fixed Cost	Total Variable Cost	Total Cost	Average Fixed Cost	Average Variable Cost	Average Total Cost	Marginal Cost
0	$50	$ 0	$ 50	$ —	$ —	$ —	$ —
1	50	80	130	50.00	80.00	130.00	80
2	50	150	200	25.00	75.00	100.00	70
3	50	210	260	16.67	70.00	86.67	60
4	50	260	310	12.50	65.00	77.50	50
5	50	320	370	10.00	64.00	74.00	60
6	50	390	440	8.33	65.00	73.33	70
7	50	470	520	7.14	67.14	74.28	80

will always intersect ATC + AVC at lowest point

| Figure 4.2 | Hypothetical Short–Run Cost Schedules for Hewlett-Packard |

Total cost includes both fixed and variable costs. Fixed costs must be paid even if no output is produced. Average total cost is the sum of average fixed cost and average variable cost. Marginal cost is the addition to total cost resulting from the production of one additional unit of output.

costs are shown in column 3 of Table 4.3 and are translated into a total variable cost curve in Figure 4.2(a).

The rate at which total variable costs rise as more printers are produced depends on the capacity limitations caused by fixed inputs. In general, total variable costs rise more slowly at low levels of output and then increase ever more rapidly. This aspect of variable costs is due to the principle of diminishing marginal productivity in the short run. As diminishing marginal productivity is encountered, each additional worker adds fewer units to the firm's output, yet the firm pays the same wage to each worker. As a result, total variable costs rise faster and faster.

Total costs are the sum of the value of all resources used over a given period to manufacture computer printers. Total costs are thus the sum of total fixed costs and total variable costs:

$$TC = TFC + TVC$$

The total costs of HP are shown in column 4 of Table 4.3 and are translated into a total cost curve in Figure 4.2(a). Notice that the vertical distance between the total cost curve and the total variable cost curve is total fixed cost.

Average Costs

Besides caring about total costs, HP managers care about *per-unit*, or *average*, costs. In the calculation of per-unit profit, average cost data are compared against price, which is always stated on a per-unit basis. Average fixed cost, average variable cost, and average total cost comprise the per-unit cost schedules of a firm, as shown in columns 5–7 of Table 4.3.

Let us begin with average fixed cost, or *AFC*, which equals total fixed cost per unit of output. Average fixed cost equals total fixed cost divided by output (*Q*), or

$$AFC = TFC/Q$$

Because total fixed cost remains the same no matter how many units are produced, average fixed cost steadily declines as output is increased. You can see by inspecting column 5 of Table 4.3 that average fixed cost decreases continually. To keep Figure 4.2(b) as uncluttered as possible, the average fixed cost curve is not shown.

Next, we look at average variable cost, or *AVC*, which is total variable cost per unit of output. Average variable cost equals total variable cost divided by output, or

$$AVC = TVC/Q$$

Column 6 of Table 4.3 shows the average variable cost of HP, which we translate into an average variable cost curve in Figure 4.2(b). According to this schedule, HP's average variable cost first decreases but eventually begins to increase as the firm produces more printers. Because a typical average variable cost schedule is shaped like the letter *U*, economists refer to this curve as U-shaped.

Finally, average total cost, or *ATC*, is total cost per unit of output. Average total cost equals total cost divided by output, or

$$ATC = TC/Q$$

This can be rewritten as

$$ATC = (TFC/Q + TVC/Q)$$

In other words, average total cost equals average fixed cost plus average variable cost, or

$$ATC = AFC + AVC$$

Column 7 of Table 4.3 shows the average total cost of HP, which we translate into an average total cost curve in Figure 4.2(b). Notice that the average total cost curve is U-shaped. Also notice that *ATC* and *AVC* become closer and closer in value as the quantity of printers rises. This is because average fixed cost gets smaller and smaller as output rises.

Marginal Cost

Businesses make decisions "on the margin." When the managers of HP consider a profit-maximization strategy, they are interested in whether the revenue earned from selling an additional printer more than offsets the cost of producing an extra printer. Because marginal means "additional," the managers will be interested in marginal cost.

Marginal cost (*MC*) refers to the change in total cost when one more unit of output is produced, or

$$MC = \Delta TC/\Delta Q$$

Marginal cost is easy to calculate; just measure how much total cost increases as another unit of output is produced. Column 8 of Table 4.3 shows the marginal cost of HP printers. As the firm increases output from zero printers to one printer, total cost rises from $50 to $130, and thus marginal cost equals $80. Producing a second printer increases total cost from $130 to $200, and thus marginal cost equals $70, and so on. We translate this marginal cost data into a marginal cost curve in Figure 4.2(b). Notice that a firm's marginal cost curve is typically U-shaped: As output expands, marginal cost decreases, eventually reaches a minimum, and then increases.

The principle of diminishing returns accounts for the U-shaped marginal cost curve. Recall that in the short run, as additional units of labor are added to machinery, the rate at which total output increases initially tends to increase. Assuming the firm pays the same wage to workers as output expands, as each additional worker adds more to total output than the previous one, the cost of each additional unit of output decreases. This extra cost is marginal cost. Therefore, as more units are produced, the marginal cost initially falls. This tendency, however, will not occur indefinitely. As more labor is applied to machinery, the marginal productivity of labor will eventually diminish. As a result, the marginal cost of production will increase. The U-shaped nature of the marginal cost curve is thus a reflection of diminishing marginal productivity in the production process.[2]

CHECK POINT

1. In general, a firm's production may take place in the short-run or the long-run period. Distinguish between these periods.

2. For a firm, distinguish between total product and marginal product.

3. As a firm adds more of a variable input to a fixed input in the short run, what happens to marginal product and total product? What accounts for this behavior?

4. Classify the following as fixed costs or variable costs per unit of time: wages, rental payments on a factory building, insurance premiums, electricity and water expenses, property taxes, transportation expenses, and advertising expenditures.

5. Why is the marginal cost curve U-shaped?

LONG-RUN PRODUCTION COSTS

So far, we have examined how costs in the short run vary as the rate of output expands for a firm of a given size. In the long run, however, all inputs under the firm's control can be varied: A firm has sufficient time to replace machinery and increase the size of a factory. Because no inputs are fixed in the long run, there are no fixed costs. All costs are therefore variable in the long run. In this section, we will examine how altering factory size, and all other inputs, influences the relationship between production and costs in the long run.

A useful way to look at the long run is to regard it as a planning horizon. When operating in today's market, HP must constantly plan and determine its strategy for the long run. For example, even before HP decides to manufacture a new type of computer printer, the firm is in a long-run situation because it can choose from a variety of types and sizes of equipment to manufacture the new printer. Once HP makes this decision, it is in a short-run situation because the type and size of equipment it owns are, mostly, frozen.

The **long-run average total cost curve** (*LRATC*) shows the minimum cost per unit of producing each output level when any desired size of factory can be constructed. Figure 4.3 shows the hypothetical *LRATC* curve of HP. Notice that this curve typically decreases with increases in output up to a certain point, reaches a minimum, and increases with further increases in output. This U-shaped appearance of the *LRATC* curve is determined

---

[2] When you inspect Figure 4.2(b), notice the relation of *MC* to *ATC* and *AVC*. *MC* intersects both *ATC* and *AVC* at their minimum points. This will always be the case. So long as the marginal cost of producing one more unit is less than the previous average cost, average cost must decrease. Conversely, average cost must increase so long as the marginal cost of producing one more unit is greater than the previous average cost. Therefore, the *MC* curve intersects the *ATC* and *AVC* curves at their lowest points.

| Figure 4.3 | Hypothetical Long-Run Average Total Cost Curve for Hewlett-Packard |

The long-run average total cost curve shows the minimum cost per unit of producing each output level when any desired size of factory can be constructed. The long-run average cost curve above is U-shaped, reflecting economies of scale in the decreasing portion and diseconomies of scale in the increasing portion. The curve also has a flat bottom as a result of an extended stage of constant returns to scale after economies of scale are exhausted.

by economies of scale and diseconomies of scale, which exist simultaneously at many different levels of output.

Economies of Scale

When a firm realizes economies of scale, the *LRATC* curve slopes downward: An increase in scale and production results in a fall in cost per unit. Here are some of the major sources of economies of scale:

- **Specialization of labor and management.** As a firm becomes larger, it may be able to benefit from greater specialization of labor and management. At Pizza Hut, some workers specialize in taking orders, others make pizza, and others wash dishes.

- **Efficient capital.** Smaller firms may not be able to acquire large, specialized machinery. For example, Wal-Mart employs sophisticated computer systems to track inventories and provide sales information to management.

- **Design and development.** Next time you purchase textbooks, compare the prices of a two-semester introductory text and a one-semester advanced text. To your surprise, you may find that the principles text does not cost much more than the advanced text. This is true even if the principles text has 250 more pages and is produced in a multicolor format compared to a black-and-white format for the advanced text. Economies of scale are present in this situation. Publishing introductory and advanced texts requires costs for development and advertising that are approximately the same per page. With introductory texts, these costs are distributed over large levels of output, say, 50,000 copies compared to only, say, 10,000 copies for an advanced text. This results in lower costs per copy and a relatively lower price per copy for the introductory text.

Do you know that when you use a prescription drug you are benefiting from the principle of decreasing long-run average cost? For prescription drugs, it takes roughly $350 million to bring the average new drug to the market. That's just for the first pill. Making the second costs about a penny. Assuming $350 million in development costs and a 1-cent marginal production cost thereafter, the average total cost of making a pill would fall from $350 million for producing just one to $350.01 for making a million to 4 cents each for sales of 10 billion. Prices fall in inverse proportion to the size of the market, as shown in Table 4.4. This example illustrates that, for pharmaceuticals, demand is not the enemy of price but its friend. The higher the demand, the lower the price because, after all, you can't have quantity discounts without quantity. *kind of, but not really*   *cost is lower*

Besides prescription drugs, many products in today's economy are produced under conditions of decreasing long-run average cost. Software, CDs, tapes, movies, and even many sophisticated electronic products are in this category.

economics
IN ACTION

From Mass Production to Lean Production

Henry Ford (1863–1947) was a noted pioneer of American industry. In 1903, Ford organized the Ford Motor Company. At first, the company manufactured only expensive automobiles, as its competitors did. However, Ford was from modest rural roots. He thought that the people who made cars ought to be able to afford one so that they too could go for a spin on a Sunday afternoon. Ford soon began developing a simple, sturdy vehicle that many people in all walks of life could afford. This car became known as the Model T, which appeared in 1908. Ford maintained that if he paid his factory workers a living wage and produced more cars in less time for less money, everyone would buy them.

In producing the Model T, Ford realized the importance of economies of mass production. He pioneered assembly line methods to slash the costs of producing automobiles. In 1908, the Model T sold for $850, which was not cheap in those days. In 1913, Ford installed moving assembly lines in his factories. The frame of the car moved through the plant on a conveyor belt. Workers on each side assembled the car by adding parts that had been brought to them by other conveyor belts. In 1914, Ford workers could assemble a Model T in a little more than 1½ hours. Building the earlier Model T had taken about 12½ hours. The big saving

of time slashed Ford's production costs. In 1916, the Model T could be sold at a profit for $400, the lowest price of any automobile. Not surprisingly, by 1921, Ford's Model T, which remained largely unchanged for 19 years, had more than 50 percent of the market. It was at this time that Ford used to make his famous announcement that "Any customer can have a car painted any color that he wants so long as it is black." Indeed, standardization, specialization, and mass production were the keys to Ford's lowering manufacturing costs, and constant price reduction was the key to attracting additional customers.

By the 1970s, however, U.S. auto manufacturers were challenged by lower costs and higher quality products from foreign firms. Japanese manufacturers like Toyota changed the rules of production from mass production to lean production. Toyota realized that it could not catch up to Ford and General Motors by using traditional mass production methods. Instead, Toyota adopted lean manufacturing, which places greater emphasis on flexibility and product quality. Instead of mass producing large numbers of identical vehicles, Toyota produces batches of similar vehicles. Toyota's goal is to have parts arrive just as they are needed, and these parts can be used interchangeably in its various models. This has allowed Toyota to manufacture higher quality vehicles at lower costs and introduce new models quickly. Toyota's success with lean manufacturing has placed great pressure on American auto firms to improve their manufacturing operations so they can compete in the global auto industry.

unions often fail to weigh short-run / long-run

Table 4.4	Average Total Cost of a Prescription Drug

Quantity of Pills	Average Total Cost
1	$350,000,000.00
10	35,000,000.01
100	3,500,000.01
1,000	350,000.01
10,000	35,000.01
100,000	3,500.01
1,000,000	350.01
10,000,000	35.01
100,000,000	3.51
1,000,000,000	0.36
10,000,000,000	0.04

Source: From *The New Paradigm*, Federal Reserve Bank of Dallas, 1999 Annual Report, p. 20.

international
ECONOMICS IN ACTION

Do U.S. Companies Have to Outsource Production to Low-Wage Countries to Remain Competitive?

In a global economy, trade with other countries tends to redirect people into the jobs that make best use of their productive abilities. Trade redirects people away from low-productive jobs in industries having cost disadvantages into high-productive jobs in industries having cost advantages. Low-productive jobs tend to disappear from the domestic economy and move abroad.

However, some economists wonder if this process always holds. It rests on the assumption that a low-skilled U.S. job shifted abroad would have remained low skilled had it stayed home. But if U.S. companies could increase the skill level for such work and perform the task more efficiently, the advantages from moving production would decline. Simply put, if work can be upgraded, it's not so obvious which countries should do the exporting. Let us consider the case of two U.S. companies, Fortune Brands and New Balance.

Fortune Brands Moves Production to Mexico

You may never have heard of Fortune Brands, but you probably are familiar with some of its products: Titleist golf clubs, Swingline staplers, Jim Beam whiskey, and Master Lock padlocks.

At the turn of the century, Fortune was implementing a cost-cutting program to improve its competitiveness. The firm expanded its manufacturing industrial park in Nogales, Mexico, which employed more than 3,000, most of them performing work Fortune used to do in the United States. Fortune moved several businesses into its 40-acre industrial park just south of the Arizona-Mexico border. For example, it brought Master Lock padlocks down from Milwaukee and Acco Industries' Swingline staplers from Queens, New York.

Locating in the Mexican industrial park was an effort to slash costs. It wasn't just a matter of taking advantage of low wages in Mexico—although that was a major factor—but of squeezing every possible cent out of costs. By constructing its own industrial park, Fortune reduced costs by obtaining its land all at once and lowered energy expenses by installing its own electric substation. Contracting single suppliers of packaging materials and components and having one waste hauler for all of the campus's plants also yielded efficiencies.

According to Fortune, the move to Nogales came at a crucial time when profit margins on its best-known products were

Diseconomies of Scale

Economies of scale are really only half the story. If they were the entire story, the question would then have to be asked: Why not manufacture autos in even larger enterprises? If Ford, DaimlerChrysler, and General Motors merged together, would they not manufacture autos more cheaply and thus realize additional profit per auto than when they produce separately. Likely not. As a firm gets larger and larger, opportunities to realize economies of scale are eventually exhausted. As a firm grows, it is likely to encounter **diseconomies of scale,** which results in increasing unit cost and the *LRATC* curve turns upward.

We can trace diseconomies of scale to the problems of managing large-scale operations. Beyond some scale of operation, the daily production routine becomes removed from the firm's top executives as additional layers of bureaucracy are added to the management team. The paperwork burden grows, and managers must control many business activities—finance, transportation, accounting, sales, research and development, personnel, and so on. The red tape and bureaucratic problems of running a large-scale operation contribute to inefficiencies and increased cost per unit.

Although the Ford Motor Company benefits from economies of scale, it has also encountered problems of large size. During the 1970s, Ford constructed a factory in Flat

under heavy pressure. Besides competition from U.S. manufacturers already in Mexico, as well as rivals in the Far East, the firm also faced demands for lower prices from its biggest customers. Buyers like Wal-Mart, Lowe's, and Home Depot increased their direct purchases of imports, forcing companies like Fortune to locate production abroad. Simply put, Fortune justified its move to Nogales on the grounds that if it didn't move abroad, its customers would find someone else who would.

New Balance Keeps Production in the United States

Now let us consider New Balance Athletic Shoe, Inc., headquartered in Boston, Massachusetts. As the firm's managers watched Nike, Reebok, and other rivals shift production abroad at the turn of the century, they came to think that producing close to their customers could give them an advantage in quick turnaround on new products and in fulfilling orders for shoe stores. How could New Balance manufacture shoes in the United States when Nike and Reebok couldn't? Mainly by using the latest production techniques adopted by American firms in higher-skilled industries.

To increase worker efficiency in New Balance's factories in the United States, workers operate shoe-stitching machines that use cameras to scan the edges of material. Working in small teams, staffers are trained to master a variety of skills. The firm also makes large capital investments in its factories, including massive robots whose arms swing around the

production floor, picking up shoe uppers, joining them with soles, and placing them on conveyor belts to be packaged. New Balance has also switched from incentive wages, based on the number of shoes workers produce, to hourly rates. Hourly rates allow staff to concentrate on training and upgrading their skills, and to internalize that the competition is workers in foreign plants, not other workers next to them. The combination of technology and small teams has reduced the cost disadvantage of manufacturing shoes in the United States.

New Balance's American workers produce a pair of shoes in just 24 minutes, versus about three hours in the Chinese factories that manufacture the same product. If the American workers were no more productive than those in China, New Balance's labor costs in the United States, where it pays $14 an hour in wages and benefits, would be a noncompetitive $44 per pair of shoes. But the company has slashed the labor cost to $4 a pair versus $1.30 in China, where wages are about 40 cents an hour. The remaining $2.70 labor cost differential is a manageable 4 percent of a typical $70 pair of shoes, and it is offset by the advantages of producing in the United States, where New Balance can fill store orders faster than rivals and respond more quickly to new footwear trends.

Sources: "Fortune Brands Moves Units to Mexico to Lower Costs," *The Wall Street Journal,* August 7, 2000, p. B2; "New Balance Stays a Step Ahead," *U.S. News & World Report,* July 2, 2001, p. 34; and "Low-Skilled Jobs: Do They Have to Move?" *Business Week,* February 26, 2001, pp. 94–95.

Rock, Michigan, to manufacture blocks for 8-cylinder engines. Ford followed the principle that large-scale production could bring lower costs per unit of output. The firm spent $200 million to build a 4-story-high factory designed exclusively to manufacture engine blocks in the fastest, most efficient way possible. By 1981, however, Ford shut down the factory and shifted production to a much older plant in Cleveland. The reason was that the Flat Rock plant was too big and inflexible. It was constructed to make engines at very large volumes, but could not be converted to produce 4- and 6-cylinder engines that became popular as gasoline prices rose. In effect, the Flat Rock plant was viewed to be an inefficient dinosaur that could not keep pace with a rapidly changing economy.

There may also be an intervening range of output over which a firm realizes **constant returns to scale**. This would occur when the firm's output changes by the same percentage as the change in all inputs. For example, a 20-percent increase in all inputs causes a 20-percent increase in the firm's output. As a result, cost per unit remains constant, and the *LRATC* curve is horizontal. This situation is consistent with many U.S. industries. For example, over an intermediate-size range, smaller firms can be as efficient as larger ones in such industries as publishing, shoes, lumber, and apparel.

SHIFTS IN COST CURVES

In discussing the general shapes of a firm's cost curves in both the short run and long run, we assumed that certain other factors—technology, resource prices, and taxes—remained constant as the firm changed its level of output. These factors are *shifters* that cause cost curves to shift upward (downward), suggesting that a given level of output can be produced at a greater (smaller) cost.

- **Technology.** As we have learned, a technological change that increases productivity shifts the total product curve and the marginal product curve upward. Because a better technology allows the same output to be produced with fewer resources, a firm's cost curves shift *downward*. For example, computers and robots reduced the number of labor hours needed to produce automobiles, and printing presses reduced the number of labor hours required to produce books and newspapers, thus resulting in lower costs.

- **Resource prices.** A decrease in the price of resources, such as materials and labor, will reduce the cost of producing each output level. Therefore, a firm's cost curves will *shift downward*. In 1997, for example, the starting price for a personal computer smashed through the $1,000 barrier as manufacturers lowered the prices of chips used to produce personal computers. Lower-priced chips resulted in falling costs for producing computers for firms such as Dell and Gateway and allowed them to slash their computer prices.

- **Taxes.** Taxes are another component of a firm's costs. Suppose that the federal government reduces the excise tax from 25 cents to 20 cents on each gallon of gasoline sold by service stations. This policy results in a decrease in the cost of doing business for a service station, which causes the firm's cost curves to *shift downward*.

Foreign Competition Forces Cost Adjustments for U.S. Steelmakers

The U.S. steel industry provides an example of changing production costs. In 1950, the U.S. steel industry was the most powerful in the world, accounting for almost one-half of world steel output. Also, the large U.S. steel companies realized a dominant position of world leadership in plant-scale and technology, a position that had gone virtually

| Table 4.5 | World Steel Cost Comparisons: Cost per Ton of Steel, 2004 |

Cost Components	United States	Japan	Germany	China
Labor cost				
Labor hours per ton	3.18	2.88	2.91	12.4
Wages and benefits per hour	× $39.00	× $42.00	× $47.00	× $1.85
Labor cost*	$ 124	$ 121	$ 137	$ 23
Material costs	307	293	333	330
Depreciation expense	22	50	40	30
Interest expense	11	6	16	10
Total cost per ton	$ 464	$ 470	$ 526	$ 393

*The product of labor hours per ton times employee cost per hour (rounded to the nearest dollar).

Source: From Peter F. Marcus and Karlis M. Kirsis, "World Steel Dynamics," *Steel Strategist #30: World Cost Curve Monitor Reference Plant Comparisons,* August 2004.

unchallenged by foreign competitors during the preceding 50 years. Moreover, the United States exported far more steel than it imported.

However, the market dominance of U.S. steelmakers did not last forever. Following World War II, Europe, Japan, and other nations rebuilt their steel industries using the latest technologies. These changes resulted in comparatively low production costs of foreign steel, which caused a stream of steel imports into the United States during the 1960s and 1970s and a flood of imports in the early 1980s. In 1982, the average total cost per ton of steel for U.S. producers was $685 per ton—52 percent higher than for Japanese producers. This cost differential was largely due to a strong U.S. dollar and higher domestic costs of labor and raw materials, which accounted for 25 percent and 45 percent, respectively, of total cost. Moreover, U.S. operating rates were relatively low, resulting in high fixed costs of production for each ton of steel.

The cost disadvantage encouraged U.S. steelmakers to initiate measures to reduce production costs and regain competitiveness. Many steel companies closed obsolete and costly steel mills, coking facilities, and ore mines. They also secured more flexible work rules, offered incentives for efficiency gains to employees, and slashed the ranks of management. Although these adjustments improved efficiency, U.S. steel companies became increasingly burdened by the benefits that had to be paid to their legions of retiring steelworkers.

Table 4.5 shows the cost of producing a ton of steel for selected nations in 2004. Notice that the labor productivity of Japanese, German, and American steel firms (measured in labor hours per ton) was much higher than for China. This factor provided a cost advantage for Japanese, German, and American steelmakers. However, steelmakers in China realized cost advantages because of lower wages and benefits. Overall, the cost of producing a ton of steel was lower in China.

COSTS AND PROFIT

An essential characteristic of the cost schedules we have observed is that they include the market value of all the resources used in the production process: land, labor, capital, and entrepreneurship. To calculate this cost, we simply identify all the resources used in production, determine their value, and then add things up.

Explicit Costs and Implicit Costs

Economists define the total costs of production as the sum of explicit costs plus implicit costs. **Explicit costs** are payments made to others as a cost of running a business. For a local Pizza Hut franchise, explicit costs would include wages paid to labor, the cost of materials and electricity, telephone and advertising expenses, rental charges for the restaurant, health insurance for employees, and the like.

Implicit costs are the costs that represent the value of resources used in production for which no monetary payment is made. For Pizza Hut, implicit costs might include the forgone salary of the owner of the restaurant who used her time to run the business. It might also include forgone interest because the owner invested her funds in the firm rather than depositing them in her savings account at the bank. If the owner used her building to house the restaurant, she also sacrificed rent that she could have received from other tenants. With implicit costs, no money changes hands. They represent the imputed value that the firm's resources could command in their best alternative uses.

like opportunity cost

Accounting Profit and Economic Profit

Consider now what the term profit means. Most people think of profit as the difference between the amount of revenues a firm takes in (total revenue) and the amount it spends for wages, materials, electricity, and so on (total cost). If costs are greater than revenues, we call such "negative profits" losses. Although this description seems clear enough, accountants and economists have different views concerning what types of costs should be included in total cost. As a result, they have different notions of profit.

To an accountant, the following formula describes profit:

$$\text{Accounting profit} = \text{Total revenue} - \text{Explicit costs}$$

We know this definition of profit as **accounting profit**. When preparing financial reports, accountants are concerned only with costs that are payable to others, such as wages, materials, and interest.

Besides caring about explicit costs, economists are interested in a firm's implicit costs, such as forgone salary, rent, and interest. **Economic profit** is total revenue minus the sum of explicit and implicit costs:

$$\text{Economic profit} = \text{Total revenue} - (\text{Explicit costs} + \text{Implicit costs})$$

Economists thus use the full cost of all resources as the figure to subtract from revenues to obtain a definition of profit.

Because accounting practice does not recognize implicit costs of owner-supplied inputs, accounting costs, as we've discussed, *underestimate* economic costs. As a result, accounting profits based on accounting costs *overestimate* profits by underestimating costs.

What does zero economic profit imply? In economics, a firm that makes zero economic profit is said to be earning a **normal profit**. It represents the minimum profit necessary to keep a firm in operation. In other words, normal profit occurs when total revenue just covers explicit costs plus implicit costs.   *like BE point*

Should the owner of a company worry if she makes only a normal profit for the past year? The answer is no. Although a normal profit may appear unattractive, the owner has realized total revenues sufficient to cover both explicit and implicit costs. If, for example, the owner's implicit cost is the forgone salary of $50,000 for managing the business of someone else, then realizing a normal profit suggests she has done as well as she could have in her next best line of employment.

This chapter considers the role of productivity and costs of production in influencing business decisions. In the next chapter, we will learn how a firm goes about maximizing economic profit. We will consider how a firm maximizes profits in a competitive market and also under a monopoly.

CHECK POINT

1. How do economies of scale and dis-economies of scale relate to a firm's long-run average total cost curve?

2. When drawing short- and long-run cost curves, we assume that certain factors remain constant. Identify these factors and their potential effects on a firm's cost curves.

3. Distinguish between explicit costs and implicit costs.

4. Why does the calculation of profit differ for an accountant as opposed to an economist?

5. Why do economists regard normal profit as a cost?

Chapter Summary

1. In general, a firm's production may take place in the short- or long-run period. The short run is a period in which the quantity of at least one input is fixed and we can vary the quantities of the other inputs. The long run is a time in which all inputs are considered to be variable in amount.

2. The relationship between physical output and the quantity of resources used in the production process is called a production function. A production function shows the maximum amount of output that we can produce with a given amount of resources.

3. According to the law of diminishing marginal returns, as a firm adds more of a variable input to a fixed input, beyond some point the marginal productivity of the variable input diminishes.

4. A firm producing goods in the short run employs fixed inputs and variable inputs. Fixed costs are payments to fixed inputs, and they do not vary with output. Variable costs are payments to variable inputs, and they increase as output expands.

5. We can describe a firm's costs in terms of a total approach: total fixed cost, total variable cost, and total cost. We can also describe them in terms of a per-unit approach: average fixed cost, average variable cost, and average total cost.

6. Marginal cost refers to the change in total cost when we produce another unit of output. The short-run marginal cost curve is generally U-shaped, reflecting the law of diminishing marginal returns.

7. The long-run average total cost curve shows the minimum cost per unit of producing each output level when we can construct any desired size of a factory. Economies of scale and diseconomies of scale account for the U-shaped appearance of this cost curve.

8. In discussing the general shapes of a firm's cost curves in the short and long run, we assume that technology, resource prices, and taxes remain constant as the firm changes its level of output. Changes in any of these factors will cause a firm's cost curves to shift upward or downward.

9. Economists define the total costs of production as the sum of explicit costs plus implicit costs.

10. According to accounting principles, profit equals total revenue minus explicit costs. Besides caring about explicit costs, economists are interested in a firm's implicit costs. Economic profit thus equals total revenue minus the sum of explicit costs and implicit costs.

11. A firm that makes zero economic profit is said to earn a normal profit. It represents the minimum profit necessary to keep a firm in operation. In other words, the firm earns just enough revenue to cover its explicit costs and implicit costs.

Key Terms and Concepts

short run (78)

fixed input (78)

variable inputs (78)

long run (78)

production (79)

production function (79)

total product (80)

marginal product (80)

law of diminishing marginal returns (81)

increasing marginal returns (81)

diminishing marginal returns (81)

total fixed cost (84)

total variable cost (84)

total cost (85)

average fixed cost (85)

average variable cost (86)

average total cost (86)

marginal cost (86)

long-run average total cost curve (87)

economies of scale (88)

diseconomies of scale (91)

constant returns to scale (92)

explicit cost (94)

implicit cost (94)

profit (94)

losses (94)

accounting profit (94)

economic profit (94)

normal profit (94)

Self-Test: Multiple-Choice Questions

1. The law of diminishing returns suggests that if increasing quantities of labor are applied to a given amount of machinery, the

   a. total product cannot be increased.
   b. total product will be decreasing.
   c. marginal product must be negative.
   d. marginal product will eventually decrease.

2. When the law of diminishing returns sets in, marginal cost must be

   a. falling at a decreasing rate.
   b. falling at an increasing rate.
   c. constant.
   d. rising.

3. The explicit costs of a firm include all of the following *except*

    a. rent paid for the use of a building.
    b. interest paid for borrowed money.
    c. money payments for the owner's self-employed resources.
    d. payments for the purchase of materials.

4. A firm's short-run production function describes how the

    a. maximum possible output varies as the quantity of labor hired varies in a given factory.
    b. minimum possible output varies as the quantity of labor hired varies in a given factory.
    c. maximum possible output varies as a firm enlarges the size of its factory.
    d. minimum possible output varies as a firm enlarges the size of its factory.

5. For U.S. Steel, the total product curve represents the

    a. maximum amount of steel attainable for each quantity of variable input hired.
    b. minimum amount of steel attainable for each quantity of variable input hired.
    c. least cost of producing various amounts of steel.
    d. maximum profit when producing and selling various amounts of steel.

6. Kaiser Aluminum's total product curve would shift upward if the firm

    a. hires additional quantities of labor and materials.
    b. pays lower wages to attract additional workers.
    c. employs more efficient technologies in aluminum production.
    d. initiates work rules leading to falling productivity of labor.

7. Marginal cost is defined as

    a. total fixed cost plus total variable cost.
    b. total cost divided by the level of output.
    c. the increase in total cost as a firm produces an additional unit of output.
    d. total cost minus total fixed cost.

8. The range over which marginal cost is decreasing is the same range over which

    a. total product is increasing.
    b. marginal product is increasing.
    c. total cost is increasing at an increasing rate.
    d. total cost is decreasing.

9. General Motors would realize diseconomies of scale if an increase in plant size causes

    a. a decrease in long-run average total cost.
    b. an increase in long-run average total cost.
    c. the short-run total product curve to shift upward.
    d. the short-run total product curve to remain constant.

10. For Boeing, technological advances in producing jetliners will tend to shift total product and marginal product curves

    a. down, and total cost and marginal cost curves up.
    b. up, and total cost and marginal cost curves down.
    c. up, and no change in total cost and marginal cost curves.
    d. down, and no change in total cost and marginal cost curves.

Answers to Multiple-Choice Questions

1. d   2. d   3. c   4. a   5. a   6. c   7. c   8. b   9. b   10. b

Table 4.6	Productivity Data	

Quantity of Labor	Total Product	Marginal Product
0	0	
1	20	
2	45	
3	65	
4	80	
5	90	

Study Questions and Problems

1. As the manager of a restaurant, you estimate the total product of labor used to cook meals, as shown in Table 4.6. Use these data to calculate the marginal product of labor.

   a. In a diagram, plot the total product and marginal product schedules.
   b. What effect does the law of diminishing marginal returns have on these schedules?
   c. What underlies the law of diminishing marginal returns?

2. South-Western/Thomson Learning has maintained data on labor input and production of economics texts, as seen in Table 4.7.

   a. Use these data to calculate the marginal product for each quantity of labor hired. Assume that when no workers are hired, output is zero.
   b. Using two figures, plot the total product curve and the marginal product curve.
   c. Identify the number of workers hired where total product is at a maximum.
   d. At which level of employment does the law of diminishing marginal returns begin?

3. Hanson Electric Co. has fixed costs of $2,000 and variable costs as shown in Table 4.8. Complete the table.

   a. In a graph, plot total fixed cost, total variable cost, and total cost. Explain the shapes of these curves in relation to one another.
   b. In another graph, plot average fixed cost, average variable cost, average total cost, and marginal cost. Explain the shapes of these curves in relation to one another.
   c. How does the law of diminishing marginal returns explain the shape of the marginal cost curve?

4. Wassink Instruments has compiled output and cost data, shown in Table 4.9, on its production of microscopes. Use these data to compute total fixed cost, total variable cost, average fixed cost, average variable cost, average total cost, and marginal cost for each output level shown.

Table 4.7	Producing Textbooks						
Labor input (workers)	3	5	1	2	4	6	7
Output of texts (total product)	380	600	100	220	520	620	580

Table 4.8		Hanson Electric Co.'s Cost of Production (in dollars)					
Output	Total Variable Cost	Total Cost	Average Fixed Cost	Average Variable Cost	Average Total Cost	Marginal Cost
1	$1,000					
2	1,600					
3	2,000					
4	2,600					
5	3,400					
6	4,800					

Table 4.9	Cost Data for the Production of Microscopes	
Output	Total Cost	
0	$ 400	
1	700	
2	900	
3	1,000	
4	1,200	
5	1,500	
6	1,900	

5. Your dry-cleaning firm currently cleans 300 shirts per day. Fixed costs for the firm are $400 per day. Variable costs are $1 per shirt. Calculate the total cost and the average total cost at the existing output level. Calculate average fixed cost. What price would your firm have to charge to realize a normal profit at the current level of output?

6. Your shoe manufacturing company estimates than whenever it triples machinery, labor, and any other inputs in the long run, its output also triples. Assuming input prices remain constant as your firm expands, construct the firm's long-run average total cost curve.

7. Some people are concerned about the decline of the small family farm and its replacement by large corporate farms. Explain how economies of scale might be a cause of this trend.

8. Increasing student population at the University of Wisconsin results in the nearby Pizza Hut restaurant realizing record sales. It is considering adding a new oven to bake additional pizzas. However, the daytime supervisor recommends simply employing more workers. How should the manager decide which course of action to initiate?

9. How will rising steel prices affect the average total cost curve and marginal cost curve of ABC Construction Inc., a builder of skyscrapers?

10. The introduction of the personal computer has decreased the number of hours required to type and edit a manuscript. How has this improvement in technology affected the average total cost curve and marginal cost curve of a publishing company?

Competition and Monopoly: Virtues and Vices

Chapter objectives

After reading this chapter, you should be able to:

1. Explain the nature and operation of a perfectly competitive firm.

2. Explain how a perfectly competitive firm achieves economic efficiency in the long run.

3. Identify factors that contribute to monopoly.

4. Describe how a monopoly goes about maximizing profits.

5. Assess the advantages and disadvantages of a perfectly competitive firm and a monopoly.

economics IN CONTEXT

Aircraft carriers have been dubbed "97,000 tons of diplomacy." But in the early 2000s, the Navy was being anything but diplomatic with its sharp criticism of Newport News Shipbuilding, Inc. Newport News, whose sprawling shipyard has hugged the St. James River in southern Virginia since it turned out its first tugboat in 1891, has long been the government's only producer of aircraft carriers. Navy officials expressed frustration with Newport News's failure to deliver promised cost savings.

The situation, Navy officials maintained, highlights what occurs in the absence of healthy competition. As a single producer, Newport News does not have to worry about staying ahead of its rivals to earn profits. Therefore, it lacks the incentive to organize production so as to minimize costs. Excess costs can be the result of ineffective supervision of employees, use of outdated equipment, payment of large bonuses to management, and the like.

However, the situation cannot easily be remedied because the work that goes into building nuclear-powered warships makes it virtually impossible for a competitor to emerge. A typical carrier takes five years to build, is 20 stories high including its tower, and carries more than 80 heavy fighter jets on a deck that covers $4\frac{1}{2}$ acres. The investment outlay required to construct another shipyard would be mammoth, which discourages others from building a shipyard to compete against Newport News. Indeed, the Navy faced a difficult issue: how to pressure Newport News into making carriers at a reasonable cost when there is no alternative supplier.

Millions of businesses operate in the U.S. economy; each behaves differently regarding its control over product price, the types of nonprice policies it uses, and its ability to realize the necessary profit to remain in business over time. Some firms have substantial control over product price, but others have little or no price-making ability. Some firms spend millions of dollars in product development or advertising, while others spend only negligible amounts on these activities. Some firms realize large economic profits over the long run, while others, no matter how well they are managed, have no such potential.

The degree of competition in a market determines the ability of a firm to control the price it charges for its product and its potential for realizing continuing economic profits. As we will see, as market competition *increases*, a firm has *less* control over product price and is *less* likely to earn continuing economic profits.

Economists have formulated four market classifications to illustrate different competitive situations: perfect competition, monopolistic competition, oligopoly, and monopoly. With perfect competition, competition is strongest; competition is nonexistent with pure monopoly. In between are monopolistic competition, which is closer to perfect competition, and oligopoly, which is closer to monopoly.

In this chapter, we will examine the virtues and vices of perfect competition and monopoly. The next chapter will consider monopolistic competition and oligopoly.

PERFECT COMPETITION

Let us begin with **perfect competition,** the most competitive market structure. A perfectly competitive market is characterized by the following:

- **Insignificant barriers to entry or exit.** New firms can enter a market if it appears profitable or exit if they expect losses. For example, lawn maintenance is an easy market to enter. To enter the market, one needs a lawnmower, an edger, and perhaps an ad in the local newspaper.

- **Many sellers and buyers.** Each sells or purchases only a negligible share of the total amount exchanged in the market.

- **A standardized product produced by firms in the industry.** For example, the wheat grown by one farmer is identical to the wheat grown by another farmer. As a result, brand preferences and consumer loyalty are nonexistent.

- **Perfect information.** All sellers and buyers are fully aware of market opportunities. That is, they know everything that relates to buying, producing, and selling the product.

(handwritten margin note: ask them to give examples of each kind)

Perfect competition is quite rare in the United States because most markets do not fulfill all of these assumptions. The usefulness of this market structure is that it serves as an important ideal against which real-world markets can be judged. Notice, however, that some markets come close to fulfilling the assumptions of perfect competition and thus provide an approximation characterized by ease of entry and exit. Examples include agricultural products, fishing industries, stock markets (such as the New York Stock Exchange), and the foreign exchange market.

The Perfectly Competitive Firm as a Price Taker

In a perfectly competitive market, each seller and buyer is so small compared to the size of the market that its decision as to what quantity to supply or purchase does not affect market price. A perfectly competitive firm is called a **price taker** because it has to "take," or accept, the price established by the market.

Figure 5.1 illustrates the hypothetical case of Puget Sound Fishing Co., which operates in a perfectly competitive market. In Figure 5.1(a), the market price of fish is $7 per pound, as determined by the intersection of the market demand curve and the market supply curve. Once the market price is established, Puget Sound Fishing Co. can sell all the fish it wants to at that price because it supplies an insignificant share of the market output. In Figure 5.1(b), the demand curve, as it appears to Puget Sound Fishing Co., is drawn as a *horizontal* line at the market price. This demand curve is also a *price line* for the firm. Note that the firm's output is much smaller than the market output. For example, hundreds of fishing firms might operate in the market, producing a combined output many times greater than that supplied by the Puget Sound Fishing Co.

Figure 5.1	**Demand and Marginal Revenue of a Perfectly Competitive Firm**

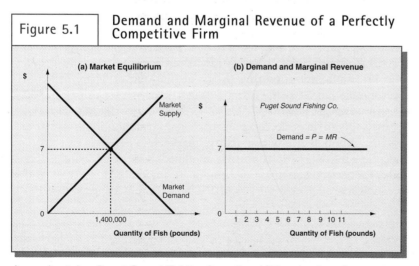

As a price taker, Puget Sound Fishing Co. sells additional units of output at a price that is determined by the market. The firm's demand schedule appears horizontal and coincides with its marginal revenue schedule.

Why won't Puget Sound Fishing Co. try to raise its price above $7? The reason is that in a perfectly competitive market many other firms sell fish at $7 per pound. If Puget Sound Fishing Co. set its price above $7, it would sell no fish. Conversely, the firm will not set its price below $7 because it can sell all the fish it wants to at the market price; thus, a lower price would decrease its revenue.

Total revenue (TR) for a perfectly competitive firm is simply the price per unit ($7 in this example) times the output level, or $TR = P \times Q$. The rate of increase in total revenue is especially important. It represents the increase in total revenue resulting from the sale of another unit of output. We call this rate of increase **marginal revenue** (MR). Mathematically, $MR = \Delta TR/\Delta Q$.

For Puget Sound Fishing Co., total revenue is zero when zero fish are sold. The sale of the first pound of fish increases total revenue from zero to $7 ($7 \times 1 = $7), so the marginal revenue is $7. The second pound increases total revenue from $7 to $14, so the marginal revenue is again $7. Marginal revenue is therefore a constant, $7, because total revenue increases by this fixed amount as each additional pound of fish is sold.

What is the relationship between price and marginal revenue for a perfectly competitive firm? In Figure 5.1(b), we see that Puget Sound Fishing Co. as a price taker sells fish at a constant price of $7 per pound. We also see that the firm's marginal revenue equals $7 for each pound sold. Therefore, in perfect competition, price (P) equals marginal revenue, or $P = MR$.

PERFECT COMPETITION: PROFIT MAXIMIZATION IN THE SHORT RUN

We have just learned about the demand and revenue schedules of a perfectly competitive firm. The next step is to combine information about the firm's revenues and costs to find the output that will maximize profits in the short run.

Marginal Revenue Equals Marginal Cost Rule

Recall that MR represents the addition to total revenue from the sale of another unit of output, and marginal cost (MC) represents the addition to total cost of producing another unit of output. If MR exceeds MC, total revenue will increase more than total cost as output rises. Because total profit is the difference between total revenue and total cost, the production of additional units that add more to total revenue than to total cost will increase total profit. Conversely, if MC exceeds MR, decreasing output will result in increased total profit. Profit maximization thus occurs at that output where $MR = MC$. This translates into economic jargon as the **marginal revenue = marginal cost rule**: Total profit is maximized where marginal revenue is equal to marginal cost. This rule applies to all firms, whether they operate in perfectly competitive markets, monopolistic markets, oligopolistic markets, or monopolistically competitive markets.

With perfect competition, the $MR = MC$ rule can be modified. Because price and marginal revenue are identical for a perfectly competitive firm, profit maximization occurs at that output where price equals marginal cost, or $P = MC$. This is simply a special case of the $MR = MC$ rule.

Perhaps you can benefit from the price = marginal cost rule the next time you purchase an automobile. The auto dealer wants to get a price that at least covers all her costs, including both variable costs and fixed costs. She might, however, be willing to sell you an automobile for only its marginal cost—that is, the wholesale price she paid for it plus a little labor time for dealer preparation of the vehicle. As long as the price exceeds

aka " equilibrium "

| Figure 5.2 | Profit Maximization for a Perfectly Competitive Firm |

In the figure, total profit of Puget Sound Fishing Co. is maximized at 2,500 pounds of fish, where marginal cost equals marginal revenue at point *A*. Total profit ($2,500) equals profit per unit ($1) multiplied by the profit-maximizing output (2,500 units).

Profit Maximization

Figure 5.2 shows the revenue and cost curves of Puget Sound Fishing Co., which operates in a perfectly competitive market. As expected, the average total cost curve and marginal cost curve are U-shaped. The demand curve is horizontal, which means that price equals marginal revenue at all levels of output.

In Figure 5.2, Puget Sound Fishing Co. maximizes total profits by selling 2,500 pounds of fish, where $MR = MC$. The firm's price equals $7 per pound, and its total revenue equals $17,500 ($7 × 2,500 = $17,500). Because the average total cost for 2,500 pounds of fish equals $6 per pound, the total cost for all 2,500 pounds is $15,000 ($6 × 2,500 = $15,000). The firm's total profit is $2,500 ($17,500 – $15,000 = $2,500). This amount is shown graphically by the shaded area in the figure.

An alternate way to calculate total profit is to multiply *profit per unit* by output. Profit per unit equals price minus average total cost $(P - ATC)$. Referring to Figure 5.2, at the profit-maximizing output of 2,500 pounds, the price is $7 and the average total cost is $6. Profit per unit thus equals $1 ($7 – $6 = $1). Multiplying this amount by 2,500 pounds gives total profit of $2,500.

Notice that Puget Sound Fishing Co. does not attempt to maximize profit per unit, where price exceeds average total cost by the greatest amount. What matters is *total* profit, not the amount of profit per unit. This is the age-old problem of selling, say, cookies at a school fund raiser. Perhaps you can maximize profit per unit by selling one box for $5, but you would make more total profit if you sold 100 boxes at a per-unit profit of only 25 cents each. The increase in volume would more than offset the reduction in profit per unit, resulting in a rise in total profit. For Puget Sound Fishing Co., total profit is at a maximum when marginal revenue equals marginal cost.

However, Puget Sound Fishing Co. is not guaranteed a profit. For example, a downturn in the economy may result in the firm realizing losses. Loss minimization for a perfectly competitive firm is discussed in "Exploring Further: 5.1" at the end of the chapter.

PERFECT COMPETITION: LONG-RUN ADJUSTMENTS AND ECONOMIC EFFICIENCY

To the owner of a business, profits are obviously desirable and losses dreadful. From the viewpoint of the overall economy, however, profits and losses play equally important roles in allocating scarce resources efficiently. Although a market economy is often referred to as a profit system, it is really a profit and loss system. Losses are equally important for the efficiency of the economy because they tell businesses what to stop producing. Let us see why this is true.

An important characteristic of perfect competition is the long-run behavior of firms in this market structure. Although the number of firms in a competitive market is fixed in the short run, freedom of entry and exit applies to the long run. Because of easy entry into and exit from a market, perfectly competitive firms operate at the *lowest possible cost,* charge the *lowest price* that they can without going out of business, and earn *no economic profit*. These characteristics are ideal from the consumer's perspective.

Let us consider again the case of Puget Sound Fishing Co. Assume the firm's cost curves are identical to all other firms in the fish market. This assumption allows us to analyze a *typical* or *average* firm, realizing that all other firms are similarly affected by any long-run adjustments that may occur.

Figure 5.3 shows the long-run position of Puget Sound Fishing Co. Notice that the firm produces at point A, where its demand curve just touches the lowest point on its long-run average total cost curve. The firm thus produces 500 pounds of fish at $5 per pound. Any other output level would result in a loss for the firm because its demand curve would be below its long-run average total cost curve.

Also notice that point A is the *minimum* point on the firm's long-run average total cost curve. This means that the firm produces at the lowest possible cost per unit in the long run. Competition forces the firm to use the least costly, and thus the most economically efficient, productive techniques. Efficient production is an important objective for society because the fundamental problem of economics is scarcity; efficiency counteracts the scarcity problem by allowing a greater amount of output to be produced with a given amount of resources. What accounts for this long-run position of a perfectly competitive firm? Freedom of entry into and exit from the market is the basis for the position of the average perfectly competitive firm in the long run.

Let us first consider the effect of entry of sellers into a perfectly competitive market. Referring to Figure 5.3(a), suppose the equilibrium price in the fish market is $6 a pound, shown at the intersection of the market supply curve (S_0) and market demand curve (D_0). With a market price of $6 per pound, the demand curve of Puget Sound Fishing Co. is located at $Demand_1$. The firm realizes an economic profit because its demand curve lies above its long-run average total cost curve. Over time, however, economic profits attract new competitors into the market. The resulting increase in market supply causes a decrease in market price and a decline in economic profits. Entry continues until the market supply reaches S_1, price falls to $5 per pound, and economic profits fall to zero for Puget Sound Fishing Co. Once economic profits disappear, entry ceases.

Now we will examine the effect of exit of sellers from a perfectly competitive market. Referring to Figure 5.3(b), suppose the equilibrium price in the fish market is $4 per

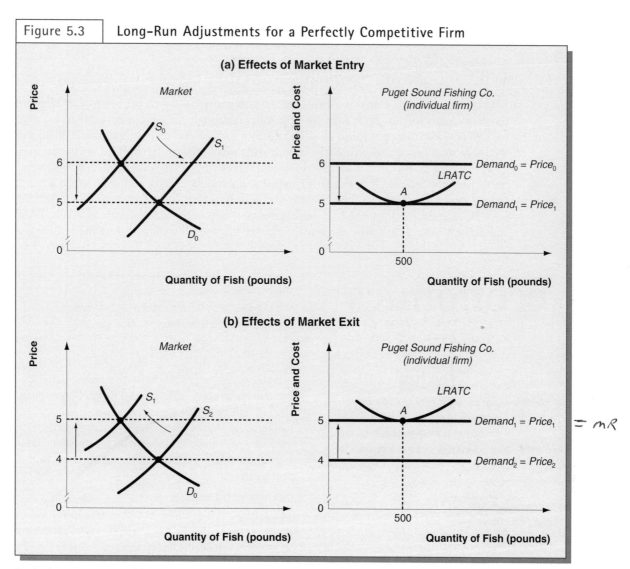

| Figure 5.3 | Long-Run Adjustments for a Perfectly Competitive Firm |

In the long run, competitive price will equal the minimum average total cost of production because short-run profits result in new firms entering a competitive industry until those profits have been competed away. Conversely, short-run losses will hasten the exit of firms from the industry until product price barely covers average cost. At the point of long-run equilibrium, price equals minimum average total cost, which allows just a normal profit.

pound, shown at the intersection of the market supply curve (S_2) and market demand curve (D_0). At this price, the average firm realizes a loss because the cost of supplying each fish exceeds the price. Less than normal profits would cause some firms to close their doors and exit the market. This results in a decrease in market supply and an increase in price. The exodus of firms would continue until the market supply reaches S_1 and the price rises to $5 per pound, at which point zero economic profits accrue for the remaining firms. Easy entry into and exit from the market thus cause a perfectly competitive firm to operate where price equals minimum average total cost, which allows only a normal profit. *aka zero*

Although production under perfect competition occurs in the long run at minimum average total cost, this result does not imply that perfectly competitive firms necessarily are more efficient than firms in others types of market structures. However, it does mean that, given the technology available to the firm, economic forces in perfect competition require producers to minimize the per-unit cost of production.

Will Online Music Startups Be Singing the Blues?

We have learned that when new firms enter a competitive market, the price decreases and the economic profit of each existing firm falls. Although the online music business that we will consider does not fulfill all of the assumptions of perfect competition, it illustrates the long-run adjustments that occur in industries with relative freedom of entry and exit.

The author of this text once asked his economics principles students if they download music from the Internet. The students laughed and virtually everyone raised his or her hand. Indeed, bootlegged services, like Napster and Kazaa, where songs can be grabbed for free, have threatened the livelihood of performers and music companies such as BMG, EMI, and Sony Music. That's why the music industry has filed lawsuits against the bootlegged

economics
IN ACTION

Steve Jobs: A Great Innovator

In market economies, whenever a new opportunity appears, innovators quickly find means to profit from it. Because innovators are free to pursue their self-interests as they see them, they profit as well from a myriad of ancillary opportunities initially undreamed of by most. Consider the case of Steve Jobs.

The next time you use your iMac computer or iPod music player, or purchase music online from iTunes, remember the name, Steve Jobs. He is a famous innovator who has brought these technologies to the masses. Born in Los Angeles in 1955, Jobs co-founded Apple Computer in 1976 with Steve Wozniak and became a multimillionaire before the age of 30.

An adopted child, Jobs gained an early appreciation of technology. At the age of 12, Jobs landed an internship at Hewlett-Packard Co. There he attended electronics lectures after school and worked during the summer. During his internship, Jobs met Steve Wozniak ("Woz"), an engineering hotshot who dropped out of the University of California at Berkeley and had a mania for inventing electronic gadgets.

After dropping out of Reed College in Portland, Oregon, in 1974, Jobs worked as a video game designer at Atari Inc. He also attended meetings of Woz's computer club and soon convinced Woz to join him and build a personal computer.

Woz and Jobs designed a computer in Jobs' bedroom, and they constructed the prototype in Jobs' garage.

This led to Jobs and Woz founding Apple Computer Inc. To raise funds for this startup, they sold their most valuable possessions: Jobs sold his Volkswagen bus, and Woz sold his Hewlett-Packard scientific calculator, which raised $1,300. With that money capital and credit obtained from local electronics suppliers, they established their first production line. Jobs thought up the name of the new company, Apple, in fond memory of a summer he had spent as an orchard worker near Portland.

In 1976, Jobs and Woz built their first computer, called the Apple I. They sold it at a price of $666 and earned revenues totaling $774,000. The following year, Jobs and Woz put together the Apple II, the first personal computer to hit it big. While the power of computing formerly had been available only to "techies," the Apple II could be delivered to offices, classrooms, and dens. Then came the development of Apple's Macintosh in 1984, the first personal computer to include the mouse, icons, and computer graphics.

Since his early years at Apple, Steve Jobs has continued to develop breakthrough products. In 2001, Jobs rocketed the music business with Apple's iPod music player, and iTunes in 2003, the first time anyone had convinced all the major record companies to market their songs online. Few doubt the innovation and marketing abilities of Steve Jobs.

Source: Laurie Rozakis and Dick Smolnski, *Steven Jobs: Computer Genius* (Vero Beach, FL: Rourke Enterprises, 1993); and Alan Deutschman, *The Second Coming of Steve Jobs* (New York: Random House, 2001).

services and their participants. To the music industry, the sharing of music files is tantamount to stealing.

During the early 2000s, the music and technology industries cast about for a legal Internet music service that would rival the bootlegged services. However, the early services were generally considered to be inadequate. They all required monthly fees, and they stressed "streaming" music, which you can listen to, but can't download. Use of their songs expired if monthly fees were not paid. Playback of songs was usually restricted to one or two PCs, and the songs often could not be used on portable music players. The ability to burn songs to CDs was either very limited or it required a per-burn payment on top of the service's monthly fee.

In 2003, however, Apple Computer launched the first really useful and legal Internet music service, the iTunes Music Store. Apple's Music Store has simpler rules. Each song costs 99 cents—no strings attached and no subscription required. You can purchase as many or as few songs as you like. Once you purchase a song, it's yours to keep. You can copy it to as many as three computers. Also, you can copy each song to an unlimited number of portable music players and burn each song to an unlimited number of homemade CDs. For each 99-cent song that Apple's Music Store sells, the music companies receive a licensing royalty of 65 to70 cents. The Music Store must also come up with another dime or so to pay for bandwidth, servers, and the staff to run them. Apple originally targeted Mac computer users, but by 2004 it had rolled out a Windows version of its Music Store.

Analysts noted that Apple's Music Store would not be able to keep an innovative edge for long. If it figured out how to make money by selling music on the Internet, rivals would be quick to follow. By 2005, Microsoft Corporation, Sony Corporation, and Yahoo Inc. had entered the online music market. The additional competition put pressure on Apple to cut prices and improve product quality to remain competitive. At the writing of this text, it was not clear whether competition would force the online startup firms to be singing the blues.

CHECK POINT

1. Identify the assumptions of a perfectly competitive market.

2. Why is a perfectly competitive firm a price taker?

3. How does a firm determine its profit-maximizing output?

4. Why does a perfectly competitive firm produce at the lowest point on its average total cost curve in the long run? Why does the firm realize zero economic profits in the long run?

MONOPOLY

If you attend a college in a small town, you might find that you can obtain textbooks from only one store. The same is often true of your college or university cafeteria. The firm that sells food in your school cafeteria is usually granted an exclusive franchise to do so by your college or university. Moreover, if you have gone to a national park or a ski resort and had lunch at one of their restaurants, you were probably purchasing food from a firm granted an exclusive franchise. As we shall learn, when a firm does not face competition, it can charge a higher price and produce output of lesser quality than if there was more competition in the market. Let us consider markets in which competition is severely restricted by barriers to entry, a situation known as *monopoly*.

economics
IN ACTION

Would Vouchers Improve the U.S. Education System?

Vouchers don't work. Smaller class size and proven academic programs do, and they are doable tomorrow. Given a choice between serving ideology and maybe helping a relative handful of children—at the expense of the rest—or responding to the legitimate demands of the vast majority of Americans and serving the needs of all children, the choice is clear. Let's do what's right and what works.

—American Federation of Teachers

Competition and the profit motive must be reintroduced into education so that teachers and school administrators will once again have a powerful incentive to meet the needs of the children and parents they serve.

—Andrew Coulson–Scholar at the Washington, DC-based Education Policy Institute

For decades, many frustrated parents have challenged one of America's near-monopolies, public education. Concerned about the poor quality of the U.S. elementary and secondary education system, as seen in a large number of school dropouts and declining reading and math skills, they ask whether it is fair to tax families, compel their children's attendance at schools, and then give them no choice between teaching methods, religious or secular education, and other matters. The question is: how do we make our educational system more productive?

One method is to reform the structure of elementary and high school education by giving parents vouchers (a stipulated amount of money) to spend on the education of their children. This would enable children to attend the public or private school of their choice. The program operates like this: Suppose the cost of education at a public school is $5,000 per student. For each school-age child, parents receive a voucher that is redeemable for $5,000 when spent on education. If a family decides to send the child to a public school, it turns in the voucher and is assessed no additional charges. The family could also decide to send the child to a different school, either public or private, and use the voucher to pay for the cost of schooling there. For example, assume the cost of educating a student at a private school is $6,000 per year. The family turns in its voucher there and is charged

A **monopoly** is a market structure characterized by a single supplier of a good or service for which there is no close substitute. With a monopoly, the firm (the monopolist) and the industry are one and the same. For many years, the suppliers of local electricity, natural gas, water, and phone service were examples of local monopolies; however, the extent of competition has increased in these industries during the past two decades.

Do you know that every time you pay for an item with paper currency, say, a dollar bill, you are using a product that comes from a near monopoly? Since 1879, virtually all of the paper purchased by the Bureau of Engraving of the Treasury Department comes from one supplier—Crane & Co., Inc., of Dalton, Massachusetts. The U.S. reliance on a single source for currency paper is not unique; most other industrial nations also rely on single domestic suppliers for their currency paper.

How does a firm become a monopoly? The first requirement is to produce a good or service that has *no close substitutes*. If a good has close substitutes, even though one firm may produce it, the firm faces competition from other firms that produce the substitute goods. Note, however, that technological change and innovation can create new products and thus weaken a monopoly's control of the market. For example, the development of e-mail and fax machines has eroded the U.S. Postal Service's monopoly of first-class

$1,000 by the school. The school turns in the voucher to the government and receives $5,000.

The voucher plan embodies the same principle as the GI bill that provides for educational benefits to military veterans. The veteran receives a voucher, good only for educational costs. He or she is completely free to choose the school at which it is used, provided that the school meets the educational standards of the state in which it is located.

Without a voucher system, public schools have a competitive advantage because they are giving away what private schools must sell. With vouchers, however, parents can send their children to the schools of their choice. Increased competition could result in a better quality of education at both the public and private schools.

Proponents maintain that with competition, innovative uses of computers and the Internet would offer new paths to learning. New methods of teaching would replace old, and costs would go down just as surely as quality would go up. This happened when parcel and message delivery was opened up to competition, when the telephone monopoly was dismembered, when air travel was deregulated, and when Japanese competition forced the U.S. automobile

industry to change its ways. Government schools would have to meet the competition or close up shop.

The teachers' unions that today control the government school monopoly would not relish that competition. However, proponents of vouchers contend that the potential winners are far more numerous. Students would benefit from an improvement in the quality of their education. Good teachers would benefit from a wider market for their services. Existing private schools would be in a far better competitive position and could use the additional funds to improve still further the education they provide.

The voucher proposal is contested by public schools that see it as a threat to the pay and job security of their faculties. Moreover, they fear that a voucher system would be ineffective in improving quality, especially in communities with less-educated parents, who would be less able to make informed decisions and be less effective in influencing school policies than would more highly educated parents. Finally, any voucher system must solve the practical problem of the extraordinary funding and programming required to educate special-needs children at the schools their parents choose. The debate over vouchers will continue as we look for ways to improve the quality of education.

letter mail. Also, the development of satellite dishes has diminished the monopoly of local cable television firms. Furthermore, technological advances in telecommunications, such as cellular telephones, have eroded the telephone monopoly on local telephone calls.

BARRIERS TO ENTRY

Another characteristic of monopoly is the existence of high barriers that make it difficult or impossible for new firms to enter an industry. **Barriers to entry** are impediments, created by the government or the firm or firms already in the market, which protect an established firm from potential competition.

Legal Barriers

Many legal barriers are created by government policy. *Patents,* for example, help prevent entry by conferring on an inventor (for example, Microsoft) the exclusive right to produce a particular good (Windows computer software) for a specified period. *Copyrights* refer to exclusive rights granted to a composer or author of artistic, musical, literary, or dramatic work. *Licenses* regulate entry into particular occupations such as medicine, law, and architecture. Finally, *public franchises* give a holder the sole legal right to supply a good or service. The U.S. Postal Service, for example, has the exclusive right to deliver first-class letter mail. Another example of a public franchise is on a freeway where particular companies are awarded the sole right to sell food and gasoline.

Taxicabs provide an example of legal barriers that shut the competition out. In New York City, government restricts the number of taxicabs to one cab for every 600 people. This results in about 13,000 yellow cabs servicing the city. To operate a taxi, one must obtain a license and place an official medallion on the taxi's hood as proof of legality. Licenses are auctioned off to the highest bidder. Although taxi drivers often complain about the unpleasant task of working more than 60 hours per week, encountering robbers, and arguing with impolite customers, they have been willing to pay more than $200,000 for a license. Why? Restricting competition decreases the supply of taxis, drives up fares, and allows remaining taxis to expand their market share. The increased profits realized by cab drivers come at the expense of travelers and excluded competitors. Operating taxis in New York City is lucrative, and drivers have no difficulty selling their licenses when they decide to leave the business.

Control over Essential Inputs

Sole control over the entire supply of raw materials and other inputs is another way to prevent a potential competitor from entering an industry. From the early 1900s until the end of World War II, Alcoa (Aluminum Company of America) monopolized the U.S. aluminum industry through its ownership of most of the bauxite mines in the world (bauxite is used to manufacture aluminum). The International Nickel Company of Canada once owned nearly all of the world's nickel. In professional sports, it is virtually impossible to compete with the National Hockey League, National Football League, and National Basketball Association. Why? NHL, NFL, and NBA teams have contracts with the best players and leases with the best arenas and stadiums. Moreover, Nintendo weakened its rivals by prohibiting game developers from designing games for anyone else, and Topps Chewing Gum established a 14-year monopoly on baseball cards by signing players to exclusive contracts. *not illegal*

Economies of Scale

Economies of scale can also cause monopoly. A **natural monopoly** occurs when one firm can supply a product for the entire market at a lower cost per unit than would be achieved by two or more firms each supplying only some of it. The monopolist can drive average total cost down by taking advantage of economies of scale over the entire range of market demand.

Figure 5.4 illustrates the hypothetical case of Northern States Power Company, a natural monopoly that supplies electricity to residents of St. Cloud, Minnesota. Suppose the market demand for electricity equals 5 million KWHs (kilowatt-hours). Given the firm's average cost total curve, *ATC*, we observe economies of scale—that is, decreasing average total cost—throughout the relevant range of production. As a single producer, Northern States Power Company can service the entire St. Cloud market at a cost of 7 cents per KWH, resulting in a total cost of $350,000 ($0.07 × 5 million KWHs = $350,000).

Instead of having a monopoly serve the St. Cloud market, suppose the market is divided evenly among five competing firms. Assume that each firm realizes a cost curve shown by *ATC*. With each firm producing 1 million KWHs, unit cost equals 11 cents. The total cost for each firm thus equals $110,000 ($0.11 × 1 million KWHs = $110,000), resulting in a total cost for the market of $550,000.

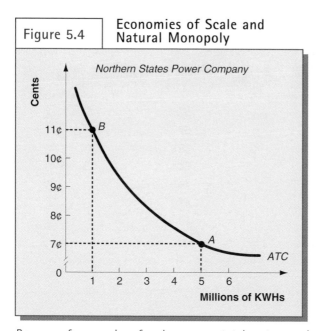

Figure 5.4 | Economies of Scale and Natural Monopoly

Because of economies of scale, average total costs may decrease over the entire range of market output. In this situation, one firm can serve consumers at lower costs than two or more firms. This is what describes a natural monopoly.

Comparing the cost of serving the St. Cloud market for Northern States Power Company and the five competing firms, we conclude that, with economies of scale, the lowest cost   — *in this case* of servicing the market occurs under monopoly. Northern States Power Company can provide 5 million KWHs of electricity at a cost of $350,000, while the cost of the five competing firms is $550,000 for the same level of service. Clearly, economies of scale serve as a barrier to entry that protects Northern States Power Company from competition, assuming that the firm is the first to operate in the market.

Many public utilities, such as natural gas, water, electric, cable television, and local telephone companies, have generally been considered to be natural monopolies. The government grants an exclusive franchise to these firms in a geographic area. With economies of scale, the firms are able to drive down average costs by producing large amounts of output. The government then regulates the monopolies to ensure that cost savings are passed through to the public in lower prices.

Barriers to Entry in the Airline Industry

The airline industry provides an example of barriers to entry protecting established firms. What types of barriers to entry exist in the airline industry? First, restricted access to takeoff and landing slots at many large airports has greatly deterred entry of competing airlines. These slots are the result of federal legislation aimed at limiting the number of takeoffs and landings during peak traffic periods. Besides restrictions on takeoff and landing slots, new entrants often have limited access to airport facilities such as gates, ticket counters, and baggage handling and storage.

Even where airport access is not a problem, airlines sometimes decline to enter new markets because the strategies of established airlines make it extremely difficult for other carriers to attract traffic. These marketing strategies include bonus commissions paid to

| Table 5.1 | Fare Differentials at Large U.S. Airports, 2000 |

Airport	Market Share of Dominant Airline	Percentage Increase in Airfares: Routes Without Low-Fare Competition versus Routes with Low-Fare Competition*
Cincinnati	Delta Air Lines/94%	57%
Pittsburgh	U.S. Airways/86%	57
Minneapolis	Northwest Airlines/80%	55
Charlotte	U.S. Airways/90%	54
St. Louis	Trans World Airlines/72%	49
Atlanta	Delta Air Lines/74%	41
Detroit	Northwest Airlines/77%	40
Denver	United Airlines/70%	29
Salt Lake City	Delta Air Lines/72%	2

*These fare differentials were derived by comparing fares at dominated hub markets in which low-fare competition exists against fares at dominated hub markets in which no low-fare competition exists. All fare comparisons were controlled for distance and density.

Source: From U.S. General Accountability Office, *Aviation Competition: Challenges in Enhancing Competition in Dominated Markets,* March 13, 2001.

travel agents, frequent-flier plans, airline ownership of the computer reservation systems used by travel agents, and code-sharing partnerships with commuter carriers. Also, established airlines often enact aggressive price-cutting policies to discourage new competitors from entering the market.   *that's ok – hurts them, helps consumers*

Research has shown that dominated airports tend to have higher airfares than airports that have more competition from other airlines. According to the U.S. General Accountability Office, passengers at major airports typically pay about 40 percent more than do their counterparts flying in markets where the dominant airline faced low-fare competition. Table 5.1 shows examples of fare differentials at airports dominated by a small number of airlines.

CABLE TELEVISION: WHY RATES ARE SO HIGH

Recall that the existence of a monopoly requires barriers to entry, be they technological, legal, or some other type. However, barriers to entry tend to break down over time and thus monopoly power erodes. This appears to be occurring for cable television companies.

Today, large companies that are well positioned to block competition dominate the cable industry. Currently, two cable companies, AT&T and Time Warner, own cable systems serving more than 50 percent of the nation's cable subscribers. The head of the Justice Department's Antitrust Division has referred to the cable industry as "one of the most persistent monopolies in the American economy."[1]

Owners of cable systems have traditionally justified their monopoly status on the grounds that cable television is a natural monopoly, much like the utilities. The central issue is one of high fixed costs. What would be the payback for a competitor to build an additional cable plant in a city. The infrastructural costs of wires and other technology are enormous.

---

[1] Statement of Joel Klein, Assistant Attorney General, May 12, 1998, announcing a Justice Department suit to block Primestar Inc. from acquiring Direct Broadcast Satellite assets of Newscorp and MCI.

Therefore, many communities decided that more than one cable system was inefficient. Most cable television companies were thus granted a monopoly franchise over the market they served. Therefore, few consumers anywhere have choice in cable television providers.

However, critics challenge the view that cable is naturally monopolistic by noting that technological developments allow companies to provide cable programming without the need for stringing or laying cable throughout a city. These technologies include direct broadcast satellite, wireless cable, and the use of common carrier lines. Also, local telephone companies could easily provide cable to people in their jurisdictions.

Potential competitors face another barrier to entry: getting quality programming. The way cable works is that an operator must obtain programming from various suppliers, such as ESPN, TNT, and the Discovery Channel. These programs make up the essential ingredients of cable service, without which it is nearly impossible to sell cable television. According to industry analysts, programmers are often reluctant to sell to competitive cable operators either because the programmers are owned outright by established cable-system operators or because the established operators use their market power to convince programmers not to sell to would-be competitors. Without such programming, competitors are at a serious disadvantage.

Although cable television companies have realized considerable monopoly power, competition from substitute goods has emerged. By the early 2000s, satellite television companies were making significant inroads on the market share of cable television firms. With growing numbers of people switching to satellite television, cable companies came under pressure to hold down rates. Several of the nation's largest cable companies also introduced cheaper packages that were intended to more effectively compete with attractive offers from satellite companies.

Competition for cable services from satellite companies and other sources should have several benefits. Competitors will reduce consumer prices, spur innovation and adoption of new technologies, and offer subscribers a wider array of choices. Just how quickly this competition will develop is still unknown.

DE BEERS: THE "GIFT OF LOVE"

The diamond industry provides another example of barriers to entry breaking down over time. Let us consider the case of De Beers.

De Beers Consolidated Mines of South Africa is one of the world's most famous monopolies. Although De Beers' mines account for approximately 15 percent of the world's diamond production, the firm monopolizes the sale of diamonds by purchasing for resale a large share of the diamonds produced by other mines throughout the world. De Beers is thus able to sell over 80 percent of the world's diamonds to a select group of manufacturers and dealers.

De Beers acts to control the price of diamonds to maximize its profits. This is accomplished by limiting the sale of diamonds to an amount that will yield prices that exceed the cost of production. In good times, De Beers' profits have surpassed 60 percent of revenues.

When the demand for diamonds decreases and prices fall, De Beers reduces sales to maintain price. The firm also advertises on television and in magazines to bolster demand. You might have seen some of these ads promoting the giving of diamonds for engagements, anniversaries, and other occasions as a "gift of love." Conversely, when the demand for diamonds strengthens, De Beers increases sales by delving into its inventories of diamonds and selling them on the market.

To defend its monopoly position, De Beers has attempted to prevent competing firms from selling diamonds. De Beers maintains inventories of diamonds that can be dumped on the market to reduce prices and thus drive any competing seller out of business. In the early 1980s, for example, Zaire attempted to sell diamonds independently of De Beers. As a result, De Beers flooded the market with diamonds, which caused the price of diamonds to decrease. Zaire thus stopped competing against De Beers and sold its diamonds to De Beers for resale on the world market.

At the turn of the century, however, several events were occurring that weakened the monopoly power of De Beers. New diamond discoveries in Angola and Canada resulted in an increasing flow of diamonds onto the market outside De Beers' control. Although Russia is part of the De Beers consortium, this poor nation ignored the dictates of De Beers and sold substantial quantities of diamonds on the world market. Also, Australian diamond producer Argyle decided to pull out of the De Beers consortium. Moreover, recent findings of diamonds in Siberia may lead to additional production, which may further undermine the monopoly power of De Beers.

In 2001, De Beers gave up on its efforts to control the supply of diamonds. It declared that it would alter its structure from a diamond consortium to a company selling high-quality diamonds under the De Beers label. Therefore, it would decrease its stockpile of diamonds and adopt a policy of increasing overall demand for diamonds through sales promotion. With its large share of the diamond market and ability to control its own production levels, De Beers will have a substantial impact on the price of diamonds in the years ahead. Even the De Beers monopoly has turned out to not be permanent.

PROFIT MAXIMIZATION FOR A MONOPOLY

In the previous section, we learned that De Beers has earned substantial profits by controlling most of the world's diamond production. Let us now consider how a monopolist goes about achieving a combination of price and output that yields maximum profits.

Price and Marginal Revenue

A perfectly competitive firm is a *price taker* that is at the mercy of the market in which it operates. The firm faces a horizontal demand curve for its product at a price established by market demand and supply. Because each additional unit of the firm's output sold adds a constant amount (price) to total revenue, the firm's marginal revenue is constant and equals product price.

In contrast, a monopolist is a *price maker* that can decide product price. Why? A monopolist is the sole producer of the product that it sells, and thus its output decisions necessarily affect product price. The firm's price will rise only if output falls; conversely, output will rise only if price falls. A monopolist, unlike a perfectly competitive firm, faces a downward-sloping demand schedule. Note that a monopolist is not completely immune from market forces in deciding price and output. Although a monopolist can charge any price it wishes, it knows that at higher prices, less output will be sold. Therefore, a monopoly faces a downward-sloping demand curve instead of a perfectly horizontal demand curve.

Table 5.2 shows the demand and revenue conditions for De Beers, assumed to be a monopoly in the sale of diamonds. Referring to columns 1 and 2 of the table, as De Beers reduces the price of diamonds, quantity demanded increases. For example, De Beers can choose a price of $3,600 and count on customers demanding one diamond, or it can reduce price to $3,200 and sell two diamonds.[2] Figure 5.5 translates this information into graphical form. The figure shows a downward-sloping demand curve for De Beers.

---

[2] In reality, De Beers sells many thousands of diamonds in a year. To keep our example as simple as possible, we assume that it sells only small quantities of diamonds.

Table 5.2	Demand and Revenue Schedules for De Beers as a Monopolist			
Quantity of Diamonds	Price (dollars)	Total Revenue (dollars)	Marginal Revenue (dollars)	
0	$4,000	$ 0		
			$3,600	
1	3,600	3,600		
			2,800	
2	3,200	6,400		
			2,000	
3	2,800	8,400		
			1,200	
4	2,400	9,600		
			400	
5	2,000	10,000		
			−400	
6	1,600	9,600		

Column 3 of Table 5.2 shows De Beers' total revenue, found by multiplying market price by the quantity of diamonds ($TR = P \times Q$). Changes in both price and quantity demanded thus result in changes in the firm's total revenue. For example, if the price of diamonds falls from $3,600 to $3,200 per diamond, resulting in an increase in quantity demanded from one diamond to two diamonds, total revenue would rise from $3,600 to $6,400.

Column 4 of Table 5.2 shows the marginal revenue schedule of De Beers. Recall that marginal revenue is the addition to total revenue when another unit of output is sold. In the table, as De Beers increases sales from, say, one diamond to two diamonds, total revenue rises from $3,600 to $6,400. The marginal revenue of the second diamond is thus

Figure 5.5	Profit Maximization for a Monopolist

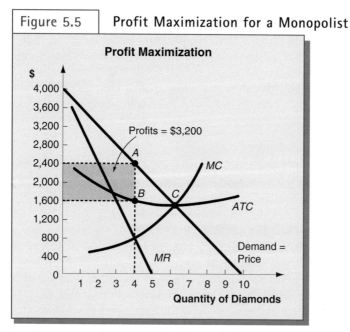

The figure shows De Beers maximizing profits by producing four diamonds, the output corresponding to the intersection of its marginal revenue and marginal cost curves. At this output, price ($2,400) exceeds average total cost ($1,600) and profit per unit equals the difference ($800); the firm's total profits ($3,200) are calculated by multiplying the profit per unit times the profit-maximizing output.

$2,800 ($6,400 − $3,600 = $2,800). Like all marginal measurements, marginal revenue is plotted midway between the quantities. Note that as De Beers lowers the price to sell additional diamonds, its marginal revenue on each additional unit sold is less than price. Translating this information into the graphical form of Figure 5.5, the monopolist's marginal revenue schedule is downward-sloping and lies beneath its demand curve.

Maximizing Profits

Although De Beers cannot dictate how many diamonds people will demand at different prices, it can select a particular price and quantity combination that will result in maximum profits. How does the firm find this combination? According to the profit-maximizing rule, as discussed earlier in this chapter, a firm will maximize total profit by selling that output where marginal revenue equals marginal cost.

Figure 5.5 shows hypothetical revenue and cost schedules of De Beers. The firm would maximize total profit by selling four diamonds, at which marginal revenue equals marginal cost. Having determined its profit-maximizing output, De Beers must now decide what price to charge for diamonds. To set product price, De Beers uses its demand curve and finds the highest price at which it can sell the profit-maximizing output. In De Beers' situation, the highest price at which it can sell four diamonds is $2,400 per diamond, shown by point A in Figure 5.5. Multiplying price ($2,400) times output (4), we calculate De Beers' total revenue to be $9,600. At the profit-maximizing output, the firm's average total cost is $1,600. Multiplying this amount by four units, we calculate total cost to be $6,400. The firm's total profit thus equals $3,200, found by subtracting total cost ($6,400) from total revenue ($9,600).

There is another method for computing total profits. First, subtract average total cost ($1,600) from product price ($2,400), which gives profit per unit ($800). Then multiply this amount by the profit-maximizing output (4) to compute total profit ($3,200).

Notice that De Beers does not charge the highest possible price for diamonds. Because De Beers is a price maker, it could have charged a price higher than $2,400 and sold less than four diamonds. However, any price higher than $2,400 does not correspond to the intersection of the firm's marginal revenue and marginal cost curves, which establishes the profit-maximizing output.

The fact that De Beers has a monopoly does not guarantee profits. Decreasing demand for diamonds can result in losses for the firm, as discussed in "Exploring Further 5.1" at the end of this chapter.

Continuing Monopoly Profits

Recall that in perfect competition, economic profits are unattainable in the long run. Because of low barriers to entry, the existence of economic profits will induce firms to enter a competitive industry until those profits have been competed away.

Sizable economic profits, however, *can* persist under monopoly—if the monopolist is protected by barriers to entry. With blockaded entry, a monopolist can charge the price that will maximize its short-run profit and still attract no rivals. The attainment of long-run economic profits is thus possible under monopoly. Remember, however, that barriers to entry are rarely complete and thus detract from the ability of a firm to realize persistently high profits. As technologies change and new products are developed, the monopolies of today evolve into firms operating in the competitive industries of tomorrow. For example, throughout the 1960s and 1970s, Boeing accounted for over two-thirds of the noncommunist world's production of jetliners. Because of the rise of Europe's Airbus during the 1980s, by 2000 Boeing's market share had declined to about 50 percent.

THE CASE AGAINST MONOPOLY

From what we have seen so far, monopoly isn't *all* bad. At times, a monopoly can fully take advantage of the economies of scale that occur under natural monopolies. Moreover, some innovative firms, such as IBM and Xerox, once had monopolies simply because each was the first to enter its industry. Why, then, do people often dislike monopoly?

Imagine an industry made up of many identical competitive firms. Suppose a single firm buys out all of the individual firms and creates a monopoly. Given identical cost conditions, a monopolist is likely to charge a *higher* price and earn *higher* profits than a competitive industry, which harms consumers. The monopolist attains excess profits by consciously *restricting* output and increasing price above the competitive level. The output restriction comes at the expense of society, which would have preferred additional output and thus additional resources devoted to the production of the good.

Figure 5.5 shows the effect of restricted output for De Beers as a monopoly. In the figure, we see that De Beers maximizes profits by producing four units of output, at which point marginal revenue equals marginal cost. At this output, the firm's average total cost is at point B. However, average total cost is at a minimum at point C. By restricting output, De Beers fails to operate at the lowest point on its average total cost curve. In contrast, firms in a competitive industry operate at the minimum point on their average total cost curves.

A monopolist also lacks the incentive to organize production so as to reduce cost. Recall that competition serves as a major source of disciplinary pressure on a firm to hold down costs to survive. But a monopolist is insulated from the rigors of competition by barriers to entry and thus does not have to produce at minimum average total cost or use inputs in the most efficient manner irrespective of the rate of output. Excess costs can be the result of ineffective supervision of employees, payment of large bonuses to management, providing company perks such as jet planes and vacation lodges, and the like.

Moreover, high-quality service is not always a characteristic of monopoly. Have you ever been frustrated trying to force (with both hands) a letter into a drive-by mailbox that is completely filled with other letters? (This author has.) How about becoming annoyed with the local cable TV company or telephone company (the only ones in town) that are agonizingly slow in providing repair service? The phrase "The customer is always right" does not necessarily apply when barriers to entry protect a firm from the discipline of competition.

Monopoly may also promote inequality in the distribution of income. To the extent that a monopolist charges a higher price than a competitive firm with identical costs, the monopolist levies a "tax" on consumers that goes into economic profits. These profits, however, are not uniformly distributed among members of society because corporate stock tends to be largely owned by the wealthy. The distribution of income is thus altered in favor of the wealthy.

Finally, government grants of monopoly, such as exclusive franchises to serve a market, encourage firms to waste resources in the attempt to secure and maintain them. Indeed, business executives often spend vast sums on political contributions and the hiring of lobbyists to convince government officials that their firm should become or remain a legal monopoly. From the perspective of economic efficiency, such expenditures are wasteful because they do not contribute to increased output.

Keep in mind, however, that monopoly may have some advantages. Recall that with natural monopoly, economies of scale are best fulfilled when one firm produces the entire market output. Also, a monopolist can eliminate certain types of duplication that are unavoidable for several small, independent firms: (1) A few large machines may replace the many small pieces of equipment used by competitive firms; (2) One purchasing agent may do a job that formerly required many buyers.

Monopolies have an advantage in pursuing research and development activities, which can result in new products, improving technologies, and falling unit cost. The vast resources (profits) of monopolies can finance expensive research and development programs. Moreover, because monopolies are sheltered from competition, they do not have to be preoccupied with day-to-day decisions regarding costs and revenues. Instead, they can take the longer view that is necessary for successful research and development.

However, the research and development argument does not consider monopoly *incentives*. Just because a monopoly has the potential to conduct research and development does not necessarily mean that it will. Instead, a monopoly may prefer to rely on existing products and technologies and earn sizable profits merely because of its monopoly power. The firm may conclude that research and development is not essential for its survival. In contrast, a competitive firm cannot continue to earn profits unless it stays ahead of its rivals; this pressure results in incentives to produce better products at a lower cost.

CHECK POINT

1. Identify the major barriers to entry that foster monopoly.

2. Compare the price-making ability of a monopoly to a perfectly competitive firm.

3. Discuss the strategy of profit maximization for a monopoly.

4. Evaluate the case for and against monopoly.

LEGAL MONOPOLY EXAMPLES

Although monopoly is relatively uncommon, it can occur when the government grants an exclusive franchise to a firm in order to provide a service. Let us consider the effects of several legal monopolies.

Central Office Supply System

For decades, the state of Washington required its state agencies to purchase office supplies and other equipment from the state's Central Office Supply System. This organization was given the exclusive franchise to serve as the monopoly seller to state agencies.

The justification for this policy was that the Central Office Supply System, as a single buyer, had the leverage to obtain office supplies at the lowest possible cost and thus pass the cost savings through to state agencies in lower prices. In this manner, government used tax dollars efficiently.

By the 1990s, the Central Office Supply System had come under increasing attack. Critics maintained that the government-run monopoly operated inefficiently because of excess layers of bureaucracy and antiquated work rules. Like other monopolies, the Central Office Supply System had no incentive to minimize its operating costs. As a result, the deliveries of the Central Office Supply System were slower, and the prices charged higher, than those of private-sector vendors.

Table 5.3 provides price comparisons for selected office supplies in 1998. Column 2 shows prices charged by the Central Office Supply System; column 3 shows the prices of like-goods

Table 5.3	Monopoly in Government Procurement			
		Central Office Supply System		
Item	Quantity	Price	Costco Price	Savings
11″ × 13″ mailing envelopes	100	$21.00	$6.49	$14.51
Neon colors laser paper	400	15.00	5.19	9.81
Liquid Paper	12	16.08	6.99	9.09
1″ × 2″ Post-It pads	48	14.24	4.79	9.45
4″ × 6″ Post-It pads	12	29.52	5.79	23.73
Paper clips (100/box)	20	4.40	2.59	1.81

Source: Data collected by author.

charged by Costco, a private-sector wholesaler. Comparing columns 2 and 3, column 4 shows that office supplies could have been purchased from Costco at substantial savings.

In 1998, the state of Washington liberalized its regulations and allowed state agencies to purchase part of their office supplies from the cheapest source. Increasingly, state colleges and other agencies have rejected the state-run monopoly and shifted to private-sector suppliers.

U.S. Postal Service

The U.S. Postal Service (USPS) is another example of a legal monopoly. The law prohibits any other firm or individual from delivering first-class mail. Competing firms also cannot deliver addressed circulars, advertisements, solicitations, mass mailings, or other third-class mail. Moreover, no one except the USPS can place anything in the mailbox of a home or business, even if the owner consents. As of 2005, about 80 percent of USPS business was protected from competition.

As a legal monopoly, the USPS is mandated to operate on a business-like basis without the benefit of government subsidies. It is subject to congressional oversight and is required to submit proposed changes in postal rates to the independent Postal Rate Commission. Unlike private carriers such as Federal Express, the USPS has a certain financial advantage: It does not have to pay taxes to the government or dividends to shareholders. However, the USPS is mandated to function as a public enterprise and provide mail service to all communities, not just those that are profitable to serve.

Proponents of the USPS's legal monopoly justify it on several grounds. A legal monopoly for the delivery of letter mail is necessary to ensure that the USPS will have sufficient revenues to carry out its public service mandates, including regular mail delivery service (typically six days a week) to all communities. Without restrictions on private delivery, "cream skimming" by private competitors in the most profitable postal markets would undermine the USPS's ability to provide universal service at reasonable, uniform rates to patrons in all areas, however remote. Moreover, the USPS as a single provider can operate at a lower cost to the nation than multiple suppliers can. This is because mail delivery fits the economic model of a natural monopoly in which lower unit cost per delivery occurs as mail volumes increase.

Critics of the USPS, however, maintain that the government-mandated postal monopoly has produced some economic problems. Because the USPS does not face the threat of competition, it lacks incentives to control costs and maintain high quality. Instead, the

USPS can overpay its postal employees in salaries, perks, and benefits while reducing work obligations for each employee. The organization does not put pressure on workers to maximize effort, reduce waste and costs, and produce the best service for consumers, as do organizations that face competition every day. Moreover, the USPS is slow to adopt cost-saving or quality-enhancing innovations because it need not be concerned about competitors adopting such innovations first. The USPS has also suffered from delivery delays, actual losses (accidental and on purpose) of mail, and excessive increases in postal rates.

Critics also question whether the USPS is a natural monopoly, as it alleges. When we think of a natural monopoly, we think of large fixed costs, such as those involved in the laying of electricity lines in a city. However, labor costs account for over 80 percent of USPS total costs, while its capital costs are modest. It is hard to comprehend such a labor-intensive industry characterized by large economies of scale. In practice, it is the USPS status as a legal monopoly, rather than a natural monopoly, that has kept it in business.

Although the USPS is a legal monopoly in the delivery of first-class and third-class mail, competition for mail delivery services has grown substantially since the 1970s. Private firms deliver urgent (overnight) mail, 2-day and 3-day letters and parcels, and unaddressed advertising circulars and periodicals. Together, these groups compete on a local, national, and international basis for portions of markets previously served only by the USPS.

In letter mail, the USPS has faced increasing competition from fax machines and electronic mail (e-mail), which gives us the opportunity to send and receive messages within minutes. Home shopping television channels, 1-800 telephone numbers, and interactive television allow us to order tickets, clothing, and merchandise with the push of a button. Even checks are not always sent in the mail anymore; often, they are sent and deposited electronically. These technological advances have reduced the USPS's share of the communications market, resulting in falling revenues. Such competition has given the USPS additional incentive to operate more efficiently.

Critics of the USPS, however, maintain that additional efforts are needed to promote competition in mail delivery. Many critics call for privatization of the USPS. One approach to privatization would be to auction the USPS to an owner who would operate it on a for-profit basis. It is argued that the resulting cost savings and quality improvements would promote reasonable prices for consumers.

In this chapter, we learned how a firm maximizes profits in a competitive market and also under monopoly. The next chapter considers how firms behave in the imperfectly competitive markets of monopolistic competition and oligopoly.

CHECK POINT

1. What is the justification for granting the Central Office Supply System or the U.S. Government Printing Office an exclusive franchise to be the sole supplier of goods and services to government agencies?

2. Why does the U.S. Postal Service have a legal monopoly on the delivery of first-class letter mail? Explain why critics of the U.S. Postal Service argue that privatization of mail delivery would result in a more efficient allocation of resources for the nation. Do you agree?

Chapter Summary

1. A perfectly competitive market is characterized by many sellers and buyers, firms that produce a standardized product, perfect information among buyers and sellers, and easy entry into and exit from a market.

2. Because a perfectly competitive firm supplies a negligible share of the market output, it has to "take" or accept the price that is determined in the market.

3. Given favorable demand conditions, a firm will maximize total profit by selling that output at which marginal revenue equals marginal cost.

4. If total revenue exceeds total variable cost, a firm would minimize short-run losses by producing where $MR = MC$ rather than shutting down. As a result, losses are less than the fixed-cost losses that would exist if the firm shut down.

5. Because of easy entry into and exit from a market, perfectly competitive firms operate at the lowest possible cost, charge the lowest price they can without going out of business, and earn no economic profit. These characteristics are ideal for the consumer.

6. Barriers to entry are impediments, created by government or by the firm or firms already in the market, which protect an established firm from potential competition. Among the major barriers to entry are legal barriers, control over essential resources, and economies of scale.

7. A monopoly differs from a perfectly competitive firm in that the monopoly's demand curve and marginal revenue curve are downward-sloping rather than horizontal. Like a perfectly competitive firm, a monopolist will maximize total profit by operating where marginal revenue equals marginal cost.

8. Given identical costs, a monopolist would find it profitable to produce a smaller output and charge a higher price than a perfectly competitive firm. Moreover, a profit-maximizing monopoly would not operate at the minimum point on its average total cost curve in the long run. However, economies of scale may make lower average total cost more attainable for a monopoly than for a competitive firm. Moreover, a monopolist generally has greater financial resources for research and development programs than a competitive firm, which make it possible for the monopolist to achieve lower cost per unit.

Key Terms and Concepts

perfect competition (102)

price taker (103)

total revenue (104)

marginal revenue (104)

marginal revenue = marginal cost rule (104)

monopoly (110)

barriers to entry (111)

natural monopoly (112)

privatization (122)

shut-down rule (128)

Self Test: Multiple-Choice Questions

1. The U.S. Postal Service has a monopoly as the result of an exclusive government franchise on the delivery of

   a. small packages.
   b. large packages.

c. express mail.

d. first-class letter mail.

2. A perfectly competitive market includes all of the following characteristics *except*

   a. freedom of entry into and exit from the market.

   b. firms in the market produce differentiated products.

   c. a large number of sellers and buyers.

   d. perfect information among buyers and sellers.

3. Barriers to entry in a market include all of the following *except*

   a. exclusive government franchises granted to producers of a good.

   b. demand curves which are highly elastic.

   c. large advertising budgets required to promote a new product.

   d. sole control over the supply of raw materials.

4. A perfectly competitive firm will maximize total profits by

   a. producing all the output it can at any particular price.

   b. setting price so that total revenue is at a maximum.

   c. setting price so that marginal revenue equals marginal cost.

   d. setting price so that price exceeds average total cost by the greatest amount.

5. A perfectly competitive firm

   a. can realize an economic profit in the short run, but not in the long run.

   b. can realize an economic profit in the long run, but not in the short run.

   c. will always realize an economic profit, irrespective of revenue and cost conditions.

   d. will never realize an economic profit, no matter how large the firm's revenues.

6. In a perfectly competitive market, if firms realize economic profits in the short run,

   a. new firms will enter the market in the long run, forcing down price and profits.

   b. firms will attempt to reduce output so as to further increase price and profits.

   c. weaker firms will exit the market before price begins to decline.

   d. increased entry of new firms will shift the market supply curve to the left.

7. Which industry best meets the assumptions of perfect competition?

   a. Automobiles

   b. Commercial aircraft

   c. Steel

   d. Agriculture

8. If in the short run, price falls below minimum average variable cost, Hodges Electric Co.

   a. should produce the output where marginal revenue equals marginal cost.

   b. should shut down and produce no output.

   c. will realize a loss but should continue to produce in the short run.

   d. will realize a profit in the short run but not in the long run.

9. Which of the following is *not* a characteristic of a pure monopoly?

   a. A demand curve that is highly sensitive to changes in price

   b. Barriers preventing the entry of other firms into the market

   c. Products for which there are no close substitutes

   d. An industry consisting of one seller

10. If the electricity market is a natural monopoly, production by a single firm is preferable to several smaller firms because

   a. profits are maximized.
   b. marginal revenue is maximized.
   c. average total cost is minimized.
   d. price is maximized.

Answers to Multiple-Choice Questions

1. d   2. b   3. b   4. c   5. a   6. a   7. d   8. b   9. a   10. c

Study Questions and Problems

1. Suppose a perfectly competitive firm sells 300 batteries at $10 each. At this output, the firm's total variable cost is $1,800 and its total fixed cost is $600. Calculate the firm's profit per unit and total profit from this information.

2. Eddy's Pizza Parlor receives $15 per pizza and sells 100 pizzas to maximize profits. Assuming the firm's variable cost is $8 per pizza and total fixed costs total $500, what is the profit per unit on a pizza at the profit-maximizing level of output? What is the firm's total profit?

3. Suppose that a monopolist can sell nine diamonds at $500 each. To sell 10 diamonds, the firm must reduce price to $475. Calculate the marginal revenue of the tenth diamond.

4. Assume that a monopolist finds that at existing output and price levels, marginal revenue is $20 and marginal cost is $15. The firm would maximize profits or minimize losses by _____ price and _____ output.

5. Table 5.4 shows the revenue and cost conditions for Johnson Electronics Inc.

   a. Graph the information contained in the table.
   b. In what market structure does this firm operate? Why?
   c. What level of output maximizes the firm's total profit? What price will be charged?
   d. Compute the firm's maximum total profit.

Table 5.4	Revenue and Cost Conditions of Johnson Electronics Inc.		
Output	P = MR	ATC	MC
10	$10	$20.80	
20	10	12.40	$4.00
30	10	9.92	5.00
40	10	9.00	6.20
50	10	8.80	8.00
60	10	9.00	10.00
70	10	9.56	13.00
80	10	10.50	17.00

Table 5.5	Revenue and Cost Data of Charette Technologies Co.

Output	Price	MR	ATC	MC
0	$35.00			
1	32.00	$32.00	$48.00	$48.00
2	29.00	26.00	30.00	12.00
3	26.00	20.00	23.34	10.00
4	23.00	14.00	21.00	14.00
5	20.00	8.00	20.00	16.00

6. Table 5.5 shows the revenue and cost data for Charette Technologies Co.

   a. Graph the information contained in the table.
   b. In what market structure does this firm operate? Why?
   c. What level of output maximizes the firm's total profit?
   d. Compute the firm's maximum total profit.

7. Table 5.6 shows the short-run revenue and cost data for a television manufacturer that sells in a perfectly competitive market.

   a. Graph the information contained in the table.
   b. Assuming the market price is $280 per television, determine the firm's profit-maximizing output and total profit.
   c. Assuming the market price is $580 per television, determine the firm's profit-maximizing output and total profits.
   d. Assuming the market price is $160 per television, will the firm continue to produce or should it shut down? Why? What if the market price is $120 per television?

8. Figure 5.6 shows the short-run cost conditions faced by a perfectly competitive firm.

   a. If the product price equals $35 per unit, the firm would maximize profits or minimize losses by producing and selling _____ units of output. At this level of output, the firm's total revenue equals _____ , total cost equals_____, and total profit (loss) equals _____.

Table 5.6	Cost Data for a Perfectly Competitive Firm

Quantity of Televisions	AFC	AVC	ATC	MC
1	$600	$200	$800	$200
2	300	150	450	100
3	200	140	340	120
4	150	146	296	160
5	120	160	280	220
6	100	180	280	280
7	86	206	292	360
8	76	238	312	460
9	66	276	342	580
10	60	320	380	720

Figure 5.6   Short-Run Cost Conditions Faced by a Perfectly Competitive Firm

b. If the product price equals $20 per unit, the firm would maximize profit or minimize losses by producing and selling _____ units of output. At this level of output, the firm's total revenue equals _____, total cost equals _____, and total profit (loss) equals _____. Why would the firm prefer to continue to produce rather than shut down?

c. If the product price equals $10 per unit, the firm would maximize profits or minimize losses by producing and selling _____ units of output. Why?

9. Figure 5.7 shows the demand and cost conditions faced by a monopolist. To maximize profits or minimize losses, the firm should produce and sell _____ units of output and charge a price of _____ per unit.

Figure 5.7   Demand and Cost Conditions Faced by a Monopolist

   a. At the profit-maximizing (loss-minimizing) level of output, the firm's average total cost equals _____ and profit (loss) per unit equals _____.

   b. At the profit-maximizing (loss-minimizing) level of output, the firm's total revenue equals _____, total cost equals _____, and total profits (losses) equal _____.

EXPLORING FURTHER 5.1: LOSS MINIMIZATION AND THE SHUT-DOWN RULE

Suppose a temporary decrease in demand depresses the price of a product below the average total cost curve of a firm. Faced with losses at all levels of output, how will the firm respond to this situation? It could temporarily produce at a loss or shut down production until the price rises. Let us first apply this situation to Puget Sound Fishing Co., a perfectly competitive firm.

If Puget Sound Fishing Co. shuts down, not only does it earn zero revenue, but it must still pay any interest on borrowed money, insurance premiums, license fees, and other fixed costs it incurs even when output is zero. Simply put, if a firm shuts down, its losses equal its total fixed costs. If, however, the firm stays in operation, it earns revenue that can be applied first to its total variable costs (wages) and then to its total fixed costs. Which situation results in the smallest loss for Puget Sound Fishing Co.?

The following shut-down rule serves as a guide for a firm that realizes losses in the short run: If *total revenue exceeds total variable cost,* the firm should continue to produce because all of its variable costs and some of its fixed costs can be paid out of revenue. If the firm shuts down, all of the fixed costs must be paid out of the owner's pocket. By producing where $MR = MC$, the firm's loss will be *less* than its total fixed cost. Conversely, a firm should shut down if total variable cost exceeds total revenue.

Referring to Figure 5.8, assume that Puget Sound Fishing Co. has total fixed costs of $3,728[3] and that the price of fish is $4 per pound. Because price lies below the firm's average total cost curve, all levels of output result in losses. Which output should the firm choose? The logic of the $MR = MC$ rule, as discussed previously, applies in this situation. At 1,600 pounds of fish, corresponding to the intersection of the firm's marginal revenue and marginal cost curves, the firm's revenues total $6,400 ($4 × 1,600 = $6,400). Moreover, average total cost equals $5.33 per pound at this output, resulting in total costs of $8,528 ($5.33 × 1,600 = $8,528). Puget Sound Fishing Co. thus loses $2,128, the difference between total revenue and total cost. Conversely, the firm would have lost $3,728 of fixed costs if it shut down.

According to our shut-down rule, Puget Sound Fishing Co. should continue to operate because total revenue exceeds total variable cost. Referring to Figure 5.8, because the firm's average variable cost is $3 at 1,600 units of output, total variable cost equals $4,800 ($3 × 1,600 = $4,800). Because total revenue ($6,400) exceeds total variable cost ($4,800), the difference ($1,600) can be used to pay off some of the firm's fixed costs. The firm thus loses a smaller amount ($2,128) by producing than by shutting down ($3,728). Keep in mind, however, that a firm cannot stay in operation when it is continually losing money; over the long run, it must at least break even.

Besides applying to a perfectly competitive firm, the shut-down rule applies to other market structures including monopoly, monopolistic competition, and oligopoly

---

[3] Total fixed cost can be calculated from the data in Figure 5.8. First, compute average fixed cost at some level of output, say 1,600 pounds of fish; the difference between average total cost ($5.33) and average variable cost ($3) gives the average fixed cost ($2.33). Next, multiply $2.33 times 1,600 pounds of fish, which gives a total fixed cost of $3,728.

Figure 5.8	Loss Minimization for a Perfectly Competitive Firm

In the figure, since average total cost always exceeds price, the firm suffers a loss at every level of output. The firm would minimize short-run losses by continuing to operate as long as price at least covers average variable cost, because some of this revenue can be applied to fixed costs.

(discussed in the next chapter). For example, suppose a temporary decrease in demand depresses the price of a product below the average total cost curve of a monopolist. If the firm can charge a price that exceeds average variable cost, it will minimize short-run losses by producing where $MR = MC$ rather than shutting down.

CHAPTER

6

Imperfect Competition

Chapter objectives

After reading this chapter, you should be able to:

1. Distinguish between monopolistic competition and oligopoly.

2. Identify the goals and effects of advertising.

3. Explain how a seller successfully practices price discrimination.

4. Discuss the major theories of oligopolistic behavior.

5. Distinguish between a horizontal merger, a vertical merger, and a conglomerate merger.

6. Explain how the threat of potential competition encourages firms to produce a high-quality product and sell it at a reasonable price to consumers.

economics IN CONTEXT

In U.S. history classes that you have taken in the past, you have learned that in 1620 the Pilgrims sailed on the *Mayflower* and landed at Plymouth Rock. What you may not have learned is that the Pilgrims intended to sail to Virginia, not Massachusetts. What caused them to modify their destination? One voyager noted in his diary that the ship's food and drink were in short supply—especially beer. Simply put, the voyage was cut short because they were running out of beer! Although historians may argue about the effect on U.S. history of the supply of beer running low on the *Mayflower*, there is no doubt that beer production has become a major industry.

From the 1930s to the 2000s, the beer industry has undergone a dramatic shakeup. Although beer sales doubled during this period, the number of breweries declined by more than 90 percent, from 404 to 29 breweries. Along with the decrease in the number of breweries came an increasing market share for these largest breweries. Today, the top five companies account for almost 90 percent of the U.S. market. These companies include Anheuser-Busch, Miller, Coors, Stroh, and Heileman. Competition in the U.S. market from foreign producers has never been a strong force in the beer industry, compared with that in markets like steel, automobiles, and consumer electronics. Indeed, the concentration of sales by the top brewers has enhanced their market power.

The beer industry does not apply to the abstract world of perfect competition, where each firm is a price taker and realizes zero economic profits in the long run. Nor does it pertain to the stable world of monopoly, where the seller can earn persistent economic profits as the result of barriers that shut potential competitors out of the market. The beer industry applies to the world of imperfect competition, which lies between the polar cases of perfect competition and monopoly.

Imperfect competition exists when more than one seller competes for sales with other sellers, each of which has some price-making ability. Individual sellers in the market can influence the price of their product by controlling its availability to buyers or by differentiating their product by either brand or quality. For example, loyal customers of PepsiCo, Inc., are willing to pay higher prices than they would for Safeway Cola, while buyers of Advil pay higher prices than they would for Kmart nonaspirin.

Imperfectly competitive markets fall into two broad categories. Monopolistic competition is a market structure in which a large number of firms compete with each other by offering similar but slightly different products. Monopolistic competition thus involves a considerable amount of competition and a small dose of monopoly power. The next market structure is oligopoly, in which a small number of firms compete with each other. Oligopoly is characterized by more monopoly power and less competition.

Some pricing power

CONCENTRATION RATIOS

Economists have developed **concentration ratios** to measure how close an industry comes to the extremes of competition and monopoly. A concentration ratio is the percent of an industry's sales accounted for by the four largest firms in that particular industry. Concentration ratios typically refer to the Top 4 firms in an industry. Concentration ranges from zero to 100 percent. A low-concentration ratio suggests a high degree of competition because the four largest firms account for a small portion of industry output and therefore compete with many other firms in the industry. On the other hand, a high-concentration ratio implies an absence of competition. In the extreme case of monopoly, the concentration ratio is 100 percent—the largest firm accounts for the entire industry output.

| Table 6.1 | Four–Firm Concentration Ratios* for Selected U.S. Manufacturing Industries |

Low-Concentration Industries (monopolistically competitive)		High-Concentration Industries (oligopolistic)	
Industry	Top 4 Ratio	Industry	Top 4 Ratio
Bakeries	4%	Batteries	98%
Metalworking machinery	7	Clothes washing machines	93
Concrete products	8	Glass containers	91
Canvas bags	9	Beer	90
Wood products	11	Lamp bulbs	88
Textiles	14	Tobacco	88
Household furniture	14	Aircraft engines	85
Apparel	18	Breakfast cereals	83
Paper	19	Automobile tires	73
Steel pipes	20	Military tanks	67

WHY? (handwritten annotation)

*Measured by value of shipments in 1997.

Source: From U.S. Bureau of the Census, *Census of Manufacturers, 1997* (Washington, D.C.: U.S. Government Printing Office), June 2001. This information can be found at http://www.census.gov.

The Top 4 concentration ratio can give us a rough idea whether an industry is monopolistically competitive or oligopolistic. When the four largest firms control 40 percent or more of industry output, the industry is generally regarded as oligopolistic. By this standard, approximately one-half of all the industries in the United States are oligopolies. When the four largest firms control less than 40 percent of industry output, the industry approximates monopolistic competition or perfect competition, depending on how low the concentration ratio is.

Table 6.1 shows the Top 4 concentration ratios for selected U.S. manufacturing industries. Column 1 of the table shows examples of low-concentration industries that are characteristic of the market structure of monopolistic competition. Column 2 shows high-concentration industries that are characteristic of oligopoly.

Be wary, however, of relying on concentration ratios alone to identify industry concentration. Most importantly, they do not take into account foreign competition and competition from substitute domestic products. For example, the U.S. automobile industry is highly concentrated. Yet it still encounters significant competition from foreign manufacturers. Because concentration ratios consider only U.S. sales by U.S. firms, they overstate the monopoly power of U.S. auto companies.

For example, the rise of foreign competition has caused U.S. firms to lose their control of the American automobile market. During the 1960s, GM sold half of the new cars purchased by Americans, while the U.S. Big Three (GM, Ford, and Chrysler) accounted for more than 90 percent of sales. At this time, GM was the industry's dominant firm and price leader. During the 1970s–2000s, however, GM's market share dwindled; by 2005, it was 26 percent of the domestic market, as shown in Table 6.2. The decline of GM was accompanied by growing Japanese competition in the U.S. market. Despite heavy U.S. import restrictions in the early 1980s, Japanese firms continued to penetrate the American market, and by 2005 they accounted for about one-third of U.S. auto sales.

U.S. companies have been forced to design more technologically advanced and fuel-efficient automobiles so as to match the features offered by the Japanese automakers.

Table 6.2	U.S. Automobile Market: Market Shares—January 2005			
Manufacturer	Percentage Share of U.S. Market	Manufacturer	Percentage Share of U.S. Market
General Motors*	26.0%	Hyundai	2.4%
Ford*	18.8	Mazda	1.6
DaimlerChrysler*	15.0	Subaru*	1.2
Toyota*	13.2	Mitsubishi	0.7
Honda*	7.6	Suzuki*	0.5
Nissan*	7.2	Other	5.8

*Vehicles built in the United States, Canada, and Mexico for sale in the United States.

Source: From *The Wall Street Journal*, February 2, 2005 p. C-8.

Pricing their vehicles competitively has required U.S. automakers to cut overhead expenses, limit wage increases, and increase output per worker. Indeed, Japanese competition has resulted in quality improvements of the autos sold to American buyers and decreased the ability of the U.S. Big Three to tacitly increase prices.

MONOPOLISTIC COMPETITION

The market structure that is closest to perfect competition is monopolistic competition. This market structure is based on a large number of firms, with each firm having a relatively small share of the total market. Although monopolistic competition typically does not include hundreds, or thousands, of firms like perfect competition, it does consist of a relatively large number of firms, say, 30 or more. With a high degree of market competition, firms do not consider the reactions of their rivals when forming their product price and output policies. Moreover, the opportunity for cooperation in ways that reduce competition is all but impossible given the large number of sellers in the market. Monopolistic competition also assumes that there is relative freedom of entry into the market and exit from the market.

Monopolistic competition differs from perfect competition in one important aspect: It assumes that the product of each firm is not a perfect substitute for the product of competing firms. Product differentiation is thus a fundamental characteristic of monopolistic competition. This gives the firm some power to control the price of its product. For example, people who believe that Nike shoes are more comfortable than other athletic shoes may be willing to pay a higher price for Nikes. Similarly, people that like the feel and look of Levi's jeans are willing to pay more for them than other jeans. Even with product differentiation, a monopolistically competitive firm does not have unlimited control over price. Because many other firms produce similar goods and services, a firm that increases price too much risks losing many of its customers.

Similar to the demand curve of a monopoly, the demand curve for a monopolistically competitive firm is downward-sloping. If the firm increases its price, it will lose some, but not all, of its sales. Conversely, price reductions result in increased sales. Because a monopolistically competitive firm faces competition from substitute goods sold by rivals, its demand curve is more sensitive to price changes (more elastic) than the demand curve of a monopoly, which does not face competition from close substitutes. This implies that if a monopolistically competitive firm raises the price of its product, it will lose a relatively large amount of sales to competitors.

Examples of monopolistic competition can be found where a large number of small retailing firms compete with each other. Restaurants compete in monopolistically competitive markets. In most towns, there are many restaurants, each offering slightly different meals. Each restaurant has many competitors, including other restaurants, fast-food outlets, and frozen-food cases at local grocery stores. Other examples of monopolistic competition are supermarkets, gasoline service stations, accounting and law firms, beauty and barbershops, auto repair shops, video rental stores, book publishers, and shoe stores.

Profit Maximization in the Short Run

Figure 6.1 shows the hypothetical revenue and cost schedules facing Fraggini's Pizza Parlor, a typical firm in the local pizza business. Fraggini's competes with Domino's, Godfather's, Pizza Hut, and many other firms in a market that has relative freedom of entry and exit. Notice that Fraggini's demand curve is downward-sloping because Fraggini's product is sufficiently better to some of its customers that a price above those of its competitors will not reduce sales to zero, at least over a small range of prices. As a result, Fraggini's marginal revenue curve is downward-sloping and lies beneath the demand schedule. To sell more pizzas, Fraggini's must reduce price, and thus the marginal revenue from additional units will be less than the price.

Refer to Figure 6.1(a). Given the marginal revenue curve, *MR*, and the marginal cost curve, *MC*, Fraggini's will maximize total profit by selling 120 pizzas per day, where marginal revenue equals marginal cost. Fraggini's demand curve indicates that the firm will charge a price of $16 per pizza to sell this quantity. Looking at the firm's average total cost

| Figure 6.1 | Market Outcomes Under Monopolistic Competition |

Given favorable demand conditions, a monopolistically competitive firm will maximize total profit in the short run by operating at that output where marginal revenue equals marginal cost. Over the long run, the existence of profits in a monopolistically competitive industry will attract new firms. With entry, there occurs a decrease in the demand curve and marginal revenue facing the typical firm, which eventually results in zero economic profit for the firm. The firm does not increase production to the output for which average total cost is at its lowest point, because it would lose money by doing so.

curve, we see that Fraggini's cost per unit is $13 at the profit-maximizing output. Fraggini's thus earns a profit of $3 per pizza, or a total daily profit of $360 ($3 × 120 = $360). Assuming Fraggini's is open every day, this amounts to yearly profits of $131,400.

The Long Run: Normal Profit and Excess Capacity

Because of the handsome economic profit earned by Fraggini's, competitors will be interested in entering the pizza business. Suppose that new firms enter the market and sell similar, but not identical, pizzas. With entry, the available supply of substitute pizzas increases. For Fraggini's, this results in a decrease in its demand and marginal revenue curves, a decline in the price at which it sells pizza, and a reduction in profits. Entry continues until Fraggini's economic profits are competed away. We conclude that because of easy entry, monopolistically competitive firms tend to earn only a *normal profit* in the long run.

Figure 6.1(b) illustrates the market position of Fraggini's in the long run. At the output where marginal revenue equals marginal cost, 90 pizzas, the average total cost curve is tangent to the demand curve. Because price ($14) just covers average total cost ($14), Fraggini' s economic profit is zero. At any smaller or larger output, the average total cost curve is above the demand curve, causing Fraggini's to operate at a loss.

Although the long-run equilibrium position of Fraggini's produces zero economic profit, the firm produces *less* than the output at which it would minimize average total cost. The difference between the output corresponding to minimum average total cost and the output produced by a monopolistically competitive firm in the long run is called **excess capacity.** Referring to Figure 6.1(b), Fraggini's long-run equilibrium output equals 90 pizzas per day. However, the firm's average total cost would be at a minimum if the firm sold 165 pizzas per day. Fraggini's excess daily capacity therefore is 75 pizzas.

Excess capacity implies that monopolistically competitive markets are crowded, with each firm using an underutilized plant. In other words, there tend to be too many pizza parlors or gasoline service stations at the corner than those required for maximum efficiency. Underutilized plants result in rising costs and higher prices for the consumer. Notice, however, that an advantage of monopolistic competition is product differentiation that results in consumers being offered a wide range of types, style, brands, and quality variants of a product. If excess capacity is the price we pay for differentiated products and increased consumer choice, is it too high a price?

DESPITE COMPETITION FROM STARBUCKS, MOST INDEPENDENT COFFEEHOUSES SURVIVE

The model of monopolistic competition can be applied to a variety of markets. Let us consider coffeehouses.[1] In1998, the news shocked the owners of the Broadway Café, a coffeehouse in Kansas City, Missouri, that Starbucks Corporation was about to open a shop in the same city block. Despite concerns that it would be wiped out by the coffee giant, the Broadway Café continued to thrive following the entry of Starbucks.

Some people feel that Starbucks crushes the independent coffeehouses—encroaching on their turf, stealing their patrons, and bankrupting their owners. However, most independents throughout the country have continued to operate—not just in spite of Starbucks, but

---

[1] "Despite the Jitters, Most Coffeehouses Survive Starbucks," *The Wall Street Journal,* September 24, 2002, pp. A1 and A11.

maybe because of it. In Kansas City, for example, nearly all of the coffeehouses in business prior to the arrival of Starbucks in 1998 continued to operate in 2002. Moreover, other independents opened, increasing their numbers well beyond the 25 stores Starbucks had in the market. Like Broadway Café, many of the independents were located within a few steps of a Starbucks shop.

the market got bigger!

Many coffeehouses have found proximity to Starbucks to be an advantage. A small Seattle chain called Tully's Coffee Corporation deliberately places its stores near a Starbucks outlet.

economics
IN ACTION

Sam Walton: King of the Discounters

Discount retailing serves as an application of the market model of imperfect competition. Consider the case of Samuel Walton, the founder of Wal-Mart.

Though it may surprise you today, discount retailing was a questionable practice when it emerged in the 1950s. Traditional retailers and manufacturers disliked discount retailers who were viewed as a threat to their dominance of the marketplace. Most states imposed restrictions on the practice of discounting.

Born in Kingfisher, Oklahoma, Samuel Walton (1918–1992) stumbled into retailing. He first learned how to compete playing high school football and basketball. As a student at the University of Missouri, Walton waited tables, managed newspaper routs, and worked as a lifeguard. After earning an undergraduate degree in economics in 1940, he contemplated pursuing an MBA degree, but could not afford it. So he accepted an offer to be a management trainee with JCPenney Co.

When discount retailing emerged in the 1960s, Walton was a wealthy individual, operating some 15 variety stores spread mostly around Arkansas, Oklahoma, and Missouri. They were traditional small-town stores that charged relatively high price markups. Being a student of retailing, Walton saw that discount stores had great potential. Walton opened his first Wal-Mart Discount City in Rogers, Arkansas, in 1962. That same year, rivals KMart and Target got their start. Discount retailing had entered the American way of life.

Once committed to discount retailing, Walton developed a business model that lasted the rest of his life: to remove costs from the merchandising system wherever they exist—in retail stores, in the manufacturers' profit margins, and with the wholesalers—all with the goal of driving prices down.

Using that model, which slashed Walton's profit margins to the bone, it was necessary that Wal-Mart increase sales at a rapid pace. It did, and Walton hit the road to open stores wherever he saw profitability. He would buzz towns in his low-flying airplane, surveying the lay of the land. When he had calibrated the proper intersection between a few small towns, he would purchase a piece of farmland at that intersection and open another Wal-Mart store.

To Walton's great delight, Wal-Mart became the world's number one retailer, surpassing the profitability of its competitors such as Sears and Kmart. Walton's extraordinary leadership skills inspired hundreds of thousands of employees to believe in what Wal-Mart could achieve, and many rode the firm's stock to wealth. Walton's cost-cutting techniques have been emulated by Home Depot, Barnes & Noble, and other retailers.

Despite Wal-Mart's success, many disgruntled small-town merchants fear that the giant retailer will drive them out of business. Also, Wal-Mart's fanatical efforts to cut costs have been attacked by unions for holding down wages and hastening the shift of production jobs overseas. However, consumers have voted heavily for Walton. He provided Americans with what they desired—low prices every day.

Source: Sam Walton and John Huey, *Sam Walton: Made in America* (New York: Bantam Books, 1993); and Daniel Gross, *Forbes Greatest Business Stories of All Time* (New York: John Wiley & Sons, Inc., 1996).

Why? Analysts maintain that Starbucks increases the overall market and attracts new customers to gourmet coffee who then patronize the independent café next door.

However, critics of Starbucks often compare it with Wal-Mart Stores. But Starbucks doesn't enjoy the advantages that have made Wal-Mart the curse of numerous Main Street retailers—lower prices, wider selection, and longer hours. The Starbucks menu isn't cheaper or broader than the independent's, and the chain's hours are often shorter. This may be why independents still dominate the industry, realizing 61 percent of industry sales in 2002.

A major reason for the success of independents is product differentiation: They are less like restaurants than like neighborhood taverns, a concept chains do not threaten. Customers often come alone to an independent in search of conversation and friendship. There they are served by familiar employees, sit in an intimate room with upholstered chairs and antique tables, and enjoy poetry readings, jazz performances, and old-movie showings. Moreover, the emergence of Starbucks has inspired independents to upgrade their cafés and broaden their menus.

Many independents are probably not as profitable as Starbucks shops. The size of its gourmet coffee orders means that Starbucks receives purchasing discounts that fatten its profit margins. But the profit margins on gourmet coffee drinks are so high that independent cafés can prosper even without volume purchasing discounts. This is especially true for coffeehouses that roast their own coffee beans because of the plunging prices of raw beans.

ADVERTISING

Product differentiation is a hallmark of many imperfectly competitive firms. Such firms often engage in advertising either to make buyers aware of the unique features of their products or to convince buyers that their product really is different from those of their competitors, or both. Advertising constantly surrounds us—in magazines and newspapers and on radio, television, and billboards. In 2003, $249 billion was spent on advertising in the United States, as shown in Table 6.3.

Many imperfectly competitive markets are characterized by brand names and continual product development and improvement as well as product promotion. For example, the brand name Prestone has become a synonym for antifreeze, while Pennzoil is a synonym

Table 6.3	Advertising Expenditures by Medium, 2003	
Medium		**Expenditure**
Television		$ 53.9 billion
Direct mail		49.1
Newspapers		45.4
Radio		19.5
Yellow pages		13.9
Magazines		11.8
Other		55.6
Total		$249.2 billion

Source: From U.S. Department of Commerce, Bureau of the Census, *Statistical Abstract of the United States,* 2004–2005, Table 1274.

| Figure 6.2 | The Effect of Advertising on Demand and Average Total Costs |

The purpose of nearly all of advertising is to increase the demand for a firm's product and to make it less sensitive to price changes (less elastic). As a result, the firm's market share increases, as does its price-making ability. By fostering an increase in market share and production, advertising can help a firm more fully realize economies of scale and decreasing unit costs.

for motor oil. The acceptance of these brands by consumers has resulted in the manufacturers of Prestone and Pennzoil charging significantly higher prices for their products than those charged for competing brands. Indeed, the market value of product brands can amount to billions of dollars.

The objective of nearly all advertising is to increase the demand for a firm's product. Consider the Coca-Cola Company, which engages in extensive advertising. By persuading consumers that Coke is really better than Pepsi and other rivals, Coca-Cola can expect to increase the amount it can sell at each price. In Figure 6.2(a), this can be shown by a rightward shift in the firm's demand curve. Prior to advertising, the Coca-Cola Company sells 6 million cases at the price of $5 per case, denoted by point A on demand curve D_0. As a result of persuasive advertising, the firm's demand curve may shift to D_1. At the $6 price, the firm can now sell 10 million cases.

Besides increasing the demand curve of Coke, persuasive advertising can make demand less sensitive to price changes (less elastic). By successfully generating brand loyalty through advertising, Coca-Cola Company convinces consumers that there exist fewer substitutes for its product. By allowing the firm to charge higher prices with a smaller loss of sales, advertising enhances the price-making ability of the Coca-Cola Company. Profits rise when advertising increases the firm's revenue more than the cost of advertising.[2]

Persuasive advertising also affects the long-run average total cost of Coke, as shown in Figure 6.2(b). Without advertising, the Coca-Cola Company's average total cost curve is

---

[2] However, not all advertising is persuasive. Sometimes, advertising can be informative. Advertising is judged to be informative when it provides trustworthy information about the quality and price of a good or service or the location of suppliers. Such advertising results in greater price elasticity of demand and less price-making ability for firms.

denoted by ATC_0. At the price of $5, the firm sells, say, 6 million cases of Coke. The firm's unit cost is $3 per case, shown by point A. To increase its market share, suppose the Coca-Cola Company decides to advertise. The advertising expenditures result in an upward shift in the firm's cost curve to ATC_1. Through successful advertising, suppose Coke's sales increase to, say, 10 million cases. By producing additional cases of Coke, the firm can take advantage of economies of scale that result in unit cost falling to $2, shown by point B. The reduction in unit cost, made possible by economies of large-scale production, more than outweighs the increase in unit cost as the result of advertising. Consumers can thus purchase Coke at a lower price with advertising than they would without.

On the other hand, what if PepsiCo, Inc., initiates an advertising campaign that offsets the demand-increasing effects of Coke's advertising campaign. In this case, the market share of each firm remains unchanged as the result of advertising. For Coca-Cola Company, advertising results in an increase in its cost curve from ATC_0 to ATC_1. Because the firm's sales remain at 6 million cases, however, unit cost rises to $5 per case (point C). The consumer thus faces a higher price because of advertising. Critics of advertising argue that this is the typical case instead of the reduction in unit cost from point A to point B. Instead, advertising expenditures could be used for hospitals, education, or other useful products that might better improve the well-being of society.

PRICE DISCRIMINATION

We have learned that imperfectly competitive firms seek to determine the price that maximizes their total profits. Sometimes, the firm may charge more than one price for a particular good. For example, golf courses often charge senior citizens a lower price than other adults to play a round of golf. Movie theaters often give discounts to students to see a movie. In these cases, the firm charges different prices to different customers for what is essentially the same product or service. These practices are known as **price discrimination,** the charging of some customers a lower price than others for an identical good even though there is no difference in the cost to the firm for supplying these consumers.

To engage in price discrimination, a seller must have price-making ability and thus operate in an imperfectly competitive market. It also must prevent significant resale of products from the lower-priced to the higher-priced market. If buyers can resell a product, price discrimination will likely be unsuccessful. Finally, the seller must divide its customers into groups, each having a different willingness and ability to pay. Price-sensitive buyers (with *more elastic* demand schedules) will pay a *lower* price than buyers who are not as sensitive to price (with less-elastic demand schedules).

Airline carriers provide an example of price discrimination. Consider a recent United Airlines flight from its hub at O'Hare International Airport in Chicago to Los Angeles. If any of the passengers had compared notes, they would have found that they had paid 27 different fares. One paid nothing, using frequent-flyer miles; another who bought a first-class ticket on the day of departure paid $1,249. And one who bought a coach ticket on the day of travel paid $108. In general, people who bought their tickets earlier paid less, but not always.

Although this pricing strategy may seem chaotic, its purpose is to squeeze as many dollars as possible out of each seat and mile flown. That means trying to project just how many tickets to sell at a discount without running out of seats for the business traveler, who usually books at the last minute and therefore pays full fare. According to the airlines, "You don't want to sell a seat to a guy for $79 when he's willing to pay $450."

Airlines use price discrimination to maximize their revenues. For airline travel, the key distinction among travelers is between leisure travel and business travel. Leisure travelers have relatively elastic demand because they can plan ahead and are flexible in their schedules.

To encourage these price-sensitive customers to fly in their planes, airlines will charge them relatively low prices and, of course, do so in a manner that prevents them from reselling their tickets to less price-sensitive passengers. Business passengers, however, have less-elastic demand because they often must travel on short notice, will not stay over weekends, and are insensitive to ticket fares. As a result, airlines charge higher fares to business travelers, who are a primary source of airline profits. But the business share of air travel is declining as electronic business communication takes the place of face-to-face business communication, a development that has contributed to falling airline profits.

Colleges also use price discrimination. In 1995, for example, Johns Hopkins University began offering aid according to the student's price elasticity of demand for attending the university.[3] Johns Hopkins wanted to attract academically gifted students who would major in humanities but might attend other universities. These students had relatively elastic demand curves for education at Johns Hopkins, given the availability of substitute universities. By granting them an extra $3,000 in aid, the university was able to increase enrollment in that group by 20 percent. However, Johns Hopkins did not worry about losing prospective pre-med students, whose demand curves for education at Johns Hopkins were relatively inelastic. Because most of these students were already hooked on its pre-med program, a price increase would not knock many out. Johns Hopkins cut this group's aid by $1,000 per student and still increased net revenue. Today, Johns Hopkins' pricing strategy is being tried out at colleges and universities all over the nation. Perhaps your relatively elastic demand for the college you are attending contributed to your receiving a scholarship.

CHECK POINT

1. Identify the characteristics of an imperfectly competitive market structure.

2. How do concentration ratios attempt to measure how close an industry comes to the extremes of competition and monopoly?

3. Explain how monopolistic competition involves a considerable amount of competition and a small dose of monopoly power.

4. How does a firm successfully practice price discrimination?

OLIGOPOLY

Oligopoly is another form of imperfect competition. In oligopoly, a small number of firms compete with each other, and each firm has significant price-making ability. Oligopoly embodies a range of market situations. It includes a situation in which there are two or three firms dominating an entire market, as well as a situation in which seven or eight firms share, say, 75 percent of the market (while a competitive fringe of remaining firms accounts for the remainder). Oligopoly also includes firms that produce standardized products as well as differentiated products. The steel and pharmaceutical industries are

---

[3] "Colleges Manipulate Financial-Aid Offers Shortchanging Many," *The Wall Street Journal*, April 1, 1996, p. A1.

generally regarded as oligopolistic. The quantity sold by an oligopolist depends not only on that firm's product price but also on the other firms' prices and quantities sold. Each firm therefore must consider the impact of its own actions on the actions of other firms. To understand the interaction between prices and sales, consider the following example. Suppose you operate one of three grocery stores in a small town. If you reduce your prices and your rivals do not reduce theirs, your sales will increase, but the sales of your two rivals will decrease. In this situation, your rivals will likely also cut their prices. If they reduce prices, your sales and profits will decline. So prior to deciding to decrease your prices, you attempt to predict how your rivals will react, and you try to estimate the impact of those reactions on your profit.

Why are some industries dominated by a few firms? We can provide some partial answers here:

- **Barriers to entry.** Oligopolistic industries may be fostered by barriers to entry such as product differentiation and advertising, patents, and the control and ownership of key resources. Historical control of raw materials explains the dominance of the Aluminum Company of America in the aluminum industry. The high costs of obtaining needed plant and equipment may also deter entry. The aircraft and cigarette industries are characterized by high investment requirements.

- **Economies of scale.** With economies of scale, a firm's average total cost declines as output expands. Smaller firms in this situation tend to be inefficient because their average total costs will be greater than those realized by a larger firm. With economies of scale, a firm may be able to drive its smaller rivals out of the market and prevent potential competitors from entering the market. Economies of scale are noticeable in the cement and rubber industries.

- **Mergers.** Another reason that oligopoly occurs is that firms combine under a single ownership or control, a practice known as merger. The merged firm becomes larger, may realize economies of scale as output expands, and usually has increased ability to control the market price of its product. In the beer industry, for example, giants such as Anheuser-Busch and Miller have grown with the acquisition of competing breweries.

RIVALRY IN THE SOFT DRINK INDUSTRY

Concerning oligopoly, one may get the impression that because there are only a few sellers in the market there is little, if any, rivalry between them. In reality, firms often fight for market share through vigorous price competition, product promotion, and improvements in product quality. Let us consider the rivalry of the Coca-Cola Company and PepsiCo, Inc., in the U.S. soft drink industry.

Historically, Coke has dominated the soft drink industry. Sales and profits have generally risen ever since Coke was first introduced to the market. Prior to the 1950s, no second-place firm was even worth considering. Consumers generally regarded Pepsi, Coke's closest competitor, to be an inferior drink.

During the 1950s, Pepsi embarked on a strategy to increase its market share. Pepsi improved the taste of its soft drink by using less sugar in its formula and establishing uniform control over local bottlers, who previously added varying amounts of carbonated water to the syrup so that Pepsi's taste varied throughout different regions of the country. Pepsi also offered consumers a 12-ounce bottle that sold for the same price as Coke's famous 6½-ounce bottle. To enhance its image, Pepsi adopted advertising campaigns featuring young women and men who drank Pepsi in high-income surroundings. The campaigns featured Pepsi as "the light refreshment," implying indirectly that Coke was "heavy." Pepsi also adopted promotional efforts to increase sales in grocery markets where Coke was comparatively weak. Moreover, Pepsi attacked Coke in the vending machine and cold-bottle segments of the market by offering financing to local bottlers who were willing to buy and install Pepsi vending machines. As Pepsi's market share increased, Coke launched retaliatory advertising campaigns. Using themes such as "The really refreshed" and "No wonder Coke refreshes best," these campaigns picked up Coke's sales. In return, Pepsi initiated two new advertising campaigns—"Be sociable" and "Think young." These campaigns especially caught on with teenagers, who account for the highest per-capita consumption of soft drinks. The youth theme suggested that Coke was an old-fashioned drink. Coke countered with its new advertising theme of "Things go better with Coke."

By the 1980s, Coke decided that it needed to compete more directly with Pepsi, which had a sweeter flavor than Coke. The firm developed a new formula for its soft drink and called it "New Coke." In spite of heavy advertising, public acceptance of New Coke was at best lukewarm and, at worst, disastrous. Several months after its introduction, Coke was forced to bring back "Classic Coke," which was based on the original formula used by Coke. It is estimated that the fiasco cost shareholders in the firm up to $500 million.

GAME THEORY AND OLIGOPOLY BEHAVIOR

A basic feature of oligopoly is that firms must weigh the impacts of their decisions on other firms and must also anticipate how those other firms will react. Basically, the behavior of an oligopoly can be viewed as a high-stakes game where the goal is to earn economic profits by outguessing your competitors. In the real world, Boeing and Airbus have been rivals in the commercial jetliner market, as have Coca-Cola and PepsiCo, Inc., in the soft drink market; Anheuser-Busch, Miller, and Coors in the beer market; Ford, General Motors, and DaimlerChrysler in the auto market; and General Mills, Post, and Kellogg's in the breakfast cereal market. These firms tend to form their price policies based on the price policies of their rivals.

We can obtain important insights into oligopolistic markets by examining a method of analysis called game theory. **Game theory** examines oligopolistic behavior by examining a series of strategies and payoffs among rival firms. A strategy is a course of action, say, to charge a high price or a low price, and the payoff is the economic profit that results from that strategy.

Consider a hypothetical market of two competing airline firms, American and United, whose goals are to increase their economic profits by price changes. Each firm makes its pricing decisions independently, without knowing in advance what its rival will do. Figure 6.3 shows the profit-payoff matrix for these firms. Each cell in the matrix shows the yearly profit that each of the two firms can expect to earn, depending on the pricing strategy that each selects and that of its rival. The top portion in each cell shows the profit of United, and the bottom portion shows American's profit.

Competitive Oligopoly and Low Prices

As shown in Figure 6.3 (on page 146), the option available to each firm is to charge either a "high price" or a "low price," and the payoff matrix shows the profit that each firm expects to earn, given its own pricing choice and that of its competitor. For example, if both firms charge high prices (cell A), each will earn a profit of $60 million. Instead, suppose United charges a low price and American charges a high price (cell B). United will then attract

economics
IN ACTION

Concentration Keeps the Beer Industry Foaming

According to anthropologists, what lured our ancient ancestors out of their caves may not have been a thirst for knowledge, but a thirst for beer. When people learned to ferment grain into beer thousands of years ago, it became one of their most important sources of nutrition. Beer gave people protein that unfermented grain couldn't supply. Besides, it tasted a whole lot better than the unfermented grain did. But in order to have a steady supply of beer, it was necessary to have a steady supply of beer ingredients. People had to give up their nomadic ways, settle down, and begin farming. Once they did, civilization was just a stone's throw away.

Today, beer is big business in the United States. The annual retail value of the brewing industry's products is currently more than $50 billion. Surveys show that approximately 88 million American men and women drink the "beverage of moderation." To meet the great demand for beer, American breweries annually produce 67 billion 12-ounce bottles or cans of malt beverages.

The brewing industry has experienced a significant transformation since the1940s, when more than 400 independent brewing companies were spread throughout the country. While the four largest brewers sold only 16 percent of the nation's beer in 1946, the top four brewers (Anheuser-Busch, SABMiller, Coors, and Pabst) currently sell 90 percent of the nation's domestically produced beer. Anheuser-Busch, with its Clydesdales and lavish Super Bowl ads, controls nearly half of all U.S. beer sales. Competition from foreign producers has never been as strong a force in the beer industry as in markets such as automobiles and consumer electronics. However, the amount of beer imported into the United States has been increasing and provides an important source of competition to the premium brands. Indeed, breweries operate in an oligopolistic market.

What led to the evolution of the beer industry from low concentration to high concentration? Referring to the supply side of the market, technological advances have increased the speed of bottling and canning lines. Today, a modern production line can produce 1,100 bottles or 2,000 cans of beer per minute. Also, automated brewing and warehousing permit large brewers to decrease labor costs. Moreover, plant construction costs per barrel are about one-third less for a 4.5 million-barrel plant than for a 1.5 million-barrel plant. Simply put, efficiencies in

customers from its rival and earn a profit of $75 million; American will earn a modest profit of $30 million. Conversely, if American charges a low price and United charges a high price, American will earn a profit of $75 million and United will earn a profit of only $30 million.

As the payoff matrix shows, each firm will realize additional profits if both firms charge a high price. However, the maximum payoff for any particular firm is to have its rival charge a high price while it alone charges a low price and then attracts customers from its rival. The minimum payoff for a particular firm is to charge a high price while its rival charges a low one, because then it will lose many sales to its rival.

The outcome of this game yields the tendency toward a low-price strategy for competitive oligopoly. If United or American charges a low price, it is doing the best that it can do, given the behavior of the other firm. Thus, once United and American reach cell D in the figure, neither firm will desire to alter its price. The market thus gravitates toward a low-price strategy for each firm. Simply put, fear of what the rival firm will do is what causes each firm to offer a low price. The low price is good for consumers, but it is not good for the firms, which realize a profit of only $40 million production appear to be a significant barrier to entry in the beer industry.

Changes on the demand side of the market have also fostered concentration. First, consumer tastes have tended to switch from the stronger-flavored beers of the small brewers to the light products of the larger brewers. Indeed, Bud Light and Miller Light are popular brands in today's market. Second, the consumption of beer has evolved away from taverns and to homes. The significance of this change is that taverns were usually supplied with kegs from local brewers; however, the acceptance of aluminum cans for home consumption made it possible for large distant brewers to compete with the local brewers.

Consumer tests confirm that many beer drinkers cannot distinguish between brands of beer. To increase sales, brewers thus vigorously advertise. Brewers that sell national brands, such as Anheuser-Busch and Miller, realize substantial cost advantages over brewers such as Pabst that have many regional brands such as Rainier and Schmidts. The reason is that national television advertising is less costly per viewer than local advertising.

Although mergers have occurred in the brewing industry, they have not been a major source of the increasing concentration. Mergers generally have represented the termination of a small, inefficient brewer that salvaged some portion of its worth by selling out to another brewer. The acquiring brewer thus gained no market power, but might have gained access to an improved distributional network or a new market. Dominant brewers, such as Anheuser-Busch and Coors, have generally expanded by vigorously advertising their main brands and by creating new brands instead of acquiring other brewers. This has sustained product differentiation as a significant barrier to entry.

A smaller brewer, producing premium beer and marketing it so as to keep transportation costs low, can survive in today's market by finding a special niche for itself. This appears to be the status of Jacob Linenkuegel Brewing Company of Chippewa Falls, Wisconsin. However, such cases are rare. In brewing, large capital-intensive plants are necessary to exploit economies of scale and survive.

Source: Kenneth Elzinga, "Beer," in Walter Adams and James Brock, editors, *The Structure of American Industry* (Upper Saddle River, NJ: Prentice Hall, 2001), pp. 85–113. See also Philip Van Munching, *Beer Blast* (New York: Random House, 1997) and Douglas Greer, "Beer: Causes of Structural Change," in Larry Duetsche, editor, *Industry Studies* (New York: M. E. Sharpe, 1998), pp. 28–64.

rather than the $60 million that each would have earned if they had both charged high prices (cell *A*).

Cooperative Behavior and Cheating

How can United and American avoid the modest profits associated with cell *D*? The answer is to cooperate with each other and decide how to set prices. For example, managers of the two firms might strike an agreement that each will charge a high price. This action will cause the firms to locate at cell *A* in the figure, where each earns profits of $60 million instead of $40 million.

Although cooperative behavior can increase the profits of each firm, the profits are not at a maximum. Therefore, each firm may be enticed to cheat on this pricing agreement and charge a low price while its rival maintains a high price. For example, if United agrees to charge a high price, but secretly charges a low price, the outcome moves from cell *A* to cell *B*, at which United earns a profit of $75 million. Similarly, if only American cheats, the outcome would move from cell *A* to cell *C*, and the firm earns a profit of $75 million. Therefore, there is a tendency for cooperative price-fixing agreements to break down.

| Figure 6.3 | Game Theory and Oligopoly Behavior |

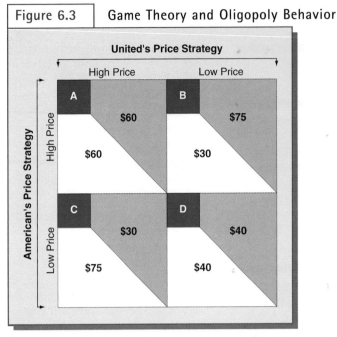

United and American would earn the largest profits if they both selected a high-price strategy. If they behave independently, either firm might realize higher profits by selecting a low-price strategy against its rival's high-price strategy. However, such rivalry tends to cause both firms to gravitate to a low-price strategy.

ARE AIRBUS' SUBSIDIES THE REASON FOR BOEING'S NOSEDIVE?

The commercial jetliner industry provides an example of oligopolistic rivalry. Consider the battle between Boeing and Airbus.

Although the Europeans developed the first commercial jetliner in the 1950s, Boeing and other U.S. manufacturers learned from European mistakes and leapfrogged ahead. Europe was concerned that competition from the Americans would wipe out its weak and divided aviation industry. Hence, European governments exercised the only option they felt was available to them: pooling their resources to establish a company that could compete against the Americans. This led to the formation of the Airbus Company in 1969.

When Airbus was first created, analysts generally doubted whether it could compete against Boeing, which enjoyed a virtual monopoly in the sale of jetliners. Maintaining that they were nurturing an "infant industry," the governments of Europe granted subsidies to Airbus. By the 1980s, Airbus was a strong competitor against Boeing, and today it accounts for more than half of the world jetliner market. According to Airbus, its success stems from providing the market with what it wants: a high-quality jetliner at a competitive price.

As Airbus has prospered, the United States has increasingly complained that Airbus' success is primarily the result of unfair subsidies from European governments, as seen in Table 6.4. U.S. officials argue that these subsidies place Boeing at a competitive disadvantage. Airbus receives loans for the development of new aircraft, which are made at below-market interest rates and can amount to 70 to 90 percent of an aircraft's development cost. Rather than repaying the loans according to a prescribed timetable as would occur in a competitive market, Airbus is allowed to repay them as it delivers an aircraft.

Table 6.4	Does Airbus Have an Unfair Advantage?

Government support of Airbus has long been a sore point for Boeing. Most of the support comes in the form of low-interest loans to develop new planes, and repayment does not begin until deliveries start. All figures below are in millions of dollars.

Airbus Aircraft Program	Government Loans	Total Cost to Airbus (with interest)	Outstanding Repayments
A300/310	$ 888	$ 0	$ 0
A320	1,480	2,101	140
A330/340	2,671	3,306	0
A340-500	2,548	3,637	3,637
A380	2,450	3,351	3,351
Total	$10,037	$12,395	$7,128

Source: European Aeronautic Defense and Space Company, Bloomberg News, Airbus, Boeing, Morgan Stanley.

Also, Airbus can avoid repaying its loans in full if sales of aircraft that are being financed fall short of forecasts. Although Airbus says that has never occurred, Boeing contends Airbus has less business risk, making it easier to obtain financing. The United States maintains that these subsidies allow Airbus to set unrealistically low prices, offer concessions and attractive financing terms to airlines, and write off development costs.

Airbus defends its subsidies on the ground that they prevent the United States from holding a worldwide monopoly in commercial jetliners. In the absence of Airbus, European airlines would have to rely exclusively on Boeing as a supplier. Fears of dependence and the loss of autonomy in an area on the cutting edge of technology motivate European governments to subsidize Airbus.

Airbus also argues that Boeing benefits from government assistance. For example, governmental research organizations support aeronautics and propulsion research that is shared with Boeing. Support for commercial jetliner innovation also comes from military-sponsored research and military procurement. Research financed by the armed services yields indirect but important technological spillovers to the commercial jetliner industry, most notably in aircraft engines and aircraft design. Boeing also receives tax breaks from the state of Washington, which houses sizable Boeing production facilities. Moreover, the Japanese government helps Boeing by providing loans to Japanese subcontractors making wings for Boeing aircraft.

In 2005, the United States and Europe entered into negotiations to resolve their differences over subsidies. It remains to be seen how the negotiations will be resolved.

COLLUSION AND CARTELS

Recall that game theory considers the possibility that oligopolistic firms may form collusive agreements with each other rather than behave as competitors. Let us further examine how oligopolies form collusive agreements, known as cartels.

A cartel is a formal organization of firms that attempts to act as if there were only one firm in the industry (monopoly). The purpose of a cartel is to reduce output and increase the price in order to increase the joint profits of its members.

A widely known cartel is the Organization of Petroleum Exporting Countries (OPEC), a group of nations that sells oil on the world market. Although OPEC has generally disavowed the term cartel, its organization consists of a secretariat, a conference of ministers, a board of governors, and an economic commission. The countries that belong to OPEC are generally from the Middle East and include countries such as Saudi Arabia, Iran, Kuwait, Qatar, and so on. OPEC has assigned production controls among its members in an attempt to make oil scarce, thus supporting prices higher than would exist under more competitive conditions.

After operating in obscurity throughout the 1960s, OPEC captured control of oil pricing in 1972–1974 when the price of oil rose from $3 to $12 per barrel. Triggered by the Iranian revolution in 1979, oil prices skyrocketed to over $35 per barrel by 1981. During this era, OPEC's success in increasing oil prices was largely due to strong consumer demand for oil and consumers being insensitive (inelastic) to price increases. Moreover, OPEC accounted for half of the world's oil production and about two-thirds of the world's oil reserves throughout this era.

By the mid-1980s, however, OPEC fell into disarray as the result of increased competition from non-OPEC nations (the former Soviet Union, Mexico, United Kingdom), conservation by the oil-importing nations, and falling oil demand caused by a downturn in the world economy. By 1986, the price of oil had tumbled to $10 per barrel, hammering industry profits and stock prices. The industry had little choice but to cut oil exploration and production budgets. By the early 2000s, the world demand for oil had rebounded. With oil inventories being low, prices shot to more than $60 per barrel in 2005, thus enhancing profits of the OPEC nations.

Although a cartel attempts to maximize the profits of its members, several obstacles may limit its success. Recall from our discussion of game theory, that once a cartel is established, incentives arise for individual member producers to leave the cartel and operate independently. If a single producer were to price below the common cartel price, this would attract additional sales to that producer, at the expense of other members, possibly increasing its profits above what they would be under the cartel. However, if other cartel members follow suit and reduce their prices, all firms will receive both lower prices and profits than they enjoyed under the cartel arrangement. Because of the incentive for individual members to leave the cartel and establish prices independently, the life span of most cartels has been short.

Besides the problem of cheating, other obstacles to forming and maintaining a cartel can arise. Among the obstacles that cartels face are the following:

- **Number of sellers.** Generally speaking, the larger the number of sellers, the more difficult it is to coordinate price and output policies among cartel members.

- **Cost and demand differences.** When cartel members' costs and demands greatly differ, it is more difficult to assign production controls and agree on price.

- **Potential competition.** Increased profits that occur under a cartel may attract new competitors, thus restricting the cartel's control of the market.

- **Economic downturn.** As market sales dwindle in a weakening economy, profits decline, thus undermining the success of a cartel.

- **Government policy.** In the United States, cartels are illegal. Business executives who are found guilty of engaging in collusion can be fined and sent to jail. This does not mean that firms do not engage in collusion. However, it is usually done secretly and is difficult to prove.

MERGERS AND OLIGOPOLY

Mergers can promote the development of oligopolistic market structures. A merger is the combining of the assets of two firms to form a single new firm. By combining their assets, the acquiring firm and the acquired firm hope to become more profitable than they were prior to the merger. Table 6.5 gives examples of mergers between U.S. firms.

Three are three types of mergers: A **horizontal merger** occurs when one firm combines with another firm that sells similar products in the same market. The merger of Jones &

Table 6.5	Selected Mergers in the United States	

Firm Acquired	Acquiring Firm	Year
Compaq	Hewlett-Packard	2002
AOL	Time Warner	2000
McDonnell-Douglas	Boeing	1997
Martin Marietta	Lachute	1994
Warner Communications	Time	1989
RCA	General Electric	1986
Gulf Oil	Chevron	1984
Getty Oil	Texaco	1984
Marathon Oil	USX (U.S. Steel)	1981

Laughlin Steel and Republic Steel to form LTV Steel is an example of a horizontal merger. A **vertical merger** is a merger between firms in the same industry, but at different stages in the production process. For example, Bridgestone (tires) has acquired rubber plantations in Indonesia and Malaysia, and Campbell Soup has acquired mushroom farms throughout the United States. Finally, a **conglomerate merger** brings together two firms producing in different industries. The merger of Greyhound (bus service) and Armor and Co. (meat products) is an example of a conglomerate merger.

Of these three types of mergers, the federal government looks most carefully at proposed horizontal mergers. The reason is that horizontal mergers can result in the uniting of formerly competing firms, thus reducing competition and increasing the monopoly power of the newly formed firm. But mergers can also contribute to cost savings and other efficiencies. For example, the newly formed firm might (1) add to industry output and promote additional competition, (2) enter markets that neither merging firm could have entered individually, or (3) realize cost reductions that would have been unavailable if each merging firm performed the same function separately. Such cost reductions could be the result of economies of scale, integration of production facilities, plant specialization, and lower transportation costs. In deciding whether a horizontal merger should be approved, the federal government weighs the benefits of increased efficiencies versus the costs of increased monopoly power.[4]

CHECK POINT

1. Oligopoly involves a considerable dose of monopoly and a small dose of competition. Explain.

2. How does game theory illustrate the mutual interdependence of firms in oligopoly?

3. Why are cartels difficult to form and operate?

4. Distinguish between a horizontal merger, a vertical merger, and a conglomerate merger.

5. Why do government regulators especially scrutinize proposed horizontal mergers?

---

[4] *Revision to the Horizontal Merger Guidelines*, Federal Trade Commission (Washington, D.C.), April 8, 1997.

Chapter Summary

1. Imperfect competition occurs when more than one seller competes for sales with other sellers, each of which has some price-making ability. Imperfect competition includes the market structures of monopolistic competition and oligopoly.

2. Economists have developed concentration ratios to tell how closely an industry comes to the extremes of competition and monopoly. A low-concentration ratio suggests a high degree of competition, and a high-concentration ratio implies a low degree of competition.

3. Monopolistic competition is characterized by a large number of sellers, each seller having a relatively small share of the total market, relative freedom of entry into the market and exit from the market, and product differentiation among sellers. Although monopolistically competitive firms tend to earn zero economic profits in the long run, they suffer from the problem of excess capacity.

4. The goal of persuasive advertising is to shift a firm's demand curve to the right and make it less sensitive to price changes. Advertising results in an upward shift in a firm's cost curve. However, economies of large-scale production made possible by increased sales volume because of advertising may lead to lower unit costs than would occur without advertising.

5. Price discrimination is the practice of charging some customers a lower price than others for an identical good or service, even though there is no difference in the cost to the firm for supplying these consumers. A firm practicing price discrimination will charge a lower price to buyers with more-elastic demand and a higher price to buyers with less-elastic demand.

6. In oligopoly, a small number of firms compete with each other, and each firm has significant price-making ability. Oligopolistic markets are characterized by high barriers to entry, economies of scale, and mergers. Because uncertainty about the interaction of competing firms in oligopoly makes it virtually impossible to formulate a single theory of oligopoly behavior, a number of different theories exist. However, game theory can be used to illustrate the mutual interdependence of firms in oligopolistic markets.

7. Rather than engage in cutthroat competition, oligopolies may decide to collude and form a cartel. The purpose of a cartel is to restrict output and drive up price, thus maximizing the joint profits of its members.

8. Oligopolies are characterized by horizontal mergers, vertical mergers, and conglomerate mergers. Of these three types of mergers, government regulators monitor proposed horizontal mergers most closely. The reason is that horizontal mergers can result in the uniting of formerly competing firms, which may increase the monopoly power of the newly formed firm.

Key Terms and Concepts

imperfect competition (132)

concentration ratios (132)

monopolistic competition (134)

product differentiation (134)

excess capacity (136)

advertising (138)

price discrimination (140)

oligopoly (141)

merger (142)

game theory (143)

cartel (147)

Organization of Petroleum Exporting Countries (OPEC) (147)

horizontal merger (148)

vertical merger (149)

conglomerate merger (149)

Self-Test: Multiple-Choice Questions

1. Retail gasoline stations provide an example of

   a. perfect competition.
   b. pure monopoly.
   c. oligopoly.
   d. monopolistic competition.

2. Which of the following is a characteristic of monopolistic competition or oligopoly, but not perfect completion?

   a. Profit-maximizing behavior according to the $MR = MC$ rule
   b. Negligible barriers to entry into an industry
   c. Relatively large number of firms in the industry
   d. Product differentiation

3. All of the following are characteristic of oligopolies *except*

   a. mergers that facilitate growth.
   b. mutual interdependence.
   c. advertising and nonprice competition.
   d. price-taking behavior among firms.

4. The operation of a cartel tends to be inhibited by

   a. economic downturns and cheating by members of the cartel.
   b. a small number of sellers in the market.
   c. relatively inelastic demand schedules.
   d. highly similar demand and cost conditions among members of the cartel.

5. Successful advertising by Pizza Hut tends to shift its demand curve

   a. rightward and make it more elastic.
   b. rightward and make it more inelastic.
   c. leftward and make it more elastic.
   d. leftward and make it more inelastic.

6. Which of the following industries is best represented by oligopoly?

   a. Farming and commercial fishing
   b. Gasoline retailing
   c. Commercial jetliners
   d. Fast-food restaurants

7. By practicing successful price discrimination, Liberty Theater will charge

   a. a relatively higher price to customers with more-elastic demand curves.
   b. a relatively higher price to customers with less-elastic demand curves.
   c. a relatively lower price to customers with more-inelastic demand curves.
   d. the same price to all customers regardless of their elasticities of demand.

8. If Coca-Cola Company and PepsiCo, Inc., agreed to divide the market for soft drinks and fix prices, what factor would limit the effectiveness of their agreement?

   a. The relatively large size of these firms in the soft drink industry
   b. The substantial economies of scale realized by these firms
   c. The degree to which large profits would attract entry of a new firm into the soft drink industry
   d. The ease of monitoring the advertising strategies and product innovation by these firms

9. Neither perfectly competitive firms nor monopolistically competitive firms can realize economic profits in the long run because

   a. substantial barriers to entry prevent established firms from realizing profits.
   b. the firms tend to encounter diseconomies of scale in the long run.
   c. free entry and competitive pricing cause prices to decline to the level of production costs.
   d. price-sensitive buyers force sellers to charge prices that just cover their average variable costs.

10. The merger of Jones & Laughlin Steel and Republic Steel to form LTV Steel is an example of a(n)

   a. integrative merger.
   b. conglomerate merger.
   c. horizontal merger.
   d. vertical merger.

Answers to Multiple-Choice Questions

1. d.   **2.** d   **3.** d   **4.** a   **5.** b   **6.** c   **7.** b   **8.** c   **9.** c   **10.** c

Study Questions and Problems

1. What is the meaning of a Top 4 concentration ratio of 20 percent? 85 percent?

2. Suppose that Don's Texaco is a typical gas station in a monopolistically competitive market. Draw a diagram showing the market position of the firm in the long run. Does the firm encounter the problem of excess capacity? Why or why not?

3. Figure 6.4 shows the short-run position of Hal's Electronics, a typical firm selling radios in a monopolistically competitive market.

   a. Hal's profit-maximizing output, price, and total revenue will be _____, _____, and _____.
   b. At the profit-maximizing output, Hal's average total cost and total cost will be _____ and _____.

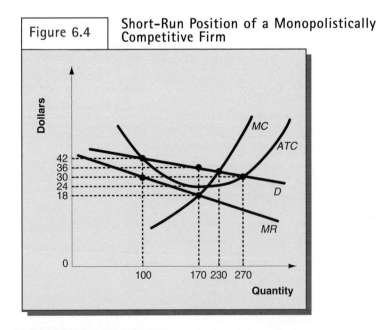

| Figure 6.4 | Short–Run Position of a Monopolistically Competitive Firm |

| Table 6.6 | Hypothetical Profit–Payoff Matrix for Nike and Reebok |

		Nike	
		High-price	Low-price
Reebok	High-price	Nike = $600 Reebok = $600	Nike = $750 Reebok = $150
	Low-price	Nike = $150 Reebok = $750	Nike = $150 Reebok = $150

    c. Hal will earn an economic profit of ____.

    d. Attracted by short-run economic profits, suppose that firms enter this industry. In the long run, what will be the effect on Hal's demand curve, marginal revenue curve, and economic profits?

4. Draw a diagram that shows how persuasive advertising affects a firm's demand curve and average total cost curve. Under what conditions will advertising result in lower cost per unit? How would you modify your diagram if advertising were assumed to be informative rather than persuasive?

5. Suppose Northwest Airlines practices price discrimination in the sale of tickets to business travelers and tourists. Discuss how price discrimination can result in higher revenues and profits for the firm than those that would occur in the absence of price discrimination.

6. Assume that Nike and Reebok are the only sellers of athletic shoes in the United States. They are contemplating how much to charge for similar basketball shoes. The only two choices are a high price and a low price. Table 6.6 shows the payoff matrix for these firms in which profits are stated in millions of dollars per year.

    a. Use the payoff matrix to discuss the interdependence that characterizes these firms.

    b. In the absence of cooperative behavior, what will be the likely pricing strategy for each firm?

    c. Why might cooperative behavior be beneficial for these firms? Why might there be an incentive to cheat on a price-fixing agreement?

7. Why do oligopolists have the incentive to fix prices? What are the obstacles to successful collusion?

CHAPTER 7

Labor Market Issues

Chapter objectives

After reading this chapter, you should be able to:

1. Explain how a firm determines the quantity of workers demanded.

2. Explain why even if U.S. wages are higher than foreign wages, U.S. labor can still be competitive if it is more productive than foreign labor.

3. Identify the advantages and disadvantages of a minimum wage law that raises the wage rate above the market equilibrium level.

4. Describe the methods used by unions to increases the wages of their members and the factors that give a union strength.

5. Explain why domestic workers are often fearful of international trade and liberal immigration policies.

economics IN CONTEXT

In 2004, Jennifer Sayles was treated like royalty. She was flown around the country on all-expense paid trips to San Francisco, Boston, New York, and Chicago. She was wined and dined at the finest restaurants, including the Rialto restaurant in Harvard Square. Such benefits used to accrue to individuals applying for high-profile jobs such as investment banking and consulting. But 26-year-old Jennifer Sayles was part of a new group of job seekers—students with a Ph.D. in economics who want to teach college students.

Traditionally, the job search for these assistant professors has been a long battle that resulted in poor pay in an ill-equipped office. At the turn of the century, however, a series of events including an increase in students desiring to learn about economics and a scarcity of Ph.D.s in economics resulted in job seekers being treated like big shots. From 1999 to 2004, pay for entry-level economics professors rose about 19 percent. In 2004, top doctoral students saw universities sweeten offers for assistant-professor jobs with light teaching loads, $15,000 in summer pay, $20,000 research budgets, and early sabbaticals. That was in addition to the $70,000 to $80,000 that they were offering for a 9-month school year. Those who specialized in finance were receiving even more lucrative packages, with many business schools offering salaries in excess of $100,000.

What explained the sizzling job market for young economists? On the demand side, college economics departments were faced with rising competition from high-paying consulting companies and business schools. Also, undergraduate enrollment in economics classes was increasing after a downturn in the early 1990s, causing schools to hire more professors. At schools like Columbia and Harvard, which don't offer undergraduate majors in business, economics is now the most popular major on campus.

And then there's the supply side. Despite the demand for economics classes by undergraduates, fewer Americans are choosing to expend the effort needed to obtain a doctorate. Students who would have pursued a Ph.D. in economics in the past now prefer law degrees and M.B.A.s because they come quicker and provide greater financial rewards. A typical doctorate takes six years to complete, which represents a big opportunity cost for a young professional. Added to that is an abundance of academic scholars who are now near retirement. Simply put, big demand and short supply means young graduates are courted like royalty.

In this chapter, we will learn about the theory of wage determination. In particular, we will learn why some workers receive higher wages than others and what methods workers have to increase their wages without losing their jobs. Table 7.1 shows the annual earnings for workers in selected occupations in 2002.

LABOR MARKET EQUILIBRIUM

Like other markets in the economy, labor markets are underlain by the forces of demand and supply. In labor markets, households are the sellers and business firms are the primary buyers. We call the price of labor the wage rate.

We can analyze a labor market and the factors that determine the wage rate and quantity in that market by using the model of demand and supply. Figure 7.1 refers to the market for apple pickers in Mt. Pleasant, Michigan. In the figure, the market demand curve for apple pickers is labeled D_0. Notice that the demand for apple pickers exists because there is a demand for the apples that apple pickers help to produce. The demand for apple pickers

Table 7.1	Annual Earnings in Selected Occupations, 2002

Occupation	Average Annual Earnings
Family practice physician	$150,267
Airline pilot	109,580
Computer engineer	70,900
Actuary	69,970
Librarian	43,090
Insurance sales agent	40,750
Social worker	33,150
Real estate agent	30,930
Word processor	26,730

Source: From U.S. Department of Labor, Bureau of Labor Statistics, *Occupational Outlook Handbook*, 2004–2005, available at http://stats.bls.gov.

is therefore a **derived demand:** It is derived from the demand of consumers for apples. An increase in the demand for apples will inspire growers to plant additional apple trees and hire more apple pickers; thus, the demand for apple pickers will increase. Conversely, a decrease in the demand for apples results in a reduced demand for apple pickers.

We would expect that apple growers would be willing to hire more apple pickers at lower wages than at higher wages. The two reasons for fewer apple pickers to be demanded as their wages rise are: (1) producers will switch to substitute resources, such as machinery; and (2) consumers will purchase fewer apples that become more expensive as the result of higher wages being paid to apple pickers, suggesting that fewer apple pickers will be needed to produce apples. "Exploring Further 7.1" at the end of this chapter further discusses the factors underlying the demand for labor.

The figure also shows the market supply curve of apple pickers, labeled S_0. As wages rise, other things remaining the same, additional workers are drawn into the labor force, thus increasing the quantity supplied.

Referring to Figure 7.1(a), the point of intersection of the labor demand and labor supply curves determines the equilibrium wage and employment level: 1,000 workers are hired at a wage of $500 per week. Any wage above $500 per week would result in a surplus of apple pickers and eventually decrease the wage to $500. Any wage below $500 per week would cause a shortage of apple pickers and impose upward pressure on the wage.

In any labor market, certain changes can occur that will result in increases or decreases in the labor supply curve or labor demand curve. When these changes take place, the equilibrium wage rate and quantity of workers demanded are affected.

Referring to Figure 7.1(b), suppose that the number of teenagers in the population rises, resulting in more workers to pick apples. Therefore, the supply curve of labor shifts rightward to S_1. As supply increases, the equilibrium wage falls from $500 per week to $400 per week, and the number of apple pickers employed increases from 1,000 to 1,200.

Let's now consider the effect of a change in the demand curve for labor. Referring to Figure 7.1(c), suppose the market demand for apples increases. Because the demand for apple pickers is derived from the demand for apples, the demand for apple pickers shifts rightward, say, to D_1 in the figure. As demand increases, the equilibrium wage rate rises from $500 per week to $600 per week, and the number of workers employed rises from 1,000 to 1,200.

Figure 7.1 | Market for Apple Pickers

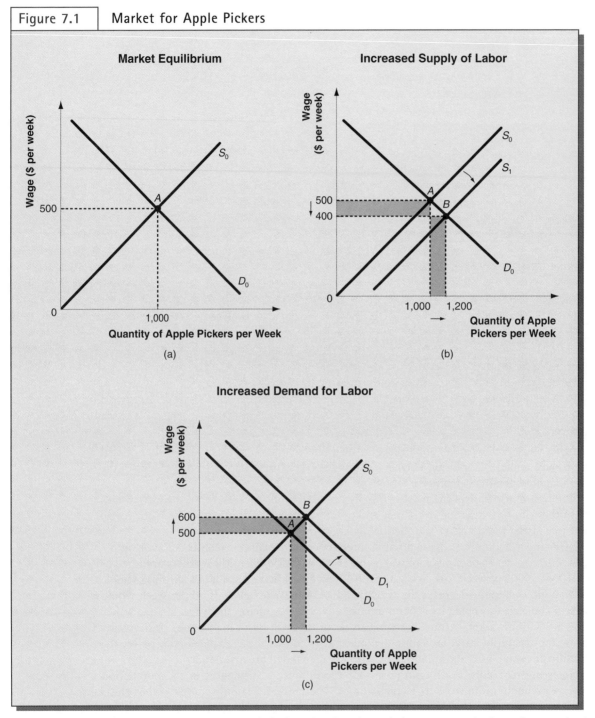

The market demand curve for labor is downward-sloping, showing that a lower wage results in an increase in the quantity of labor demanded. The market supply for labor is upward-sloping, implying that higher wages cause the quantity supplied of labor to increase. The point of intersection between the labor demand and labor supply curves determines the equilibrium wage and employment level. An increase in the market supply of labor results in a fall in the wage rate and an increase in the amount of labor employed. An increase in the market demand for labor causes a rise in the wage rate and an increase in the amount of labor employed.

We will next apply the theory of labor markets to some contemporary labor issues—the minimum wage law, labor unions, outsourcing, and immigration.

CHECK POINT

1. Explain how the demand for labor is derived from the product that labor helps produce.

2. How is equilibrium determined in the labor market?

3. What factors cause the market demand curve for labor or the supply curve of labor to increase or decrease?

4. What effect does an increase in the market supply curve of labor have on the wage rate and the quantity of labor demanded? How about an increase in the market demand curve for labor?

DO THE MINIMUM WAGE LAWS HELP WORKERS?

To help the working poor, in 1938 Congress passed *The Fair Labor Standards Act*. This law established a federal **minimum wage**, the smallest amount of money per hour that an employer can legally pay a worker. Proponents maintained that a national standard for wages was essential to restore wages to the barest minimum and to prevent any further cuts below it.

As seen in Table 7.2, the first federal minimum wage was set at 25 cents an hour in 1938. Over the years, the minimum wage has risen. The most recent increase in the minimum wage occurred in 1997, resulting in a wage floor of $5.15 an hour.

Table 7.2	Federal Minimum Wage Rates		
Effective Date	**Hourly Rate**	**Effective Date**	**Hourly Rate**
1938	$0.25	1975	$2.10
1939	0.30	1976	2.30
1945	0.40	1978	2.65
1950	0.75	1979	2.90
1956	1.00	1980	3.10
1961	1.15	1981	3.35
1963	1.25	1990	3.80
1967	1.40	1991	4.25
1968	1.60	1996	4.75
1974	2.00	1997	5.15

Source: From U.S. Employment Standards Administration, *Minimum Wage History*, available at http://www.dol.gov. See also U.S. Department of Commerce, Bureau of the Census, *Statistical Abstract of the United States* (Washington, D.C.: U.S. Government Printing Office).

Figure 7.2 | Effects of a Minimum Wage

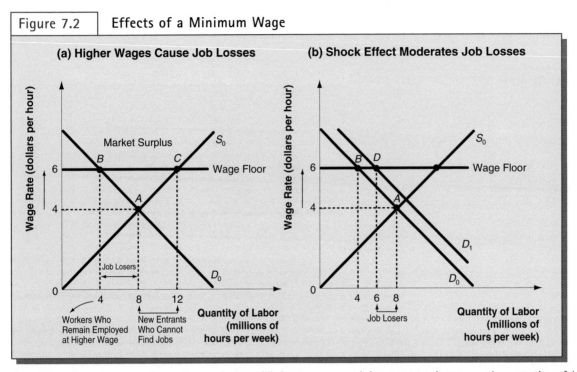

(a) Higher Wages Cause Job Losses

Wage Rate (dollars per hour)

Market Surplus

S_0

B

C

6   Wage Floor

A

4

Job Losers

D_0

0

4   8   12

Workers Who   New Entrants   **Quantity of Labor**
Remain Employed Who Cannot   **(millions of**
at Higher Wage   Find Jobs   **hours per week)**

(b) Shock Effect Moderates Job Losses

Wage Rate (dollars per hour)

S_0

B D

6   Wage Floor

A

4

D_1

D_0

0

4   6   8

Job Losers   **Quantity of Labor**
                (millions of
                hours per week)

By raising the wage rate above the market equilibrium wage, a minimum wage increases the quantity of labor supplied but decreases the quantity of labor demanded. Some workers realize higher wages, but others remain or become unemployed. If a wage hike causes the marginal productivity of labor to increase, the demand for labor would increase and unemployment would decline.

Federal minimum wage legislation now covers more than 80 percent of the nonagricultural labor force. Besides federal legislation, about 40 states have passed their own minimum wage legislation. Most states set lower minimum wages than those set by federal legislation, and 12 states plus the District of Columbia set them higher. In any state where there are differing state and federal minimum wage laws, the employee is entitled to the higher of the two. To government officials, raising the minimum wage is an attractive method of reducing poverty because it does not require an increase in government welfare payments and an accompanying tax increase.

Is the minimum wage a good means of improving the standard of living of the working poor? Figure 7.2 illustrates the market for low-skill workers, a group whose equilibrium wage rate is likely to be below the minimum wage. In a competitive labor market, suppose the equilibrium wage equals $4 per hour, shown at the intersection of the market supply curve (S_0) and market demand curve (D_0). At the equilibrium wage, workers supply 8 million hours of labor a week, and businesses demand 8 million hours of labor a week.

Suppose the federal government imposes a minimum wage of $6 per hour, higher than the market equilibrium wage. What are the effects of this wage floor? First, consider the impact of the wage hike on the quantity of labor demanded. A profit-maximizing employer will hire a worker only if the value of the output she produces is greater than the wage. As a result, the quantity demanded of labor will decrease in response to a wage increase. In Figure 7.2(a), as the wage rises from $4 to $6 per hour, the quantity of labor hours demanded falls from 8 million hours to 4 million hours. Put simply, raise the wage, and you price workers above the value they can add. An excessive price for labor yields a reduced quantity of jobs.

In Figure 7.2(a), also notice what happens on the supply side. The rise in wages from $4 to $6 per hour attracts people into the labor market. As a result, the quantity of labor supplied rises from 8 million hours to 12 million hours per week. Everybody prefers one of those higher paying jobs. At the minimum wage of $6 per hour, there is a *surplus* of labor equal to 8 million hours per week (12 million − 4 million = 8 million). In other words, there are 8 million hours of labor that people wish to provide at the minimum wage, but are unable to provide. With more job seekers than jobs, *unemployment* results.

The minimum wage benefits workers who are fortunate enough to find work at a wage level that exceeds the market equilibrium wage. However, it harms many workers, including teenagers and young adults, who seek employment at the higher wage, but cannot. Critics maintain that the minimum wage law can be described as saying to the potential worker: "Unless you can find a job paying at least the minimum wage, you may not accept employment." When it is put this way, it is hard to understand why anyone would think such a law is a good idea.

In the short run, firms may not reduce their workforce by much in response to an increase in the minimum wage. Over time, however, the increased costs due to an increased minimum wage may force smaller firms out of business, and it is here that the reduction in employment is apparent.

The minimum wage tends to have its greatest impact on unskilled workers, especially teenagers. Because teenagers are often the least experienced and least skilled members of the labor force, their market equilibrium wage is low. Teenagers, chiefly minorities, are therefore the most likely to lose jobs as a result of increases in the minimum wage.

However, some economists argue that the minimum wage may improve labor productivity. By raising the incomes of workers, a minimum wage may inspire them to become more productive. A minimum wage may also shock firms into upgrading their technology, improving their management, and using labor more efficiently. If the productivity of labor increases, the demand for labor shifts to the right, thus lessening the employment-reducing effects that the minimum wage might cause. This so-called **shock effect** is illustrated in Figure 7.2(b) where we assume that the minimum wage leads to the demand for labor increasing from D_0 to D_1. The increase in the demand for labor moderates some of the unemployment which otherwise would have occurred; the quantity of labor demanded declines by only 2 million hours per week rather than by 4 million hours.

An example of the shock effect occurred in 1914 when Ford Motor Company offered to double the wages of its employees from $2.50 to $5 per day.[1] At that time, the prevailing wage in manufacturing was only $2 to $3 per day. The offer to increase wages was motivated by the high rates of absenteeism and quitting that occurred among workers at Ford's factories. Ford apparently hoped that an increase in wages would improve the morale of workers and result in their working harder to keep their high-paying jobs. As a result, labor productivity would increase. Immediately following the wage hike, more than 10,000 workers applied for employment with Ford. According to analysts, Ford's tactic was successful. Employees remained on the job and worked harder, resulting in labor productivity gains exceeding 50 percent.

Finally, many businesses pay wages higher than the minimum wage. Indeed, the turnover of workers is the biggest expense for many businesses. What business owners might save in payroll expenses by paying a lower wage may be more than offset by the cost of

---

[1] Daniel Raff and Lawrence Summers, "Did Henry Ford Pay Efficiency Wages?" *Journal of Labor Economics,* October 1987, pp. S57–S86.

recruitment and lost investment in training people to perform a job when they will be gone in a few months. Simply put, retaining workers and reducing absenteeism are strong motivations for paying higher wages.

POPEYES' RESTAURANTS FRET OVER HOW TO HANDLE A MINIMUM-PAY RISE

In 1996, the minimum wage was a hot issue, pitting business against labor. To increase the wages of less-skilled workers, the U.S. government announced an increase in the minimum wage from $4.25 to $5.15 per hour in a 2-step move. David Rosenstein, owner of 13 Popeyes Chicken & Biscuits fast-food restaurants, staunchly opposed the wage hike, characterizing it as a bad idea. He indicated that the managers at his restaurants would not be able to cope with the wage rise.

The $4.78 wage was the average hourly wage earned by the 20 or so employees at the Popeyes' restaurant in West Philadelphia, Pennsylvania. These were the fry cooks, biscuit makers, floor sweepers, and cash-register jockeys doing some of the jobs at the bottom of the economic pyramid. For workers here, the $5.15 minimum wage would mean a raise.

For store manager, Mohammed Isah, however, the extra 37 cents an hour was a big deal. "Where is the extra productivity going to come from?" asked Mr. Isah. He was mapping contingency plans to cut some jobs when the higher wage was imposed. And in Falls Church, Virginia, the controlling shareholder in 13 franchised Popeyes' restaurants didn't like the prospect either. David Rosenstein calculated that if the minimum wage went up, operating profits would decline 25 percent or more in some of his stores. To Rosenstein, the minimum wage increase was a bad idea.

Popeyes' managers faced this economic issue: Could the workers generate enough extra output to offset an automatic raise for much of the staff? Mr. Rosenstein found the whole issue difficult. In the end, a rise in the minimum wage could leave him with the following three basic choices:

- **Accept lower profits.** He ruled that out. The company was trying to pay off debt from restaurants acquired earlier and needed funds to remodel and expand.

- **Cut staff.** But, in his view, he already operated with a bare-bones staff in most of his restaurants. Cutting more could degrade service and drive away customers.

- **Raise prices.** This is what Mr. Rosenstein planned to do, even if his managers preferred labor cutbacks. But he acknowledged that raising prices could be risky, especially in some Philadelphia stores. "If we raise our prices too high, transactions would decrease," he said. Yet if higher wage costs forced his fast-food competitors to raise prices, too, Mr. Rosenstein's profits could escape much damage.

By 1997, despite two hikes in the minimum wage, Mr. Rosenstein's restaurants were prospering. Operating profits were up 11 percent from 1996 on a 10-percent rise in sales. Mr. Rosenstein raised prices, opened a new store, and doubled the size of his spacious office. "The economy is good. Business is good," says Mr. Rosenstein. What about the minimum wage increase? "I think we saw it in more dire terms than it worked out," he said.

Indeed, the minimum wage increase turned into one of the nonevents of 1997, thanks mostly to the economy's continuing strength. Low-wage Americans got a raise. But amid the prosperity at that time, hardly anybody noticed.[2]

---

[2] Excerpted from "A Popeyes Chain Frets Over How to Handle a Minimum-Pay Rise," *The Wall Street Journal*, April 24, 1996, p. A-1; and "Minimum Wage Is Up, But a Fast-Food Chain Notices Little Impact," *The Wall Street Journal*, October 27, 1997, p. A-1. Reprinted with permission.

economics
IN ACTION

Big Air Carriers Fly Belly Up, Resulting in Overhaul of Labor Contracts

In 1978, the Airline Deregulation Act was passed in response to pressure from consumer groups and free-market advocates. It promoted additional competition in the airline industry by providing free entry and competitive pricing. Following the passage of the act, a number of discount carriers such as Southwest Airlines entered the industry. Compared to major airlines, discount carriers squeeze more seats on board, sell more than half of their tickets on the Internet, have shorter flight turnaround times, don't serve meals, and thus can reduce fares by 20 to 40 percent, or more. Table 7.3 shows airlines' flight operation costs in 2002.

By 2002, major U.S. airlines such as United, U.S. Airways, and Delta were pummeled by the worst downturn in aviation history. This was the result of a poor economy, terrorism jitters, the Internet—which makes it much easier to find cheap tickets, and the specter of war. Making matters worse, the big airlines were being swamped by expanding competition from low-cost carriers such as Southwest Airlines, JetBlue Airways, and AirTran Airways.

Consider the case of United Airlines. In 1994, it began a bold experiment in employee ownership. In exchange for deep pay cuts, the pilots, mechanics, ground workers, and management received 55 percent of United's shares. The dream was that those employees would moderate their future pay demands for the good of the company they mostly owned. But the concept was flawed from takeoff. The unions, especially the pilots' union, soon realized that they could extract more wealth from United by driving up salaries than by earning stock dividends. This led to United's having the highest labor costs in the industry, with pilots earning up to $300,000 a year for 80 hours of work per month. Moreover, United's unit operating costs (one seat flown one mile) were 170 percent of Southwest's. Simply put, big U.S. airlines have traditionally had higher labor costs than many of the smaller, low-fare operators. But the high cost structure of the big airlines could not hold up in a weak market, and they scrambled for ways to slash billions in costs without destroying the route networks and service to business customers who pay premium prices.

By 2005, the nation's giant carriers were able to wring massive pay concessions from pilots and flight attendants and thus cut operating costs. This allowed them to mount effective challenges against the discount carriers. For example, Delta Air Lines slashed its most expensive fares by as much as 50 percent, instantly erasing the price advantage of its discount competitors. Moreover, discount carriers began to find themselves tormented at the low end by a new crop of even cheaper upstarts. Indeed, fortunes can swiftly change in the modern U.S. economy.

Table 7.3 Same Route, Same Plane, Yet United's Flight Costs More to Operate than JetBlue's		
	JetBlue 112 (discount airline)	United 235 (major airline)
Route	Washington, D.C. to Oakland	Washington, D.C. to Oakland
Plane model	Airbus A320	Airbus A320
Crew size	2 pilots, 4 flight attendants	2 pilots, 4 flight attendants
Seats per plane	162	138
Flights per day	2 roundtrip	2 roundtrip
One-way ticket price	$129 to $307.50	$129 to $1951
Cost to operate plane one way	$14,546	$23,690

Source: From "The Companies, Unisys Corp's R2A Transportation Management Consultants." See also "Costly Race in the Sky," *The Wall Street Journal*, September 9, 2002, p. B1.

Analysis   Raising the minimum wage during a period of general prosperity and tight labor markets helps mask the adverse effects of a higher minimum wage. If the demand curve for labor remains constant, a higher wage results in a decrease in the quantity of labor demanded. If the demand curve for labor shifts rightward, however, labor employment increases.

During the 1990s, many employers' demand curves for labor increased with the rise in business sales and profits. The increased demand for labor offset some of the employment reduction effects of a higher minimum wage. Moreover, many firms had to pay wages above the minimum wage in order to attract scarce labor in a fully employed economy, thus lessening the adverse effects of a higher minimum wage. Simply put, a period of general prosperity and strong demand for labor is most conducive for increasing the minimum wage.

ARE WORKERS BETTER OFF WITH LABOR UNIONS?

Throughout this chapter, we have assumed that individual workers actively compete in the sale of their services. In some markets, workers form **unions** so as to sell their services collectively. Unions exist because workers realize that acting together provides them with more bargaining power than would acting individually and being at the mercy of their employers. You are probably familiar with unions such as the United Auto Workers, the United Steel Workers, and the Teamsters.

In 1970, about 25 percent of the U.S. labor force belonged to unions. Only about 13 percent are members today, as seen in Table 7.4. With the declining role of manufacturing jobs in the workforce, union success hinges on penetrating the service sector. That's very difficult to organize. Service workers tend to be in many different locations, and many jobs in the service sector are transient.

The chief aim of a labor union is to improve the wages, hours, working conditions, and job security of its members. Unions act on behalf of workers to bargain with employers on matters relating to employment, a process known as **collective bargaining**. This process allows one negotiator to act as the workers' agent rather than having each worker negotiate his own labor contract.

Table 7.4	Percent of Wage and Salary Workers Belonging to Unions, 2003	

Salary Worker	Wage and Salary Workers
Agriculture	1.6%
Mining	9.1
Construction	16.0
Manufacturing	13.5
Transportation and utilities	26.2
Financial activities	2.1
Professional and business people	2.3
Education and health services	8.3
Government	37.2
All workers	12.9

Source: From U.S. Department of Commerce, Bureau of the Census, *2004–2005 Statistical Abstract of the United States* (Washington, D.C.: U.S. Government Printing Office), Tables 638 and 639.

Most disagreements between labor and management involve wages, hours, or other conditions of employment. If labor and management cannot settle their differences, they may receive outside help called mediation. If the two parties still cannot agree, they may submit to a process known as arbitration. A person called an arbitrator listens to both sides of a dispute and makes a decision that is binding on both sides. Strikes may also occur when workers feel that stopping work is the best way to pressure their employer into granting their demands. Before a union calls a strike, it must put the question to a vote by its members. Generally, a strike cannot be called unless a majority of the voting members support it.

Increasing Union Wages

Indeed, economic researchers estimate that, on average, union workers earn about 15 percent more than nonunion workers. To increase the wages of their members, unions use several strategies: (1) increase the demand for labor, (2) restrict the supply of labor, and (3) impose an above-equilibrium wage floor on the market. Let us consider each of these strategies.

Increase the Demand for Labor   From the perspective of a labor union, the preferable technique for increasing wages is to increase the demand for labor. As seen in Figure 7.3(a), an increase in the demand for labor causes an increase in both the wage rate and the quantity of labor demanded. Employment and incomes thus rise for union members, a most favorable outcome.

Unions adopt several strategies to increase the demand for the labor of their members.

- **Increase the demand for the good they help produce and thus the derived demand for their own labor services.** One way to increase product demand is to advertise and persuade the public to purchase only those goods manufactured by union workers. Another approach might be to pressure Congress to impose restrictive tariffs or quotas on, say, steel imported from South Korea, so that U.S. consumers will demand more steel produced by U.S. workers. Moreover, teachers' unions often lobby for increased government spending on public education, and aerospace workers push for increased spending on national defense.

- **Support increases in the minimum wage laws to increase the cost of unskilled labor.** A rise in the wage rate of unskilled labor results in a decrease in the quantity demanded of unskilled labor and an increase in the demand for more skilled, union workers.

- **Increase the productivity of union members.** By establishing grievance procedures, unions may reduce turnover and promote stability in the workforce—conditions that enhance workers' productivity, thus increasing the demand for union workers.

Decrease the Supply of Labor   Another way of promoting wage increases is to restrict the supply of labor. As seen in Figure 7.3(b), a decreased supply of labor results in a higher wage rate, although it reduces the quantity of labor demanded. Those workers who keep their jobs receive higher incomes, but fewer workers will be employed.

Craft unions, such as bricklayers and electricians, have often adopted restrictive membership policies such as high initiation fees, long apprenticeship programs, and limitations on the union's membership. *Professional associations,* such as the American Bar Association or the American Medical Association, are similar to craft unions in terms of their restrictive impact on the supply of labor. Entry into a profession is limited through certification requirements and control over professional schools.

Impose an Above-Equilibrium Wage Floor   Rather than organizing the workers of a particular occupation, an *industrial union* represents all workers in a specific industry,

| Figure 7.3 | Union Methods to Increase Wages |

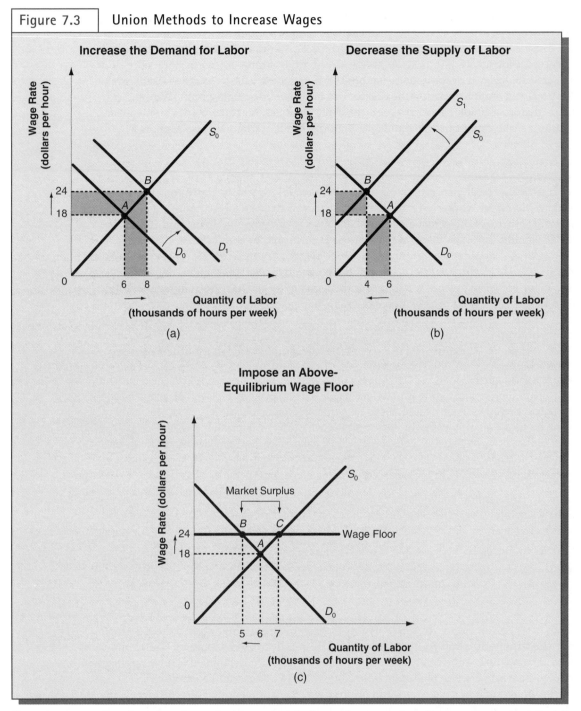

From the perspective of a union, the preferable method for increasing wages is to increase the demand for labor. An increase in the demand for labor causes an increase in both the wage rate and the quantity of labor demanded. Another way to increase wages is to restrict the supply of labor. Those workers who keep their jobs receive higher incomes, but fewer workers will be employed. A successful industrial union will impose an above-equilibrium wage floor on the market for its members. Although the wage hike increases the incomes of those members having jobs, some members may be priced out of the market.

regardless of their skills or craft. Examples of industrial unions are the United Auto Workers (UAW) and the United Postal Workers. Similarly, public employee unions represent the workers in a given profession, such as teaching. The National Education Association, for example, is a powerful union representing teachers throughout the United States.

The purpose of an industrial union or public employee union is to bring all workers in an industry into a union, resulting in a strong bargaining position. Industrial unions must also organize workers at most of the firms in an industry. Otherwise, nonunion firms might gain a cost advantage by paying lower wages to their employees and thus undersell the union-organized firms. In practice, industrial unions may fail to organize an entire industry. In automobiles, for example, the UAW has organized Ford, General Motors, DaimlerChrysler (the U.S. Big Three), and also several foreign firms with assembly plants in the United States. However, workers at other foreign assembly plants have chosen not to affiliate with the UAW.

Figure 7.3(c) shows the impact of the UAW on the market for autoworkers. The competitive wage and employment are $18 per hour and 6,000 hours of labor demanded per week, as seen at point A in the figure. Suppose the UAW organizes the U.S. Big Three auto companies and bargains for a wage rate of $24 per hour. The bargained wage rate has the effect of an above-equilibrium wage floor imposed on the labor market. Although the wage hike results in increased incomes for those workers who remain employed, the quantity of labor demanded falls from 6,000 hours to 5,000 hours per week. The push for higher wages thus prices some workers out of a job. Generally, unions adhere to the policy of "last hired, first fired." Workers with the least amount of seniority will be the first ones to lose their jobs. Also, the higher wage increases the quantity supplied of labor to 7,000 hours per week, resulting in a surplus of labor equal to 2,000 per week.

What Gives a Union Strength?

Not all unions are able to increase the wages of their members. What factors allow unions to obtain large wage increases while suffering only modest reductions in employment?

If nonunion workers are good substitutes for union workers, an employer may turn to these substitutes and reduce its demand for union labor as it becomes more costly. Higher union wages will therefore price union workers out of the market, resulting in a sharp decline in their employment. For this reason, unions have lobbied against liberal immigration policies and the importation of goods produced by foreign workers. Unions have also attempted to obtain contracts with a **union shop** provision. This would require that all employees join the recognized union within a specified length of time (usually 30 days) after their employment with the firm begins. Each state has the option to accept or reject union shops.

Besides substituting nonunion for union labor, firms may substitute other factors of production for union workers as their wages are pushed upward. For example, General Motors may automate various production operations, replacing people with robots. When machines are good substitutes for labor, the bargaining power of labor declines.

The strength of a union also depends on the number of substitutes available for the product that its members help produce. For example, during the 1980s, the U.S. trucking industry was deregulated in an attempt to foster additional competition and a more efficient use of resources. Unionized firms in the trucking industry therefore began to compete with nonunion firms having lower labor costs. The labor-cost advantage allowed many nonunion trucking firms to slash prices to win a larger share of the market. The result was a decline in the market share of unionized trucking firms and a loss of more than 100,000 jobs for Teamsters' members. The sharp decline in employment eventually led to the union's agreeing to a 30-percent cutback in wages and fringe benefits in an attempt to save jobs.

The experience of the U.S. auto industry illustrates how nonunion workers can threaten the employment levels and wage structures of union workers. For decades, the UAW has represented workers at the U.S. Big Three—Ford, GM, and DaimlerChrysler—whose factories are located in the northern states where the UAW is strong. Being an effective bargainer, for decades the UAW pushed its members' wages above the levels of the average American manufacturing worker. By the 1980s, however, nonunion Japanese companies established automobile assembly plants in the southern part of the United States, where unions are not strong. Lower wages combined with more efficient workers have given the Japanese a labor-cost advantage in the production of automobiles. This has allowed them to capture an increasing share of the U.S. auto market, causing fewer sales for the U.S. Big Three and job losses for UAW members. As the number of nonunion workers in the auto industry grows, the UAW's power to set wages and working conditions weakens.

CHECK POINT

1. Explain why an increase in the minimum wage may be beneficial to some workers but harmful to others.

2. How might an increase in labor productivity offset the adverse effects of a higher minimum wage?

3. Identify the methods that labor unions use to increase the wages of their members. Which method is most preferable to a union?

4. What factors underlie the ability of a union to increase the wages of its members?

OUTSOURCING OF JOBS: THREAT OR OPPORTUNITY FOR U.S. WORKERS?

In discussions about jobs, recent attention has focused on international trade and terms such as "outsourcing." The concern is that a free-trade environment allows good jobs to drain from the U.S. economy and wind up in China, India, and other countries where workers command much lower salaries. In the extreme, some would like to see restraints on trade to protect those jobs and halt the globalization trend. Let us consider the nature and effects of outsourcing.

In its broadest sense, **outsourcing** is simply contracting out functions that had been done in-house, a longtime practice. When a car manufacturer in Michigan buys brake pads from an intermediate supplier in Ohio rather than produce them in-house, that's outsourcing. When a company replaces its cleaning and cafeteria workers with an outside contractor who performs the same services more cheaply, that's outsourcing. Clearly, outsourcing can result in job losses if the outside supplier is more efficient and uses fewer workers.

Instead of turning to domestic providers, firms may decide to purchase a good or service from overseas providers because of lower costs. Outsourcing, too, has a long history in U.S. manufacturing; for example, firms in Mexico supply seat covers and wiper blades to Detroit automakers. What appears to be new about outsourcing is its effect on workers in the service sector who never expected to see foreign competition for their jobs—data managers, computer programmers, medical transcribers, and the like.[3]

What Prevents U.S. Jobs from Being Outsourced Abroad?

In today's global economy, job security is of vital concern for many workers. Indeed, many Americans fear that U.S. companies will relocate production in Mexico, Malaysia, Singapore, or other developing countries where wages are much lower than in the United States. Thus, U.S. workers will be displaced by, say, Mexican workers.

Although this concern is real, can we be sure that jobs will flow to the country with low wages? Suppose you are the manager of El Paso Radio Company, a firm located in the United States. Wouldn't you want to locate your assembly plant in Mexico, where labor is cheaper? The answer is that firms are interested in more than just the wages that they must pay to workers. They are also interested in the marginal product of labor in different nations.

For example, suppose a typical radio assembler in the United States earns $9 per hour and a radio assembler in Mexico earns $4 per hour. Also assume that the marginal product of the U.S. assembler is 18 radios per hour and that the marginal product of the Mexican assembler is four radios per hour. Therefore, we have higher productivity in the United States but lower wages in Mexico. Where will the El Paso Radio Company locate its assembly plant?

The answer is in the United States because more radios are produced per every dollar paid to labor than in Mexico. To illustrate, with a marginal product of 18 radios and a wage rate of $9 per hour, the U.S. worker assembles two radios per every dollar that he is paid (18/9 = 2). In contrast, with a marginal product of four radios and a wage rate of $4 per hour, the Mexican worker assembles one radio for every dollar that she is paid (4/4 = 1). Because the firm receives more output for every dollar spent on assemblers in the United States than in Mexico, the firm will find it less costly, and hence more profitable, to hire U.S. workers rather than Mexican workers. The conclusion is that even if U.S. wages are higher than Mexican wages, if U.S. labor is more productive than Mexican labor, U.S. labor can still be competitive.

Effects of Outsourcing

Proponents of outsourcing emphasize how it can help increase productivity growth in the United States. For example, technologies such as computers and the Internet have made the U.S. service sector a candidate for outsourcing on a global scale. High-tech companies such as IBM can easily outsource software programming to India, and American medical centers are relying on Indian doctors to process data.

Proponents of outsourcing maintain that it can create a win-win situation for the global economy. Obviously, outsourcing benefits a recipient country, say, India. Some of its people work for, say, a subsidiary of Delta Air Lines of the United States and make telephone reservations for Delta's travelers. Moreover, incomes increase for Indian vendors supplying goods and services to the subsidiary, and the Indian government receives additional tax revenue. The United States also benefits from outsourcing in several ways:

- **Reduced costs and increased competitiveness for Delta,** which hires low-wage workers in India to make airline reservations. Also, whereas in the United States many of the outsourced jobs

---

[3] Robert Parry, "Globalization: Threat or Opportunity for the U.S. Economy?" *Economic Letter*, Federal Reserve Bank of San Francisco, May 21, 2004, pp. 1–3.

are viewed as relatively undesirable or of low prestige, in India they are often considered attractive. Thus, Indian workers may be highly motivated to outproduce their counterparts in the United States. Higher productivity of Indian workers leads to falling unit costs for Delta.

- **New exports.** As business expands, Delta's Indian subsidiary may purchase additional goods from the United States, such as computers and telecommunications equipment. These purchases result in increased earnings for U.S. companies such as Dell and AT&T and additional jobs for American workers.

Simply put, proponents of outsourcing contend that if U.S. companies cannot locate work abroad they will become less competitive in the global economy as their competitors reduce costs by outsourcing. This will weaken the U.S. economy and threaten more American jobs. They also note that job losses tend to be temporary and that the creation of new industries and new products in the United States will result in more lucrative jobs for Americans. As long as the U.S. workforce retains its high level of skills and remains flexible as companies improve their productivity, high-value jobs will not disappear in the United States.

Critics, however, note that if outsourcing were a limited practice driven by domestic scarcity of a few specific skills, the United States might benefit from outsourcing. However, outsourcing is a problem because many U.S. jobs in manufacturing and service industries can be transferred abroad. The higher the wages paid to Americans, the greater the incentive to outsource work to China or India, where enormous excess supplies of labor guarantee relatively low wages for years to come. Faith that new industries and occupations will rise to replace lost ones is troublesome, because the same incentive will encourage replacement industries to be outsourced as well.

Of course, the benefits of outsourcing to the United States do not eliminate the burden on Americans who lose their jobs or find lower-wage ones due to foreign outsourcing. This is why American labor unions often lobby Congress to prevent outsourcing, and several U.S. states have considered legislation to severely restrict their governments from contracting with companies that move jobs to low-wage developing countries. Indeed, getting the American public to accept outsourcing will likely require giving workers a safety net in the form of income assistance and training to qualify for the jobs being created in the United States. Education is the bedrock of the U.S. edge in productivity and technology and the key to producing workers with the flexibility to learn new skills as markets evolve.

DO LIBERAL IMMIGRATION LAWS HARM AMERICAN WORKERS?

Besides jobs outsourcing, immigration has been a controversial issue for American workers. Historically, the United States has been a favorite target for international migration. Because of the vast inflow of migrants, the United States has been described as the "melting pot" of the world. Migrants have been motivated by better economic opportunities and by noneconomic factors such as politics, war, and religion.

Although migration of foreign workers into the United States can enhance the nation's productivity, many Americans prefer restrictions on immigration. They argue that open immigration tends to reduce their employment opportunities and wages. For example, responding to higher wages, low-skilled Mexican workers may migrate to the United States. This leads to a reduction in the Mexican labor supply and an increase in the U.S. labor supply. Wage rates fall in the United States while rising in Mexico, which has an equalizing effect. In particular, U.S. labor unions tend to support restrictions on immigration because competition from foreign workers reduces their members' jobs and wages.

international
ECONOMICS IN ACTION

Nike and Reebok Respond to Sweatshop Critics: But Wages Remain at Poverty Level

Prodded by controversy over exploitation in foreign factories that make much of America's clothes and shoes, Nike, Reebok, and other U.S. corporations have pushed for sweatshop reforms. A sweatshop is characterized by the systematic violation of workers' rights that have been certified in law. These rights include the right to organize and bargain collectively and the prohibition of child labor. Also, employers must pay wages that allow workers to feed, clothe, and shelter themselves and their families. Table 7.5 provides examples of abusive labor conditions in Chinese factories producing for U.S. companies.

For example, a 1997 audit by the firm of Ernst & Young, commissioned by Nike, was leaked to reporters. The audit found that employees in a large Vietnam factory were exposed to cancer-causing toluene and had a high incidence of respiratory problems. The audit also found that employees were required to work as long as 65-hour weeks, sometimes in unsafe conditions. Also, in 1999 Reebok released a study of two large Indonesian factories.

The study uncovered substandard working conditions, sex bias, and health problems among workers.

Pressured by sweatshop critics, in 1999 Nike and Reebok initiated improvements in the wages and working conditions of its foreign workers. Nike and Reebok increased wages and benefits in their Indonesian footwear factories, which employed more than 100,000 workers, making base compensation 43 percent higher than the minimum wage. Also, Nike agreed to end health and safety problems at its 37 factories in Vietnam and other nations. However, critics argued that these reforms left much to be desired.

In the late 1990s, dozens of U.S. universities jumped on the anti-sweatshop bandwagon, reacting to a growing student protest movement, and took steps to bar labor abuses in the manufacture of clothes that bear college logos. This led to a new White House-sponsored alliance, the Fair Labor Association (FLA), which consisted of 56 universities and corporations such as Nike, Reebok, Liz Claiborne, and Phillips-Van Hausen. The alliance is intended to set up an elaborate, worldwide factory-monitoring system to attempt to eliminate sweatshop abuses. Under its provisions, participating companies can use the FLA logo on their labels and in their advertising, which helps to portray the firms as ethical corporate citizens.

Sources: Robert Collier, "U.S. Firms Reducing Sweatshop Abuses: But Wages Still at Poverty Level," *San Francisco Chronicle*, April 17, 1999; and "Reebok Finds Ills at Indonesian Factories," *The Wall Street Journal*, October 18, 1999.

Table 7.5 Sweatshop Conditions in Chinese Factories Producing for U.S. Companies	
U.S. Company/Product	**Labor Problems in Chinese Factory**
Huffy/bicycles	15-hour shifts, 7 days a week. No overtime pay.
Wal-Mart/handbags	Guards beat workers for being late.
Kathie Lee/handbags	Excessive charges for food and lodging mean some workers earn less than 1 cent per hour.
Stride Rite/footwear	16-year-old girls apply toxic glues with bare hands and toothbrushes.
Keds/sneakers	Workers locked in factories behind 15-foot walls.
New Balance/shoes	Lax safety standards, no overtime pay as required by Chinese law.

Source: From National Labor Committee, *Made in China*, May 2000, New York.

No substantial restrictions were placed on immigration into the United States until the passage of the Quota Law of 1921. This law set quotas on the number of immigrants based upon the country of origin. The Quota Law primarily restricted immigration from eastern and southern Europe. The Immigration and Nationality Act Amendments of 1965 eliminated the country-specific quota system and instead established a limit on the maximum number of immigrants allowed into the United States. Under this act, preferential treatment is given to those who immigrate for the purpose of family reunification. Those possessing exceptional skills are also given priority. No limit, however, is placed upon the number of political refugees allowed to immigrate into the United States. Not all immigrants, of course, enter the country through legal channels. Individuals often enter on student or tourist visas and begin working in violation of their visa status. Other individuals enter the country illegally without a valid U.S. visa. The Immigration Reform and Control Act of 1986 addresses the issue of illegal immigration by imposing substantial fines on employers that hire illegal immigrants.

The Illegal Immigration Reform and Immigrant Responsibility Act of 1996 provided several new restrictions to immigration. Host families could only accept immigrants if the host family receives an income that is at least 125 percent of the poverty level. This act also required that the Immigration and Naturalization Service maintain stricter records of entry and exit by nonresident aliens.

However, even the less-skilled immigrants contribute to our economy and our lives by working in jobs most Americans do not want, such as cleaning offices, cooking in restaurants, and ringing up purchases in the grocery store. They also buy homes, clothes, and groceries. The wonderful cultural diversity brought to the United States by immigrants has become secondary to their willingness to work hard and become part of today's America.

Moreover, the infusion of foreigners into the United States does not include only people with minimal skills and education. The United States also reaps a bonanza of highly educated newcomers who enhance the competitiveness of its firms. America's high-tech industries, from biotechnology to semiconductors, depend on immigrant scientists, engineers, and entrepreneurs to remain competitive. In Silicon Valley, the jewel of U.S. high-tech centers, much of the workforce is foreign-born. With their bilingual skills, family ties, and knowledge of how things get done overseas, immigrants also contribute to the export of made-in-USA goods and services. Moreover, they help revitalize America by establishing new businesses and generating jobs, profits, and taxes to pay for social services. These benefits must be weighed against the economic disruptions caused by the infusion of less-educated and less capable people into the nation.

This chapter examined the market for labor and the determination of wages. The next chapter will consider the role of government in the market economy.

CHECK   POINT

1. What methods do labor unions use to improve the economic well-being of their members?

2. What factors underlie the strength of a labor union?

3. Does outsourcing benefit American workers? Why are some workers fearful of outsourcing?

4. Although the United States has been described as the "melting pot" of the world, many Americans are fearful of liberal immigration policies. Why?

Chapter Summary

1. As in other markets, the forces of demand and supply underlie labor markets. The point of intersection of the labor demand and labor supply curves determines the equilibrium wage and level of employment. The demand for labor is derived from the demand for the product that labor helps produce.

2. In a competitive market, a firm will maximize profits by hiring workers up to the point where the value of the marginal product of labor equals the wage rate. Moreover, the value of the marginal product curve of labor constitutes a firm's demand curve for labor.

3. Even if U.S. wages are higher than Mexican wages, if U.S. labor is more productive than Mexican labor, U.S. labor can still be competitive.

4. An increase in the market supply curve of labor causes the equilibrium wage to decrease and the quantity of labor demanded to increase. As the market demand curve for labor increases, both the equilibrium wage and the quantity of labor supplied increase.

5. To help the working poor, in 1938 Congress established a federal minimum wage, the smallest amount of money per hour that an employer may legally pay a worker. The minimum wage benefits workers who can find work at a wage level that exceeds the market equilibrium wage. However, it harms workers who seek employment at the higher wage, but cannot find jobs. To the extent that a higher wage causes labor to become more productive, the demand for labor increases, thus offsetting the unemployment effects caused by the minimum wage.

6. Labor unions use several strategies to increase the wages of their members: increase the demand for labor, restrict the supply of labor, and impose an above-equilibrium wage floor on the market. The ability of a union to increase the wages of its members is threatened by nonunion labor, by other factors of production (machinery) that may be substituted for labor, by the availability of good substitutes for the product that members help produce, and when labor's share of production costs is high.

7. In the discussion about jobs, much attention has focused on outsourcing. The concern is that a free-trade environment allows good jobs to drain from the U.S. economy and wind up in China, India, and other countries where workers command much lower salaries.

8. Although migration of foreign workers into the United States can enhance the nation's productivity, many Americans prefer restrictions on immigration. They argue that open immigration tends to reduce their employment opportunities and wages.

Key Terms and Concepts

derived demand (157)

minimum wage (159)

shock effect (161)

unions (164)

collective bargaining (164)

mediation (165)

arbitration (165)

strikes (165)

union shop (167)

outsourcing (168)

marginal product of labor (178)

value of the marginal product of a worker (178)

demand curve for labor (178)

Self-Test: Multiple-Choice Questions

1. The ability of the United Steel Workers' union to increase the wages of its members is enhanced by a(n)

   a. decrease in the demand for steel by U.S. auto companies.
   b. decrease in tariffs on steel imported by the United States.
   c. elastic demand for the labor of U.S. steelworkers.
   d. inelastic demand for the labor of U.S. steelworkers.

2. By increasing the wages of their members, unions tend to

   a. cause employers to seek substitutes for union labor.
   b. increase the wages of nonunion workers.
   c. increase the productivity of all workers.
   d. shift the demand for labor to the right.

3. If the demand for labor in the United States is inelastic, the migration of workers from Mexico to the United States will

   a. decrease the total amount of wage earnings received by U.S. workers.
   b. increase the total amount of wage earnings received by U.S. workers.
   c. leave unchanged the total amount of wage earnings received by U.S. workers.
   d. cause the demand curve for U.S. workers to shift to the right.

4. In a competitive labor market, the demand curve for labor is the curve showing the

   a. value of the marginal product of labor.
   b. marginal physical product of labor.
   c. value of the total product of labor.
   d. total physical product of labor.

5. A rightward shift in the supply curve of labor would be caused by

   a. a reduction in the value of the marginal product of labor.
   b. lower available wages in other industries.
   c. quotas placed on the number of immigrants who can enter the country.
   d. a decrease in the total physical product of labor.

6. As an industrial union, the United Auto Workers would be most successful in improving the wages, jobs, and working conditions of its members if it could

   a. shift the supply curve of autoworkers to the right.
   b. unionize all the firms in the auto industry.
   c. initiate policies that cause the demand for autos to decrease.
   d. collect membership dues from all of its workers.

7. If the federal government imposes a minimum wage that is above the market equilibrium wage, we can expect a

   a. decrease in the wage costs of employers.
   b. decrease in the number of workers that participate in the labor market.
   c. shortage of labor.
   d. surplus of labor.

8. With a competitive market for aerospace workers, a reduction in the price of jetliners will result in

   a. lower employment and a lower wage.
   b. lower employment and a higher wage.

c. higher employment and a higher wage.

d. higher employment and a lower wage.

9. Assume that a union shop applies to the electricians' market. If the electricians' union reduced the supply of its members, all of the following would occur *except*

a. wages of union electricians would increase.

b. employment of union electricians would decrease.

c. the cost of construction projects would increase.

d. the demand for nonunion electricians would decrease.

10. Proponents of higher minimum wage laws maintain that they will

a. inspire workers to become more productive, thus increasing the demand for labor.

b. increase the mobility of workers among occupations subject to the minimum wage.

c. result in shortages of workers, which impose extra upward pressure on wages.

d. make less-skilled workers less desirable for part-time employment.

Answers to Multiple-Choice Questions

1. d   2. a   3. a   4. a   5. b   6. b   7. d   8. a   9. d   10. a

Study Questions and Problems

1. Draw a figure showing how the intersection of the market demand curve for labor and the market supply curve of labor determines the equilibrium wage rate and employment level. How are the equilibrium wage rate and employment level affected by:

a. An increase (decrease) in the market supply curve of labor?

b. An increase (decrease) in the market demand curve for labor?

2. Explain how U.S. labor can be competitive with Mexican labor, even if U.S. wage rates are higher than Mexican wage rates.

3. Table 7.6 pertains to the hiring decision of Youngquist Strawberry Co., which hires workers and supplies strawberries in competitive markets.

Table 7.6	Labor Data for Youngquist Strawberry Co.				
	Labor Input (workers per week)	Total Product (boxes of berries per week)	Marginal Product of Labor (boxes of berries per week)	Product Price	Value of the Marginal Product of Labor
	0	0			
	1	100		$8	$
	2	190		8	
	3	270		8	
	4	340		8	
	5	400		8	
	6	450		8	

| Table 7.7 | Market for Less-Skilled Labor |

Wage Rate (dollars per hour)	Quantity of Labor Supplied (thousands of hours)	Quantity of Labor Demanded (thousands of hours)
$1.00	10	70
2.00	20	60
3.00	30	50
4.00	40	40
5.00	50	30
6.00	60	20
7.00	70	10

    a. Complete the remaining columns of the table.

    b. In a figure, draw the firm's demand curve for labor.

    c. If the wage rate is $560 per week, how many workers will the firm hire? What if the wage rate is $400 per week?

4. Table 7.7 shows the market for less-skilled workers.

    a. In a figure, plot the market demand curve for labor and the market supply curve of labor. Find the equilibrium wage rate and the level of employment.

    b. Suppose the government enacts a minimum wage of $6 per hour. How much labor will be supplied and demanded at this wage rate? Will the level of employment be higher or lower than the employment level that exists in the absence of a minimum wage? By how much?

    c. Suppose the minimum wage inspires workers to become more productive. Draw a new demand curve for labor that results in the same level of employment as that which occurs in the absence of a minimum wage.

5. In a figure, draw the market supply curve of labor and the market demand curve of labor. What techniques do labor unions use to raise their members' wages? Assuming these techniques succeed in raising wages, what effect do they have on the quantity of labor demanded? Show the effects graphically. Which technique is most favorable for a union?

6. What factors underlie the extent to which the UAW will, or will not, increase its demand for higher wages?

7. In a figure, draw the market supply curve and the market demand curve of autoworkers. Assume that the UAW organizes U.S. auto firms. In your figure, show the effects of the following situations:

    a. The UAW imposes an above-equilibrium wage floor on the market for autoworkers.

    b. Japanese firms export additional autos to the United States, which causes a decrease in the demand for domestic autos and also a decrease in demand for members of the UAW. Concerning jobs and wages, what options does the UAW have to minimize the adverse effects of the decreased demand for its members? What is the limitation of each option?

8. Explain verbally, and show graphically, why domestic workers may be apprehensive about liberal immigration policies.

EXPLORING FURTHER 7.1: A FIRM'S HIRING DECISION

Concerning a firm's demand curve for labor, consider how the Mt. Pleasant Apple Company, a typical apple producer, chooses the quantity of workers demanded. Suppose that the firm sells apples in a competitive market and so cannot affect the price it gets for the sale of apples. Also assume that the firm hires workers in a competitive market and therefore has no influence on the wages it pays to apple pickers. Finally, assume the firm is a profit maximizer, caring only about the difference between the total revenue obtained from the sale of apples minus the total cost of producing them.

When hiring apple pickers, the Mt. Pleasant Apple Company must know how much workers contribute to its output. Figure 7.4 gives a numerical example. Referring to Figure 7.4(a), the first column of the table shows the number of apple pickers. The second column shows the amount of apples harvested each week by the workers. The firm's production data suggest that one worker can harvest 90 boxes of apples per week, two workers can harvest 170 boxes, and so on. The third column in the table gives the

Figure 7.4 | A Firm's Demand Schedule for Labor

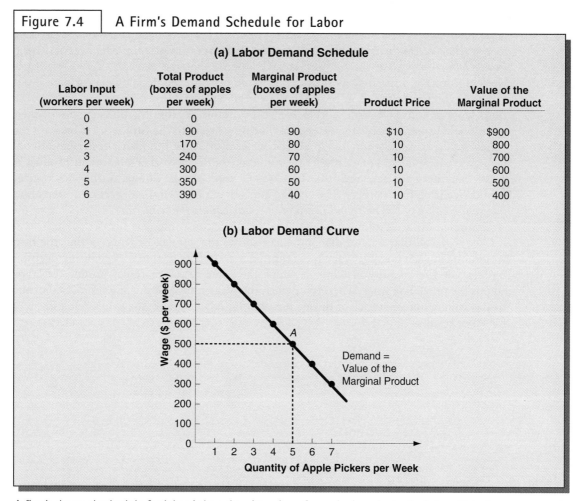

(a) Labor Demand Schedule

Labor Input (workers per week)	Total Product (boxes of apples per week)	Marginal Product (boxes of apples per week)	Product Price	Value of the Marginal Product
0	0			
1	90	90	$10	$900
2	170	80	10	800
3	240	70	10	700
4	300	60	10	600
5	350	50	10	500
6	390	40	10	400

(b) Labor Demand Curve

A firm's demand schedule for labor is based on its value of marginal product schedule, which decreases as extra workers are employed.

marginal product of labor, the *additional* output from hiring each worker. When the firm increases the number of workers from, say, 1 to 2, the amount of apples harvested rises from 90 boxes to 170 boxes. The marginal product of the second worker is thus 80 boxes (170 − 90 = 80). Similarly, the marginal product of the third worker is 70 boxes of apples (240 − 170 = 70), and so on. Consistent with the law of diminishing returns, as discussed in Chapter 4, the marginal product decreases as the firm hires more workers. In this example, diminishing marginal productivity sets in with the first worker hired.

Besides needing to know about the amount of apples harvested by an additional worker, the Mt. Pleasant Apple Company needs to know about the worker's contribution to revenue. The **value of the marginal product of a worker** is the increase in revenue to a firm resulting from hiring an additional worker. In other words, the value of the marginal product is the dollar value of a worker's contribution to production.

We *calculate the value of the marginal product by multiplying the marginal product of a worker times the price of apples.* Referring to Figure 7.4(a), suppose the price of apples is $10 per box. The value of the first worker's product equals $900, found by multiplying his marginal product times the price of apples (90 × $10 = $900). Similarly, the value of the second worker's productivity is $800 (80 × $10 = $800). The value of the marginal product schedule of labor is shown graphically in Figure 7.4(b).

How many workers should the Mt. Pleasant Apple Company hire? *The firm will hire additional labor as long as doing so adds more to revenue than to cost—that is, as long as the value of the marginal product is greater than the wage rate. The firm will stop hiring labor only when the two are equal.* Suppose that the market wage is $500 per week. In this case, the first worker is profitable because the dollar value of his output ($900) is greater than the cost of hiring the worker ($500). Hiring the second worker, the third worker, and the fourth worker is also profitable because the dollar value of their additional outputs exceeds the wage rate. Hiring stops with the fifth worker because the value of her marginal product equals the wage rate. After the fifth worker, additional hiring is unprofitable. For example, the value of the sixth worker's marginal product is $400, but the wage rate is $500. The Mt. Pleasant Apple Company thus maximizes profits by hiring five workers. The conclusion is that *a firm hires workers up to the point where the value of the marginal product of labor equals the wage rate.*

The value of the marginal product of labor curve constitutes the firm's **demand curve for labor.** Recall that a labor demand curve shows the number of workers that the firm would hire at each possible wage rate that might exist. The firm makes its hiring decision by selecting the quantity of labor at which the value of the marginal product of labor equals the prevailing wage. Therefore, when the wage rates and the amounts of labor the firm is willing to hire at each of those rates are plotted in a graph, the firm's demand curve for labor results.

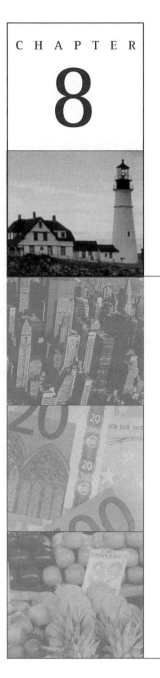

CHAPTER

8

Government and Markets

Chapter objectives

After reading this chapter, you should be able to:

1. Explain why markets sometimes fail to allocate resources efficiently.

2. Describe the nature and operation of antitrust policy.

3. Assess the advantages and disadvantages of economic regulation versus social regulation.

4. Explain why public utilities, such as electricity and cable television, have traditionally been provided an exclusive franchise to serve a local community.

5. Identify the factors that contribute to the failure of the market system.

economics IN CONTEXT

For decades, individuals have made tape recordings of live musical performances or musical performances sold on records, tapes, or CDs. These recordings were often copied and traded with friends and other collectors. However, taped copies were of a lower quality than the original, which reduced the possibility for widespread tape copying of music files as an alternative to purchasing music from recording companies. By the 1990s, technological improvements made it possible to record music files off the Internet. As a result, musical recordings could be compressed into a compact file that could be played back at near-CD quality.

In 1999, Shawn Fanning, a freshman at Northwestern University, introduced the Napster program and service. Through the Internet, Napster allowed users to swap music files with other users of this service. Napster provided the software that located and downloaded music files and maintained a central directory containing the addresses of computers that contained such files.

However, a significant share of the music traded through Napster involved illegal transfers of copyrighted music. In 2000, the Recording Industry of America initiated a lawsuit against Napster, claiming that Napster was involved in copyright violation. According to the music industry, Napster had no rights to its recordings and was therefore preventing the music industry from making money on its recordings. However, Napster argued that its service allowed new musicians to distribute music to a wide audience at virtually no cost. It also argued that the existing system of music distribution provided the recording companies with a monopoly control over the distribution of a given artist's music. This resulted in high prices and profits for these companies, but only limited rewards to most musicians. Napster contended that it was difficult for new artists to break into the market under the existing system.

Agreeing with the music industry, the court ruled against Napster, thus shutting down the free distribution service it provided. In spite of the Napster trial, online distribution of music is a low-cost alternative to the existing system of selling music on CDs and cassette tapes. The recording industry faces the challenge of developing a business model that allows it to take advantage of the low-cost distribution mechanism provided by the Internet while remaining profitable. The advent of Apple Computer's Music Store in 2003, discussed in Chapter 5, may be a viable business model.

In this chapter, we will examine the role of government in the market economy. As we will see, in some cases unregulated markets may not provide the best answers to the fundamental economic questions of society. Whenever that occurs, government intervention is needed to temper the market's operation and make it conform to the interests of society.

MARKET FAILURE

The U.S. economy relies mainly on the market system to determine what goods and services are produced, in what quantities, and at what prices. Americans have generally accepted the market system as the most effective way of allocating resources to meet the needs and wants of households and families. The market system provides firms with strong incentives to produce the goods that consumers want at the lowest possible cost and to find innovative ways of meeting consumer demands. Firms that efficiently produce the goods that consumers desire will prosper; others will be driven out of business, and the resources they employ will be reallocated to more highly valued uses. The interaction between many producers and many consumers results in the production and consumption of an ideal quantity of each good. Markets are also flexible and accommodate change well.

Changes in technology and consumer demands are quickly registered in the market, re-arranging the types, prices, and quantities of goods and services that are offered for sale. The quest for profits encourages firms to develop new products and cheaper ways of producing existing products.

Some markets, however, fail to allocate resources efficiently—a situation called **market failure**. When a monopoly serves a market, for example, it makes output artificially scarce and sets the price higher than would occur in a more competitive market in order to maximize profits. In other markets, some people affected by the production or consumption of a good are not able to influence those choices. For example, a steel mill may ignore the pollution problems it creates, or a toy manufacturer may not provide full information about the risks of using its product—information consumers may need to make the best decision. Such market failures provide a legitimate reason for governments to consider intervening in the private sector through such means as regulation. Sources of market failure include the following:

- Monopoly power

- Spillovers or externalities

- Public goods

- Inadequate information

- Economic inequality

Let us consider the nature of these problems and then see why government intervention is desirable in each situation.

MONOPOLY POWER

Although competition generally results in the most efficient use of a nation's resources, an individual firm would prefer to conduct business in an environment that is more akin to monopoly. If allowed, some competing firms may attempt to create a monopoly environment by colluding with rivals, merging with rivals, or driving rivals out of business.

As we have learned, a monopoly tends to produce much less desirable outcomes than a competitive market. Given the same costs, a monopoly maximizes profit by selling a smaller output and charging a higher price than would a competitive market. Also, substantial barriers to entry may shelter a monopoly from the pressure of competition, which results in the monopoly's costs being greater than their lowest possible level. Lack of competition also suggests that there is no external pressure for advancements in technology in monopoly. Simply put, monopoly results in market failure because the monopoly uses too few resources to produce goods at an artificially higher price.

ANTITRUST POLICY

What can the government do to counteract monopoly power? One approach is to adopt a rigorous antitrust policy. **Antitrust policy** is the attempt to foster a market structure that will lead to increased competition and to curb anticompetitive behavior that harms consumers. Antitrust laws are designed to prevent unfair business practices that restrain trade, such as price-fixing conspiracies, corporate mergers likely to reduce the competitive vigor of particular markets, and predatory acts designed to achieve or maintain monopoly power.

By the late 1800s, large corporations began to dominate many U.S. industries, including oil, railroads, and banking. These firms were run by the so-called *robber barons,* which attempted to drive competitors out of business, monopolize markets, and gouge consumers. They realized their monopoly power by forming *trusts,* the nineteenth century name given to cartels and other business agreements intended to restrain competition. In the oil industry, for example, Standard Oil of New Jersey acquired small, competing firms and eventually accounted for 90 percent of sales in the domestic market. In tobacco, American Tobacco controlled up to 90 percent of the market for tobacco products.

Concern about the growing monopoly power of these firms led to the federal government's intervention into the economy's private sector in order to prevent the acquisition and exercise of monopoly power and to encourage competition in the marketplace. These efforts culminated in the passage of the **Sherman Act of 1890,** the cornerstone of federal antitrust law. This act prohibits contracts and conspiracies in the restraint of trade as well as monopolization and the threat to monopolize an industry. For example, conspiracies such as collusive agreements among competing sellers to fix prices and control markets are outlawed. Firms found in violation of the Sherman Act could be broken up, and parties responsible for illegal conduct could be fined and imprisoned. Moreover, parties harmed by illegal monopoly behavior could sue for three times the amount of monetary injury inflicted upon them.

Although the Sherman Act attempted to provide a solid foundation for government action against business monopolies, its vague language allowed the courts wide latitude in interpreting the meaning of its sections. The **Clayton Act of 1914** was enacted to make explicit the intent of the Sherman Act. The Clayton Act outlaws price discrimination, certain types of mergers, and tying (exclusive) contracts between a supplier and a buyer that substantially lessen competition. It also prohibits interlocking boards of directors among competing companies.

The Justice Department and the Federal Trade Commission enforce federal antitrust laws. The Justice Department, exclusively, is responsible for enforcing the Sherman Act and, with the Federal Trade Commission, is responsible for enforcing the Clayton Act. The majority of antitrust cases initiated by these agencies are settled by an agreement between them and the defendant. This saves the federal government time and money.

Music Industry Pays Millions for Price Fixing

The music industry provides an example of companies violating U.S. antitrust laws. In 2002, the five top distributors of compact discs and three large music retailers agreed to pay $143 million in cash and CDs to settle charges that they cheated consumers by fixing prices of CDs between 1995 and 2000. The companies broke state and federal antitrust laws, costing consumers millions of dollars. The settlement resulted in $67.3 million cash being distributed to the states to compensate consumers who overpaid for CDs. It also required 5.5 million CDs valued at $75.7 million to be distributed to public entities and nonprofit organizations in each state to promote music programs.

Three national music retail chains participated in the deal: Trans World Entertainment, Tower Records, and Musicland Stores. Also participating were several music distributors: Bertelsmann Music Group, EMI Music Distribution, Warner-Elektra-Atlantic Corporation, Sony Music Entertainment, and Universal Music Group. The lawsuit alleged that the companies, upset with low prices charged by some stores, conspired with retailers to set music prices at a minimum level, effectively raising the retail prices consumers paid for CDs. However, this action is a violation of the Sherman Act, which outlaws price-fixing agreements.

Music industry officials noted that the settlement did not include any admission of wrongdoing. However, antitrust authorities stated that the settlement was of major importance, and it addressed years of illegal price fixing. They also noted that the agreement would provide consumers with substantial refunds and result in the distribution of a wide variety of recordings for use in the nation's schools and communities.

ECONOMIC REGULATION AND DEREGULATION

Is our best approach for improving the performance of markets the vigorous enforcement of the antitrust laws? Or should we consider more extreme intervention in the marketplace? If market forces fail to establish prices equal to the cost of production, why not enact direct government regulation and mandate prices to be set that way?

Besides using antitrust laws to regulate business behavior, the federal government can enact **economic regulation** to control the prices, wages, conditions of entry, standards of service, or other important economic characteristics of particular industries. Industries made subject to economic regulation have included airlines, trucking, railroads, banking, communications, and energy.

Industries were originally made subject to economic regulation for many and varied reasons. One example was the objection to the so-called "natural monopoly" enjoyed by an industry with such large economies of scale that meaningful competition was impossible. In other instances, fear of "destructive competition" provided the primary rationale for regulation. Extending the scope of service was yet another aim behind government intervention.

By the late 1970s, however, the tide of opinion was turning against economic regulation. It became obvious that the growth of the economy and technological progress had eroded many former natural monopolies, converted infant industries into mature ones, and created conditions conducive to reliable competitive services. Because the existing economic regulations were applicable to outdated economic conditions, it was time for a change.

Recognizing the problems of economic regulation, in the late 1970s, the federal government initiated steps to dismantle regulations in several industries where the existing regulations had outlived their usefulness—airlines, trucking, railroads, energy, telecommunications, and banking. The purpose of such **deregulation** was to increase price competition and provide incentives for companies to introduce new products and services. Economic research has shown that by making markets work better, deregulation has led to technical and operating innovations that have been accompanied by price reductions for consumers.

PUBLIC UTILITY REGULATION

Economic regulation involves the regulation of public utilities like electricity, gas pipelines, telephones, and cable television. Rather than promoting competition in these industries through the use of antitrust laws, the U.S. government has traditionally allowed public utilities to operate as private monopolies subject to government regulation of price and output policies. Some nations have tried government ownership as an alternative; with few exceptions, these have proven to be less effective than private ownership and regulation.

Usually, the stated reason for resorting to regulation of a monopoly rather than promoting competition through antitrust is that the industry in question is believed to be a *natural monopoly*—an industry in which product demand can be supplied most efficiently by a single firm. In such cases, the judgment may be made that competition is not workable and that the market is best served by a single monopoly firm that can fully exploit the advantage of economies of scale, but that would be prevented by price regulation from exercising monopoly power over customers.

Figure 8.1 | Public Utility Regulation of Natural Monopoly

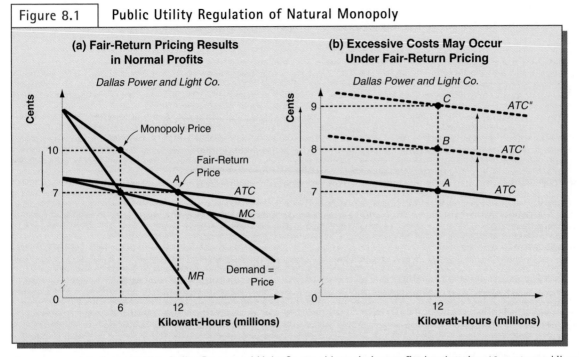

As an unregulated monopolist, Dallas Power and Light Co. would maximize profits by charging 10 cents per kilowatt-hour of electricity. Public utility commissioners would typically require the firm to charge a price equal to 7 cents, the fair-return price. Although this eliminates excess profit, the firm can still earn a normal profit for its stockholders. Critics of fair-return pricing contend that it reduces incentives for public utilities to innovate or to contain costs because the firm realizes essentially the same profits regardless of its efforts.

Figure 8.1 shows the hypothetical cost and revenue curves for Dallas Power and Light Co., assumed to be a natural monopolist in the electricity industry. As an unregulated monopolist, Dallas Power and Light Co. would maximize profits by applying the familiar $MR = MC$ rule. Referring to Figure 8.1(a), the firm's price and output would thus be 10 cents per kilowatt-hour of electricity and 6 million kilowatt-hours, respectively. Because price exceeds average total cost at 6 million kilowatt-hours, the firm realizes an economic profit.

Suppose that the legislature decides to impose public-utility regulation on Dallas Power and Light Co. In addition to overseeing service and entry into and exit from the industry, public-utility regulation determines the price of the monopolist. Legislatures have traditionally allowed a regulated firm to receive a **fair-return price** in which the firm can charge a price only high enough to cover average total cost. In our example, Dallas Power and Light Co. will set its price where its demand curve intersects its average total cost curve; the fair-return price is thus 7 cents per kilowatt-hour. Recall that average total costs include a "normal" or "fair" profit. Although fair-return regulation eliminates the excess profit for Dallas Power and Light Co., it allows the firm to earn a fair profit for its stockholders.

But what type of costs should be included in the average total cost of Dallas Power and Light Co.? When economists construct average total cost curves, like the ones in Figure 8.1(b), and conclude that, for 12 million kilowatt-hours of electricity, it costs 7 cents per unit to provide electricity, they are referring to only the least possible cost. It is possible to produce 12 million kilowatt-hours at 8 or 9 cents—as shown by points B and C in the figure.

Cost curves are drawn as they are because we usually assume that profit-seeking firms will use the most efficient methods available. In situations where public-utility regulators set rates that cover average total cost, however, the incentive to hold costs down may not be very great. What is to prevent the managers from awarding themselves large salaries and forcing the customers to foot the bill? Should the utility be allowed to have prices that cover obviously foolish expenditures such as the purchase of fuel from one supplier at a price twice as high as what could have been obtained elsewhere? In short, fair-return regulation tends to reduce the incentives for public utilities to innovate or to contain costs, because the firm realizes essentially the same profits regardless of its efforts.

PARTIAL DEREGULATION OF ELECTRICITY SHOCKS CALIFORNIANS

California's electricity market illustrates the problems that can arise when attempting to regulate electric utilities.[1] For decades, government officials in California regulated the prices charged by electric utilities. But critics maintained that the utilities were incredibly expensive and provided horrible service to their customers. Because the utilities could easily pass on costs to customers, they lacked incentives to utilize capacity more efficiently or to offer innovative services. California business leaders pushed for deregulation because they were paying 50 percent more for power than their counterparts in other states.

In 1996, California restructured its electricity industry, allowing consumers to obtain electricity from out-of-area (often out-of-state) power suppliers. Local utilities were forced to sell their power-generation plants and purchase power on the wholesale market from other suppliers. By breaking the power-generation monopoly of local utilities, state officials anticipated decreases in electricity costs.

However, California's plan had a major flaw: State officials opted for partial deregulation rather than complete deregulation of electric utilities. Although California opened its generation market to competition, it did not permit the free entry of new power plants into the market. Environmental concerns were a significant factor that checked the development of new electricity-generation facilities. Moreover, state officials tried to assure California voters access to cheap electricity by freezing retail prices for consumers. Yet wholesale prices of electricity were not regulated; they varied according to changing conditions in the national market.

Most aspects of California's electricity problems can be illustrated with supply and demand curves, as seen in Figure 8.2. First, consider the market before deregulation. California's electricity supply comes from lower-cost plants whose electric turbines operate continuously and are powered by water, coal, or nuclear fuel. During periods of surging demand, California's electricity supply comes from higher-cost oil- and natural gas-fired plants and power purchased from plants in other states (which results in added transportation costs). Higher prices support production at more facilities, and, therefore, more electricity is available at higher prices along supply curve S_0. As demand curve D_0 shows, consumers are willing to purchase more electricity at lower prices. Together, supply and demand establish a market-clearing price and quantity at 8 cents per kilowatt-hour and 100 kilowatt-hours, respectively.

When California deregulated its electricity-generation market, policymakers hoped competition between power plant owners would shift the supply curve outward, but they also imposed a price ceiling (at 10 cents) to maintain stable retail prices. However, rising prices of oil and natural gas and the reduced availability of production capacity and power imported from plants in other states curtailed electricity supply in California to S_1.

[1] This section is drawn from "Power Struggle," *Fedgazette*, Federal Reserve Bank of Minneapolis, January 2001, pp. 1–3.

Figure 8.2   California's Electricity Woes

Although government officials in California deregulated their electricity-generation market, they maintained a ceiling on the retail of electricity that was below the wholesale cost of electricity. This contributed to losses for utilities and intensified shortages of electricity in California.

At the same time, strong economic growth boosted electricity demand to D_1. These changes should have established a new market-clearing price and quantity at 30 cents and 140 kilowatt-hours, respectively.

If we stopped here, we would have a classic shortage at the price ceiling. But electric utilities have a duty to serve under the law. Consequently, California's utilities were legally obligated to supply all the electricity consumers wanted to purchase, 190 kilowatt-hours, at the price ceiling. To do so, utilities were forced to pay a much higher price (40 cents) for electricity on the wholesale market. This resulted in losses for California's utilities. In practice, California's utilities did not succeed in obtaining all the electricity customers wanted at the ceiling price. The result was a combination of shortages and utilities paying higher prices for electricity than they could sell it for to their own customers.

PEAK-LOAD PRICING: BUYING POWER BY THE HOUR

Another aspect of public utility pricing involves peak-load pricing. For decades, power economists have recognized that consumers do not have the incentive to conserve electricity at times when they should conserve. To promote conservation of electricity, many utilities have enacted a variable pricing system called **peak-load pricing** or time-of-use pricing. To understand how peak-load pricing works, let us first consider the costs of producing electricity.

Producing electricity entails fixed costs and variable costs. Fixed costs mainly consist of the costs of electric power generators, the costs of the plants that house them, and the costs of transmission lines. These costs do not vary with changes in electricity production. Variable costs include the costs of labor, coal, natural gas, and diesel fuel. As more power is produced, more of these inputs are needed to operate the generators.

For a typical utility, fixed costs are very high relative to total costs in electricity production. Also, power plants generally operate most of the time with a large amount of excess capacity. Therefore, customers who buy power during the peak periods cause electric companies to incur very high costs—the cost of constructing and operating generators that are used only during the peak period and that stay idle at other times.

Moreover, the variable costs of producing electricity change substantially throughout the day. During the night, the demand for electricity is smallest, and the variable costs of producing electricity are lowest because the utility uses very efficient plants that operate 24 hours a day. These plants use coal or nuclear fuel to boil water to turn the electrical turbines, which take a long time to rev up. As demand climbs, say around midafternoon on a summer afternoon, additional plants—more expensive to operate—are called into operation to supply power for people's air conditioners. These "peak-load" plants usually use gas turbines that run on exhaust gases instead of boiling water. Although they can be brought online almost instantly, they use expensive fuels (diesel and natural gas). The variable costs of providing peak service are thus greater than those of providing off-peak service.

Apparently, those who purchase electricity during the middle of the night should pay a lower price per kilowatt-hour than those who purchase electricity during the afternoon. But often, they do not. Most of us pay a constant price per kilowatt-hour, whether we use expensive hours or cheap ones. So we have no reason for conserving power during hours of high demand. Peak-load pricing changes all of this.

With peak-load pricing, prices reflect the difference in the cost of providing electricity during peak hours and off-peak hours. Therefore, consumers are charged more for electricity during peak demand periods when it costs more to provide power. The higher price encourages consumers to switch part of their use to the cheaper off-peak periods. The shift in demand is achieved in several ways. For example, people may purchase timers that operate air conditioners, water heaters, and space heaters only during off-peak periods. Similarly, they may avoid using washing machines, clothes dryers, and dishwashers during the peak period. The effect of such consumption shifts is that a utility can serve its customers with much smaller generating capacity.

The state of Wisconsin provides an example of peak-load pricing for electricity. In 2003, Wisconsin households had the option of purchasing all the electricity they needed during a week at a fixed price of 7.09 cents per kilowatt-hour. They could also choose a peak-load system option. From Monday through Friday, the price of electricity purchased during the off-peak period (8 P.M.–8 A.M.) was 3.2 cents per kilowatt-hour; a price of 13.6 cents per kilowatt-hour was charged for purchases during the peak period (8 A.M.–8 P.M.). The off-peak price was also applied to weekend consumption of electricity. The large differential between the peak and off-peak prices provides considerable motivation for households to shift consumption to the off-peak times of the day.

CHECK POINT

1. How does monopoly power contribute to market failure?

2. How do the Sherman and Clayton acts attempt to combat monopoly power?

3. Why have public utilities traditionally been granted an exclusive franchise to serve a local community? Identify the problems of public-utility regulation.

4. How does peak-load pricing attempt to spread the available power around throughout the day?

SPILLOVER EFFECTS

We have learned that monopoly power can result in market failure. Another source of market failure involves what economists refer to as spillover effects.

A **spillover,** or **externality,** is a cost or benefit imposed on people other than the producers and consumers of a good or service. For example, if a smelter pollutes the air or water, and neither the firm nor its customers pay for the harm that pollution causes, the pollution becomes a **spillover cost** for society. In some cases, however, spillovers can be desirable. For example, the development of laser technology has had beneficial effects far beyond whatever gains its developers captured, improving products in industries as diverse as medicine and telecommunications. Laser technology is an example of a **spillover benefit.**

How does the market system fail when the production of a good or service entails spillover effects? When the production of some good results in spillover costs, *too much* of it is produced and resources are *overallocated* to it. Conversely, *underproduction* and *underallocation* of resources arise from spillover *benefits.* Let us show these conclusions graphically.

Spillover Costs

How can spillover costs cause failure in a market for chemicals? Referring to Figure 8.3, the market demand curve for chemicals is shown by D_0, and S_0 denotes the market supply curve. Notice that the market supply curve includes the firms' private marginal costs of producing chemicals, such as labor and material costs. In equilibrium, 900 pounds of chemicals are sold at a price of $80.

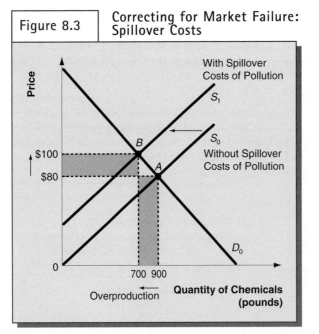

Figure 8.3	Correcting for Market Failure: Spillover Costs

With pollution, market failure occurs because the firm fails to take into account the spillover costs. As a result, too much output will be produced at too low a price. To correct this market failure, government could require the firm to install pollution-abatement equipment or pay a tax on pollution.

Now suppose that the production of chemicals results in toxic wastes. If firms can dump these wastes into the waterways and thus pass their pollution costs on to the public, their private marginal costs of producing chemicals are lower. Referring to Figure 8.3, market supply curve S_0 includes only the firms' private marginal costs of producing chemicals. Therefore, it lies too far to the right of such a supply curve that would include all costs (both private costs and spillover costs of pollution). This means that the equilibrium output, 900 pounds, exceeds the optimal output of 700 pounds. Simply put, the market supply curve does not reflect all of the costs resulting from the production of chemicals. Therefore, the market produces too many chemicals and thus overallocates resources to their production.

How can government force the market to decrease its pollution? The approach that has dominated public policy in the United States to date involves **command-and-control regulations** that impose restrictions on the amount of the polluting activity that can occur, as well as stipulating how the goal will be fulfilled. Clean air and water laws restrict the amount of pollutants that firms can place into the air, rivers, and lakes. Moreover, toxic-waste legislation specifies special procedures and dumpsites for the disposal of contaminated solvents and soils.

By mandating that chemical firms be responsible for pollution abatement, such laws increase the firms' private marginal cost of production. In Figure 8.3, the market supply curve thus shifts from S_0 to S_1. The price of chemicals rises from $80 to $100, and the equilibrium output falls from 900 pounds to 700 pounds. In this manner, the overallocation of resources to chemical production is corrected.

Another way to reduce spillover costs is to establish **incentive-based regulations,** which set an environmental objective but are flexible because producers can find ways to achieve the objective. Companies that are unable to fulfill the objective pay penalties in the form of taxes, but they are not rewarded for exceeding the objective. For example, the government may levy an excise tax on the production of chemicals in order to encourage firms to reduce pollution. Facing this tax, firms must decide whether to pay it or expend additional funds to develop new methods to reduce pollution. In either case, the tax will increase the private marginal cost of producing chemicals, again shifting the market supply curve from S_0 to S_1 in Figure 8.3. Any tax revenue resulting from the regulations could be used to compensate those harmed by the pollution.

Economists generally favor incentive-based regulations over command-and-control regulations. A main problem of command-and-control regulations is that regulators lack the detailed knowledge of individual production facilities and processes and of alternative production and abatement methods that would be necessary to implement an efficient regulatory program by command and control. It can also be costly to monitor and enforce the regulations. However, incentive-based regulation makes it profitable for firms to develop the most efficient techniques to reduce pollution.

Trading Emission Certificates Clears Skies of Acid Rain

The trading of emission certificates provides an example of incentive-based regulations. As part of a science project, sixth grade students at Glens Falls Middle School in New York removed 330 tons of sulfur dioxide from the air. Conducting bake sales, raffles, and auctions over a 3-year period, they raised $25,000 to purchase 330 pollution certificates in the U.S. Environmental Protection Agency's acid-rain-emissions trading program. Each certificate allows the owner to emit one ton of sulfur dioxide into the air. Public utilities trade the certificates—some purchase them to comply with air-quality regulations while others sell them for a profit. However, the sixth graders decided to keep these certificates so that the air will be that much cleaner.

Developed in 1995, trading pollution certificates is a market-oriented solution to the problem of acid rain. The basic idea of the sulfur dioxide program is simple. The EPA set a cap on the total amount of the pollutant it would allow in the air, starting in 1995 and declining thereafter. It then issued a limited number of certificates that gave the holder, say, an electric utility, the right to emit some part of the total amount of pollution. Such certificates are sold by the EPA at auction and can be resold by owners. The EPA auction and the private resale market thus establish a price on the use of the environment. The more pollution a user engages in, the more certificates it would have to buy, thus raising its costs of production. The polluter has the incentive to put cleaner technologies in place.

By giving polluters a financial incentive to reduce acid rain in the least expensive possible way, emissions trading decreases the costs of environmental protection. Firms with high pollution-control costs can buy permits from firms with low pollution-control costs. Therefore, firms find it profitable to reduce their emissions and sell their surplus permits. As a result, greater responsibility for reducing pollution is allocated to those firms that can do so at the least expense. Moreover, conservation groups also have a direct method of affecting the environment. They can buy and hold some of the pollution certificates, which directly reduces the amount of pollution allowed and increases the cost of pollution.

Emissions trading encourages a firm to hunt for the most cost-efficient ways to reduce pollution. For Milwaukee-based Wisconsin Electric Power Co., the 1995 EPA limit meant it had to reduce sulfur dioxide emissions from its five power plants by about 30,000 tons. The company calculated that it could remove 20,000 tons relatively cheaply by switching to low sulfur coal. Removing the remaining 10,000 tons would be difficult. The firm would have to purchase two $130 million machines called "scrubbers." Because other electric utility companies had decreased their emissions well below the EPA's limit, the market was flooded with cheap pollution certificates. Wisconsin Electric Power Co. then bought 10,000 of them, resulting in a cost saving of over $100 million.

Spillover Benefits

Recall that in the case of spillover costs, the market supply curve understates the total costs associated with the production of a good. Now we will see that the market demand curve understates the total benefits associated with the purchase and consumption of a good, which entails spillover benefits.

Assume that a new drug, called "Cold Free," is developed; this drug cures the common cold. In Figure 8.4(a), the market demand curve, D_0, shows the price that private individuals would be willing to pay for Cold Free to receive the benefits of having fewer colds. The market supply curve, S_0, shows the quantity of Cold Free offered for sale at different prices. At equilibrium point A, 50 packages of Cold Free are sold at a price of $6.

Because of spillover benefits, however, this equilibrium point fails to achieve an optimum allocation of resources. Why? When buyers take Cold Free, other people who do not purchase the drug also benefit because the virus is less likely to spread. For society in general, taking Cold Free results in a healthier population, yielding widespread output and income benefits. The market demand curve, D_1, consists of the private benefits from Cold Free plus the extra, or spillover, benefits accruing to society in general. With market demand curve D_1, the optimal equilibrium at point B is established, shown by the intersection of D_1 and S_0. We conclude that with spillover benefits, the actual equilibrium output, 50 packages, is less than the optimal output, 70 packages. The market fails by not producing enough Cold Free and thus underallocating resources to its production.

How can government prevent market failure in this instance? One approach would be for government to require all citizens to purchase and use Cold Free each year. In Figure 8.4(b), such a policy would result in the market demand curve increasing from D_0 to D_1. This

| Figure 8.4 | Correcting for Market Failure: Spillover Benefits |

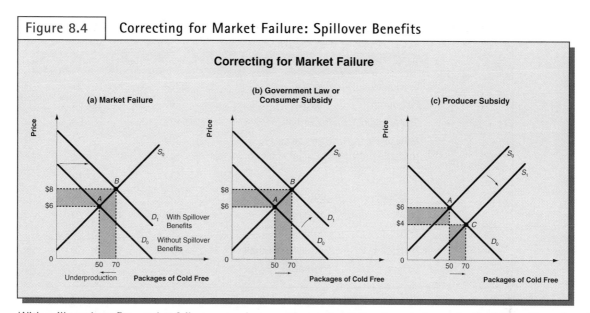

With spillover benefits, market failure occurs because the market demand curve does not reflect the spillover benefits of a good. As a result, the good is underproduced and underconsumed. Government could correct this market failure by requiring consumers to purchase additional units of the product, granting subsidies to consumers to finance purchases of the product, or subsidizing producers so that they could supply additional units of the product at a lower price.

explains why all children must receive diphtheria, tetanus, pertussis, polio, and other vaccines before entering primary school. Another solution would be for government to provide subsidies to individuals to help them pay for the cost of Cold Free, again shifting the market demand curve rightward.

Alternatively, government might grant subsidies to the producers of Cold Free. Such a subsidy would lower the producers' cost of production so that the market supply curve would increase from S_0 to S_1 in Figure 8.4(c). Producers could thus offer more Cold Free to consumers at a lower price.

In practice, subsidies are granted for a number of activities that yield spillover benefits. Education receives large subsidies. Students in public schools, from kindergarten through high school, receive an education that is virtually free. Moreover, the cost of a student's education at a state college or university is only partially paid for out of student tuition and fees, with the remainder coming from government tax dollars. The government also provides subsidies for public television, mass transit, and medical programs, as well as for the construction of stadiums for professional sports. Are these subsidies justified?

SHOULD GOVERNMENT SUBSIDIZE PROFESSIONAL SPORTS?

Are large governmental subsidies of new sports stadiums a good investment for cities? Many professional sports teams have insisted that the local community grant subsidies to them if they are to operate in the community. For example, government funds are often used to finance a substantial portion of the construction or renovation of a sports stadium. Since all of the major sports leagues (baseball, football, basketball, and hockey) tightly control both the creation of new franchises and the relocation of teams, cities' demand for teams far

Table 8.1	Publicly Financed Major League Stadiums and Arenas		
City	**Sport**	**Cost (millions)**	**Public Funds**
Cincinnati	Baseball	$334	91%
Pittsburgh	Baseball	262	85
San Antonio	Basketball	175	84
Milwaukee	Baseball	394	77
Denver	Football	400	75
Seattle	Baseball	517	72
Pittsburgh	Football	252	70
Seattle	Football	420	70
Houston	Football	367	69
Dallas	Hockey/basketball	330	38
Detroit	Football	325	35

Source: From Street and Smith's *Sports Business Journal*, March 27, 2000, May 8, 2000, and July 17, 2000.

exceeds the supply. Hence, the price cities must pay to acquire teams has gone up. Table 8.1 provides examples of publicly financed major league stadiums and arenas.

Often, subsidies are justified by claims that attracting or retaining sports teams more than pays for itself in increased local tax revenue by creating new jobs and more spending. Also, local officials often view a downtown stadium project as an important part of the revitalization of the central city's urban core. Advocates of this approach point to Coors Field in Denver and Camden Yards in Baltimore as models of how stadium-based development can work.

However, many economists who study pro sports have concluded that not only are teams marginal contributors to local economies, but that local governments, in their zeal to keep and attract teams, have also sustained one of the largest corporate welfare systems in the country. Such concerns led the Federal Reserve Bank of Minneapolis to recommend national legislation that would stop cities from competing for teams. Consider the views of the Federal Reserve Bank on this matter:

If Congress is concerned about sports fans, it should prohibit the city and state funding that supports team moves. Team owners, as well as the leagues, would be forced to rely upon the economics of fan support rather than public subsidies. While states spend millions of dollars to retain and attract businesses, state and local governments struggle to provide such public goods as schools, libraries, roads, and public health services that are critical to the success of any community.

Many state and local governments have forgotten that their business is public, not private, goods and the funding of professional sports and all other private businesses should be left to the marketplace. When franchises are enticed to relocate, there appears to be no net loss to the overall economy; however, on closer examination, we see that this is not just a zero-sum game. Fewer public goods will be produced in the overall economy because, in the aggregate, states will have less revenue. In addition to this loss of public goods, the overall economy becomes less efficient because output will be lost as businesses are enticed to move from their best locations. Simply put, nothing is added to the area's economy; instead, leisure spending is merely shifted around. Although owners of the sports franchises and players benefit—the latter often by 8-digit annual incomes—taxpayers often receive little but increases in the price of tickets, food, and drink.

Researchers at the Brookings Institution have found that the promised stadium-driven booms generally turn out to be disappointments. At best, they have a tiny, and sometimes even a negative, impact on local employment. Whatever good may be achieved is more than canceled by the cost of taxes levied to subsidize them. Looking at personal income trends in 37 cities over 26 years, Brookings found that sports stadiums actually reduce per-capita income in their hometowns.

Why? Subsidies for sports stadiums mean that taxes must rise or that local governments must reduce other spending. That money could have been used to dredge a harbor, fund education, or provide more police, all of which would make the economy more productive and produce more local spending than a stadium. Also, subsidized stadiums use taxpayer money to generate more wealth for owners and players, who do not tend to spend a large portion of their income in the local area. Meanwhile, the new faculty siphons money away from other local establishments. When more people fill the seats in an expanded stadium, fewer dollars are spent on other entertainment, such as bowling, golf, or theater.[2]

However, proponents of subsidies contend that the critics miss a basic issue: Pro sports teams add to residents' quality of life in cities that host teams. People may obtain benefits from having a local sports team even if they never go to a game. They root for local athletes, look forward to reading about their success or failure in the newspaper, and share in the citywide joy when the home team wins a championship. If people benefit from having a pro sports franchise in their community, they are presumably willing to pay for it—if not directly through the purchase of tickets, then indirectly through higher taxes. Thus, residents should think of a pro sports team in the way they think of a new art museum or new symphony hall, which receive public subsidies.

Simply put, subsidy proponents maintain that professional sports yield spillover benefits similar to quality of life benefits such as clean air and scenic views. If the value of these spillover benefits is large enough, they alone might justify the subsidies that local taxpayers grant to teams. However, measuring these spillover benefits is difficult and subject to criticism.[3]

SOCIAL REGULATION

We have learned that government implements economic regulation by setting standards for prices, wages, conditions of entry, and standards of service in particular industries. Since World War II, the government has assumed an ever-increasing role in regulating the quality of life for society. **Social regulation** is intended to correct a variety of undesirable side effects in a market economy that relate to health, safety, and the environment—effects that markets, left to themselves, often ignore. Markets do not respond well to these problems, primarily because only a very small fraction of any benefits from lessening these problems accrues to those who produce the side effects. Incentives to take

---

[2] Melvin Burstein and Arthur Rolnick, "Congress Should End the Economic War for Sports and Other Businesses," *The Region*, Federal Reserve Bank of Minneapolis, June 1996; Roger Noll and Andrew Zimbalist, editors in *Sports, Jobs, and Taxes: The Economic Impact of Sports Teams and Stadiums* (Washington, D.C.: The Brookings Institution, 1997); Raymond Keating, *Sports Pork: The Costly Relationship Between Major League Sports and Government* (Washington, D.C.: Cato Institute, 1999); Dennis Coates and Brad Humphreys, "The Stadium Gambit and Local Economic Development," *Regulation*, Volume 23, No. 2, 2000; and Rodney Fort, *Sports Economics* (Upper Saddle River, NJ: Prentice Hall, 2003).

[3] Gerald Carlino and Edward Coulson, "Should Cities Be Ready for Some Football? Assessing the Social Benefits of Hosting an NFL Team," *Business Review*, Federal Reserve Bank of Philadelphia, Quarter 2, 2004, pp. 7–17.

action or collect information leading to health, safety, and environmental improvements are thus lacking in the private business sector.

Whereas economic regulation governs the conditions of doing business in a particular industry, social regulation addresses the conditions under which goods are produced in a variety of industries. Social regulation applies to a particular issue (environmental quality) and affects the behavior of firms in many industries (automobiles, steel, chemicals, and the like). Consider the following examples of social regulation:

- The Environmental Protection Agency regulates the amount of pollutants that firms can discharge into the air, lakes, and rivers.

- The Consumer Product Safety Commission removes dangerous products from the marketplace. It can also establish standards for product safety, such as controls that automatically shut off the engine of a lawnmower when the operator lets go of the handle.

- The National Highway Transportation Safety Administration requires that automobiles be equipped with seat belts and brake lights.

- The Food and Drug Administration approves the sale of both prescription and nonprescription drugs.

- The Occupational Safety and Health Administration establishes standards that are intended to decrease workers' exposure to injury and to health risks, such as those associated with asbestos.

As with other types of government regulation, not everyone agrees on the merits of social regulation. Some people claim that compliance with social regulations results in higher operating costs for firms striving to meet them. These higher costs are similar to a tax. Suppose that the imposition of health and safety regulations increases a firm's costs by $10 per unit. The firm's supply curve therefore shifts upward by that amount, which results in higher prices and a decrease in output. Like other taxing situations, the consumer absorbs part of the regulatory tax in the form of a higher price, while a firm's revenues are reduced by the remainder of the tax.

Proponents of social regulation, however, contend that although the costs are high, the benefits are even higher. They may claim, for example, that government regulations on asbestos lead to 2,000 fewer people dying from cancer each year; that highway fatalities would be 30 percent higher in the absence of auto safety features required by regulation; and that mandated child proof lids result in 85 percent fewer child deaths caused by accidental swallowing of poisonous substances. Although social regulation results in higher consumer prices, is this too much of a burden when compared to an improved quality of life for society?

Although social regulation based on a careful balancing of costs and benefits can sometimes improve market performance, policymakers often ignore the fact that the government is an imperfect regulator. Critics of social regulation, for example, claim that regulators often lack accurate information about an industry and cannot always predict the effects of specific regulations. Although the decision to regulate may be well intentioned, the regulations themselves can have adverse and unintended consequences.

Corporate Fuel Economy Standards

The U.S. government's fuel economy standards on automobile manufacturers illustrate some of the problems of social regulations. Originally enacted in 1975, **corporate average fuel economy standards (CAFÉ)** represent the foundation of U.S. energy conservation policy. Applying to all passenger vehicles sold in the United States, the standards are based on the average fuel efficiency of all vehicles sold by all manufacturers. Since 1990, the CAFÉ requirement for passenger cars has been 27.5 miles per gallon. Manufacturers whose average fuel economy falls below this standard are subject to fines.

During the 1980s, CAFÉ requirements were used not only to promote fuel conservation but also to protect jobs of U.S. autoworkers. The easiest way for U.S. car manufacturers to improve the average fuel efficiency of their fleets would have been to import smaller, more fuel-efficient vehicles from their subsidiaries in Asia and Europe. However, this would have decreased employment in an already depressed industry. The U.S. government thus enacted *separate but identical* standards for domestic and imported passenger cars. Therefore, General Motors, Ford, and DaimlerChrysler, which manufactured vehicles in the United States and also sold imported cars, would be required to fulfill CAFÉ targets for *both* categories of vehicles. U.S. firms thus could not fulfill CAFÉ standards by averaging the fuel economy of their imports with their less fuel-efficient, domestically produced vehicles. By calculating domestic and imported fleets separately, the U.S. government attempted to force domestic firms not only to manufacture more efficient vehicles but also to produce them in the United States! In short, social regulations sometimes place effective import barriers on foreign commodities, whether they are intended to do so or not, thus aggravating foreign competitors.

PUBLIC GOODS

So far, we have analyzed market failure in terms of monopoly power and spillover effects. Another source of market failure is public goods. Let us consider the nature of private goods and public goods and see why the latter contribute to market failure.

Private goods, which are produced through the market system, are *divisible* in that they come in units small enough to be purchased by individual consumers. For example, we can go to McDonald's and buy one (or several) Big Macs and a small, medium, or large-sized Coke. Also, private goods are subject to the *exclusion principle,* the notion that only those who have the ability to pay can purchase the good, while those who do not possess the ability to pay are excluded from consumption. Moreover, the *principle of rival consumption* applies to private goods. When I eat a Big Mac, you cannot eat the same one. So you and I are rivals for that hamburger. In general, the market system works well in producing private goods in accordance with the needs of consumers.

An entire class of goods is not considered private goods and thus is not provided by the market system. These are called **public goods** and include things such as national defense, highways, lighthouses, and air-traffic control. These goods are *indivisible* because they cannot be produced and sold very easily in small units. For example, you cannot go down to the local store and purchase $10 worth of national defense. Moreover, the exclusion principle does not pertain to public goods. For example, all households are protected by national defense even if they don't have the money to pay for it. Finally, more people can use public goods at no extra cost. Once money has been spent to construct a lighthouse, the benefit you receive does not lessen the amount of protection received by anyone else.

The reason the market system fails to supply public goods efficiently is that the exclusion principle does not apply. Consider the snow removal system of Buffalo, New York. Such a system is justified if the benefits of improved transportation exceed the costs of buying and operating snowplows, dump trucks, and the like. However, the benefit received by each individual motorist would not justify the cost of such a large and indivisible product. Once the snowplows clean the streets, there is no practical method to exclude certain motorists from their benefits. As a result, why should any motorist voluntarily pay for benefits received from clean streets? Clean streets are available for everyone, and a motorist cannot be excluded from driving on them if he decides not to pay.

Economists call this the **free-rider problem:** Because it is impossible to exclude you from consumption of a public good whether or not you pay for the good, you can let others pay for it, and you can still consume it. Of course, if everyone behaves in this manner, no money will be spent on public goods, and entrepreneurs will not have the incentive to supply them to the market. We conclude that the market system fails by *underproducing* public goods!

Because of the free-rider problem, government is looked upon to provide public goods through the use of tax financing. Of course, there is no guarantee that public goods, such as national defense and pollution control, will be provided in optimal amounts.

INADEQUATE INFORMATION

Another source of market failure is inadequate information, a less visible type of market failure than monopoly power, externalities, and public goods. This inefficiency occurs when either sellers or buyers have incomplete or inaccurate information about price, quality, or another aspect of the good or service. Without adequate information, markets may give false signals, incentives may get distorted, and sometimes markets may simply not exist. In such cases, government may decide to step in and correct the market failure.

Lack of information often arises in the sale of used cars. Sellers of used cars know the flaws of their cars, while buyers often do not. Because owners of the worst cars are more likely to sell them than are the owners of the best cars, car buyers may be fearful of purchasing a "lemon." Therefore, many people refuse to purchase cars in the used-car market.

Let us examine market failure by considering how inadequate information about sellers and their goods can disrupt the operation of the gasoline market. Suppose there was no government inspection of gas pumps, no system of weights and measures established by law, and no laws against false advertising. Each gas station could announce that its gas has a minimum octane rating of 87 when in actuality it is only 80. Moreover, the gas station could calibrate its pumps to show that they are pumping, say, 10 gallons of gas, when in fact they pump only nine gallons. In this situation, the cost to the motorist of obtaining reliable information would be very high. Each motorist would have to purchase samples of gas from various stations and have them analyzed for levels of octane. Motorists would also have to pump gas into, say, 5-gallon containers to make sure that a station's pump was calibrated correctly. Because of the high costs of obtaining information about the seller, many motorists might prefer to opt out of this chaotic market. More realistically, government might step in and correct the failure of the market. It could pass legislation against false advertising, hire inspectors to check the accuracy of pumps, and establish a system of weights and measures.

Inadequate information about sellers disrupts the efficient operation of a market but so can inadequate information about buyers. In the labor market, an employer has several economic incentives to provide a safe workplace. A safe workplace fosters higher worker productivity by reducing job accidents, thus decreasing the costs of training new workers. It also entails lower insurance premiums for a firm that, by law, must provide insurance against job injuries. These factors would reduce a firm's costs and thus increase its profit. Conversely, providing safe equipment and protective gear results in additional costs, which reduces the firm's profit. When deciding how much safety to provide, a firm will consider the extra benefits and extra costs associated with a safe workplace.

In a competitive market, if workers have complete information about the workplace safety of firms, they will be reluctant to work for those firms with unsafe workplaces. The supply of labor to those firms thus decreases, forcing the firms to increase their wages to attract additional labor. The increased wages reduce the firm's profits and give it an extra incentive to provide a safe workplace.

Instead, suppose that workers are unaware of the safety at various workplaces. Because of inadequate knowledge, the employer will not have to pay higher wages to attract additional workers. The incentive of the employer to eliminate safety hazards diminishes, and society does not receive the desirable amount of workplace safety. Indeed, market failure can impose hardships on workers.

How can government intervene to correct the problem of inadequate information in the labor market? It can require that firms give information to workers about known workplace dangers and can mandate standards of workplace safety that are enforced by inspection and fines. Government can also give information to workers about the workplace safety records of various firms.

ECONOMIC INEQUALITY

As we have learned, monopoly power, spillover effects, public goods, and inadequate information all cause market failure. Where these phenomena occur, the market system fails to produce the optimal mix of output for society. Besides being concerned about what goods to produce, we also care about for whom output is to be produced. Does the market system result in a distribution of output that is fair to all members of society?

In a market economy, output is disproportionately distributed to people with the most income. Although this may be efficient, it is not necessarily equitable. Persons who are disabled or elderly, for example, may not be able to earn as much income. However, they are still considered "worthy" of receiving goods and services.

In some situations, society may desire to modify the market system's answer concerning how goods should be distributed. Rather than relying exclusively on the individual's ability to pay for these goods, society provides income transfers. Transfer payments are payments from the government to households and firms for which no goods or services are currently rendered. Transfer payments include payments such as unemployment compensation, food stamps, Aid to Families with Dependent Children, Medicare, and business subsidies. They are intended to supplement the income of those for whom the market system itself provides too little. Recipients of transfer payments can therefore obtain a greater share of the nation's output.

To finance the costs of its transfer payment programs, the government enacts graduated taxes on households and businesses and channels these funds to the needy. Through this system of taxation and transfer payments, income is redistributed from the wealthier to the less wealthy.

This chapter discussed the role of government in the market economy. The next chapter will broaden our understanding of government by considering the mixed economy of the United States.

CHECK POINT

1. Explain how the market system fails to allocate resources efficiently when the production of some good entails spillover costs or spillover benefits. What can government do to correct for market failure in these situations?

2. What is the purpose of social regulation? Identify some government agencies involved in social regulation. Why are people sometimes critical of social regulators?

3. How does the market system fail to allocate resources efficiently in the case of public goods? How about when society experiences economic inequality?

4. How does inadequate information cause market failure?

Chapter Summary

1. In some cases, unregulated markets may not provide the best answers to the fundamental economic questions of society. Whenever that occurs, government intervention is needed to temper the market's operation and make it conform to the interests of society.

2. Some markets fail to allocate resources efficiently, a situation called market failure. The main sources of market failure include monopoly power, spillovers or externalities, public goods, inadequate information, and economic inequality.

3. Antitrust policy is the attempt to curb anticompetitive behavior and foster a market environment that will lead to increased competition. The Sherman Act of 1890 and the Clayton Act of 1914 are the foundations of federal antitrust policy.

4. Besides using antitrust laws to regulate business behavior, the federal government sometimes enacts economic regulation to control the prices, wages, conditions of entry, and standards of service of an industry. Industries made subject to economic regulation have included airlines, trucking, railroads, banking, communications, and energy. By the late 1970s, however, it was generally agreed that many economic regulations were no longer suited to prevailing economic conditions. As a result, the federal government initiated steps to dismantle many economic regulations, a process known as deregulation.

5. Public utilities have traditionally been subject to economic regulation on the grounds that they are natural monopolies. In return for being granted an exclusive franchise to serve a local market, the utility is subject to price regulation according to the fair-return principle. Although fair-return pricing allows a utility to realize a price that covers average total cost, it does not provide the incentive for a utility to minimize its costs.

6. A spillover is a cost or benefit imposed on people other than the producers and consumers of a good or service. When the production of some good results in spillover costs, too much of it is produced, and there is an overallocation of resources to its use. Conversely, underproduction and underallocation of resources arise from spillover benefits.

7. Social regulation attempts to correct a variety of undesirable side effects in a market economy that relate to health, safety, and the environment—effects that markets, left to themselves, often ignore. Among the federal government agencies involved in social regulation are the Environmental Protection Agency, the Consumer Product Safety Commission, the Food and Drug Administration, and the Occupational Safety and Health Administration.

8. Public goods, such as national defense, are indivisible and are not subject to the exclusion principle. As a result, the market system fails to supply public goods efficiently.

9. Without adequate information, markets may give false signals, incentives may get distorted, and sometimes markets may simply not exist. In such cases, government may decide to step in to correct the market failure.

10. Because an unregulated market may fail to provide a fair distribution of income and output for society, government modifies the distribution of income through taxation and transfer payment programs.

Key Terms and Concepts

market failure (181)

antitrust policy (181)

Sherman Act of 1890 (182)

Clayton Act of 1914 (182)

economic regulation (183)

deregulation (183)

fair-return price (184)

peak-load pricing (186)

spillover (188)

externality (188)

spillover cost (188)

spillover benefit (188)

command-and-control regulations (189)

incentive-based regulations (189)

social regulation (193)

corporate average fuel economy standards (CAFÉ) (194)

private goods (195)

public goods (195)

free-rider problem (195)

Self-Test: Multiple-Choice Questions

1. The attempt to curb anticompetitive behavior that harms consumers and foster a market structure that will lead to increased competition is called

    a. social regulation.
    b. economic regulation.
    c. antitrust policy.
    d. command-and-control regulation.

2. The Clayton Act does *not* outlaw

    a. profit maximization according to the $MR = MC$ rule.
    b. tying (exclusive) contracts between a seller and a buyer.
    c. mergers that substantially lessen competition.
    d. price discrimination not justified by cost differences.

3. Which of the following has been used to control the prices, conditions of entry, and standards of service for industries such as airlines, trucking, and railroads?

    a. Fair-return regulation
    b. Economic regulation
    c. Social regulation
    d. Command-and-control regulation

4. With spillover benefits, the market fails because the demand curve does not reflect all of the benefits of a good. Therefore, all of the following are true *except*

    a. the good is underproduced and underconsumed.
    b. the good is overproduced and overconsumed.
    c. government could correct the market failure by granting subsidies to consumers to finance the purchase of the good.
    d. government could correct the market failure by subsidizing producers so that they can supply more of a product.

5. Sources of market failure include all of the following *except*

    a. monopoly power.
    b. spillovers or externalities.
    c. inadequate information.
    d. private goods.

6. Concerning electric utilities, peak-load pricing is considered to be a method of

   a. allowing utilities to earn exorbitant rates of return on invested capital.
   b. encouraging electricity consumption during the peak periods of the day.
   c. more evenly distributing the demand for electricity throughout the day.
   d. conserving power by charging lower rates to big industrial buyers.

7. Usually, the stated reason for resorting to regulation of a monopoly, rather than promoting competition through antitrust policy, is that the industry in question is believed to be

   a. perfectly competitive.
   b. monopolistically competitive.
   c. a pure monopoly.
   d. a natural monopoly.

8. Suppose that market failure occurs when Kaiser Aluminum Co. does not take into account spillover costs. Thus, the firm produces too

   a. much aluminum and charges too high a price.
   b. much aluminum and charges too low a price.
   c. little aluminum and charges too high a price.
   d. little aluminum and charges too low a price.

9. Economists generally maintain that the least-cost method of decreasing pollution by, say, the steel industry is to

   a. require that all steel companies reduce their pollution by the same percentage.
   b. require that steel companies with the greatest profits decrease pollution the most.
   c. require that all steel companies with the lowest profits exit the market.
   d. provide incentives for companies with the lowest cost of decreasing pollution to make relatively large reductions.

10. If the government adopts command-and-control regulations to reduce acid rain,

    a. a tax is imposed on factories for each unit of pollutant emitted.
    b. a lump-sum tax is imposed on polluters irrespective of the extent that they pollute.
    c. restrictions are imposed on the amount of pollutants emitted by a factory.
    d. subsidies are granted to firms to help them finance the cost of pollution.

Answers to Multiple-Choice Questions
1. c   2. a   3. b   4. b   5. d   6. c   7. d   8. b   9. d   10. c

Study Questions and Problems

1. Table 8.2 shows hypothetical demand and cost data for New England Power and Light Co., a monopolist that sells electricity in Massachusetts.

   a. Draw a figure that contains the firm's demand curve, marginal revenue curve, marginal cost curve, and average total cost curve.
   b. As an unregulated monopolist, the firm would maximize economic profits by producing _____ units of electricity and selling them at a price of $_____. The firm's total revenue equals $_____, total cost equals $_____, and total profit equals $_____.
   c. Suppose the legislature imposes public-utility regulations on the firm and sets the price of electricity according to the fair-return principle. Such regulations result in the firm

| Table 8.2 | Hypothetical Demand and Cost Data for New England Power and Light Co. |

Quantity of Electricity	Price	Marginal Revenue	Average Total Cost	Marginal Cost
0	$52.50			
1	48.00	$48.00	$72.00	$72.00
2	43.50	39.00	45.00	18.00
3	39.00	30.00	35.00	15.00
4	34.50	21.00	31.50	21.00
5	30.00	12.00	30.00	24.00
6	25.50	3.00	29.25	25.50

producing _____ units of electricity and selling them at a price of $_____. The firm's total revenue equals $_____, total cost equals $_____, and total profit equals $_____.

d. Why might fair-return regulation result in inefficiencies for the firm?

2. Under what conditions do unregulated markets fail to allocate resources efficiently?

3. How do the antitrust laws attempt to combat the problem of monopoly power?

4. By the late 1970s, many economic regulations were being removed in industries such as trucking, airlines, and communications. Comment on the advantages and disadvantages of such deregulation.

5. By the 1990s, deregulation was spreading to the electricity and cable television industries. Explain why this occurred.

6. Why does the government regulate markets that generate spillover costs and spillover benefits?

7. Compare and contrast social regulation versus economic regulation. Give examples of each.

8. Why does the market system provide goods such as Pepsi-Cola, while the government provides goods such as highways and lighthouses?

9. How does the government attempt to correct the failure of markets resulting from economic inequality?

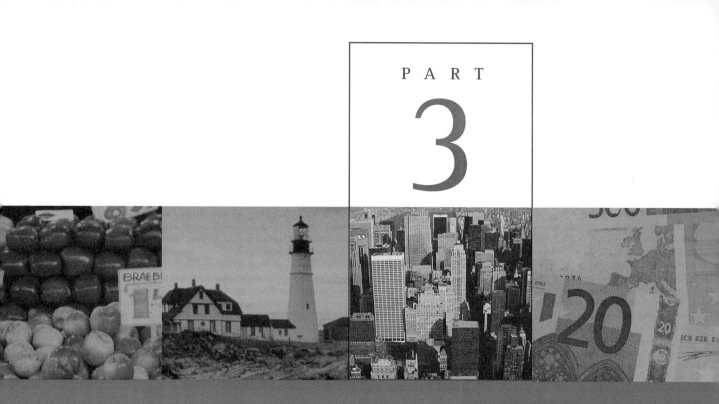

PART 3

the
Macroeconomy

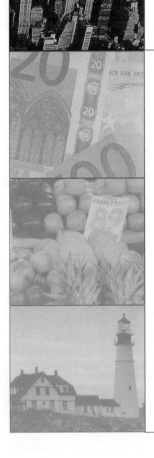

The Mixed Economy of the United States

Chapter objectives

After reading this chapter, you should be able to:

1. Distinguish between the functional distribution of income and personal distribution of income and identify the sources of income inequality.

2. Identify the major sources of revenue and expenditures of the federal government and also of state and local governments.

3. Evaluate various proposals for reforming the Social Security system.

4. Assess the strengths and weaknesses of the U.S. tax system.

5. Identify the merits of a flat-rate income tax, a value-added tax, and a national sales tax.

economics IN CONTEXT

inevitable

A t the turn of the century, the nation's economy was performing at peak levels. The number of workers employed was at an all-time high, the unemployment rate was at a 30-year low, and inflation-adjusted wages were increasing after years of stagnation. Single women with children, immigrants, and minorities, whose economic status had not improved in the past decades, were experiencing progress. Besides spreading the benefits of economic growth more widely, a robust economy generated other benefits. It contributed to a decrease in welfare caseloads, allowing government to focus increased resources on designing and implementing welfare reform. Moreover, low unemployment and, especially, the rise in average wages were contributing to a reduction in crime. Simply put, maintaining prosperity is of vital concern for all sectors of the economy.

However, a thriving economy does not always ensure prosperity for all households. Some groups have experienced declines in employment and income even as the overall economy prospers. In fact, for the last 20 years, the gap in income between rich and poor has increased. What accounts for the recent increases in income inequality in the United States? Economists cite different and varying reasons for this phenomenon, including changing technology, increased trade competition from low-wage countries, increased immigration, declines in the inflationary-adjusted minimum wage, and declines in unionism. Indeed, few issues resonate more with Americans than income and poverty.

In previous chapters, we have emphasized the private sector of the economy, which includes households and businesses. By adding the role of government to our discussion, we will now examine the **mixed economy**. In the mixed economy of the United States, the private sector consists of the millions of households and businesses in the nation. The public sector includes the federal, state, and local governments found in the United States. These two sectors will illustrate a few pertinent facts concerning our mixed economy.

HOUSEHOLDS AS INCOME RECEIVERS

Everyone knows that there are many rich and poor people in our society. **Distribution of income** is the way income is divided among members of society. It reflects the manner in which people share in the rewards from the production of goods and services. Income distribution can be analyzed in two ways.

The functional distribution of income shows the shares of a nation's income accruing to the *factors of production*—land, labor, capital, and entrepreneurship—as rent, wages, interest, and profits. Here income is shared by the factors of production according to the function they perform. Table 9.1 illustrates the functional distribution of income for the United States in 2002. Note that the largest source of the nation's income accrued to labor as wages and salaries.

How do *individual households* share the nation's income? This issue is addressed by the personal distribution of income, as seen in Table 9.1. The table indicates the share of before-tax annual money income received by *quintiles*—that is, each one-fifth of families, ranked from lowest to highest. In 2002, for example, the poorest 20 percent of all families received 4.2 percent of total money income; this is in contrast to the 20 percent they would have received if income were equally distributed. Conversely, the richest 20 percent of families

Table 9.1	Distribution of Income in the United States, 2002	
Functional Distribution of Income		
Wages and salaries		72%
Interest		8
Proprietor income		9
Corporate profit		9
Rents		2
Personal Distribution of Income		
Lowest 20%		4.2%
Second 20%		9.7
Middle 20%		15.5
Fourth 20%		23.0
Top 20%		47.6

Source: From U.S. Department of Commerce, *2004–2005 Statistical Abstract of the United States* (Washington, D.C.: U.S. Government Printing Office), Table 672.

[handwritten: — Compare with taxes paid on pg. 220]

received 47.6 percent of total money income. The richest fifth of all families thus received more than 11 times as much of the before-tax money income as the poorest fifth. Note, however, that the distribution of income is not the same thing as the distribution of wealth. A complete account of a family's wealth would also include things such as bank savings deposits, houses, land, cars, pensions, Social Security, and stocks and bonds. Moreover, human skills can be thought of as a type of wealth.

SOURCES OF INCOME INEQUALITY

Concerning the personal distribution of income, income inequality decreased significantly between the 1930s and 1950. Since 1970, however, income inequality has increased somewhat. Why do some people earn more income than others? Among the most important determinants of income differences are age, differences in productive resources, investment in human capital, inheritance, and discrimination.

[handwritten: Secondarily / Correlation is not causation]

Age is a determinant of income because with age comes, generally, more education, more training, and more experience. Income is usually lower when people start working at age 18; it then rises to a peak at around age 45 to 50, and then gradually decreases as people approach retirement age. When individuals begin working at a young age, they usually have little work-related experience and earn less than older workers with more experience. As workers become older, they develop additional work skills, become more productive, work longer hours, develop seniority, and thus earn increased income. At the age of 45 to 50, the productivity of workers usually peaks. As workers reach retirement age, their number of hours worked usually declines, along with decreases in stamina and strength. These factors detract from the income-earning ability of older workers.

Other determinants of income are the quantity and quality of resources possessed by an individual. In a market economy, those who use their human and physical resources to produce many things that are highly valued by others have high incomes. Shaquille O'Neal, the star basketball player of the Miami Heat, earns millions of dollars leading his team to victories. The connection between personal reward and productivity provides individuals with a strong incentive to use their resources efficiently and to figure out better ways of doing things.

People are not born with equal amounts of potential raw talent or intelligence. Inherited differences in people can be magnified or offset by acquired skills. Sharpening productive talents or acquiring new skills is called investment in human capital. People invest in their education, training, and health care for self-improvement that leads to higher productivity and higher income. If you invest in yourself by going to college instead of going to work after high school and earning more current income, you will likely be rewarded in the future with a more interesting job or a better paying job, or both.

Inheritance also affects income. It is not unusual to inherit cash, stocks, bonds, homes, or land that generate profits, interest, and rental income. Such gifts represent the benefits of someone else's labor or investments rather than the benefits of your own labor or investments.

Finally, discriminatory labor markets can influence income. Economic discrimination occurs whenever female or minority workers who have the same education, training, abilities, and experience as white male workers earn lower wages or receive less access to jobs or promotion. African-American and other minorities have encountered discrimination in the acquisition of human capital. For example, the amount and quality of schooling offered to black Americans has often been inferior to that offered to whites. Moreover, many women have maintained that they have been forced to accept low-paying jobs such as secretaries, janitors, and food service because other jobs were closed to them. In some cases, occupations predominantly held by women offer low pay despite the fact that similarly skilled, predominantly male occupations pay much higher incomes.

HOUSEHOLDS AS SPENDERS

Besides receiving income, householders are spenders. Part of household income flows into consumption expenditures, while the rest is used to pay taxes or is saved.

Table 9.2 illustrates the disposition of household income in 2004. The table shows that more than four-fifths of household income was used for consumption expenditures. Consumer purchases include durable goods, such as computers and automobiles; nondurable goods, such as food and clothing; and services, including the work done by doctors and lawyers for consumers. The U.S. economy is service oriented, with more than half of household consumption expenditures used for services in 2004.

Table 9.2	Disposition of Household Income, 2004		
		Amount	Percent of Total
Personal consumption expenditures		$8,282 billion	88%
Durable goods		1,007	11
Nondurable goods		2,387	25
Services		4,888	52
Personal taxes		1,044	11%
Personal savings		43	1
Total		9,369	100%

Source: From *National Economic Accounts*, Bureau of Economic Analysis, U.S. Department of Commerce, available at http://www.bea.doc.gov/bea/dnl.htm.

Besides spending money as consumers, households allocate a portion of income for taxes, of which the federal personal income tax is the most important component. As seen in Table 9.2, 11 percent of household income was used to pay taxes in 2004.

The amount of household income that is not used for consumption expenditures, or to pay taxes, is saved. In 2004, households saved 1 percent of their income, as seen in Table 9.2. Household savings are put into bank accounts, stocks and bonds, insurance policies, and the like. The motivation to save is usually underlain by the desire to provide a nest egg for unforeseen adversities such as poor health, education savings for children, or for retirement. People also save for speculation. For example, an individual might purchase stock in IBM with the hope of selling it in the future at a higher price, thus realizing a handsome profit.

THE BUSINESS SECTOR   *households was first*

Business is the second component of an economy's private sector. A business is an organization established for producing and selling goods and services. In the United States, there are more than 25 million businesses. Many are small firms, such as local gas stations or grocery stores. Others are large firms such as automobile and computer manufacturers.

A business firm can be organized in one of three ways: as a sole proprietorship, a partnership, or a corporation. The structure chosen determines how the owners share the risks and liabilities of the firm and how they participate in the making of decisions. Table 9.3 shows the importance of these three business types for the United States. Although sole proprietorships are numerically dominant, corporations account for the largest share of total sales.

A **sole proprietorship** is a firm owned and operated by one individual. These establishments are typically small, such as a local espresso stand or pizza business. A sole proprietorship is relatively easy to organize and operate, and its owner is not responsible or answerable to anyone. The size of a sole proprietorship, however, is limited by the proprietor's wealth and credit standing, as well as by business profits. The greatest disadvantage of a sole proprietorship is a proprietor's unlimited liability; that is, the personal assets of the owner are subject to use for payment of business debt. Almost everything that a proprietor owns, such as an automobile, may be sold to pay a firm's debts if it fails or is held liable for damages in a lawsuit.

A **partnership** form of business organization is an extension of the sole proprietorship. Rather than being owned by one individual, a partnership has two or more owners who pool their financial resources and business skills. Many doctors, for example, form partnerships. This allows them to share office expenses and reduces the need to be "on call" 24 hours a day, seven days a week. Lawyers and accountants also tend to organize along partnership lines. In a partnership, each partner has unlimited liability. One partner's poor business decisions may

Table 9.3	U.S. Business Firms in 2001			
Form of Business	Number of Firms (millions)		Business Receipts (billions)	
	Number	Percent	Dollars	Percent
Proprietorships	18.3	71%	$ 1,017	4%
Partnerships	2.1	8	2,569	11
Corporations	5.2	21	19,308	85
Totals	25.6	100%	$22,894	100%

Source: From U.S. Commerce Department, Bureau of the Census, *2004–2005 Statistical Abstract of the United States* (Washington, D.C.: U.S. Government Printing Office), Table 716.

impose significant losses on the other partners, a problem that the sole proprietor need not worry about. Also, decision making is usually more cumbersome in a partnership than a proprietorship because there are more people involved in making decisions. Moreover, termination of a partnership usually occurs when a partner dies or voluntarily withdraws from the business.

A corporation is a "legal person" that conducts business just as an individual does. Corporations can produce and sell output, make contracts, pay fines, and sue and be sued. General Motors, IBM, Boeing, and Microsoft are examples of corporations that have become household names.

Stockholders own corporations and receive the profits of the firms through dividend checks. For large corporations, such as General Electric, the number of stockholders may include hundreds of thousands of people; however, some corporations have only a few stockholders. The stockholders vote, according to the amount of stock they own, for a board of directors. The board, in turn, appoints officers to run the corporation according to the guidelines established by the board.

Limited liability is an advantage for the stockholders of a corporation. With corporate bankruptcy, a stockholder can lose only the money used to purchase the firm's stock. Moreover, corporations can obtain funds through the sale of shares of stock or borrowing money. Corporations borrow by issuing bonds to investors or by obtaining loans directly from banks and other financial institutions. In contrast, loans are the only option for obtaining outside funding available to sole proprietorships and partnerships. Finally, corporations are efficient in transferring ownership. When a stockholder of a corporation wishes to give up ownership rights, she can sell her stock to other investors.

Corporations, however, have several drawbacks. The first is the double taxation of income. Profits of a corporation are first subject to corporate income taxes. Then, if any of the after-tax profits are distributed to stockholders as dividends, these payments are taxed as personal income. Corporation profits are thus taxed twice under our tax system; the profits of proprietorships and partnerships are taxed only once as personal income. In 2003, the top tax rate on dividends was cut to 15 percent from 38.6 percent, thus reducing the burden of double taxation of income.

Corporations can also suffer from the problem of separation of ownership and control. Stockholders of a corporation often have little to do with its actual operation. Instead, officers, who may own little or no corporate stock, manage the firm. The objective of stockholders is to maximize the dividends they receive from their stock ownership in the firm. Unless the officers receive compensation in corporate stock, their motivations may differ from that of stockholders. For example, officers may reward themselves with extravagant salaries or lavish offices, both of which are not necessary for the efficient operation of the company. Such luxuries increase the cost of doing business and decrease the dividends of stockholders.

CHECK POINT

1. Distinguish between the functional distribution of income and the personal distribution of income.

2. Identify the determinants of an individual's income and how income is spent.

3. Describe the advantages and disadvantages of the three legal forms of business organization.

GOVERNMENT IN THE MIXED ECONOMY

The activities of government have a major influence on our lives. In a mixed economy, the government provides an appropriate legal and social framework, promotes competition, alters the distribution of income by taxing income away from some people and giving it away to others, provides public goods such as national defense, encourages businesses to produce goods entailing spillover benefits (public television), discourages companies from polluting the environment, and initiates policies to promote price stability and high employment for the nation. These functions require government expenditures that are financed by taxes paid by households and businesses.

Government expenditures or outlays consist of purchases and transfer payments, including federal, state, and local government. Government purchases are expenditures on goods and services. They include such items as street lighting, sewage systems, city playgrounds, national parks, county roads, police cars, fire trucks, tanks, computers, and jet planes. Government also purchases the labor services of engineers, teachers, accountants, and lawyers to produce goods ranging from highway construction to college education. When government purchases goods and services, fewer resources are available to produce goods and services used in the private sector.

Government expenditures also include transfer payments, which are payments of income from taxpayers to individuals who make no contribution to current output for these payments. Transfer payments thus provide a *safety net* of income security for the poor and needy. The major governmental transfer payment programs have included the following:

- **Unemployment compensation** provides temporary income support for unemployed workers. The amount an unemployed worker receives each week and the number of weeks an unemployed worker is allowed to receive benefits vary among the states.

- **Food stamps** are given to the poor, elderly, and disabled so that they can acquire nutritionally adequate products. Recipients receive a quantity of stamps monthly; these stamps are redeemable for goods at most grocery stores.

- **Supplemental security income** payments are made to the disabled, blind, and elderly who are unable to work.

- **Aid to Families with Dependent Children** consists of payments to surviving spouses with small children and also to single-parent families. These families are usually headed by women who cannot work because they must care for their young children.

- **Medicaid** provides health care payments to low-income families and also the blind, elderly, and disabled.

- **Housing and energy subsidies** are granted to low-income families to help them afford the cost of a dwelling.

- **Agricultural assistance** to farmers consists of subsidies and grants such as minimum price supports and low-interest-rate loans to farmers who have difficulty in obtaining credit elsewhere. Such assistance attempts to stabilize farm incomes and thus provide consumers with a stable supply of food.

The United States has devised a system of taxes and transfer payments to alter the distribution of income in favor of the poor—economically advantaged "Peter" is taxed to help economically disadvantaged "Paul." Critics of the system, however, maintain that many transfer payments are doled out without concern for need. Moreover, the welfare system has contained powerful disincentives against work and personal responsibility, which promotes continued welfare.

In 1996, the *Personal Responsibility and Work Opportunity Reconciliation Act* was passed by Congress and signed into law by President Bill Clinton. The act established the principle that individuals and families are no longer automatically entitled to government support just because they are poor. Specifically, the law established a "workfare" requirement by stipulating that recipients must give up most welfare benefits unless the family head begins to work within two years. Families can spend more than one spell on welfare, but lifetime benefits are limited to five years. The law also decentralized welfare policy through federal lump-sum grants to state governments that are free to operate their own welfare programs. Moreover, the law tightened welfare payments to immigrants who are noncitizen legal aliens. The reforms were intended to force welfare parents to get even modest jobs, thereby providing new hope and motivation for their children. Indeed, the pros and cons of workfare have been widely debated, and it will be many years before the long-run effects on the efficiency and coverage of welfare systems can be known.

REFORMING OUR SOCIAL SECURITY SYSTEM

The major source of growth in transfer payments has been in Social Security and Medicare.

Social Security is the largest retirement and disability program in the United States. Social Security was created in 1935 as a means of providing income security upon retirement to people who would not otherwise have that form of security. As of 2005, it provided cash benefits to more than 50 million retired and disabled workers and to their dependents and survivors.

In 1965, the federal government added a health insurance program, Medicare, to the Social Security system. Its objective is to reduce the financial burden of illness on the elderly. Medicare covers physician fees, hospitalization, outpatient care, and skilled nursing at home. As of 2005, Medicare provided more than 42 million people with health insurance.

Social Security is a *pay-as-you-go* system financed by payroll taxes. In 2005, workers paid a flat-rate tax of 6.2 percent for old-age, survivors, and disability insurance, on their wages up to $90,000, which was matched by their employers. Also, employees and employers each paid a 1.45-percent tax on all wages to finance Medicare. Social Security taxes flow into the U.S. Treasury, with each program's share credited to separate trust funds—one for retirement and survivors, another for disability, and two others for Medicare. Social Security and Medicare are mandatory for most wage earners whether they like it or not.

Contrary to popular belief, the Social Security trust funds themselves do not hold money to pay benefits. They are simply accounts that are located at the U.S. Treasury. These balances, like those of a bank account or a government savings bond, represent a promise (IOU) from the government. It pledges to obtain resources in the future, equal to the value of the trust-fund accounts, if funds are needed to pay Social Security benefits. Any surplus of taxes in the Social Security system is used to purchase U.S. Treasury securities. The federal government then uses these funds as part of its operating cash that is used to pay for any of the many functions of government such as national defense and unemployment compensation benefits.

For more than three decades after Social Security was created, the system's income routinely exceeded its outgo, and its trust funds grew. Beginning in the 1970s, however, the trust funds started to decline. This was largely due to benefit increases. Not only were the number of beneficiaries growing, but benefits were also periodically adjusted to keep pace with inflation. By the 1980s, Social Security benefits were automatically raised annually to reflect inflation. These cost-of-living adjustments, or COLAs, also contributed to revenue shortfalls.

Another concern of Social Security is that the number of workers paying Social Security taxes has declined relative to the number of Social Security beneficiaries. An aging post-World War II "baby boom" generation, falling birth rates, and increasing life expectancies have all contributed to this decline. In 1945, for each worker collecting benefits there were 46 workers paying payroll taxes. By 1996, there were only three workers for every beneficiary. Estimates suggest that there will be only 2.4 workers for every beneficiary by the year 2050. The bottom line is that there will be relatively fewer people of working age to support a growing elderly population. Simply put, the declining ratio of young to old foretells serious solvency problems for Social Security. Economists estimate that the Social Security system's trust funds will be depleted in 2042 and only 73 percent of its benefits would be payable then with incoming receipts. Take a male who was born in 2000 and makes the average income over his working life. He will be promised $290,900 in today's dollars. But the system will only have the resources to pay him $211,700.

From the 1940s to the 1980s, Social Security recipients received a good deal for the taxes they paid to support the system. Most recipients received more than the value of the taxes they paid. However, because Social Security tax rates have increased over the years and the age for full benefits has risen, it is becoming increasingly apparent that Social Security will be less of a good deal for many future recipients. Workers who earned average wages and retired in 1980 at age 65 took 2.8 years to recover the value of the retirement portion of the combined employee and employer shares of their payroll taxes plus interest. For their counterparts retiring at age 65 in 1996, it took 14 years. For those retiring in 2025, it will take a projected 23 years.

Concerns about Social Security's financing problems and survival have led to proposals to reform the system. One option that has been used is to increase the Social Security tax rates paid by current employees. However, wage earners may resist future increases. Because Social Security is a pay-as-you-go system, not a penny of the tax goes into the accounts of those who make contributions. To them, Social Security may be viewed as a program offering little in return. Instead of raising the payroll taxes of current wage earners, why not decrease the benefits of the elderly? Consider these options:

- **Adopt means testing.** Social Security recipients must qualify on the basis of financial need similar to other welfare programs such as food stamps and Medicaid. Because many of the elderly are wealthy, they could easily forego Social Security benefits.

- **Remove the income cap.** As of 2005, workers paid Social Security taxes on only the first $90,000 they earned in a year. So those who earn millions a year paid the same tax as a worker earning only $90,000 a year. Removing the income cap would create more tax revenue without further taxing strained paychecks.

- **Raise the retirement age.** Congress did this; but under current law, the retirement age won't rise from 65 to 67 until 2027. A revised law should phase in this change at an earlier date. By 2020, the retirement age should be 70 or higher, reflecting the increased life expectancy of the coming generations of elderly.

- **Decrease the COLA.** Social Security benefits are raised annually to reflect inflation. Benefit levels are adjusted each year according to the change in average U.S. wages. Over the long term, wages have outpaced consumer prices by roughly 1 percent a year, which causes Social Security benefits to be too large. The formula could be switched so that benefits keep pace with prices instead of wages.

- **Fully tax Social Security benefits.** Rather than partially taxing Social Security benefits, treat them as ordinary income subject to full taxation.

None of these options is politically popular with senior citizens. Many of them lived through the Depression and World War II, and they view the wolf to be always at the door. Their generation took care of their parents and frequently lived with and supported them in an extended family. Why shouldn't the next generation do the same? Given the voting power of the American Association of Retired Persons, it is not difficult to see why the president and Congress have been reluctant to cut Social Security benefits.

However, critics see Social Security as an anachronism, built on depression-era concerns about high unemployment and widespread dependency among the aged. They see the prospect of reform today as an opportunity to modernize the way society saves for retirement. Believing government-run, pay-as-you-go systems are unsustainable in aging societies, they prefer a system that lets workers acquire wealth by investing for their retirement, rather than the current system that must impose tax hikes on future workers to meet promised benefits.

Can the Stock Market Help Save Social Security?

During his 2005 inaugural address, President George W. Bush proposed that workers under 55 be allowed to divert four percentage points of their 12.4-percent annual Social Security payroll tax into personal investment accounts. This approach would allow participants to take advantage of the superior growth prospects offered by the stock market. Today, promised benefits of Social Security work out to about a 2-percent annual return on payroll taxes. The same funds invested in a balanced portfolio of stocks might earn 6 percent.

Private investment accounts have several advantages. They would allow retirement plans to be tailored to individual needs and preferences. Individuals who can bear more risk, perhaps because they own their houses outright, would prefer to hold retirement portfolios that are more heavily weighted with stocks. Private accounts would also allow healthy persons who like their jobs to work past the usual retirement age without having to sacrifice part of their retirement incomes. Simply put, private accounts would allow individuals to be able to save for retirement with their preferred mix of stocks and securities, and they would also choose their own best time to retire.

However, critics of private investment accounts argue that the funds going into them would be removed from the social insurance system. Therefore, they would no longer be available to pool risk and transfer income between high- and low-wage workers, between families with and without children, between the able and the disabled during retirement. Rather than being a guaranteed government benefit, Social Security payments to individual workers would depend on asset values, interest rates, and investment strategies as well as lifetime earnings.

Critics also note that adding private accounts to Social Security doesn't absolve us of the promises still outstanding to retirees. Maintaining existing benefits would be just as much a cost of privatized Social Security as it is of the current system. For example, suppose a privatized program places 4 percent of your Social Security tax into a private investment account. The rest continues to pay current beneficiaries, except now there's less revenue to cover the same bill. The money has to come from somewhere, so taxes must be increased, money borrowed, or benefits cut.

Finally, there is the cost of moving from the existing Social Security system. If workers shift, say, four percentage points of payroll tax into their individual retirement accounts, the government would have to find some other money to pay benefits to current retirees. The transition cost over the next decade could easily cost $1–2 trillion. To come up with the money, government would have to either raise taxes or borrow money. At the writing of this textbook, it remains to be seen how our Social Security system will be reformed.

GOVERNMENT FINANCE

We will now compare the expenditures and receipts of the federal, state, and local units of government. Table 9.4 gives a breakdown of the federal budget for fiscal year 2004. Indeed, the preparation of the federal government's annual budget is a complicated process, as seen in Figure 9.1. It may be surprising that the largest component of federal spending was not national defense. Instead it was *income transfer programs* such as Social Security, Medicare, and public assistance to the poor and disabled. These items comprised 48 percent of federal expenditures in 2004. The next largest expenditure in that year was *national defense,* which accounted for 20 percent of federal spending.

Another category of federal expenditures is *interest on the public debt.* In the past, the federal government has often incurred a budget deficit, the amount by which expenditures exceed tax revenues. The national or *public debt* is the total accumulation of the federal government's combined deficits occurring over many years. To finance its debt, the federal government sells securities (U.S. savings bonds) to investors. When a security matures, investors are paid its face value plus the accumulated interest. Federal expenditures for interest on the public debt stood at 7 percent of government expenditures in 2004. As the government uses more tax dollars to pay for interest on the public debt, fewer tax dollars are available for public education, police and fire protection, and other governmental programs.

Table 9.4	Government Receipts and Expenditures, Percent of Total

Federal Government (2004)

Receipts		Expenditures	
Personal income taxes	43%	Social Security, Medicare, income security	48%
Social Security, Medicare, retirement taxes	39	National defense	20
Corporate income taxes	10	Net interest on the public debt	7
Excise taxes	4	Health	10
Other	4	Other	15
	100%		100%

State and Local Government (2002)

Receipts		Expenditures	
Sales and excise taxes	20%	Education	34%
Revenue from the federal government	19	Public welfare	16
Property tax	17	Highways	7
Personal income tax	13	Other	43
Corporate income tax	2		100%
Other	29		
	100%		

Source: From Office of Management and Budget, *The Budget for Fiscal Year 2006, Historical Tables* and *Economic Report of the President,* 2005.

| Figure 9.1 | Preparation of the Federal Government's Annual Budget |

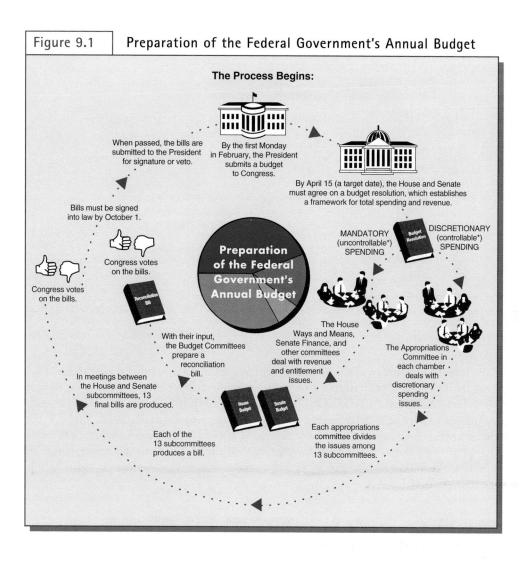

Where does the federal government obtain its funds? Table 9.4 gives a breakdown of federal government receipts in 2004. We see that the largest share of revenue came from the *personal income tax* (43 percent), which is paid by households, sole proprietorships, and partnerships. This was followed by *Social Security* contributions, or *payroll taxes* (39 percent). The federal government also levied *corporate income taxes* on corporate profits (10 percent) and consumption taxes taking the form of *excise taxes or sales taxes* on goods such as gasoline, tobacco, and alcohol (4 percent). Other miscellaneous taxes consisted of death and gift taxes, customs duties, and licenses.

The expenditures and receipts of government vary among the different government units. Referring again to Table 9.4, we see that state and local governments allocated 34 percent of their expenditures to *public education* in 2002. *Public welfare* was the second most important expenditure of state and local governments (16 percent), followed by expenditures on highways (7 percent). On the revenue side, state and local governments relied primarily on *sales and excise taxes* (20 percent) and *property taxes* (17 percent) in 2002. Personal income taxes accounted for only 13 percent of state and local revenue. This is unlike the federal government, which relies primarily on the personal income tax as its main revenue source. Besides collecting tax revenues, state and local governments receive grants from the federal government, which amounted to 19 percent of state and local receipts in 2002.

Table 9.5	Total Tax Receipts as a Percent of Gross Domestic Output, 2003

Nation	Average Tax Rate
Sweden	59.3%
France	50.4
Austria	50.4
Italy	45.8
Germany	45.3
Canada	41.2
Australia	37.0
United Kingdom	33.9
United States	31.0
Japan	30.9

Source: From U.S. Department of Commerce, Bureau of the Census, *2004–2005 Statistical Abstract of the United States* (Washington, D.C.: U.S. Government Printing Office), Table 1344.

How does the tax burden of the United States compare to that of other nations? Table 9.5 presents total tax receipts at all levels of government as a share of gross domestic output for 10 industrial nations in 2003. This measures the size of the entire tax burden in each nation relative to its economic output and is equivalent to an average tax rate for the nation as a whole. As can be seen in the table, the United States had an average tax rate of 31.0 percent of domestic output. Sweden topped the list with an average tax rate of 59.3 percent. By international standards, U.S. citizens are among the lighter taxed people in the industrialized world. *but others get way more bennies*

TAXATION PRINCIPLES: BENEFITS–RECEIVED VERSUS ABILITY TO PAY

Much of the public debate on taxation, as reported in the press, concerns the issue of equity. Is a tax fair? People are generally more likely to comply voluntarily with tax policies if they believe that the policies are reasonable and equitable. A fair tax system is usually regarded as being based on people's ability to pay taxes, although some have contended that taxes should instead be based on how much people benefit from public expenditures.

According to the benefits-received principle of taxation, taxes should be paid in proportion to the benefits that taxpayers derive from public expenditures. Just as people pay private dollars in proportion to their consumption of private goods, such as food and clothing, an individual's taxes should be related to his or her use of public goods, like parks or roads. From this viewpoint, the ideal tax would be a *user charge*, such as those that would be established if business firms provided the public goods.

The *gasoline tax* is consistent with the benefits-received principle. Gas taxes are used to finance the construction and maintenance of roads and other transportation systems. The number of gallons of gas you buy is an indicator of the amount of transportation services used; the larger the number of gallons bought, the greater the tax paid. Also, *taxes on airline tickets* are used for airport traffic control, airport operations, and airport security. Frequent fliers obtain greater benefits from the airline transportation system and thus pay higher taxes to fund its operation. Moreover, if the construction of a new bridge is financed by *tolls* on the bridge, this payment method follows the benefits-received principle because you pay for the bridge only if you use it.

Difficulties arise, however, in attempting to apply the benefits-received principle to many important categories of government spending, such as national defense, police and fire protection, and public education. How could we calculate the benefit that particular individuals get from these goods, and how much tax should they have to pay? We cannot make such a calculation! Moreover, it is even more difficult to apply the benefits-received principle to programs that redistribute national income. For example, it does not make sense to force unemployed workers, who receive unemployment compensation, to pay all the taxes to finance their welfare benefits. Although there are instances where the benefits-received principle applies, it has historically played a minor role in the development of the U.S. tax system.

The ability-to-pay principle sharply contrasts with the benefits-received principle. Ability-to-pay taxation is founded on the notion that people with greater income and wealth should be taxed at a higher rate because their ability to pay is presumably greater. Most people would find it reasonable for Bill Gates, the founder of Microsoft Corporation and one of the wealthiest people in the United States, to pay more taxes than those with modest income; he should also pay a higher proportion of his income in taxes! As we will see in the next section, progressive income taxation incorporates the ability-to-pay concept.

A limitation of the ability-to-pay principle is that there is no precise way to calculate one's fair ability to pay taxes. How much higher should the tax rate be for those with higher incomes? The answer seems to be based on guesswork and on the government's need for revenue.

PROGRESSIVE, REGRESSIVE, AND PROPORTIONAL TAXES

Recall that governments raise revenues from a variety of taxes such as income taxes, property taxes, Social Security taxes, and sales taxes. These taxes fit into one of three types of taxation systems—*proportional* taxation, *progressive* taxation, and *regressive* taxation. Taxes are proportional if they take a constant fraction of income as income rises, progressive if they take a larger fraction of income as income rises, and regressive if they take a smaller fraction of income as income rises.

Table 9.6 shows the average tax rate and marginal tax rate under these tax systems. Column 1 shows different levels of total income earned by an individual. Column 2 shows the total taxes due at various levels of income. Column 3 shows the average tax rate, which is equal to total taxes due divided by total income:

$$\text{Average tax rate} = \frac{\text{Total taxes due}}{\text{Total income}}$$

Column 4 shows the marginal tax rate, which is the fraction of additional income paid in taxes:

$$\text{Marginal tax rate} = \frac{\text{Change in taxes due}}{\text{Change in income}}$$

Let us first calculate the average tax rate under a *progressive* tax system. Referring to the upper portion of Table 9.6, at an income of \$100, the average tax rate is 5 percent (\$5/\$100 = 0.05); at an income of \$200, the average tax rate is 10 percent (\$20/\$200 = 0.10); at an income of \$300, the average tax rate is 15 percent (\$45/\$300 = 0.15).

Table 9.6	Progressive, Proportional, and Regressive Taxes

	Total Income	Taxes Due	Total Average Tax Rate	Marginal Tax Rate	
Progressive Tax	$ 0	$ 0	—	—	*In a progressive tax system, the average tax rate and marginal tax rate rise as income increases.
	100	5	5%	5%	
	200	20	10	15	
	300	45	15	25	
Regressive Tax	$ 0	$ 0	—	—	*In a regressive tax system, the average tax rate and marginal tax rate fall as income increases.
	100	30	30%	30%	
	200	50	25	20	
	300	60	20	10	
Proportional Tax	$ 0	$ 0	—	—	*In a proportional tax system, the average tax rate and marginal tax rate remain the same as income increases.
	100	10	10%	10%	
	200	20	10	10	
	300	30	10	10	

As these figures show, this tax system is progressive because the average tax rate increases as income rises.

Now we will compute the marginal tax rate under a progressive tax system. Referring to Table 9.6, as income increases in the first bracket, from $0 to $100, taxes due rise from $0 to $5. The marginal tax rate of the first bracket thus equals 5 percent ($5/$100 = 0.5). Moving to the second bracket, as income rises from $100 to $200, taxes due increase from $5 to $20, and the marginal tax rate equals 15 percent ($15/$100 = 0.15). As income increases by another $100, taxes due rise by $25, and the marginal tax rate equals 25 percent. Our tax system is progressive because the marginal tax rate increases as an individual moves to higher brackets of income. We conclude that in a progressive tax system, both the average tax rate and marginal tax rate rise as income increases. Progressive taxation is thus consistent with the ability-to-pay principle of taxation.

Next, we consider a *regressive* tax. With regressive taxation, a smaller fraction of income is taken in taxes as income increases. Refer to the regressive tax shown in Table 9.6. As income increases, taxes due also rise. The tax is regressive, however, because the average tax rate and marginal tax rate fall as income increases. A regressive tax thus imposes a relatively larger burden on the poor than on the rich and thus contradicts the ability-to-pay principle of taxation.

Finally, there is the *proportional* tax, also called a *flat-rate* tax. Proportional taxation means that as an individual's income rises, taxes due rise by the same fraction. Refer to the proportional tax shown in Table 9.6. As income rises, the average tax rate is 10 percent applied to each tax bracket, and the marginal tax rate turns out to be 10 percent also.

What is the relationship between a proportional tax and the ability-to-pay principle of taxation? Consider a 20-percent tax that collects $2,000 from Joe Smith, who earns $10,000 a year and $20,000 from Helen Miller, who earns $100,000 a year. Although each individual pays an identical tax rate of 20 percent, the tax imposes a greater burden on Joe than Helen. After paying the tax, Joe has little income left to buy groceries for his family; Helen can live comfortably after paying her tax. One can argue that Helen is not paying a fair share of her income in taxes according to the ability-to-pay principle.

THE U.S. TAX STRUCTURE

Let us now try to understand the principles by which the U.S. tax system is constructed. What can be said about the progressivity, regressivity, or proportionality of the major taxes in the United States?

Federal Personal Income Tax

The most important tax in the U.S. economy is the federal personal income tax. All U.S. citizens, resident aliens, and most others who earn income in the United States are required to pay federal taxes on all taxable income. Taxable income is gross income minus exemptions, deductions, and credits:

Gross Income (wages, salaries, tips, bonuses, and so on)
— **Exemptions** (an allowance for each household member)
— **Deductions** (home mortgage interest payments, business expenses, charitable contributions, medical expenses, certain state and local taxes)
— **Credits** (child care, elderly and disabled, low-income allowance)

Taxable Income

Table 9.7 shows the federal income tax rates for a single taxpayer in 2005. The federal income tax is *progressive* with the average tax rate and marginal tax rate increasing as an individual moves into higher brackets of taxable income. Table 9.8 is also consistent with the progressive impact of the federal income tax. The table shows the share of federal income taxes paid by various income groups in 2001. For example, the top 1 percent of tax filers paid 34 percent of federal taxes, while the top 10 percent of tax filers paid 65 percent. These data must be kept in mind when evaluating proposals to revise the tax system. Simply put, the tax shares already paid by various income groups largely determine the distributional outcomes of most major tax proposals, not the tax rate structure of the legislation itself.

| Table 9.7 | Federal Income Tax Rates for a Single Taxpayer, 2005 |

Tax Bracket		Taxes Due*	Average Tax Rate	Marginal Tax Rate
Over	Up to			
$ 0	$ 7,300	$ 730	10%	10%
7,300	29,700	4,090	14	15
29,700	71,950	14,653	20	25
71,950	150,150	36,549	24	28
150,150	326,450	94,728	29	33
326,450 and over				35

*Computed at the top of the six taxable income brackets.
Source: From Internal Revenue Service, *2005 Tax Rate Schedules.*

Table 9.8	Share of Federal Personal Income Tax Paid by Various Income Groups, 2001		
	Percentiles Ranked by Adjusted Gross Income	Adjusted Gross Income Threshold on Percentiles	Percentage of Federal Personal Income Tax Paid
	Top 1%	$292,913	34%
	Top 5%	127,904	53
	Top 10%	92,754	65
	Top 25%	56,085	83
	Top 50%	28,528	96
	Bottom 50%	Less than 28,528	4

Source: From *New IRS Data on Income and Tax Shares*, Joint Economic Committee, September 2003, available at http://www.house.gov/jec.

Federal Corporate Income Tax

After a corporation has determined its annual income and met all its expenses, it must pay part of its income to the federal government. The corporate income tax is essentially a *proportional* tax with a flat rate of 35 percent for almost all corporations.

Social Security Tax

As of 2005, the Social Security tax was imposed on an individual's *wage income* up to $90,000. The Social Security tax (excluding Medicare) equaled 12.4 percent, split evenly between employee and employer (6.2 percent each).

The Social Security tax is largely a *proportional* tax because it taxes a fixed percentage of wage earnings. It does have some *regressive* features, however, since it is higher on low wages than on high wages. For example, in 2005 a worker's Social Security tax rate was 6.2 percent, which was applied to the *first* $90,000 of wage income. A worker earning exactly $90,000 would pay a Social Security tax of $5,580 (0.062 × $90,000 = $5,580). However, a worker earning twice as much, $180,000, would also pay a Social Security tax of $5,580, resulting in a tax rate of only 3.1 percent ($5,580/$180,000 = 0.031). We conclude that the Social Security tax becomes regressive once wage income exceeds $90,000.

The regressivity of the Social Security tax is magnified by the inclusion of *nonwage* income such as dividends and interest that tend to be received more by higher-income individuals. In the previous example, suppose our worker with wage income of $180,000 also received dividends of $100,000. The Social Security tax would then amount to only 2 percent ($5,580/$280,000 = 0.02) of total income.

Sales, Excise, and Property Taxes

States obtain most of their revenue from general sales taxes on goods and services. Also, states usually add their excise taxes to the federal excise taxes on gasoline, liquor, and cigarettes. As for local governments, most of their revenue comes from property taxes.

Sales taxes are *regressive* because lower-income families generally spend a large fraction of their income to purchase consumption items that are subject to sales and excise taxes. Higher-income families, however, generally save a portion of their income and thus devote a smaller fraction of their income to consumption goods subject to sales and excise taxes.

Assume the state of Wisconsin imposes an 8-percent sales tax on all purchases and that the Miller family earned $30,000 during the last year while the Jefferson family earned $100,000. The Millers, with a $30,000 income, spend their entire income on food and other necessities, while the Jeffersons, with a $100,000 income, spend $40,000 on food and other necessities and save the remainder. Since each family pays an 8-percent sales tax, the lower-income Millers pay taxes of $2,400 (0.08 × $30,000 = $2,400), which is about 1/12 of their income. The higher-income Jeffersons, however, pay taxes of $3,200 (0.08 × $40,000 = $3,200), which is about 3/100 of their income. Although the wealthier Jeffersons pay more taxes than the poorer Millers, the sales tax is regressive because the Jeffersons' average tax rate is lower than that of the Millers.

Excise taxes, like those on cigarettes, are also *regressive*. Cigarettes are widely recognized as an inferior good—consumption decreases as income increases. Individuals with lower incomes thus tend to spend more on cigarettes than those with higher incomes. Cigarette taxes paid by low-income people account for a larger fraction of their incomes than do cigarette taxes paid by high-income people.

Property taxes are levied mainly on real estate—buildings and land. Each locality establishes an annual tax rate that is applied to the assessed value of property. Economists generally agree that property taxes on real estate are *regressive* for similar reasons as sales taxes: As a fraction of income, property taxes are higher for the poor than the wealthy because the poor must spend a larger share of their income for housing.

but this is a choice

Overall U.S. Tax System

As we have seen, the federal tax system (especially the personal income tax) is somewhat progressive. However, state and local governments rely mainly on sales, excise, and property taxes, which are regressive. Most economists argue that when federal, state, and local taxes are combined, the overall effect is roughly *proportional*. The overall tax system itself does not significantly affect the distribution of the nation's income, because the rich and poor alike pay roughly the same fraction of their income as taxes.

Although the U.S. tax system does not substantially redistribute income from the rich to the poor, the U.S. system of transfer payments does decrease income inequality. Transfer payments to the poorest fifth of American families are almost four times as much as their combined incomes. The U.S. tax-transfer payment system is therefore more progressive than the U.S. tax system by itself.

Do Q. 5 in groups

CHECK POINT

1. Distinguish between government expenditures and transfer payments.

2. Identify the major sources of revenue and expenditures of the federal government and also state and local governments.

3. Which of the following taxes is consistent with the ability-to-pay principle, and which is consistent with the benefits-received principle? Federal income tax. Gasoline tax. Tolls used to finance the construction of a bridge.

4. Define a proportional tax, a progressive tax, and a regressive tax. Classify the major federal taxes, and also state and local taxes, according to these tax systems.

SHOULD THE U.S. TAX SYSTEM BE REFORMED?

Because the distribution of income in the United States is quite unequal, many people look to the federal income tax to redistribute income. Recall that the federal income tax is designed to be *progressive,* bearing down harder on the rich than the poor. It fulfills this objective by defining six brackets of taxable income and taxing each at progressively higher rates ranging from 10 percent to 35 percent.

In reality, however, federal tax burdens are not so progressively distributed. Legal tax rates pertain only to taxable income. Much income is nontaxable due to various tax loopholes established by Congress. Tax loopholes include exemptions, deductions, and credits, as previously discussed.

Suppose Helen Smith earns a salary of $50,000. She is unmarried with no children, lives in a rented apartment, has no retirement plan, and doesn't benefit from any tax shelters. Helen puts all of her savings in a certificate of deposit (CD) at a local bank. In this situation, she could not take advantage of any tax loopholes. When determining her taxable income, Helen could benefit from only the personal exemption ($2,000). This would decrease her taxable income to $48,000 and would lead to a tax bill of $10,400.

Now suppose that Helen alters her financial position. She borrows money from a savings and loan institution to purchase a house, sets up an individual retirement account (retirement plan) at her bank, and donates money to her church. Helen still earns $50,000, but she now has several tax loopholes.

Helen again uses the personal exemption of $2,000, which decreases her taxable income to $48,000. From this amount, she can also deduct the interest payments on her home mortgage ($8,000), contributions to her individual retirement account ($2,000), and charitable contributions ($1,000). Helen's taxable income now totals $37,000, which results in a tax bill of $7,300. By taking advantage of these loopholes, Helen can decrease her average tax rate from 21 percent ($10,400/$50,000 = 0.21) to 15 percent ($7,300/$50,000 = 0.15). In short, the various exemptions, deductions, and credits permitted by the Internal Revenue Service *decrease the progressivity* of the federal income tax system.

Critics of the federal income tax system maintain that it is unfair and inefficient. They contend that the federal income tax favors the rich, who are able to shelter much of their income by using tax loopholes. Is it fair that some wealthy individuals pay little or no taxes? Second, it is argued that the federal income tax system is costly for taxpayers, who must keep records and fill out tax forms. Given the complexity of federal regulations, an estimated 40 percent of all taxpayers pay for professional help devoted to legal tax avoidance. Such costs could be avoided given a simpler tax system. Third, it is maintained that progressive tax rates can discourage saving and investment that promote economic growth. Finally, the tax system violates the principle that people with the same income pay the same taxes. Depending on the composition of a particular taxpayer's household, Americans with identical incomes pay wildly different taxes.

These concerns have prompted proposed reforms of the federal tax system. Any reasonable reform would reduce loopholes, lower rates, and abolish the tax bias against saving and investment. The result would be a simpler system, easy for taxpayers to figure out, and transparent so that the costs of government services were readily visible. Three of the most widely discussed reforms have been a proposed flat-rate income tax, a value-added tax, and a national sales tax.

Flat-Rate Income Tax

In its purest form, a **flat-rate income tax** system would junk the existing array of five different tax rates on personal income and replace them with a single tax rate. In addition,

| Figure 9.2 | Replacing the Progressive Income Tax with a Flat-Rate Tax |

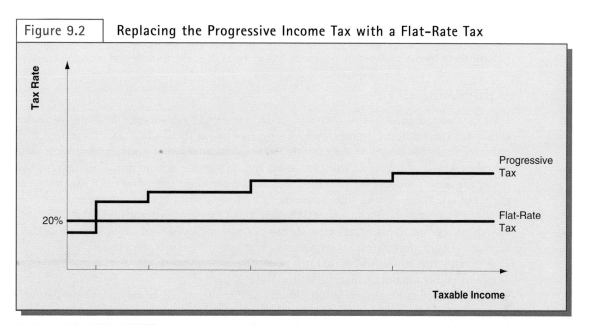

Replacing the progressive income tax with a flat-rate tax of 20 percent would decrease the tax burdens of higher income individuals while increasing the tax burdens of the poor and lower middle class. The poor could be protected by giving them some tax loopholes such as a standard deduction and personal exemptions for dependents.

all exemptions, deductions, and credits would be abolished. By eliminating tax loopholes, all income, regardless of its source, would be taxed at the same rate, ending complaints that many taxpayers, especially the rich, are able to shelter much of their income by using tax loopholes. A flat tax system would also be designed to generate the same revenue as the current progressive income tax. It is estimated that a flat tax of about 20 percent would yield identical revenue.

As seen in Figure 9.2, replacing the progressive income tax with a flat-rate tax would have a dramatic impact on the distribution of the U.S. tax burden. Holding tax revenue constant, a flat-rate tax would reduce the tax burdens on higher-income individuals while increasing the burdens on the poor and lower middle class. Because such an income redistribution is widely perceived as unfair, the various proposals for a flat tax include some tax loopholes to protect the poor.

Proponents of a flat tax contend that it simplifies the tax system and thus reduces the cost of keeping records and filling out tax forms. The gains in simplicity are immense. Families and businesses could file their returns on forms the size of postcards. The numbers entered on these forms would be clear and easy to calculate. Opportunities for cheating would be minimized.

In spite of the advantages of a flat-rate income tax, several difficulties remain. One problem is the costly transition it would involve. Individuals and corporations have made major decisions and investments designed to maximize income based on certain deductions and tax rates under the current tax structure. Thus, the introduction of a flat tax, and the elimination of tax loopholes, would alter long-standing tax rules sharply. A flat tax would also alter the distribution of income and wealth by increasing taxes on some income groups and decreasing taxes on others. The elimination of all deductions likely would encounter opposition from special interest groups representing churches, schools, state and local governments, housing industries, and the elderly who benefit from tax deductions.

A less extreme reform of the federal tax system would be to close tax loopholes while retaining the current progressive income tax. Advocates of this reform argue that there are plenty of loopholes that don't make economic sense. Tax breaks for second homes and lavish deductions of business expenses, for example, could be eliminated to cut taxes on working families. Nobody likes taxes. But if we are to have public services, doesn't it make sense to pay for them by taxing wealthy people at higher rates than the middle and working classes?

Value-Added Tax

Like the flat-rate income tax, the value-added tax (VAT) is proposed by some as a substitute for current federal taxes. A VAT operates like a retail sales tax except that it is collected from businesses at the various *stages of production* of goods and services. For a loaf of bread, the VAT is collected from the farmer for wheat production, from the miller for flour production, from the baker at the cooking stage, and from the grocer at the retail sale stage. A VAT thus amounts to a *national sales tax* on consumer goods.

hidden tax!

Many European nations, such as Sweden and Germany, currently use the VAT as a source of revenue. This is reflected in Table 9.9, which illustrates taxes on goods and services as a fraction of total tax revenues for selected nations.

A major virtue of the VAT is that it is a tax on consumption rather than a tax on saving. Many economists maintain that the United States should increase saving by changing its tax structure toward one based on consumption and away from one based on income. Nations that save more also tend to invest more, which ultimately promotes growth in productivity and living standards. Another advantage of the VAT is that tax avoidance is extremely difficult, which partially accounts for its popularity in Europe. This is because tax-paying businesses leave a paper trail, which reduces the potential for tax evasion.

VATs, however, are not without problems. Because VATs are largely hidden, final customers may be unaware of the VAT included in the price of a product. Voters may thus underestimate true tax burdens and thus support additional spending made possible by the expansion of tax revenues. Another objection is that the VAT is a regressive tax that takes a larger share of poor people's incomes than it takes from the rich.

National Sales Tax

Another alternative to the current federal income tax is a national sales tax. This system would entail a federal consumption tax collected at the retail level by businesses. Used items are not taxed. The national sales tax would equal a set percentage of the retail price

Table 9.9	Taxes on Goods and Services as a Share of Total Tax Revenues	
Country	**Taxes on Goods and Services as a Percent of Total Tax Revenue, 2001**	
United Kingdom	31.3%	
Germany	28.8	
Italy	25.6	
France	25.2	
Canada	24.7	
Japan	19.0	
United States	16.1	

Source: From U.S. Department of Commerce, Bureau of the Census, *2004–2005 Statistical Abstract of the United States* (Washington, D.C.: U.S. Government Printing Office), Table 1345.

of taxable goods and services. Retail businesses would collect the tax from individuals and remit tax revenue to the federal government.

Proponents argue that a national sales tax is a fair and simple alternative to the current federal income tax. The national sales tax is a voluntary consumption tax in which the more you buy, the more you pay in taxes; the less you buy, the less you pay in taxes. Also, this system would collect taxes from everyone living in the United States, including aliens, illegal aliens, and the underground cash economy and thus add billions to the nation's treasury. To make sure that a national sales tax would not bear down excessively on low-income families, who spend almost every penny they earn on subsistence items, tax rebates would be provided on poverty level expenditures.

However, critics maintain that rates would be crushing if a national sales tax were established to generate the same amount of revenue that occurs under the current federal income tax. The national sales tax rate could be 50 percent, or more, and be out of proportion with any existing state sales tax. The temptation to evade the national sales tax would thus become overwhelming, according to critics.

This chapter examined the mixed economy of the United States. The next chapter will focus on how productivity influences the U.S. economy by considering its gross domestic product.

CHECK POINT

1. Do tax loopholes make the federal income tax more or less progressive? Why?

2. Why do critics of the current federal income tax system maintain that it is unfair and inefficient?

3. How does a flat-rate income tax differ from a progressive income tax?

4. Explain how a value-added tax and a national sales tax are taxes on consumption.

Chapter Summary

1. The way income is divided among members of society is known as the distribution of income. There are two approaches for analyzing income distribution. The functional distribution of income shows the shares of a nation's income accruing to land, labor, capital, and entrepreneurship as rent, wages, interest, and profits. The personal distribution of income shows the share of income received by poor, middle-income, and wealthy families.

2. Household income flows into consumption expenditures, taxes, and savings. The United States is a service-oriented economy with over half of household consumption expenditures currently used for services.

3. A business firm can be organized in one of three ways: as a sole proprietorship, a partnership, or a corporation. Although sole proprietorships are numerically dominant in the United States, corporations account for the largest share of total business sales.

4. Government expenditures include federal, state, and local government purchases of goods and services and also transfer payments. Transfer payments have been the main source of the increasing size of government in the past four decades.

5. Social Security is the largest retirement and disability program in the United States. It is a pay-as-you-go system financed by payroll taxes levied on employees and their employers. Social Security is mandatory for most workers, who must belong whether they like it or not. Social Security's financial problems largely stem from liberal benefit increases and a declining number of workers paying Social Security taxes compared to an increasing number of beneficiaries.

6. For the U.S. government, the personal income tax is the major source of revenue; income transfer programs—such as Social Security and Medicare—are the major expenditure. State and local governments rely primarily on sales taxes, excise taxes, and property taxes as revenue raisers. Education is their major expenditure.

7. The U.S. tax system is founded upon the benefits-received and ability-to-pay principles. Taxes fit into one of three types of systems: proportional taxation, progressive taxation, and regressive taxation. The federal tax system is somewhat progressive; state and local tax systems tend to be regressive.

8. Tax loopholes—including exemptions, deductions, and credits—decrease the progressivity of the federal income tax. Critics of the federal income tax contend that it favors the rich, who can shelter much of their income by using tax loopholes. Proposed reforms of the federal tax system include the flat-rate income tax, the value-added tax, and the national sales tax.

Key Terms and Concepts

mixed economy (205)

distribution of income (205)

functional distribution of income (205)

personal distribution of income (205)

human capital (207)

sole proprietorship (208)

partnership (208)

corporation (209)

government expenditures (210)

government purchases (210)

transfer payments (210)

Social Security (211)

Medicare (211)

cost-of-living adjustment (COLA) (211)

benefits-received principle (216)

ability-to-pay principle (217)

average tax rate (217)

marginal tax rate (217)

taxable income (219)

flat-rate income tax (222)

value-added tax (VAT) (224)

national sales tax (224)

Self-Test: Multiple-Choice Questions

1. The U.S. Social Security system

   a. is essentially a pay-as-you-go system financed out of payroll taxes.
   b. is a welfare system financed out of personal income taxes.
   c. requires all workers to have personal investment accounts with the system.
   d. earns a profit that is turned over to state and local governments.

2. The functional distribution of income shows how

   a. income is divided up among land, labor, capital, and entrepreneurship.
   b. income is divided up among the low-, middle-, and high-income groups in society.

   c. households divide their income among consumption, saving, and taxes.

   d. households divide their income among durable goods, nondurable goods, and services.

3. The Social Security tax is

   a. proportional at low incomes and progressive at high incomes.

   b. proportional at low incomes and regressive at high incomes.

   c. regressive at low incomes and progressive at high incomes.

   d. progressive at low incomes and regressive at high incomes.

4. For a value-added tax, all of the following are true *except* it is

   a. essentially a national sales tax on consumer goods and services.

   b. used more widely in the United States than in Europe.

   c. collected at various stages of production of goods and services.

   d. a tax on consumption rather than a tax on saving.

5. All of the following taxes tend to be regressive *except*

   a. sales taxes of state governments.

   b. excise taxes of state governments.

   c. property taxes of local governments.

   d. income tax of the federal government.

6. The Personal Responsibility and Work Opportunity Reconciliation Act of 1996

   a. terminated all federal welfare assistance to the needy.

   b. reduced federal payments by 10 percent to all recipients.

   c. limited the time that households can be on welfare.

   d. increased welfare payments to immigrants of the United States.

7. In its purest form, a _____ would eliminate all exemptions, deductions, and credits so that a person's gross income would equal taxable income.

   a. value-added tax

   b. consumption tax

   c. flat-rate tax

   d. regressive income tax

8. The ability-to-pay principle is most evident in

   a. tolls used to finance the construction and operation of a bridge.

   b. taxes on airline tickets that are used to finance airport security.

   c. gasoline taxes used to finance the construction and maintenance of roads.

   d. the progressive income tax of the federal government.

9. The largest source of revenue of the federal government is the

   a. corporate income tax.

   b. Social Security tax.

   c. sales tax.

   d. personal income tax.

10. For state and local governments, the largest sources of revenue are

   a. sales taxes and property taxes, respectively.

   b. excise taxes and license fees, respectively.

   c. personal income taxes and property taxes, respectively.

   d. corporate income taxes and excise taxes, respectively.

Answers to Multiple-Choice Questions

1. a   2. a   3. b   4. b   5. d   6. c   7. c   8. d   9. d   10. a

Study Questions and Problems

1. Compare the advantages and disadvantages of a sole proprietorship, a partnership, and a corporation.

2. Distinguish between the benefits-received principle of taxation and the ability-to-pay principle of taxation. Which principle is more evident in the U.S. tax system?

3. Describe the progressivity, proportionality, or regressivity of the major taxes of the federal government and also of state and local governments.

4. The U.S. tax system alone is more progressive than the U.S. system of taxes and transfer payments combined. Do you agree with this statement?

5. Table 9.10 gives four levels of taxable income and the taxes to be paid at each of the income levels.

   a. Calculate the average tax rate and the marginal tax rate at each level of taxable income.
   b. Indicate whether the tax is progressive, proportional, or regressive.

Table 9.10	Hypothetical Tax Data		
Total Taxable Income	Total Taxes Paid	Average Tax Rate (%)	Marginal Tax Rate (%)
$10,000	$3,500	35	—
20,000	6,000	30	25
30,000	7,500	25	15
40,000	8,000	20	5

Table 9.11	Hypothetical Sales Tax Data		
Income	Consumption Expenditures	Sales Tax Paid	Average Tax Rate (%)
$10,000	$10,000	$ 800	8
11,000	10,800	864	7.9
12,000	11,600	928	7.7
13,000	12,400	992	7.6

they do

6. Assume the state of California levies an 8-percent sales tax on all consumption expenditures. Consumption expenditures for four income levels are illustrated in Table 9.11.

   a. Calculate the sales tax paid at the four income levels.
   b. Calculate the average tax rate at these incomes.
   c. If income were used as the tax base, the sales tax would be classified as a _____ tax.

discuss

7. Do the proposed flat-rate income tax, value-added tax, or national sales tax lead to a more fair and efficient tax system than the current federal income tax?

also :   how is it unfair if all pay 20% tax —

shald rich be punished ?

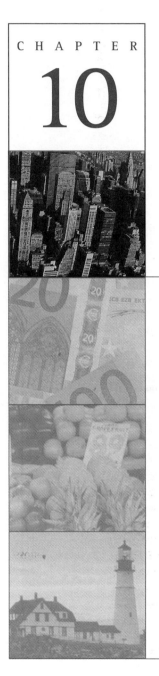

Gross Domestic Product and Economic Growth

Chapter objectives

After reading this chapter, you should be able to:

1. Discuss the nature of gross domestic product and how it is calculated.

2. Distinguish between nominal gross domestic product and real gross domestic product.

3. Describe the factors that underlie a nation's rate of economic growth in the long run.

4. Discuss the possible policies that government might enact to speed up economic growth.

5. Distinguish between traditional growth theory and new growth theory.

economics IN CONTEXT

Has the growth in technological innovation affected the economy as a whole? Yes, by increasing productivity for the economy. Labor productivity in manufacturing, retail and wholesale trade, finance, business services, and other sectors of the economy has risen due to technological advances, improving organizational practices, and increased global competition. As we have learned, increasing efficiency allows the economy to produce more output with a given amount of resources.

The changes witnessed in the steel industry exemplify these changes in production processes and management practices. The fundamental processes of steelmaking remain much as they always were: melting raw material, forming it into an intermediate product, and shaping and treating that product into final goods. But a number of technological advances, many incorporating computer technology to measure, monitor, and control these processes, have affected almost every step in steel production.

As recently as 1990, steelmaking involved extensive manual control and setup and relied heavily on operators' experience, observation, and intuition in determining how to control the process. Computer processing of data from sensors, using innovative software, has improved the ability to control the process, allowing faster, more efficient operation.

For example, the availability of computing power to quickly process data has enabled steelmakers to reduce both energy consumption and wear and tear on the equipment. The setup to cast the molten steel into an intermediate product has changed from a process

in which several operators would "walk the line," setting the controls for every motor and pump, to one in which a single operator uses an automatic control system that synchronizes and sets the equipment. The rolling process now incorporates sensors that constantly inspect for deviations from the desired shape, allowing operators to make corrections before material is wasted. Operators can remotely control the speed and clearance of the rolls using computer-controlled motors to correct problems as they develop.

The result of this computer integration has been a significant improvement in steelmaking performance. Together with other technological changes, such as larger furnaces and improvements in casting practices, and the closing of older, inefficient plants, the new technologies have also contributed to higher product quality and productivity. Steelmakers today use less than four worker-hours to produce a ton of steel, down from six worker-hours in 1990. The best-performing mills have achieved results of less than one worker-hour per ton.

In this chapter, we will learn how productivity influences the performance of not only a particular industry, but also the economy as a whole. Just as a doctor gives a physical exam to determine how well a patient is, so do economists use statistics to get a quantitative measure of the economy's performance. This chapter introduces the broadest measure of the total output of an economy—that is, the gross domestic product. The chapter also discusses the factors that determine the long-run growth rate of an economy.

MEASURING AN ECONOMY'S OUTPUT

The output of an economy includes millions of different goods. We could tabulate how much of each product the economy produced in a given year: 3,600,224 houses; 2,436,789 radios; 40,987,345 apples; and so forth. Although such data may be useful for some purposes, they do not accurately measure the economy's output. Suppose next year the output of houses falls by 4 percent, the output of radios falls by 8 percent, and the output of apples rises by 2 percent. Has total output increased or decreased? By how much?

We need a single statistic to measure the output of an economy. But how do we add up the houses, radios, apples, and millions of other goods produced in the economy? To make such a calculation, we compute what is known as gross domestic product, or GDP.

GROSS DOMESTIC PRODUCT

What exactly is GDP? GDP is the *market value of all final goods and services produced within a country in a given year*. All of the words in this definition are important.

- **"GDP is the market value"**
  You have likely heard the expression, "You can't compare apples and oranges." However, GDP makes such a comparison. GDP combines the different types of goods and services into a single measure of economic activity. To do this, it uses the total "market value" of the economy's output. Total market value means that we take the quantity of goods produced, multiply them by their respective prices, and add up the totals. For example, if an economy produced 200 apples at $0.20 an apple and 400 oranges at $0.15 an orange, the market value of these goods would be calculated as follows:

$$(200 \times \$0.20) + (400 \times \$0.15) = \$100$$

  Adding the market value of all goods and services gives the total market value, or GDP. The reason we multiply the quantity of goods times their respective prices is that we cannot simply add the number of apples and the number of oranges. Using prices permits us to express everything in a common standard of value, in this case, dollars.

- **"of all final goods and services"**
  GDP is a comprehensive measure of a nation's output. It measures the market value of not only apples and oranges but many other goods, such as jetliners, calculators, and clothing, as well. GDP also includes intangible services, such as banking, engineering, medical, and legal. When you purchase a video of your favorite rock concert, you are purchasing a good, and the purchase is part of GDP. When you go to a football game, you are buying a service, and the ticket price is also part of GDP.

  Note that only "final" goods and services are included in GDP. Many goods and services are purchased for use as inputs in producing other goods. McDonald's buys ground beef to make Big Macs. If we counted the value of the ground beef and the value of the Big Mac, we would be counting the ground beef twice and thus overstating the value of the production. Final goods therefore are finished goods and services produced for the ultimate consumer.

- **"produced"**
  GDP measures the current production of an economy. Many financial transactions take place, but they do not directly generate current output, and so they must be excluded from GDP. These include transfer payments such as welfare payments and Social Security payments that government makes to individuals. They also include a college student's yearly subsidy from his family to finance his college education. Moreover, purchases and sales of stocks and bonds are not part of GDP because they do not represent the production of new goods and services.

- **"within a country"**
  GDP includes the value of production within the boundaries of a country. When a Mexican citizen works temporarily in the United States, her production is part of U.S. GDP. When General Motors owns an assembly plant in Canada, the autos produced at that plant are part of Canada's GDP rather than U.S. GDP.

- **"in a given year"**

  Because GDP is expressed as a rate of current production, goods produced in previous years would not be included in this year's GDP. If you sell your 1975 Chevy Nova to a relative, this transaction is not included in this year's GDP because no current production is occurring.

CHECK POINT

1. How do economists define gross domestic product (GDP)?

2. What is the significance of the following definitional characteristics of GDP?

a. Market value.
b. Final goods and services.
c. Produced within a country.
d. In a given year.

THE COMPONENTS OF GDP

The GDP of an economy can be reached by totaling the expenditures on goods and services produced during the current year. National income accountants refer to this method of calculating GDP as the **expenditure approach**. When derived by the expenditure approach, the four components of GDP are: (1) personal consumption expenditures, (2) gross private domestic investment, (3) government purchases of goods and services, and (4) net exports to foreigners.[1] Table 10.1 shows the components of GDP for the United States in 2004. Let us examine each of these components.

Personal consumption expenditures (C) are purchases of final goods and services by households and individuals. Some items are durable goods, such as refrigerators, that last for a number of years. Nondurable goods are items that consumers use soon after purchase, such as gasoline and food. Services include intangible items, such as services of mechanics and engineers. For the United States, personal consumption expenditures typically account for two-thirds or more of GDP.

Gross private domestic investment (I), commonly known as gross investment, consists of all private-sector spending for investment. Gross investment includes the purchase of capital equipment and structures, such as an IBM assembly plant, as well as purchases of new homes by households, a type of capital good. Moreover, gross investment includes changes in business inventories during the year. When GM's automobile inventories increase from one year to the next, they are added to investment. Increases in business inventories represent goods that have been produced during the current year but have not been sold to buyers in the market. Conversely, decreases in business inventories during the year are counted as negative investment.

Government purchases of goods and services (G) include spending on final output by federal, state, and local governments. Each tank, filing cabinet, calculator, and desk purchased by government is part of the government purchases portion of GDP. Also included is the entire payroll of all governments, representing the purchases of labor services by government. Recall that government purchases exclude transfer payments, such as welfare payments and Social Security payments, because they do not represent newly produced goods.

---

[1] GDP can also be reached by the *income approach*. This approach calculates GDP by adding together the income payments to the resource suppliers and the other costs of producing those goods and services.

Table 10.1	Gross Domestic Product, 2004 (billions of dollars)		
	Component	Amount	Percent of Total
1	Personal consumption expenditures:	$ 8,231.1	70%
	Durable goods	995.6	
	Nondurable goods	2,376.5	
	Services	4,859.0	
2	Gross private domestic investment:	$ 1,922.4	16
	Fixed investment (plant, equipment)	1,879.3	
	Business inventories	43.1	
3	Government purchases of goods and services:	$ 2,183.8	19
	Federal	810.0	
	State and local	1,373.8	
4	Net exports of goods and services:	$ (609.3)	(5)
	Exports	1,170.3	
	Imports	(1,779.6)	
	Gross domestic product	$11,728.0	100%

Source: From *Economic Report of the President*, 2005, pp. 208–209.

Net exports $(X - M)$ comprise the last component of GDP. Sales of a country's goods and services to foreigners during a particular time period represent its exports (X). For the United States, exports include the sale of an IBM computer to a Mexican buyer or the purchase of a ticket to Disneyland by a tourist from Germany. Purchases of foreign-produced goods and services by a country's residents constitute its imports (M). U.S. imports include the purchase of an Airbus jetliner by United Airlines, or a stay in a Toronto motel by the New York Yankees baseball team. Subtracting imports from exports yields net exports.

As shown in Table 10.1, in 2004, foreign buyers purchased $1,170.3 billion of goods and services from the United States. That same year, Americans purchased $1,779.6 billion of goods and services from foreign countries. The difference between these two figures, −$609.3 billion, represents the net exports of the United States in 2004. Net exports were *negative* because imports exceeded exports. Conversely, net exports would be positive if exports exceed imports. In the past three decades, U.S. net exports have consistently been negative.

A Formula for GDP

GDP is the sum of purchases by the four sectors of the economy. Therefore, we can write the following equation for GDP:

$$GDP = C + I + G + (X - M)$$

Applying this formula for the year 2004, the U.S. GDP equals $11,728.0 billion.

$$\$11,728.0 = \$8,231.1 + \$1,922.4 + \$2,183.8 - \$609.3$$

This equation is a key element in analyzing macroeconomic problems and formulating macroeconomic policy. When economists analyze the economy at large, they apply this equation to predict the behavior of the major sectors of the economy: households, business, government, and foreign commerce.

WHAT GDP DOES NOT MEASURE

GDP is our best single measure of the value of output produced by an economy. Yet, it is not a perfect measure. You need to be aware of several flaws in the construction of GDP. First, GDP ignores transactions that do not take place in organized markets. If you grow your own vegetables, repair your car, paint your house, clean your apartment, or perform similar productive household activities, your labor services add nothing to GDP, because no market transaction is involved. Such nonmarket productive activities are sizable—10 percent of total GDP, or more.

GDP also ignores the underground economy in which unreported barter and cash transactions take place outside recorded market channels. For example, owners of flea markets may make "under the table" cash transactions with their customers. The underground economy also includes transactions involving illegal goods and services, such as prostitution, gambling, and drugs. These illegal goods and services are final products that are not part of GDP. Estimates of the value of the transactions that take place in the underground economy are as high as one-third of GDP.

GDP does not value changes in the environment that arise through the production of output. Pollution and other aspects of industrial activity impose costs on society. However, these costs are not subtracted from the market value of final goods when GDP is calculated. For example, suppose a chemical firm produces $1 million worth of output but pollutes the water and decreases its value by $2 million. Rather than indicating a loss to society, GDP will show a $1 million increase.

GDP excludes leisure, a good that is valuable to each of us. Suppose that Canada achieves a $25,000 per-person GDP, with an average workweek of 35 hours. Germany might achieve the identical per-person GDP with a 40-hour workweek. With regard to economic well-being, Canada would be better off, because it generates additional leisure while producing the same output per person. However, GDP does not account for this fact.

Another problem of using GDP as a measure of well-being is that it does not show how much output is available per person. For example, suppose that Nigeria and Kuwait have the same GDP, say, $40 billion. Kuwait has a population of 2 million people, and Nigeria has a population of 124 million people. This suggests that people in Kuwait will have more than 60 times as many goods per person. In Kuwait, the $40 billion GDP must be divided among 2 million people, resulting in $20,000 worth of GDP per person ($40 billion/ 2 million = $20,000). In Nigeria, however, there would be just $323 worth of GDP per person ($40 billion/124 million = $323). The people in Kuwait, on average, would be better off than the people in Nigeria, even though the total value of GDP is the same for both nations.

The distribution of goods among different people in a nation also poses a problem for GDP. If most of a nation's GDP is consumed by a very small fraction of the people, there will be few rich people and many poor people. If the GDP of a nation is more evenly distributed, however, the number of poor people will be smaller and a larger middle class will appear. GDP is blind as to whether a small fraction of the citizenry consumes most of the nation's GDP or consumption is evenly divided.

Finally, GDP does not reflect the quality and kinds of goods that make up a nation's output. Today, new cars are safer and more fuel efficient than new automobiles of 30 years ago. Dental services are usually less annoying than they were 20 years ago. Moreover, the efficiency of the workplace has been improved by new products, such as personal computers, scanners, fax machines, and the Internet. In short, GDP is a quantitative, rather than a qualitative, indicator of the output of goods and services.

In spite of these limitations, GDP is a reasonable estimate of the rate of output in the economy. GDP was never intended to be a complete measure of economic well-being or happiness of a nation's residents.

REAL GDP VERSUS NOMINAL GDP

We often want to compare GDP figures from year to year. Many people think that we are economically better off if GDP increases from one year to the next. However, we must exercise caution when making such a comparison.

So far, we have expressed GDP figures in terms of the prices existing in the year in which the goods and services were produced. Such an expression gives what is known as nominal GDP, or current-dollar GDP. To make comparisons over time when prices are changing, we must adjust nominal GDP so that it reflects only changes in output and not changes in prices. Real GDP, or constant-dollar GDP, is nominal GDP adjusted to eliminate changes in prices. It measures actual (real) production and shows how actual production, rather than the prices of what is produced, has changed. Real GDP is thus superior to nominal GDP for assessing the performance of the economy, especially rates of economic growth.

Suppose, for example, that in 2003 a computer cost $3,000. The identical computer in 2004 cost $3,200. When the computer was counted in GDP in 2004, each computer added $200 more to GDP than in 2003. Even if the same number of computers were sold in 2004, GDP would have increased in 2004. The actual amount of goods available in the economy would not have increased, but the dollar value would have risen. The increase in the GDP would thus be the result of a rise in prices rather than an increase in output. When using GDP to assess growth, we must realize that part of the growth may be the result of rising prices.

In order to convert nominal GDP to real GDP, it is necessary to have a measure of price changes over the years. Economists use a price index to adjust GDP figures so that the figures only show changes in actual output. The broadest price index to calculate real GDP is called the GDP deflator.[2] It equals the ratio of the cost of buying all final goods and services in the current year to the cost of buying the identical goods at base-year prices. The GDP deflator is a weighted average of the prices of all final goods and services produced in the economy: consumer goods, business investment, government purchases of goods and services, and net exports. It is a weighted average because the various goods and services are not of equal importance. In the base year, the GDP deflator has a value of 100. Currently, the base year for the GDP deflator is 2000.

Now let's calculate real GDP, the GDP adjusted for price changes. To do so, we value the current-year output at the base-year prices. Thus, we divide the nominal GDP for a given year by the GDP deflator for that year, and then multiply that answer by 100.

$$\text{Real GDP for a given year} = \frac{\text{Nominal GDP for a given year}}{\text{GDP deflator for that year}} \times 100$$

Table 10.2 shows the nominal GDP, real GDP, and the GDP deflator for the United States during the 1990–2004 period. Let us first calculate real GDP in 2000, the base year.

---

[2] In more technical jargon, the GDP deflator is known as the GDP chain price index. This index is a moving average of a price level's "deflator" index calculated by a complex chain-weighted geometric series.

Table 10.2	Nominal GDP, Real GDP, and GDP Deflator, 1990–2004		
Year	Nominal GDP (billions)	Real GDP (billions)	GDP Deflator (2000 = 100)*
1990	$ 5,803.1	$ 7,112.5	81.6
1992	6,337.7	7,336.6	86.4
1994	7,072.2	7,835.5	90.3
1996	7,816.9	8,328.9	93.9
1998	8,747.0	9,066.9	96.5
2000	9,817.0	9,817.0	100.0
2002	10,487.0	10,074.8	104.1
2004	$11,728.0	$10,837.2	108.2

*The amounts in this column have been rounded to the nearest tenth.

Source: From *Economic Report of the President*, 2005, pp. 208, 210.

To calculate real GDP, we divide nominal GDP in 2000 ($9,817.0 billion) by the GDP deflator in 2000 (100.0), and multiply that answer by 100, as follows:

$$\text{Real GDP} = \frac{\$9,817.0 \text{ billion}}{100.0} \times 100 = \$9,817.0 \text{ billion}$$

Real GDP in 2000 was $9,817.0 billion, the same as nominal GDP in that year. In the base year, real GDP will always equal nominal GDP.

Now we will calculate real GDP in 2004. To compute real GDP, we divide nominal GDP in 2004 ($11,728.0 billion) by the GDP deflator in 2004 (108.2), and multiply that answer by 100, as follows:

$$\text{Real GDP} = \frac{\$11,728.0 \text{ billion}}{108.2} \times 100 = \$10,837.2 \text{ billion}$$

From 2000 to 2004, nominal GDP increased from $9,817.0 billion to $11,728.0 billion. However, the GDP deflator increased from 100.0 to 108.2 over this period, which suggests an 8.2-percent increase in prices. To calculate real GDP in 2004, we must thus subtract the increase in prices that occurred from 2000 to 2004. As a result, real GDP increased from $9,817.0 billion to only $10,837.2 billion over this period. This example clearly illustrates the usefulness of real GDP as a measure of economic growth. It is apparent that real GDP grew from 2000 to 2004, but not as much as was suggested by the growth in nominal GDP.

CHECK POINT

1. How do economists calculate GDP according to the expenditure approach?

2. What are the major weaknesses of GDP as an indicator of economic well-being?

3. Distinguish between nominal GDP and real GDP. Which measure of GDP is superior for assessing the performance of the economy, especially rates of economic growth?

LONG-RUN ECONOMIC GROWTH

In the past 25 years, we have seen the development of many new products, such as personal computers, cellular phones, and fax machines. Indeed, new products are a reflection of our economic progress. Over time, we produce not only more goods and services, but new and better goods and services as well. As a result, our material standard of living increases.

A nation realizes economic growth when it increases its full production level of output over time. Recall from Chapter 1 that economic growth can be expressed in terms of the production possibilities model. With economic growth, a nation's production possibilities curve shifts outward, or to the right. Economic growth is a *long-run* objective that can be achieved over a period of time.

Although economic growth suggests an increase in full production output over time, a more accurate definition is a rise in full production output *per person* over time. Suppose that output rises by 10 percent over time, but population grows at 12 percent over time. As a result, output per person would decrease. Even with more goods and services available, the average person would be worse off.

Rate of Economic Growth

Let us now calculate the rate of growth in the economy. The rate of economic growth is the percentage change in the level of economic activity from one year to the next. Typically, analysts look at the rate of growth in an economy's real GDP.

The rate of economic growth is simply the change in real GDP between two periods divided by real GDP in the first period. To illustrate, suppose that in year 1 real GDP is $1,000 and in year 2 real GDP is $1,100. Hence, the rate of growth between years 1 and 2 would be:

$$\text{Rate of growth} = \frac{\text{Year 2 real GDP} - \text{Year 1 real GDP}}{\text{Year 1 real GDP}}$$

$$= \frac{\$1,100 - \$1,000}{\$1,000}$$

$$= 0.1$$

Thus, the rate of growth for the economy between years 1 and 2 would be 10 percent.

A useful rule of thumb can help us appreciate the power of growth rates. Suppose that you knew the constant rate of growth of real GDP, but you wanted to know the number of years it takes the level of real GDP to double. The answer is given by the rule of 70: *or 72*

$$\text{Years to double} = \frac{70}{\text{Percentage growth rate}}$$

As an example, suppose that real GDP grew at 3 percent a year. Thus, it would take about 23 years for the real GDP to double (70/3 = 23 1/3).

How fast can the U.S. economy grow on a sustainable basis? Most mainstream analysts believe that real GDP can grow about 2.5 percent per year. However, some analysts have asserted that much more rapid growth, possibly as fast as 5 percent per year, may be sustainable. The answer to this question has profound implications for the future well-being of the American people. If the mainstream view is correct, real output will double only every 28 years or so according to the rule of 70. But if the alternative view is correct, real output could double every 14 years. Figure 10.1 shows how long it took for several nations to double their output beginning in 1960.

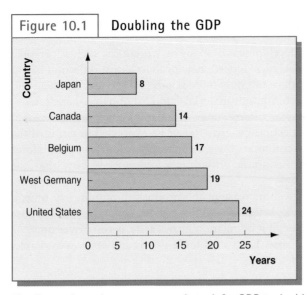

Figure 10.1 Doubling the GDP

The figure shows how many years it took for GDP to double, starting in 1960, for selected nations.

Source: From Angus Madison, *Dynamic Forces in Capitalist Development* (New York: Oxford University Press, 1991).

why shorter for them?

WHAT DETERMINES ECONOMIC GROWTH?

The output level of an economy is determined by the level of inputs (land, labor, capital, and entrepreneurship) used and the production methods used to convert the inputs into goods and services. Output can only be increased through additional inputs or more efficient use of the available inputs. How fast we can increase inputs is limited, however: Land is essentially fixed. Population growth and participation rates determine the size of the labor force.

In less-developed economies such as Mexico or China, a large fraction of inputs are under-utilized and the level of capital is usually low. These economies can grow rapidly by increasing inputs and/or increasing production efficiency—for example, by moving toward state-of-the-art technology and raising the level of education. A developed economy, like the United States or Germany, which is starting from a higher level of input use and efficiency has more difficulty sustaining high rates of economic growth. Innovation and improvements in existing technology are the keys to increased growth rates.

In the final analysis, the keys to long-run economic growth are the incentives that induce individuals to work and firms to invest in production technology, within the limits imposed by demographics and the rate of technological advances. Let us consider the major determinants of economic growth.

*examples
finding oil*

Natural Resources

The first pillar of economic growth is natural resources, which are gifts of nature that are usable in the production process. Resources such as mineral deposits, land, forests, and rivers come under this classification. Some natural resources, such as oil, are nonrenew-able. Because it takes nature thousands of years to produce oil, there is a limited supply. When a barrel of oil is extracted from a well, it is impossible to produce more. Other natural resources, such as a forest, are renewable. When we cut down a tree, we can replace it by planting a seedling in the ground to be harvested in the years ahead.

international
ECONOMICS IN ACTION

Why Are Some Countries Rich and Others Poor?

As seen in Table 10.3, there are great discrepancies in living standards throughout the world. If we ask a simple question such as "Why are some economies rich and others poor?" we get a simple answer: Rich economies have greater resources per capita—they have more human capital (skills) and physical capital (machinery) and better technology. But this answer only begs another question: "Why do some economies have high levels of capital and technology, while others do not?"

It is a nation's choice of institutions that greatly impacts wealth and development. What separates economic "haves" from "have-nots" is whether an economy's institutions, especially its public institutions, facilitate or confiscate the production of wealth.

What elements must a government put in place to allow an economy to take full advantage of possible gains from trade? Economists note that a well-functioning economy requires a foundation of enforceable property rights, generally accepted accounting principles, sound financial institutions, a stable currency, and the like.

Throughout the world, there are great disparities in these institutions, which tends to promote differences in living

Table 10.3	Comparisons of Living Standards Throughout the World
Country	Gross National Income per Person, 2003*
United States	$37,500
Switzerland	32,030
Canada	29,740
Japan	28,620
Mexico	8,950
Russia	8,920
Togo	1,500
Zambia	850
Ethiopia	710
Sierra Leone	530

*Measured at purchasing power parity.

Source: From The World Bank, *World Development Indicators Database*, September 2004, available at http://www.worldbank.org/data/. Scroll to "Quick reference tables."

Haiti - vs - D.R.

standards. A key question is how a government can create the sort of environment in which people find it worthwhile to accumulate human and physical capital and carry out technological development, thus creating economic prosperity.

Although countries rely on natural resources as productive inputs, a domestic supply of natural resources is not crucial for an economy to produce goods and services. For example, Japan is a highly productive and wealthy nation, even though it has few natural resources. International trade allows Japan to be a productive nation. Japan imports natural resources, such as iron ore and oil, and transforms them into steel, automobiles, electronics, and other manufactured goods to be exported to nations abundant in natural resources.

You may wonder if natural resources are a limit to growth. If the world has a fixed supply of nonrenewable resources, how can production, population, and standards of living continue to increase in the years ahead? Won't the supplies of resources eventually dry up, thus stopping economic growth and causing living standards to decrease?

Although such arguments are appealing, most economists are optimistic concerning the capacity of the economy to grow. They contend that technological progress often provides alternatives to the scarcity of resources. Comparing our current economy to the one of years ago, we see many ways in which resources are better utilized. More productive oil rigs have increased the amount of oil harvested from a well. Modern automobiles have more efficient engines that allow them to run on less gasoline. New houses are better insulated and require less energy to cool or heat them. Recycling oil, aluminum, tin, plastic, glass, cardboard, and paper permits conservation of resources. Technological progress has also allowed us to substitute abundant resources for scarce resources. For example, plastic has replaced tin as an input used to manufacture food containers, and telephone calls often travel over fiber-optic cables that are made from sand. In short, technological progress has contributed to a more efficient use of crucial resources.

Physical Capital

The second pillar of economic growth is increases in physical capital, which enable workers to produce more goods and services. No matter how educated workers are, they still need computers, machinery, and other equipment to produce goods and services. Capital investment is thus a key determinant of both productivity and growth. For example, when workers build a house, they use saws, hammers, electric drills, and other tools. Additional investment provides workers with more and better tools.

Productivity increases through capital investment have often involved exploiting economies of large-scale production. Industries such as electricity generation, food processing, and beverages are cases in point. In the beverage industry, for example, high-speed canning lines have raised productivity, but their contribution has been made possible in part by the development of large markets. To operate efficiently, these lines must produce nearly 500 million cans per year!

Of course, investment is not a free gift of nature; an opportunity cost is involved. When additional resources are used to produce equipment and manufacturing plants, fewer resources are available for the production of current-consumption goods such as hamburgers. However, those who save and invest will be able to produce more in the future.

Besides the economy's private sector, government is also a source of physical capital for the economy. Historically, investment in public capital, such as roads, bridges, airports, and utilities, has made a significant contribution to the nation's productivity growth. Such public capital is called infrastructure.

Human Capital

A third pillar of economic growth is improvements in human capital: the knowledge, experience, and skills of the workforce. As the economy has changed, the demands imposed on the brainpower of the American workforce have increased enormously. Increases in the hourly output of the average worker can reflect an improvement in the characteristics that allow workers to accomplish the same tasks in less time, to adapt to changing situations with greater flexibility, and to become engineers of change themselves.

The importance of human capital can be seen in shipbuilding that took place during World War II. Between 1941 and 1944, U.S. shipyards produced more than 2,500 units of a cargo ship, known as the *Liberty Ship*, to a standardized design. In 1941, it required 1.2 million labor-hours to construct a ship. By 1943, it required only 500,000. Thousands of workers learned from experience and attained human capital that more than doubled their productivity in two years.

Providing individuals with a formal education is one way to increase their human capital, thus contributing to aggregate productivity growth. Estimates suggest that investment in U.S. education boosted U.S. labor productivity about 0.3 percentage points per year, on average, between 1963 and 1995. Another way of increasing human capital is training workers on the job. Research has found that companies offering more training enjoy higher rates of productivity growth.

| Table 10.4 | Annual Rates of Growth in U.S. Labor Productivity and Real Compensation per Hour in the Business Sector, 1960–2004 | |

Year	Labor Productivity Growth Rate	Real Compensation per Hour Growth Rate
1960s (ave.)	3.2%	2.9%
1970s (ave.)	1.8	1.3
1980s (ave.)	1.2	0.2
1990s (ave)	1.9	1.2
2000–2004 (ave.)	3.5	1.8

Source: From *Economic Report of the President*, 2005, p. 270.

The returns from receiving an education, as measured by the difference in incomes between college and high school graduates, have risen sharply in the last 20 years. Today, the average college graduate can expect to earn between 5 and 15 percent more than the average high school graduate. Much of this difference probably reflects the increasing importance of computer skills in the workplace. Moreover, the payoff to formal training, including apprenticeships, can be quite substantial: A year of training typically provides returns of a similar magnitude to those offered by a year of formal schooling. Perhaps it would be worthwhile if you obtained a summer internship with a local employer.

Productivity

A fourth pillar of growth is greater **productivity**. Economists think of productivity as a ratio that measures the quantity of output produced relative to the amount of work required to produce it. Mathematically, it appears as follows:

$$\text{Productivity} = \frac{\text{Total output}}{\text{Hours worked}}$$

An increase in productivity occurs when total output increases faster than the amount of work required to produce it. For example, an increase in the quantity of output with no increase in hours worked would be an increase in productivity.[3]

Rearranging the terms can help illustrate the significance of productivity for economic growth as follows:

$$\text{Total output} = \text{Productivity} \times \text{Hours worked}$$

This shows that total output depends on both work and productivity. Any increase in total output must thus come about as the result of increases in either hours worked or productivity.

As seen in Table 10.4, U.S. productivity growth has been erratic. During the 1960s, productivity grew by 3.2 percent per year. But during the next three decades, productivity growth fell to less than 2 percent per year only to improve at the turn of the century.

---

[3] The most popular measure of productivity for the U.S. economy is average labor productivity. Labor productivity is measured in terms of average output per hour. It is a ratio of the quantity of output to the hours of work done. The quantity of output is based on real GDP, as discussed in this chapter.

economics
IN ACTION

Productivity Gains: Working Smarter, Not Harder

Compare America today with earlier times and one fact stands out: We live better. Give most of the credit to productivity. Through it, we get more goods and services from each bit of work. Through it, we secure economic progress and earn bigger paychecks. We've taken plenty of our added productivity as material gains—more cars, bigger and better-equipped houses, sophisticated computers, etc. Also, we work less. Over the past few generations, the typical worker has gone from a 6-day workweek with little vacation to an average of 34 hours plus three weeks off. Indeed, the power of productivity has made the United States a rich nation. Consider these examples of productivity gains:

- With ATMs, electronic fund transfers, and the Internet, banks can handle more transactions using fewer tellers and support staff. Output per hour in commercial banking has doubled since 1970.

- Electronic telephone switches have taken over much of the nation's long-distance and toll-call traffic. Calls per operator rose from 17 per day in 1950 to about 2,100 today.

- At auto assembly plants, computers and robots now handle welding and many other tasks once done by hand. Although today's cars are vastly more complex, annual production per employee increased from 10 vehicles in 1950 to 14 in 2003.

- Dr Pepper/Seven Up Bottling Group Inc. grew more productive with huge machines that fill and package 800 bottles or 1,500 cans per minute, almost double the previous generation.

Day in and day out, markets encourage companies to push for greater output per hour. Do the job faster.

Reduce inputs. Improve quality. Trim a few cents off the cost of production. The relentless march of productivity comes in myriad ways, limited only by technology and human ingenuity.

To survive in a competitive market, U.S. airlines have scrambled to find ways to reduce costs and make flying more convenient for passengers facing tighter security. For Continental Airlines and other carriers, one answer was check-in kiosks that allow passengers with electronic tickets to bypass lines at the counters. Kiosks allow passengers to get boarding passes without going to ticket agents, meaning that airlines need fewer ticket agents to load their planes. Self-service check-ins cost airlines 16 cents per passenger, compared with $3.68 for ticket counter agents.

Indeed, as productivity reorganizes the economy, it changes how we use our innate skills and talents in the workplace. Each generation of inventions produces tools to take on more of the tasks once done by human beings. Americans adjust by taking jobs that put our other talents to work. Over time, our work moves up a hierarchy of human talents, focusing on new tasks that require higher-order skills, ones that machinery can't do as well. By redefining the way we work, the economy creates a new and more productive mix of technology and human talents. For example, workers once used muscle power to dig with picks and shovels. Over time, ever-larger digging and loading machines have allowed a single operator to do what once required legions of laborers.

This serves as a lesson for today's college students. Americans who want to prepare for the better jobs of the future will concentrate on developing skills that allow them to ascend the hierarchy of human talents. A college education is a window of opportunity that can help improve your productivity.

Source: Drawn from W. Michael Cox and Richard Alm, "A Better Way: Productivity and Reorganization in the American Economy," *2003 Annual Report*, Federal Reserve Bank of Dallas, pp. 3–23.

Higher rates of productivity growth permit rising real compensation for labor, as this table illustrates.

What factors contribute to changes in productivity? Clearly, technological advancement has much to do with productivity gains. During the past century, the development of power-driven machines, such as tractors; improvements in transportation, such as railroads and airlines; and the growing stock of computers have increased the productivity of workers.

Obviously, technological advancement requires invention, the discovery of a new process or product. Yet, it also encompasses innovation, the successful introduction and adoption of a new process or product. Henry Ford did not invent the automobile; instead, he was an innovator who pioneered assembly-line production techniques that allowed workers to produce more automobiles in an hour's time, resulting in falling costs for each automobile produced.

Improving the productivity of the economy is not just a matter of improving technology. How the economy is organized plays an important role in creating incentives for firms to use their capital and labor as efficiently as possible. If the market economy is to deliver on its promise of growth and prosperity, markets have to be competitive, because it is competition that motivates firms to be efficient and innovative. Firms, however, often find it easier to increase profits by reducing competition than by improving efficiency in response to competition. Monopolies and oligopolies not only can charge inefficiently high prices and restrict output, but may also have a diminished drive to innovate.

Another source of increasing productivity in the economy is reorganization resulting from international trade. As competition forces producers to seek comparative advantage in the marketplace, resources shift to their best uses, creating a more efficient deployment of labor for the economy. As the economy reorganizes to produce more, it also lowers prices relative to wages, so that our paychecks buy more. Indeed, international trade can be every bit as powerful as technology in making us productive. Trade's productivity gains provide a strong justification for open markets. Economists widely agree that enormous benefits are lost when countries bow to their producers' narrow interests and enact protectionist measures that block imports or raise their price.

Economists at Harvard University and the Federal Reserve Bank of New York have examined the sources of U.S. productivity growth during the 1990s. They analyzed three classic sources for productivity growth: capital investment, labor quality, and technological progress. They found that major gains came from technological progress. Then they broke that down and found that 44 percent of the gains from technological progress directly related to productivity gains in the information technology sector—including computers, software, and communications equipment.[4]

The Significance of Technological Innovation

We have learned how technological gains result in increased productivity. Over the long run, economic progress in advanced countries such as the United States hinges largely on technological progress. Each of the great industrial revolutions of the past was founded on innovation. The late 1800s and early 1900s, for example, witnessed the invention and general usage of electricity, the radio and the telephone, the internal combustion engine and the automobile, the factory assembly line, and the airplane. The surge of innovation in the late1900s was powered by the microprocessor, which gave rise to information technology and rapid growth in productivity.

Growth without technological advance winds up becoming sluggish. If you continue to produce the same goods even with modest improvements, the result is stagnation. Without technological breakthroughs, the strategy of improving and refining existing production methods runs into diminishing returns and eventually fizzles out. Simply put, it's the jump into a new technology, such as computers or perhaps solar power, that radically improves people's lives.

If the pace of technological advance dwindles, there will be less need for college-educated workers. Jobs will be routinized, and companies will replace expensive college-educated

---

[4] Dale Jorgenson and Keven Stiroh, *Raising the Speed Limit: U.S. Economic Growth in the Information Age*, Federal Reserve Bank of New York, May 1, 2000.

economics
IN ACTION

Intel's Microprocessor and the Computer Revolution

The computer revolution of the late 1900s is often cited as a source of economic growth. Indeed, increased computing power has raised the productivity of households, business, and government.

What spurred the computer revolution was the development of the microprocessor by Intel Corporation. A microprocessor is a tiny electronic device that serves as a computation engine. It consists of millions of transistors on a silicon chip as small as a fingernail. The microprocessor is often called a "computer on a chip."

Intel's first microprocessor was produced in 1971 for use in handheld calculators. The chip contained 2,300 transistors and was capable of executing 60,000 operations in one second. These calculators were very expensive, and few people could afford them. However, advanced manufacturing techniques soon decreased the cost of manufacturing microprocessors. The low cost, small size, and modest power requirements of microprocessors soon led to their use in hundreds of other products besides calculators. These products included microwave ovens, digital watches, telephones, sewing machines, and video games. Microprocessors also made possible the computerization of store checkout lines, bank records, gasoline pumps, medical instruments, and many other products that made the economy more productive. By the early 1980s, the microprocessor made possible the personal computer (PC).

Intel saw great potential for its technological breakthrough. If a bundle of transistors could be made to fit on a silicon chip, ways could be found to double the capacity of a single chip, and then redouble it. Intel's goal has been to double the power of memory chips about every two years. Early microprocessors could execute up to 100,000 instructions per second. Today, microprocessors carry out more than 7,000 million instructions per second.

Because Intel was the first firm to produce microprocessors, it initially could charge a premium price that resulted in large profit margins. By the1980s, however, firms such as Motorola and Texas Instruments, as well as Japanese companies, developed microprocessors. Silicon chips thus become a commodity, with many different companies manufacturing them. This resulted in lower chip prices and falling profits for Intel.

The advent of competition has forced Intel to operate as if it were a research institution. The firm ploughs much of its profit into product development to stay ahead of the competition. Like a jogger running on an accelerating treadmill, Intel has to run faster just to maintain its position, and even faster just to stay ahead of its competitors.

Source: Tim Jackson, *Inside Intel* (New York: Plume Books, 1997); Andrew Grove, *Only the Paranoid Survive* (New York: Doubleday, 1996); and T. R. Reid, *The Chip: How Two Americans Invented the Microchip and Launched a Revolution* (New York: Random House, 1985).

---

workers with cheaper workers with associate degrees or even less education. Companies will also have greater incentive to source routine jobs to foreign workers whose wages are a fraction of domestic workers. Advances in technology create better paying jobs that require analytical reasoning, imagination, creativity, and people skills.

Economists often quote an old saying: "There's no such thing as a free lunch." The notion is that you generally only receive what you pay for. However, technological gains provide an exception to the free-lunch concept, furnishing a stimulus to growth and higher living standards. Simply put, rising productivity makes it easier to pay for things like Social Security, better education, and other goods that improve our quality of life.[5]

---

[5] Michael Mandel, *Rational Exuberance* (New York: HarperCollins Publishers, Inc., 2004).

The Role of Government

Without a doubt, the future rate of increase in the economy's productive capacity will largely be determined by the decisions of the millions of individual businesses and households in the private sectors of the economy. In addition, government can help promote the growth of an economy. Let us consider government policies that might speed up economic growth.

- **Boosting productivity by increasing domestic saving.** Historically, nations that have saved the most have also invested the most, and investment has been strongly correlated with productivity. To stimulate national saving, government can reduce its spending, thus freeing resources to be used for investment. Government can also induce the private sector to save more by providing tax incentives.

- **Improving the skills of the workforce.** To help workers invest in skill acquisition, the government adopts policies to promote lifelong learning. By funding basic education and setting high standards in basic skills such as mathematics, science, and language, the government can improve the nation's production capabilities.

- **Stimulating research and development.** Increasing investment in R&D is one way to promote technological innovation and productivity growth. Since the 1800s, the U.S. government has sponsored research about agricultural practices and advised farmers how best to manage their land. The government has also supported aerospace research through NASA and the Air Force and has provided tax breaks for firms practicing R&D.

- **Working to reduce trade barriers.** Economists have found that economic growth rates are closely related to openness to trade, education, and communications infrastructure. As the graph in Figure 10.2 shows, a country can raise its growth rate by increasing its openness to

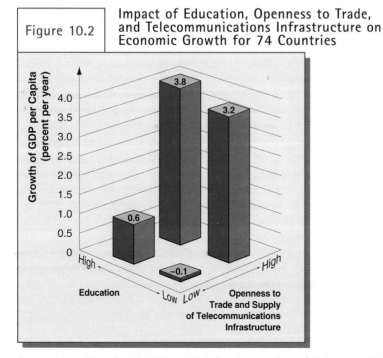

Figure 10.2   Impact of Education, Openness to Trade, and Telecommunications Infrastructure on Economic Growth for 74 Countries

would you buy only in mishawaka?

1970's car market

Source: Adapted from The World Bank, *World Development Report* (Washington, D.C., The World Bank, 1999), p. 23.

international trade, the education of its people, and its supply of telecommunications infrastructure. The impact on growth can perhaps be as much as four percentage points for a country that moves from significantly below the average to significantly above the average on all of these indicators. As a result, economists generally argue for the reduction of trade barriers and the opening of markets to global competition.

- **Improving the efficiency of regulation.** In many cases, an improvement in government regulation can simultaneously promote the more effective attainment of policy objectives and increase the efficiency of the economy. For example, a traditional approach to the problem of reducing pollution from the air might have entailed mandatory investment in costly new pollution-reduction equipment by all polluters. Instead, a system based on tradable emissions certificates (see Chapter 8) can achieve the same results while encouraging the efficient allocation of the task of reducing pollution across polluters.

CHECK POINT

1. Describe the concept of long-run economic growth. How do economists measure the rate of economic growth?

2. Of what significance is the rule of 70 for economic growth?

3. Identify the major determinants of economic growth.

4. What policies might government enact to speed up economic growth?

THEORIES OF ECONOMIC GROWTH

The traditional theory of economic growth has its origins in the writings of Adam Smith, who wrote *The Wealth of Nations* in 1776.[6] Smith saw progress in economic activity as flowing from larger markets. According to Smith, larger markets encourage individuals to specialize in different parts of the production process and coordinate their labor. In turn, specialization is the chief engine of increased productivity. It fosters productivity gains by permitting the saving of time that is commonly lost in passing from one type of work to another. Smith saw the inventive activity that improved production techniques as being a by-product of specialization, since, because a worker concentrated attention on one activity, time-saving inventions often came to mind. Of course, even in the 1700s, when Smith was writing, the activity of inventors was evident in the economy. But the flow of payments to creative work was minuscule compared with those that flowed to the labor, land, and capital that directly produced products.

Simply put, Smith's principles of economic growth emphasized two resources—labor and capital. Technology was discussed, but only in a superficial manner. Technological progress was viewed as being outside the scope of economic theory and thus something that we simply accept as a given.

---

[6] Adam Smith, *The Wealth of Nations* (New York: Modern Library, 1937).

New Growth Theory and Creative Destruction

In the early 1900s, economists began formulating a different theory of economic growth. Considering technological progress to be within the scope of economic theory, they viewed innovation and creativity as an economic activity. This perspective on economics has found its foremost advocates in a Harvard professor named Joseph Schumpeter (1942) and professor Paul Romer of Stanford University in the 1980s.[7]

Schumpeter constructed a theory of economic growth in which technological innovation was the prime source of growth in a modern economy and profits were the fuel. He argued that what is most important about a capitalist market system is precisely that it rewards change by allowing those who create new products and processes to capture some of the benefits of their creations in the form of monopoly profits. These monopoly profits provide entrepreneurs with the means to (1) fund creative activities in response to perceived opportunities, (2) override the natural conservatism of other parties who must cooperate with the new product's launch as well as the opposition of those whose markets may be harmed by the new products, and (3) widen and deepen their sales networks so that new products are quickly made known to a large number of customers. Competition, if too vigorous, would deny these rewards to creators and instead pass them on to consumers, in which case firms would have scant reason to create new products.

The drive to temporarily capture monopoly profits promotes, in Schumpeter's phrase, creative destruction, as old technologies, goods, and livelihoods are replaced by new ones. Thus, while Smith saw monopoly profits as an indication of economic inefficiency, Schumpeter saw them as evidence of valuable entrepreneurial activity in a healthy, dynamic economy. Indeed, Schumpeter's view was that new technologies and products are so valuable to consumers that governments of countries should encourage entrepreneurs by granting temporary monopolies over innovations and inventions. Thus, in contrast to Smith, Schumpeter argued that government action to prevent or dismantle monopolies might harm growth and the consumer in the long run.

Why Are the Forces Opposing Creativity So Strong?

Although technological innovation tends to provide benefits to consumers, why are the forces opposing creativity so strong? The answer is that creating, making, competing against, and buying new products are very risky endeavors. All activities are at risk in an environment of creative destruction.

One factor limiting creativity is that it puts existing products at risk. An example is the personal computer, whose power and speed have been rising at rapid rates for over 20 years. In the competition to supply components of the personal computer, such as modems or memory, any firm that wants to play the game has to invest in creating new, faster, and smaller versions of the component. To earn profits to justify this investment and its uncertainties, the resulting innovation must leapfrog the competition by creating a new generation. The first firm to market with the new generation can often grab the bulk of the entire market and, with it, almost all the profits to be had. Of course, this typically wipes out the profitability of the previous generation and sets the stage for the next leapfrogger, who will then destroy the profits of the current leader.

Also, being creative is inherently risky. You don't know what will work until you try it. Although successful new products may earn immense returns, others inevitably fail and create losses for their creators and supporters. An example of a product that was expected

---

[7] Joseph Schumpeter, *Capitalism, Socialism, and Democracy* (New York: Harper, 1942); and Paul Romer, "Economic Growth," *The Fortune Encyclopedia*, ed., David R. Henderson (New York: Warner Books, 1993).

to fare well in the marketplace, but did not, was Betamax, which looked like a technology winner to most experts when videocassette recorders were invented in the late 1970s. Beta was competing with VHS, and insiders knew that Sony had the opportunity to develop either Beta or VHS and had chosen Beta as the superior technology. But the corporations that developed VHS were able to more rapidly lengthen videocassette playback times. Consumers who did adopt Beta eventually found that they had to switch to VHS, as Sony was forced to abandon the system by the greater availability of prerecorded videocassettes on VHS. Simply put, when consumers do choose a system, the system's rivals may suffer irreversible setbacks, as the Beta system did. Moreover, VHS was being replaced by DVD systems by 2000.

IS ECONOMIC GROWTH DESIRABLE?

Our analysis of economic growth in this chapter makes it appear to be beneficial. Is it?

The main justification for economic growth is that it allows a nation to realize rising material abundance and increased standards of living. Expanding output and rising incomes allow households to purchase additional medical care, education, recreation and travel, and higher-quality consumer goods. Growth is also an avenue for supporting more of the arts, including theater, music, and drama. The high living standard that growth permits increases our leisure and provides additional time for self-fulfillment.

Growth also helps generate more resources for national defense, police and fire protection, care of the disabled and sick, and improvements in our nation's infrastructure, such as roads and communications. In today's world, additional jobs made possible by economic growth may be the only achievable method for decreasing poverty, given society's reluctance to increase the amount of national income shared with the poor.

Although economic growth may provide benefits, it can also entail costs. Some individuals maintain that additional economic growth results in more pollution, more crowded cities, excessive emphasis on materialism, and psychological problems that result in suicide and drug usage. They contend that the country would be better off with less growth rather than with more. What's wrong with a slower and more peaceful life?

Antigrowth advocates also contend that economic growth has not solved society's problems, such as poverty, discrimination, and homelessness. According to the antigrowth view, poverty in the United States is largely due to the distribution of the nation's income rather than the growth of production and income. To alleviate poverty, society must be willing to adopt policies to redistribute income and wealth in favor of the poor rather than making investment in new technologies more profitable for the rich.

Another concern is the relationship between economic growth and the availability of resources. Recall that many people argue that continued increases in population and the size of the economy will cause us to run out of scarce resources. At some point, the time will come when there is no more clean air and pure water, no more natural resources, and no more open space wherein to live comfortably. As a result, the nation's living standard will decline. These people contend that we must reduce the rate of economic growth and conserve our scarce resources.

Others argue that economic growth does not cause these problems. They maintain that growth brings about many favorable things, such as higher real income, less poverty, and greater economic security. Moreover, if the government would strictly enforce environmental laws, pollution would not be a major problem. Finally, we are not running out of natural resources. If and when the scarcity of resources becomes a barrier to growth, rising relative prices of these resources will force households to conserve them and develop alternative resources. As you can see, there are no simple answers to the question of the optimal rate of economic growth.

This chapter considered the U.S. economy's gross domestic product and the role of economic growth. The next chapter will examine the impacts of the business cycle, unemployment, and inflation on the economy.

C H E C K   P O I N T

1. Distinguish between the traditional theory of economic growth and new growth theory.

2. Describe the principle of creative destruction. Why are the forces opposing creativity so strong?

3. Identify some possible disadvantages of economic growth.

Chapter Summary

1. Economists have developed a single statistic to measure the output of an economy. This statistic is known as gross domestic product, or GDP. GDP is the market value of all final goods and services produced within a country in a given year.

2. The GDP of an economy can be calculated by adding the expenditures on goods and services produced during the current year. When derived by the expenditure approach, there are four components of GDP: personal consumption expenditures, gross private domestic investment, government purchases of goods and services, and net exports to foreigners. For the United States, personal consumption expenditures have been the largest component of GDP, typically accounting for two-thirds or more of GDP.

3. Although GDP is our best single measure of the value of the output produced by an economy, it is not a perfect measure of economic well-being. For example, GDP ignores transactions that do not take place in organized markets. GDP also ignores the underground economy as well as changes in the environment that arise through the production of output. Furthermore, GDP neither accounts for leisure, nor does it show how much output is available per person. Finally, GDP does not reflect the quality and kinds of goods that compose a nation's output.

4. Nominal GDP, or current-dollar GDP, is expressed in terms of the prices existing in the year in which goods and services were produced. Real GDP, or constant-dollar GDP, is nominal GDP adjusted to eliminate changes in prices. It measures actual (real) production and shows how actual production, rather than the prices of what is produced, has changed. Real GDP is superior to nominal GDP for assessing rates of economic growth.

5. An economy realizes economic growth when it increases its full production level of output over time. The rate of economic growth is the percentage change in the level of economic activity from one year to the next. Typically, analysts look at the rate of growth in an economy's real GDP.

6. The keys to long-run economic growth are the incentives that induce individuals to work and firms to invest in production technology, within the limits imposed by demographics and the rate of technological advances. Among the major determinants of economic growth are natural resources, physical capital, human capital, and economic efficiency. Government may enact policies that also foster economic growth, such as boosting productivity by increasing domestic

saving, stimulating research and development, working to reduce trade barriers, and improving the efficiency of regulation. Governments may also target and subsidize specific industries that might be especially important for technological progress.

7. According to the traditional theory of economic growth as pioneered by Adam Smith, the model of perfect competition is the main spur to economic efficiency. Traditional growth theory emphasized two resources—labor and capital. Technological progress was viewed as being outside the scope of economic theory, and thus something that we accept as a given.

8. According to the new growth theory, as pioneered by Joseph Schumpeter, technological progress is within the scope of economic theory, and creativity is an economic activity. According to Schumpeter, ideas and creativity are the prime sources of growth in a modern economy and profits are the fuel. The drive to capture monopoly profits promotes creative destruction, as old goods and livelihoods are replaced by new ones. Thus, while Adam Smith saw monopoly profits as an indication of economic inefficiency, Schumpeter saw them as evidence of valuable entrepreneurial activity in a healthy, dynamic economy.

9. Although economic growth may provide benefits for a nation, it can also entail costs. Critics maintain that additional economic growth can promote more pollution, more crowded cities, excessive emphasis on materialism, and psychological problems that result in suicide and drug usage. Economic growth may also cause depletion of scarce resources, eventually resulting in a decline in the nation's standard of living. However, proponents argue that economic growth does not cause these problems but rather fosters higher real income, less poverty, and greater economic security.

Key Terms and Concepts

gross domestic product (GDP) (233)

expenditure approach (234)

personal consumption expenditures (234)

gross private domestic investment (234)

government purchases of goods and services (234)

net exports (235)

underground economy (236)

nominal GDP (237)

real GDP (237)

price index (237)

GDP deflator (237)

economic growth (239)

rate of economic growth (239)

rule of 70 (239)

infrastructure (242)

human capital (242)

productivity (243)

creative destruction (249)

Self-Test: Multiple-Choice Questions

1. Economists measure nominal GDP in _____ prices and real GDP in _____ prices.
   a. domestic, foreign
   b. final, intermediate
   c. current year, base year
   d. base year, current year

2. GDP is calculated as the sum of

   a. transfer payments, interest, rent, and profits.
   b. personal consumption, gross investment, government purchases, and net exports.
   c. wages and salaries, unemployment compensation benefits, and gross investment.
   d. intermediate goods and final goods.

3. Real GDP best measures the

   a. market value of all intermediate goods.
   b. level of real output.
   c. standard of living of domestic households.
   d. level of society's welfare.

4. Suppose that in 1998 the nominal GDP was $1,000 billion and the price index was 100; in 2000, the nominal GDP was $1,200 billion and the price index was 110. On the basis of this information, we can say that real GDP equaled

   a. $1,000 billion in 1998 and $1,091 billion in 2000.
   b. $1,000 billion in 1998 and $2,010 billion in 2000.
   c. $1,000 billion in 1998 and $991 billion in 2000.
   d. $1,000 billion in 1998 and $889 billion in 2000.

5. In GDP accounts, all of the following are final products *except*

   a. a tank bought by the U.S. Department of Defense.
   b. a computer bought by Stanford University.
   c. steel bought by General Motors.
   d. a refrigerator bought by Memorial Hospital.

6. GDP is the sum of the market value of

   a. final goods and services.
   b. intermediate goods and services.
   c. industrial production and business services.
   d. normal goods and services.

7. According to the rule of 70, if real GDP grows at 4 percent per year, it will take about _____ for the real GDP to double.

   a. 10 years
   b. 14 years
   c. 18 years
   d. 22 years

8. The major determinants of economic growth include all of the following *except*

   a. tastes and preferences of households.
   b. natural resources.
   c. physical capital.
   d. technological advancement.

9. If investors purchased $200 million of Microsoft stock on the New York Stock Exchange, this would

   a. be included in GDP as gross investment.
   b. be included in GDP as domestic investment.
   c. be included in GDP as retail services.
   d. not be included in GDP.

10. According to the economic growth theory of Adam Smith,

   a. the model of pure monopoly is the main spur to economic efficiency.
   b. economic growth is primarily the result of creativity and new ideas.
   c. technological progress is something that we accept as a given.
   d. smaller markets encourage firms to specialize and reduce costs.

11. The new growth theory as pioneered by Joseph Schumpeter maintains that

   a. monopoly profits are an indication of economic inefficiency.
   b. ideas and creativity are the prime sources of growth in a modern economy.
   c. a highly competitive economy best enhances long-run economic growth.
   d. creative destruction leads to declines in output and economic activity.

Answers to Multiple-Choice Questions

1. c   2. b   3. b   4. a   5. c   6. a   7. c   8. a   9. d   10. c   11. b

Study Questions and Problems

1. Which of the following are included in calculating this year's GDP?

   a. Interest received on a security of the U.S. government.
   b. The purchase of a new automobile.
   c. The services of a gardener in weeding her garden.
   d. The purchase of a life insurance policy.
   e. The money received by John when he sells his computer to Mary.
   f. The purchases of new office equipment by the U.S. government.
   g. Unemployment compensation benefits received by a former autoworker.
   h. A construction firm builds a new apartment building.
   i. People in Canada travel to the United States to visit Disneyland.

2. Table 10.5 shows hypothetical GDP data for the United States. On the basis of this information, calculate GDP.

3. Table 10.6 shows the nominal GDP and the GDP deflator for the United States for selected years. On the basis of this information, calculate real GDP.

Table 10.5	Gross Domestic Product Data	
	Government purchases of goods and services	$360 billion
	Compensation of employees	210
	U.S. imports of goods and services	40
	Interest and dividend income	23
	Personal consumption expenditures	720
	Social Security earnings	13
	Gross private domestic investment	77
	Household savings	12
	U.S. exports of goods and services	28
	Household taxes	45

| Table 10.6 | Calculation of Real Gross Domestic Product |

Year	Nominal GDP (billions)	GDP Deflator	Real GDP (billions)
1990	$6,139	93.6	
1991	6,079	97.3	*do any 1*
1992	6,244	100.0	
1993	6,386	102.6	
1994	6,609	105.0	

maybe discuss   **4.** Assume that the average workweek declines by 20 percent because U.S. citizens decide to take life a little easier. How will this affect GDP for the United States? How will it affect the welfare of the United States?

5. Assume that the United States produces only radios and calculators. In 1999, it produced 100 radios at a price of $25 and 50 calculators at a price of $30. In 2000, the United States produced 120 radios at a price of $30 and 60 calculators at a price of $35. Calculate the nominal GDP for each year.

discuss   **6.** Why do economists prefer to compare real GDP figures for different years instead of nominal GDP figures?

7. If real GDP is $8,880 billion and nominal GDP is $9,988 billion, what does the GDP deflator equal?

8. Suppose that GDP for a given year equals $9,650 billion. What does this mean?

9. Why would removing a barrier to trade, such as a tariff, result in more rapid economic growth?

discuss   **10.** Explain how higher saving can promote a faster rate of economic growth.

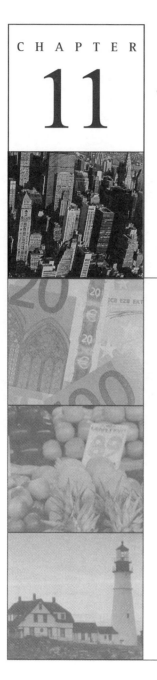

The Business Cycle, Unemployment, and Inflation

Chapter objectives

After reading this chapter, you should be able to:

1. Discuss the four phases of the business cycle.

2. Explain what the unemployment rate means and how it is calculated.

3. Identify the various types of unemployment and their costs on the economy.

4. Discuss the importance of the consumer price index as a measure of inflation.

5. Identify who benefits and who is hurt from inflation.

6. Describe the causes of inflation.

economics IN CONTEXT

In the late 1990s, computer makers were boosting already robust sales by marketing elegant new hardware designs and faster processors. By the early 2000s, however, things had become ugly in the personal–computer (PC) market: The PC market witnessed a brutal price war in which dealers rapidly slashed retail prices and provided generous rebates and lots of freebies. Dell Computer Corporation, which initiated the price battle, tossed in a free printer, free delivery, and free Internet access to customers who purchased a PC through its Web site.

Although that was good for customers, computer makers winced as the intensifying competition sliced into profits. Compaq Computer Corp., the world's largest PC maker, downsized operations and laid off workers to help compensate for new price reductions. Other computer makers slashed jobs and warned investors of reduced sales. The focal point of the industry's problems was a dramatic slowdown in revenue growth. Fears of recession hurt sales as consumers and many companies held on to their

computers longer. PC producers announced that if demand continued to decline and PC prices fell, the resulting squeeze could trigger a wave of consolidation among the biggest PC makers, as seen in the merger between Hewlett-Packard (HP) and Compac in 2002.

Indeed, the history of U.S. capitalism is one of recurrent periods of boom and bust. Sometimes business conditions are robust, with plenty of job vacancies, factories working near maximum capacity, and strong profits. The 1990s was a period of sustained economic expansion for the United States. At other times, goods are not sold and pile up as excess inventories, jobs become scarce, and profits are low. Sometimes a downturn is mild; at times, like the Great Depression of the 1930s, a downturn is prolonged and traumatic.

In this chapter, we explore the nature and effects of macroeconomic instability. First, we gain an overview of the business cycle, the recurrent periods of recession and expansion characterizing our economy. Then we examine the nature and causes of unemployment and inflation.

BUSINESS CYCLES

In an ideal economy, real GDP would increase over time at a smooth and steady pace. Moreover, the price level would remain constant or only increase slowly. However, economic history shows that the economy never grows in a smooth and steady pattern. Instead, it has been interrupted by periods of economic instability, as shown in Figure 11.1.

The economy may realize several years of expansion and prosperity. Then national output declines, profits and real incomes decrease, and the unemployment rate increases to uncomfortably high levels as many workers lose their jobs. Eventually, the economic contraction vanishes and recovery begins. The recovery may be slow or fast. It may be partial, or it may be so strong as to result in a new era of prosperity. Or it may be characterized by escalating inflation, soon to be followed by another downturn. The upward and downward movements in output, employment, and inflation form the business cycle that characterizes all market economies.

Phases of the Business Cycle

The term business cycle refers to recurrent ups and downs in the level of economic activity extending over several years. Although business cycles vary in intensity and duration, we divide each into four phases, as shown in Figure 11.2.

GDP

Figure 11.1	Historical Business Fluctuations in the United States

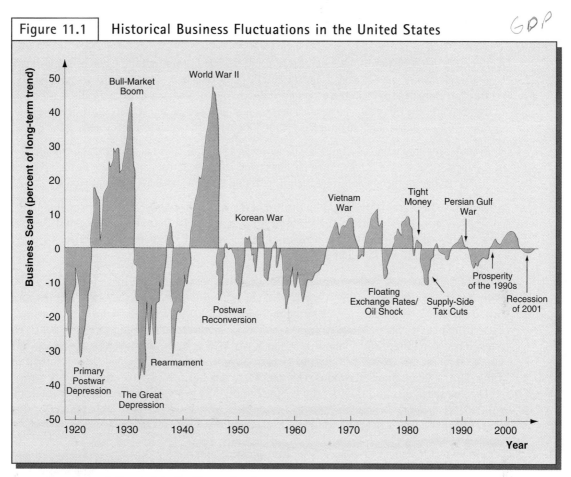

Source: From *Economic Report of the President*, various issues.

Figure 11.2	The Business Cycle

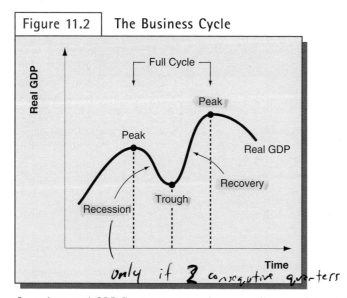

only if 2 consecutive quarters

Over time, real GDP fluctuates around an overall upward trend. Such fluctuations are called the business cycle.

- **Peak.** At the peak of a business cycle, real GDP is at a temporary high. Employment and profits are usually strong.

- **Recession.** A recession is a period of significant decline in total output, income, employment, and trade, which usually lasts from six months to a year and is marked by widespread contraction of many sectors in the economy. The recession begins at a peak and ends at a trough. For example, the U.S. economy began a recession after it peaked in February 2001. The recession was short lived, lasting only until November 2001 when the economy recovered.

- **Trough.** The low point of real GDP, just before it begins to turn up, is called the trough of a business cycle. At the trough, unemployment and idle productive capacity are at their highest levels relative to the previous recession. The trough may be short-lived or quite long.

- **Recovery.** Recovery is the upturn in the business cycle during which real GDP rises. During the recovery or expansion phase of the business cycle, industrial output expands, profits usually increase, and employment moves toward full employment. The expansion of 1991–2001 is the longest on record for the United States.

Note that business cycle patterns are erratic. Business cycles are like mountain ranges with different valleys and hills. Some valleys are deep and long, as in the Great Depression; others are shallow and narrow, as in the recession of 2001. We measure the entire business cycle from peak to peak. Usually, business cycles have averaged four to five years, although a few have been longer and some shorter. Since World War II, the average U.S. expansion has averaged about 3½ years; the average recession has lasted about 10 months, as shown in Table 11.1. During these recessions, U.S. real GDP has fallen by an average of 2.5 percent.

Despite these ups and downs, the U.S. economy has grown significantly over the long run, so the growth during expansions more than offsets the decline during recessions. Output has increased over the long run because of increases in the amount and quality of resources, better technology, and improvements in methods of production.

Although business cycles are not duplicates, they do have similar characteristics. When the economy encounters a recession, we can usually expect the following. First, consumer expenditures decrease abruptly, while business inventories of steel, automobiles, and

Table 11.1	Post–World War II Recessions for the United States		
Period		Duration in Months	Percentage Decline in Real GDP
1949–1949		11	−2.0%
1953–1954		10	−3.7
1957–1958		8	−3.9
1960–1961		10	−1.6
1969–1970		11	−1.1
1973–1975		16	−4.9
1980		6	−2.4
1981–1982		16	−3.4
1990–1991		8	−1.8
2001		8	−0.5
Average		10.4	−2.5

Source: From National Bureau of Economic Research, available at http://www.nber.org/. Select "Data" and then scroll down to "Business Cycle Dates."

other durable goods rise unexpectedly. As businesses react by curtailing production, real GDP declines. Soon thereafter, business investment in plant and equipment falls. Second, the demand for labor decreases. This is first seen in a reduction in the average workweek, followed by layoffs and increased unemployment. Third, as output falls, the demand for materials, services, and labor decreases, which may result in a decline in their prices or a slowdown in their rate of price increases. Finally, business profits decline in recessions. In anticipation of this, stock prices generally drop as investors become pessimistic about the decline in business activity. Moreover, because the demand for credit decreases, interest rates usually also decline in recessions.

What is the difference between a recession and a depression? Recall that analysts describe a recession as a decrease in real GDP for at least two quarters. A **depression** is a

economics
IN ACTION

Does the Downsizing of Jobs Promote Increases in Productivity?

Workers fear it. Firms ponder its benefits. Financial markets celebrate it. Some politicians want the government to shield us from it. The media portrays it as the scourge of the market economy. *Downsizing.* To some people, downsizing signifies a breakdown in the loyalty that once held the company and its workers together. To others, it signifies personal defeat—a verdict that we, as workers, are no longer valuable human resources. Viewing layoffs as a malfunction, some of capitalism's critics go so far as to propose that the government reward "good" companies that don't cut jobs and punish "bad" ones that do with taxes, sanctions, and regulations.

According to researchers at the Federal Reserve Bank of Dallas, such views are incomplete, if not wholly incorrect. Layoffs aren't a sign of failure, not for the economy, not even for most workers. Job losses hurt American workers and their families, no doubt about that, but downsizing cannot be understood apart from a broader view of the economy's health and well-being. More often than not, labor force turnover reflects positive market forces at work. Companies develop new or cheaper products, entrepreneurs pursue opportunities, and factories and offices become more productive. In the process, new jobs inevitably replace old ones. This is how the economy grows: through a relentless process of turmoil, a continuous churn of what

Table 11.2 Downsizing and Productivity Among the Top Corporate Job Cutters, 1990–1995		
Company	Jobs Cut	Productivity Gain or Loss
Sears	185,000	−10.3%
IBM	121,601	28.1
General Electric	76,000	32.2
General Dynamics	70,400	5.6
Digital Equipment	62,300	59.9
Boeing	56,700	−6.8
General Motors	52,400	21.0
GTE	48,000	30.3

Source: From "The Upside of Downsizing," *Southwest Economy*, Federal Reserve Bank of Dallas, November–December 1996, p. 7.

economists call "creative destruction." As Table 11.2 shows, most companies that resorted to downsizing in the 1990s emerged to become more productive and competitive.

Downsizing has been going on for centuries. In 1800, for example, it took nearly 95 of every 100 Americans to feed the country. In 1900, it required 40. Today, it takes just three. The downsizing of agriculture, however, hasn't left the country hungry. Quite the contrary, the United States enjoys agricultural abundance. Moreover, the workers no longer needed on the farm are available to provide new homes, computers, medical assistance, and many other goods and services. The country today would have far fewer goods and services if farming had not endured one of history's most drastic times of downsizing.

very deep and prolonged recession. Because no subsequent recession has approached the severity of the Great Depression, the term "depression" is often used as a reference to the pronounced and long recession of the 1930s. How severe was the Great Depression for the United States? During that slump, the unemployment rate skyrocketed to 25 percent of the labor force, and industrial output fell by over 40 percent over a 3-year period, which hampered business activity for over a decade.

In summary, business cycles have three main characteristics.

- Fluctuations in the economy are irregular and unpredictable. Sometimes, recessions are close together, as seen in the recessions of 1980 and 1980; sometimes, economic expansions continue many years, such as the expansion of 1991–2001.

- Most macroeconomic variables that measure some aspect of production, income, or spending fluctuate together throughout the business cycle. When real GDP decreases during a recession, so do national income, business profits, household expenditures, investment spending, industrial production, auto sales, retail sales, and the like.

- Fluctuations in the economy's output of goods and services correspond strongly to changes in the rate of unemployment. When real GDP decreases, unemployment rises, and vice versa.

Theories of the Business Cycle

Over the years, economists have debated the sources of the business cycle. What causes the economy to turn downward or upward?

Many economists believe that a change in total spending (demand) is the immediate determinant of domestic output and employment. Recall that total spending in the economy includes expenditures for final goods by households, businesses, government, and foreign buyers.

Why do changes in total spending explain fluctuations in economic activity? If total spending decreases, businesses may find it unprofitable to produce the existing level of output. As they decrease production, they employ less land, labor, and capital. Thus, reductions in total spending result in decreases in national output, employment, and incomes. These decreases, in turn, can cause a recession for the economy. Conversely, an increase in total spending results in a rise in national output, employment, and incomes. These increases, in turn, promote economic expansion.

Besides being explained by changes in the economy's total spending, business cycles may also be caused by changes in the supply side of the market. For example, the development of a new technology might result in new investment spending, thus causing an economic expansion. Conversely, a decrease in the availability of natural resources could cause an increase in the costs of production that results in a recession. Also, shocks may foster recession. Although the September 11 terrorist attacks did not cause recession for the U.S. economy in 2001 (the recession actually began in March of that year), they were clearly a factor that deepened the downward spiral of economic activity.

As we continue our study of macroeconomics, we will learn more about the causes of business cycles. Using aggregate demand and aggregate supply curves, we will learn why changes occur in national output, employment, income, and the price level.

Do Economic Expansions Die of Old Age?

One question that has intrigued economists is whether each economic expansion contains the seeds of its own destruction. Is it true that the longer an expansion lasts, the more likely it is to end in the next quarter or the next year? Studies find no compelling evidence that postwar expansions possess an inherent tendency to die of old age. Instead, they appear to fall victim to specific events related to economic disturbances or government policies.

For example, the Iraqi invasion of Kuwait, which led to a doubling of oil prices in the fall of 1990, contributed to the decline in economic activity during the recession of 1990–1991. American consumers, having suffered through the tripling of oil prices in 1973–1974 and their subsequent doubling in 1979, anticipated negative repercussions on the U.S. economy, and consumer confidence declined sharply and consumption fell, resulting in a decline in total spending.

The 1990s expansion provides another example of cyclical slowdown. Beginning in 1991, the U.S. economy rebounded from recession, only to operate at very high levels at the turn of the century. During 2000 and 2001, however, several factors contributed to economic slowdown: the decline in stock market wealth, the surge in energy prices, an increase in interest rates, the collapse of the high-technology sector, and the lingering effects of preparations against the year-2000 (Y2K) computer bug. With all this backdrop setting the stage for sluggish growth, the subsequent decline in consumer and business confidence in 2001 was sufficient to tip the nation into recession.

CHECK POINT

1. Identify the four phases of a business cycle.

2. What factors cause the economy to turn upward or downward?

3. Do economic expansions die of old age?

UNEMPLOYMENT

One reason we want to avoid recessions and depressions is that they result in hardship among individuals. During a recession, not only does real GDP decline, but also fewer people can find jobs. Economists define the **unemployed** as those individuals who do not have jobs but who are actively seeking work.   *also   under employment*

Besides imposing costs on individuals, unemployment generates a cost for the economy as a whole because it produces fewer goods and services. When the economy does not provide enough jobs to employ all those individuals who are seeking work, the productivity of that unemployed labor is forgone. This lost output, combined with the hardship that unemployment imposes on individuals and their families, is the real cost of unemployment.

Measuring Unemployment

The unemployment rate is a closely watched measure of an economy's health. How is the unemployment rate calculated, and what does it mean?

Every month, the Bureau of Labor Statistics conducts a nationwide random survey of about 60,000 households to gather information on labor market activities. The survey divides the adult (16 years old and over) population into three categories.

- Those who have jobs are classified as employed.

- Those who don't have jobs but are looking for them and are available for work are classified as unemployed.

- Those who don't have jobs and are not looking for work are not classified as members of the labor force.

The **unemployment rate** is the number of people unemployed divided by the labor force—the number of people holding or seeking jobs.

$$\text{Unemployment rate} = \frac{\text{Number of persons unemployed}}{\text{Number of persons in the labor force}}$$

In 2004, the unemployment rate was 5.5 percent:

$$\text{Unemployment rate} = \frac{8,149,000}{147,401,000} = 5.5 \text{ percent}$$

Although the Bureau of Labor Statistics takes great care in calculating the unemployment rate, it is subject to several shortcomings. Part-time employment represents one problem. Although some part-time workers work less than a full week because they want to, others do so only because they cannot find a suitable full-time job. Nevertheless, a worker who has been cut back to part-time work is still counted as employed, even if that worker would prefer to work full time. During a recession, workers may find that their work hours are reduced from 40 to 30 a week because of slack demand for the product their employer produces. Because the statistics don't measure the "underemployment" of these workers, they tend to *underestimate* the actual extent of unemployment in the economy.

Unemployment statistics also suffer from the problem of discouraged workers. A **discouraged worker** is a person who is out of work, would like to work, and is available for work, but who has stopped looking because of lack of success in finding a job. Discouraged workers are not part of the labor force because they do not actively seek employment. As a result, we do not count them as unemployed. Because the official unemployment rate does not include discouraged workers, the actual degree of unemployment in the economy tends to be underestimated.

Although the overall unemployment rate in 2004 was 5.5 percent, the burdens of unemployment were not equally distributed. As seen in Table 11.3, unemployment rates tend to vary considerably for different groups in society. In particular, unemployment rates among blacks have roughly been double that of whites. This may be the result of the concentration of blacks in less-skilled occupations or the inner city, where job opportunities are negligible and there is discrimination in employment and education. Moreover, teenagers tend to have much higher unemployment rates than adults. This is largely because teenagers have relatively modest job skills, have little geographic mobility, and more frequently leave their jobs than adults.

Three Kinds of Unemployment

Not everyone who is unemployed is unemployed for the same reason. Unemployment is classified into three types based on its causes. As you will see, some kinds of unemployment may not be as important as others.

Some people are unemployed because they cannot currently find work that matches their qualifications. For example, think of college students majoring in accounting or computer science. When they finish school, they will look for jobs that match their skills, but finding such jobs may take time. Yet, the students will likely find jobs soon because their skills are marketable. This unemployment is temporary. Economists refer to this type of unemployment as frictional unemployment. **Frictional unemployment** is the unemployment that arises

Table 11.3	The Burdens of Unemployment in 2004

Unemployment Rates by Demographic Characteristics (percent)	
Overall	5.5
Gender:	
Male	5.6
Female	5.4
Race:	
White	4.8
Black	10.4
Age:	
Males:	
16–19 years	18.4
20 years and over	5.0
Females:	
16–19 years	15.5
20 years and over	4.9
Average duration of unemployment	19.6 weeks

Source: From *Economic Report of the President*, 2005, and Bureau of Labor Statistics, available at http://www.bls.gov.

from normal labor turnover—that is, from people being "between jobs." Frictional unemployment is not of much concern when dealing with the national unemployment problem.

However, not all unemployment is short lived. **Structural unemployment** is unemployment caused by skills that do not match what employers require or from being geographically separated from job opportunities. Substantial structural unemployment is found quite often side by side with job vacancies, because the unemployed lack the skills required for newly created jobs. For example, there may be vacancies for electrical engineers while truck drivers are unemployed. Moreover, there may be worker shortages in the Southwestern states that are undergoing economic growth and unemployment in states that are suffering economic contraction, as in the Midwest during the era of weak demand for U.S. automobiles in the 1980s. Because both skill and location problems are usually of long duration, structural unemployment is perhaps the most serious type of unemployment.

Cyclical unemployment is the fluctuating unemployment that coincides with the business cycle. Cyclical unemployment is a repeating short-run problem. The amount of cyclical unemployment increases when the economy goes into a slump and decreases when the economy goes into an expansion. A steelworker who is laid off because the economy enters a recession and gets rehired several months later when the upswing occurs has experienced cyclical unemployment. Government policymakers are especially interested in decreasing both the frequency and extent of this type of unemployment by reducing the frequency and extent of the recessions that account for it. Government also attempts to lessen the impact of recession by providing unemployment compensation for those temporarily laid off.

Mitigating the Costs of Unemployment

The U.S. government has many policies and programs at its disposal to reduce the costs that unemployment imposes on some workers. The main policy instrument that addresses some of the immediate needs of workers who lose their jobs is the unemployment insurance system.

Other policies, such as mandatory advance notice of layoffs, may provide short-run benefits as well. Still other policies, such as education and training programs, attempt to improve the longer-term fortunes of those hurt by unemployment.

Unemployment insurance was established in the United States as part of the Social Security Act of 1935. This system helps support consumer spending during periods of job loss and provides economic security to workers through income maintenance. Another potential benefit of the unemployment insurance system is that it provides an individual with the financial resources to prolong his job search until he receives an offer appropriate to his skills. Although the federal government maintains control over the broad design of the unemployment insurance system, individual states have considerable autonomy in tailoring the program's features within their jurisdictions.

Unemployment insurance provides weekly benefits to workers who have been laid off or who have lost their jobs for reasons other than misconduct or a labor dispute. Only workers with a sufficiently long employment history—usually six months of significant employment—are eligible. Benefits are a fraction of average weekly earnings on the job that was lost, up to a maximum dollar amount, and paid up to 26 weeks in most states. This fraction is typically between 50 and 70 percent. Benefits are financed, in most states, by a payroll tax levied on firms.

Although the unemployment insurance system has benefited millions of workers over the years, these benefits do not come without costs. Many economists contend that higher unemployment benefits lead to longer unemployment spells. Providing benefits to unemployed workers reduces their incentive to search intensively for a new job. Research suggests that a 10-percentage-point increase in unemployment benefits results in an additional 1 to 1.5 weeks of unemployment, when an average insured unemployment spell lasts roughly 15 weeks. Job finding rates also increase somewhat as the exhaustion of benefits approaches.[1]

so? of course they would

What Is Full Employment?

Indeed, a high-employment economy provides benefits for society. But what do economists mean by full employment? Does full employment mean zero unemployment?

Recall that total unemployment in an economy consists of frictional, structural, and cyclical unemployment. We call the level of unemployment at which there is no cyclical unemployment the **natural rate of unemployment.** In other words, the natural rate of unemployment is the sum of frictional and structural unemployment, which economists consider as essentially unavoidable. The natural rate of unemployment is economists' notion of **full employment.** Therefore, we define full employment as something less than 100-percent employment of the labor force.

In the United States today, most economists estimate that the natural rate of unemployment is between 4 and 6 percent. In 2000, the U.S. economy realized an unemployment rate of 4 percent, suggesting that there was little, if any, slack in the economy. Put simply, the economy was at "full employment" for all practical purposes.

Notice that the natural rate of unemployment can vary over time. Changes in the natural rate of unemployment occur in response to shifting demographics of the labor force or changes in society's customs and laws. In the early 1990s, for example, structural unemployment increased as the result of corporate downsizing and decreases in defense spending. These changes increased the natural rate of unemployment. However, aging of the workforce in the 2000s will likely decrease the amount of frictional unemployment because older workers are less likely to quit their jobs than are younger workers. This will cause the natural rate of unemployment to decrease. Not only can the natural rate of unemployment change

---

[1] *Economic Report of the President,* 1997, p. 159.

over time, but it also tends to differ among countries. In Europe, for example, estimates of the natural rate of unemployment put it between 7 and 10 percent.

International Comparisons of Unemployment

Unemployment rates vary greatly among countries over specific periods because different countries have different natural rates of unemployment and may be in different phases of the business cycle. Many economists argue that, compared to the United States, the natural rate of unemployment is likely to be higher in Europe. Let us consider some labor practices that affect these countries' natural rates of unemployment.

Europe   Europe's approach to labor markets has generally been to protect workers, especially low-skilled workers, which keeps their wages relatively high and penalizes firms for firing them. Europe was the birthplace of the welfare state, and countries like The Netherlands, France, and Sweden have legislated generous welfare benefits and unemployment insurance. This allows people a longer duration of time to conduct a job search, thus increasing the natural rate of unemployment. Moreover, companies pay high

international
ECONOMICS IN ACTION

Inflexible Labor Market Costs Jobs for Western Europeans

Wolfgang Mueller didn't say he felt burned out as he embarked on the first of two 3-week vacations he planned in 2004. The 35-year-old machinist at a Volkswagen assembly plant in Frankfurt, Germany, knocks off work each day at 3 p.m. in the course of a 35-hour workweek. Typically, he works only 13 to15 days a month.

Western Europeans generally consider a healthy dose of leisure as part of what distinguishes them from Americans. They maintain that spending too much time working results in less time with family, less social cohesion, and more fertile ground for crime. Western Europeans also argue that a shorter workweek fosters job growth by spreading the same amount of work among more people. Moreover, it motivates people to become more productive, squeezing more work into less time.

Although Western Europe has enacted strict laws against firing and restrictions on the workweek, such policies have made its labor markets inflexible to future changes. Companies like Caterpillar that conduct business in Western Europe are aware of the problems of inflexible labor markets. Even though Western Europe has high-skilled,

well-trained, and educated workers, companies say the shorter work hours result in additional costs that reduce their competitiveness in a global economy. Simply put, an engineer who works only 35 hours is not worth it for Volkswagen. As a result, many companies are reluctant to hire Western European workers, even if demand is strong. Instead, they establish manufacturing subsidiaries in other parts of the world where labor markets are more flexible and workers are less expensive to hire. Inflexible labor markets also help explain why Western Europe hasn't become as attractive a home for foreign investment as the United States.

For example, in 2004, Mercedes-Benz threatened its German auto workers that if they did not agree to lower pay and more hours of work, the firm would move production to the Czech Republic or Poland where workers earn less than a third the average wage in Germany. Yes, German workers were more productive. But workers in Eastern and Central Europe, with the help of state-of-the-art plants, were becoming more productive, too.

As a result, some labor leaders in Western Europe have begun to make concessions in hopes of saving jobs. The change could revolutionize labor relations in Europe, fostering a trend toward more flexible labor rules and weaker unions. That would enhance Europe's competitiveness, which has dwindled because of high labor costs and an opposition to reforms, but could also increase social tension as workers encounter the possibility of losing jobs, taking lower pay, and working longer hours.

employment taxes to help the welfare state. This adds to the cost of hiring labor, which decreases the quantity demanded.

Another factor affecting unemployment is unionization. Compared to the United States, the percent of Europe's labor force that is unionized is two to three times as high. To the degree that strong unions in Europe force wages above market-equilibrium levels and decrease wage flexibility, they increase the natural rate of unemployment. Moreover, many European governments maintain minimum wages that are at or above equilibrium wage rates in various industries and occupations. This results in wage inflexibility and in a higher natural rate of unemployment.

Besides adding to the cost of hiring labor, many European nations, hoping to thwart job losses, have saddled companies with burdensome rules on when and how they can dismiss workers. The red tape and reproach involved in cutting jobs makes firms wary of hiring new workers in the first place. With few new opportunities opening up, workers cling to existing jobs. As a result, too many of Europe's labor resources remain frozen, and companies cannot respond quickly and aggressively to changes in the market. Europe may have managed to save a few existing jobs, but at a high cost in economic performance.

United States   Although the United States has had an inferior record when compared to Europe in the growth of real wages and productivity in the past three decades, it has done better in achieving growth of jobs and maintaining a relatively low unemployment rate. Compared to Europe, U.S. policies are more laissez faire and leave labor market arrangements to employers and employees. Therefore, U.S. workers are in a different bargaining position than European workers.

In the United States, we see relatively weak unions, a relatively low minimum wage, and substantial competition for low-skilled jobs from foreign workers and immigrants. This results in a weaker bargaining position of labor in the United States, which makes it easier and cheaper for American firms to hire workers. Also, there are less generous unemployment and welfare benefits in the United States, which makes welfare even less attractive compared to work. Job security for U.S. workers has also been threatened by company downsizing.

Indeed, labor markets are more flexible in the United States than in Europe. We can understand the differences between the labor markets of these countries in terms of Figure 11.3. Europe's more rigid labor market is shown in Figure 11.3(a), while the more flexible U.S. labor market is shown in Figure 11.3(b). The labor market equilibrium is shown by point *A* in the figures, the equilibrium wage being $24 per hour. Suppose that the demand for labor declines in each market because of a business recession. The market rigidities of Europe prevent wages from declining to the new equilibrium at point *C*, the result being a relatively large decrease in the quantity of labor demanded at point *B*. In the more flexible U.S. market, however, wages fall during the recession. Although the quantity of labor demanded declines during the slump, it does not decrease to point *C* as in Europe. Put simply, the rigidity of Europe's labor market results in a relatively large decline in the quantity of labor demanded and involuntary unemployment.

JOBLESS EXPANSIONS: THE PRODUCTIVITY AND JOBS CONNECTION

Ask any economist and he or she will tell you that faster productivity growth leads to higher real wages and improved living standards. Yet, a quite different picture of productivity growth has dominated the news in recent years. Numerous newspaper articles have blamed strong productivity growth for a "jobless recovery" following the recessions of 1991 and 2001. As economic output grew, the economy continued to experience prolonged periods in which employment did not grow. Faster productivity growth, according to this view, allows firms to increase production without increasing employment.

| Figure 11.3 | Rigid Wages Can Result in Involuntary Unemployment |

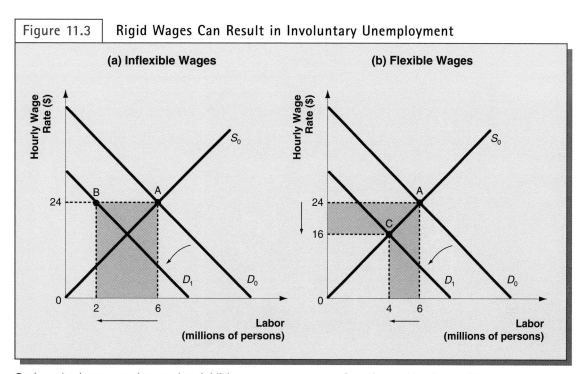

During a business recession, market rigidities may prevent wages from decreasing, the result being involuntary unemployment for labor. In a flexible labor market, wages decrease during the recession. The wage reduction clears the market of involuntary unemployment. Many believe that the labor market of Europe is more rigid while the U.S. labor market is more flexible.

These two views of productivity growth seem dramatically inconsistent. If higher productivity allows firms to shed workers, how can it raise wages and living standards? If productivity does lead to improved wages and living standards, why do workers often feel that productivity growth leaves them behind? To answer these questions, we must consider the short- and long-run effects of changes in productivity.[2]

Concerning the short run, if firms see the demand for their products rise, they respond by expanding production. And if labor productivity is unchanged, then typically they need to hire more workers to increase production. But if labor productivity is increasing, then it has the potential to reduce employment growth, because firms will be able to satisfy demand using fewer workers. Likewise, if overall demand in the economy has not expanded, then an increase in labor productivity could lead to a fall in unemployment in the short run. In this case, faster productivity growth might lead to an increase in job loss without a corresponding increase in job creation in new and expanding industries. Eventually, employment catches up, even to the increased levels of output made possible by productivity growth. However, the problem can remain for some time.

In the long run, however, income and employment depend not on demand but instead on supply factors including the economy's stock of capital, labor force, and technology. While the short-run perspective emphasizes the impact of productivity on the number of workers needed to produce a *given* level of output, the long-run perspective emphasizes that an increase in labor productivity *increases* potential output. It does so directly by allowing more output to be produced with the same level of employment, but it also

[2] Carl Walsh, "The Productivity and Jobs Connection: The Long and the Short Run of It," *Economic Letter*, Federal Reserve Bank of San Francisco, July 16, 2004.

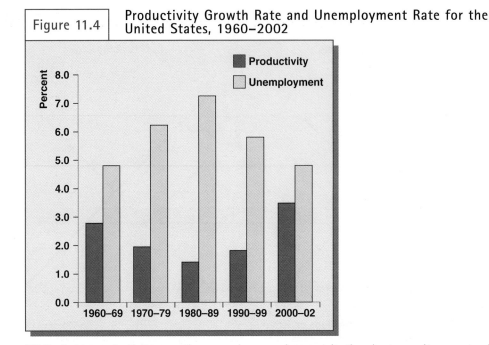

Figure 11.4 — Productivity Growth Rate and Unemployment Rate for the United States, 1960–2002

While faster productivity growth may reduce employment in the short run, it promotes higher employment and wages in the long run.

increases employment because it decreases the cost of labor to firms.[3] As the new technological innovations that boost productivity occur, new industries arise, along with the creation of new jobs. The increased demand for labor will tend to boost wages, as firms compete to hire additional workers, and raise total employment.

There is little debate among economists about the long-run effect of productivity on employment: Faster productivity growth should translate into an increase in the overall demand for labor in the economy. This, in turn, will lead real wages to rise, just as an increase in the demand for a typical good or service acts to bid its price up. Figure 11.4 shows the relationship between productivity growth and the unemployment rate. It suggests that while faster productivity growth may reduce employment in the short run, it promotes employment in the long run. However, this process can be costly and painful for the workers whose skills are no longer in demand.

CHECK POINT

1. What is meant by the "unemployment rate," and how is it calculated?

2. Economists classify unemployment according to its causes. Explain.

3. What is meant by "full employment," and how is it measured?

4. What factors explain unemployment rate differences in the United States and Europe?

---

[3] For firms, the relevant cost of labor is not measured simply by the wages and benefits paid to the workers. Rather, it is measured by the costs of these wages and benefits *relative* to the output the workers are able to produce. Just as a rise in wages increases labor costs if worker productivity remains constant, a rise in labor productivity lowers the cost of labor at a given level of wages and benefits. And if higher productivity makes labor less costly, then firms will find it profitable to expand employment.

Table 11.4	The Impact of Inflation on the Real Value of $10,000, 2000–2010				
	Annual Inflation Rate				
Year	2 Percent	4 Percent	6 Percent	8 Percent	10 Percent
2000	$10,000	$10,000	$10,000	$10,000	$10,000
2002	9,610	9,250	8,900	8,570	8,260
2004	9,240	8,550	7,920	7,350	6,830
2006	8,880	7,900	7,050	6,300	5,640
2008	8,530	7,310	6,270	5,400	4,670
2010	8,200	6,760	5,580	4,630	3,860

INFLATION

Since the end of World War II, the United States has experienced almost continuous inflation. We can define **inflation** as a sustained or continuous rise in the general price level. We should note several things about this definition. First, inflation refers to the movement in the general level of prices. However, some prices may fall. During the 1990s, the prices of computers fell, while the prices of many other goods increased. In an inflationary period, rising prices outweigh falling prices, causing the average level of prices to increase. Second, the rise in the price level must be substantial and continue over a period longer than a day, week, or month.

When there is inflation, the purchasing power of a given amount of money will decrease. Table 11.4 shows what would happen to the real value of $10,000, from January 1, 2000, to January 1, 2010, at different rates of inflation. At 2-percent inflation, $10,000 would purchase only $8,200 of goods in 2010. At 10-percent inflation, that same $10,000 would be worth only $3,860.

The average price level may decrease or increase. We refer to a continuing fall in the average price level as **deflation**. It occurs when price reductions on some goods and services outweigh price rises on all others. The last deflation in the United States occurred during the Great Depression of the 1930s.

Measuring Inflation: The Consumer Price Index

The most frequently cited indicator of inflation is the **consumer price index (CPI)**. The CPI is calculated by the Bureau of Labor Statistics through its sampling of thousands of households and businesses. When a news report says that the "cost of living" rose by, say, 3 percent, it is usually referring to the CPI.

In constructing the CPI, the Bureau of Labor Statistics selects a "market basket" of about 400 goods and services that are assumed to be most crucial to the spending of the typical American consumer. Then it assigns weightings to these goods and services according to past patterns of consumer expenditures. Every month, surveyors log the prices of the goods and services in cities throughout the United States to compute the current cost of the market basket. Because buying patterns change, the market basket is revised about once each decade.

The Bureau of Labor Statistics arbitrarily sets the average value of the goods and services in the market basket for some base period, currently 1982–1984 = 100. Referring to Table 11.5, we see that the CPI was 188.9 in 2004. This means that prices in 2004 were almost 89 percent higher than the prices in the base period. A typical bundle of

Table 11.5	Consumer Price Index and Rate of Inflation for Selected Years (1982–1984 = 100)	
Year	CPI	Yearly Percentage Change in CPI (annual rate of inflation)
1997	160.5	2.3
1998	163.0	1.6
1999	166.6	2.2
2000	172.2	3.4
2001	177.1	2.8
2002	179.9	1.6
2003	184.0	2.3
2004	188.9	2.7

Source: From *Economic Report of the President,* 2005.

goods and services that was worth $1,000 in the base period would have cost about $1,889 in 2004 ($1,000 × 1.889 = $1,889).

Once we have the CPI for selected years, we can calculate the rate of inflation between years. We use the following formula:

$$\text{Rate of inflation} = \frac{\text{CPI}_{\text{Given year}} - \text{CPI}_{\text{Previous year}}}{\text{CPI}_{\text{Previous year}}} \times 100$$

For example, suppose we wanted to compute the rate of inflation between 2003 and 2004. Referring to Table 11.5, we see that in 2003 the CPI equaled 184.0 and in 2004 it equaled 188.9. The rate of inflation between the two years thus equals 2.7 percent, calculated as follows:

$$\text{Rate of inflation} = \frac{188.9 - 184.0}{184.0} \times 100 = 2.7 \text{ percent}$$

- The CPI can be used to calculate how prices have changed over the years. Let's say you have $10 to purchase some goods and services today (year 2004). How much money would you have needed in 1950 to buy the same amount of goods and services in 2004?

Given

1. The CPI for 1950 = 24.1

2. The CPI for 2004 (today) = 188.9

Use the following formula to compute the calculation:

$$1950 \text{ Price} = 2004 \text{ Price} \times \frac{1950 \text{ CPI}}{2004 \text{ CPI}}$$

$$= \$10.00 \times \frac{24.1}{188.9}$$

$$= \$1.28$$

You would have needed $1.28 in 1950 to buy the same amount of goods and services in 2004.

The CPI is the principal source of information concerning trends in consumer prices and inflation in the United States. The CPI is used as the basis for making cost-of-living adjustments to the wages paid to millions of union workers, payments to Social Security recipients and retirees of the federal government and military, and entitlement programs such as food stamps and school lunches. Also, many banks link the interest rates they charge on mortgages, automobile loans, and personal loans to the CPI. Moreover, individual income tax brackets and personal exemptions are adjusted upward to account for the rate of inflation. Finally, the Federal Reserve bases its monetary policy on the rate of inflation as measured by the CPI.

Although the CPI is used as a measure of the cost of living for a typical urban family, it is really an imperfect measure. One weakness of the CPI is that people's buying patterns change, so that the change in what people actually spend on "living" deviates from measured increases in bacon and eggs. As some prices rise, people switch to cheaper goods. Thus, the CPI overstates the actual cost of living.

Another problem with the CPI is that its fixed market basket fails to keep pace with the development of better products, such as computers offering greater memory and faster speeds. The price of a new computer may be higher, but its capabilities may be much better than those of an older model. Part of a price increase may reflect higher quality rather than simply a higher price for the same product. To the extent that product quality improves, the CPI will overstate the rate of inflation.

Finally, the CPI ignores price discounting. New types of discount stores, such as Office Max, Costco, Home Depot, and Wal-Mart, have gained an increased share of the market by offering lower prices than competitors. Again, the CPI overstates the rate of inflation. For these reasons, most economists maintain the CPI will overstate inflation, but there is no consensus about the amount of overstatement.

WHO BENEFITS FROM AND WHO IS HURT BY INFLATION?

Why are economists concerned about inflation? As we will see, inflation can greatly affect the national standard of living. It can also influence economic behavior and lead to significant impacts on the operation of the economy.

Inflation and the Purchasing Power of Income

No matter what the rate of inflation rate is, it is interesting to know whether you are beating inflation or whether inflation is beating you. In other words, has your nominal income increased by a smaller percentage, the same percentage, or a greater percentage than the inflation rate?

To answer this question, we must adjust nominal income for changes in the price level. **Nominal income** is the actual number of dollars of income received during a year. **Real income** is the actual number of dollars received (nominal income) adjusted for any change in price. Real income therefore measures your real purchasing power, the amount of goods and services that can be purchased with your nominal income. Real income is computed as follows:

$$\text{Real income} = \left(\frac{\text{Nominal income}}{\text{CPI}} \right) \times 100$$

This formula can help us determine whether we beat inflation.

Table 11.6	The Price of a Big Mac, December 2004

Country	Big Mac Price (in dollars)
Switzerland	$5.46
Denmark	4.97
Britain	3.61
United States	3.00
Japan	2.50
Australia	2.46
Brazil	1.99
Russia	1.49
China	1.26

Source: From "Big Mac Currencies," *The Economist*, December 26, 2004.

For example, assume that Emily's nominal income rises from $50,000 in 2003 to $56,000 in 2004, an increase of 12 percent. Also, suppose the CPI rises from 184.0 in 2003 to 188.9 in 2004, an increase of 2.7 percent. Because Emily's nominal income has risen by a greater percentage than the inflation rate, she has more than kept up with inflation. In other words, her real income has risen from 2003 to 2004. Using the preceding formula, we can calculate her real income, stated in terms of the base year, for the two years, as follows:

$$\text{Real income}_{2003} = (\$50,000/184.0) \times 100 = \$27,174$$

$$\text{Real income}_{2004} = (\$56,000/188.9) \times 100 = \$29,645$$

Emily's real income has risen from $27,174 in 2003 to $29,645 in 2004.

The preceding example helps us see how inflation affects real purchasing power. Conclusion: If your nominal income increases by a greater percentage than the inflation rate, then your purchasing power rises. But if the inflation rate rises faster than your nominal income, then your purchasing power falls.

Concerning the purchasing power of income, have you ever wondered what a "Big Mac" hamburger sandwich, sold by McDonald's, costs throughout the world? Every year, *The Economist* publishes the so-called Big Mac Index, as shown in Table 11.6. For example, the cheapest burger on the chart is in China, at $1.26, compared with an average American price of $3.00. American tourists traveling to China would find Big Macs to be a good buy.

Redistribution of Wealth from Lenders to Borrowers

What is the impact of inflation on lenders and borrowers? To the extent that inflation is unanticipated, it creates winners and losers among these groups. If inflation is higher than anticipated, the winners are all those who agreed to borrow at an interest rate that did not reflect the higher inflation. The losers are all of those who agreed to lend at that interest rate. In other words, unanticipated inflation benefits people who are in debt because the purchasing power of dollars will decrease over the life of the loan. Borrowers thus pay back principal and interest with dollars that are less valuable than when they incurred the loan. As a result, unanticipated inflation results in a decrease in purchasing power for lenders.

The federal government is another debtor that has benefited from unanticipated inflation. Historically, the federal government has financed its budget deficits by borrowing from the public through the sale of Treasury bills and other securities. Unanticipated inflation has allowed the federal government to pay off its loans with dollars that have less purchasing power than the dollars it originally borrowed. Therefore, unanticipated inflation decreases the real burden of the public debt to the federal government.

Indeed, unanticipated inflation may cause a redistribution of wealth from lenders to borrowers. However, if inflation is steady and predictable, many people may correctly anticipate its effects on the purchasing power of money and thus can avoid the decline in real income that inflation will cause. For example, if the lending officer at Wells Fargo Bank correctly anticipates inflation, she can avoid the unwanted impact on her bank's real income by attaching an inflation premium to the nominal interest rate she charges for new auto or real estate loans. The additional nominal interest rate compensates the bank for the loss in the purchasing power of money due to inflation.

Inflation and Real Interest Rates

Inflation may also hurt savers and investors. For example, suppose you have a 2-year certificate of deposit that yields 6 percent per year. If inflation is 10 percent per year, you will lose on your savings each year. Although you will receive interest payments of 6 percent, they will not keep pace with 10-percent inflation. The result will be a decline in your purchasing power.

The interest that the bank pays is called the **nominal interest rate**, and the interest rate that is adjusted for inflation is called the **real interest rate**. The relationship between the nominal interest rate and the real interest rate is given by the following formula:

$$\text{Real interest rate} = \text{Nominal interest rate} - \text{Inflation rate}$$

The real interest rate is the difference between the nominal interest rate and the inflation rate. Although the nominal interest rate is always positive, the real interest rate can be positive or negative. When the real interest rate is negative, savers and lenders are hurt because interest does not keep pace with inflation. Table 11.7 shows the real and nominal interest rates for the United States from 1995 to 2004.

Because inflation threatens people's financial well-being by reducing the purchasing power of money, they take great pains to find investments where returns exceed the inflation rate, such as stocks, bonds, and many other financial instruments. When returns are corrected for inflation, however, investors sometimes see negative numbers.

In 1996, the U.S. government made financial history by announcing its intention to issue the first U.S. securities indexed to the rate of inflation. Dubbed Treasury inflation-protection

| Table 11.7 | Nominal and Real Interest Rates, 1995–2004 |

	Nominal Interest Rate*	Inflation Rate	Real Interest Rate
1995	5.5	2.5	3.0
1997	5.0	1.7	3.3
1999	4.7	2.7	2.0
2001	4.6	2.8	1.6
2003	1.0	2.3	−1.3
2004	1.4	2.7	−1.3

*3-month Treasury bills.

Source: From various issues of *Economic Report of the President* and *Statistical Supplement to the Federal Reserve Bulletin.*

securities (TIPS), the indexed securities were first sold in 1997. Now, U.S. investors can purchase a financial instrument that provides a guaranteed hedge against the loss of purchasing power that accompanies increases in the consumer price index.

Inflation and Taxpayers

Inflation hurts taxpayers because it pushes up tax bills without any explicit changes in the tax laws. The reason: Part of our country's tax system is based on nominal income instead of real income.

We will first consider the federal income tax system that existed prior to 1985. During this era, the progressive structure of the individual income tax assured that, as incomes rose during a time of inflation, the average rate of tax paid by most taxpayers went up. In other words, tax bills didn't just rise as fast as inflation—they actually rose *faster*.

To illustrate, suppose the average price level rises by 10 percent from year 1 to year 2. Suppose also that Alice has a cost-of-living provision in her labor contract that results in her nominal wages increasing by 10 percent from year 1 to year 2. On the surface, it appears that she broke even with inflation. Yet, this does not account for the fact that a 10-percent rise in nominal income will push Alice into a higher tax bracket with a higher tax rate. Although Alice's nominal income keeps pace with inflation, her real income falls because inflation results in her paying a higher tax rate. Alice's real income is redistributed to the government and ultimately to those who benefit from government spending. Notice that Alice's higher tax rate occurs without congressional action to increase taxes. Critics refer to this situation as "taxation without representation."

To prevent the redistribution of real income through the federal personal income tax system, in 1985, the U.S. government indexed the federal personal income tax. Each year, tax brackets and personal exemptions are corrected for the rate of inflation. Therefore, households are pushed into a higher tax bracket only if their real incomes increase rather than by inflation alone.

Home Ownership as a Hedge Against Inflation

One potential hedge against inflation is home ownership. As you complete your college education and enter the workforce, you may decide that buying a house is a good investment instead of paying rent year after year to live in a dwelling that will never be yours. Table 11.8 shows the median costs and financial terms for buying a new house in 2004.

If you decide to buy a house, you must consider what you can afford to buy and how much you can borrow. Most mortgage lenders require you to have at least 10 percent of the purchase price as a down payment, plus enough cash on hand for closing costs. Closing costs include filing fees, mortgage and real estate taxes, attorneys' fees, and points, which are an up-front interest charge paid to the lender. A point is 1 percent of the mortgage amount, and paying two to three points is typical. If you borrow $100,000 for a mortgage, you may pay $3,000 as a service fee (points) for the loan.

Lenders generally assume you can afford to spend 28 percent of your total income on your mortgage, property taxes, and homeowner's insurance. Even if you meet this requirement, you may still be rejected if your mortgage expenses and other regular debt payments (student and auto loans) are more than 36 percent of your total income.

If you borrow from a mortgage lender, you will have the option of a fixed-rate mortgage or an adjustable-rate mortgage (ARM). The best choice for you will depend on your available cash, how frequently you move, and most important of all, whether you think interest rates will go up or down.

| Table 11.8 | Buying a New Home |

Mortgage on Average New Home, 2004		Loan	Interest Rate on Mortgage		
			7.00%	7.50%	8.00%
Terms		$100,000	$665	$699	$734
Purchase price	$297,600	150,000	998	1,049	1,101
Amount of loan	218,700	200,000	1,331	1,398	1,468
Loan-to-price ratio	76%	250,000	1,663	1,748	1,834
Maturity	29 years	300,000	1,996	2,098	2,201
Fees and charges (percent of loan amount)	0.47%	400,000	2,661	2,797	2,935
		500,000	3,326	3,496	3,669
Interest rate	5.75%	600,000	3,991	4,195	4,403

Use this chart to estimate what your monthly principal and interest payments would be based on your mortgage loan amount and interest rate.

Source: From *Statistical Supplement to the Federal Reserve Bulletin*, February 2005.

Fixed-rate or *conventional* mortgages have been around since the 1930s. The total interest and monthly payments are set at the closing. You repay the principal and interest in equal (usually monthly) installments over a 15-, 20-, or 30-year period. You will always know what you will pay and for how long. Even if interest rates increase, your monthly mortgage will not go up. However, you won't benefit if interest rates fall.[4]

ARMs were introduced in the 1980s to help more borrowers qualify for mortgages and to protect lenders by letting them pass along higher interest costs to borrowers. An ARM has a variable interest rate that changes on a regular basis, say, once a year, to reflect fluctuations in the cost of borrowing. Lenders tie the variable interest rate to another interest rate such as the rate on 1-year U.S. Treasury securities. As the rate on Treasury securities fluctuates, so does the rate on your mortgage and also your monthly mortgage payment.

Compared to fixed-rate mortgages, ARMs are usually offered at lower initial rates and with lower closing costs. Also, the interest rate on your ARM will decrease if other interest rates decline. Keep in mind, however, that you will have to pay more interest if the rate on your ARM goes up. However, ARMs have limits, or caps, on the amount of the interest rate that can be charged over the life of a contract.

EFFECTS OF SEVERE INFLATION

During periods of severe inflation, when the annual rate of inflation is 10 percent or higher, economic behavior may change. Many people feel discouraged because their income cannot keep up with rising prices. They cannot plan for future expenses because they do not know how much their money will buy later. *3rd world*

---

[4] If interest rates decline, are you stuck with your fixed-rate loan for, say, the next 25 years? No. You may want to refinance your fixed-rate loan to get a lower rate. This will reduce your monthly payment and the overall cost of the mortgage. However, refinancing usually requires you to again bear the closing costs on a mortgage. Refinancing a mortgage requires an application and credit check, new survey, title search and insurance, an appraisal and inspection, and attorneys. Refinancing may thus force you to pay sizable closing costs and up-front fees again, even if your mortgage is only several years old. Although every situation is different, the general rule is that it pays to refinance if you can obtain an interest rate of at least two percentage points lower than you're currently paying.

Some consumers fight the effects of inflation by purchasing more than usual during an inflationary period. Many consumers borrow money or use credit for large expenses, instead of purchasing later when prices will probably have risen even further. Moreover, some consumers may barter their services, do their own home repairs, and make their own clothing.

Some people attempt to protect themselves against inflation by investing in items that quickly increase in value. Such items include gold bars, rare stamps, gold and silver coins, diamonds, and art objects. Many people purchase real estate during inflationary periods because the value of land and buildings tends to increase rapidly at such times.

Some businesses may prosper during periods of inflation. They include discount stores, credit card agencies, and agencies that collect overdue debts. Businesses that lease items such as large appliances and automobiles, which many people cannot afford to purchase, also thrive at these times.

It is possible that a country may experience **hyperinflation,** a rapid and uncontrolled inflation that destroys its economy. For example, hyperinflation caused the collapse of the German economy after World War I ended in 1918. The German government printed large amounts of currency to finance itself after the war. Therefore, prices in Germany increased more than 1 trillion percent from August 1922 to December 1923. In 1923, $1 in U.S. currency was worth over 4 trillion marks! Many Germans took to burning their paper money because it was a cheaper source of fuel than firewood.

The hyperinflation left a traumatic impression on the German economy. Business owners discovered the impossibility of rational economic planning. Profits declined as employees demanded frequent increases in wages. Workers were often paid daily and sometimes two and three times a day, so that they could purchase goods in the morning before the inevitable afternoon increase in prices. Workers became demoralized and were reluctant to work as their money became worthless or virtually worthless. Also, patrons at restaurants found that they had to pay more for their meals than was listed on the menu when they ordered. Also, speculation became rampant, which disrupted production. The result was a 600-percent increase in unemployment between September 1 and December 15, 1923. As the hyperinflation intensified, people could not find goods on the shelves of retailers. Indeed, hyperinflation crushed the middle class of Germany and left an imprint on Germany that affects its governmental policy to this day.

CAUSES OF INFLATION

Recall that inflation is an increase in the general level of prices and that prices are the result of the interaction of buyers' demand and sellers' supply decisions. Therefore, forces taking place on either the buyers' side of the market or the sellers' side of the market may cause inflation. Inflation originating from upward pressure on the buyers' side of the market is called **demand-pull inflation.** Inflation caused by upward pressure on the sellers' side of the market is termed **cost-push inflation.**

The most familiar type of inflation is demand-pull inflation, which occurs when buyers' demands to purchase goods and services outrun sellers' capacities to supply them, thus forcing up prices on what is available. Businesses cannot respond to this excess demand because all available resources are fully employed. Demand-pull inflation is often described as a situation in which "too much money chases too few goods."

However, some economists argue that inflation is caused on the sellers' side of the market. When businesses raise their prices in response to cost increases, the result is cost-push inflation. Workers then may demand higher wages to keep up with rising prices, and a wage-price spiral occurs. If wages and prices rise but production does not, the supply of goods and services cannot meet the demand for those items.

Cost-push inflation also occurs if a limited number of businesses control the supply of certain products. The increase of oil prices during the 1970s provides a good example. During this period, the Organization of Petroleum Exporting Countries (OPEC) limited the supply of oil to drive prices up and thus earn higher profits. Because oil is a resource used to make other goods, the cost of those items also rose, resulting in cost-push inflation.

This chapter considered the impacts of the business cycle, unemployment, and inflation on the economy. In the next chapter, we will use aggregate demand curves and aggregate supply curves to analyze the causes of macroeconomic instability.

C H E C K   P O I N T

1. What is meant by inflation, and how is it measured?

2. Who is helped or hurt by inflation?

3. What are the sources of inflation?

Chapter Summary

1. The business cycle refers to recurrent ups and downs in the level of economic activity extending over several years. Although business cycles vary in intensity and duration, we divide each into four phases: peak, recession, trough, and recovery.

2. When real GDP decreases for at least two consecutive quarters, we say that the economy is in a recession. A depression is a very deep and prolonged recession. Because no subsequent recession has approached the severity of the Great Depression, the term "depression" is often used as a reference to the slump of the 1930s.

3. Many economists believe that a change in total spending is the immediate determinant of domestic output and employment. However, other economists maintain that business cycles are caused by changes in the supply side of the market, such as the development of better technologies or decreases in natural resources.

4. The unemployment rate is the number of people unemployed divided by the number of persons in the labor force. Although economists take great care in calculating the unemployment rate, it suffers from problems involving part-time employment and discouraged workers.

5. Not everyone who is unemployed is unemployed for the same reason. In describing labor markets, economists refer to frictional unemployment, cyclical unemployment, and structural unemployment. To mitigate the costs of unemployment, government has many programs such as education and training programs and also unemployment insurance.

6. Economists call the level of unemployment at which there is no cyclical unemployment the "natural rate of unemployment." The natural rate of unemployment is the sum of frictional and structural unemployment and is the economist's notion of "full employment." Most economists estimate the natural rate of unemployment to be between 4 and 6 percent of the labor force.

7. Inflation is a sustained or continuous rise in the general price level; deflation is a continuing fall in the average price level. The most frequently cited indicator of inflation is the consumer price index.

8. Inflation results in a decrease in the purchasing power of a fixed amount of income, a redistribution of wealth from creditors to debtors, declining real interest rates on savings, and higher tax revenues for the government.

9. Inflation may be caused by forces taking place on the buyers' side of the market or the sellers' side of the market. Inflation originating from upward pressure on the buyers' side of the market is called demand-pull inflation. Cost-push inflation is caused by upward pressure on the sellers' side of the market.

Key Terms and Concepts

business cycle (258)

peak (260)

recession (260)

trough (260)

recovery (260)

depression (261)

unemployed (263)

unemployment rate (264)

discouraged worker (264)

frictional unemployment (264)

structural unemployment (265)

cyclical unemployment (265)

unemployment insurance (266)

natural rate of unemployment (266)

full employment (266)

inflation (271)

deflation (271)

consumer price index (CPI) (271)

nominal income (273)

real income (273)

nominal interest rate (275)

real interest rate (275)

hyperinflation (278)

demand-pull inflation (278)

cost-push inflation (278)

Self-Test: Multiple-Choice Questions

1. A turning point of the business cycle is the

   a. peak.
   b. recession.
   c. depression.
   d. recovery.

2. If the consumer price index increases by 5 percent and Helen Osborne's nominal income increases by 3 percent, her real income

   a. increases by 8 percent.
   b. increases by 2 percent.
   c. decreases by 2 percent.
   d. decreases by 8 percent.

3. Although all segments of the economy feel the business cycle, it tends to affect _____ industries the most.

   a. durable good
   b. nondurable good

    c. business services

    d. consumer services

4. The unemployment rate is the percentage of the

    a. labor force unemployed.

    b. total population unemployed.

    c. labor force that has been fired or laid off.

    d. total population that has been fired or laid off.

5. Upon graduation from college, John Smith begins his job search. Two months later, Hewlett-Packard hires him as a systems analyst. During this period, John Smith encounters

    a. structural unemployment.

    b. cyclical unemployment.

    c. frictional unemployment.

    d. seasonal unemployment.

6. The natural rate of unemployment, which is the economist's notion of full employment, is the sum of

    a. frictional unemployment and structural unemployment.

    b. frictional unemployment and cyclical unemployment.

    c. structural unemployment and cyclical unemployment.

    d. none of the above.

7. Compared to the United States, Europe has experienced a higher unemployment rate in recent years. Which of the following is *not* a plausible reason for this discrepancy?

    a. Relatively high wages in the nonunion sectors of the European economy

    b. Relatively high wages in the union-controlled sectors of the European economy

    c. Relatively high minimum wage laws in Europe

    d. Relatively low welfare benefits in Europe

8. The most frequently cited indicator of inflation in the United States is the

    a. wholesale price index.

    b. business price index.

    c. consumer price index.

    d. producer price index.

9. Assume that you have $10 to purchase goods and services in 2004, the consumer price index in 1960 equals 24.1, and the consumer price index in 2004 equals 160.5. You would need _____ in 1960 to buy the same amount of goods and services in 2004.

    a. $1

    b. $1.25

    c. $1.50

    d. $1.75

10. Assume that in 1950 it cost 25 cents to go to a baseball game, the consumer price index equals 24.1 in 1950, and the consumer price index equals 160.5 in 2004. What would attending a baseball game in 2004 be worth in 2004 dollars?

    a. $1.27

    b. $1.41

    c. $1.53

    d. $1.67

Answers to Multiple-Choice Questions

1. a   **2.** c   **3.** a   **4.** a   **5.** c   **6.** a   **7.** d   **8.** c   **9.** c   **10.** d

Study Questions and Problems

1. Suppose the Bureau of Labor Statistics announces that of all adult Americans, 129 million are employed, 7 million are unemployed, 3 million are not in the labor force, and 2 million are part-time workers looking for full-time jobs. What is the unemployment rate?

2. Discuss how the following individuals would be affected by inflation of 9 percent per year.

   a. A student heavily indebted with loans.
   b. A retired nurse receiving a fixed pension.
   c. An individual with a savings account paying an interest rate of 4 percent per year.
   d. An autoworker who has a cost-of-living adjustment included in his labor contract.

3. If the consumer price index was 155 last year and 160 this year, what was this year's rate of inflation?

4. How can you realize an increase in nominal income and a decrease in real income at the same time?

5. Suppose the interest rate on your passbook savings account is 4 percent per year and this year's inflation rate is 5 percent. Are you better off or worse off as a saver?

6. Assume that the consumer price index in 1960 equaled 50 while in 1990 it equaled 150. Suppose you had $60 in 1990 to purchase goods and services. How much money would you have needed in 1960 to buy the same amount of goods and services?

| Table 11.9 | Inflation and Real Wages | | | |

Year	CPI	Inflation Rate	Nominal Wage	Real Wage
2000	100	_____	$12.00	_____
2001	106	_____	14.00	_____
2002	110	_____	15.00	_____
2003	112	_____	15.50	_____

| Table 11.10 | Nominal and Real Interest Rates | | |

Year	Inflation Rate	Nominal Interest Rate	Real Interest Rate
2001	6%	8%	_____
2002	3	3	_____
2003	5	4	_____

7. In 1914, Henry Ford paid his employees $5 a day. If the consumer price index was 11 in 1914 and 161 in 1997, how much is the Ford paycheck worth in 1997 dollars?

8. In Table 11.9, compute the inflation rate for 2001, 2002, and 2003. Also compute the real wage in each year.

9. In Table 11.10, compute the real interest rate for 2001, 2002, and 2003. Assume that the CPI refers to the price level at the end of each year.

10. How can hyperinflation result in depression?

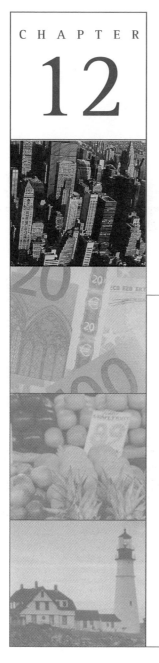

Macroeconomic Instability: Aggregate Demand and Aggregate Supply

Chapter objectives

After reading this chapter, you should be able to:

1. Explain why the classical economists felt that the economy would automatically move to full employment and why John Maynard Keynes argued that the market economy is inherently unstable.

2. Develop the macroeconomic model of aggregate supply and aggregate demand to understand how prices and output are determined in the short run.

3. Use the model of aggregate supply and aggregate demand to analyze the origins of recession and inflation.

4. Distinguish between demand-pull inflation and cost-push inflation.

5. Identify the policies that government might use to counteract recession or inflation.

economics IN CONTEXT

For American consumers, the late 1990s were about as good as it gets: Unemployment was down, while real wages were growing. With higher incomes, consumers went on a spending spree.

Consider Mary Ann Turnquist, a typical American consumer. In 2000, she and her husband Fred purchased a 4-bedroom home for $198,000 in Boulder, Colorado. They then spent $1,500 in cash on a new bedroom set and $4,000 on new kitchen and laundry appliances. The couple, she a clerk in the state court and he a truck mechanic, were not concerned about their job security or paying off their mortgage. With a strong economy in 2000, they had every right to feel secure. So did most Americans.

Indeed, consumers had plenty of cash to spend, which supported their spending sprees. For example, steady pay increases prompted Pam Miller of Pittsburgh to buy a new Ford Taurus to replace her Mercury Sable. Nothing was wrong with the 5-year-old vehicle, but Pam said that having extra cash gave her an itch for new wheels.

Paychecks went a lot further at the turn of the century, thanks to a low inflation rate that was reinforced by cheap imports from Asia as a result of its economic crisis. Also, low mortgage rates allowed more families to own homes. Furthermore, consumer installment debt as a percent of take-home pay had declined, thus giving consumers more freedom to take out home equity loans to use for computers, college tuition, and vacation. Finally, the stock market's "bull run" continued to increase household wealth.

However, the economy's dependence on consumers did have its risks. A sudden shock, such as a big decrease in stock prices, could cause consumers to feel less wealthy and snap shut their pocketbooks, leaving businesses with too much inventory and too many workers. Another risk was that all of the consumer buying could become too much of a good thing. Excess spending could result in an overheating economy, where more competition for workers could push labor costs above gains in productivity, resulting in inflation. If that trend continued and businesses started increasing prices, the Federal Reserve might slam on the monetary brakes, perhaps pushing the economy into recession.

Indeed, the growth performance of the U.S. economy has been uneven. In most years, the output of goods and services rises as a result of increases in the capital stock, increases in the labor force, and advances in technological knowledge. In some years, however, economic growth does not take place. Firms find themselves unable to sell the goods and services that they have produced so they shut down factories and lay off workers. As a result, the economy's real GDP declines.

The central focus of macroeconomics is on what causes short-run fluctuations in economic activity and what, if anything, the government can do to promote full employment without inflation. To answer these questions, we need a model of the macroeconomy. Most economists use the model of aggregate demand and aggregate supply. In this chapter, we develop aggregate demand and aggregate supply curves that will assist us in analyzing the problems of recession and inflation.

STABILITY OF THE MACROECONOMY

Indeed, the stability of the macroeconomy is of concern to households, businesses, and government. Let us examine the views of classical economists and John Maynard Keynes concerning this topic.

Classical View

Prior to the Great Depression of the 1930s, a group of economists known as the classical economists dominated economic thinking. According to classical economists, the market economy automatically adjusted to ensure the full employment of its resources. Although an economic downturn might force producers to decrease their output and lay off workers, the downturn would be short-lived. Because classical economists thought economic downturns were temporary, they argued that government should not interfere in economic affairs.

The optimism of classical economists was founded on the assumption of freely flexible wages and flexible prices. If some workers became unemployed during an economic slump, they would make themselves attractive to employers by offering their services at lower wages. As wages fell, firms would find it more profitable to hire workers. As a result, the downward adjustment in wages would guarantee that everyone who wanted a job would find one.

Flexible prices would also help eliminate an economic downturn, according to classical economists. During a recession, firms realize a decrease in demand for products. To clear the market of any excess supply, they would be willing to accept price reductions. If prices would decline enough, all the output produced could be sold. Therefore, workers would not have to be laid off because of declining consumer demand.

Classical economists also contended that the economy would never suffer from a level of spending that would be inadequate to purchase the full-employment level of output. This contention was based on **Say's Law,** attributed to the nineteenth-century economist Jean Baptiste Say. According to Say's Law, "supply creates its own demand." Whatever was produced (supplied) would create the income necessary to purchase that production. Say's Law thus suggests that there will be enough spending to buy the full-employment output. Overproduction is therefore an impossibility according to classical economists. Simply put, the classical model attempted to explain the long-run behavior of the economy whereby powerful forces existed to drive the economy to full employment.

The Great Depression

Although classical economists advocated the impossibility of long-run unemployment, the Great Depression was a stunning blow to their theory. The depression was a global economic downturn that lasted for more than a decade. It ranked as the worst and longest period of low business activity and high unemployment in modern times. It even caused some nations to change their leader and type of government.[1] The Great Depression began in October 1929, when stock values in the United States declined sharply. Thousands of stockholders lost huge amounts of money, and many went bankrupt. Factories, banks, and stores shut down and left millions of people jobless and penniless. Many Americans had to depend on charity or the government for food and other basic necessities. The Great Depression affected almost every nation. It ended after nations increased their output of war goods at the beginning of World War II. The rising level of production provided jobs and put large sums of money back into circulation.   *Proving Say's Law*

The depression was caused by several factors. During the 1920s, many bank failures, together with low incomes among farmers and factory workers, set the stage for the depression. Farmers were hit hard by slumping prices of agricultural goods. Although industrial production dramatically rose in the 1920s, incomes of factory workers rose far more slowly. Thus, these workers could not purchase products as fast as industry

---

[1] John K. Galbraith, *The Great Crash,* 1929 (New York: Houghton Mifflin, 1979) and Robert Stobel, "The Great Depression," *World Book Encyclopedia* (Chicago, IL: World Book Inc., 1988), pp. 363–367.

produced them. Most economists agree that the stock market crash of 1929 triggered the depression. The crash was the result of rampant speculation in which people bought stocks in hopes of making larger profits following future price increases. When stock values decreased dramatically in 1929, many investors panicked and sold huge amounts of stock at losses.

In 1925, about 3 percent of the nation's workers were unemployed. The unemployment rate rose to 9 percent in 1930 and 25 percent in 1933. Many Americans who maintained or found jobs had to absorb wage reductions. In 1932, wage cuts averaged about 18 percent. Many people, including college graduates, felt lucky to find any job. In 1932, the New York City Police Department estimated that 8,000 persons over the age of 17 sold pencils or shined shoes for a living. A popular song of the 1930s called "Brother, Can You Spare a Dime?" symbolized the despair of Americans.

Herbert Hoover was president when the depression began. He thought that business, if left alone to operate without government regulation, would correct the economic downturn. He vetoed several bills intended to combat the depression because he believed they provided the federal government with too much power. Instead, he felt that it was the states' responsibility to provide assistance for the poor. Since most Americans thought that Hoover performed inadequately in combating the depression, they elected Franklin D. Roosevelt to be president in 1932.

Roosevelt thought the federal government had a major responsibility of combating the Great Depression. He called Congress into special session to enact legislation to help the needy. Roosevelt called his program the New Deal. These laws gave states money for the poor and provided jobs in the construction of such public projects as highways, parks, schools, bridges, and dams. The federal government also fostered recovery by spending large amounts of money and increased trade by lowering tariffs on imported goods, in return for other nations lowering tariffs on products they purchased from the United States. Congress also created agencies to supervise banks, prevent unfair labor practices, and protect investors from purchasing unsafe stocks and bonds. In 1935, Congress passed the Social Security Act to provide money for retired and unemployed people. Although the New Deal did not end the depression, it did provide economic relief and renewed the confidence of Americans in the federal government.

The Great Depression altered the opinions of many Americans toward business and the federal government. Prior to the depression, most people considered bankers and business executives to be the nation's leaders. After the stock market crashed and these leaders could not promote prosperity, many Americans lost confidence in them. They thought that the government, not business, had the responsibility of stabilizing the economy. The stage was set for John Maynard Keynes, and his emphasis on an activist government, to influence economic thinking and policymaking.

Keynesian View

In 1936, in the midst of the Great Depression, British economist **John Maynard Keynes** formed a theory that provided an explanation for prolonged depressed conditions.[2] According to Keynes and his followers, the market economy is inherently unstable, and the Great Depression was no accident; adverse shocks that occur in one sector of the economy can quickly affect other sectors, causing reductions in total output and employment. Although classical economists might explain the economy's operation in the long run, the long run could be a very long time in arriving according to Keynes. Keynes thus

---

[2] John M. Keynes, *The General Theory of Employment, Interest, and Money* (New York: Harcourt, Brace and Company, 1936).

developed a macroeconomic model that focused on the causes of economic fluctuations in the short run.

A main disagreement that Keynes had with classical economists was that prices and wages did not appear sufficiently flexible to guarantee the full employment of resources. *true* According to Keynes, prices and wages were rather inflexible, or sticky, in a downward direction. Even when demand was weak, Keynes argued that powerful labor unions and large businesses would resist wage and price reductions. Therefore, output and employment would fall during an economic downturn.

The essence of Keynesian economics is simple. The level of economic activity depends on the total spending of consumers, businesses, and government. If business expectations are pessimistic, investment spending will be reduced, resulting in a series of decreases in total spending. If this should occur, the economy can move into a depression and remain there.

Because the market economy is unstable, Keynes argued that an activist government must intervene to protect jobs and income. To avoid a depression, Keynes recommended that government increase spending, promote lower interest rates, and make more money available for loans. These actions, he maintained, would encourage investment and consumption spending, which result in a greater increase in national output, employment, and income. Simply put, Keynes was a champion of the modern mixed economy in which government increases its spending during downturns to increase the overall level of demand and, thus, employment.

Keynes' ideas altered the thinking of many economists and became increasingly accepted in colleges and government agencies in the 1940s and 1950s. By the 1960s, most of the economics profession had adopted his theory. Macroeconomics became Keynesian economics, and the classical model was subsequently eliminated from most economics textbooks.

However, a counterrevolution to Keynesian economics emerged by the 1970s and 1980s. Today, many economists who find classical theory inadequate in explaining economic fluctuations in the short run find it useful in explaining long-run economic trends. The policy prescriptions of Keynesian economics will be further discussed in Chapters 13 and 15.

CHECK POINT

1. Why did classical economists maintain that the market economy automatically ensured the full employment of its resources?

2. According to John Maynard Keynes, the market economy is inherently unstable and the Great Depression was no accident. Explain.

3. What was the proper role for government in the economy according to classical economists and John Maynard Keynes?

AGGREGATE DEMAND AND AGGREGATE SUPPLY

In the tradition of Keynes, let us develop a model of aggregate demand and aggregate supply that we can use to understand how output and prices are determined in the short run.

Just as we analyze an individual market with a market demand curve and a market supply curve, we analyze fluctuations in the economy as a whole with the model of

Figure 12.1 | **Macroeconomic Equilibrium**

The economy is in equilibrium when aggregate supply equals aggregate demand. This intersection determines the equilibrium price level and output for the economy.

aggregate demand and aggregate supply. This model is shown in Figure 12.1. On the vertical axis is the average price level in the economy, as measured by the consumer price index. On the horizontal axis is the total quantity of goods and services. Because we are adding together many different kinds of products, their dollar value is used to represent quantity in Figure 12.1. To keep out the effects of inflation, this quantity is in *real* terms—that is, real GDP.

In Figure 12.1, the aggregate demand curve shows the total demand of all people for all final goods and services produced in an economy. The aggregate supply curve is the total supply of all final goods and services in an economy. The economy is in equilibrium when aggregate demand equals aggregate supply. This is where the two lines cross at point *A*. To understand the nature of macroeconomic equilibrium, let us examine the forces that shape the aggregate demand and aggregate supply curves.

AGGREGATE DEMAND

An aggregate demand curve shows the total amount of final goods and services (real GDP) that buyers will purchase at alternative price levels during a given year. Recall that the total amount of final goods and services can be divided into the amounts spent for consumption, investment, government purchases, and net exports. The aggregate quantity demanded is the quantity of final output that buyers will purchase at a given price level.

As seen in Figure 12.1, the aggregate demand curve may look like a market demand curve, but it's really different. Instead of showing the relationship between the price and quantity demanded of a single good, say, motorcycles, the aggregate demand curve describes the relationship between the price level and the aggregate quantity of all final goods and services demanded in the economy.

Movements Along an Aggregate Demand Curve

Referring to Figure 12.1, notice that the aggregate demand curve is downward sloping. As the price level *falls,* other things equal, the total amount of final goods and services purchased *rises.* What explains this relationship?

The price level is a determinant of the amount of money demanded. As the price level declines, households need to hold less money to purchase the goods and services they desire. Households thus try to decrease their holdings of money by lending it out as the price level falls. For example, a household might place its excess money in an interest-bearing savings account at a bank. The increased supply of savings drives interest rates downward, thereby encouraging borrowing by households who wish to invest in new housing or by businesses that want to invest in new plant and equipment. Put simply, a lower price level decreases interest rates, which results in additional spending on investment goods and so increases the aggregate quantity of goods and services demanded.[3]

The downward slope of the aggregate demand curve suggests that, other things equal, a decrease in the price level increases the aggregate quantity of goods and services demanded. Movements along the aggregate demand curve are thus caused by a change in the price level of the economy.

Shifts in an Aggregate Demand Curve

So far, we have found that changes in the price level induce changes in the level of spending of consumers, businesses, government, and foreigners. However, the spending patterns of these sectors are affected by factors other than the price level. If one or more of these other factors changes, the aggregate demand curve shifts.

A change in aggregate demand is shown by a rightward or leftward shift in the aggregate demand curve. An *increase* in aggregate demand is represented by a *rightward* shift in the aggregate demand curve. When aggregate demand increases, a greater quantity of goods and services is demanded at each alternative price. Conversely, a *decrease* in aggregate demand is denoted by a *leftward* shift of the aggregate demand curve.

Many possible examples of events can shift the aggregate demand curve. Here are a few.

- Due to expectations of a future economic recession, U.S. business firms do not think they can sell all of their current output. Therefore, they decrease their purchases of machines and equipment, which results in a leftward shift in the aggregate demand curve.

- Economic weakness in Japan slows its economic growth, thereby depressing demand for U.S. exports of beef, lumber, and chemicals. As a result, the aggregate demand curve will shift leftward for the United States.

- Because of political tensions in the Middle East, Congress decides to increase purchases of new weapons systems. As the overall quantity of goods purchased increases, the aggregate demand curve shifts rightward.

- With the prices of stocks and homes rising, Americans who own these items suddenly become less concerned about saving for retirement and increase their current consumption. Because the quantity of goods and services demanded increases at each alternative price level, the aggregate demand curve shifts rightward. Just how much can a soaring stock market drive up consumer spending? The rule of thumb is that consumers spend 4 cents more for each dollar in personal wealth. Figure 12.2 shows the relationship between stock prices and changes in

---

[3] This explanation of the downward-sloping aggregate demand curve is known as the *interest rate effect.* Other explanations include the so-called *real wealth effect* and the *foreign trade effect,* which can be found in more advanced textbooks on macroeconomics.

| Figure 12.2 | The Wealth Effect: Stock Prices Versus Change in Consumer Spending, Inflation-Adjusted Annual Rate |

According to the wealth effect, rising stock prices result in increased household wealth and thus a rise in consumption spending.

*The Wilshire 5000 is the broadest measure available for the U.S. stock market, measuring the values of more than 6,500 stocks that it contains.

Source: Data taken from U.S. Department of Commerce and Wilshire Associates.

consumer spending for the period 1997–2001. As the figure suggests, consumers strongly react to rising and falling stock portfolios.

THE MULTIPLIER EFFECT

According to Keynesian economics, if an increase in demand occurs in the economy, then the final effect on national output will be much greater. In other words, there will be a multiple expansion of output. How does this happen?

Suppose the U.S. government purchases additional uniforms for members of the military. When clothing production increases, the demand for the textiles used in that production also rises. Increasing textile production then strengthens the demand for fibers, aiding the chemical manufacturer, cotton farmer, and sheep rancher alike. And when those producers are able to sell their goods, the providers of production equipment, parts, fuel, and seed are also able to sell theirs. Moreover, the commercial support services feel the prosperity: the software specialists, engineers, architects, bankers, insurance companies, truckers, railroaders, utilities, and construction workers. With U.S. factories in operation, countless small businesses then prosper: the car dealerships, dry cleaners, barbershops, and restaurants, among many local services. Simply put, an increase in one part of the economy moves throughout its length and breadth, aiding owners, workers, suppliers, distributors, communities, states, and ultimately the whole nation. In other words, an improvement in economic activity in one sector of the economy multiplies as it flows through the economy. But these forces also operate in reverse: A decline in one sector of the economy results in a magnified contractionary effect on the overall economy. Economists call this the **multiplier effect.**

A good analogy to understand the multiplier effect is that of someone throwing a rock into a pond: there is an initial splash (the increased spending on military uniforms), then additional ripples as the recipients of the initial money spend it, and so on, until the ripples decline in strength as they reach the bank.

Figure 12.3	Aggregate Supply Curve

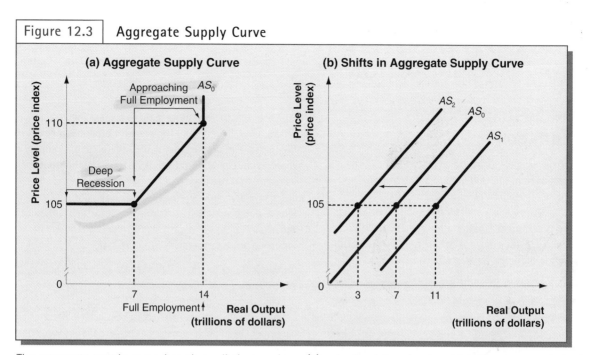

The aggregate supply curve has three distinct regions: (1) a horizontal region in which the economy is in deep recession or depression, (2) an upward-sloping region in which the economy approaches full employment, and (3) a vertical region in which the economy is at full employment. An increase (decrease) in aggregate supply is denoted by a rightward (leftward) shift of the aggregate supply curve.

The multiplier effect begins by recognizing that all economies experience fluctuations in aggregate demand that can be caused by autonomous changes in spending on consumption, investment, government purchases, and net exports.[4] For example, a rise in aggregate demand of $100 million gives rise to further increases through the impact of higher incomes on consumer spending. This results in, say, a $300 million increase in national output. The **multiplier** is the ratio of the change in national output to the change in aggregate demand; in this example, the multiplier equals 3 (300/100 = 3). It indicates the extent to which the change in aggregate demand is "multiplied" into changes in larger output. The mechanics of the multiplier effect are discussed in "Exploring Further 12.1" at the end of this chapter.

The multiplier effect is of great importance for economic policymakers. To combat a weak economy, policymakers may inject a stimulus by increasing government expenditures. Such a policy results in an increase in aggregate demand, which can lead to a magnified increase in the economy's output, employment, and income. Indeed, the multiplier effect is an integral part of economic policymaking, as discussed in the next chapter.

AGGREGATE SUPPLY

Now let's turn to the aggregate supply curve. The aggregate supply curve shows the relationship between the level of prices and amount of final goods and services (real GDP) that will be produced by the economy in a given year. The **aggregate quantity supplied** is the quantity of final output that will be supplied by producers at a particular price level. Figure 12.3 shows the economy's aggregate supply curve. When drawing the aggregate

---

[4] An autonomous variable is one that is assumed not to depend on the state of the economy—that is, it does not change when the economy changes.

economics
IN ACTION

Is Productivity a Cure for Inflation?

In 2000, government policymakers struggled to apply what happened in the United States to traditional economic models. Growth was robust, stocks were soaring, job markets were tightening—yet inflation was nowhere to be found. Quarter after quarter, the pattern held. And try as they did, policymakers couldn't explain it by using the old rules. So they stopped trying.

Instead, they rallied around a new consensus view: The United States was in the midst of a technology-driven boom that allowed the economy to grow faster than once thought possible without igniting growth-inhibiting wage and price increases. Indeed, unemployment stood at a 29-year low, the economic expansion appeared inexhaustible; and the money supply was growing rapidly. But with inflation in check, these indicators could no longer be interpreted in the same manner.

The key to the new thinking was the belief that productivity growth, which had languished at 1 percent during the 1970s and 1980s, had taken a long-term leap to 2 percent or more as companies used technology to become more efficient. Policymakers embraced the argument that the adoption of productivity-enhancing technology changed the way the economy operates. However, was the increase in productivity a change in the trend?

The possibilities of a long-term productivity rate of 2 percent were enormous for policymakers. It meant that they could live with stronger growth without fearing resurgent inflation.

Analysis

Traditional theory suggests that the relationship between the economy's price level and real output is such that as production increases from low employment toward full-employment levels, the price level increases more rapidly as full employment is approached. Figure 12.4 shows this relationship. Given aggregate supply curve AS_0, as

aggregate demand increases from AD_0 to AD_1 to AD_2, the price level rises more rapidly as full employment is approached.

Suppose that the economy realizes a sharp increase in productivity. By reducing the per-unit production cost, the increase in productivity causes the aggregate supply curve to shift rightward from AS_0 to AS_1. Real output increases and the price level remains unchanged as aggregate demand increases from AD_0 to AD_1 to AD_2. Simply put, productivity growth is a factor that underlies the expansion of aggregate supply and is a moderating influence on the economy's inflation rate.

Although higher productivity increases aggregate supply, which dampens inflation, it can also increase aggregate demand, which aggravates inflation. The reason? Productivity advances affect stock prices, which affect consumer spending. If investors anticipate that productivity will continue to increase, they will bid up stock prices today in the expectation that more productive companies will earn higher profits in the future. As investors feel richer, they will spend more on everything from computers to vacations. Increased consumption spending boosts aggregate demand, which can aggravate inflation.

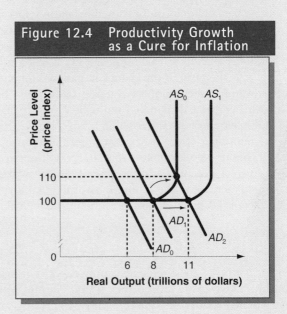

Figure 12.4   Productivity Growth as a Cure for Inflation

supply curve, we assume that all resource prices and the availability of resources in the economy are constant. We also assume that the level of technology remains fixed during the current period.

Movements Along an Aggregate Supply Curve

Referring to Figure 12.3, notice that the aggregate supply curve has three segments: a horizontal range at price level 105, a positively sloped range from price level 105 to price level 110, and a vertical range from price level 110 and above.

Along the horizontal segment of the aggregate supply curve, the economy is assumed to be in recession. Notice that the full-employment level of real output is at $14 trillion, far beyond the output levels of the horizontal region of the aggregate supply curve. Recall that during a deep recession or depression there is much excess capacity and many unemployed resources in the economy. Therefore, producers are willing to sell additional output at current prices, while workers are willing to work extra hours at current wages. Because excess capacity places no upward pressure on prices and wages, changes in aggregate demand cause changes in real output, but no change in the price level, along the horizontal segment of the aggregate supply curve.

Throughout the positively sloped region of the aggregate supply curve, higher price levels provide an incentive for companies to produce and sell additional real output, while lower price levels decrease real output. Therefore, the relationship between the price level and the amount of output firms offer for sale is positive or direct. Consequently, as the price level rises from 105 to 110, firms find it profitable to increase real output from $7 trillion to $14 trillion. As companies increase production, they hire additional workers, which causes the unemployment rate to decline.

However, there is a physical limit to the amount of output that can be produced in a given year. Once the economy reaches its full-employment output level, $14 trillion in this illustration, the aggregate supply curve becomes vertical. At that point, it is impossible to hire the labor and other resources needed to expand output further. Any rise in the price level will not call forth extra output because the economy is already operating at maximum capacity. Individual companies may attempt to increase output by offering higher wages to attract workers from other companies. This will raise production costs and ultimately prices. However, the extra workers and output that one company gains will be forgone by other companies that lose workers. Therefore, despite the increase in wage rates and price level, real output will not expand for the economy when it is at full employment.

that's why its cyclical

Shifts in an Aggregate Supply Curve

The aggregate supply curve shows the quantity of goods and services that companies produce and sell at alternative price levels. However, the amount that firms will produce does not depend on the price level alone. Many events can induce shifts in the aggregate supply curve.

A change in aggregate supply is shown by a rightward or leftward shift in the aggregate supply curve. Referring to Figure 12.3, an *increase* in aggregate supply is represented by a *rightward* shift in the aggregate supply curve. When aggregate supply increases, a greater quantity of output is supplied at each possible price. Conversely, a *decrease* in aggregate supply is represented by a *leftward* shift in the aggregate supply curve.

Recall that we draw the aggregate supply curve under the assumption that the level of all resource prices, the availability and quality of resources, and technology are fixed.

A change in one or more of these factors will cause the aggregate supply curve to shift. Here are a few examples of events that result in a shift in the aggregate supply curve.

- Wages and salaries are the largest expense for many companies, typically accounting for 70 to 75 percent of total costs. Therefore, an increase in wages and salaries results in a significant cost increase. With unit costs rising, a firm will not be able to produce as much output at any given price. Therefore, a wage or salary increase causes the aggregate supply curve to shift leftward. A rise in the price of other resources will also cause the aggregate supply curve to shift leftward.

- To encourage the economy to increase its stock of capital goods, suppose the government reduces taxes for businesses. Because the tax cut increases the profitability of investment, businesses purchase new, superior equipment that causes productivity to increase. By reducing per-unit production costs, the increase in productivity allows firms to offer more output at each price level, thus shifting the aggregate supply curve to the right.

- Suppose that entrepreneurs such as Bill Gates develop new technologies that increase the economy's productive capacity. This would decrease per-unit costs of production and allow more output to be produced at each price. Therefore, the aggregate supply curve shifts rightward.

CHECK   POINT

1. What factors account for the inverse relationship between the aggregate quantity demanded and the price level? Give examples of events that would cause the aggregate demand curve to shift rightward or leftward.

2. What is the multiplier effect? What accounts for the size of the multiplier?

3. Why does the aggregate supply curve have a horizontal region, an upward-sloping region, and a vertical region? Give examples of events that would cause the aggregate supply curve to shift rightward or leftward.

THE ORIGINS OF RECESSION

Now that we have introduced the model of aggregate demand and aggregate supply, we have the tools we need to analyze short-term fluctuations in economic activity. We will first apply the aggregate demand and aggregate supply model to the problem of recession, and then to inflation.

Decreases in Aggregate Demand

Referring to Figure 12.5, assume the economy is in equilibrium at point *A*, whereby the price level is 100 and real output is at $12 trillion. Suppose that for some reason a wave of pessimism hits the U.S. economy. The source might be an economic crisis in East Asia, an outbreak of war abroad, or a crash in the stock market. Because of this disturbance, many Americans lose confidence in the future and modify their behavior. Households curtail purchases of dishwashers and furniture, and companies postpone purchases of new equipment and machinery.

How does this wave of pessimism affect the economy? Such an event decreases the aggregate demand for goods and services. This means that at any given price level, households and companies now desire to purchase a smaller quantity of goods and services.

Figure 12.5 | The Origins of Recession

In the short run, a decrease in aggregate demand may cause the economy to move into recession. Government policymakers might attempt to offset the recession by increasing government spending in order to increase aggregate demand. A recession may also be caused by some event, say, rising oil prices, that leads to a decrease in aggregate supply. With a given aggregate demand curve, a decrease in aggregate supply can cause stagflation—a combination of recession and inflation.

As aggregate demand shifts leftward from AD_0 to AD_1 in the figure, the economy moves to equilibrium at point B, whereby real output falls to 9 trillion and the price level declines to 90. As real output decreases, companies lay off workers and unemployment rises. The decrease in real output suggests that the economy moves into a contraction because of the reduction in aggregate demand. Therefore, the pessimism that triggered the reduction in aggregate demand is, to some degree, self-fulfilling: Pessimism about the future results in declining economic activity.

What should policymakers do when confronted with such a recession? According to John Maynard Keynes, policymakers should increase government spending or make more money available for loans. These actions would shift the aggregate demand curve rightward, thus causing an increase in output, employment, and income for the economy.

The recession of 2001 provides an example of a demand shock plaguing the U.S. economy. Prior to 2001, companies eagerly invested in equipment necessary to develop new technologies, including the Internet. New businesses that used the Internet were established to sell electronics, books, clothing, and prescription drugs. They needed office buildings, capital equipment, and warehouses, which resulted in increased investment spending. By 2001, such investment caught up with the needs of the market, and the level of investment spending began to decline. Another factor contributing to falling investment was the terrorist attacks on the World Trade Center and Pentagon on September 11, 2001. The uncertainty and fear that gripped Americans following the attacks caused investment in jet airliners, hotels, and other goods to decrease. Although consumption spending continued to increase, partly due to a 10-year cut in income taxes that took place in June 2001, the decrease in investment more than offset the increase in consumption spending. This resulted in a decrease in the AD curve. As the negative multiplier effect took place, real GDP and employment declined, and the economy fell into recession. The recession lasted from March to November of 2001. Chapters 13 and 15 will discuss the role of fiscal policy and monetary policy in counteracting this recession.

Decreases in Aggregate Supply

Just as a decrease in aggregate demand can force the economy into recession, so can a decrease in aggregate supply. Referring to Figure 12.5, assume the economy is in equilibrium at point A', where the price level is 100 and real output is $12 trillion. Now suppose that firms realize an increase in production costs. It might result from an increase in the level of wages not matched by productivity increases or from a rise in the price of a key resource such as oil.

What is the macroeconomic effect of such an increase in production costs? At any given price level, firms will be willing to offer a smaller quantity of goods to the market. Therefore, as Figure 12.5 shows, the aggregate supply curve shifts leftward from AS_0 to AS_1. The decrease in aggregate supply moves the economy from its initial equilibrium at point A' to a new equilibrium at point B'. The real output of the economy decreases from $12 trillion to $9 trillion, and the price level rises from 100 to 110. The decline in aggregate supply is especially detrimental because it results in falling output, increased unemployment, and rising prices. Such an event is called **stagflation**, that is, recession (stagnation) with inflation.

The recession of 1990–1991 provides an example of a supply shock that burdened the U.S. economy. In 1990, Saddam Hussein and his Iraqi army invaded Kuwait, a major oil producer. Within six hours, Iraq occupied the entire country. Although the United States and its allies were able to oust the Iraqi army from Kuwait, during the conflict the oil produced by both Kuwait and Iraq was taken off the world market. The decrease in the supply of oil resulted in oil prices rising from $14 to $27 per barrel. Consistent with what our AS-AD model predicts, rising oil prices caused the AS curve to decrease, while the AD curve remained relatively constant. This resulted in a 1.5-percent decrease in real GDP during the first quarter of 1991 and a rise in the unemployment rate. Also, the consumer price index increased more rapidly as the recession gripped the nation.

THE ORIGINS OF INFLATION REVISITED

We will now apply the model of aggregate demand and aggregate supply to the types of inflation introduced in the previous chapter: demand-pull inflation and cost-push inflation.

Demand-Pull Inflation

Recall that *demand-pull inflation* is the increase in the average price level caused by an excess of total spending, that is, aggregate demand. The expression "too many dollars chasing too few goods" is often used to describe this type of inflation. "Too many dollars" suggests that the total spending in the economy is excessive. "Too few goods" suggests that the total supply of goods in the economy is too low in relation to that demand.

When firms cannot supply all the goods and services demanded by buyers, they respond by increasing prices. The average price level is thus pulled up by the total spending of buyers. A general increase in the availability of money and credit in the economy is a common cause of demand-pull inflation.

The degree to which an increase in aggregate demand pulls up the price level depends on how the close the economy is to the level of real output that corresponds to full employment. Suppose there is considerable unused capacity in the economy and significant unemployment during the year. Such a situation puts downward pressure on the prices charged by companies and workers' wages. In this situation, the main effect of an increase in aggregate demand will be a rise in real output, with little or no upward pressure on the price level.

Now suppose, instead, that factories and offices are operating around the clock and there is little, if any, slack capacity or unemployment. In this situation, the main effect of a rise in aggregate demand will be on the price level; there will be little, if any, impact on real output. As seen in Figure 12.6(a), an increase in aggregate demand from AD_0 to AD_1 will pull the price level from 105 to 110, a considerable increase. The price level increase that is associated with the rise in aggregate demand comprises demand-pull inflation because the shift in aggregate demand pulls up the price level. To generate continuous demand-pull inflation, the aggregate demand curve would have to keep shifting out along a given aggregate supply curve.

What should policymakers do when confronted with demand-pull inflation? To reduce inflation, policymakers must decrease the growth in aggregate demand by, say, a reduction in the growth rate of the money supply or a decrease in government spending. As aggregate supply grows over time, slower growth in aggregate demand will reduce the inflation rate.

like that could happen

However, a policy to reduce aggregate demand is not without problems. Although decreasing the growth rate of aggregate demand reduces the inflation rate, it is likely to be accompanied by a rise in unemployment in the short run. A reason for the rise in unemployment is the contractual obligations of companies to pay higher wages. Such contracts were presumably signed when it seemed that inflation would accelerate. As inflation decreases, firms will see that the prices of their goods will rise less rapidly, if not at all. Therefore, firms may have to lay off workers so as to fulfill their contractual obligations to those workers still employed. Such layoffs cause the unemployment rate to increase.

| Figure 12.6 | The Origins of Inflation |

When buyers' demands to purchase goods and services exceed sellers' capacities to supply them, prices are forced up on what is available, and demand-pull inflation occurs. Demand-pull inflation tends to arise when the economy is close to or at full employment. When price increases are caused by pressures from the sellers' side of the market, cost-push inflation occurs. Cost-push inflation can be caused by bargaining power by resource owners, limited availability of resources, declining productivity, or chance events.

Increases in unemployment often accompany decreases in inflation. During the late 1970s, inflation accelerated in the United States, reaching a level of 13.5 percent in 1980. To reduce inflation, the Federal Reserve (see Chapter 15) sharply decreased the growth rate of the money supply in 1981. This policy reduced the growth rate in aggregate demand and resulted in a dramatic decline in the inflation rate. By 1983, the inflation rate was only 3.2 percent. However, the unemployment rate rose from 7.6 percent in 1981 to 9.6 percent in 1983, causing much hardship for many households. If the Federal Reserve had not pursued its anti-inflation policy in 1981, the inflation rate would have likely continued to accelerate. This would have required an even tougher anti-inflation policy, which would have caused more unemployment than what occurred during 1981–1983.

Cost-Push Inflation

Although economists widely agree that inflation can be caused by demand-pull forces, some economists argue that inflation can be the result of events on the supply side of the market. Recall that *cost-push* inflation arises from events that increase the cost of production at each price level. Two events that result in cost-push inflation are increases in wages and increases in the prices of nonlabor inputs such as energy and raw materials. With an increase in the costs of production, the aggregate supply curve shifts leftward while the aggregate demand curve remains unchanged. A decrease in aggregate supply usually leads not only to a higher price level but also to a falling level of output, a combination that is identified in Figure 12.6(b) as *stagflation*.

We can show the nature of cost-push inflation in Figure 12.6(b). The economy is initially assumed to be located at point A', where the price level is 105 and real output equals $10 trillion. Suppose that workers are able to secure increases in wages that exceed gains in productivity. As wages and unit production costs rise, the aggregate supply curve shifts leftward from AS_0 to AS_1. The price level therefore increases from 105 to 110, as shown by point B' in the figure.

Cost-push inflation results in a dilemma for government policymakers. If aggregate demand remains unchanged at AD_0 in Figure 12.6(b), real output will fall from $10 trillion to $8 trillion because of the leftward shift in aggregate supply, resulting in a new equilibrium at point B'. Government may attempt to offset the decline in real output by enacting policies to increase aggregate demand, say, to AD_1. Such a policy, however, would further intensify inflation by raising the price level from 110 to 115, at point C'. Therefore, cost-push inflation forces policymakers to choose between stable prices and high levels of aggregate output and employment.

CHECK POINT

1. Use the aggregate demand and aggregate supply model to show the origins of recession.

2. What do economists mean by "stagflation," and why is it a problem for economic policymakers?

3. Use the aggregate demand and aggregate supply model to show the origins of inflation.

4. If the government enacts policies to counteract demand-pull inflation, adverse side effects may ensue. Explain.

5. Why does cost-push inflation pose a dilemma for economic policymakers?

Chapter Summary

1. The growth of the U.S. economy has been uneven. Although the output of goods and services has risen in most years, in some years economic growth has not occurred. The central focus of macroeconomics is what causes short-run fluctuations in economic activity and what, if anything, the government can do to promote full employment without inflation.

2. Prior to the Great Depression of the 1930s, classical economists dominated economic thinking. According to classical economists, the market economy automatically ensured full employment of all of its resources. The optimism of classical economists was largely based on the assumption of freely flexible wages and prices.

3. During the 1930s, John Maynard Keynes formed a theory that provided an explanation for the Great Depression. According to Keynes, the level of economic activity depends on the total spending of the economy. If business expectations are pessimistic, investment spending will be reduced, resulting in a series of decreases in total spending. If this should occur, the economy can move into a depression and remain there. Because the market economy is inherently unstable, Keynes argued that government must intervene to protect jobs and income.

4. The model of aggregate demand and aggregate supply can be used to show how output and prices are determined in the short run. An economy is in equilibrium when aggregate demand equals aggregate supply.

5. The aggregate demand curve shows the total amount of real output that buyers will purchase at alternative price levels during a given year. Movements along an aggregate demand curve are caused by changes in the price level of the economy. Shifts in the aggregate demand curve are caused by changes in nonprice factors that affect household consumption expenditures, business investment, government expenditures, and net exports of goods and services.

6. According to the multiplier effect, a change in any one of the components of aggregate demand (consumption, investment, government spending, or net exports) tends to result in a magnified impact on national output and income. The size of the multiplier depends on the spending and saving habits of consumers and businesses.

7. The aggregate supply curve shows the relationship between the level of prices and amount of real output that will be produced by the economy in a given year. The aggregate supply curve is horizontal when the economy is in deep recession or depression, upward sloping when the economy approaches full employment, and vertical when the economy achieves full employment. Changes in factors such as resource prices, resource availability, and the level of technology will cause the aggregate supply curve to shift to a new location.

8. The aggregate demand and aggregate supply model can be applied to the problems of recession and inflation. According to this model, decreases in aggregate demand or decreases in aggregate supply can result in a recession for the economy; inflation may be the result of increases in aggregate demand or decreases in aggregate supply. An economy experiences "stagflation" when there is both recession and inflation.

Key Terms and Concepts

classical economists (287)

Say's Law (287)

John Maynard Keynes (288)

aggregate demand curve (290)

aggregate supply curve (290)

aggregate quantity demanded (290)

multiplier effect (292)

multiplier (293)

aggregate quantity supplied (293)

stagflation (298)

marginal propensity to consume (MPC) (305)

marginal propensity to save (MPS) (305)

Self-Test: Multiple-Choice Questions

1. According to Say's Law,

   a. demand creates its own supply.
   b. supply creates its own demand.
   c. prices are inflexible in a downward direction.
   d. prices are inflexible in an upward direction.

2. According to classical economists,

   a. the market economy automatically ensures full employment of its resources.
   b. because economic downturns are usually permanent, government needs to intervene in economic affairs.
   c. inadequate consumer demand often causes workers to become permanently laid off.
   d. inflexible prices of commodities help sustain the buying power of households, which promotes maximum consumption and full employment.

3. In the Keynesian macroeconomic model,

   a. the market economy is inherently unstable and unemployment is no accident.
   b. the labor market will always be in equilibrium at full employment.
   c. flexible prices guarantee that overproduction of goods will not occur.
   d. active government intervention cannot move the economy toward full employment.

4. The aggregate demand curve would shift to the left if

   a. households become more optimistic about their future income.
   b. government expenditures increase on roads, dams, and bridges.
   c. businesses invest more in plant and equipment.
   d. government increases personal income taxes.

5. If the cost of resources declines, the

   a. aggregate supply curve shifts to the left.
   b. aggregate supply curve shifts to the right.
   c. aggregate demand curve shifts to the left.
   d. aggregate demand curve shifts to the right.

6. Given an upward-sloping aggregate supply curve, an increase in aggregate demand results in a(n)

   a. decrease in the price level and a decrease in the level of output.
   b. increase in the price level and an increase in the level of output.
   c. decrease in the price level and an increase in the level of output.
   d. increase in the price level and a decrease in the level of output.

7. According to the _____, if government increases demand in the economy, then the final effect on national output will be much greater.

   a. multiplier effect
   b. foreign trade effect
   c. interest rate effect
   d. real balances effect

8. The marginal propensity to save

   a. is the fraction of income that people desire to save.
   b. is the fraction of additional income that people desire to save.
   c. equals 1 plus the marginal propensity to consume.
   d. equals the marginal propensity to consume minus 1.

9. If the *MPC* equals 0.9, then an increase in income will cause consumption to increase by

   a. nine times the increase in income.
   b. 10 times the increase in income.
   c. 0.9 of the increase in income.
   d. 0.1 of the increase in income.

10. Assume the economy has idle resources and a constant price level. If the marginal propensity to consume is 0.8, the multiplier equals

   a. 4.
   b. 5.
   c. 8.
   d. 10.

Answers to Multiple-Choice Questions
1. b   **2.** a   **3.** a   **4.** d   **5.** b   **6.** b   **7.** a   **8.** b   **9.** c   **10.** b

Study Questions and Problems

1. According to classical economists, flexible prices and flexible wages guaranteed that all output produced could be sold and everyone who wanted a job would have a job. Explain. Why did John Maynard Keynes believe that prices and wages were not sufficiently flexible to guarantee the full employment of resources?

2. What explains the inverse relationship between the aggregate quantity demanded and the price level?

3. What accounts for the shape of the aggregate supply curve?

4. Explain whether each of the following events increases, decreases, or has no effect on the short-run aggregate demand curve:

   a. A decrease in the U.S. price level results in American goods becoming more attractive to foreign buyers.
   b. Households decide to consume a larger share of their income.
   c. Worsening profit expectations cause firms to decrease their expenditures on new machinery and equipment.
   d. As the price level declines, the purchasing power of currency increases, and thus Americans increase their purchases of computers and office equipment.
   e. Because of decreasing political tensions in North Korea, the U.S. Congress reduces purchases of jet fighters and tanks.
   f. Economic expansion in Europe results in an increase in the European demand for Boeing jetliners.
   g. Fearing a future economic downturn, households decide to save a larger fraction of their income.

5. Suppose the marginal propensity to consume in the economy is 0.75. Assuming that prices are constant, what effect would a $50 million increase in investment spending have in the equilibrium real GDP?

| Table 12.1 | Aggregate Demand and Aggregate Supply Data |

Real Domestic Output Demanded (billions)	Price Level (price index)	Real Domestic Output Supplied (billions)
$ 6,000	130	$16,000
8,000	120	16,000
10,000	110	14,000
12,000	100	12,000
14,000	90	10,000
16,000	90	8,000

6. Suppose that the marginal propensity to save in the economy is 0.1. Assuming that prices are constant, what effect would a $20 million decrease in net exports have on the equilibrium real GDP?

7. Explain whether the following events increase, decrease, or have no effect on the short-run aggregate supply curve:

   a. A tornado damages factories in Wisconsin and Minnesota.
   b. Because of expectations of a booming economy, auto companies invest in more efficient machinery and equipment.
   c. New technologies result in declining prices of crude oil.
   d. The United Steel Workers Union wins a large increase in wages with domestic steel companies.
   e. Workers participate in retraining programs that enhance their productivity.

8. Table 12.1 shows the short-run aggregate supply and aggregate demand schedules for a hypothetical economy.

   a. What are the economy's equilibrium price and quantity of real output?
   b. The full-employment segment of the economy's aggregate supply schedule is associated with what level of real output?
   c. If the economy is in the horizontal segment of its aggregate supply schedule, what will be the impact of an increase in aggregate demand?
   d. Given the initial data in the table, suppose the quantity of real output supplied rises by $4,000 at each given price level. What will the new equilibrium price level and real output be?

9. Why is an increase in aggregate supply "doubly beneficial" and a decrease in aggregate supply "doubly detrimental"?

10. Use the aggregate supply and aggregate demand model to show the differences between demand-pull inflation and cost-push inflation.

EXPLORING FURTHER 12.1:
THE NATURE AND OPERATION
OF THE MULTIPLIER EFFECT

According to the multiplier effect, an autonomous change in aggregate demand has a magnified effect on the economy's income and output. Why is there a multiplier effect for the economy?

Table 12.2	The Multiplier Process		
Spending Rounds	**Increased Income and Output**	**Increased Consumption (spend 80%)**	**Increased Saving (save 20%)**
Original increase in investment	$100.0	$ 80.0	$ 20.0
Second round	80.0	64.0	16.0
Third round	64.0	51.2	12.8
Fourth round	51.2	41.0	11.2
	etc.	etc.	etc.
	500.0	400.0	100.0

The basic idea is quite simple, as seen in Table 12.2. Suppose that General Electric constructs a factory in your town at a cost of $100 million. Also suppose that people spend 80 percent of their additional income and save 20 percent. According to the table, the increase in investment of $100 million, when spent, becomes income of $100 million for the owners of the construction firm and for the workers who build the factory. Suppose that these people save 20 percent of their additional income, or $20 million, and use the rest, $80 million, to purchase new Ford automobiles. The $80 million becomes income to the owners of Ford Motor Company and its workers. These people, in turn, spend 80 percent of the $80 million ($64 million), say, on food, and save the remaining $16 million. This results in $64 million in income for food producers. This process of receiving income and then respending the money, which generates income for others, continues until the original amount of money ($100 million) is all held in saving by the various individuals. At that time, no more income will be created. Through this process, the initial investment of $100 million results in an increase of $500 million in income and output. Therefore, in this example the multiplier has a value of 5.

The multiplier effect also works in reverse. Suppose that consumers become more thrifty and reduce consumption spending. According to the multiplier effect, national output and income decline by an amount greater than the initial decrease in consumption spending.

Calculating the Value of the Multiplier

As you examine Table 12.2, notice that the size of the multiplier depends on the spending and saving patterns of individuals and businesses in the economy. In the jargon of economists, the multiplier depends on the marginal propensity to consume and the marginal propensity to save.

The **marginal propensity to consume (MPC)** is the fraction of additional income people spend. Referring to Table 12.2, we assumed that people spend 80 percent of additional income. This means that the $MPC = 0.8$. Similarly, the **marginal propensity to save (MPS)** is the fraction of additional income that is saved. Referring to the table, we assumed that people save 20 percent of their additional income. Thus, the $MPS = 0.2$. Notice that the MPS and MPC always add up to 1 because all consumer income that is not spent on goods and services must be saved.

The formula for the multiplier is as follows:

$$Multiplier = 1/(1 - MPC)$$

To illustrate this formula, if the *MPC* equals 0.8, then the multiplier is $1/(1 - 0.8)$, or 5.

Because $MPC + MPS = 1$, it follows that $MPS = (1 - MPC)$. Therefore, we can restate the multiplier formula as:

$$Multiplier = 1/MPS$$

To illustrate this formula, if *MPS* equals 0.2, the multiplier is $1/0.2 = 5$.

If aggregate demand changes, the equilibrium income and output will change by the amount of the change in aggregate demand times the multiplier. This process is summarized as follows:

$$Aggregate\ demand \times Multiplier = Equilibrium\ income$$

For example, if investment spending rises by $100 million, and the multiplier is 5, equilibrium output and income will rise by $500 million ($100 million × 5 = $500 million).

Graphical Illustration of the Multiplier Effect

Figure 12.7 shows the full multiplier effect of a $100 million increase in investment spending. The direct effect of the increase in investment spending is to shift the aggregate demand curve rightward by $100 million, from AD_0 to AD_1. Moreover, aggregate demand gets an additional boost from the extra consumption spending induced through the process of people receiving income and then respending it. This results in aggregate demand increasing by $400 million, from AD_1 to AD_2. The total effect of the $100 million increase in investment

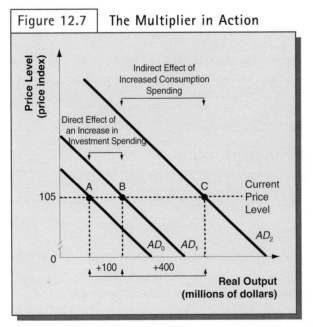

Figure 12.7   The Multiplier in Action

An increase in investment spending initially shifts aggregate demand rightward from AD_0 to AD_1. Aggregate demand gets an extra boost from the additional consumption resulting from people receiving income and respending it. Because of the multiplier effect, aggregate demand increases from AD_1 to AD_2.

spending is to shift aggregate demand from AD_0 to AD_2, which causes national output to increase by $500 million.

For the full multiplier effect to occur, some idle resources in the economy must cause a constant price level, as shown in Figure 12.7. If an increase in aggregate demand occurs when the economy is already at, or close to, full employment, consumers and others bid up prices by attempting to purchase more output than the economy is capable of producing. This results in inflation, suggesting an increasing price level that offsets the multiplier effect. Therefore, without idle resources and a constant price level, the multiplier effect is impeded. Simply put, price level increases weaken the multiplier.

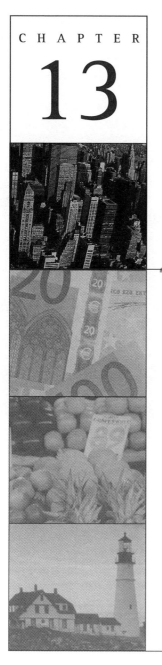

CHAPTER
13

Fiscal Policy and the Federal Budget

Chapter objectives

After reading this chapter, you should be able to:

1. Identify the operation of fiscal policy and the problems it encounters.

2. Explain how discretionary fiscal policy attempts to combat the problems of recession and inflation.

3. Describe how automatic stabilizers help cushion an economy during a recession.

4. Evaluate the strengths and weaknesses of supply-side fiscal policy.

5. Identify the potential effects of the federal debt.

economics IN CONTEXT

Once upon a time, tax cuts commanded almost universal support among economists as the desired method of combating recessions. When Congress passed the Kennedy–Johnson tax cuts in 1964, such enthusiasm was at its peak. As time passed, however, changes in taxes and spending gradually lost favor to changes in interest rates by the Federal Reserve.

As the U.S. economy slowed in 2001, companies such as Hewlett-Packard, Nortel, and Cisco stated that the high-tech economy was so bad that they did not foresee profits for the year. Moreover, job losses would likely occur for thousands of Americans. As a result, they lobbied for a fiscal boost in the form of a tax cut. In response to the weakening economy, President George W. Bush assaulted the conventional wisdom by implementing a reduction in taxes in 2002. He argued that the United States needed a tax cut because the federal government was pulling too much money out of the private economy, and this was a drag on U.S. growth. This was followed by another tax cut in 2003.

√ it worked

Those who believe that the economy is inherently unstable often urge the government to intervene to protect jobs and income. Government can help stabilize the economy through its use of government spending and tax policies, as discussed in this chapter.

Before we proceed to government stabilization policies, recall that the federal budget consists of two components: government expenditures and tax revenues or receipts. When government spending exceeds tax revenues during a given year, a budget deficit occurs. When the budget is in deficit, the federal government must borrow funds by issuing securities such as Treasury bills, notes, and bonds. If tax revenues exceed government spending, a budget surplus exists. When the federal government incurs a budget surplus, it can use the excess revenue to pay off some of its debt. Finally, if government spending equals tax revenues, a balanced budget exists.

FISCAL POLICY

Recall from Chapter 12 that John Maynard Keynes believed that the Great Depression was caused by insufficient aggregate demand. Because he thought that prices and wages were inflexible in a downward direction, Keynes maintained that the classical economists' optimism of an economy moving automatically and quickly to full employment was incorrect. To Keynes and his followers, an activist government must increase aggregate demand to protect jobs and income. In other words, expansionary fiscal policy initiated by the federal government was the way to stabilize the economy.

Fiscal policy is the use of government expenditures and taxes to promote particular macroeconomic goals such as full employment, stable prices, and economic growth. Government expenditures consist of purchases of goods and services, such as the procurement of jet aircraft from Boeing, and transfer payments, such as unemployment compensation and food stamps. In the United States, Congress and the president set fiscal policy. It is therefore a reflection of a collective decision-making process. Table 13.1 shows recent examples of U.S. fiscal policies.

Fiscal policies may be expansionary or contractionary. An *expansionary fiscal policy* increases real output, employment, and income. Such a policy can be used to move the economy out of recession. A *contractionary fiscal policy* decreases real output, employment, and income. It can be used to combat the problem of inflation.

| Table 13.1 | Examples of U.S. Fiscal Policies |

Year	Economic Problem	Policy
1964	Recession	With the economy in a slump, Presidents Kennedy/Johnson enact permanent tax cuts for individuals and corporations. The top tax rate for individuals is cut from 91 to 70 percent.
1968	Inflation	To dampen inflationary pressures, President Johnson orders a temporary tax increase. This one-time surcharge of 10 percent is added to individual income tax liabilities. *dumb!*
1969	Inflation	Facing an overheated economy, President Nixon orders reductions in government expenditures.
1975	Recession	Fearing a recession caused by the oil-price hikes of OPEC, President Ford orders a temporary tax reduction of 10 percent. The tax cut is enacted immediately by Congress.
1981	Recession	In response to a sluggish economy, President Reagan calls for a sharp cut in individual income taxes and an increase in defense spending. The top tax rate for individuals is cut from 70 to 28 percent.
1992	Recession	President Bush orders a reduction in withholding rates in order to raise take-home pay in 1992 and to increase consumption.
1993	Recession	In response to unacceptably high levels of unemployment, President Clinton calls for a $16 billion jobs program consisting of government expenditures and tax reductions intended to increase investment. The measure is turned down by Congress.
2001	Recession	President Bush convinces Congress to pass reductions in taxes.

Fiscal policies have been used to alter the economy's aggregate demand curve and aggregate supply curve in order to promote full employment and stable prices. Let us analyze both possibilities, beginning with the use of fiscal policy to shift the aggregate demand curve.

FISCAL POLICY AND AGGREGATE DEMAND

Let us pick up where we left off in Chapter 12 by discussing the use of discretionary fiscal policy, as Keynes urged, to help stabilize the economy. Discretionary fiscal policy is the deliberate use of changes in government expenditures and taxation to affect aggregate demand and influence the economy's performance in the short run. Recall that aggregate demand has four components: consumption, investment, government spending, and net exports.

Combating a Recession

Referring to Figure 13.1, suppose the economy suffers from recession at equilibrium point A, where the aggregate demand curve intersects the aggregate supply curve. In equilibrium, the level of output is $700 billion, below the full-employment output of $900 billion. Here, the economy can be improved by following Keynesian economics and shifting the aggregate demand curve rightward, say, from AD_0 to AD_1. Therefore, the economy's output increases from $700 billion to $800 billion. Notice that the price level remains constant given the abundance of idle resources in the economy.

How can government increase aggregate demand? It has three fiscal policy options: (1) increase government spending, (2) cut taxes, or (3) combine the two in some manner. If the federal budget is initially balanced, fiscal policy should move toward a *budget deficit* (government spending in excess of tax revenues) to combat a recession.

Figure 13.1 | Expansionary Fiscal Policy

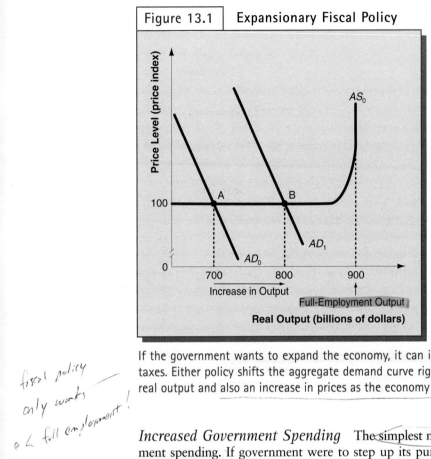

If the government wants to expand the economy, it can increase government spending or lower taxes. Either policy shifts the aggregate demand curve rightward, which results in an increase in real output and also an increase in prices as the economy approaches full employment.

fiscal policy only works @ < full employment!

Increased Government Spending   The simplest method would be to increase government spending. If government were to step up its purchases of jet planes, highways, and other goods, the increased spending would add directly to aggregate demand. According to the multiplier effect discussed in the previous chapter, aggregate demand will rise by more than just the added government spending.

eg Bush $600 refund

If the government purchases, say, $25 billion of jet aircraft from Boeing, this is the beginning of the multiplier process. The initial effect of the increased demand from the government is to stimulate employment and profits at Boeing. As the workers realize fatter paychecks and the firm owners realize higher dividends, they respond to the increased income by increasing their own spending on autos, appliances, and the like. Therefore, government purchases from Boeing increase the demand for products of many other companies such as Ford, Whirlpool, and General Electric. Therefore, these firms hire more workers and realize higher profits. Higher earnings and profits lead to increased consumer spending once again, and so on. Each round of added spending increases aggregate demand a little more. When all of these effects are combined, the total impact on the quantity of goods and services demanded can be much larger than the initial stimulus from increased government expenditures. Referring to Figure 13.1, government purchases of $25 billion increase aggregate demand by $100 billion. See "Exploring Further 13.1" for additional information about fiscal policy and the multiplier effect.

Ever since the days of Franklin Roosevelt, the federal government has implemented public-works projects to combat downturns in the economy and to create jobs. During the Depression of the 1930s, Roosevelt established the *Works Project Administration,* or WPA. The WPA provided jobs building highways, streets, dams, bridges, schools, courthouses, parks, and other projects intended to have long-range value. It also created work for artists, writers, actors, and musicians. The WPA employed an average of 2 million workers annually between 1935 and 1941. Roosevelt also established the *Civilian Conservation Corps* (CCC) from 1933 until 1942. The CCC gave work and training to 2¹/₂ million young people. It achieved great success with its programs for flood control, forestry, and soil. These government projects cost a great deal of money, much more than the government was collecting through taxes. The deficit was made up partly by raising taxes and partly by borrowing. As a result, the national debt rose higher than ever before.

In recent years, the federal government has provided public-works spending for mass transit, highways, and other transportation projects. When President George H. Bush signed a $151 billion transportation bill in 1991, he declared that the effect would be "jobs building roads, jobs building bridges, and jobs building railways."

Besides providing long-term public-works projects, the federal government has enacted public-employment projects. The notion underlying these programs is clear: If the economy suffers from high unemployment, why not create jobs directly. Public-employment projects are intended to hire unemployed workers for a limited period in public jobs, after which people can take jobs in the economy's private sector. During the 1970s, for example, the *Comprehensive Employment and Training Act* (CETA) provided public-service jobs for more than 700,000 hard-core unemployed and young people. These workers did everything from working in theaters and museums to raking leaves.

Decreased Taxes   Other than increasing spending, is there any other way the government could cause aggregate demand to increase? Another expansionary fiscal policy intended to increase aggregate demand is for the government to reduce taxes.

Lowering *taxes on personal income* increases the amount of take-home pay people have. If take-home pay goes up, we can expect households to save more and consume more than they did prior to the tax reduction. The initial consumption spending induced by the tax cut starts the multiplier process in motion. The new consumer spending creates additional income for owners of firms and workers, who will then use the additional income to increase their own consumption. This results in a cumulative increase in aggregate demand that exceeds the initial increase in consumption. Put simply, the multiplier effect makes tax reductions a powerful tool of fiscal policy.[1]

A reduction in the *tax rate on corporate profits* also tends to stimulate aggregate demand. After a tax reduction, firms have additional funds to spend on new machinery and equipment. They may also distribute more money to shareholders who, in turn, would spend at least a portion of it.

Another type of tax cut for business is an *investment tax credit*. Such a policy allows a company to decrease its tax liability by a fraction of the investment it initiates during a particular period. Suppose the investment tax credit is 10 percent. If Microsoft purchases $10 million worth of new equipment during a year, its tax liability would fall by $1 million for that year. The purpose of an investment tax credit is to make investment more profitable

---

[1] However, the multiplier effect for a change in taxes is smaller than for an equivalent change in government spending. For example, assume that the economy's MPC is 0.75, which suggests that the expenditures multiplier is 4—multiplier = $1/(1 - MPC) = 1/(1 - 0.75) = 4$.

Suppose that the federal government cuts personal income taxes by $25 billion. With more spendable income, households will increase consumption spending by $18.75 billion ($25 billion × 0.75 = $18.75 billion) and save $6.25 billion. If the economy's prices remain constant, aggregate demand will increase by $75 billion as a result of the multiplier effect (4 × $18.75 billion = $75 billion).

Instead, suppose that the government increases spending by $25 billion. According to the multiplier effect, aggregate demand will increase by $100 billion (4 × $25 billion = $100 billion) as a result of the increased government spending.

Comparing these examples, we see that the increase in government spending results in a larger increase in aggregate demand, and thus real output, than the decrease in personal income taxes. This is because part of the tax reduction increases saving rather than consumption.

Table 13.2	Discretionary Fiscal Policies	
Economic Problem:	**Recession**	**Inflation**
Solution:	Expansionary Fiscal Policy	Contractionary Fiscal Policy
	1. Increased government spending	1. Decreased government spending
	2. Decreased taxes	2. Increased taxes

and thus to promote additional private-sector investment. As a result, aggregate demand rises, causing an increase in real output, employment, and income. The investment tax credit was used during the 1960s as a method of stimulating a sluggish economy.

As seen in Table 13.2, tax reductions and spending increases are expansionary fiscal policies. Both the level of government spending and taxation affect output and employment in the short run through their influence on the demand for goods and services in the economy. But which fiscal policy is most effective?

The goal of an expansionary fiscal policy is to increase spending, and fiscal policies can differ in the extent to which they induce spending. While a fiscal stimulus delivered through a direct increase in government expenditures has a relatively straightforward effect, a fiscal stimulus delivered via a personal tax cut tends to have a more muted effect on the economy, because only part of it will be spent. The smaller the share spent, the smaller the stimulus. There is also a fear that consumers who feel uncertainty about the future will not spend a tax cut. Therefore, a tax reduction must be somewhat larger than an increase in government expenditures if it is to yield an identical amount of stimulus to the economy.

Combating Inflation

The preceding example showed how expansionary fiscal policy moves an economy closer to full employment. Suppose, however, that aggregate demand exceeds the economy's capacity to produce, resulting in demand-pull inflation. In this case, a contractionary or restrictive fiscal policy may help control it.

Referring to Figure 13.2, suppose a stock market boom boosts household wealth. This causes the aggregate demand curve to shift rightward from AD_0 to AD_1 so that the economy operates at point B on the full-employment range of the aggregate supply curve, AS_0. The increase in aggregate demand has raised the price level from 110 to 120. However, we want stable prices. If government desires to combat this inflation, it may adopt a contractionary fiscal policy to reduce aggregate demand. The cost of doing this could be a lower level of real output and a higher rate of unemployment.

To decrease aggregate demand, the government has three fiscal options: (1) cut government spending, (2) increase taxes, or (3) combine the two in some manner. When the economy encounters demand-pull inflation, fiscal policy should move toward a *budget surplus* (tax revenues in excess of government spending).

FISCAL POLICY IN ACTION

Although the basic elements of Keynesian fiscal policy were developed during the Great Depression, it took many years before politicians accepted these principles. In particular, they feared the consequences of the large budget deficits that might result from an increase in government spending or a decrease in taxes.

Figure 13.2	Contractionary Fiscal Policy

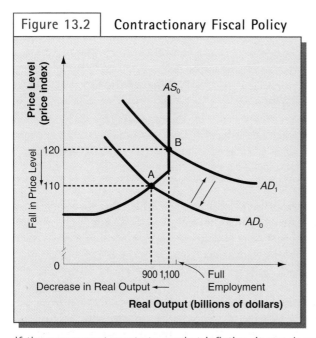

If the government wants to combat inflation, it can decrease government spending or increase taxes. Either policy shifts the aggregate demand curve leftward. Although inflation may decline as a result of a contractionary fiscal policy, real output may fall and unemployment may rise.

By the early 1960s, Keynesian fiscal policy came to be accepted as one of the country's main weapons for combating recession or inflation. When President John F. Kennedy entered office, the unemployment rate stood at 6.7 percent. However, analysts estimated that the unemployment rate at full employment was about 4 percent. Also, they noted that the federal deficit in 1961 was negligible, less than 1 percent of GDP. As a result, President Kennedy proposed substantial tax cuts to boost the economy out of a slump.

In 1962, the government enacted legislation that provided for a 7-percent tax credit on investment in new equipment and machinery, therefore strengthening the incentives of businesses to invest. In 1964, the government provided permanent tax reductions for individuals and corporations. Following the tax cuts, the economy grew rapidly, and unemployment declined from 5.2 percent in 1964 to 4.5 percent in 1965.

During this period, another expansionary force developed: the Vietnam War buildup. Escalation of the Vietnam War resulted in a 40-percent rise in government spending on national defense during 1965–1967. Another 15-percent increase on war-related expenditures took place in 1968. As military spending increased, unemployment declined. By 1969, the unemployment rate was 3.5 percent, and analysts worried that the economy was overheating and inflationary pressures would ensue.

To dampen inflationary momentum, Congress enacted a temporary, 1-year tax surcharge of 10 percent so that consumption spending would decrease. However, the surcharge did not cause consumer spending to fall as much as analysts forecasted. Because the tax increase was temporary, households were only marginally affected and thus continued to engage in consumption spending. The result was a rise in inflation from 1.9 percent in 1965 to 5.6 percent in 1970. Put simply, the temporary tax surcharge had little, if any, effectiveness in combating inflation.

During the 1970s, many changes were made in government spending and taxes, but not in major fiscal policy initiatives. The 1980s, however, ushered in a new fiscal era. In 1981,

economics
IN ACTION

Bush Cuts Taxes to Stimulate Economy

In response to the recession of 2001, President George W. Bush signed into law two sweeping tax cuts. The rationale of the tax cuts was partly economic and partly philosophical. The president wished to slash taxes to help offset a cyclical downturn in the short run and promote economic growth in the long run. Also, tax cuts remove revenues from Washington and thus keep Congress from spending them. President Ronald Reagan understood this point when he pushed for income tax cuts in the1980s.

To provide a quick fix to a sluggish economy, the legislation cut individual income taxes by lowering tax withholding and sending rebate checks to households. By boosting the purchasing power of households, the tax cut was intended to provide an immediate stimulus to consumption spending and aggregate demand. The legislation also reduced marginal income tax rates over several years, slashed income taxes on dividends, and allowed businesses to write off more of their investment expenditures. These tax reductions were intended to stimulate long-term growth by providing for additional incentives for saving, investment, and capital accumulation, thus shifting the economy's aggregate supply curve to the right.

However, skeptics were concerned that the tax cuts were unjustified for several reasons. First, federal deficits might occur because the tax cuts ignored the rising costs of the war against terrorism, Social Security, Medicare, and Medicaid, which would place additional pressure on the budget in the years ahead. Moreover, the tax cuts provide disproportionately large benefits to the highest income households, while providing meager benefits to households in the bottom half of the income distribution. Finally, the tax cuts would not significantly add

higher multiplier effect

Congress enacted the fiscal policy of President Ronald Reagan, which called for sharp tax reductions, a large increase in defense spending, and a few reductions in civilian expenditure programs. These measures helped nudge the economy out of the deep recession of 1981–1982 and into a rapid expansion of the economy. However, the Reagan fiscal policy led to a sharp rise in the government's budget deficit.

When President Bill Clinton entered office in 1993, he faced a major dilemma. The government's deficits continued to be high, but the economy was stagnating and the level of unemployment was unacceptably high. Should the president confront the deficit by reducing government spending and raising taxes, which would suggest a contractionary fiscal policy? Or should the president worry that a contractionary fiscal policy might throw the economy into a major slump. In the end, the president decided that the budget deficit was the main priority. The Budget Act of 1993 led to fiscal measures that reduced the deficit by about $150 billion over the next five years. As things turned out, the economy did not slump. Instead, it continued on an expansionary path throughout the 1990s.

By 2001, the economy was weakening. As a result, President George W. Bush signed into law a sweeping $1.35 trillion tax cut to bolster the economy. This was followed by another tax cut in 2003 (see "Economics in Action" above).

mandatory's rising

AUTOMATIC STABILIZERS

Recall that discretionary fiscal policy entails the changing of spending and taxes by government to promote full employment, stable prices, and economic growth. "Discretionary" implies that changes in government spending programs and tax rates are at the option of Congress and the White House.

to long-term economic growth if people were too afraid to invest.

One policy lesson of the Bush tax cuts is that both the kind and pace of tax cuts are significant. In order to get his first round of tax cuts passed in 2001, Bush agreed to the proposal to put money in consumers' hands more quickly, resulting in a tax rebate. The theory was that poor and middle-class people spend money, while rich folks save it, so cut taxes for them but not for the rich. So under the tax cuts of 2001, only small reductions were immediately implemented, with the rest being phased in over several years. However, the stimulus from the tax rebates was minor. They gave a short-run boost to aggregate demand, as Keynesian theory suggests, but once the money was spent, the effect dwindled. Referring to the supply side, because most of the tax cuts were deferred, investors and businesses postponed much of their economic activity until a later date when tax rates were lower. Thus, the slow recovery from the 2001 recession may have been, in part, due to the lack of stimulus provided by the phased-in nature of the income tax reductions.

However, the second round of Bush tax cuts went into effect immediately. The 2003 cut accelerated the marginal rate cuts first passed in 2001 and also provided immediate cuts in dividend rates. The immediate nature of the tax cuts provided incentives for production and investment to rise, thus affecting behavior on the supply side. Once this tax cut was implemented, the economy began to gain genuine momentum. Simply put, evidence proves that tax cuts stimulate the economy more when they are permanent and immediate rather than when they are phased in. It is important to recognize, however, that other things also contributed to the economic recovery, notably an expansionary monetary policy by the Federal Reserve, the ebbing of corporate scandals, and business adjustment to terrorism.

Source: Christopher House and Matthew Shapiro, *Phased-In Tax Cuts and Economic Activity*, National Bureau of Economic Research, Cambridge, MA, Working Paper 10415, April 2004.

Unlike discretionary fiscal policy, **automatic stabilizers** consist of changes in government spending and tax revenues that occur automatically as the economy fluctuates. The automatic stabilizers prevent aggregate demand from decreasing as much in bad times and rising as much in good times, thus stabilizing the economy. It is important to note that automatic stabilizers operate silently in the background and do their job without requiring explicit policy changes by Congress or the White House. Economists estimate that automatic stabilizers can offset about 8 percent of an economic shock to GDP.[2]

The most important automatic stabilizer is the tax system. The personal income tax depends on the earnings of households, the corporate income tax depends on companies' profits, and the Social Security tax depends on workers' wages. When the economy goes into a recession, income, profits, and wages all decline, which results in a decrease in tax collections for the government. This automatic decline in tax revenues bolsters aggregate demand and reduces the severity of the recession.

[margin note: wrong; restricts supply; so closes the gap]

Government transfer payments also serve as an automatic stabilizer. When the economy goes into a recession and workers are laid off, they become eligible for unemployment insurance benefits, food stamps, and other welfare benefits. This automatic increase in transfer payments supports consumption spending and aggregate demand, which helps offset the decline in economic activity. The automatic stabilizers in the U.S. economy are not sufficiently strong to eliminate recessions completely. However, they provide a cushion for the economy as it goes into a slump.

[2] Alan Auerback and Daniel Feenberg, "The Significance of Federal Taxes as Automatic Stabilizers," *National Bureau of Economic Research, Working Paper No. 7662*, April 2000.

Table 13.3	Automatic Stabilizers During the Recession of 1973–1975			
	Year	Unemployment Rate	Percentage Change in Personal Income Tax Collections	Percentage Change in Transfer Payments
	1974	5.6	14.2	11.8
Trough of the recession	1975	8.5	3.9	29.1
	1976	7.7	7.6	17.0
	1977	7.1	21.3	8.3

Source: From *Economic Report of the President*, 1990.

During economic prosperity, tax collections automatically rise and transfer payments automatically decline. The increase in tax collections and the decrease in transfer payments slow the growth of aggregate demand, thus controlling the upward pressure on the price level when the economy is expanding. In this manner, the automatic stabilizers help prevent an economy from overheating.

The recession of 1973–1975 provides an example of the workings of the automatic stabilizers.[3] During that slump, real GDP declined by 4.9 percent, and the unemployment rate jumped from 4.9 percent to 8.5 percent. As seen in Table 13.3, the personal income tax and transfer payments provided a stabilizing role during this period. As the economy fell toward its trough, which occurred in 1975, tax collections grew at a diminishing rate while transfer payments grew at an increasing rate. These factors helped offset the economic downturn. As the economy rebounded in 1976 and 1977, tax collections grew faster and transfer payments grew slower, thus imposing a constraint on inflationary pressures.

CHECK POINT

1. What are the tools of fiscal policy?

2. How does discretionary fiscal policy attempt to combat recession? How about inflation?

3. What impact does an expansionary fiscal policy have on the budget of the federal government? How about a contractionary fiscal policy?

4. How do the automatic stabilizers help cushion the economy during a recession? What are some examples of automatic stabilizers?

PROBLEMS OF FISCAL POLICY

Although Keynesians usually view fiscal policy as effective in combating recession and inflation, other economists are concerned about the shortcomings of fiscal policy. Let us examine some of these concerns.

---

[3] The recession of 1973–1975 provides a good example of the impact of automatic stabilizers because government spending programs and tax rates were largely unchanged during this period.

Timing Lags

In theory, Congress and the president should work together to enact timely and effective fiscal policies. In practice, however, it takes months and often years for fiscal policies to be enacted and to have an impact on the economy. In particular, three timing lags constrain the operation of fiscal policy:

- **Recognition lag.** The recognition lag refers to the time between the beginning of inflation or recession and the recognition that it is actually occurring. For example, if the economy goes into a slump in March, the decline may not be apparent for three or four months. Once policymakers become aware of a problem in the economy, they rarely enact policies immediately. Instead, they want to be sure that the problem is more than a short-term disturbance.

- **Administrative lag.** The way Congress operates makes it difficult to get quick action on fiscal policy. Much debate occurs before fiscal policy can change. This process can take months.

- **Operational lag.** Once enacted, a fiscal policy measure takes time to be put into operation. Although changes in tax rates can be implemented quickly, increased spending for public-works programs will require construction firms to submit bids for the work, negotiate contracts, and so on.

Most postwar recessions in the United States have been short, lasting on average just under 11 months. By the time a fiscal program is starting to boost business and consumer demand—that is, after policymakers recognize that economic growth has slowed, propose a fiscal package, debate it, pass it, and send it to the president for his signature, the economy is already likely to be recovering. For this reason, discretionary fiscal policy in the United Sates is generally viewed as too unwieldy for dealing with the typical, mild recessions experienced in recent decades.

For example, evidence appeared in late 2000 that the U.S. economy was slowing. Congress did pass a tax cut in 2001, but this was part of President George W. Bush's legislative agenda before any hint of an economic slowdown. It took Congress until March 2002 to pass the Economic Recovery Act to provide further stimulus to the economy. Simply put, many economists are skeptical of fiscal policy as a stabilization tool, particularly through the mechanism of tax cuts. Because of decision-making lags and administrative lags in getting tax cuts to individuals, a fiscal stimulus enacted through a tax cut can be poorly timed.

Irreversibility

Fiscal policy also suffers from the problems of irreversibility. Under our political system, it is difficult to reverse changes in government spending or taxes. Expenditure programs that create new government departments or expand existing ones tend to become permanent, or at least difficult to downsize or eliminate. Many temporary tax changes become permanent as well. The government is never pleased to reverse a tax increase that provides it with additional revenues, and the public is never pleased to reverse a tax cut that reduces its tax bills. These inflexibilities hinder the operation of fiscal policy.

Crowding-Out Effect

Not all economists believe that an expansionary fiscal policy can stimulate the economy the way we have described. Their concern comes under the heading of the **crowding-out effect**. With crowding out, private spending (consumption spending or investment) falls as a result of increased government expenditures and the subsequent budget deficits. The source of the decline in private spending is higher interest rates generated by budget deficits.

For example, suppose that the government enacts an expansionary fiscal policy, say, an increase in defense spending. The policy must be financed either by increased taxes or through the borrowing of funds to finance the enlarged federal deficit. If the government borrows funds to finance the deficit, the total demand for funds will increase as the government competes with the private sector to borrow the available supply of funds. The additional government borrowing thus increases the demand for funds and pushes up interest rates. Because of higher interest rates, businesses will delay or cancel purchases of machinery and equipment, residential housing construction will be postponed, and consumers will refrain from buying interest-sensitive goods, such as major appliances and automobiles. Therefore, the higher interest rates caused by government borrowing squeeze out private-sector borrowing. In other words, crowding lessens the effectiveness of an expansionary fiscal policy.

Although most economists accept the logic of the crowding-out argument, they also recognize that government deficits don't necessarily squeeze out private spending. In recessions, the main problem is that people are not spending all of the available funds. Typically, consumers are saving more than businesses intend to invest. Such a shortage of spending is the main motivation for increased government spending. In this recessionary situation, deficit-financed government spending doesn't crowd out private spending. Moreover, even government spending that does squeeze out private spending does not necessarily retard economic growth. The government may use the borrowed funds to build airports, highways, or other infrastructure that increases the productive capacity of the nation.

FISCAL POLICY AND AGGREGATE SUPPLY

We have seen that by influencing the aggregate demand curve, fiscal policy can affect the economy's short-run performance. Fiscal policy can also influence the economy's long-run performance through its effect on aggregate supply.

Supply-Side Effects of Changes in Taxes

When Congress alters tax rates, they affect the incentive of people to work, save, and invest. From a supply-side perspective, the *marginal tax rate* is of crucial importance. Recall from Chapter 10 that the marginal tax rate is the fraction of additional income paid in taxes. A decrease in marginal tax rates increases the reward stemming from extra work, saving, and investment.

According to advocates of supply-side economics, a policy that reduces marginal tax rates will increase productivity because individuals will work harder and longer, save more, and invest more. As the total supplies of labor and capital in the economy expand, the aggregate supply curve shifts rightward, which will lead to higher real output. Besides cutting marginal tax rates for individuals, the government can promote increases in aggregate supply by enacting tax breaks that subsidize investment and by eliminating burdensome regulations on business.

Figure 13.3 shows possible effects of fiscal policy on aggregate supply. Referring to Figure 13.3(a), if an expansionary fiscal policy can shift the economy's aggregate supply curve from AS_0 to AS_1, prices will decline and output will expand. Policymakers will have succeeded in reducing inflation, raising real output, and lowering unemployment at the same time. Hence, the trade-off between unemployment and inflation will have been defeated. This is the objective of supply-side policies.

Although proponents consider supply-side policies to be a painless remedy for our economic problems, critics consider it as wishful thinking. Their first objection is that supply-side policies are too optimistic. The hoped-for favorable impacts of a tax cut on incentives to work, save, and invest may not be nearly as large as supply-side advocates maintain. Just because cutting tax rates increases the returns on work does not mean people will actually work more. As a result of an increase in after-tax wages, people may work less, not more.

do on board
☆

| Figure 13.3 | Supply–Side Fiscal Policy |

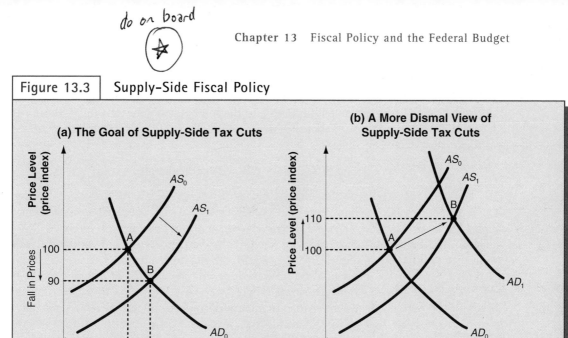

The goal of a supply-side tax cut is to shift the aggregate supply curve rightward, resulting in a lower price level and increased real output. The tax cut, however, also shifts the aggregate demand curve rightward. If the increase in aggregate demand more than offsets the increase in aggregate supply, the result will be a higher price level.

The reason is that, with higher after-tax wages, an individual may be able to work fewer hours while still maintaining or even improving his standard of living. Similarly, if cutting tax rates increases the return on savings, people may find their savings objectives more easily fulfilled and respond by saving less. As a result, the aggregate supply curve may shift rightward by only a modest amount in response to a tax cut. Supply-side policies may thus cause, at most, only a small increase in real output. *So ?!*

Second, supply-side advocates underestimate the effects of tax cuts on aggregate demand. If personal taxes are reduced, individuals may possibly work more, but they will surely spend more, which would shift the aggregate demand curve to the right. The demand-side effects of tax reductions are likely to be much larger than the supply-side effects, especially in the short run. *So ? thats what the dems are trying to do anyway!*

The implications of these two concerns are shown in Figure 13.3(b). In response to a tax cut, there may be a small rightward shift in the aggregate supply curve, which reflects the first concern, and a large rightward shift in the aggregate demand curve, which reflects the second concern. As a result, the economy's equilibrium moves from point A to point B following a decrease in taxes. Prices thus rise as output increases. This situation contradicts the view that supply-side economics is a painless remedy for our economic problems. According to critics, supply-side policies should not be considered a substitute for short-run stabilization policy. It is best suited for promoting economic growth in the long run. *exactly !*

Do Cuts in Tax Rates Cause Tax Revenues to Rise (Fall)?

If income tax rates were cut, would tax revenues rise or fall? Most people think that the answer is obvious: Declining tax rates result in lower tax revenues. Supply-side advocate Arthur Laffer, however, maintained that this may not be true.

To illustrate how tax rates influence tax revenue, we will use a simple device, the **Laffer curve,** named after Arthur Laffer. The Laffer curve shows the relationship between the income tax rate that a government imposes and the total tax revenue that the government collects. The amount of revenue that the government collects depends on both the tax rate and the level of taxable income:

Tax revenue = Tax rate × Taxable income

The essence of the Laffer curve is that high tax rates may cause tax revenue to decline. Taxable income falls when tax rates are too high because people are discouraged from working, saving, and investing—taxable income decreases, which results in falling tax revenue.

Figure 13.4 illustrates the Laffer curve. On the vertical axis are hypothetical tax revenues, measured in billions of dollars per year. On the horizontal axis are hypothetical tax rates from 0 to 100 percent. Zero tax revenues will be collected at two tax rates—0 and 100 percent. Obviously, no tax revenues will be collected if the tax rate is zero. If the tax rate is 100 percent, the incentive to earn income disappears, and tax revenues are again zero. As the tax rate rises above 0 percent, total revenues will rise until at some tax rate they finally begin to fall toward zero. This occurs when the high tax rate discourages so many people from seeking work that employment declines, the result being a smaller amount of taxable income. If the decrease in taxable income exceeds the increase in the tax rate, total tax revenues will fall.

In Figure 13.4, the maximum revenues collected are $300 billion per year. They can be generated by a tax rate of 48 percent. After this point, a rise in tax rates actually decreases total tax revenues. For example, at a tax rate of 85 percent, revenues will have fallen from a maximum of $300 billion to $200 billion. Put simply, the Laffer curve provides a reminder to the White House and Congress that increases in tax rates may be counterproductive, causing a decline in economic activity and also a decrease in total tax revenues.

Such thinking provided the intellectual underpinnings of the economic policies of the Reagan administration (1981–1988). President Ronald Reagan dramatically cut the personal

| Figure 13.4 | The Laffer Curve |

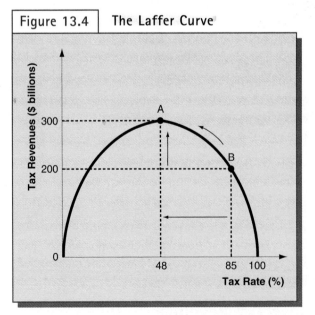

The Laffer curve is a graphical illustration of the relationship between tax rates and the total tax revenues raised by taxation. According to the Laffer curve, if tax rates are high enough it may be possible to increase tax revenues by cutting those tax rates.

income tax rate in order to foster increased economic activity and perhaps increase tax revenues. The Reagan tax cut lowered the top tax rate from 70 to 28 percent. Subsequent history, however, fails to confirm that the Reagan tax cuts resulted in higher total tax revenues. When Reagan reduced taxes, the result was falling tax revenue. Revenue from personal income taxes (per person, adjusted for inflation) declined by 9 percent from 1980 to 1984, even though average income (per person, adjusted for inflation) increased by 4 percent during this era. Because the tax cut could not generate enough revenue to finance government spending, the government ran large budget deficits during the Reagan administration.

FEDERAL DEFICIT AND FEDERAL DEBT

Recall that the main mechanism of fiscal policy is the federal government's budget. As we have learned, changes in federal taxes or spending are the tools for shifting the aggregate demand curve and aggregate supply curve. The use of the federal budget to stabilize the economy suggests that the budget will often be *unbalanced*. To combat a recession, the federal government will increase spending or reduce taxes, giving rise to a budget deficit. Conversely, counteracting inflation means decreasing government spending or increasing taxes, resulting in a budget surplus. From the viewpoint of economic stabilization, budget deficits and surpluses are a common feature of fiscal policy.

Notice that the **federal deficit** (surplus) is the difference between total federal spending and revenue in a *given year*, as seen in Figure 13.5. To cover this gap, the government borrows from the public. Each yearly deficit adds to the amount of debt held by the public. Referring to the figure, we see that the federal government's budget has generally been in deficit. Also, the term **federal debt** represents the cumulative amount of outstanding

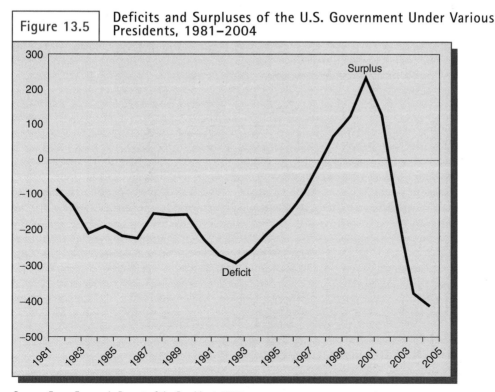

Figure 13.5 | **Deficits and Surpluses of the U.S. Government Under Various Presidents, 1981–2004**

Source: From *Economic Report of the President*, 2005.

Table 13.4	Federal Debt Held by the Public	
Year	Federal Debt (billions)	Federal Debt as a percent of GDP
1940	$ 43	44%
1945	236	106
1955	227	57
1965	261	38
1975	395	25
1985	1,500	36
1995	3,603	49
2000	3,410	35
2004	4,721	37

(handwritten margin notes: "so, prob is deficits and unfunded mandates")

Source: From *Economic Report of the President*, 2005, p. 304.

borrowing from the public over the nation's history. It has been rising because of the persistent federal deficits that have occurred on an annual basis.

The main measure of the U.S. federal debt is the *debt held by the public*. This is the measure most commonly used because it reflects how much of the nation's wealth is absorbed by the federal government to finance its obligations and, thus, best represents the current impact of past federal borrowing on the economy. As seen in Table 13.4, the federal debt held by the public was about $4.7 trillion in 2004. In contrast, the federal debt was only $43 billion in 1940.

The amount of a borrower's debt by itself is not a particularly good indicator of the debt's burden. If size were the only thing that mattered, a wealthy individual with a large mortgage would be judged to have a greater debt burden than a person of modest means with a smaller mortgage. In order words, a borrower's income and wealth are also important in assessing the burden of debt. Therefore, to get a better sense of the burden represented by the federal debt, debt should be viewed in relation to the nation's income. A commonly used measure of national income is GDP. Comparing the debt to GDP provides a better indicator of the debt burden than the debt's dollar value, because it captures the capacity of the economy to sustain the debt.

As of 2004, the federal debt equaled 37 percent of GDP. Although this level is high by historical standards, it is not as high as the debt levels of many other nations where debt may equal 60 percent of GDP, or more. In the past, the debt–GDP measure of the United States has only risen substantially as a result of wars and recessions. The peak period in U.S. history was reached immediately after World War II when, as a result of wartime borrowing, the federal debt was 106 percent of GDP, meaning that it exceeded the annual output of the economy. After the war, spurred by economic growth and inflation, this measure fell dramatically over the next three decades to a postwar low of 24 percent in 1974. Since the mid-1970s, the debt–GDP ratio has generally crept upward.

The federal government is not the only borrower that has increased its debt since the 1980s. The borrowing of individuals, businesses, and state and local governments all rose significantly during this period, but not as much as the federal debt.

Sales and Ownership of Federal Debt

How does the federal government borrow? The federal government borrows by issuing securities, mostly through the Treasury Department. Most of the securities that constitute debt held by the public are marketable, meaning that once the government issues them, they can be resold by whoever owns them. These marketable securities consist of Treasury bills, notes, and bonds with a variety of maturities ranging from three months to 30 years. The mix of outstanding securities changes regularly as new debt is issued.

The mix of securities is important because it can have a significant influence on interest payments. For example, a long-term Treasury bond typically carries a higher interest rate than a short-term Treasury bill due to the investors' perceptions that longer-term securities are subject to greater risks, such as higher inflation in the future. However, long-term bonds offer the certainty of knowing what your payments will be over a longer period.

Who lends to the federal government? The federal debt held by the public is owed to a wide variety of investors. In 2004, 42 percent of the federal debt was owned by the U.S. Treasury and other federal agencies, 25 percent by private domestic investors, 24 percent by foreign investors, and 9 percent by Federal Reserve banks.

A Treasury security can be purchased by anyone. Although debt ownership is concentrated among businesses and other institutions, many small investors also own debt securities. For example, anyone who owns a U.S. savings bond holds a portion of the federal debt. Further, many pension funds own debt securities, so small investors are also represented indirectly through these holdings.

The United States benefits from foreign purchases of government securities because, as foreign investors fill part of our borrowing needs, more domestic saving is available for private investment, and interest rates are lower than they otherwise would be. However, to service this foreign-owned debt, the U.S. government must send interest payments abroad, which adds to the income of citizens of other countries rather than to U.S. citizens.

IS THE FEDERAL DEBT GOOD OR BAD?

What are the economic consequences of federal borrowing? Borrowing has both benefits and costs.

Many believe that borrowing is appropriate under certain circumstances. For example, some believe that automatic increases in federal borrowing during recessions help the economy by maintaining income and spending levels. Wartime borrowing is also widely considered to be beneficial, because such borrowing allows a government to increase defense spending without enacting large tax increases that could be disruptive to the economy. Moreover, federal borrowing may also be appropriate for investment spending, such as building roads, training workers, or conducting scientific research. If an investment is well chosen, it can ultimately boost worker productivity and economic growth in the long term, producing a larger economy from which to pay the interest on borrowed funds.

However, if federal borrowing is not used for any of the purposes mentioned earlier, many believe that the costs outweigh the benefits. In this case, the benefits of any increased federal spending are likely to be more concentrated in the short term while the costs tend to occur mainly in the long term. This timing difference can have important implications for different generations. The impact of today's increased borrowing will be felt by tomorrow's workers and taxpayers, who may not fully share in the benefits of the additional spending made possible by the borrowing. To the extent that deficits reduce national investment, they also slow the growth in living standards for future generations.

Federal borrowing can reduce the funds that are available for private investment and put upward pressure on interest rates. Because the federal government competes with private investors for scarce capital, federal borrowing can reduce the amount available for other investors. Government borrowing can be large enough to affect the overall level of interest rates, making borrowing more expensive for individuals and families who take out loans for homes, cars, and college.

Since the 1970s, the large amounts of federal borrowing have been particularly troublesome because private saving has been declining as a share of the U.S. economy. These two trends have had a significant impact on the economy: Federal deficits are eating up a larger portion of a shrinking pool of private savings, sharply reducing the amount of this saving that is available for private investment. However, part of the decline in national saving has been offset by increased borrowing from foreign investors.

How does borrowing affect the federal budget? Although borrowing allows the government to provide more services today than it could otherwise afford, the cost is borne tomorrow in the form of interest payments. To make these payments while avoiding larger deficits, the government has to forgo spending money on other national priorities. It also means less is available for unexpected needs.

SHOULD THERE BE A BALANCED-BUDGET AMENDMENT?

Although federal budget surpluses briefly appeared at the end of the 1990s, skeptics are concerned that the U.S. government has a bias toward overspending. Therefore, they call for Congress to enact laws to force the federal government to eliminate its deficit. In the United States, 49 states have balanced-budget requirements. Why not require the federal government to achieve what most states require for state governments?

One approach would be to enact a constitutional amendment to balance the budget. The rule most commonly proposed includes several provisions. Each year, the president must submit a balanced budget to Congress in which tax revenues match expenditures. Congress then works on the budget. A budget deficit can be approved only by 60 percent of the members of Congress on a roll-call vote, name by name. In the event of war or national emergency, the balanced-budget requirement can be suspended.

Proponents of the balanced-budget amendment note that Congress lacks the willpower to exercise fiscal restraint. Although it might make sense in principle to have a deficit when the economy enters a downturn, the reality is that the budget has often been in deficit irrespective of underlying economic conditions. Only the power of a constitutional rule can permanently make the government live within its means over the long haul.

However, critics of this rule argue that it could make recessions more frequent and severe. A balanced-budget requirement would make recessions longer and more painful, first by eliminating the automatic stabilizers that protect people in a downturn and, second, by instead requiring measures to cut spending or increase taxes during slowdowns when the economy is already suffering from lack of demand.

Critics of the balanced-budget amendment also maintain that even if it were enacted Congress would figure out ways to escape its restrictive provisions. For example, Congress might use things like "off-budget" expenditures and unrealistic budget projections in order to avoid the amendment's discipline.

This chapter discussed fiscal policy as a possible solution for macroeconomic instability. The next chapter will consider the roles of money and the economy's banking system.

CHECK POINT

1. Identify the major shortcomings of fiscal policy.

2. Why do proponents of supply-side fiscal policy consider it a painless remedy for our economic problems?

3. The federal debt entails both benefits and costs for the economy. Explain.

4. Identify advantages and disadvantages of a balanced-budget amendment for the federal government.

Chapter Summary

1. Fiscal policy is the use of government expenditures and taxes to promote particular macro-economic goals such as full employment, stable prices, and economic growth. In the United States, Congress and the president conduct fiscal policy. An expansionary fiscal policy attempts to nudge the economy out of a recession, and a contractionary fiscal policy attempts to combat inflation.

2. Discretionary fiscal policy is the deliberate use of changes in government expenditures and taxation to affect aggregate demand and influence the economy's performance in the short run. To combat a recession, the government can slash taxes and/or increase expenditures in order to boost aggregate demand. The government can combat inflation by increasing taxes and/or cutting expenditures, thus decreasing aggregate demand.

3. Unlike discretionary fiscal policy, automatic stabilizers consist of changes in government spending and tax revenues that occur automatically as the economy fluctuates. The automatic stabilizers prevent aggregate demand from decreasing as much in bad times and rising as much in good times, thus moderating fluctuations in economic activity. Automatic stabilizers include the personal income tax, the corporate income tax, and transfer payments such as unemployment insurance benefits and food stamps.

4. Although Keynesians usually view fiscal policy as effective in combating recession and inflation, other economists are concerned about its shortcomings. Among the problems of discretionary fiscal policy are timing lags, inflationary bias, the crowding-out effect, and the foreign-trade effect.

5. Besides having potential effects on aggregate demand, fiscal policy can also influence the level of economic activity through its effect on aggregate supply. According to supply-side fiscal policy, a reduction in marginal tax rates will cause productivity to increase because individuals will work harder and longer, save more, and invest more. Therefore, the aggregate supply curve will shift rightward, which leads to higher real output.

6. During the early 1980s, supply-side economists argued that a cut in tax rates would enhance incentives to work, save, and invest, which would promote an increase in economic activity and national income. In theory, the enlarged income would cause total tax revenues to rise even though tax rates would be lower. However, evidence from the 1980s does not support this outcome.

7. The federal deficit is the difference between total federal spending and tax revenue received in a given year. The federal debt represents the cumulative amount of outstanding borrowing from the public over the nation's history. The federal government borrows by issuing securities, mostly through the Treasury Department.

8. Federal borrowing may entail both benefits and costs. Many believe that federal borrowing is beneficial when it helps the economy by supporting income and spending levels, when it is used to increase defense spending, and when it helps finance investment spending on roads, dams, bridges, and the like. Critics of federal borrowing fear that it will slow the growth in living standards of future generations and reduce private consumption and investment expenditures. As a result, critics prefer laws to force the federal government to refrain from deficit spending.

Key Terms and Concepts

Fiscal policy (310)

Discretionary fiscal policy (311)

Automatic stabilizers (317)

Recognition lag (319)

Administrative lag (319)

Operational lag (319)

Crowding-out effect (319)

Laffer curve (322)

Federal deficit (323)

Federal debt (323)

Self-Test: Multiple-Choice Questions

1. _____ refers to the use of government expenditures, transfer payments, and taxes to promote full employment, stable prices, and economic growth.

   a. Industrial policy
   b. Commercial policy
   c. Monetary policy
   d. Fiscal policy

2. Assume that the economy has idle resources and a constant price level. Also suppose taxes are constant and $MPC = 0.75$. If government expenditures increase by $10 billion, then real GDP will increase by

   a. $10 billion.
   b. $20 billion.
   c. $30 billion.
   d. $40 billion.

3. When tax receipts fall short of government expenditures, government must

   a. increase transfer payments.
   b. increase tax rates.
   c. reduce its spending.
   d. borrow funds.

4. Crowding out tends to occur when government

   a. restricts certain types of business investments.
   b. increases personal income tax rates.
   c. finances a deficit by printing new money.
   d. finances a deficit by borrowing.

5. The creation of public debt is burdensome for the economy for all of the following reasons *except* that it

   a. results in crowding out.
   b. is held largely by domestic investors instead of foreigners.
   c. reduces the supply of capital goods.
   d. creates inflation.

6. Countercyclical fiscal policy can best be exemplified by a(n)

   a. increase in government spending and an increase in tax rates during recessions.
   b. increase in government spending and a decrease in tax rates during recessions.
   c. decrease in government spending and an increase in tax rates during recessions.
   d. decrease in government spending and a decrease in tax rates during recessions.

7. Automatic stabilizers include all of the following *except*

   a. national defense spending.
   b. welfare payments such as food stamps.

  c. unemployment compensation payments.
  d. the federal income tax.

8. Suppose that the economy's aggregate demand is $400 billion below its full-employment output. If the marginal propensity to consume is 0.8, how much would government expenditures have to increase to push aggregate demand to the full-employment output?

   a. $40 billion
   b. $60 billion
   c. $80 billion
   d. $100 billion

9. During the Great Depression of the 1930s, President Herbert Hoover initiated a fiscal policy that resulted in a balanced budget instead of a budget deficit. According to Keynesian economics, a balanced budget was inappropriate during a depression because it

   a. resulted in more inflation for the economy.
   b. caused declines in economic activity, thus increasing unemployment.
   c. contributed to only minor gains in economic activity and employment.
   d. decreased personal savings more than business investments.

10. Countercyclical fiscal policy suggests that government should combat a recession by

   a. running a budget surplus, thus increasing aggregate demand.
   b. running a budget surplus, thus decreasing aggregate demand.
   c. running a budget deficit, thus increasing aggregate demand.
   d. running a budget deficit, thus decreasing aggregate demand.

Answers to Multiple-Choice Questions
1. d   2. d   3. d   4. d   5. b   6. b   7. a   8. c   9. b   10. c

Study Questions and Problems

1. Explain how each of the following fiscal policies affects aggregate demand.

   a. The government increases its expenditures on highways and bridges by $10 billion.
   b. Personal income tax rates are increased by 10 percent across the board.
   c. Expenditures on the food-stamp program are increased by 15 percent in order to help the poor.
   d. The government slashes national defense expenditures as peace spreads throughout the world.

2. In each of the following situations, explain whether discretionary fiscal policy is expansionary or contractionary.

   a. The government increases tax rates for households and corporations.
   b. The government increases funding for unemployment insurance benefits.
   c. The government approves funding for highway improvements in the Pacific Northwest.
   d. Due to increased expenditures, the government's budget shows a deficit.

3. Tax reductions tend to affect both aggregate demand and aggregate supply. Does it matter which is affected more? Use the aggregate demand and aggregate supply model to explain your answer.

4. Some economists argue in favor of using discretionary fiscal policy to combat recession and inflation, while some argue against it. Discuss the advantages and disadvantages of using discretionary fiscal policy to stabilize the economy.

Table 13.5	Hypothetical Tax Data for the United States	
	Tax Rates (percent)	Tax Revenues (billions of dollars)
	0%	$ 0
	10	90
	15	150
	20	180
	25	150
	30	90
	35	0

5. Explain how changes in government spending and taxes can have a multiplied effect on aggregate demand and real output.

6. The following questions are based on Table 13.5.

   a. What two points indicate zero tax revenues? How can this occur?
   b. What tax rate results in maximum tax revenues for the government?
   c. Suppose the economy imposes a tax rate of 25 percent, which yields tax revenues of $150 billion. What will happen to tax revenues if the tax rate rises to 30 percent? Why might this occur?
   d. Suppose the economy imposes a tax rate of 10 percent, which yields tax revenues of $90 billion. What will happen to tax revenues if the tax rate rises to 15 percent? Why might this occur?

7. Using the aggregate demand and aggregate supply model, describe the destabilizing effects of fiscal policy if a constitutional amendment mandating an annually balanced budget were enacted.

8. Keynesian economists emphasize the aggregate demand effects of fiscal policy, while supply-side economists focus on the aggregate supply effects. Discuss the process by which a tax reduction might result in an increase in real output and employment according to these two approaches. If tax reductions are beneficial for the economy, why doesn't the government slash taxes to zero?

9. Why is crowding out an important issue in the debate over the merits of discretionary fiscal policy? Is crowding out equally likely to occur during all phases of the business cycle?

10. If the government today decides that aggregate demand is deficient and is causing a recession, what is it likely to do? What if the government decides that aggregate demand is excessive and is causing inflation?

11. Expansionary fiscal policy can combat recessions, but it usually results in a cost in terms of higher inflation. This dilemma has led to interest in "supply-side" tax cuts intended to stimulate aggregate supply. Use the aggregate demand and aggregate supply model to explain the purpose of supply-side economics. Identify the problems associated with supply-side tax cuts.

12. Assume that the economy's marginal propensity to consume is 0.8. To combat a recession, suppose the federal government increases its expenditures by $50 billion. If prices remain constant, what impact will this policy have on the economy's aggregate demand and real

output? Instead, suppose that prices increase as the economy's aggregate demand increases. What effect would this have on your answer?

13. Assume that the economy's marginal propensity to consume is 0.67. To combat a recession, suppose the federal government is considering whether to reduce personal income taxes by $40 billion or to increase government expenditures by $40 billion. Assuming a constant price level for the economy, what effect would each of these policies have on aggregate demand and real output? Which policy is more expansionary? Why?

EXPLORING FURTHER 13.1: FISCAL POLICY AND THE MULTIPLIER

Recall from the previous chapter that the formula for the multiplier is $1/(1 - MPC)$, where MPC is the economy's marginal propensity to consume. If the MPC is 0.75, the value of the multiplier is 4: $1/(1 - 0.75) = 4$. In our example of an expansionary fiscal policy, we assume that government purchases increase by $25 billion. Given a multiplier of 4, the aggregate demand curve will shift rightward by four times the distance of the initial $25 billion increase in government purchases. Indeed, the multiplier makes government spending a very powerful policy tool for stimulating output and production.

To illustrate this multiplier effect, refer to Figure 13.6. The direct effect of the increase in government purchases is to shift the aggregate demand curve rightward by $25 billion, from AD_0 to AD_2. According to the multiplier process, the indirect effect of increased consumption spending is shown by a rightward shift in aggregate demand by an additional $75 billion, from AD_2 to AD_1. Altogether, the $25 billion increase in government purchases results in a $100 billion increase in aggregate demand, shown by the shift from AD_0 to AD_1. This fourfold increase in aggregate demand is due to the multiplier effect.

Notice that this particular increase in aggregate demand takes place within the horizontal region of the aggregate supply curve, where the economy's price level is constant. Thus, real output will increase by the full amount of the multiplier. Moreover, unemployment will decline as firms employ workers who were laid off during the recession.

Figure 13.6   Fiscal Policy and the Multiplier Effect

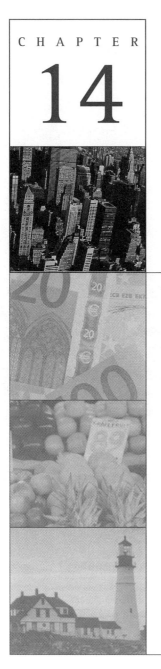

Money and the Banking System

Chapter objectives

After reading this chapter, you should be able to:

1. Define money and identify the functions of money.

2. Describe the collection process a check goes through.

3. Describe the major depository institutions in our economy.

4. Explain how banks attempt to make a profit for their stockholders.

5. Discuss the process of money creation by the banking system.

6. Identify the purposes of the Federal Deposit Insurance Corporation.

economics IN CONTEXT

In 2000, the United States introduced its eighth dollar coin. The new dollar coin is gold in color and bears the image of Sacagawea—the only woman on the Lewis and Clark expedition. Proponents of the dollar coin point out that the widespread use of dollar coins would result in considerable savings to the government. On average, coins have a projected life of 30 years, compared with about 18 months for the dollar bill. Although dollar bills cost about 3.5 cents to produce, compared to 12 cents for the dollar coin, the relatively short life of dollar bills makes them more expensive in the long run.

Dollar coins, however, have never found wide use for day-to-day transactions in the United States. One possible explanation for this is simply that people find coins inconvenient relative to paper currency. Accordingly, dollar coins would replace notes only if the public has no choice. Despite a $45 million ad campaign, approximately half of the new coins remained in the vaults of Federal Reserve Banks and the U.S. Mint a year after the coin was first introduced. The other half was in "circulation." However, many of these coins were apparently being hoarded because few of them were observed in day-to-day transactions.

According to the saying, money makes the world go around. As far back as 300 B.C., Aristotle maintained that everything had to be accessed in money because this always allows people to exchange their services, and so makes society possible. Indeed, money is an integral part of our everyday life.

In this chapter, we will examine money and the role it plays in the economy. We will focus on the nature of money, the operation of our banking system, and the process through which money is created.

Throughout this chapter, we will refer to the Federal Reserve System. The Federal Reserve System is the *central banking system* in the United States. The Federal Reserve supplies the banks[1] with currency, operates a nationwide clearing mechanism for checks, serves as a lender of last resort for troubled banks, supervises and examines member banks for safety and soundness, provides checking accounts for the Treasury, issues and redeems government securities, and conducts monetary policy for the nation. We will discuss the nature and operations of the Federal Reserve System more fully in the next chapter.

THE MEANING OF MONEY

When you go to Pizza Hut to purchase a dinner, you obtain something of value—a pizza and a soft drink. To pay for these items, you might hand the waiter some cash or a personal check. The restaurant is happy to accept either of these pieces of paper, which, in themselves are worthless. Nevertheless, they are considered to be money.

We begin with a simple question: What is **money?** Money is the set of assets in the economy that people regularly use to purchase goods and services from other people. Gold and silver were once the most common forms of money. But today, money consists primarily of paper bills, coins made of various metals, and checking account deposits.

Each country has its own system of money. In the United States, for example, the basic unit of money is the U.S. dollar. Canada uses the Canadian dollar, Mexico uses the peso, Japan uses the yen, and so on. We call the money in use in a country its **currency.**

---

[1] The U.S. economy has an array of banks, including commercial banks, savings and loan associations, mutual savings banks, and credit unions. We call these institutions depository institutions: They accept deposits from people and provide checking accounts that are part of the money supply.

Money has three functions in the economy: It is a medium of exchange, a unit of account, and a store of value. These functions distinguish money from other assets such as stocks, bonds, and real estate.

Medium of Exchange

anything could be this

First, money is a **medium of exchange**: It is something that people are willing to accept in payment for goods and services. In the United States, a penny, a dime, a quarter, or a $1 bill are mediums of exchange because people are willing to accept these items in payment, realizing that they can be used for other purchases. The transfer of money from the buyer to the seller allows the transaction to occur.

Without a medium of exchange, people would have to trade their goods or services directly for other goods or services. If you wanted a motorcycle, you would have to find a motorcycle owner willing to trade. Suppose the motorcycle owner wanted a computer in exchange for the motorcycle, and you did not own a computer. You would then have to find something that an owner of a computer wanted and trade it for a computer to give to the owner of the motorcycle.

Such trading, called *barter,* is inefficient because you could spend days running around looking for someone who has what you want and wants what you have. Also, some items, like animals, simply are not divisible, and deals must be struck at uneven rates of exchange. Finally, barter restricts productive capacities. As societies become more sophisticated and produce a greater range of goods, the exchange process becomes too complicated for barter alone. However, a medium of exchange, or money, removes the problems of barter. Wants need not coincide because every person one deals with is willing to accept money in return for goods or services.

Unit of Account

this is easy too! but excludes rocks

A second function of money is that it serves as a **unit of account.** People state the prices of goods and services in terms of money. In the United States, people use dollars to specify price. When you go shopping, you might observe that a pair of pants costs $40 and a 12-pack of Pepsi costs $4. The unit of account function of money allows us to compare the relative values of goods. If a pair of pants costs $40 and a 12-pack of Pepsi costs $4, then one pair of pants equals ten 12-packs of Pepsi ($40/$4 = 10). Put simply, people use money to specify price, just as they use kilometers to measure distance or hours to express time.

Store of Value

we have first money

A third function of money is as a **store of value.** People can save money and then use it to make purchases in the future. Of course, money is not the only store of value in the economy. Other stores of value include gold, real estate, paintings, jewels, or even baseball cards. However, money does have the advantage of being immediately usable by people in meeting financial obligations.

The store of value function of money helps us appreciate how severe and prolonged inflation can weaken an economy. With inflation, the ability of money to serve as a store of value deteriorates. Thus, people may be unwilling to save money if they expect that its future purchasing power will erode because of increasing prices. Moreover, borrowing money for productive investment may be hampered if lenders expect that the repaid loans will have less purchasing power.

Any object or substance that serves as a medium of exchange, a unit of account, and a store of value is money. To be convenient, however, money should have several other characteristics. It should be portable so that people can carry enough money to purchase

also needs to be portable and in limited supply

what they need. It should come in pieces of standard value so that it does not have to be weighed or measured every time it is used. It should be durable and not easily wear out. Finally, it should divide into small units so that people can make small purchases and receive change.

Are Credit Cards Money?

Most people think of credit cards, such as MasterCard and VISA, as "plastic money." After all, credit cards serve as a convenient form of financing transactions.

Are credit cards money? Not at all! MasterCard may be accepted as readily as money. However, the reason that merchants honor these cards is that they expect to be paid by the financial institution that issued the card. Eventually, you must pay off your bill by writing a check to the financial institution that issued the card. Yet, without an adequate amount of funds in your checking account, MasterCard would soon discover that the credit receipt it received with your signature on it was virtually worthless. Put simply, if you use your MasterCard to make a purchase, you obtain a short-term loan from the financial institution that issued the card. Credit cards are thus a method of postponing payment for a brief period.

Credit cards are often more convenient than writing checks or making payment in cash. People who have credit cards can pay many of their bills all at once at the end of the month, instead of sporadically as they make purchases. Therefore, people who have credit cards tend to hold less cash on average than people who do not have credit cards. Thus, the increased usage of credit cards may decrease how much money that people desire to hold.

SHOPPING FOR A CREDIT CARD

This year, you may receive a few invitations to get a new credit card. Card companies mail billions of unsolicited credit offers to U.S. households during a year and make tens of millions of telephone calls to sell their cards. Today, some large issuers, such as First USA Bank with 12 million cards in circulation, are banks in name only. Credit cards are their primary business. The business can be highly profitable as long as cardholders stay in debt. Today, the typical U.S. adult has a credit card account with a balance of more than $1,800. Table 14.1 provides a comparison of selected bank credit cards.

Credit associations, like VISA or MasterCard, sign up banks that offer cards to consumers; firms like Discover and American Express offer cards directly to consumers. How does the amount on your charge slip end up on your monthly statement and get paid along the way?

Suppose you go to Wal-Mart and purchase a CD player with your VISA card. The cashier runs the card through an electronic approval machine to see if the card is valid and if you have enough credit for the purchase. You sign the receipt, which becomes your agreement to repay. Within five business days, Wal-Mart sends the receipt to VISA, which serves as a clearinghouse for all sales receipts. VISA contacts Wal-Mart's bank, which pays the store the sales price minus a fee, which is generally around 3 percent, depending on the store's monthly sales volume and other considerations. Merchants can't increase prices to consumers to cover the bank's fees, but they can offer discounts to customers who pay by cash or check. Then, VISA clears the receipt from its books by charging the bank that issued the card. Your bank immediately pays Wal-Mart's bank the entire amount. Your bank then mails you a statement for the full amount of the purchase and for any other purchases you made during the period.

No credit card will fulfill all the needs and usage patterns of every consumer. You'll have to do some homework if you want to take advantage of the best available terms.

| Table 14.1 | How Bank Credit Cards Compare, 2005 | | | |

Card Issuer	Annual Percentage Rate	Type of Interest Rate	Grace Period (days)	Annual Fee
Citibank (VISA)	15.24%	Variable	20	None
Wells Fargo Bank (VISA)	15.35%	Variable	20	None
Chase MasterCard	15.24%	Variable	20	None
Discover Bank DiscoverCard	17.99%	Variable	20	None
Evans National Bank (VISA)	15.20%	Fixed	25	$20
Wells Fargo (VISA)	20.50%	Variable	25	None

Source: From *Credit Card Rankings* at http://www.creditcardrankings.com/. Other Internet sites that provide similar information include http://www.creditcardcatalog.com and http://www.cardweb.com.

For example, in the disclosure form from the credit card issuer, a key credit term to consider is the *annual percentage rate* (APR). A low APR can make a big difference if you often carry a balance from month to month. Unfortunately, credit card issuers with low APRs of around 10 percent are very particular as to whom they extend credit; they may turn down people with sizable credit card debts—the very folks who would benefit most from a lower rate.

Equally important is the *grace period*—the time between your purchases and when you have to pay to avoid finance charges. Also, remember that if you exceed your credit line, the bank may charge an *over-limit* fee of, say, $15. If your minimum payment is overdue, there is often a *late payment fee* as well. Moreover, most banks also charge *cash advance fees* for money withdrawn from an automatic teller with your credit card. Don't forget that you begin paying interest on cash advances immediately. There is no grace period.

How do I get a better rate on my credit card? It might sound crazy, but experts say consumers should just ask for one. Past experience and consumer studies show that credit card issuers are often willing to negotiate with their best customers in order to keep them from switching to a rival. As a word of caution, if you call a bank and say that you've gotten a better credit card offer elsewhere, be prepared for the fact that they might call your bluff. The wisest use of a credit card, by far, is to pay off your debt every month and avoid high interest costs. Consider making it your top financial priority.

CHECK POINT

1. What is money?

2. Identify the functions of money.

3. Why are credit cards not a component of the basic money supply?

4. As a consumer, what factors should you watch for when comparing credit cards?

U.S. MONEY SUPPLY

Money is anything that people agree to accept in exchange for the things they sell or the work they do. Gold and silver were once the most common types of money. Today, however, money consists mainly of currency and checking account deposits. Let us first examine the currency of the United States.

U.S. currency consists of coins and paper money. Under federal law, only the Federal Reserve System issues paper currency, and only the U.S. Treasury issues coin. The Federal Reserve issues paper currency called *Federal Reserve notes*. All U.S. currency carries the nation's official motto, "In God We Trust."

Coins

Coins come in six denominations: pennies (one cent), nickels (five cents), dimes (10 cents), quarters (25 cents), half-dollars (50 cents), and $1.

The U.S. Mint—with satellites in Philadelphia, Denver, West Point, and San Francisco—makes coins for circulation. All U.S. coins typically bear a mint mark showing which mint produced them. Coins minted in Philadelphia bear a *P* or no mint mark; those minted in Denver, a *D*; in San Francisco, an *S*; and in West Point, a *W*. All of the U.S. coins currently minted portray past U.S. presidents. All U.S. coins now issued bear the motto "In God We Trust" in a form similar to that used on other nations' money.

All coins consist of alloys (mixtures of metals). Pennies are copper-coated zinc alloyed with less than 3-percent copper. Nickels are a mixture of copper and nickel. Dimes, quarters, half-dollars, and dollars consist of three layers of metal. The core is pure copper, and the outer layers are an alloy of copper and nickel. Federal law requires that coins be dated with the year that they were made. Coins also must bear the word *Liberty* and the Latin motto *E Pluribus Unum*, meaning *out of many, one*. This motto refers to the creation of the United States from the original 13 colonies.

When producing coins, the U.S. Mint rolls ingots of metal alloys into flat sheets of proper thickness. Blanks are punched from the metal sheets, and the good blanks are sorted from the scrap. After being softened and washed, blanks are put in a machine that gives them a raised edge. Blanks are then weighed and inspected before stamping. Front and back are stamped simultaneously at pressures exceeding 40 tons. Finally, the coins are weighted, counted, and shipped to the Federal Reserve Banks for distribution.

Why do coins have ridges? When coins were made of gold and silver, subtle cheating was a common occurrence. People would shave the edges of their coins before spending them, eventually collecting enough shavings to use as money. Milled edges, the ridges, were devised to discourage these cheaters. Today, gold and silver are no longer used to make coins, but the style still remains. Placing ridges on coins also helps blind people recognize certain denominations. For example, the ridges on a dime distinguish it from a penny, which has a smooth edge.

Paper Money

Federal Reserve notes make up all the paper money issued in the United States today.[2] They come in seven denominations: $1, $2, $5, $10, $20, $50, and $100. The notes are issued by the 12 Federal Reserve Banks in the Federal Reserve System. Each note has a letter, number, and seal that identify the bank that issued it. Moreover, each note bears

---

[2] The other small part of paper currency consists of *U.S. notes,* which are still in circulation but are no longer issued. These notes, which were issued in the denomination of $100, are the descendants of Civil War *greenbacks.*

the words *Federal Reserve note* and a green Treasury seal. It costs about 4 cents to produce a Federal Reserve note.

The Bureau of Engraving and Printing in Washington, D.C., is responsible for designing and printing our paper currency. There is also a satellite production facility in Fort Worth, Texas. All notes bear the words *Washington, D.C.,* below the upper-right serial number on the face of the note. Notes printed in Forth Worth also show the letters *FW* immediately to the left of the plate serial number in the lower-right corner of the note's face.

The new paper money is shipped to the 12 Federal Reserve Banks, which pay it out to commercial banks, savings and loan associations, and other depository institutions. Customers of these institutions withdraw cash as they need it. Once people spend their money at grocery stores, department stores, and so on, the money is redeposited in depository institutions. As notes wear out or become dirty or damaged, depository institutions redeposit them at the 12 Federal Reserve Banks.

Money wears out from handling, and it is sometimes accidentally damaged or destroyed. The average life of a $1 bill, for example, is about 18 months. For a $5 bill, the average life is 15 months; for a $20 bill, two years. The $10 bill has about the same life as a $1 bill. The larger bills, $50s and $100s, last longer than the smaller denominations because they don't circulate as often. A $50 bill usually lasts five years, and a $100, eight and one-half years.

Banks send old, worn, torn, or soiled notes to a Federal Reserve Bank to be exchanged for new bills. The Federal Reserve Banks sort the money they receive from commercial banks to determine if it is "fit" or "unfit." Fit (reusable) money is stored in their vaults until it goes out again through the commercial banking system. The Federal Reserve Banks destroy worn-out paper money in shredding machines and burn the shredded paper into a mulch; they return damaged and worn coins to the U.S. Treasury.

Paper money that we have mutilated or partially destroyed may be redeemable at full face value. Any badly soiled, dirtied, defaced, disintegrated, limp, torn, or worn-out currency that is clearly more than half the original note can be exchanged at a commercial bank, which processes the note through a Federal Reserve Bank. More seriously damaged notes, those with not clearly more than half the original surface, or those requiring special examination to determine their value, must be sent to the U.S. Treasury for redemption.

Checking Accounts

In the U.S. economy, the supply of money includes more than dollar bills and coins. Most people realize this when they offer to pay for goods with a check instead of currency. The "money balances" you have in your checking account can be used to purchase goods and services, pay debts, or be retained for future use. Because checking accounts perform the same functions as currency, we must include checking account balances in our notion of money.

With a checking account, you use checks to withdraw money from the account that you have deposited in it. Therefore, you have quick, convenient, and, if needed, frequent access to your money. Typically, you can make deposits into the account as often as you choose. Many institutions will allow you to withdraw or deposit funds at an automated teller machine (ATM) and to pay for purchases at stores with your ATM card.

Some checking accounts pay interest; others do not. A regular checking account, frequently called a **demand deposit account**, does not pay interest. The money in the account is available to the account holder "on demand"—by writing a check, making a withdrawal, or transferring funds. Another type of checking account is a **negotiable order of**

consumer
ECONOMICS IN ACTION

The Dollar Bill

Have you ever stopped to examine the features of the dollar bill, as seen in Figure 14.1? It is more than a piece of paper printed with green and black ink. Take a look at a dollar bill—it probably is a Federal Reserve note. To the left of the portrait of George Washington is a seal of the Federal Reserve Bank that issued the note. The seal bears the name and the code letter of that bank. Which Federal Reserve Bank issued your currency? To the right of the portrait is the Treasury seal, which is overprinted on the face of each note. The dollar bill also contains the signatures of the treasurer of the United States and the secretary of the Treasury, as well as the expression that the dollar bill is *legal tender for all debts, public and private.*

The serial number appears on the upper-right and lower-left corners of a dollar bill. No two dollar bills have the same serial number. Counterfeiters are often caught when they make batches of a bill bearing the same serial number. Businesses and banks may have lists of dollar bills with certain serial numbers that are known to be counterfeit.

The Great Seal of the United States, adopted in 1782, appears on the back of a dollar bill. The face of the seal,

on the right-hand side of the bill, shows the American bald eagle with wings and claws outstretched. Above the eagle's head is a "glory," or burst of light, containing 13 stars. The number 13 represents the original 13 colonies. The eagle's right claw holds an olive branch with 13 leaves, representing peace, and the left, a bundle of 13 arrows, symbolizing war. The eagle's head is turned toward the olive branch, indicating a desire for peace. The shield (with 13 stripes) covering the eagle's breast symbolizes a united nation. The top of the shield represents Congress; the head of the eagle, the executive branch; and the nine tail feathers, the Supreme Court. A ribbon held in the eagle's beak bears the Latin motto *E Pluribus Unum* (13 letters), which means "Out of Many, One."

The back of the Great Seal, on the left-hand side of the dollar bill, depicts a pyramid, a symbol of material strength and endurance. The pyramid is unfinished, symbolizing a striving toward growth and a goal of perfection. Above the pyramid a glory, with an eye inside a triangle, represents the benevolent gaze of God and places the spiritual above the material. At the top edge is the 13-letter Latin motto *Annuit Coeptis,* meaning "He Has Favored Our Undertakings." The base of the pyramid bears the year 1776 in Roman numerals. Below is the motto *Novus Ordo Seclorum,* "A New Order of the Ages."

---

withdrawal (NOW) account, which does pay interest but typically requires a larger minimum balance. Credit unions offer accounts that are similar to checking accounts at other depository institutions, but have different names. Credit union members have share draft accounts rather than checking accounts.

Institutions may impose fees on checking accounts, in addition to the charge for the checks you order. Fees vary among institutions. Some institutions charge a maintenance or flat monthly fee regardless of the balance in your account. Other institutions charge a monthly fee if the minimum balance in your account drops below a certain amount. Some charge a fee for every transaction, such as for each check you write or for each withdrawal you make at an ATM. Many institutions impose a combination of these fees.

Although a checking account that pays interest may appear more attractive than one that does not, it is important to look at fees for both types of accounts. Often, checking accounts that pay interest charge higher fees than do regular checking accounts, so you could end up paying more in fees than you earn in interest.

The next time you write a check, take a close look at the electronic codes that appear on the face side of the check. Do you know what these numbers stand for? Figure 14.2 gives you the answer.

Figure 14.1	The Dollar Bill

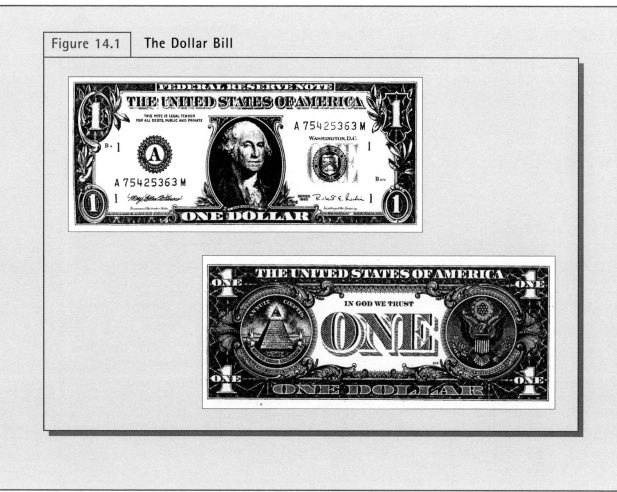

Special Types of Checks

For most personal financial transactions, a check drawn on a personal checking account is an acceptable form of payment. In certain situations, though, a special type of check that carries a greater guarantee of payment may be needed.

Certified checks are usually used when called for by a legal contract, such as real estate or automobile sale agreements. Certified checks are considered less risky than personal checks because the bank on which they are drawn has certified that the funds are available to the payee. To certify a check, a bank uses the following procedures: (1) A bank officer or other authorized employee verifies the check writer's signature and determines that there are sufficient funds in the checking account to pay the check and (2) The authorized employee signs the check and certifies it by marking, stamping, or perforating it so that it will be less likely to be altered. By certifying the check, the bank guarantees payment and becomes liable for the amount certified, and the check writer no longer has access to the funds.

A less expensive alternative to a certified check is a **cashier's check.** The purchaser of a cashier's check does not need to have a checking account. He or she merely goes to the

Figure 14.2 | Electronic Codes of a Check

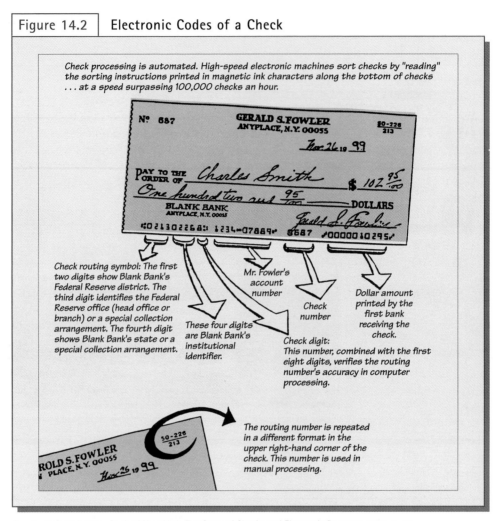

Check processing is automated. High-speed electronic machines sort checks by "reading" the sorting instructions printed in magnetic ink characters along the bottom of checks . . . at a speed surpassing 100,000 checks an hour.

Check routing symbol: The first two digits show Blank Bank's Federal Reserve district. The third digit identifies the Federal Reserve office (head office or branch) or a special collection arrangement. The fourth digit shows Blank Bank's state or a special collection arrangement.

These four digits are Blank Bank's institutional identifier.

Mr. Fowler's account number

Check number

Dollar amount printed by the first bank receiving the check.

Check digit: This number, combined with the first eight digits, verifies the routing number's accuracy in computer processing.

The routing number is repeated in a different format in the upper right-hand corner of the check. This number is used in manual processing.

Source: Federal Reserve Bank of New York, The Story of Checks and Electronic Payment, 1983, p. 15.

bank, requests a cashier's check for a certain amount, and pays the bank that amount plus a service charge. In some financial transactions, the payee may prefer a cashier's check to a personal check. A cashier's check has a better guarantee of payment because it is drawn by a bank against itself.

For people who do not maintain a checking account or who prefer not to make payments with cash, **money orders** often serve the same function as personal checks. Money orders can be purchased at banks, some retail establishments, and the U.S. Postal Service. They are usually issued in smaller amounts and are cheaper than cashier's checks. Often, only the amount is filled in at the time the money order is issued. Until the blanks for the payee's name, the date, and the purchaser's signatures are filled in, the money order is as risky as cash to the purchaser. For this reason, some banks require that the blank spaces be filled in when the money order is issued.

Travelers wanting to protect their money against loss or theft can purchase **traveler's checks** through banks and travel companies. Traveler's checks are usually issued in $20, $50, $100, and $500 denominations. The usual cost is the check's face value plus a small percentage. Widely accepted both in the United States and abroad, traveler's checks are nearly as convenient to use as cash. The purchaser of traveler's checks signs them at the time of purchase and again when they are cashed. This practice protects both the user and the cashing party. The issuing company will replace lost or stolen traveler's checks.

Check Processing and Collection: The Federal Reserve

The check collection system in the United States is efficient, but the collection process a check goes through may be complicated. A check written on a particular bank, say, Chase Manhattan Bank, and cashed by or deposited into the same bank would be handled and processed within that one bank. Checks of this type—called "on us" checks—account for about one-third of all checks. The remaining two-thirds are known as "transit checks" because they must move between different banks, sometimes passing through several banks in different parts of the country.

The Federal Reserve (sometimes called the Fed), headquartered in Washington, D.C., is the largest nationwide processor of transit checks. There are 46 Federal Reserve check-processing facilities: 11 of the 12 Federal Reserve Banks, their branches, and 11 regional check-processing centers. All financial institutions that accept deposits can purchase Federal Reserve check collection and other payments services. Law requires the Federal Reserve to charge these institutions a fee for its services to cover its expenses. However, the Fed's large volume of checks, extensive automation, and speedy processing allow it to keep check collection costs, and prices, low. Checks are moved efficiently across the country from one Federal Reserve check-processing region to another using the Fed's Interdistrict Transportation System, an air transit network. The Federal Reserve Banks also are linked electronically through the Interdistrict Settlement Fund in Washington, D.C. The fund keeps track of the districts' net balances as they exchange checks for settlement. Figure 14.3 provides an example of how a check clears.

Many bankers once believed that sophisticated electronic technology would make paper checks obsolete. Yet, a "checkless society" still seems far away. Although the use of automated teller machines and electronic payment methods, such as funds transfers and debit cards, has been growing each year, check volume has not declined but has actually increased slightly. At some point in the future, the use of checks may begin to dwindle as electronic payment methods become less expensive and more accessible and familiar to consumers. Meanwhile, checks remain a convenient, popular way of making payments.

WHAT BACKS THE MONEY SUPPLY?

If you ask your friends "What backs our money supply?" you may get answers such as "Gold or silver backs our money." No! Gold and silver were removed from our monetary system decades ago. We must look elsewhere to see what backs our money supply.

Recall that the major components of our money supply—paper currency and checking deposits—are promises to pay, or debts. Paper currency is the circulating debt of the Federal Reserve System, and checking deposits are the debt of depository institutions. These items have no intrinsic value. A $20 bill is simply a piece of paper; a checking account is an accounting entry; and a 25-cent piece has less value as metal than its face value.

What underlies the value of a $10 bill or a $500 checking account? Currency and checking accounts are money because we widely accept them in payment for goods and services. We accept money in exchange because we are confident that others will be willing to accept money when we spend it. Put simply, money is anything that we generally accept as a medium of exchange.

The law reinforces our confidence in the acceptability of currency. All U.S. currency, including paper money and coins, is designated as **legal tender;** that is, the federal government mandates its acceptance in transactions and requires that dollars be used in payment

Figure 14.3 | How the Payments System Works

People and organizations move money among themselves by using depository institutions, such as commercial banks, as their switching mechanism. Depository institutions, in turn, use clearing-houses, correspondent banks, or Federal Reserve Banks as their switching mechanism. Federal Reserve Banks use the Interdistrict Settlement Fund in Washington, D.C. as their switching mechanism. The fund settles net amounts due between Federal Reserve Banks daily. Let's trace a check through the Federal Reserve System's clearing and collection facilities to see how the Fed links the payments system.

Source: Federal Reserve Bank of New York, *The Story of Checks and Electronic Payment*, 1983, p. 13.

of taxes. However, this does not mean that a particular type of currency must always be accepted. For example, a convenience store may legally refuse to accept bills having denominations more than $20, or an automobile dealer may refuse to be paid only in pennies.

Although the legal tender pledge reinforces the general acceptability of currency, it does not apply to other types of money. For example, government has not mandated checks to be legal tender. Nevertheless, checking accounts are the largest component of the basic money supply. Although checks are a generally accepted medium of exchange, we may legally turn them down for the payment of goods and services. Perhaps you have attempted to buy gasoline from an establishment that has a sign next to the cash register saying: "No out-of-town checks!"

Table 14.2	The M$_1$ Measure of U.S. Money Supply, January 2005

Component	In Billions of Dollars	Percent of Total
Currency	$ 687.7	51%
Demand deposits	318.4	24
Other checkable deposits	327.4	24
Traveler's checks	7.6	1
Total	1,341.1	100

Source: From *Federal Reserve Bulletin*, January 2005.

MEASURING THE MONEY SUPPLY: M$_1$ MONEY SUPPLY

So far in this chapter, we have discovered many forms of money. Let us now consider how the money supply is measured in the United States.

There are two approaches to defining and measuring money: the *narrow* definition of the money supply, which emphasizes the role of money as a *medium of exchange,* and the *broader* definitions of the money supply, which emphasize the role of money as a *temporary store of value.*

Table 14.2 lists the components of the U.S. money supply according to its narrowest definition, the **M$_1$ money supply.** Included in this measure of the money supply are currency in the hands of the public, demand deposits, other checkable deposits (NOW and share draft accounts), and traveler's checks. M$_1$ is expressed in a formula as follows:

$$M_1 = \text{Currency in the hands of the public} + \text{Demand deposits}$$
$$+ \text{Other checkable deposits} + \text{Traveler's checks}$$

In our definition of money, we include currency only if it is *in the hands of the public.* Some cash is kept in bank vaults and is released only when customers withdraw cash from their vaults. Other cash is kept on deposit at a Federal Reserve Bank, which stores the funds for future use. Until this cash is released by banks or a Federal Reserve Bank, it is not part of the money supply.

Notice that the components of M$_1$ are highly *liquid* (immediately spendable) money that can be used to finance transactions. Coins and paper currency are as liquid as money can be. Checking accounts? Banks are legally obligated to make the money in your checking account available to you upon demand. Traveler's checks, too, are immediately spendable money that we widely accept as payment for goods and services.[3]

As seen in Table 14.2, the M$_1$ money supply equaled $1,341.1 billion in January 2005. Of this amount, 51 percent was issued by the U.S. Treasury and the Federal Reserve Banks as coin and paper currency, 48 percent was issued by our banking system as

---

[3] Economists use broader measures of the money supply to account for other financial assets. The M$_2$ measure of the money supply includes the various components of M$_1$. It also includes (small denomination) time deposits, money market deposit accounts, and money market mutual funds. M$_3$, still a broader measure of the money supply, includes the various components of M$_2$ plus large time deposits, which are less easily converted into spendable money.

checking account money (demand deposits and other checkable deposits), and 1 percent came from traveler's checks. Put simply, checking accounts are a significant component of the M_1 money supply.

Why are checking accounts a widely used type of money? First, making large payments by check is convenient. Imagine how much paper money, say, $20 bills, that we would need to purchase a new house. Second, checks provide records of payment, thus making it unnecessary to keep receipts for purchases of goods and services. Finally, checking accounts provide an element of safety. If you lose your checkbook, you can instruct your bank to stop payment on any future checks that are written on your account.

CHECK POINT

1. For the United States, who issues coins? How about paper currency?

2. How do checks clear from one bank to another?

3. What "backs" the U.S. money supply?

4. Identify the components of the U.S. money supply according to the M_1 money supply.

HOW YOUR MONEY GROWS OVER TIME: COMPOUND INTEREST

In 1624, Native Americans sold Manhattan Island to Peter Minuit, governor of the Dutch West India Company. He paid for it with beads, cloth, and trinkets worth $24. If at the end of 1624, the Native Americans had invested their $24 at 8-percent interest and reinvested the principal and accumulated interest, it would be worth more than $89 trillion by 2000, 376 years later. With $89 trillion in the bank, the Native Americans could have repurchased all Manhattan, for probably $85 to $90 billion, and had plenty left over. This story illustrates the incredible power of compound interest.

When you add to your savings account at a bank, you will receive repayment of the principal amount saved and also payment of interest. By not spending a dollar today and saving it, you obtain more than a dollar to spend in the future. The interest rate is the percentage of your money added to your account each time you are paid interest. Simply put, the interest rate is the reward for saving. To a saver, the key is whether the interest is compound and how it is compounded.

Suppose you have just won $10,000 in a lottery. You would like to save the winnings so that you can eventually purchase a house. You place the money in a savings account at your bank, which offers you 5-percent interest each year. After one year, you have a total of $10,500, or your original $10,000 plus interest of $500 ($10,000 × 1.05 = $10,500).

What happens if you hold your savings deposit for two years? If the interest rate remained constant at 5 percent and you reinvested your principal and accumulated interest, you would earn 5-percent interest on your accumulated savings each year. This process of earning interest on the interest, as well as on the principal, is known as compounding. At the end of two years, you would have $11,025 ($10,500 × 1.05 = $11,025). Notice that your interest increased to $525 the second year ($11,025 − $10,500 = $525), which is $25 more than the $500 interest that you earned during the first year. Why do you earn more interest during the second year than you did during the first? Simply because you can now earn interest on the sum of the original principal and the interest you earned in the first year. You are now earning interest on interest, which is the concept of compound interest.

It is easy to use the concept of compound interest to calculate the value of your savings for any number of years. As seen in Figure 14.4, at the end of three years the value of your savings would have grown to $11,576; at the end of four years, the value of your savings would have growth to $12,155; and at the end of five years, the value of your savings would have grown to $12,763. Indeed, compound interest really does make a difference.

Until now, we have assumed that the compounding period is always annual. However, banks sometimes compound interest on a quarterly or daily basis. What happens to the future value of your money when the compounding period is less than a year? You earn more money faster. The sooner your interest is paid, the sooner you start earning interest on it, and the sooner you realize the benefits of compound interest. For example, if a bank decided to switch from paying interest annually to paying interest daily, the number of compounding periods per year increases from one period to 365 periods. Your money grows faster as the number of compounding periods increases. For a given interest rate and identical saving period, the more frequent the compounding, the larger the future value of money. This explains why banks like to advertise daily compounding rather than

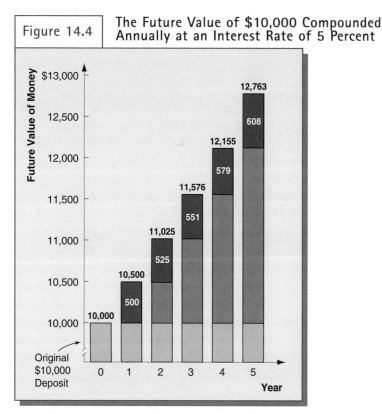

| Figure 14.4 | The Future Value of $10,000 Compounded Annually at an Interest Rate of 5 Percent |

According to the concept of compound interest, a savings deposit earns "interest on interest." This means that interest earned in earlier periods is reinvested to earn interest in future periods. In this manner, the amount of interest you earn grows, or compounds. As seen in the figure, a $10,000 savings deposit compounded annually at an interest rate of 5 percent will have a future value of $12,763 at the end of the fifth year.

annual or quarterly compounding. Also, it's not just time that adds to the future value of money. It's also the interest rate. Obviously, a higher interest rate earns you more money.

Let's again consider the Native Americans' sale of Manhattan Island to Peter Minuit. If the Native Americans had invested their $24 at 10-percent interest compounded annually at the end of 1624, they would have about $129 quadrillion by the end of 2004. If they had invested the $24 at a slightly lower interest rate, say, 8 percent, they would have had only $121 trillion by the end of 2004.

THE BUSINESS OF BANKING

A commercial bank is a corporation that seeks to make profit for its stockholders. How does a bank operate? To understand more clearly the business of banking, we can look at a bank's balance sheet, a tool used by accountants.

A Bank's Balance Sheet

A balance sheet is a 2-column list that shows at a specific date the financial position of a bank. It shows everything of value that it owns (assets), the debts that it owes (liabilities), and the amount of the owners' investment (net worth) in the bank. The difference between a bank's assets and liabilities is its net worth. When a bank is started, its owners must place their own funds into the bank. These funds are the bank's initial net worth. If a bank makes profits, its net worth will rise. Conversely, the bank's net worth falls if it incurs losses.

Table 14.3 shows the consolidated balance sheet for all commercial banks in the United States as of December 2004. We will use this picture of the entire banking system to get an idea of what a commercial bank does and the importance of the various assets and liabilities to an average or typical commercial bank in this country.

Let us consider the assets of the commercial banking system, which we see on the left side of Table 14.3. First are the banks' reserves, which total $324.3 billion. Reserves are deposits that banks have received but have not lent out. Reserves can be kept either in vault cash or deposits at a Federal Reserve Bank, neither of which earn interest for the bank.

Table 14.3	Consolidated Balance Sheet for All U.S. Commercial Banks, December 2004 (billions of dollars)		
Assets		**Liabilities and Net Worth**	
Reserves	324.3	Deposits:	5,220.6
Loans:	4,801.1	Checking deposits	719.9
Commercial/industrial	901.0	Savings/time deposits	4,500.7
Real estate	2,490.2	Borrowings	1,595.4
Consumer	670.2	All other liabilities	530.3
Other	739.7	Total liabilities	7,346.3
Securities:	1,908.7	Net worth (assets − liabilities)	615.5
U.S. government	1,141.4		
Other	767.3		
All other assets	927.7		
Total assets	7,961.8		

Source: From *Statistical Supplement to the Federal Reserve Bulletin*, March 2005.

Since banks do not earn any interest on their reserves, why do they maintain holdings of reserves? Wouldn't a profit-seeking bank want to hold most of its assets in loans and securities that generate interest income? One reason for holding reserves is that on a particular day, some of a bank's customers might want to withdraw more cash than other customers are depositing. The bank must be able to fulfill its obligation for withdrawals, so it must have cash on hand to meet this commitment. Also, law requires banks to hold a fraction of their checking deposits as reserves, as will be discussed later.

Next come the $4,801.1 billion of loans and $1,908.7 billion of securities owned by the commercial banking system. Loans are IOUs signed by households and businesses. Examples include commercial and industrial loans, real estate loans, and consumer loans for automobiles and other durable goods. Securities are IOUs issued by a government agency or a corporation when it borrows money. Both loans and securities provide interest income for the bank. Finally, banks have "other" assets such as the value of their office buildings and equipment.

On the right side of the banks' balance sheet are liabilities. The major liability is deposits, which equal $5,220.6 billion and include both checking deposits and a variety of savings deposits and time deposits. Why are deposits liabilities? Because the customers of banks have the right to withdraw funds from their deposit accounts. Until they do, the banks owe them these funds. Another liability is bank borrowings. At a particular point in time, a bank may find that its reserves are inadequate to meet the withdrawal of deposits by its customers, and thus may borrow reserves. A bank may borrow reserves from another bank or from a Federal Reserve Bank.

Also on the right side of the balance sheet is the banks' net worth, $615.5 billion, which represents the difference between assets ($7,961.8 billion) and liabilities ($7,346.3 billion). If a bank were to go out of business, selling all of its assets and using the proceeds to pay off all of its liabilities, the excess would go to the bank's stockholders—its owners.

Reserve Requirement

By law, all banks are required to hold a certain percentage of their checking deposits on reserve either in the form of vault cash or deposits at the Federal Reserve. Banks are not pleased to make such holdings because vault cash and deposits at the Federal Reserve do not pay interest.

Required reserves are the minimum amount of vault cash and deposits at the Federal Reserve that must be maintained by a bank. **Actual reserves** are what the bank is holding. If a bank is holding more than required, it has **excess reserves,** which can be used to make loans or purchase government securities. Therefore, actual reserves are the sum of its required and excess reserves, calculated as follows:

$$\text{Actual reserves} = \text{Required reserves} + \text{Excess reserves}$$

For example, U.S. Bank may have $80 million of actual reserves, of which $8 million must be held in required reserves. The remainder, $72 million, is the bank's excess reserves.

The **required reserve ratio** is a specific percentage of checking deposits that must be kept as vault cash or deposits at the Federal Reserve. It is established by the Federal Reserve System and directly limits the ability of banks to grant new loans. For example, a required reserve ratio of 10 percent on checking deposits suggests that a bank must have an amount on reserve equal to 10 percent of the value of the checking deposits it is holding. If Chase Manhattan Bank has $50 million in checking accounts and a 10-percent required reserve ratio, it must maintain at least $5 million in actual reserves ($50,000,000 × 0.10 = $5,000,000).

THE PROCESS OF MONEY CREATION

If you were to ask friends where our money comes from, they might have a simple answer: "The government prints it." They might even have toured the U.S. Mint in Philadelphia or Denver and seen pennies and nickels being stamped or have visited the Bureau of Engraving and Printing in Washington, D.C., and seen dollar bills being printed. As we have learned, however, most of our money comes from checking accounts issued by banks rather than from the government. Let us examine how banks create money.

Suppose that you walk into Wells Fargo Bank and deposit $1,000 cash into your checking account. The deposit of cash, which the bank keeps in its vault, results in a $1,000 decrease in the money supply (recall that currency held by a bank is not part of the economy's money supply). However, the checking account component of the money supply rises by $1,000 because of the deposit. Thus, the total supply of money does not change. However, Wells Fargo Bank will not earn a profit by keeping all of the cash that it receives in its vault. It will want to make loans to the public.

Let's suppose that the required reserve ratio is 10 percent, suggesting that a bank must keep 10 percent of its checking deposits as required reserves. Wells Fargo Bank will keep $100 in required reserves ($1,000 × 0.10 = $100) and make loans of $900. When Wells Fargo Bank makes these loans, the supply of money increases. Why? As a depositor, you still have your checking account of $1,000, but now the borrowers hold $900 in their checking accounts. Therefore, the money supply equals $1,900. Figure 14.5(a) shows the change in the balance sheet of Wells Fargo Bank after it has made the loan.

Suppose that Wells Fargo Bank makes a loan to a computer software company that wants to purchase some equipment. The company buys $900 of equipment from another firm that deposits the check in its account at U.S. Bank. Figure 14.5(b) shows what happens to the balance sheet of U.S. Bank. Its checking deposits increase by $900 because of the deposit. The bank must maintain $90 of required reserves ($900 × 0.10 = $90), and it can lend out $810. Suppose the bank lends $810 to the owner of an espresso stand and opens a checking account for him. In this way, U.S. Bank creates an additional $810 of money. The espresso stand owner then purchases supplies from a wholesaler who deposits the check in her account at Rainier Bank, which keeps $81 in reserve ($810 × 0.10 = $81) and makes $729 in loans. Figure 14.5(c) shows what happens to the balance sheet of Rainier Bank.

Figure 14.5	Process of Money Creation

(a) Wells Fargo Bank

Assets		Liabilities
Required Reserves = $100		Checking Deposits = $1,000
Loans =	$900	

(b) U.S. Bank

Assets		Liabilities
Required Reserves = $90		Checking Deposits = $900
Loans =	$810	

(c) Rainier Bank

Assets		Liabilities
Required Reserves = $81		Checking Deposits = $810
Loans =	$729	

The process goes on and on. Each time we deposit a check and a bank makes a loan, more money is created. We can determine how much money is eventually created by the banking system by adding the money created by each bank:

$$
\begin{array}{lr}
\text{Original checking deposit} = \$ & 1{,}000 \\
\text{Wells Fargo Bank loan} \quad = & 900 \\
\text{U.S. Bank loan} \quad\quad\quad = & 810 \\
\text{Rainier Bank loan} \quad\quad = & 729 \\
\qquad\qquad\bullet & \bullet \\
\qquad\qquad\bullet & \bullet \\
\qquad\qquad\bullet & \bullet \\
\hline
\text{Total money supply} = & \$10{,}000
\end{array}
$$

The process of money creation can continue forever. If we added the infinite sequence of numbers in our example, we find that the initial checking deposit of $1,000 results in a total money supply of $10,000. Put simply, the money supply can be increased by a *multiple* of the initial checking deposit for the banking system.[4]

We call the maximum amount of money the banking system generates with each dollar of reserves the **money multiplier.** In our example, where the initial $1,000 of reserves leads to a money supply totaling $10,000, the money multiplier is 10.

What determines the size of the money multiplier? The money multiplier is the reciprocal of the required reserve ratio, calculated as follows:

$$\text{Money multiplier} = 1/\text{Required reserve ratio}$$ *only in theory*

In our example, the required reserve ratio is 10 percent, so the money multiplier is 10 ($1/0.10 = 10$). If the required reserve ratio is 20 percent, the money multiplier is 5 ($1/0.20 = 5$).

Notice that our formula tells us the *maximum* amount of money the banking system can generate with each dollar of reserves. In the real world, however, the money creation ability of the banking system is smaller than our formula suggests. The main reason is that our formula assumed that all loans made their way directly into checking accounts. In reality, people may hold part of their loans as currency. Currency kept in a person's purse or wallet or safe-deposit box remains outside the banking system and cannot be held by banks as reserves from which to make loans. The greater the currency holdings, the smaller the actual money expansion multiplier.

THE FEDERAL DEPOSIT INSURANCE CORPORATION

Indeed, banks can affect the economy through their ability to create money. Therefore, there is much concern about the stability of our banking system. If many depositors lose confidence in a bank's financial position, they may attempt to rapidly withdraw funds from the bank. One source of confidence for our banking system is the Federal Deposit Insurance Corporation.

---

[4] The basic money supply (M_1) is the sum of currency held by the public plus checking accounts issued by banks. Thus, the *change* in the money supply will equal the change in currency held by the public plus the change in checking accounts. Although in our example of money creation, checking accounts increased by $10,000, the public now has $1,000 less currency because they deposited the currency in the bank. The money supply thus *increased* by $9,000 ($10,000 − $1,000 = $9,000).

The Federal Deposit Insurance Corporation (FDIC) has been insuring deposits and promoting safe and sound banking practices since 1933. The FDIC sign, posted in insured financial institutions across the country, has become a symbol of confidence. Let us first consider circumstance that led to the creation of the FDIC.

The Great Depression of the 1930s caused financial chaos in the United States. More than 9,000 banks closed between the stock market crash of October 1929 and March 1933, when President Franklin Roosevelt took office. For all practical purposes, the nation's banking system had shut down completely even before Roosevelt (less than 48 hours after his inauguration) declared a "banking holiday," suspending all banking activities until stability could be restored. Among the actions taken by Congress to bring order to the system was the creation of the FDIC in June 1933. The intent was to provide a federal government guarantee of deposits so that customers' funds, within certain limits, would be safe and available to them on demand. After the introduction of federal deposit insurance, the number of bank failures declined sharply. Since the formation of the FDIC, not one depositor has lost a cent of insured funds because of bank failure.

Bank examinations are the front line of the FDIC's operations to promote and maintain the safety and soundness of banks. Through bank examinations, the FDIC determines the condition of each bank and obtains a better understanding of the risks the FDIC assumes in insuring the bank's deposits.

The FDIC also provides for a system of national deposit insurance. All types of bank deposits received are insured, currently to a limit of $100,000. To protect depositors when an insured bank fails, the FDIC pays depositors up to the $100,000 insurance limit and recovers as much money as possible from the failed institution's assets—primarily loans, real estate, and securities. To help prevent bank failure, the FDIC sometimes arranges a merger between a sound bank and a failing bank; this allows the failing bank to keep its doors open, thus preserving the confidence of the banking public.

This chapter examined the nature of money and the operation of our banking system. The next chapter broadens our understanding of these topics by considering the Federal Reserve and monetary policy.

CHECK POINT

1. Identify the major assets and liabilities for a typical commercial bank.

2. How do banks create money? Why does the banking system have a money multiplier?

3. How does the Federal Deposit Insurance Corporation promote stability in the nation's banking system?

Chapter Summary

1. Money is the set of assets in the economy that people regularly use to purchase goods and services from other people. Money has three functions in the economy: It is a medium of exchange, a unit of account, and a store of value. These functions distinguish money from other assets such as stocks and bonds, real estate, and the like.

2. Are credit cards money? Not at all! If you use your credit card to make a purchase, you obtain a short-term loan from the financial institution that issued the card. Credit cards are

thus a method of postponing payment for a brief period. In shopping for a credit card, a person should consider features such as the card's annual percentage rate, the grace period, whether the issuer may charge an over-limit fee or a late payment fee, and the annual cost of the card.

3. The basic money supply (M_1) consists of coins, paper money, checking accounts, and traveler's checks. Under federal law, only the U.S. Treasury issues coin and the Federal Reserve System issues paper currency. Checking account money is created by the banking system.

4. The check collection system in the United States is efficient, but the collection process that a check goes through may be complicated. The check-processing system is conducted by local clearinghouses, correspondent banks, and the Federal Reserve System's check collection network.

5. The U.S. economy has an array of banks, including commercial banks, savings and loan associations, mutual savings banks, and credit unions. We call these institutions depository institutions because they accept deposits from people and provide checking accounts that are part of the money supply.

6. If you save money in a bank, you have alternatives such as money market deposit accounts, savings accounts, and certificates of deposit. In shopping for an account, it is important to look at features such as the interest rate, the method of interest compounding, the annual percentage yield, the timing of interest earned, and fees.

7. A commercial bank is a corporation that seeks to make a profit for its stockholders. Among the most important assets of a bank are its reserves, loans, and government securities. Deposits and borrowings are a bank's major liabilities.

8. Most of our money comes from checking accounts issued by banks, rather than currency. Through the process of lending reserves, banks create money. The money multiplier is used to calculate the maximum amount of money the banking system generates with each dollar of reserves. The money multiplier is the reciprocal of the required reserve ratio.

9. The FDIC has been insuring deposits and promoting safe and sound banking practices since 1934. The FDIC insures deposits up to $100,000 in virtually all U.S. banks. Since the start of FDIC insurance, not one depositor has lost a cent of insured funds because of bank failure.

Key Terms and Concepts

Money (334)

currency (334)

medium of exchange (335)

unit of account (335)

store of value (335)

demand deposit account (339)

negotiable order of withdrawal (NOW) account (339)

certified check (341)

cashier's check (341)

money order (342)

traveler's check (342)

legal tender (343)

M_1 money supply (345)

compound interest (346)

balance sheet (348)

reserves (348)

required reserves (349)

actual reserves (349)

excess reserves (349)

required reserve ratio (349)

money multiplier (351)

Federal Deposit Insurance Corporation (FDIC) (352)

Self-Test: Multiple-Choice Questions

1. The functions of money include all of the following *except*

   a. medium of exchange.
   b. store of value.
   c. unit of account.
   d. measure of productivity.

2. All of the following are components of the basic (M_1) money supply *except*

   a. coins.
   b. paper currency.
   c. demand deposits.
   d. savings deposits.

3. Which type of checking account provides interest income to its holders?

   a. Negotiable order of withdrawal
   b. Time deposit
   c. Certificate of deposit
   d. Demand deposit

4. A _____ is generally considered to have the *least* guarantee of payment.

   a. personal check
   b. certified check
   c. cashier's check
   d. traveler's check

5. A commercial bank's balance sheet includes all of the following assets *except*

   a. government securities.
   b. loans to businesses and households.
   c. vault cash and deposits at the Federal Reserve.
   d. checking accounts and savings deposits.

6. Your savings account provides you the most interest income if interest compounding is conducted on a

   a. daily basis.
   b. weekly basis.
   c. monthly basis.
   d. yearly basis.

7. If Tom and Barb Jacobs have individual savings accounts and a joint savings account at Wells Fargo Bank, the maximum amount of FDIC insurance coverage that they can have is

   a. $100,000.
   b. $200,000.
   c. $300,000.
   d. $400,000.

8. If the Federal Reserve sets the required reserve ratio at 20 percent, the money multiplier is

   a. 0.2.
   b. 5.
   c. 10.
   d. 20.

9. The M$_1$ money supply places primary emphasis on money as a

   a. medium of exchange.
   b. standard of debt.
   c. store of value.
   d. measure of inflation.

10. The U.S. banking system includes all of the following *except* the

   a. Yakima Federal Savings and Loan Association.
   b. Central Washington University Credit Union.
   c. American National Bank.
   d. New York Stock Exchange.

Answers to Multiple-Choice Questions
1. d   2. d   3. a   4. a   5. d   6. a   7. c   8. b   9. a   10. d

Study Questions and Problems

1. Analyze each of the following assets in terms of their potential use as a medium of exchange, a unit of account, and a store of value. Which use is most appropriately associated with each asset?

   a. A VISA credit card
   b. A $20 Federal Reserve note
   c. Ten shares of Microsoft stock
   d. A 90-day Treasury bill
   e. A certificate of deposit at a commercial bank
   f. A checking account at a savings and loan association
   g. $20 worth of dimes

2. Table 14.4 shows hypothetical money supply data for the United States. Compute the basic (M$_1$) money supply.

3. For a commercial bank, which of the following items represent assets and which represent liabilities?

   a. Certificates of deposit
   b. Borrowings from a Federal Reserve Bank
   c. Bank office equipment
   d. Loans to businesses and households

Table 14.4	Hypothetical Money Supply Data (billions of dollars)	
	Money market deposit accounts	20
	Checking deposits	150
	Coin	10
	Paper currency	90
	Certificates of deposit	25
	Traveler's checks	5
	Mutual funds	15

Table 14.5	Balance Sheet of the Bank of Ohio .

Assets		Liabilities	
Reserves	$55,000	Checkable deposits	$110,000
Loans	90,000	Savings deposits	75,000
Securities	28,000	Borrowings from other	8,000
Other	20,000	banks	

    e. Holdings of government securities

    f. Checking deposits

    g. Deposits with a district Federal Reserve Bank

4. If borrowers take a portion of their loans as cash rather than checkable deposits, what happens to the money multiplier of the commercial banking system?

5. If Jennifer Gray deposits a $100 bill into her checking account, and her bank has a required reserve ratio of 5 percent, how much will the bank's required reserves increase? What happens to excess reserves?

6. Suppose the Federal Reserve sets the required reserve ratio at 15 percent. If the banking system has $10 million in excess reserves, what amount of checkable deposits can be created?

7. American National Bank has reserves of $100,000 and checking deposits of $500,000. The required reserve ratio is 20 percent. Suppose households deposit $50,000 cash into their checking deposits at American National Bank, which then adds this amount to its reserves. What amount of excess reserves does the bank now have?

8. Suppose that the banking system has reserves totaling $50 billion. Also assume that required reserves are 25 percent of checking deposits, and that banks hold no excess reserves and households hold no cash. What is the money multiplier?

9. Assume that you take $2,000 cash and deposit it in your bank checking account. If this $2,000 remains in the banking system as reserves and if banks hold reserves equal to 20 percent of checking deposits, by how much does the total amount of checking deposits in the banking system increase?

10. Table 14.5 shows the hypothetical balance sheet of the Bank of Ohio. Assuming that the required reserve ratio on checkable deposits equals 10 percent, answer the following questions:

    a. Bank of Ohio must maintain required reserves of _____.

    b. Bank of Ohio has excess reserves in the amount of _____.

    c. The maximum that Bank of Ohio can increase the money supply by lending is _____. If Bank of Ohio actually lends the maximum amount it is able to lend, what will happen to its excess reserves?

    d. Instead, suppose that the balance sheet pertains to the entire commercial banking system. The maximum that the banking system could increase the money supply by lending is _____.

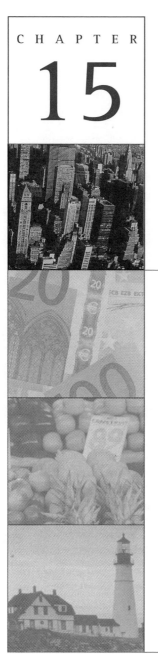

The Federal Reserve and Monetary Policy

Chapter objectives

After reading this chapter, you should be able to:

1. Describe the structure and operation of the Federal Reserve System.

2. Identify the services that the Federal Reserve System provides for the U.S. economy.

3. Explain the purpose and operation of monetary policy.

4. Assess the advantages and disadvantages of monetary policy.

5. Evaluate whether Congress should reduce the independence of the Federal Reserve.

economics IN CONTEXT

In 2001 and 2002, developing gloom lay heavy and thick on the U.S. economy like smog in the air. Consumers, who account for two-thirds of economic activity, had lost a significant amount of their wealth as the value of their stocks fell in a sagging market. Increasingly, consumers put off their purchases, which resulted in falling sales and declining profitability for businesses. Economists feared that eroding profit expectations would dampen capital spending. Add in the slower growth in much of the world economy, and the prospects for U.S. exporters were also becoming grim.

To bolster a weakening economy, the Federal Reserve cut its interest rate 12 times during 2001–2002. Its actions were aimed at Americans like Jim Riley, who owns a small construction firm in Fort Collins, Colorado. Mr. Riley was contemplating starting a new business that wouldn't experience the winter downturns that construction does. He thought about manufacturing new homes using an indoor facility; these homes

could then be transported to a building site in any season. By 2002, his enthusiasm for the project had dwindled as the economy waned.

Indeed, few issues in economics evoke more emotion than the conduct of monetary policy. Critics have maintained that the Federal Reserve System—also known as the Fed—has sometimes destabilized the economy by causing inflation or recession. However, proponents of the Fed argue that it has done a credible job in promoting economic stability. They maintain that severe economic shocks—such as stock market crashes, wars, rising oil prices, and foreign competition—have unsettled the economy, and that the Fed has done the best it could to maintain a stable economy.

In this chapter, we will examine the nature and operation of the Fed. We will begin by considering its structure and how it attempts to control the money supply and interest rates to stabilize the economy.

THE FEDERAL RESERVE SYSTEM

The Federal Reserve System (Fed) is the central bank of the United States. It was legislated by Congress and signed into law by President Woodrow Wilson in 1913 to provide the nation with a safer, more flexible, and more stable monetary and financial system. All major countries have a central bank whose functions are broadly similar to those of the Fed. These central banks include the Bank of England, the Bank of Canada, and the Bank of Japan.

Before Congress created the Fed, periodic financial panics had plagued the nation. These panics contributed to many bank failures, business bankruptcies, and general economic downturns. A particularly severe crisis in 1907 prompted the eventual passage of the Federal Reserve Act in 1913.

Structure of the Federal Reserve System

The Fed has a structure designed by Congress to give it a broad perspective on the economy and on economic activity in all parts of the nation. At the head of its formal organization is the Board of Governors, located in Washington, D.C. The 12 regional Federal Reserve Banks make up the next level. *+25 branch banks* The organization of the Fed also includes the Federal Open Market Committee and three advisory councils. These bodies and other policymaking committees provide additional avenues for regional and private-sector participation in the Fed's activities.

Board of Governors   The Board of Governors administers the Fed. The board consists of seven members who are appointed by the president and confirmed by the Senate to serve 14-year terms of office. Members may serve only one full term, but a member who has been appointed to complete an unexpired term may later be reappointed to a full term. These long terms help to insulate the decisions of the board from day-to-day political pressure. The president designates, and the Senate confirms, two members of the Board of Governors to be chair and vice chair, for 4-year terms. Only one member of the board may be selected from any one of the 12 Federal Reserve districts. In making appointments, the president is directed by law to select a fair representation of the financial, agricultural, industrial, and commercial interests and geographic divisions of the country.

As head of the nation's central bank, the chair appears before Congress to report on Federal Reserve policies, the System's views about the economy, financial developments, and other matters. The chair also meets from time to time with the president of the United States and regularly confers with the secretary of the Treasury and the chair of the Council of Economic Advisors.

Board members usually meet several times a week. As they carry out their duties, members of the board routinely confer with officials of other government agencies, representatives of banking industry groups, officials of the central banks of other countries, members of Congress, and academicians.

Federal Open Market Committee   The Federal Open Market Committee (FOMC) is the Fed's most important policymaking body for controlling the growth of the money supply. To do so, the FOMC oversees the purchases and sales of U.S. government securities. These operations are conducted by the New York Reserve Bank, which serves as the agent for the FOMC. The FOMC members include the seven members of the Board of Governors, the president of the Federal Reserve Bank of New York, and four other Reserve Bank presidents who serve 1-year terms on a rotating basis.

The Reserve Banks   The day-to-day operations of the Fed are carried out by the 12 Federal Reserve Banks. As seen in Figure 15.1, each of the Federal Reserve Banks serves a certain region of the country and is named after the location of its headquarters—Atlanta, Boston, Chicago, Cleveland, Dallas, Kansas City, Minneapolis, New York, Philadelphia, Richmond, San Francisco, and St. Louis. Also, there are 25 Federal Reserve branch banks located throughout the country.

Although the Federal Reserve Banks are not motivated by profit, they do earn substantial revenues on the Fed's large holdings of income-producing government securities acquired in the process of implementing monetary policy. Also, the Federal Reserve Banks charge banks for check collection and other services. Almost all of these revenues are turned over to the U.S. Treasury. Moreover, the Fed receives no funding from the government.

The Federal Reserve Banks are owned by the banks that are members of the Federal Reserve System. That is, the member banks are the stockholders of the Fed. Each Federal Reserve Bank has its own board of nine directors chosen from outside the Bank.

Finally, at the bottom of the Fed's organizational structure is the U.S. banking system, which consists of commercial banks, mutual savings banks, savings and loan associations, and credit unions.

Independence of the Fed

Congress structured the Fed to be independent within the government—that is, although the Fed is accountable to Congress, it is insulated from day-to-day political pressures. This reflects the conviction that the people who control the country's money supply should be independent of the people who frame the government's spending decisions. Most studies *reflects the reality of where banking happens*

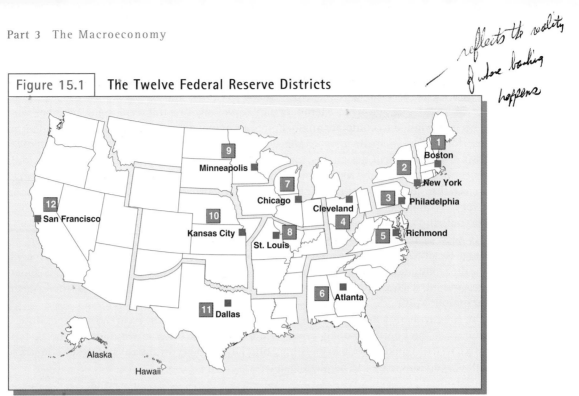

Figure 15.1   The Twelve Federal Reserve Districts

The day-to-day operations of the Federal Reserve are carried out by the 12 Federal Reserve Banks, which are located throughout the United States.

economics
IN ACTION

Federal Funds Rate

Banks such as Chase Manhattan Bank and BankAmerica actively trade reserves held at the Federal Reserve among themselves. Such a market for reserves is called the federal funds market. Those banks with surplus balances in their accounts transfer reserves to those in need of boosting their balances.

Typically, a federal funds transaction takes the form of an overnight loan. Arrangements are agreed upon by telephone between the lending bank and the borrowing bank and confirmed later by mail. The actual transfer of the reserves is normally accomplished via a phone call from the lending bank to the Federal Reserve Bank, instructing the latter to transfer the agreed-upon amount from its reserve account

to that of the borrower. Generally, the Federal Reserve Bank will reverse the transaction on the following day.

The benchmark rate of interest charged for this short-term use of these funds is called the federal funds rate. The federal funds rate is not an administered rate; instead, it is a market-determined rate, fluctuating continuously depending on the relationship between the demand for loans, by banks who need to borrow, and the supply from banks who want to lend. For example, an increase in the amount of reserves supplied to the federal funds market causes the funds rate to fall; a decrease in the supply of reserves raises that rate. Indeed, the federal funds rate closely reflects the basic supply and demand conditions in the market for bank reserves that are influenced by the Fed's monetary policies. Therefore, analysts pay close attention to the federal funds rate for signals of changes in monetary policy.

of central bank independence rank the Fed among the most independent in the world. Three structural features make the Fed independent: the appointment procedure for governors, the appointment procedure for Reserve Bank presidents, and funding.

The seven members of the Board of Governors are appointed by the president of the United States and confirmed by the Senate. Independence derives from several factors. First, the appointments are staggered to reduce the chance that a single U.S. president could "stack" the board with appointees. Second, their terms of office are 14 years—much longer than elected officials' terms.

Also, each Reserve Bank president is appointed to a 5-year term by that respective Bank's Board of Directors, subject to final approval by the Board of Governors. This procedure adds to independence because the directors of each Reserve Bank are not chosen by politicians but are selected to provide a cross-section of interests within the region—including banks, businesses, labor, and the public.

Finally, the Fed is structured to be self-sufficient in the sense that it meets its operating expenses primarily from the interest earnings on its holdings of government securities. Thus, it is independent of congressional decisions about appropriations.

Although the Fed is independent of congressional funding and administrative control, it is ultimately accountable to Congress and comes under government audit and review. The chair, other governors, and Reserve Bank presidents report regularly to Congress on monetary policy and regulatory policy, and meet with government officials to discuss the Federal Reserve's and the federal government's economic programs.

Functions of the Federal Reserve System

The Federal Reserve, as the overseer of the nation's monetary system, has a variety of important duties. Some important functions of the Fed are as follows:

- Controlling the money supply through policies that affect the quantity of reserves that banks use to make loans.

- Lender of last resort to banks in order to forestall financial panics.

- Regulating and supervising banks in order to maintain financial responsibility.

- Supplying services to banks such as check processing and electronic transfers of funds.

- Supplying services to the government such as the transportation of currency, issuance and redemption of Treasury securities, and maintenance of the Treasury's checking account.

consumer
ECONOMICS IN ACTION

What Does a Quarter-Point Decrease in Interest Mean?

In 2001–2002, the Fed reduced interest rates 12 times in order to bolster a weakening economy. These reductions ranged from one-quarter of a percentage point to one-half of a percentage point at a time. How would a measly one-quarter of 1-percentage point decrease in interest rates bolster the economy?

In an economy built on credit, a decrease in borrowing costs may have an immediate and pronounced economic effect. Housing provides an illustration, because it is quickly affected by changes in interest rates. Homes are generally

re-fi

(continued)

built with borrowed money: They are purchased with mortgages. Their sale therefore depends on the availability and price of borrowed money.

About two-thirds of American households own their home. Those with fixed-rate mortgages, about 70 percent of the households in 2002, are not affected by interest-rate decreases. However, the remaining 30 percent of households with adjustable-rate mortgages are affected. That small decrease in interest rates by the Fed could translate into one-quarter of a percentage point reduction on many mortgages with adjustable rates. For some, the lower rates could begin within weeks following a rate drop ~~hike~~ by the Fed.

A one-quarter-point decrease on a $100,000 adjustable rate mortgage might reduce it to 6.25 percent from 6.5 percent, resulting in a smaller monthly payment of $25, or $300 a year out of pocket. On a $150,000 mortgage, the cost reduction would be about $450. This money could be spent on other goods such as electronics, clothing, and transportation.

The effect on housing construction could also be immediate, with builders increasing commitments because of money costs or availability. Also, homeowners might increase their remodeling and repairs, a $115 billion per year business in 2002. Because of the lower rates, the National Association of REALTORS® estimates that perhaps 50,000 additional home sales would occur within 18 months of the Fed's action. At an average 2002 price of $145,000, that's about

$7 billion. The impact on new single-family sales could be equal or greater. Assuming that it is equal—50,000 units—it would mean another $12 billion or so in additional transactions, since the average new-home price was about $260,000.

Besides increasing single-family sales, a reduction in interest rates stimulates business for several sectors of the economy. For example, housing construction is a $275 billion per year industry, one the National Association of Home Builders describes as "a vital sector of local, state and national economies, creating jobs and generating taxes and wages." Based on its estimates, the construction of 50,000 single-family houses generates 122,400 jobs in construction and construction-related industries; $4 billion in wages; and $800 million in federal, state, and local tax revenues and fees. Moreover, the Association says, in the first 12 months after buying a newly built home, owners spend an average of $7,500 on furnishings, decorations, and improvements. And buyers of existing homes spend $2,500.

The effects spread widely, from local masons, plumbers, and carpenters to retailers, distributors, manufacturers, and suppliers of raw materials—to distant lumber producers and paint makers, and to producers of electrical wiring, carpeting, and shingles. Indeed, a modest decrease in interest rates can have a pronounced effect on the economy.

Sources: National Association of Home Builders, *Economic and Housing Data*, http://www.nahb.com/facts. See also National Association of REALTORS® at http://www.realtor.org/.

Although some of these functions are routine activities or have a service aspect, the major task of the Fed is to manage the nation's money supply in order to stabilize the economy. Let us consider the nature and operation of monetary policy.

CHECK POINT

1. What is the Fed, and why was it established?

2. Describe the organizational structure of the Fed.

3. Which committee is the Fed's most important policymaking body for controlling the growth of the money supply?

4. What are the major functions of the Fed?

MONETARY POLICY

Monetary policy consists of changing the economy's money supply to assist the economy in achieving maximum output and employment and also stable prices. In order to carry out monetary policy, the Fed acts as the economy's "money manager." It tries to balance the flow of money and credit with the needs of the economy. Too much money in the economy can result in inflation; too little can stifle economic activity. The Fed seeks to strike a balance between these two extremes.

In order to balance the flow of money, the Fed influences the ability of banks to create checking account money through loans. This is accomplished by increasing or decreasing the volume of bank reserves. As we will see, by adding to bank reserves, the Fed can stimulate an increase in the money supply; by letting bank reserves fall, the Fed can induce a reduction in the money supply.

The Fed uses several important policy instruments to influence bank reserves and the money supply: open market operations, the discount rate, and the reserve requirement. Let us examine each of these policy tools.

Open Market Operations

Open market operations are the most useful and important of the Fed's policy tools. They refer to the purchase or sale of securities by the Fed. When the Fed conducts an open market operation, it makes a transaction with a bank or some other business or individual, but it does not effect a transaction directly with the federal government.

Each purchase or sale of securities by the Fed directly affects the volume of reserves in the banking system and, in the process, the economy as a whole. When the Fed wants to *increase* the flow of money and credit, it *buys* government securities from banks and businesses; when it wants to *restrict* the flow of money and credit, it *sells* government securities.

Open market operations occur largely through auctions in which security dealers are requested to submit bids to buy or offers to sell securities of the type and maturity that the Fed has elected to sell or to buy. The dealers' bids or offers are arranged according to price, and the Fed accepts amounts bid or offered in sequence, taking the highest prices bid for its sales and the lowest prices offered for its purchases, until the desired size of the whole transaction is reached.

The Fed's purchase of government securities can be illustrated by using balance sheets. Referring to Figure 15.2, suppose the Fed buys $10 million of securities from Seafirst Bank. The Fed would pay for the securities by increasing Seafirst's deposits at the Fed—its reserves by $10 million. Seafirst's excess reserves increase by the full amount of the transaction.[1] With more excess reserves, it can make more loans and increase its checking deposits.

The process does not stop here. As deposit holders spend their newly acquired funds, the deposits will move to other banks. These institutions will set aside part of their new funds as reserves to back their new deposits, but they can lend the remainder. The resulting loans create additional new deposits, which will move in part to other depository institutions to expand loans and deposits in the same manner. By the time the process stops, checking deposits usually will have risen by several times the amount of reserves created by the Fed's original action. Put simply, a purchase of securities by the Fed results in a multiple expansion of the money supply.

We saw in Chapter 14 how a change in bank reserves would result in a multiplied change in the money supply. If the required reserve ratio is 20 percent, the $10 million

---

[1] Because this transaction does not affect Seafirst's checking deposits, against which the reserve requirement applies, its required reserves do not change. As a result, the bank's total reserves and excess reserves change by the same amount.

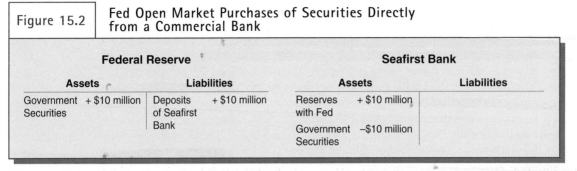

Figure 15.2 — Fed Open Market Purchases of Securities Directly from a Commercial Bank

Federal Reserve		Seafirst Bank	
Assets	**Liabilities**	**Assets**	**Liabilities**
Government +$10 million Securities	Deposits +$10 million of Seafirst Bank	Reserves +$10 million with Fed	
		Government −$10 million Securities	

When the Fed buys securities from a bank, the Fed pays for the securities by increasing the bank's deposits at the Fed (its reserves). The bank's excess reserves increase by the full amount of the transaction. With more excess reserves, the bank can make more loans and increase its checking deposits.

banks, etc. buy the securities because they pay interest; but then there is no multiplier

purchase of securities from banks will result in a $50 million increase in the economy's money supply. Virtually the same result can be achieved if the Fed purchases securities from businesses or individuals, because these sellers generally deposit the money received from the sale of securities in banks. Conversely, if the Fed wanted to decrease the money supply, it would sell securities to banks, businesses, or individuals.

A main advantage of open market operations is flexibility: The Fed can purchase or sell government securities in large or small amounts. Also, open market operations have a speedy effect on bank reserves. As a result, open market operations are the main instrument of monetary policy.

As we have learned, the Federal Open Market Committee oversees the purchases and sales of U.S. government securities. The FOMC meets about every six weeks, more often if necessary, to establish policy. FOMC meetings generally fall into four parts—a review of recent actions by the managers of the Fed accounts, a discussion of general economic conditions, a discussion of financial conditions and monetary policy alternatives, and finally, a vote on monetary policy by FOMC members. Discussion is quite free, and there often is considerable diversity of opinion. Twice each year, in accordance with law, the FOMC establishes its long-term goals for monetary policy and reports them to Congress.

Between meetings, the various members of the FOMC stay in touch through written and electronic correspondence. Moreover, an FOMC member talks daily with the New York Federal Reserve Bank, which carries out the buying and selling of government securities. Telephone meetings of the entire FOMC may be called on very short notice, if necessary, and any member is free to object at any time to the manner in which the New York Federal Reserve Bank is carrying out the instructions of the FOMC.

The Discount Rate

Another policy tool of the Fed is the discount rate—the rate Federal Reserve Banks charge for loans to banks. An important purpose of the Fed is to serve as the "lender of last resort" to banks. By lending funds to banks through its discount window, the Fed can help protect the safety and soundness of the nation's financial system.[2]

---

[2] Banks once borrowed from Federal Reserve Banks by bringing securities and other asset documents to a teller's cage, or "window." The amount loaned was the face value of the security, minus a "discount." Today, banks still borrow from Federal Reserve Banks. However, the term "discount window" is simply an expression for Fed loans that are repaid with interest at maturity, arranged by telephone, and recorded along with pledged collateral such as U.S. government securities.

Financially sound banks can borrow from the Fed with few restrictions. Such loans are often made to banks that experience unexpected withdrawals of deposits or spikes in loan demand. However, the Fed expects that banks will not rely on the discount window as a regular source of funding. Discount window loans can also be made to help troubled banks that are on the verge of bankruptcy. The Fed closely monitors such loans, and troubled banks must demonstrate that they are conforming to the Fed's regulatory requirements.

Changes in the discount rate are initiated by the individual Federal Reserve Banks and must be approved by the Board of Governors. This coordination generally results in almost simultaneous changes at all 12 Federal Reserve Banks.

Discount rate changes have important effects on bank credit conditions. An increase in the discount rate, for example, makes it more costly for banks to borrow from Federal Reserve Banks. The higher cost may encourage banks to obtain funds by selling government securities rather than using the discount window. Also, it may force banks to screen their customers' loan applications more carefully and slow the growth of their loans. Thus, if the Fed raises the discount rate, banks would be discouraged from borrowing reserves because borrowing becomes more costly. Conversely, lowering the discount rate will induce banks to borrow additional reserves.

In principle, the Fed can use the discount rate as a tool of monetary policy: *reducing* the discount rate to *increase* bank reserves and the money supply and *increasing* the discount rate to *decrease* bank reserves and the money supply. In practice, changes in the discount rate have only minor effects on bank borrowing and the money supply. This is because the Fed expects that banks will not rely on the discount window as a regular source of funding.

usually only those in trouble

Reserve Requirement

Changing reserve requirements can also affect bank lending and the money supply. Recall that banks are required to maintain a fraction of their checking deposits in reserve, either as cash in their vaults or as deposits at the Federal Reserve. This fraction is known as the required reserve ratio, and it is applied to a bank's total checking deposit liabilities to determine the dollar amount of reserve assets that must be held. For example, a bank whose depositors' own checking accounts equal to $100 million would need to have cash plus reserve accounts at the Fed equal to $10 million if the required reserve ratio were 10 percent.

Table 15.1 shows the required reserve ratios of banks as of January 2005. Notice that required reserve ratios are structured to bear relatively less heavily on smaller banks than on larger banks. To provide banks with flexibility in meeting their reserve requirements, the Federal Reserve stipulates that banks must hold an average amount of reserves over a period of only two weeks rather than a specific amount on each day. Also, required reserve ratios pertain only to checking deposits rather than savings and time deposits.

Table 15.1	Required Reserve Ratios of the Fed	
Type of Deposit	**Required Reserve Ratio (percent)**	
Checking deposit:		
$0 million–$6.6 million	0	
$6.6 million–$45.4 million	3	
More than $45.4 million	10	
Savings and time deposits	No required reserve ratio	

Source: From *Statistical Supplement to the Federal Reserve Bulletin*, February 2005.

As we learned in the previous chapter, the ability of the banking system to create checking deposit money is dependent on the required reserve ratio. A required reserve ratio of 10 percent requires a bank that receives a $100 deposit to maintain $10 in required reserves and thus lend out only $90 based on that deposit. If the borrower then writes a check to someone who deposits the $90, the bank receiving that deposit will receive reserves of $90 when the check clears through the system. It can then lend $81 and must keep $9 in reserve. As the process continues, the banking system will expand the initial deposit of $100 into a maximum of $1,000 of money ($100 + $90 + $81 + $72.90 . . . = $1,000). If the required reserve ratio were 20 percent, the banking system would be able to expand the initial $100 deposit into a maximum of $500 ($100 + $80 + $64 + $51.20 + . . . = $500). Therefore, a *lower* required reserve ratio should result in an *increase* in the money supply; a *higher* required reserve ratio should result in a *decrease* in the money supply.

In principle, changes in required reserve ratios can be a useful tool of monetary policy. However, required reserve ratios currently play a relatively limited role in money creation in the United States. Why? Because even small changes in the required reserve ratio can substantially affect required reserves; adjustments to required reserve ratios are not well suited to the day-to-day implementation of monetary policy. Also, because required reserve ratios are an important factor in banks' business calculations, frequent changes in them would unnecessarily complicate financial planning by these institutions. Therefore, the Fed changes required reserve ratios only infrequently.

SHIFTING AGGREGATE DEMAND

Let us now examine the economic effects of monetary policy. In the short run, when prices are temporarily fixed, the Fed has the ability to affect the level of interest rates in the economy. When the Fed increases the money supply in order to reduce interest rates, aggregate demand increases, which results in an increase in output and employment. Conversely, a decrease in the money supply that increases interest rates will decrease aggregate demand, output, and employment. In the long run, however, a change in the money supply by the Fed affects only prices and not the level of output and employment. Using Figure 15.3, we will examine the sequence of events that occurs when the Fed conducts monetary policy.

Expansionary Policy

Suppose the economy is in a recession, producing less than its full-employment potential. This situation is seen in Figure 15.3(a), where the equilibrium level of output is $60 trillion. The goal of the Fed in this situation is to stimulate the economy, increasing the level of output to $70 trillion.

We learned in Chapter 13 that fiscal policy can help promote the desired expansion. If the government reduced taxes, households would have more income to spend for consumption, and the aggregate demand would shift to the right. Similarly, an increase in government expenditures would also shift the aggregate demand curve rightward.

Monetary policy may also be used to shift aggregate demand. To combat a recession, the Fed would adopt an *expansionary (easy)* monetary policy by *purchasing* more government securities on the open market, *decreasing* the discount rate, or *reducing* reserve requirements. As a result, bank reserves will increase. In turn, banks will attempt to use the extra reserves to make more loans. By offering lower interest rates, banks can encourage people to borrow additional money to purchase goods that are sensitive to interest cost, such as residential housing, automobiles, and large household appliances. Lower interest rates will also stimulate the demand for business investment in equipment and factories. In this manner, the expansionary monetary policy causes a rightward shift in the aggregate demand curve. In Figure 15.3(a), as aggregate demand increases from AD_0 to AD_1, the

Figure 15.3	Effects of Monetary Policy on the Economy

To combat an expansionary monetary policy, the Fed would purchase more government securities on the open market, decrease the discount rate, or reduce reserve requirements. This results in an increase in bank reserves. Banks will attempt to use the extra reserves to make more loans to businesses and households, thus increasing aggregate demand and the level of economic activity.

economy moves to the full-employment level of output. Table 15.2 shows the strategy for using the Fed's monetary tools for combating recession (inflation).

Although the short-run effect of the expansionary monetary policy will be to stimulate output and employment, the action also has important long-term effects. In the long run, an expansionary monetary policy may result in both increased expectations of inflation, which cause higher long-term interest rates, and also higher rates of inflation caused by an acceleration in the growth of the money supply. These effects may persist for many years and may have a greater effect on the economy than do the initial effects of the Fed's action.

yes, but we're not talking about accelerating the growth

Restrictive Policy

Monetary policy may also be used to combat demand-pull inflation. Recall that demand-pull inflation occurs when buyers' demands to purchase goods and services outrun sellers' capacities to supply them, thus forcing up prices on what is available.

tight $ decreases demand

Table 15.2	Using Monetary Policy to Combat a Recession or Inflation

Economic Problem/Policy	Open Market Operations	Discount Rate	Reserve Requirement
Recession (easy money)	Buy securities	Decrease	Decrease
Inflation (tight money)	Sell securities	Increase	Increase

The objective of monetary policy in this situation is to decrease aggregate demand. Thus, the Fed will initiate a *restrictive (tight)* monetary policy by selling government securities on the open market, raising the discount rate, or increasing reserve requirements. All of these actions will decrease bank reserves, which will drive interest rates upward. The combination of a smaller supply of loanable funds and higher interest rates will reduce consumption and investment spending. As seen in Figure 15.3(b), the aggregate demand curve will shift to the left, which eliminates the excess spending and demand-pull inflation.[3]

When the Fed lowers the rate of growth in the money supply, the intended outcome is price stability, a long-run objective. Yet, what are the consequences of this action in the short run? In the short run, the decrease in the rate of growth of the money supply causes a decline in aggregate demand and thus a fall in output and employment. This is why the Fed may be severely criticized when it attempts to combat inflation: Nobody wants to have his business shut down or be thrown out of work as a result of a restrictive monetary policy. Over time, however, price stability contributes to low interest rates and increased confidence of consumers, savers, and investors, and thus tends to promote economic expansion. Therefore, the Fed must consider whether the short-run side effects of combating inflation, which are adverse, are outweighed by the long-run benefits of price stability.

For example, in the early 1980s, the Fed successfully used a restrictive monetary policy to fight double-digit inflation. The Fed sold securities on the open market to reduce reserves in the banking system so as to increase the interest rate and slow the growth of borrowing and spending. As a result, short-term interest rates were driven up to about 16 percent. The tight monetary policy helped bring inflation down from 13.5 percent in 1980 to 3.2 percent three years later, thus building Fed credibility as an inflation fighter. Lowering the inflation rate, however, was not painless. By decreasing the money supply, the Fed contributed to the 1981–1982 recession during which the unemployment rate rose to 9.7 percent, the highest level since the Great Depression. Indeed, millions of unemployed Americans suffered as the economy moved toward price stability.

THE RECESSION OF 2001 AND THE FEDERAL RESERVE

In Chapter 12, we learned about the origins of the recession of 2001, which lasted from March to November of that year. A rapid decrease in investment spending caused a reduction in aggregate demand, which combined with the multiplier effect, triggered a fall in output and employment. However, we did not address an important question: What actions did the Fed take to cushion the economy from the recession?

In mid-2000, several months before the start of the recession, investment spending abruptly slowed, and that bothered the Fed. Although the economy was operating at full employment, investment spending was declining in high-tech equipment such as computers, software, and communications equipment. The fall in investment spending had started a negative multiplier effect, which was gripping the economy and had the potential to result in a recession. The Fed also feared that a sharp fall in stock prices had destroyed billions of dollars in household wealth. As a result, consumption spending might decrease, contributing to recession.

Moreover, Fed policy itself may have hastened the recession of 2001. During the late 1990s, the Fed worried that the investment boom and consumer optimism were increasing the aggregate demand curve too rapidly, signaling that the economy would overheat and inflation would intensify. The Fed reacted by curtailing the money supply and increasing interest rates. From mid-1999 to mid-2000, the Fed increased the federal funds rate six times by a combined two percentage points. In hindsight, the Fed may have

the fed guesses in order to prevent, instead of reacting

---

[3] In the real world, the objective of tight money is to prevent inflation—that is, halt further increases in the price level.

economics
IN ACTION

Attack on America: How the Fed Defended the Financial System

It was a day like no other in U.S. history. September 11, 2001, marked the end of American global innocence, the onset of recession, and perhaps even the fading of the country's anything-is-possible economic exuberance. A devastating terrorist attack hit at the heart of the nation's economic and military power: the World Trade Center near Wall Street in New York City and the Pentagon in Washington, D.C., just miles from the White House.

In addition to causing thousands of lives to be lost, the attacks forced immediate changes to the way business is conducted. Following the attack, travel was suspended, sporting events were canceled, business offices were closed, and financial markets were shut down. Corporations, such as United Airlines and Boeing, announced layoffs of thousands as sales plummeted. Indeed, the attack seriously shook the nation's confidence and economists feared that it could throw the United States into despair and recession.

The initial impact of the terrorist attacks on the U.S. financial system is reminiscent of the beginnings of crises during the late 1800s and early 1900s. On September 11 and the following days, the system encountered a significant shock to the demand for liquidity. The disruptions in communications and transportation associated with the attacks conjure up the limited communications and transportation capabilities of the banking era of the previous century. However, one major difference is that during this modern crisis, an ultimate provider of liquidity to the financial system existed. *It existed during great depression, but didn't act!* Officials at the Fed realized that the future economic outlook depended on how U.S. consumers and businesses behave. Typically, their response to a crisis is to freeze. Spending stops, and decisions about the future are put on hold. If fear and uncertainty prevail, how can people be expected to spend and invest for the future? If hijackers can steal commercial jets and crash them into high-profile buildings, how safe can people feel to fly or even work in ordinary skyscrapers?

While efforts were being made to rescue victims of the attack, the immediate job ahead for the Federal Reserve was clear: It must address this national crisis and restore confidence as quickly as possible. As news spread about the nation's catastrophe, banks faced soaring demand for cash as nervous depositors began to pull money out of their accounts. The Fed quickly announced that it would keep its discount window open to any bank that needed it.

The provision of liquidity following September 11 was unprecedented in Federal Reserve history. On September 12, discount window borrowing by financial institutions peaked at over $45 billion, relative to around $100 million on a typical day. On the same day, the Federal Reserve injected $38 billion in liquidity through open market operations, compared to a typical daily action of $3.5 billion. The Federal Reserve also extended swap lines of credit with the European Central Bank, the Bank of England, and the Bank of Canada in an attempt to provide liquidity to international markets. Simply put, the Fed sent a clear message to financial markets that it would provide sufficient liquidity to keep them operating in an orderly fashion.

Having restored confidence in the financial system, the Fed turned its attention to the disaster's impact on the economy. The Fed quickly cut the federal funds rate, its target for short-term interest rates, by one-half percentage point. Several large U.S. commercial banks responded to the Fed rate by reducing their lending rates to business and household customers.

As the situation eased, the Fed kept the financial system flush with cash but at much lower levels than in previous days. Although the United States suffered a major blow, the financial system proved to be quite resilient with markets and companies functioning better than one might expect.

increased interest rates too much, even after the aggregate demand curve ceased shifting rightward. And the impact of this policy may have lasted into 2001, aggravating the fall in investment spending that was taking place for other reasons. Therefore, the Fed's contractionary monetary policy may have helped trigger the recession.

When the economy showed signs of weakening, the Fed decided to take action. During 2001, the Fed rapidly increased the money supply and cut the federal funds rate 11 times for a total reduction of almost five percentage points. When the economy failed to gain much forward momentum, the Fed continued to slash interest rates in 2002 and 2003. The increased money supply and lower interest rates had the effect of bolstering aggregate demand, thus making the recession less severe.

Figure 15.4 illustrates this situation. Initially, the economy was at point A, with output equaling $92 trillion in the first quarter of 2001. The Fed worried that if it refrained from action, the investment decline would cause the aggregate demand curve to decrease from AD_0 to AD_2; this would move the economy to equilibrium point C, where output equals, say, $88 trillion. When the Fed enacted an expansionary monetary policy, aggregate demand instead fell to AD_1, and the decline in output was smaller. Although the Fed's aggressive monetary policy did not completely offset the recession, it reduced its depth and duration.

The Fed's policy of cutting interest rates was helpful in bolstering new-home construction, a component of investment spending that is quite responsive to interest rates. Falling interest rates also perked up consumption spending on big-ticket items such as automobiles. Moreover, lower interest rates fueled an enormous wave of mortgage refinancing in which homeowners exchange their mortgages with higher interest rates for new mortgages with lower interest rates. After a refinance, monthly mortgage payments decrease, setting free cash to be spent on discretionary goods. Increased spending on homes and mortgage refinancing helped support aggregate demand during the recession of 2001.

But what about the effect of the Fed's actions on the price level? Here, we must realize that there is a discrepancy between what Figure 15.4 shows and what actually occurred. According to the figure, the price level will decline following a decrease in aggregate demand. During most of the 2001 recession, however, prices actually rose. The reason is that inflation tends to have momentum: When inflation has been increasing at some rate for a period of time, then, left alone, it will proceed at that same rate. However, the decrease in aggregate demand implies that inflation was not left alone in 2001. The decrease in aggregate demand

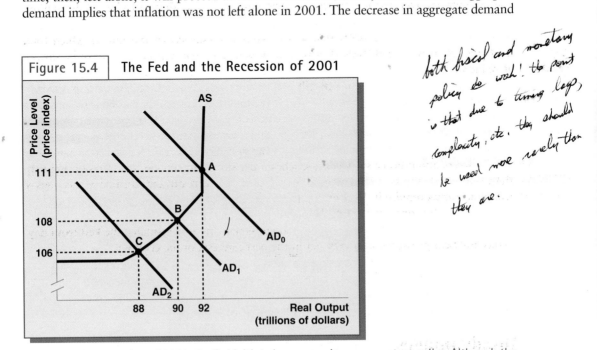

Figure 15.4   The Fed and the Recession of 2001

To combat the recession of 2001, the Fed initiated an expansionary monetary policy. Although the policy could not eliminate the recession, it made it less severe. Because of the expansionary policy, the economy moved from point A to B rather than from point A to C, and the decline in output was smaller.

put downward pressure on the price level. Although inflation initially increased during 2001, it moderated as the year continued. That is what our aggregate supply-aggregate demand model suggests.

CHECK POINT

1. Describe the nature and operation of monetary policy.

2. Identify the instruments that the Fed uses to control the money supply.

3. Discuss how changes in the money supply by the Fed can result in changes in output, employment, and prices.

4. How would the Fed combat a recession in the economy? How about inflation?

MONETARY POLICY: ADVANTAGES AND DISADVANTAGES

Most economists consider monetary policy to be an important tool for stabilizing the economy. Let us evaluate how well monetary policy works.

Advantages of Monetary Policy

One strength of monetary policy is that it interferes very little with the freedom of the market, although market imperfections sometimes intensify the effects of policy upon particular sectors of the economy. A restrictive monetary policy cuts down the rate at which total spending can increase, but it does not dictate which particular expenditures must be slowed or reduced. If a restrictive monetary policy forces interest rates up from 6 to 8 percent, for example, you, the typical consumer, still have the option of borrowing money to purchase a new home, a car, or a major appliance. The expenditures you cut in response to higher borrowing costs are the ones to which you attach the lowest priorities. Similarly, an expansionary monetary policy stimulates total spending, but the market also dictates its form.

Another strength is that monetary policy is flexible. The Federal Open Market Committee usually meets about every six weeks, reaches a decision, and acts on that decision immediately. Moreover, the Federal Open Market Committee can call extraordinary meetings if economic events require it. In contrast, the application of fiscal policy can be postponed for many months by congressional deliberations.

Finally, and perhaps most important, Congress has carefully insulated the Fed from day-to-day political pressures so it may act in the best interests of the economy. As a result, the Fed can base its policy actions almost entirely upon economic considerations rather than political considerations. This allows the Fed to engage in unpopular policies that might be necessary for the long-term health of the economy. Of course, it also empowers the Fed to pursue correct policies in spite of pressures to do otherwise.

government spending is in best interest of congressmen / women

Disadvantages of Monetary Policy

Formulating monetary policy is a difficult task, and policies have definite limitations. Promoting economic stability requires not only wise monetary policy, but sound fiscal policy, as well. It also requires sufficient competition throughout the economy so that

true, but not a disadvantage

Also requires free markets

individual prices are free to move <u>down</u> as well as up. Obviously, trouble can develop in all three areas, so it is difficult to achieve perfect stability.

Policy trade-offs present another problem for the Fed. Basically, the Fed has one policy instrument: the money supply. Does this mean that the Fed can pursue only one goal? Consider the goals of price stability and full employment. As we have learned, combating inflation requires the Fed to decrease the money supply. However, a decrease in the money supply results in declining economic activity and rising unemployment. Conversely, combating unemployment calls for an increase in the money supply, which may intensify inflation. Indeed, the short-run trade-offs between price stability and full employment make it difficult for the Fed to formulate policy.[4] *same as with fiscal policy*

Finally, the extent to which monetary policy can revive a sagging economy has been long debated. Some economists argue that monetary policy is largely powerless to revive economic activity after a downturn. Recall that during a downturn the Fed will adopt an expansionary monetary policy by increasing banks' excess reserves. However, this does not guarantee that banks will actually make loans. If businesses are pessimistic about future profits, they may be unwilling to borrow excess reserves, thus frustrating the expansionary monetary policy.[5]

monetary policy is slower + less dramatic

Fixed Rules or Discretion?

The weaknesses of monetary policy highlight a crucial policy debate. Should the Fed try to fine-tune the economy with constant changes in the money supply? Or should the Fed instead keep the money supply growing at a steady rate? *how can you when it is slow acting?*

The case for active monetary intervention is founded on the notion that the economy is constantly affected by recessionary or expansionary forces. Without an active monetary policy, it is feared that the economy would oscillate in unacceptably wide swings. To decrease such instability, it is said that the Fed can "lean against the wind" by stimulating the economy when it becomes sluggish or restraining the economy when it overheats.

However, critics argue that active changes in the money supply by the Fed may destabilize the economy. They note that the Fed does not have up-to-the-minute, reliable information about the state of the economy and prices. Information is limited because of lags in the publication of data. Also, the Fed has a less-than-perfect understanding of the way the economy works, including the knowledge of when and to what extent policy actions will affect aggregate demand. The operation of the economy changes over time and with it the response of the economy to policy measures. These limitations add to uncertainties in the policy process and make determining the appropriate setting of monetary policy instruments more difficult.

Those who believe that active monetary policy is destabilizing argue that the time required for this process to work itself out is very long—so long, indeed, that policy measures undertaken to combat ongoing inflation are only likely to cut aggregate demand some months after the inflationary pressure has disappeared and the economy has turned to recession. In that situation, the monetary policy will only make the recession worse.

Similarly, critics maintain that an expansionary monetary policy undertaken to increase aggregate demand to combat recession can also be expected to make matters worse. By the

[4] The U.S. government faces similar policy conflicts when it formulates fiscal policy.

[5] Economists at the Fed have examined the effects of monetary policy by estimating the cumulative response in output in the two years following a 1-percent change in the federal funds rate. They found that a 1-percentage point increase in the federal funds rate decreases quarterly output growth over the following two years by 1.2 percentage points. However, only a 0.5-percentage point increase in output occurs in response to a 1-percentage point decline in interest rates. Apparently, monetary policy tightening has more effect on output that monetary easing. See "Pushing on a String," *Monetary Trends,* Federal Reserve Bank of St. Louis, March 2003.

time aggregate demand is actually increased by monetary measures taken many months previously, the economy may have recovered and be well on the road to inflation. The antirecession policy would thus merely magnify the succeeding inflation.

SHOULD CONGRESS REDUCE THE INDEPENDENCE OF THE FEDERAL RESERVE?

Recall that when the Federal Reserve was created, Congress carefully insulated it from day-to-day political pressures so that it could act in the best interest of the country. Congress made the Fed responsible to itself rather than to the president or party in power. The Fed is governmental, but it is independent within government.

The primary argument for Fed independence is that monetary policy—which affects inflation, employment, and economic growth—is too important to be determined by politicians. Because elections occur frequently, politicians may be mainly concerned with the short-run benefits rather than the long-run costs of their economic policies. Put simply, politicians may put reelection, rather than the long-run health of the economy, first in their decision making.

The most sensitive aspect of the economy over which short- and long-run interests clash is inflation. Supporters of the Fed's independence maintain that monetary policy tends to become too expansionary if left to policymakers with short-run horizons, thus intensifying inflationary pressures. However, the Fed cannot assume that the goals of politicians reflect public sentiment. The public may prefer that officials at the Fed, rather than politicians, formulate monetary policy.

However, critics of the Fed's independence contend that, in a democracy, elected officials should formulate public policy. Because the voting public holds elected officials responsible for their economic policies, the president and Congress should exercise more control over monetary policy. Moreover, critics also maintain that placing the Fed under control of elected officials could result in benefits by coordinating monetary policy with the government's fiscal policy. Finally, critics argue that the Fed has not always used its independence well. For example, they note that monetary policy was too expansionary during the inflationary era of the 1970s and too restrictive during the recessionary era of the early 1990s.

This chapter considered the Federal Reserve and monetary policy as a possible solution to macroeconomic instability. The next chapter will broaden our focus by discussing the United States in the global economy.

CHECK POINT

1. Identify the major strengths and weaknesses of monetary policy.

2. Why do some economists argue that the Fed should keep the money supply growing at a steady rate rather than actively manage the money supply in order to fine-tune the economy?

3. Why was the Fed structured so as to have a high degree of independence from the federal government? Discuss the advantages and disadvantages of such independence.

Chapter Summary

1. The Federal Reserve System, often simply called the Fed, is the central bank of the United States. It was created through an act signed by President Woodrow Wilson in 1913 to provide the nation with a safer, more flexible, and more stable monetary and financial system.

2. The Fed has a structure designed by Congress to give it a broad perspective on the economy. At the head of the Fed's formal organization is the Board of Governors. The 12 regional Federal Reserve Banks make up the next level. The organization of the Fed also includes the Federal Open Market Committee and three advisory councils. The Federal Reserve has as stockholders the commercial banks that are members of the Fed.

3. The Fed, as the overseer of the nation's monetary system, has many important duties: serving as the lender of last resort, regulating and supervising banks, supplying services to banks and to the government, foreign-exchange operations, and controlling the money supply and interest rates.

4. The main responsibility of the Fed is that of formulating and implementing monetary policy, which consists of changing the economy's money supply to help the economy in achieving maximum output and employment and also stable prices. The Fed uses three policy instruments to influence the money supply: open market operations, the discount rate, and the reserve requirement.

5. In the short run, when prices are temporarily fixed, the Fed has the ability to affect the level of interest rates in the economy. When the Fed increases the money supply in order to reduce interest rates, aggregate demand increases, which results in an increase in output and employment. Conversely, a decrease in the money supply that increases interest rates will decrease aggregate demand, output, and employment. In the long run, a change in the money supply by the Fed affects only prices and not output and employment.

6. One strength of monetary policy is that it is highly impersonal: Monetary policy interferes very little with the freedom of the market. Monetary policy is also flexible and can be implemented quickly in response to changing economic circumstances. Finally, the Fed is insulated from day-to-day political pressures, so it can act in the best interests of the economy. This allows the Fed to engage in unpopular policies that might be necessary for the long-run health of the economy.

7. Critics of the Fed, however, argue that active changes in the money supply by the Fed can and do destabilize the economy. They note that the Fed does not have up-to-the-minute, reliable information about the state of the economy and prices. Timing lags also limit the effectiveness of monetary policy. As a result, critics call for the elimination of activism in monetary policy in favor of a law requiring a fixed rate of increase in money each year.

Key Terms and Concepts

Federal Reserve System (Fed) (358)

Board of Governors (359)

Federal Open Market Committee (FOMC) (359)

federal funds market (360)

federal funds rate (360)

monetary policy (363)

open market operations (363)

discount rate (364)

discount window (364)

Self-Test: Multiple-Choice Questions

1. The main policymaking body of the Federal Reserve System is the

   a. Federal Advisory Council.
   b. Council of Economic Advisors.
   c. Board of Governors.
   d. Federal Open Market Committee.

2. The functions of the Federal Reserve System include all of the following *except*

   a. controlling the money supply.
   b. regulating and supervising banks.
   c. supplying check-processing services to banks.
   d. issuing deposit insurance to banks.

3. The most important monetary tool of the Fed is

   a. open market operations.
   b. the reserve requirement.
   c. the discount rate.
   d. the margin requirement.

4. It is common for commercial banks with surplus balances in their accounts to lend reserves overnight to banks with deficiencies of reserves. The interest rate that pertains to these loans is the

   a. discount rate.
   b. prime rate.
   c. federal funds rate.
   d. commercial loan rate.

5. To counteract a recession, the Fed would adopt a(n)

   a. contractionary monetary policy that shifts the aggregate demand curve rightward.
   b. contractionary monetary policy that shifts the aggregate demand curve leftward.
   c. expansionary monetary policy that shifts the aggregate demand curve rightward.
   d. expansionary monetary policy that shifts the aggregate demand curve leftward.

6. To counteract demand-pull inflation, the Fed would

   a. decrease the discount rate, decrease the required reserve ratio, and buy securities in the open market.
   b. decrease the discount rate, decrease the required reserve ratio, and sell securities in the open market.
   c. increase the discount rate, increase the required reserve ratio, and buy securities in the open market.
   d. increase the discount rate, increase the required reserve ratio, and sell securities in the open market.

7. If the Fed decreases the required reserve ratio, all of the following are true *except* that the banking system's

   a. total reserves will remain unchanged.
   b. required reserves will decline and excess reserves will rise.
   c. money multiplier will increase.
   d. federal funds rate will increase.

8. If the Fed reduces the required reserve ratio from 25 to 20 percent, the value of the money multiplier

   a. increases from 4 to 5.
   b. increases from 5 to 6.
   c. decreases from 5 to 4.
   d decreases from 6 to 5.

9. To shield the Federal Reserve from political pressure, members of the Board of Governors

   a. have lifetime appointments.
   b. are elected by the stockholders of the Fed.
   c. are appointed to 14-year terms.
   d. are elected by the voting public.

10. Concerning the short-run effects of monetary policy, an increase in the money supply works mainly through decreases in

   a. interest rates that result in additional investment and an increase in aggregate supply.
   b. interest rates that result in additional investment and an increase in aggregate demand.
   c. the purchasing power of money that result in declining consumption and a decrease in aggregate demand.
   d. the purchasing power of money that result in declining consumption and a decrease in aggregate supply.

Answers to Multiple-Choice Questions

1. c   2. d   3. a   4. c   5. c   6. d   7. d   8. a   9. c   10. b

Study Questions and Problems

1. Who is the current chair of the Board of Governors of the Federal Reserve System? Why has the chair of the Board of Governors of the Federal Reserve System been characterized as the second most powerful person in Washington, D.C., next to the president?

2. If the Fed's independence was restricted so that it became subordinate to the president and Congress, would this affect the ability of monetary policy to combat recession or inflation?

3. When the Fed purchases government securities from commercial banks, businesses, or individuals, the nation's money supply increases. Explain how this works.

4. What is the discount rate, and how can the Fed use it to influence the nation's supply of money?

5. How can a decrease in the reserve requirement by the Fed result in an increase in the money supply?

6. Which is the most frequently used monetary instrument of the Fed? Why?

7. If the Fed wants to increase the value of the dollar in terms of other currencies, what should it do? What should the Fed do if it wants to decrease the foreign-exchange value of the dollar?

8. Suppose the economy is suffering from a prolonged and deep recession. What changes in open market operations, the discount rate, and the reserve requirement would the Fed likely enact? Explain in each case how the change would affect bank reserves, the money supply, interest rates, and aggregate demand.

9. Suppose the Fed adopts a restrictive monetary policy in order to combat demand-pull inflation. Assuming the economy is closed to international trade, use the aggregate demand

and aggregate supply model to show the events that follow the Fed's policy. Assume the economy is open to international trade. How will changes in the international value of the dollar affect the performance of the economy? Now, answer the same set of questions by assuming that the Fed adopts an expansionary monetary policy to combat recession.

10. Why do some economists maintain that an active monetary policy of the Fed is counterproductive?

11. Explain how the Fed is structured to have certain checks and balances within it to limit the power any one group inside or outside the Fed can wield.

12. Why do critics argue that the Fed has aggravated the income gap between the rich and the poor?

13. Suppose the required reserve ratio on checking deposits is 15 percent and the Fed purchases $10 million of U.S. securities from the commercial banking system. What is the maximum amount of new money that the banking system could create?

14. Pioneer Bank has checking deposits of $10 million and total reserves of $7.5 million; the required reserve ratio is 10 percent. If the Fed sells $1.5 million of government securities to the bank, what will happen to its total reserves and excess reserves?

15. Figure 15.5 shows the balance sheet for the commercial banking system. Answer the following questions on the basis of this information.

    a. If the Fed set the required reserve ratio at 10 percent, the banks would have required reserves of _____ and excess reserves of _____; the money multiplier would equal _____ , and the maximum amount of new money that the banking system could create would equal _____.

    b. If the Fed decreased the required reserve ratio to 5 percent, banks would have _____ of excess reserves; the money multiplier would equal _____ , and the maximum amount of new money that the banking system could create would equal_____.

16. Figure 15.6 shows the balance sheet of Wisconsin National Bank. Assume that the Fed has set the required reserve ratio at 10 percent.

    a. Wisconsin National Bank would have required reserves of _____ and excess reserves of _____. The maximum amount of new money that the bank could create would equal _____.

    b. Suppose the Fed sells $10 million in government securities to Wisconsin National Bank. After the sale, the bank would have _____ of required reserves and _____ of excess

Figure 15.5	Combined Balance Sheet of All Commercial Banks (billions of dollars)

Assets		Liabilities	
Cash in Vault	$ 300	Checking Deposits	$3,600
Reserves with	150	Due to Other	850
Federal Reserve		Banks and Fed	
Banks			
Loans	3,000		
Government	1,000		
Securities			

| Figure 15.6 | Wisconsin National Bank's Balance Sheet (millions of dollars) |

Assets		Liabilities	
Reserves with Fed	$90	Checking Deposits	$120
Loans	10		
Government Securities	20		

reserves. Because of this transaction, Wisconsin National Bank's ability to create additional money would increase/decrease by _____.

c. Instead, suppose the Fed buys $10 million in government securities from Wisconsin National Bank. Because of this transaction, Wisconsin National Bank's ability to create additional money would increase/decrease by _____.

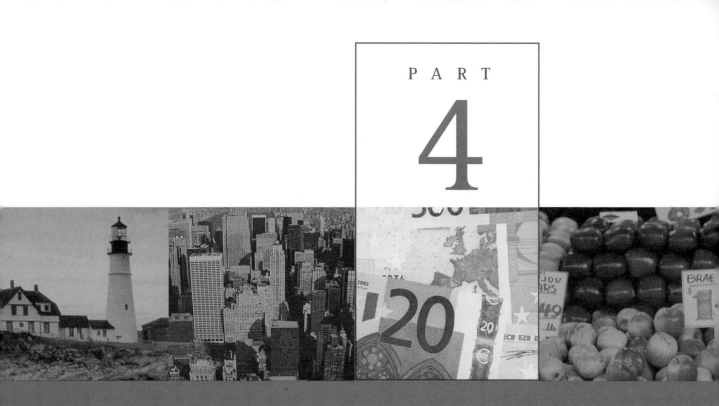

the
International
Economy

16

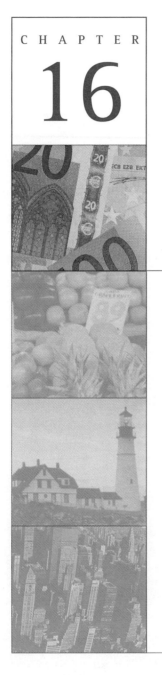

The United States and the Global Economy

Chapter objectives

After reading this chapter, you should be able to:

1. Describe the United States as an open economy.

2. Discuss the advantages of specialization and trade.

3. Explain why free trade is controversial.

4. Identify the effects of import tariffs and the arguments for trade restrictions.

5. Assess the advantages and disadvantages of the World Trade Organization and the North American Free Trade Agreement.

economics IN CONTEXT

U.S. sheep producers have long been dependent on government. Burdened with high costs and inefficiencies, and facing domestic competition from beef, chicken, and pork, at the beginning of the new millennium sheep producers attempted to limit foreign competition by petitioning the U.S. government for import restrictions.

Almost all U.S. lamb imports come from producers in New Zealand and Australia, who provide strong competition for U.S. producers. These producers have invested substantial resources in new technology and effective marketing, making them among the most efficient producers in the world. These cost savings were passed on to American consumers in the form of low-priced lamb.

[handwritten: not govt. subsidised like in Japan]

In response to increasing imports of lamb, the American Sheep Industry Association complained that domestic producers were being seriously injured by foreign competition. As a result, the U.S. government imposed restrictions on lamb imports. This policy outraged farmers in Australia and New Zealand, who relied on exports to the United States for their livelihood. Moreover, American consumers complained that the

[handwritten: we don't want them doing it but we do with farmers]

trade restrictions prevented them from purchasing low-priced foreign lamb. Simply put, consumers felt that they were "fleeced" by the import restrictions on lamb.

The United States has generally recognized that open domestic markets and an open global trading system are superior to trade protection and isolationism when it comes to promoting broad-based growth and prosperity. For decades, our open economy has generated important benefits for the American people in the form of stronger growth and improved employment opportunities. The opportunity to acquire goods and services from abroad both encourages us as producers to stay competitive and allows us as consumers to raise our standard of living.

Although most people benefit from an open global trading system, some are hurt. The unequal distribution of benefits and burdens of an open global system are reasons why nations impose restrictions on international trade.

In this chapter, we will examine the benefits and costs of an open trading system. In particular, we will consider the effects on consumers, producers in exporting industries, and producers in import-competing industries.

THE UNITED STATES AS AN OPEN ECONOMY

Indeed, the U.S. economy has become increasingly integrated into the world economy (become an open economy) in recent decades. Such integration involves a number of dimensions, including trade of goods and services, financial markets, the labor force, ownership of production facilities, and dependence on imported materials.

As a rough measure of the importance of international trade in a nation's economy, we can look at the nation's exports plus imports as a percentage of its gross domestic product (GDP). In 2004, the United States exported 10 percent of its GDP, while imports were 15 percent of GDP; the openness of the U.S. economy to trade thus equaled 25 percent. The relative importance of international trade to the U.S. economy has increased by about 50 percent during the past century.

[handwritten: they want our $:)]

The United States exports a variety of goods, including grain, chemicals, scientific equipment, machinery, automobiles, computers, and commercial aircraft. It also imports many goods such as steel, oil, automobiles, textiles, shoes, rubber, and foodstuffs such as

Table 16.1	The Fruits of Free Trade: A Global Fruit Basket

On a trip to the grocery store, consumers can find goods from all over the globe.			
Apples	New Zealand	Limes	El Salvador
Apricots	China	Oranges	Australia
Bananas	Ecuador	Pears	South Korea
Blackberries	Canada	Pineapples	Costa Rica
Blueberries	Chile	Plums	Guatemala
Coconuts	Philippines	Raspberries	Mexico
Grapefruit	Bahamas	Strawberries	Poland
Grapes	Peru	Tangerines	South Africa
Kiwifruit	Italy	Watermelons	Honduras
Lemons	Argentina		

Source: From "The Fruits of Free Trade," *Annual Report*, Federal Reserve Bank of Dallas, 2002, p. 3.

bananas, tea, and coffee. With which nations does the United States conduct trade? Canada, Japan, Mexico, and China head the list. Other leading trading partners of the United States are Germany, the United Kingdom, South Korea, Singapore, Belgium, and Luxembourg.

The significance of international trade for the U.S. economy is even more noticeable when specific products are considered. For example, we would have fewer personal computers without imported components, little aluminum if we did not import bauxite, no tin cans without imported tin, and no chrome bumpers if we did not import chromium. Students taking an 8 A.M. course in economics might sleep through the class (do you really believe this?) if we did not import coffee or tea. Moreover, many of the products we buy from foreigners would be much more costly if we were dependent on domestic production. Imagine the cost of greenhouse coffee! Table 16.1 provides examples of fruits that the United States imports.

THE ADVANTAGES OF SPECIALIZATION AND TRADE

The idea of being self-sufficient may be appealing. You might even desire to live by yourself in an isolated region in northern Idaho or British Columbia. But consider the problems of self-sufficiency. If you lived by yourself, you could only consume the items that you produced. The food that you eat, the shirts and pants that you sew, and the house that you construct would not be anything like the items you currently purchase. You would not be able to obtain many products—computers, telephones, televisions, automobiles, and medicines. Because of the limitations of self-sufficiency, most people choose to specialize and trade with each other.

Specialization and trade pertain not only to individuals but also to groups of individuals. Imagine what would occur if the people of your state desired to be self-sufficient and refused to trade with other regions in the country. Residents of the state of Idaho could produce their own apples and wheat, but where would they get oranges and oil? Conceivably, they could grow oranges in greenhouses and drill for oil, but obtaining these items would come at great cost. Therefore, it is not practical for each of the 50 states to be self-sufficient. The founders of the United States realized this. That is why they pro-hibited the imposition of trade barriers on interstate commerce. What is true for states is also true for countries. National specialization and trade can result in a more efficient use of the world's resources.

Specialization increases productivity for several reasons. First, specialization avoids the time it takes for workers to switch from one job to another. Also, specialization allows production processes to be divided so that workers can practice and perfect a par-ticular skill; this process is called the division of labor. People who practice a particular activity, like hitting a baseball or keyboarding, tend to become a lot better than those who do not practice. In like manner, a country that specializes in machine tools tends to become highly productive in this activity. Finally, the division of labor fosters invention and innovation. As a worker learns a task very well, she might figure out ways to perform it better—inventing a new machine and/or a routine to do it. Specialization and invention thus reinforce each other. However, the very nature of specialization can limit its benefits because repetitive jobs can result in bored and unproductive workers.

Indeed, the degree to which specialization can be practiced is limited by the size of the market. For many mass-produced items, producing for the world market provides greater scope for specialization than producing for the domestic market. Boeing is an example; it has sold about 70 percent of its jetliners overseas in recent years. Without exports, Boeing would have found it difficult to cover the large design and tooling costs of its jetliners, and the jets might not have been produced at all.

bigger market = efficiency !

Proponents of free trade contend that if each country produces what it does best and allows trade, over the long run all will enjoy lower costs and prices and also higher levels of output, income, and consumption than could be achieved in isolation. In a dynamic world, market forces are constantly changing owing to shifts in technologies, input pro-ductivities, and wages, as well as tastes and preferences. A free market compels adjustment to take place. Either the efficiency of, say, the aluminum industry must improve, or else resources will flow to a broad range of industries in which productivity is higher.

COMPARATIVE ADVANTAGE AND INTERNATIONAL TRADE

To visualize the advantages of specialization and trade, let us consider a world of two countries—the United States and France—that each produces only two goods—autos and computers. Also assume that resources in each country are equally suited to producing autos or computers. As a result, the production possibilities schedule of each country appears as a straight line in Figure 16.1.[1]

Comparing the production possibilities schedules of the two countries, we see that the United States can produce more autos and more computers than France. If the United States devotes all of its resources to auto production, it can produce 100 autos a day. France, on the other hand, can produce a maximum of 80 autos a day because it has less efficient production skills than the United States. Similarly, by devoting all of their respective resources to producing a single good, the United States could produce a maximum of 200 computers a day and France could produce 80 computers a day. Again, the United States can outproduce France in computers because of its superior produc-tion skills.

---

[1] This implies that the law of increasing costs, as discussed in Chapter 1, is replaced with the assumption of constant costs.

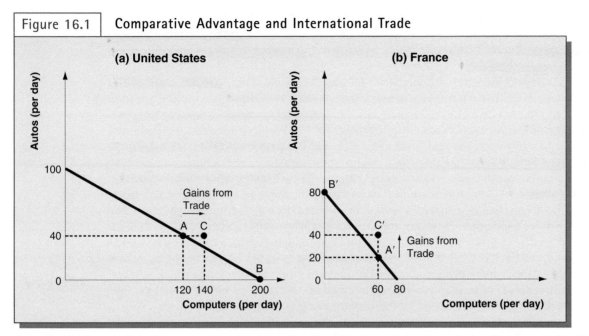

| Figure 16.1 | Comparative Advantage and International Trade |

According to the principle of comparative advantage, countries should specialize in producing those goods in which they are relatively more efficient. Such specialization allows countries to realize gains in production and consumption.

Production and Consumption Without Specialization and Trade

Without trade, the production possibilities schedule of each country defines the maximum amount of two goods that are available for consumption. In other words, a country can consume only what it produces when there is no trade. Without trade, suppose the United States decides to produce and consume 120 computers and 40 autos, shown by point *A* in Figure 16.1(a). Also suppose that France decides to produce and consume 60 computers and 20 autos, shown by point *A'* in Figure 16.1(b). Because we assume that the United States and France are the only two countries in the world, the world output of these goods totals 180 computers (120 + 60 = 180) and 60 autos (40 + 20 = 60).

Production and Consumption with Specialization and Trade

Now assume that the United States specializes in the production of computers and France specializes in the production of autos. As seen in Figure 16.1(a), the United States moves down along its production possibilities schedule until it produces 200 computers, shown by point *B*. Similarly, France slides up along its production possibilities schedule until it produces 80 autos, shown by point *B'* in Figure 16.1(b). Comparing the total world output that occurs before and after specialization, we see that specialization increases output by 20 computers (200 − 180 = 20) and 20 autos (80 − 60 = 20). Clearly, specialization is desirable because it results in resources being used more efficiently.

Because specialization entails more efficient production, larger quantities of output are available to both countries. Referring to Figure 16.1(a), assume the United States specializes in computer production at point *B* and agrees to import 40 autos from France in

what if we demand more?

exchange for 60 of its computers. Are <u>consumers</u> in the United States better off with trade? Yes. At point *B*, the United States produces 200 computers. Subtracting the 60 computers it exports to France leaves the United States with 140 computers; however, the United States imports 40 autos from France. The United States winds up consuming at point *C* in the figure. Comparing points *A* and *C*, we see that the United States can consume the same number of autos and 20 more computers because of trade. Clearly, U.S. consumers are better off with trade.

France also gains from trade. After exchanging 40 of its autos for 60 computers, France moves from point *A′* to point *C′* in Figure 16.1(b). French consumers thus have the same number of computers but 20 more autos than without trade.

Trade between the United States and France allows both countries to gain because they can consume a combination of goods that exceeds their production possibilities schedules.[2] The effect of international specialization and trade is thus equivalent to having more and better resources or discovery of improved production techniques. By reallocating production assignments so that France produces 60 more autos at the sacrifice of only 60 computers, and the United States produces 80 additional computers at the sacrifice of only 40 autos, total auto production rises by 20 units (60 − 40 = 20) and total computer output rises by 20 units (80 − 60 = 20)—a win-win outcome occurs.

Comparative Advantage

In our trading example, we assume that the United States is more efficient than France at producing both computers and autos. The possession of superior production skills is called having an *absolute advantage*. If the United States has an absolute advantage in the production of both goods, why does it specialize in the production of computers? Why does France, with absolute disadvantages in both goods, specialize in auto production? The answer lies in the principle of **comparative advantage,** which states that individuals and countries specialize in producing those goods in which they are *relatively*, not absolutely, more efficient. In other words, comparative advantage is the ability of a country to produce a good at a lower opportunity cost than some other country.

we can't do everything!

Let us return to our trading example in Figure 16.1 to determine the opportunity costs of producing computers and autos for the United States and France. Because workers in the United States can produce 200 computers or 100 autos, the opportunity cost of one computer is 0.5 auto (100/200 = 0.5). In France, because workers can produce 80 computers or 80 autos, the opportunity cost of one computer is one auto (80/80 = 1). Thus, the opportunity cost of computers is lower in the United States than in France. Therefore, the United States has a comparative advantage in producing computers, because it has a lower opportunity cost: That is, producing computers "costs" fewer autos. Similarly, France has a comparative advantage in producing autos, because its opportunity cost in that industry is lower.

According to the principle of comparative advantage, mutually beneficial trade between any two countries is possible whenever one country is relatively better at producing an item than the other country. Being relatively better suggests having the ability to produce an item at a lower opportunity cost—that is, at a lower sacrifice of other items forgone.

some countries can't do much besides sugar

---

[2] How much some country gains from trade depends on the rate at which autos exchange for computers. The United States gains more from trade when a given quantity of its computers exchanges for larger quantities of French autos. In contrast, France gains more from trade when a given quantity of its autos trades for larger quantities of U.S. computers. Supply and demand conditions in the two countries determine the rate of exchange and thus the distribution of the gains from trade.

economics
IN ACTION

Babe Ruth and the Principle of Comparative Advantage

Babe Ruth was the first great home-run hitter in baseball history. His batting talent and vivacious personality attracted huge crowds wherever he played. He made baseball more exciting by establishing homers as a common part of the game. Ruth set many major league records, including 2,056 career bases on balls and 72 games in which he hit two or more home runs. He had a .342 lifetime batting average and 714 career home runs.

George Herman Ruth (1895–1948) was born in Baltimore. After playing baseball in the minor leagues, Ruth started his major league career as a left-handed pitcher with the Boston Red Sox in 1914. In 158 games for Boston, he compiled a pitching record of 89 wins and 46 losses, including two 20-win seasons—23 victories in 1916 and 24 victories in 1917. He eventually added five more wins as a hurler for the New York Yankees and ended his pitching career with a 2.28 earned run average. Ruth also had three wins against no losses in World Series competition, including one stretch of 29 2/3 consecutive scoreless innings. Ruth evolved to become the best left-handed pitcher in the American league.

Although Ruth had an absolute advantage in pitching, he had even greater talent at the plate. Simply put, Ruth's comparative advantage was in hitting. As a pitcher, Ruth had to rest his arm between appearances, and thus could not bat in every game. To ensure his daily presence in the lineup, Ruth gave up pitching to play exclusively in the outfield.

In Ruth's 15 years with the Yankees, he dominated professional baseball. He teamed with Lou Gehrig to form what became the greatest one-two hitting punch in baseball. Ruth was the heart of the 1927 Yankees, a team regarded by some baseball experts as the best in baseball history. That year, Ruth set a record of 60 home runs; at that time, a season had 154 games as compared to 162 games of today. He attracted so many fans that Yankee Stadium, which opened in 1923, was nicknamed "The House That Ruth Built." The Yankees released Ruth after the 1934 season, and he ended his playing career in 1935 with the Boston Braves. In the final game he started in the outfield for Boston, Ruth hit three home runs.

The advantages to having Ruth switch from pitching to batting were enormous. Not only did the Yankees win four World Series during Ruth's tenure, but they also became baseball's most renowned franchise. Ruth was elected to the Baseball Hall of Fame in Cooperstown, New York, in 1936.

Sources: Paul Rosenthal, *America at Bat: Baseball Stuff and Stories* (National Geographic, 2002); Geoffrey Ward and Ken Burns, *Baseball: An Illustrated History* (Knoph, 1994); and Keith Brandt, *Babe Ruth: Home Run Hero* (Troll, 1986).

There are many examples of comparative advantage. Brazil is a major exporter of coffee because its soil and climate are relatively better for coffee than for other crops. China, with its abundance of low-skilled labor, has a comparative advantage in producing shirts that require much handiwork. Saudi Arabia has a comparative advantage in producing oil because its vast oil reserves can be harvested at low cost. Canada is a major exporter of lumber because its forested land is relatively unproductive in nonforest crops. Table 16.2 provides other examples of comparative advantage.

But endowments of natural resources are not the only source of comparative advantage. For example, Japan has few natural resources, yet it is a major exporter of autos, steel, and electronics. The basic ingredients that go into the production of autos, such as iron ore, are imported by the Japanese. Japan's auto industry highlights the importance of acquiring comparative advantage through saving and accumulating capital and constructing

Table 16.2	Examples of Comparative Advantages in International Trade

Country	Product
Canada	Lumber
Israel	Citrus fruit
Italy	Wine
Jamaica	Aluminum ore
Mexico	Tomatoes
Saudi Arabia	Oil
China	Textiles
Japan	Automobiles
South Korea	Steel, ships
Switzerland	Watches
United Kingdom	Financial services

efficient factories. Moreover, countries can develop comparative advantages in goods requiring a skilled labor force, such as scientific instruments, by channeling resources to education.

Superior knowledge also results in comparative advantage. Many years ago, Switzerland developed a comparative advantage in watches because the people of the country have superior knowledge and expertise in manufacturing watches. Similarly, semiconductor equipment is an export product of the United States given the technical expertise of firms such as Intel Corp.

CHECK POINT

1. How does specialization promote increases in productivity?

2. How does the principle of comparative advantage explain the pattern of world trade?

3. What determines comparative advantage?

4. Discuss the argument for free trade.

WHY ARE FREE TRADE AND GLOBALIZATION CONTROVERSIAL?

Although nations can benefit from specialization and trade, why do some people object to free trade? The answer is not hard to find. Despite the gains to the overall economy, some groups within the economy are likely to lose from free trade while others gain much more. Opening up trade thus results in a list of losers and winners across the economy, as seen in Table 16.3.

Table 16.3	Advantages and Disadvantages of Globalization and Free Trade

Advantages	Disadvantages
Productivity increases faster when countries produce goods and services in which they have a comparative advantage. Living standards can increase more rapidly.	Millions of Americans have lost jobs because of imports or shifts in production abroad. Most find new jobs that pay less.
Global competition and cheap imports keep a constraint on prices, so inflation is less likely to disrupt economic growth.	Millions of other Americans fear getting laid off, especially at those firms operating in import-competing industries.
An open economy promotes technological development and innovation, with fresh ideas from abroad.	Workers face demands of wage concessions from their employers, which often threaten to export jobs abroad if wage concessions are not met.
Jobs in export industries tend to pay about 15 percent more than jobs in import-competing industries.	Besides blue-collar jobs, service and white-collar jobs are increasingly vulnerable to operations being sent overseas.
Unfettered capital movements provide the United States access to foreign investment and maintain low interest rates.	American employees can lose their competitiveness when companies build state-of-the-art factories in low-wage countries, making them as productive as those in the United States.

Clearly, those industries that produce goods in which the home country has a comparative advantage gain from free trade. For example, Boeing's production of jetliners expands when orders increase from foreign airline companies. Also, Boeing's workers find that the demand for their labor increases along with the level of production. Moreover, firms supplying engines, landing gear, and other inputs that are used to produce Boeing jetliners realize increased sales and employment for their workers. Indeed, people in the state of Washington, who account for a significant amount of the production of Boeing jetliners, benefit from international trade.

The consumer is another beneficiary of free trade. We have learned that competition among firms leads to increased output and lower prices. This also pertains to competition between domestic and foreign firms. Because international trade keeps markets from being dominated by one or a few domestic firms, more competition exists. This forces domestic firms to charge lower prices and to produce goods of higher quality—two factors that consumers value. Clearly, American Airlines and its passengers are better off when Boeing and Airbus compete for the jetliner purchases of American Airlines. Also, trade can increase the diversity of products available to consumers. U.S. auto buyers, for example, can purchase Fords, Chevys, and Chryslers and also Toyotas, Hondas, and Mitsubishis.

Reducing restrictions on trade, however, does not benefit everyone. Firms and their workers in import-competing industries face declining sales, profits, and employment levels as foreign-produced goods displace their goods. Many workers who lose their jobs in import-competing industries do not have the skills needed to allow them to be easily re-employed at a comparable wage level. Also, the firms and their workers who supply inputs to these industries suffer because of foreign competition. Both management and labor in these industries are likely to oppose free trade and seek government protection against imports. Seekers of protectionism are often established firms in an aging industry that has lost its comparative advantage. High costs may be due to lack of modern technology, inefficient management procedures, outmoded work rules, or high wages paid to domestic workers. In the United States, industries seeking protectionism have included shoes, textiles, steel, oil, and automobiles.

Figure 16.2   Economic Effects of a Tariff

explain graph on board

A tariff placed on an imported good is shifted to the domestic consumer via a higher product price. As a result, imports of the product decrease from their pretariff level. This reduction can be attributed to falling domestic consumption and rising domestic production. The effect of a tariff is to protect domestic producers from foreign competition.

Government officials must balance the opposing interests of consumers and firms/workers in exporting industries against firms and workers in import-competing industries when setting the course for changes in international trade policy.

LIMITING FOREIGN COMPETITION: TARIFFS

For centuries, governments have used tariffs to raise revenues and protect domestic producers from foreign competition. A **tariff** is a tax imposed on imports. For example, the United States imposes a tariff of 2.9 percent on autos. If a foreign car costs $30,000, the amount of the tariff will equal $870 ($30,000 × 0.029 = $870), and the domestic price including the tariff will be $30,870.[3]

We can use supply and demand analysis to understand the economic effects of tariffs. Figure 16.2 shows the steel market for the United States. The domestic supply and demand curves for steel are denoted by $S_{U.S.}$ and $D_{U.S.}$, respectively. In the absence of international trade, the equilibrium price of steel is $500 per ton, the quantity of steel supplied by U.S. producers is 10 million tons, and the quantity of steel demanded by U.S. consumers is 10 million tons.

---

[3] Another way to restrict foreign competition is to impose a quota. A quota is a physical restriction on the quantity of goods traded each year. For example, a quota might state that no more than 1 million kilograms of cheese or 2 million kilograms of ice cream could be imported during the current year.

Suppose that the U.S. economy is opened to international trade, and the rest of the world has a comparative advantage in steel. Assume that the world price of steel is $250 per ton. For simplicity, we will also assume that the United States takes the world price of steel as given.[4] At the price of $250, domestic consumption is 15 million tons and domestic production is 5 million tons. The quantity of imported steel, 10 million tons, reflects the horizontal difference between the U.S. demand curve and U.S. supply curve at the price of $250.

Compared to the situation before trade, free trade results in a fall in the domestic price from $500 to $250. As a result, consumers increase their purchases from 10 million tons to 15 million tons. Clearly, domestic consumers are better off because they can buy more steel at a lower price. However, domestic producers now sell less steel at a lower price than they did before trade. As production falls from 10 million tons to 5 million tons for domestic steel firms, profits decline and unemployment rises for domestic steelworkers.

In response to pleas for protection against imports by the domestic steel industry, assume the U.S. government imposes a tariff of $150 per ton on steel that is imported into the United States. This will increase the price of steel from $250 to $400. Therefore, domestic consumption will decline from the 15 million tons in the free-trade equilibrium to 12 million tons after the tariff is imposed. Also, domestic production will increase from 5 million tons to 8 million tons, and the quantity of imports falls from 10 million tons to 4 million tons. Thus, a tariff will tend to raise the price, lower the amounts consumed and imported, and increase domestic production.

Clearly, the tariff benefits domestic steel firms and their workers at the expense of domestic consumers. Because of the tariff, consumers pay more for farm equipment, refrigerators, and other steel-using products. Steel-using firms such as Ford (autos) and Caterpillar (tractors) will realize higher costs and a loss of sales because of the tariff on steel. As production declines for these firms, they will lay off some of their workers.

Another effect of a tariff is the revenue that it raises for the government. In our example, we assume that the tariff equals $150 per ton of steel that is imported. Multiplying this amount times the quantity of imports, 4 million tons, gives tariff revenues of $600 million. This tariff revenue is a transfer of income from U.S. steel consumers to the U.S. government.

Also, U.S. exporters are indirectly impeded by a tariff. Because a tariff causes sales of imported steel to decrease in the United States, the rest of the world will earn fewer dollars with which to purchase U.S. exports of computers, chemicals, and wheat. U.S. export industries, which have a comparative advantage, will thus decrease production. Also, if the imposition of the import tariff by the United States causes foreign nations to retaliate[4] and impose tariffs on imports, U.S. export industries will suffer. Simply put, tariffs foster the growth of inefficient industries that do not have a comparative advantage and promote the decline of efficient industries that do have a comparative advantage. By causing resources to move from high-efficiency industries to low-efficiency industries, tariffs reduce the standard of living for people.

For example, the U.S. government has imposed tariffs to limit imports of steel. In the 1950s, U.S. steelmakers dominated the world market, accounting for half of global steel output. Since the 1960s, however, foreign steelmakers have made significant inroads into the American market, turning the United States into a net importer of steel. To protect domestic producers, the U.S. government has consistently limited steel imports by imposing tariffs, quotas, and other barriers to trade. One such policy occurred in 2002 when President George W. Bush imposed tariffs on imported steel for a 2-year period. The tariffs ranged from 8 to 30 percent on a variety of steel products. Bush hoped that the tariff relief would buy time for

(handwritten margin notes: workers are still laid off, just different ones!; why would we want to do that?!; that's not good — state 3)*

---

[4] This assumption implies that the United States is a small economy compared to the rest of the world. Although the small-economy assumption is not necessary to analyze the effects of international trade, it greatly simplifies the analysis.

steel companies so they could bring their labor costs down and upgrade equipment so as to become competitive with producers in other nations. However, critics noted that protecting steel placed a heavy burden on American steel-using industries such as automobiles and earth-moving equipment. Although the tariffs would temporarily save roughly 6,000 jobs, the cost to U.S. consumers and steel-using firms of saving these jobs was between $800,000 and $1.1 million per job. Moreover, the steel tariffs would cost as many as 13 jobs in steel-using industries for every one steel job protected.[5]

ARGUMENTS FOR TRADE RESTRICTIONS

Although the free-trade argument is very persuasive, virtually all nations have imposed restrictions on international trade. Let us examine the main arguments for trade restrictions.

Job Protection

The issue of jobs has been a dominant factor in motivating government officials to levy trade restrictions on imported goods. During periods of economic recession, workers are especially eager to point out that cheap foreign goods undercut domestic production, resulting in a loss of domestic jobs to foreign labor. Alleged job losses to foreign competition historically have been a major force behind the desire of most U.S. labor leaders to reject free-trade policies.

This view, however, has a serious omission: It fails to acknowledge the dual nature of international trade. Changes in a nation's imports of goods and services are closely related to changes in its exports. Nations export goods because they desire to import products from other nations. When the United States imports goods from abroad, foreigners gain purchasing power in dollars that will eventually be spent on U.S. goods, services, or financial assets. U.S. export industries then enjoy gains in sales and employment, whereas the opposite occurs in U.S. import-competing industries. Rather than promoting overall unemployment, imports tend to generate job opportunities in some industries as part of the process by which they decrease employment in other industries. However, the job gains due to open trade policies tend to be less visible to the public than the readily observable job losses stemming from foreign competition. The more conspicuous losses have enabled many U.S. business and labor leaders in import-competing industries to combine forces in their opposition to free trade.

Protection Against Cheap Foreign Labor

One of the most common arguments used to justify trade restrictions is that tariffs are needed to defend domestic jobs against cheap foreign labor. As indicated in Table 16.4, production workers in Norway, Germany, and the United States are paid much higher wages, in terms of the U.S. dollar, than workers in countries such as Mexico and Taiwan. So it could be argued that low wages abroad make it difficult for U.S. producers to compete with producers using cheap foreign labor and that, unless U.S. producers are protected from imports, domestic output and employment levels will decrease.

Indeed, a widely held view maintains that competition from goods produced in low-wage countries is unfair and harmful to American workers. Moreover, companies that produce goods in foreign countries to take advantage of cheap labor should not be allowed to dictate the wages paid to American workers. A solution: Impose a tariff on

---

[5] Robert Carbaugh and John Olienyk, "U.S. Steelmakers in Continuing Crisis," *Challenge*, January–February 2004, pp. 86–106.

Table 16.4	Hourly Compensation Costs in U.S. Dollars for Production Workers in Manufacturing, 2003	

Country	Hourly Compensation (dollars/hour)
Norway	$31.55
Germany	31.25
United States	21.97
Japan	20.09
Canada	19.28
South Korea	10.28
Singapore	7.41
Taiwan	5.84
Mexico	2.48

Source: From U.S. Department of Labor, Bureau of Labor Statistics, *International Comparisons of Hourly Compensation Costs for Production Workers in Manufacturing*, November 2004, at http://stats.bls.gov/news.release/ichcc.t02.htm/.

goods brought into the United States that makes up for the wage differential between foreign workers and U.S. workers in the same industry. That way, competition would be confined to who makes the best product, not who works for the least amount of money. Therefore, if Calvin Klein wants to manufacture sweatshirts in Pakistan, his firm would be charged a tariff equal to the cost difference between the earnings of a Pakistani worker and a U.S. apparel worker.

Although this viewpoint may have widespread appeal, it fails to recognize the links among efficiency, wages, and labor. Labor cost per unit of output reflects not only the wage rate, but also the productivity of labor. Even if domestic wages are, say, twice as much as foreign wages, if the productivity of domestic labor is more than twice as much as the productivity of foreign labor, domestic unit labor costs will be lower. For example, in 1990 wages in Malaysia were 10 percent of wages in the United States. But Malaysian labor productivity was also about 10 percent of the U.S. level in 1990. This means that unit labor costs were approximately the same in Malaysia and the United States because the difference in productivity almost exactly offset the difference in wages between the two countries.

Fairness in Trade: A Level Playing Field

Fairness in trade is another reason given for protectionism. Business firms and workers often argue that foreign governments play by a different set of rules than the home government, giving foreign firms unfair competitive advantages. Domestic producers contend that import restrictions should be enacted to offset these foreign advantages, thus creating a level playing field on which all producers could compete on equal terms.

U.S. companies often allege that foreign firms are not subject to the same government regulations regarding pollution control and worker safety as U.S. companies; this is especially true in many developing nations (such as Mexico and South Korea), where pollution enforcement has been lax. Moreover, foreign firms may not pay as much in corporate taxes or have to comply with employment regulations such as affirmative action, minimum wage, and overtime pay. Also, foreign governments may erect high trade barriers that effectively

so why don't we charge?! ~ If we like these things, of course there is a cost!

close their markets to imports, or they may subsidize their producers so as to enhance their competitiveness in world markets.

Infant Industry

One of the more commonly accepted cases for tariff protection is the infant industry argument. This argument does not deny the validity of the case for free trade. However, it contends that for free trade to be meaningful, trading nations should temporarily shield their newly developing industries from foreign competition. Otherwise, mature foreign businesses, which are at the time more efficient, can drive the young domestic businesses out of the market. Only after the young companies have had time to become efficient producers should the tariff barriers be lifted and free trade take place.

Although there is some truth to the infant industry argument, it must be qualified in several respects. First, once a protective tariff is imposed, it is very difficult to remove, even after industrial maturity has been achieved. Special-interest groups can often convince policymakers that further protection is justified. Second, it is very difficult to determine which industries will be capable of realizing comparative-advantage potential and thus merit protection. Third, the infant industry argument generally is not valid for mature, industrialized nations such as the United States, Germany, and Japan.

Noneconomic Arguments

Noneconomic considerations also enter into the arguments for protectionism. One such consideration is national security. The national security argument contends that a country may be put in jeopardy in the event of an international crisis or war if it is heavily dependent on foreign suppliers. Even though domestic producers are not as efficient, tariff protection should be granted to ensure their continued existence. An application of this argument involves the major oil-importing nations, which saw several Arab nations impose oil boycotts on the West to win support for the Arab position against Israel during the 1973 Middle East conflict. The problem, however, is stipulating what constitutes an essential industry. If the term is defined broadly, many industries may be able to win import protection, and the argument loses its meaning. *— besides, one effects all*

Another noneconomic argument is based on cultural considerations. New England may desire to preserve small-scale fishing; West Virginia may argue for tariffs on hand-blown glassware, on the grounds that these skills enrich the fabric of life; certain products such as narcotics may be considered socially undesirable, and restrictions or prohibitions may be placed on their importation. These arguments constitute legitimate reasons and cannot be ignored.

PURSUING TRADE LIBERALIZATION

Since the 1940s, advanced nations have significantly lowered their trade restrictions. Such trade liberalization has stemmed from two approaches. *our standard of living has gone way up*

The first is a reciprocal reduction of trade barriers on a nondiscriminatory basis. The 148 members of the World Trade Organization (WTO) acknowledge that tariff reductions agreed on by any two nations will be extended to all other members. Such an international approach encourages a gradual relaxation of tariffs throughout the world.

A second approach to trade liberalization occurs when a small group of nations, typically on a regional basis, forms a regional trading arrangement. Under this system, member nations agree to impose lower barriers to trade within the group than with nonmember nations. The North American Free Trade Agreement (NAFTA) is an example of a regional trading arrangement.

Proponents of regional trading arrangements maintain that small blocs of nations with many similar interests are more likely to liberalize trade dramatically than the vast number of dissimilar nations. Critics, however, maintain that the members of a regional trading arrangement may not be greatly interested in global liberalization, but only in liberalization among themselves. Let us examine two trading arrangements—the World Trade Organization and the North American Free Trade Agreement.

WORLD TRADE ORGANIZATION

Established in 1995, the World Trade Organization is headquartered in Geneva, Switzerland. The main purpose of the WTO is to promote freer international trade. It does this by administering international trade agreements, facilitating trade negotiations to lower tariffs and quotas, resolving trade disputes, and providing technical assistance and training to developing countries. The WTO is not a government; individual nations remain free to set their own appropriate levels of environment, labor, health, and safety protections.

One of the most useful roles of the WTO is adjudicating trade disputes. The dispute-settlement mechanism of the WTO provides for the formation of a dispute panel once a case is brought and sets time limits for each stage of the process. The decision of the panel may be taken to an appellate body, but the accused party cannot block the final decision.

For example, during the 1990s, the United States complained that governments in Europe prevented U.S. producers from selling their beef in Europe. After consulting with experts, the WTO found that Europe had engaged in unfair trade. Europe therefore had the choice of desisting from this practice or facing retaliation from the United States. As things turned out, the United States imposed 100-percent tariffs on imports of selected European goods to pressure Europe to open its markets to U.S. beef.

Since the inception of the WTO, the trade dispute framework has proved useful to the United States. As a complaining party, the United States prevailed in 22 out of 24 cases from 1995 to 2000. Yet, the WTO also handed the United States several major defeats. One such defeat occurred in 2000 when the WTO ruled that U.S. tax law provided illegal subsidies for American exporters.

Although the WTO attempts to promote freer international trade, it has become a magnet for resistance to globalization by protectionists and critics of free trade. Protectionists include American steelworkers who complain that the free-trade policies of the WTO allow cheap Russian steel to flood the U.S. market, resulting in Russian workers taking away their jobs. Also, critics of free trade are incensed that, as economies become more closely intertwined, trade policy is increasingly impinging on such sensitive issues as social justice, product safety, and the environment.

For example, American environmentalists were outraged during the 1990s when the WTO ruled against a U.S. ban on imports of Malaysian shrimp from countries using nets that trap turtles and a ban on imports of Mexican tuna caught in ways that drown dolphins. Also, U.S. labor unions insist that Indonesian firms must pay livable wages to their workers and improve the working conditions in their "sweatshop" factories if they are to sell their goods in the United States. Finally, some church leaders declare that the international debts of poor nations be forgiven.

In spite of pressure for reform, the WTO has remained a centerpiece of the world trading system. Its policies are based on the notion that when countries can trade freely with each other, without import tariffs or other measures aimed at protecting the domestic market from competition, the world economy grows and everyone in general benefits. However, free trade can impose costs on firms and workers in import-competing industries. The protesters of the WTO are a reminder that the policies of the WTO must be weighed in a broader context of the world community and social justice, not just increased economic growth.

NORTH AMERICAN FREE TRADE AGREEMENT

The notion of a U.S.-Canadian-Mexican free-trade area has a long tradition. During the 1900s, the three nations considered the free-trade issue several times. However, because of the urgency of nation building and apprehensions concerning political sovereignty, the nations maintained restrictionist stances. With the weakening of its position of world leadership in the 1980s, the United States appeared more willing to pursue trade negotiations with Canada and Mexico. Also, because Canada and Mexico had grown increasingly dependent on the United States, a free-trade area appeared to be in their interests.

In 1993, the North American Free Trade Agreement (NAFTA) was approved by the governments of the United States, Mexico, and Canada. The pact went into effect in 1994. By removing trade restrictions among themselves, the members hoped to gain better access to the others' markets, technology, labor, and expertise. In many respects, there were remarkable fits between the nations: The United States would benefit from Mexico's pool of cheap and increasingly skilled labor, while Mexico would benefit from U.S. investment and expertise. Moreover, U.S.-Canada trade was also expected to increase because of free trade. However, negotiating the free-trade agreement was difficult because it required meshing two large advanced economies (the United States and Canada) with that of a sizable developing nation (Mexico).

NAFTA proponents maintain that the agreement benefits the U.S. economy overall by expanding trade opportunities, reducing prices, increasing competition, and enhancing the ability of U.S. firms to attain economies of large-scale production. The United States produces more goods that benefit from large amounts of physical capital and a highly-skilled workforce, including chemicals, plastics, cement, sophisticated electronics and communications gear, machine tools, and household appliances. U.S. companies, particularly larger ones, get better access to cheaper labor and parts. Moreover, the United States benefits from a more reliable source of petroleum and less illegal Mexican immigration, as new jobs became available in Mexico and wages increased. In spite of these benefits, the overall economic gains for the United States are estimated to be modest, because the U.S. economy is 25 times the size of the Mexican economy.

But even ardent proponents of NAFTA acknowledge that it has inflicted pain on some segments of the U.S. economy. On the business side, the losers have been industries such as citrus growing and sugar that rely on trade barriers to limit imports of low-priced Mexican goods. Other major losers are unskilled workers, such as those in the apparel industry, whose jobs are most vulnerable to competition from low-paid workers abroad.

U.S. labor unions have been especially concerned that Mexico's low wage scale encourages U.S. companies to locate in Mexico, resulting in job losses in the United States. Cities such as Muskegon, Michigan, which has thousands of workers cranking out such basic auto parts as piston rings, are especially vulnerable to low-wage Mexican competition. Indeed, the hourly manufacturing compensation for Mexican workers has been a small fraction of that paid to U.S. and Canadian workers. Although studies have shown that wages are not necessarily the driving factor in business-location decisions, the huge disparity between U.S. and Mexican wages cannot be ignored.

Another concern is Mexico's environmental regulations, criticized as being less stringent than those of the United States. U.S. labor and environmental activists fear that polluting Mexican plants might cause plants in the United States, which are cleaner but more expensive to operate, to close down. Environmentalists also fear that increased Mexican growth will bring increased air and water pollution.

Thomas Friedman
McDonalds
Dell

It is in politics, not economics, that NAFTA has had its biggest impact. The trade agreement has come to symbolize a close and perhaps irreversible embrace between the United States and Mexico. Given the history of hostility between the two countries, this embrace is remarkable. Its cause was the realization by U.S. officials that their chance of curbing the flow of illegal immigrants and illegal drugs would be far greater if their southern neighbors were wealthy instead of poor. Put simply, the United States bought itself an ally with NAFTA.

In short, NAFTA is not the solution to all the economic problems of North America, but it is not the disaster that critics claimed it would be.

This chapter considered the United States as an open economy and the importance of international trade. The next chapter will discuss the U.S. balance of payments and the markets in which Americans exchange dollars for other currencies.

CHECK POINT

1. Why do tariffs result in benefits for domestic producers but costs for domestic consumers?

2. What are the major arguments for trade restrictions? Explain the flaw in each argument.

3. How does the World Trade Organization attempt to improve the efficiency of the world trading system?

4. Is the North American Free Trade Agreement good for people in the United States? How about people in Mexico or Canada?

Chapter Summary

1. The U.S. economy has become increasingly integrated into the world economy in recent decades. Such integration involves a number of dimensions, including the trade of goods and services, financial markets, the labor force, ownership of production facilities, and dependence on imported materials.

2. Specialization and trade pertain to individuals, but also to groups of individuals and nations. By increasing productivity, specialization can result in a more efficient use of resources and an increase in output. However, the very nature of specialization can limit its benefits because repetitive jobs can result in bored and unproductive workers.

3. Proponents of free trade contend that if each country produces what it does best and allows trade, over the long run all will enjoy lower costs and prices and also higher levels of output, income, and consumption than could be achieved in isolation. A free market compels firms and their workers to adjust to forces such as shifts in technologies, input productivities, and tastes and preferences.

4. The principle of comparative advantage underlies patterns of world trade. This principle states that countries should specialize in producing those goods in which they are relatively, not absolutely, more efficient. In other words, comparative advantage is the ability of a country to produce a good at a lower opportunity cost than some other country. Among the

sources of comparative advantage are natural endowments of resources, a skilled labor force, and superior knowledge.

5. Although economies can benefit from specialization and free trade, some people object to free trade. This is because some groups in the economy lose from free trade, while others gain. Consumers and those firms and their workers that produce goods in which the home country has a comparative advantage gain from free trade. However, firms and their workers in import-competing industries suffer. Government officials must thus consider the opposing interests of these groups when setting the course for international trade policy.

6. To protect firms and their workers from foreign competition, governments can impose tariffs and other trade restrictions. These devices, however, tend to foster the growth of inefficient industries that do not have a comparative advantage and promote the decline of efficient industries that do have a comparative advantage, thus reducing the standard of living for the nation.

7. Among the arguments for trade restrictions are job protection, protection against cheap foreign labor, fairness in trade, infant industry, national security, and preservation of culture.

8. Since the 1940s, advanced nations have significantly lowered their trade barriers. Such trade liberalization has stemmed from the World Trade Organization and regional trading arrangements such as the North American Free Trade Agreement.

Key Terms and Concepts

division of labor (383)

comparative advantage (385)

tariff (389)

quota (389)

level playing field (392)

infant industry argument (393)

World Trade Organization (WTO) (393)

North American Free Trade Agreement (NAFTA) (394)

Self-Test: Multiple-Choice Questions

1. Countries that trade on the basis of comparative advantage have _____ than countries that don't.

   a. more goods and services available to them
   b. higher production costs and transportation costs
   c. lower levels of product quality from which to choose
   d. lower levels of labor productivity

2. The major determinants of comparative advantage include all of the following *except*

   a. national income.
   b. climate.
   c. labor-force skills.
   d. capital per worker.

3. Free trade and specialization tend to result in

   a. higher wages for workers in import-competing industries.
   b. higher product prices for domestic consumers.
   c. a smaller range of product availability for domestic consumers.
   d. increased profits for firms in export industries.

4. Trade between countries results in

   a. lower living standards.
   b. higher product prices.
   c. increased specialization.
   d. greater self-sufficiency.

5. Which of the following is *not* cited as a justification for trade restrictions?

   a. Permitting infant industries to mature and become competitive
   b. Increasing jobs for workers in import-competing industries
   c. Maintaining self-sufficiency for the nation's military
   d. Fostering specialization based on the principle of comparative advantage

6. Protectionist pressures in the United States have been caused by all of the following *except*

   a. deficits in the U.S. balance of trade.
   b. unemployment of U.S. workers.
   c. rising national income in developing nations.
   d. falling profits of U.S. manufacturers.

7. The imposition of a tariff on steel imports is *least* likely to result in a(n)

   a. increase in the production cost of steel-using industries.
   b. decrease in the quantity of steel imports.
   c. increase in the price of domestic steel.
   d. increase in productivity in the domestic steel industry.

8. Free traders maintain that an open economy is advantageous in that it provides all of the following *except*

   a. increased competition for world producers.
   b. a wider selection of products for consumers.
   c. the utilization of the most efficient production methods.
   d. relatively high wages for all domestic workers.

9. A sudden shift from import tariffs to free trade may induce short-term unemployment in

   a. import-competing industries.
   b. industries that only export to foreign countries.
   c. industries that sell domestically as well as export.
   d. industries that neither import nor export.

10. Recent economic research supports the notion that productivity performance in industries is

    a. directly related to globalization of industries.
    b. inversely related to globalization of industries.
    c. not related to globalization of industries.
    d. none of the above.

Answers to Multiple-Choice Questions

1. a   2. a   3. c   4. c   5. d   6. c   7. d   8. d   9. a   10. a

Study Questions and Problems

1. Table 16.5 shows the hypothetical production possibilities tables of Japan and South Korea. Use this information to answer the following questions.

| Table 16.5 | Production Possibilities Schedules of Japan and South Korea | | | | | | |

	Japan			South Korea		
	TVs	VCRs		TVs	VCRs
A	0	80	A'	0	120
B	8	64	B'	6	96
C	16	48	C'	12	72
D	24	32	D'	18	48
E	32	16	E'	24	24
F	40	0	F'	30	0

a. What is the opportunity cost of producing a TV for Japan and for South Korea?

b. Which country has a comparative advantage in producing TVs?

c. In the absence of trade and specialization, suppose that Japan produces and consumes at combination *B* and South Korea produces and consumes at combination *E'*. If these countries specialize according to the principle of comparative advantage, how much will total output increase?

d. Show how consumers in each country can share the gains in total output that result from specialization.

2. The United States tends to have a comparative advantage over other nations in the production of high-technology goods. What would be the likely sources of this advantage?

3. Which individuals in the nation might gain from a tariff placed on imported textiles? Which might lose?

4. Why do economists maintain that trade barriers lead to a misallocation of resources for the world?

5. Although people may grow grapefruit in Idaho, why do they purchase most of their grapefruit from California and Florida?

6. Suppose the U.S. government imposes a quota on cheese imported from Europe. Who would likely be helped and hurt?

7. What is NAFTA, and what have been its effects to date?

8. Explain the impact of trade with low-wage countries on jobs in the United States. How can the United States pay its workers higher wages than foreign nations and still be competitive in foreign markets?

9. Suppose that Canada can produce 160 machine tools by using all of its resources to produce machine tools and 120 calculators by devoting all of its resources to calculators. Comparative figures for Brazil are 120 machine tools and 120 calculators. According to the principle of comparative advantage, in which product should each country specialize?

10. Draw a supply and demand diagram for autos in the United States, a product in which the United States has a comparative disadvantage. Show the effect of Japanese imports on the domestic price and quantity. Now show a tariff that cuts the level of auto imports in half. Show the effects of the tariff on U.S. producers and consumers.

Table 16.6	Australia's Computer Market	
Price of Computers	Quantity Demanded	Quantity Supplied
$4,000	10	40
3,500	15	35
3,000	20	30
2,500	25	25
2,000	30	20
1,500	35	15
1,000	40	10

11. Table 16.6 shows the demand and supply schedules of computers for Australia. On the basis of this information, answer the following questions:

a. In the absence of trade, what are the equilibrium price and quantity of computers for Australia?

b. Suppose that the world price of computers is $1,500 per unit and that Australia takes this price as given. How many computers will Australia produce, consume, and import?

c. To protect its producers from world competition, suppose the Australian government imposes a tariff of $500 per unit on computer imports. What is the effect of the tariff on the price of computers in Australia, the quantity of computers supplied by Australian producers, the quantity of computers demanded by Australian consumers, and the quantity of imports? How much revenue will the Australian government gain because of the tariff?

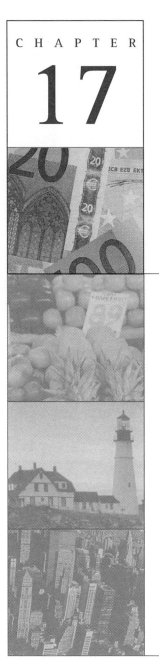

International Finance

Chapter objectives

After reading this chapter, you should be able to:

1. Explain what a current account deficit or surplus means.

2. Understand the foreign exchange quotations as presented in major newspapers.

3. Identify the factors that determine the dollar's exchange rate.

4. Discuss the features of the major exchange rate systems of the world.

economics IN CONTEXT

During the early 2000s, the U.S. balance of payments (current account) reached record deficits, sparking fears of a flight from the dollar with wrenching consequences for U.S. economic prosperity. Nothing is intrinsically wrong with a country running such a deficit. But the United States has run a string of deficits for the past 20 years, and foreigners now hold unprecedented financial claims on the United States. At some point, foreigners might become reluctant to hold these dollars and set into motion a series of corrective economic adjustments including sharply rising interest rates and recession for the U.S. economy.

Although international trade is an important component of the global economy, it is just part of the picture. International finance is another part. The balance of payments is an important dimension of international finance, as is the financing of international trade.

In this chapter, we will examine the U.S. balance of payments and the markets in which Americans exchange dollars for other currencies. We will also expand our understanding of foreign currency markets by analyzing the advantages and disadvantages of various exchange rate systems.

THE BALANCE OF PAYMENTS

Every year, Americans conduct many transactions with foreigners such as the following examples:

- Sears imports shirts from Hong Kong.
- General Motors exports minivans to Brazil.
- Holiday Inn supplies rooms to German tourists visiting San Francisco.
- Ayako Ozawa, a student at Stanford, receives gifts from her family in Japan.
- American investors receive dividends from their investments in Germany.
- Edgar Valdez, a resident of Mexico, purchases U.S. Treasury bills.
- George Thomas, who lives in Philadelphia, purchases stock in Sony Corp. of Japan.

The U.S. government compiles a statistical record of these and other transactions. This record is called the balance of payments. The **balance of payments** is a record of a country's international trading, borrowing, and lending. In the balance of payments, *inflows* of funds from foreigners to the United States are noted as *receipts*, with a plus sign. *Outflows* of funds from the United States to foreigners are noted as *payments*, with a minus sign. The balance of payments has two components, the current account and the capital and financial account, which we will now examine.

Current Account

The first component of the balance of payments is the **current account**, which includes, as the name suggests, the dollar value of U.S. transactions in currently produced goods and services, investment income, and unilateral transfers.

The most widely reported component of the current account is the balance of trade, also known as the trade balance. This balance includes all of the goods (merchandise) that the United States exports or imports: agricultural products, machinery, autos, petroleum, electronics, computer software, jetliners, textiles, and the like. Combining the exports and imports of goods gives the balance of trade. When exports exceed imports, the trade balance is a *surplus;* when imports exceed exports, the trade balance is a *deficit.*

Another component of the current account are exports and imports of services. Examples of internationally traded services include tourism, airline and shipping transportation, construction, architecture, engineering, consulting, information management, banking, insurance, medical, and legal. When exports exceed imports, the services balance is a surplus; when imports exceed exports, the services balance is a deficit.

Broadening the current account, we also include flows of income. This item consists of the net earnings (dividends and interest) on U.S. investments abroad—that is, earnings on U.S. investments abroad less payments on foreign investments in the United States. It also includes the net compensation of employees.

Finally, the current account includes unilateral transfers. These items, gifts, include transfers of goods and services or money between the United States and the rest of the world for which nothing is given in exchange—hence, unilateral. Examples of private transfers are gifts that Americans make to their families in Europe or living allowances that Japanese families send to their sons and daughters who attend college in the United States. The economic and military aid that the U.S. government provides to other governments is an example of a governmental unilateral transfer.

The current account balance is the sum of the trade balance, the services balance, net investment income, and net unilateral transfers. If the monetary inflows on these accounts exceed the monetary outflows, the current account balance is a *surplus*. But if the monetary outflows on these accounts exceed the monetary inflows, the current account balance is a *deficit*.

Capital and Financial Account

The second component of the balance of payments is the capital and financial account. Capital and financial transactions in the balance of payments include all international purchases or sales of assets such as real estate, corporate stocks and bonds, and government securities. Changes in foreign asset holdings by governments and central banks are also included in the capital and financial account.

When an American sells an asset (a golf course, a share of stock, or a bond) to a Japanese investor, the transaction is recorded in the capital and financial account as an inflow, because funds flow into the United States to purchase the asset. When an American purchases a skyscraper in Switzerland, the transaction is recorded in the capital and financial account as an outflow because funds flow from the United States to purchase the asset.

The capital and financial account balance is the amount of inflows minus outflows. The capital and financial account balance is a *surplus* if those in the United States sell more assets to foreigners than they purchase from foreigners. The capital and financial account balance is a *deficit* if those in the United States buy more assets from foreigners than they sell to foreigners.

What Does a Current Account Deficit (Surplus) Mean?

The current account and the capital and financial account are not unrelated; they are essentially reflections of one another. Recall that each international transaction represents an exchange of goods, services, or assets among households, businesses, or governments.

Thus, the two sides of the exchange must always balance. This means that, sign ignored, the current account balance equals the capital and financial account balance, as shown in the following equation:

$$\text{Current account balance} = \text{Capital and financial account balance}$$

It follows that any current account *deficit* must be balanced by a capital and financial account *surplus*. Conversely, any current account *surplus* must be balanced by a capital and financial account *deficit*.

To better understand this notion, assume that in a particular year your spending is greater than your income. How will you finance your "deficit"? The answer is by borrowing or selling some of your assets. You might liquidate some real assets (for example, sell your personal computer) or perhaps some financial assets (sell a U.S. government security that you own). In like manner, when a nation experiences a current account deficit, its expenditures for foreign goods and services are greater than the income received from the international sales of its own goods and services, after making allowances for investment income flows and gifts to and from foreigners. The nation must somehow finance its current account deficit. But how? The answer lies in selling assets and borrowing. In other words, a nation's current account *deficit* is financed essentially by a net *inflow* of capital in its capital and financial account. Conversely, a nation's current account *surplus* is financed by a net *outflow* of capital in its capital and financial account.

Although the current account balance always equals the capital and financial account balance, the figures gathered on international transactions are not 100 percent accurate or complete. Consequently, an adjustment for measurement errors, the **statistical discrepancy**, is reported in the capital and financial account component of the balance of payments. Economists generally believe that the statistical discrepancy is primarily the result of large hidden capital and financial flows (for example, unidentified borrowing from the rest of the world or tax evasion), and so the item has been placed in the capital and financial account component of the balance of payments.

THE U.S. BALANCE OF PAYMENTS

Table 17.1, shows the balance of payments accounts for the United States during 1980–2004. Items in the current account and capital and financial account that provide inflows of funds from foreigners to the United States are "plus" items that result in flows of funds from the United States to other nations have a minus sign.

Let us consider the U.S. balance of payments for 2004. As seen in the table, the United States had a merchandise trade deficit of –$665.5 billion, resulting from the difference between U.S. merchandise exports and merchandise imports. The United States was thus a net importer of merchandise. The table also shows that the United States has consistently realized merchandise trade deficits since 1980.

Discussions of U.S. competitiveness in merchandise trade often give the impression that the United States has consistently performed poorly relative to other nations. However, the merchandise trade deficit is a narrow concept, because goods are only part of what the world trades. Another part of trade is services. Table 17.1 shows that in 2004 the United States realized a surplus of $48.4 billion on services transactions with foreigners. In recent decades, the United States has consistently generated a surplus in its services account, as seen in the table. The United States has been especially competitive in transportation, construction, engineering, finance, and certain health-care services.

Adjusting the merchandise trade balance and services balance for net investment income flows and net unilateral transfers gives the balance on current account. As Table 17.1

| Table 17.1 | U.S. Balance of Payments: 1980–2004 (in billions of dollars) |

Year	Merchandise Trade Balance	Services Balance	Income Flows, Net	Unilateral Transfers, Net	Current Account Balance	Capital and Financial Account Balance
1980	−25.5	6.1	30.1	−8.3	2.4	−2.4
1984	−112.5	3.3	30.0	−20.6	−99.8	99.8
1988	−127.0	12.2	11.6	−25.0	−128.2	128.2
1992	−96.1	55.7	4.5	−32.0	−67.9	67.9
1996	−191.4	82.8	14.2	−40.5	−134.9	134.9
2000	−449.9	81.0	−13.3	−53.2	−435.4	435.4
2004	−665.5	48.4	24.1	−72.9	−665.9	665.9

Sources: From U.S. Department of Commerce, *Survey of Current Business*, various issues. See also U.S. Department of Commerce, Bureau of Economic Analysis, at http://www.bea.doc.gov.

shows, the United States had a current account deficit of −$665.9 billion in 2004. Because our exports were insufficient to pay for our imports, we either borrowed from foreigners or sold them assets such as corporate stock, golf courses, real estate, and skyscrapers to make up the difference. The capital and financial account tells us how much. In 2004, the net borrowing and sale of assets by the United States was $665.9 billion. Since 1982, the United States has realized current account deficits.

Indeed, we buy much more from foreigners than they buy from us. Therefore, foreigners lend or give us the funds to make up the difference between our imports and our exports. It would not be an overstatement to say that we borrow so much from foreigners to finance our current account deficits that we sell them pieces of America, so to speak. Those pieces consist primarily of real estate and corporate stock. However, foreigners also lend us billions of dollars each year in the form of purchases of government and corporate securities and other debt instruments.

Are U.S. Current Account Deficits Bad?

In both the media and popular opinion, current account deficits are often portrayed negatively, being blamed on either the unfair trading practices of our trading partners or a lack of U.S. competitiveness in world markets. Some have even suggested that growing current account deficits would eventually cause the demise of the expansion of the U.S. economy.

When a nation realizes a current account deficit, it becomes a net borrower of funds from the rest of the world. Is this a problem? Not necessarily. The benefit of a current account deficit is the ability to push current spending beyond current production. However, the cost is the debt service that must be paid on the associated borrowing from the rest of the world.

Is it good or bad for a country to get into debt? The answer obviously depends on what the country does with the money. What matters for future incomes and living standards is whether the deficit is being used to finance more consumption or more investment. If used exclusively to finance an increase in domestic investment, the burden could be slight. We know that investment spending increases the nation's stock of capital and expands the economy's capacity to produce goods and services. The value of this extra output may be sufficient to both pay foreign creditors and also augment domestic spending. In this case, because future consumption need not fall below what it otherwise would have been, there would be no true economic burden. If, on the other hand, foreign borrowing is used to finance or increase domestic consumption (private or public), there is no boost given to future productive capacity. Therefore, to meet debt service expense, future consumption must be reduced below what it otherwise would have been. Such a reduction represents the burden of borrowing. This is not necessarily bad; it all depends on how one values current versus future consumption.

In the past two decades, the United States has run continuous deficits in its current account. Can the United States run deficits indefinitely? Because the current account deficit arises mainly because foreigners desire to purchase American assets, there is no economic reason why it cannot continue indefinitely. As long as the investment opportunities are large enough to provide foreign investors with competitive rates of return, they will be happy to continue supplying funds to the United States.

However, the consequence of a current account deficit is a growing foreign ownership of the capital stock of the United States and a rising fraction of U.S. income that must be diverted overseas in the form of interest and dividends to foreigners. Whether the United States can sustain its current account deficit over the foreseeable future depends on whether foreigners are willing to increase their investments in U.S. assets. The current account deficit puts the economic fortunes of the United States partially in the hands of foreign investors.

Do Current Account Deficits Cost Americans Jobs?

The sizable U.S. current account deficits that have occurred in recent years have prompted concerns that American jobs are in jeopardy. Increasing competition in the domestic market from low-cost Asian imports could put pressure on U.S. firms to lay off workers. Exporters such as Ford, whose sales decline as a strong dollar raises the price of its autos in foreign markets, could also move to restrict employment. Finally, jobs in export-oriented firms such as Boeing were hurt by the 1997–1998 recession in Asia, which weakened the demand for U.S. goods. Adding to concerns about the employment effects of the current account deficit is the fear that increasing numbers of U.S. firms will shut down domestic operations and shift production to other countries, largely to take advantage of lower labor costs. Do current account deficits cost Americans jobs?

According to economists at the Federal Reserve Bank of New York, the U.S. current account deficit is not a threat to employment for the economy as a whole.[1] A high current account deficit may indeed hurt employment in particular firms and industries as workers are displaced by increased imports or by the relocation of production abroad. At the economy-wide level, however, the current account deficit is matched by an equal inflow of foreign capital, which finances employment-sustaining investment spending that would not otherwise occur. When viewed as the net inflow of foreign investment capital, the current account deficit produces jobs for the economy as a whole, both from the direct effects of higher employment in investment-oriented industries and from the indirect effects of higher investment spending on economy-wide employment. Viewing the current account deficit as a capital inflow thus helps to dispel misconceptions about the adverse consequences of economic globalization on the domestic job market.

---

[1] Matthew Higgins and Thomas Klitgaard, "Viewing the Current Account Deficit as a Capital Inflow," *Current Issues and Economics and Finance*, Federal Reserve Bank of New York, December 1999, pp. 1–6.

FOREIGN EXCHANGE MARKET

Now that we have learned about international flows of exports, imports, investment, and income, let us consider how these transactions are financed. Financing these transactions involves the purchase and sale of foreign currencies such as the Mexican peso and Japanese yen.

In most cases, the buying and selling of currencies takes place in the **foreign exchange market.** The currencies of most advanced and many developing economies are traded in this market. The foreign exchange market does not involve sending large loads of currency from one country to another. Typically, it involves electronic balances. Dollar-denominated balances in computers in the United States or other countries are traded for computer-housed balances around the world that are denominated in Japanese yen, British pounds, Swiss francs, or any dozens of other commonly traded monies. In short, when "currency" is traded, paper and metal are not the usual media of exchanges. Foreign exchange exists mainly in the world of cyberspace.

Most daily newspapers publish foreign exchange rates for major currencies. The **exchange rate** is the price of one currency in terms of another—for example, the number of dollars required to purchase one United Kingdom (U.K.) pound. For example, the dollar price of the pound may be $2 = 1 pound. It is also possible to define the exchange rate as the number of units of foreign currency required to purchase one unit of domestic currency. For example, the pound price of the dollar may be 0.5 pound = $1. Of course, the pound price of the dollar is the reciprocal of the dollar price of the pound, calculated as shown:

$$\text{Pound price of the dollar} = 1/\text{Dollar price of the pound}$$
$$0.5 = 1/2$$

Therefore, if $2 is required to buy 1 pound, 0.5 pound is required to buy $1.

Table 17.2 shows examples of exchange rates for Friday, January 28, 2005. In columns 2 and 3 (*U.S. Dollar Equivalent*) of the table, the selling prices of foreign currencies are listed in dollars. The columns state how many dollars are required to purchase one unit of a given foreign currency. For example, the quote for the Swiss franc for Friday was 0.8433. This means that $0.8433 (about 84 cents) was required to purchase one franc. Columns 4 and 5 (*Currency per U.S. Dollar*) show the foreign exchange rates from the opposite perspective, telling how many units of a foreign currency are required to buy a U.S. dollar. Again referring to Friday, it would take 1.1858 Swiss francs to purchase one U.S. dollar.

In a free market, exchange rates can and do change frequently, usually within a very narrow range. When the dollar price of pounds increases—for example, from $2.00 = 1 pound to $2.01 = 1 pound, the dollar has depreciated (weakened) relative to the pound. Currency **depreciation** means that it takes *more* units of a nation's currency to purchase a

Table 17.2	Foreign Exchange Quotations

Exchange Rates (Friday, January 28, 2005)				
Country	U.S. Dollar Equivalent Friday	Thursday	Currency per U.S. Dollar Friday	Thursday
Argentina (peso)	0.3417	0.3419	2.9265	2.9248
Canada (dollar)	0.8059	0.8077	1.2408	1.2381
China (yuang)	0.1208	0.1208	8.2781	8.2781
Japan (yen)	0.009674	0.009699	103.37	103.10
Mexico (peso)	0.0889	0.0886	11.2473	11.2931
Russia (ruble)	0.03562	0.03563	28.074	28.066
Switzerland (franc)	0.8433	0.8440	1.1858	1.1848
United Kingdom (pound)	1.8880	1.8878	0.5297	0.5297
Euro	1.3406	1.3035	0.7665	0.7672

Source: From Reuters, Currency Calculator, at http://www.reuters.com. See also, Federal Reserve Bank of New York, "Foreign Exchange Rates," available at http://www.newyorkfed.org/markets/fxrates/tenAm.cfm.

unit of some foreign currency. Conversely, when the dollar price of pounds decreases, say, from $2.00 = 1 pound to $1.99 = 1 pound, the value of the dollar has appreciated (strengthened) relative to the pound. Currency appreciation means that it takes *fewer* units of a nation's currency to purchase a unit of some foreign currency.

Referring to Table 17.2, look at columns 2 and 3 (*U.S. Dollar Equivalent*). Going forward in time from Thursday (January 27) to Friday (January 28), we see that the dollar cost of the euro increased from $1.3035 to $1.3406; the dollar thus depreciated against the euro. This means that the euro appreciated against the dollar. To verify this conclusion, refer to columns 4 and 5 of the table (*Currency per U.S. Dollar*). Going forward in time from Thursday to Friday, we see that the euro cost of the dollar decreased from 0.7672 euros = $1 to 0.7665 euros = $1. In similar fashion, we see that from Thursday to Friday the dollar appreciated against the Argentina peso from $0.3419 = 1 peso to $0.3417 = 1 peso; the peso thus depreciated against the dollar from 2.9248 pesos = $1 to 2.9265 pesos = $1.

IS A STRONG DOLLAR GOOD?
IS A WEAK DOLLAR BAD?

Is a "strong" U.S. dollar good? Is a "weak" dollar bad? When the dollar strengthens (appreciates) in the foreign exchange market, its value rises in relation to one or more other currencies. A strong dollar will buy more units of a foreign currency than previously. When the dollar weakens (depreciates) in the foreign exchange market, it will buy fewer units of a foreign currency than previously.

One result of a significantly stronger dollar is that the prices of foreign goods and services decrease for U.S. consumers. This may allow Americans to take that long-postponed vacation to Austria or Japan, or to buy a flashy Mercedes Benz that used to be too expensive.

Although U.S. consumers benefit from a strong dollar, U.S. exporters are hurt. A strong dollar means that IBM computers or Ford autos are more expensive for Europeans who, as a result, tend to purchase fewer U.S. products. Because it takes more of a foreign currency to purchase strong dollars, any product priced in dollars is more expensive overseas.

A weak dollar also hurts some people and benefits others. When the value of the dollar depreciates significantly in relation to another currency, prices of goods and services from that country rise equally significantly for U.S. consumers. Because it now takes more dollars to purchase the same amount of foreign currency to buy goods and services, U.S. consumers and U.S. firms that import products have reduced purchasing power. Therefore, they tend to buy fewer foreign goods.

At the same time, a weak dollar means prices for U.S. goods decline for foreigners, benefiting U.S. manufacturers. With a weak dollar, it takes fewer units of, say, British pounds to buy the right amount of U.S. dollars to purchase tractors produced by Caterpillar, Inc. Thus, consumers in Britain can buy tractors with less money and their purchases of tractors tend to increase.

Weak Dollar Is Bonanza for European Tourists

Jackie Murphy held up a white pair of jogging shoes for her husband, Edward, to examine in a Nike store aisle piled high with boxes of shoes. She smiled when she saw the price tag. "They're only $55!" said Murphy, a tourist from London, England. "Do you like them? Try them on."

Although Murphy is an experienced shopper—it is one of her favorite pastimes back home—she was shocked at her purchasing power on a vacation to Orlando in 2004. The power came primarily from a currency exchange rate that had the British pound approaching twice the value of the U.S. dollar. "The exchange rate is fantastic," said Edward Murphy, who sells electronics in London. "We couldn't have timed it better to come over on our vacation." In 2004, the dollar reached a record low against the euro and an 11-year low against the pound.

Many European and Canadian visitors followed the Murphy example, in part because of the inexpensive U.S. dollar. The American tourist industry was delighted about this situation. Because of the cheaper dollar, tourists could afford to stay longer, stay at nicer and more expensive hotels, take more tours, eat at more restaurants, and shop with bargain-basement enthusiasm. Adding to the bonanza for Europeans, air fares to and from the United States declined.

For example, the cheap dollar encouraged 15-year-old Molly Sanders of Liverpool, England, to purchase six heavy-metal T-shirts during a visit to Orlando, and her parents decided they could afford a road trip to Miami. The family booked hotel reservations and purchased theme park tickets in the United States rather than in Britain. By obtaining the tickets in dollars instead of pounds, they saved about $21 each day they went to the parks. The weaker dollar also allowed Molly to buy a large cup of Starbucks coffee in Miami for $1.80 rather than paying $2.80 in London. Similarly, an Apple iPod sold for $300 in Miami and $425 in London.

The exchange rate also led the British travel firm Virgin Holidays to renegotiate prices with the U.S. car rental companies and hotels that it uses. The new prices permitted the firm in 2004 to offer a package of airfare to Orlando, seven nights' accommodations, and rental car for 399 pounds, or 130 pounds less than what it previously offered. At the prevailing exchange rate, the discounted price was equal to $718, for about $234 in savings.[2]

EXCHANGE RATE DETERMINATION

What determines the equilibrium exchange value of a currency? Let us consider the exchange rate from the perspective of the United States—in dollars per unit of foreign currency. Like other prices, the exchange rate in a free market is determined by both supply and demand conditions.

---

[2] "Coming to America: Exchange Rate Attracts Foreign Visitors," *Yakima Herald Republic*, March 18, 2004, p. 6-A and "As Dollar Declines, Europeans See U.S. as Big Half-Off Sale," *The Wall Street Journal*, December 6, 2004, p. A1.

Figure 17.1 | Exchange Rate Determination

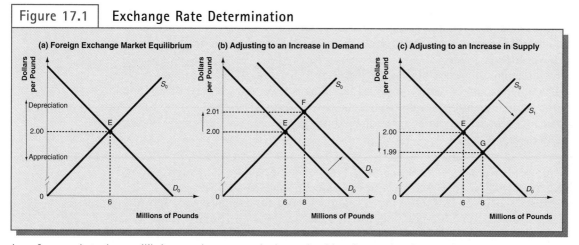

In a free market, the equilibrium exchange rate is determined by the market forces of supply and demand. In the figure, market equilibrium occurs at point *E*, where S_0 and D_0 intersect. All else being equal, an increase in the demand for foreign currency causes a depreciation of the dollar; an increase in the supply of foreign currency results in an appreciation of the dollar.

Figure 17.1 shows the market for the British pound. The demand curve for pounds, denoted by D_0, stems from the desire of Americans to purchase British goods, services, and assets. Like most demand schedules, the U.S. demand for pounds varies inversely with price. As the dollar price of the pound rises, British goods become more expensive for Americans, who thus purchase smaller quantities. Therefore, fewer pounds are demanded in the foreign exchange market.

The supply curve of pounds, denoted by S_0 in the figure, shows the quantity of pounds that will be offered to the market at various exchange rates. The British supply pounds to the market in order to purchase American goods, services, and assets. As the dollar price of the pound rises (and hence the pound price of the dollar falls), American goods become cheaper to the British, who are induced to purchase additional quantities. Therefore, more pounds are offered in the foreign exchange market to buy dollars with which to pay U.S. exporters.

As long as central bankers do not attempt to influence exchange rates, the **equilibrium exchange rate** is determined by the market forces of supply and demand. In Figure 17.1(a), exchange market equilibrium occurs at point *E*, where S_0 and D_0 intersect. Six million pounds will be traded at a price of $2 per pound. The foreign exchange market is precisely cleared, leaving neither an excess supply nor an excess demand for pounds.

With given supply and demand schedules of pounds, there is no reason for the pound's exchange rate to deviate from the equilibrium level. In reality, it is unlikely that the equilibrium exchange rate will remain very long at the existing level. This is because the forces that underlie the location of the supply and demand schedules tend to change frequently, causing shifts in the schedules.

Referring to Figure 17.1(b), suppose that an increase in the quantity of British goods demanded by Americans causes the demand for pounds to increase. Therefore, the dollar price of the pound will increase, which means that the dollar will *depreciate* against the pound. Conversely, a *decrease* in the demand for pounds causes the dollar to *appreciate*.

Now we will consider the effect of a change in the supply of pounds on the equilibrium exchange rate. Referring to Figure 17.1(c), suppose that expanding U.S. exports to the United Kingdom results in an *increase* in the supply of pounds on the foreign exchange market. This causes the dollar price of the pound to decrease, suggesting that the dollar will *appreciate* against the pound. Conversely, a *decrease* in the supply of pounds causes the dollar to *depreciate*.

We have learned that a shift in the demand or supply curve of a currency causes changes in the equilibrium price of the currency. What factors will induce shifts in these curves, causing the currency to depreciate or appreciate? We can analyze the behavior of exchange rates from two time periods, the long run and short run.

Long-Run Determinants of Exchange Rates

Changes in the long-run value (one, two, even five years) of the exchange rate are due to reactions of traders in the foreign exchange market to changes in four key factors: relative price levels, relative productivity levels, consumer preferences for domestic or foreign goods, and trade barriers. Note that these factors underlie trade in domestic and foreign goods and thus changes in the demand for exports and imports.

- **Relative prices.** Suppose the domestic price level increases rapidly in Mexico and remains constant in the United States. Mexican consumers will desire low-priced computers produced by Dell and Gateway, therefore increasing the supply of pesos. At the same time, U.S. consumers will buy fewer tomatoes from Mexico, reducing the demand for pesos. This combination of an increase in the supply of pesos and a decrease in the demand for pesos will cause the dollar price of the peso to fall, meaning the dollar has appreciated.

- **Relative productivity levels.** If German CD manufacturers become more productive than Canadian manufacturers, they can produce CDs more cheaply than their Canadian competitors can. Thus, Germany's exports of CDs to Canada tend to increase and its imports from Canada decrease. This results in an appreciation of Germany's euro against Canada's dollar.

- **Consumer preferences.** If preferences of Americans change in favor of Swiss watches, the demand for the Swiss franc will increase as Americans import more watches, causing a depreciation of the dollar against the franc.

- **Trade barriers.** Suppose that the U.S. government imposes tariffs on Toyota automobiles. By making Toyotas more expensive, the tariff discourages Americans from purchasing them. This results in a decrease in the demand for Japanese yen and an appreciation of the dollar against the yen.

Short-Run Determinants of Exchange Rates

Economists believe that the determinants of exchange rate fluctuations are rather different in the short run (a few weeks or even days) than the long run. Thus, we will consider the short-run time frame when analyzing exchange rates. In the short run, foreign-exchange transactions are dominated by transfers of investment funds (bank deposits and Treasury securities) that respond to differences in interest rates and to shifting expectations of future exchange rates; such transactions have a major influence on short-run exchange rates.

- **Relative interest rates.** A country with relatively *high* interest rates tends to find its currency's exchange value *appreciating*. You've already learned that a rise in interest rates makes an asset, such as a Treasury bill, more attractive to investors. Suppose that a tight monetary policy causes interest rates to be high in the United States, while an easy monetary policy causes interest rates to be low in Switzerland. Therefore, Swiss investors find the United States to be an attractive place to purchase Treasury bills. The increase in the demand for U.S. Treasury bills results in an increase in the supply of Swiss francs and thus a decrease in the dollar price of the franc. The dollar therefore appreciates against the franc.

- **Expectations of future exchange rates.** Suppose that an unanticipated rise in the growth rate of the U.S. money supply is interpreted as a signal that the U.S. inflation rate will rise, which in turn signals a possible depreciation in the dollar's exchange rate. This set of expectations causes Americans who intend to make purchases in Sweden to obtain krona prior to the antic-ipated depreciation of the dollar (when the krona would become more expensive in dollars). Accordingly, the demand for krona increases in the foreign exchange market. The increased demand for krona results in a depreciation of the dollar.[3]

EXCHANGE RATE SYSTEMS

We have learned that exchange rates are determined by actions of investors, exporters, tourists, and importers who participate in the foreign exchange market. However, govern-ments can also affect exchange rates. The extent and nature of government participation in foreign exchange markets define the various systems of exchange rates including floating exchange rates and fixed exchange rates.

Floating Exchange Rates

In a **floating exchange rate** system, governments and central banks do not participate in the foreign exchange market. Instead, currency values are established daily in the foreign exchange market by supply and demand conditions. With floating exchange rates, an equi-librium exchange rate equates the demand for and supply of the home currency. Changes in the exchange rate will ideally correct a payments imbalance by bringing about shifts in imports and exports of goods, services, and capital. The exchange rate depends on relative income levels among nations, relative interest rates, relative prices, and the like.

One advantage claimed for floating exchange rates is their adjustment efficiency. Floating exchange rates respond quickly to changing supply and demand conditions, clearing the market of shortages or surpluses of a given currency. Thus, governments will not have to restore balance in international payments through painful adjustments in fiscal policy or monetary policy. Instead, they can use these policies to combat domestic unemployment and inflation.

Although there are strong arguments in favor of floating exchange rates, this system is often considered to be of limited usefulness for bankers and businesspeople. Critics of floating exchange rates maintain that an unregulated market may lead to wide fluctua-tions in currency values, discouraging foreign trade and investment. Moreover, the greater freedom for domestic policymakers provided by floating exchange rates may result in their being more inclined to overspend, which contributes to inflation.

Fixed Exchange Rates

Rather than allowing exchange rates to be determined by market forces, governments sometimes attempt to maintain completely fixed exchange rates.[4] Today, **fixed exchange rates** are used primarily by developing nations that maintain ties to a key currency such as the U.S. dollar. A key currency is one that is widely traded on world money markets, has

---

[3] Concurrently, the Swedes, who hold the same set of expectations, will be less willing to give up krona in exchange for dollars that will soon decrease in value. The supply of krona offered in the foreign exchange market decreases. The increased demand for krona and the decreased supply of krona thus result in a depreciation of the dollar. In this way, future expectations of a currency's depreciation can be self-fulfilling.

[4] How do central banks attempt to maintain fixed exchange rates? For example, to prevent the dollar from depre-ciating against the euro, the Federal Reserve could purchase dollars on the foreign exchange market, drawing on its holdings of euros. The increase in the demand for the dollar thus promotes an increase in the exchange value of the dollar against the euro. Instead, the Fed could adopt a contractionary monetary policy that will increase domestic interest rates and attract European purchases of American securities. As more dollars are demanded by Europeans, the value of the dollar will rise against the euro.

demonstrated relatively stable value over time, and has been accepted as a means of international settlement. Fixed exchange rates are also used when a group of countries form an economic bloc, such as the European Monetary Union, discussed later in this chapter.

One reason why nations choose to tie their currencies to a key currency is that it is used as a means of international settlement. Consider a Venezuelan importer who wants to purchase Argentine beef over the next year. If the Argentine exporter is unsure of what the Venezuelan bolivar will purchase in one year, he might reject the bolivar in settlement. Similarly, the Venezuelan importer might doubt the value of Argentina's peso. One solution is for the contract to be written in terms of a key currency, such as the U.S. dollar.

Maintaining ties to a key currency provides several benefits for developing nations. First, the prices of many developing nations' traded products are determined primarily in the markets of industrialized nations such as the United States. By linking their currencies, say, to the dollar, these nations can stabilize the domestic currency prices of their imports and exports. Second, many developing nations with high inflation have linked to the dollar (the United States has relatively low inflation) in order to exert restraint on domestic prices and reduce inflation. By making the commitment to stabilize their exchange rates against the dollar, governments hope to convince their citizens that they are willing to adopt the responsible monetary policies that are necessary to achieve low inflation.

The exchange rate system used by the United States is a combination of fixed and floating exchange rates. Known as a **managed floating exchange rate**, the system allows the dollar to generally float in the foreign exchange market according to the market forces of supply and demand. However, governmental intervention may be used to stabilize the dollar's value when the foreign exchange market becomes disorderly and disruptive to international trade and investment.

MONETARY INTEGRATION FOR EUROPE AND THE UNITED STATES

The globalization of economies has promoted opportunities and challenges for the international monetary system. Let us consider two challenges that are important for the new century.

The Euro: A Common Currency for Europe

One important challenge for the international monetary system is the development of the European Union. The **European Union (EU)** is a regional economic bloc consisting of 25 European nations. The primary objective of the EU has been to create an economic bloc in which trade and other transactions take place freely among member nations. From the 1950s to the 1990s, the EU succeeded in eliminating trade restrictions among member countries, allowing for the free movement of labor and capital within the union, and adopting common policies toward competition and agriculture.

In 1991, the EU agreed to achieve monetary unification in 1999 for those nations eligible to participate. Participation in the monetary unification would require nations to fulfill economic goals concerning inflation, public finances, interest rates, and exchange rates. Nations that participate in the EU would have a common currency, a single exchange rate, a single monetary policy, and a single central bank to oversee the monetary policy.

In 2002, eleven European countries united in the **European Monetary Union (EMU)** replaced their individual currencies, such as the German mark and French franc, with a single currency, the **euro**. At that point, the euro became the single currency in circulation throughout the monetary union. If the monetary union expands according to plans, in two or three decades, the euro will be in use throughout most of western and central Europe.

international
ECONOMICS IN ACTION

Euro Facts

2002 was a momentous year in Europe because it marked the introduction of euro notes and coins into the member economies of the European Monetary Union. What are the characteristics of the euro?

Referring to the above euro note, the sign for the new single currency looks likes an *E* with two horizontal parallel lines across it. It was inspired by the Greek letter epsilon, in reference to the cradle of European civilization and to the first letter of the word "Europe." The parallel lines represent the stability of the euro.

What do euro notes look like? The designs of euro notes are symbolic and closely related to the historical phases that make up Europe's architectural heritage. Windows and gateways dominate the front side of each banknote as symbols of the spirit of openness and cooperation in the EU. The reverse side of each banknote features a bridge from a particular age, a metaphor for communication among the people of Europe and between Europe and the rest of the world.

Like U.S. currency, euro notes and coins come in a variety of denominations. There are seven euro notes and eight euro coins. The denominations of the notes range from 500 to 5 euro, and the coins range from 2 euro to 1 euro cent. Vending machines and other coin- or note-operated automatic machines in the participating member countries have been adapted for use with euro notes and coins.

The euro could prove a strong alternative to the U.S. dollar as a key currency for the global financial system. Financial markets will conduct transactions in euros, and central banks will want to hold some of their reserves in these currencies.

The EMU also resulted in the creation of a new **European Central Bank** to take control of monetary policy and exchange rate policy for the member countries. This central bank alone controls the supply of euros, sets the euro interest rate, and maintains permanently fixed exchange rates for the member countries. With a common central bank, the central bank of each participating nation would perform operations similar to those of the 12 regional Federal Reserve Banks in the United States.

For Americans, the benefits of a common currency are easy to understand. Americans know they can walk into a McDonald's or Burger King anywhere in the United States and purchase hamburgers with dollar bills in their purses and wallets. The same is not true in European countries. Because each is a distinct nation with its own currency, a French person cannot buy something at a German store without first exchanging French francs for German marks. This would be like someone from St. Louis having to exchange Missouri currency for Illinois currency each time she visits Chicago. To make matters worse, because marks and francs float against each other within a range, the number of marks the French traveler receives today will probably differ from the number he would have received yesterday or tomorrow. On top of exchange rate uncertainty, the traveler also must pay a fee to exchange the currency, making a trip across the border a costly proposition indeed. Although the costs to individuals may be limited because of the small quantities of money involved, firms can incur much larger costs. By replacing the various European currencies with a single currency, the euro, the EMU can avoid such costs.

On the downside, a lack of exchange rate flexibility and a loss of national monetary policy may prolong regional economic downturns. A country cannot lower interest rates when it goes into recession unless all the other countries agree that this is a good policy, perhaps prolonging a localized recession. For example, the fact that Texas could not lower interest rates when a collapse in oil prices sent its economy into recession in 1986 may have extended Texas's recession.

Indeed, the EMU is a groundbreaking monetary experiment. Never before have politically independent nations with histories of monetary independence and longstanding central banks given up that independence to form a common central bank and adopt a single currency. The success of the EMU remains an open question.

The Dollar: A Common Currency for the Americas?

Another challenge for the international monetary system is the integration of the U.S. dollar into the monetary systems of other countries in North America and South America.

Many developing economies such as Ecuador have experienced high and unstable inflation rates when their governments increased the money supply to finance higher levels of government spending. High and unstable inflation rates result in a more unstable investment climate and a lower rate of economic growth. When people lose faith in the domestic currency, it is not uncommon for another currency to be used as a medium of exchange in the domestic economy. Because of its relative stability and use as an international currency, the U.S. dollar frequently is used for this purpose. **Dollarization** is said to occur when the U.S. dollar replaces the domestic currency as the official medium of exchange.

Advocates of dollarization suggest that developing economies that replace their less stable domestic currency with the U.S. dollar experience a lower and more stable inflation rate. A lower and more stable inflation rate, in turn, is expected to lead to a higher level of investment and a faster rate of economic growth. This benefit is larger when the domestic monetary authorities have established a poor track record in maintaining a stable domestic money supply.

Opponents of dollarization note that the domestic monetary authorities have no control over the domestic money supply under this policy. The government of a dollarized economy will not be able to use discretionary monetary policy to deal with domestic macroeconomic problems. If the domestic economy experiences a business cycle that closely corresponds to the U.S. economy's business cycle, this may present less of a problem because the U.S. Federal Reserve might engage in appropriate monetary policy responses. Even if the Federal

Reserve can be trusted to engage in "appropriate" policy responses, many countries are still reluctant to cede their control over domestic macroeconomic policy to a foreign agency. Countries that replace their national currencies with the dollar will also lose the profit made by governments that issue money (profit exists because the purchasing power of coin and paper money exceeds the cost of producing the money).

Many U.S. policymakers argue that dollarization is an indication of the relatively high rate of success that the Federal Reserve has experienced in maintaining a stable currency in recent years. There is some concern, though, that foreign governments will attempt to exert political pressure to encourage the Federal Reserve to pursue monetary policies that are not consistent with U.S. monetary policy objectives. In the future, the dollarization debate is likely to be a major policy issue in the United States and in countries experiencing currency instability.

This chapter examined the U.S. balance of payments and the markets in which Americans exchange dollars for other currencies. The next chapter will broaden our understanding of globalization by considering alternative economic systems and the economic problems of developing countries.

CHECK POINT

1. What is the foreign exchange rate? What does it mean when a currency depreciates (appreciates) in the foreign exchange market?

2. Identify the major factors that determine the exchange value of the dollar in the long run and the short run.

3. Discuss the major features of floating exchange rates and fixed exchange rates.

4. What are the advantages and disadvantages of the European Monetary Union's replacement of its currencies with the euro?

Chapter Summary

1. The balance of payments is a record of a country's international trading, borrowing, and lending. In the balance of payments, inflows of funds from foreigners to the United States are noted as receipts; outflows of funds from the United States to foreigners are noted as payments.

2. The balance of payments has two components, the current account and the capital and financial account. The current account includes the dollar value of transactions in currently produced goods and services, investment income, and unilateral transfers. If the monetary inflows on these accounts are greater (less) than monetary outflows, the current account balance is a surplus (deficit). The second component of the balance of payments is the capital and financial account, which includes international purchases or sales of assets such as real estate, corporate stocks and bonds, and government securities. The capital and financial account balance is a surplus (deficit) if domestic residents sell more (fewer) assets to foreigners than they purchase from foreigners. Because the current account balance and capital and financial account balance always equal each other, any current account deficit (surplus) must be balanced by a capital and financial account surplus (deficit).

3. In recent years, the United States has realized a deficit in its current account. Thus, foreigners lend or give us the funds to make up the difference between our imports and our exports. It would not be an overstatement to say that we borrow so much from foreigners to finance our

current account deficits that we sell them pieces of America. Those pieces consist primarily of real estate and corporate stock. However, foreigners also lend us billions of dollars each year in the form of purchases of government and corporate securities and other debt instruments.

4. The buying and selling of currencies generally takes place in the foreign exchange market. This market does not involve sending large loads of currency from one country to another. Typically, it involves electronic balances. Dollar-denominated balances in computers in the United States or other countries are traded for computer-housed balances around the world that are denominated in yen, pounds, francs, and the like. In short, when currency is traded, paper and metal are not the usual media of exchange.

5. Most daily newspapers publish foreign exchange rates for major currencies. The exchange rate is the price of one currency in terms of another. Currency depreciation (appreciation) means that it takes more (fewer) units of a nation's currency to purchase a unit of some foreign currency. Among the major factors that determine the equilibrium exchange rate in a free market are productivity levels, consumer preferences, relative prices, trade barriers, relative interest rates, and expectations of future exchange rates.

6. Although exchange rates are determined by supply and demand, governments can affect exchange rates in various ways. The extent and nature of government participation in foreign exchange markets defines the various systems of exchange rates. These systems include floating exchange rates and fixed exchange rates.

7. As part of its strategy for forming a regional economic bloc, the European Union has pursued monetary integration. For participating nations, monetary integration implies a common currency, a single exchange rate, a single monetary policy, and a single central bank to oversee the monetary policy.

Key Terms and Concepts

balance of payments (402)

current account (402)

balance of trade (trade balance) (403)

services (403)

income (403)

unilateral transfers (403)

current account balance (403)

capital and financial account (403)

capital and financial account balance (403)

statistical discrepancy (404)

foreign exchange market (407)

exchange rate (407)

depreciation (407)

appreciation (408)

equilibrium exchange rate (410)

floating exchange rate system (412)

fixed exchange rates (412)

managed floating exchange rates (413)

European Union (EU) (413)

European Monetary Union (EMU) (413)

euro (413)

European Central Bank (414)

dollarization (415)

Self-Test: Multiple-Choice Questions

1. The current account of the balance of payments includes all of the following *except*

   a. flows of international investment.
   b. unilateral transfers.

    c. trade in merchandise.
    d. trade in services.

2. A surplus on the current account

    a. results in a surplus on the capital and financial account.
    b. results in a deficit on the capital and financial account.
    c. has no relation to the capital and financial account.
    d. none of the above.

3. Which of the following will *not* increase the demand for dollars in the foreign exchange market?

    a. Exports of Boeing jetliners to China
    b. Travel by Swiss tourists in the United States
    c. The desire of German investors to purchase U.S. Treasury bills
    d. Imports of Honda Accords from Japan

4. If the United States sells more assets to foreigners than it purchases from foreigners, the U.S.

    a. capital and financial account balance shows a surplus.
    b. services balance shows a deficit.
    c. current account balance shows a surplus.
    d. unilateral transfers balance shows a deficit.

5. American tourists in Mexico would prefer

    a. a depreciation of the dollar against the peso.
    b. an appreciation of the dollar against the peso.
    c. no change in the value of the dollar against the peso.
    d. none of the above.

6. Under a system of floating exchange rates, the exchange value of the dollar would depreciate if

    a. the U.S. economy grows more slowly than the rest of the world.
    b. U.S. consumer preferences worsen for goods of the foreign country.
    c. the United States has a higher inflation rate than the rest of the world.
    d. the United States has higher interest rates than the rest of the world.

7. The broadest account of the balance of payments is the

    a. unilateral transfers account.
    b. current account.
    c. merchandise trade account.
    d. investment income account.

8. Which of the following would give rise to a flow of funds from foreigners to the United States?

    a. Sears purchases shirts from a manufacturer in Taiwan.
    b. French investors collect interest on their holdings of U.S. Treasury bills.
    c. A German student spends a year studying at Boston University.
    d. Tom Sullivan makes a remittance to his relatives in Ireland.

9. If a Toyota automobile costs 4 million yen in Japan and the yen price of the dollar is 133.33 yen = $1, the dollar cost of the Toyota is

    a. $25,000.
    b. $30,000.
    c. $35,000.
    d. $40,000.

10. In the short run, the dollar's exchange value is determined by

    a. tariffs and quotas.
    b. productivity levels.
    c. consumer preferences for domestic and foreign goods.
    d. relative interest rates.

Answers to Multiple-Choice Questions

1. a   **2.** b   **3.** d   **4.** a   **5.** b   **6.** c   **7.** b   **8.** c   **9.** b   **10.** d

Study Questions and Problems

1. Indicate whether each of the following items represents a monetary inflow or outflow on the U.S. balance of payments:

   a. A U.S. importer purchases a shipload of French wine.
   b. A Japanese automobile firm builds an assembly plant in Kentucky.
   c. A British manufacturer exports machinery to Taiwan on a U.S. vessel.
   d. A U.S. college student spends a year studying in Switzerland.
   e. U.S. charities donate food to people in drought-plagued Africa.
   f. Japanese investors collect interest income on their holdings of U.S. government securities.
   g. A German resident sends money to her relatives in the United States.
   h. Lloyds of London sells an insurance policy to a U.S. firm.
   i. A Swiss resident receives dividends on his IBM stock.

2. Concerning a country's balance of payments, when would its current account be in surplus (deficit)? What would a current account surplus (deficit) imply for the capital and financial account? Is a current account deficit necessarily bad?

3. Why are some economists concerned that the United States borrows too much from abroad?

4. Table 17.3 summarizes hypothetical transactions, in billions of U.S. dollars, that took place during a given year.

   a. Calculate the U.S. merchandise trade and current account balances.
   b. Which of these balances pertains to the net borrowing (lending) position of the United States? How would you describe that position?

Table 17.3	International Transactions of the United States (billions of dollars)
U.S. capital inflow	100
Merchandise exports	375
Services imports	−20
Income receipts from abroad	35
Statistical discrepancy	30
Merchandise imports	−450
Unilateral transfers, net	−45
Services exports	55
Income payments abroad	−25
U.S. capital outflow	−55

Table 17.4	Supply of and Demand for British Pounds	

Quantity of Pounds Supplied	Dollars per Pound	Quantity of Pounds Demanded
50	$2.50	10
40	2.00	20
30	1.50	30
20	1.00	40
10	0.50	50

5. Table 17.4 shows supply and demand schedules for the British pound. Assume that exchange rates are flexible.

   a. The equilibrium exchange rate equals _____. At this exchange rate, how many pounds will be purchased, and at what cost in terms of dollars?

   b. Suppose the exchange rate is $2.00 per pound. At this exchange rate, there is an excess (supply/demand) of pounds. This imbalance causes (an increase/a decrease) in the dollar price of the pound, which leads to (a/an) _____ in the quantity of pounds supplied and (a/an) _____ in the quantity of pounds demanded.

   c. Suppose the exchange rate is $1.00 per pound. At this exchange rate, there is an excess (supply/demand) for pounds. This imbalance causes (an increase/a decrease) in the price of the pound, which leads to (a/an) _____ in the quantity of pounds supplied and (a/an) _____ in the quantity of pounds demanded.

6. If the exchange rate changes from $1.70 = 1 pound to $1.68 = 1 pound, what does this mean for the dollar? For the pound? What if the exchange rate changes from $1.70 = 1 pound to $1.72 = 1 pound?

7. Table 17.5 gives hypothetical dollar/franc exchange values for Wednesday, May 1, 2003.

   a. Fill in the last two columns of the table with the reciprocal price of the dollar in terms of the franc.

   b. On Wednesday, the price of the two currencies was _____ dollars per franc, or _____ francs per dollar.

   c. From Tuesday to Wednesday, the dollar (appreciated/depreciated) against the franc; the franc (appreciated/depreciated) against the dollar.

   d. On Wednesday, the cost of buying 100 francs was _____ dollars; the cost of buying 100 dollars was _____ francs.

8. Assuming market-determined exchange rates, use supply and demand schedules for pounds to analyze the effect on the exchange rate (dollars per pound) between the U.S. dollar and the British pound under each of the following circumstances:

Table 17.5	Dollar/Franc Exchange Values			

	U.S. $ Equivalent		Currency per U.S.$	
	Wed.	Tue.	Wed.	Tue.
Switzerland (franc)	0.7207	0.7225		

a. Voter polls suggest that Britain's conservative government will be replaced by radicals who pledge to nationalize all foreign-owned assets.
b. The British economy and U.S. economy slide into a recession, but the British recession is less severe than the U.S. recession.
c. The Federal Reserve adopts a tight monetary policy that dramatically increases U.S. interest rates.
d. The United Kingdom encounters severe inflation while price stability exists in the United States.
e. Fears of terrorism reduce U.S. tourism in the United Kingdom.
f. The British government invites U.S. firms to invest in British oil fields.
g. The rate of productivity growth in the United Kingdom decreases sharply.
h. An economic boom occurs in the United Kingdom, which induces the British to purchase more U.S.-made autos, trucks, and computers.
i. Ten-percent inflation occurs in both the United Kingdom and the United States.

9. Explain why you agree or disagree with each of the following statements:

a. A nation's currency will depreciate if its inflation rate is less than that of its trading partners.
b. A nation whose interest rate falls more rapidly than that of other nations can expect the exchange value of its currency to depreciate.
c. A nation whose economy grows more slowly than its major trading partners can expect the exchange value of its currency to appreciate.
d. A nation's currency will appreciate if its interest rate rises relative to that of its trading partners and its income level falls relative to that of its trading partners.

10. Suppose the United States has a system of managed floating exchange rates. What policies could the Federal Reserve use to prevent the dollar from depreciating beyond acceptable levels? How about appreciating beyond acceptable levels? What are the weaknesses of these policies?

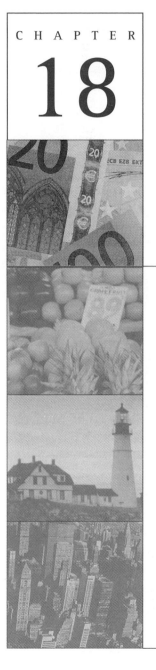

Economic Systems and the Developing Countries

Chapter objectives

After reading this chapter, you should be able to:

1. Discuss how a market economy, command economy, and mixed economy answer the so-called fundamental economic questions.

2. Explain why the transition economies began moving toward capitalism beginning in the 1990s.

3. Discuss the obstacles to economic growth faced by developing nations.

4. Identify sources of aid for developing countries.

economics IN CONTEXT

If Rip Van Winkle woke up in 2005 after a 30-year sleep, he would be surprised about the world. In 1974, at the beginning of his slumber, about one-third of the world's population lived under Chinese-style or Soviet-style central planning dictated by the Communist party leadership. Although these economies were not wealthy, they were muddling along without immediate fear of disintegration.

Imagine Rip Van Winkle's shock on waking in 2005. The Soviet empire has collapsed. Germany has reunited. China has embraced capitalism and has realized phenomenal growth. Many developing countries of Latin America, Eastern Europe, and East Asia are attracting large sums of investment. In spite of these changes, however, about 3 billion people, or nearly half the world's population, live on $2 or less a day.

In this chapter, we discuss the various economic systems that nations prefer to implement and what underlies their choices. We also examine why some nations are rich and others are poor, consider obstacles that have prevented poor nations from developing, and identify policies that might be formed to help them increase their growth rates.

ECONOMIC SYSTEMS AND THE FUNDAMENTAL ECONOMIC QUESTIONS

Every society, regardless of its wealth and power, must make certain decisions regarding the production and distribution of goods and services: (1) *What* goods will be produced, and in what quantities? (2) *How* shall these goods be produced? (3) *For whom* shall the goods be produced? These questions are known as the **fundamental economic questions.**

The first economic decision, what goods to produce, is influenced by the problem of scarcity, which means that society cannot have all the goods that it would like to have. Producing more of one good requires producing less of another good. In the United States, most production is geared toward consumer goods, while less effort is devoted to the production of military goods. In the former Soviet Union, a relatively large share of national output went to military goods, which led to the frustration of Soviet consumers. Japan has emphasized investment in plants and equipment to produce goods such as autos and consumer electronics while allocating a negligible share of national output to military equipment.

After deciding what goods to produce, a society must determine how to combine scarce resources and technology to produce these goods. For example, a shoe can be manufactured primarily by hand (labor), primarily by machine (capital), or partially by hand and machine. Which production method uses society's scarce resources most efficiently? Should college students be taught in large classes by professors (highly skilled labor) or in small sections by graduate teaching assistants (less-skilled labor)?

Another business decision involves the location of production. The growth of the global economy, coupled with technological advances, enables many companies to move production easily around the world. For example, Toyota, Inc., shifts the assembly of its autos between its plants in Japan and the United States in response to changing market conditions. Also, Kellogg's Company (of Battle Creek, Michigan) produces breakfast cereals in more than 20 countries and sells them in more than 150 countries. Moreover, U.S.

companies haven't made televisions for years. The last U.S. producer, Zenith, Inc., shifted television assembly to Mexico in the 1980s to cut labor costs. By deciding to close its U.S. factories, Zenith admitted that its U.S.-made televisions could not compete against lower-cost foreign competitors.

The final decision, for whom to produce, refers to the distribution of output among different groups within society. Who should receive the computers, VCRs, automobiles, and other goods produced by our economy? Should the distribution of goods and services among households be based on their ability to buy them? For example, students majoring in engineering generally find jobs that pay much higher incomes than students majoring in education or sociology. So engineers get more goods and services than teachers. Although there are significant exceptions, whites tend to earn more than minorities; men tend to earn more than women; and college graduates tend to earn more than high school graduates. Moreover, Americans generally earn more than Africans and Asians. The income inequality around the world contributes to greatly different standards of living. Instead of distributing goods on the basis of ability to pay, would "need" be a better criterion?

The manner in which these decisions are made depends on a society's economic system. The three broad types of economies are the market economy, the command economy, and the mixed economy. Let us consider the main features of each type of economy.

Market Economy

A **market economy**, also called **capitalism**, is a free-enterprise system rooted in private property and markets. Individuals and businesses have the freedom to possess and dispose of goods, services, and resources as they choose. Buyers and sellers are brought together in markets. Buyers come to markets expressing their desire to purchase property in the form of goods, services, and resources at various prices. Sellers come to markets expressing their desire to supply property in the form of goods, services, and resources at various prices. In this manner, property is exchanged at freely negotiated prices.

Because proponents of a market system contend that it leads to production efficiency, high employment, and economic growth, the need for governmental control is small. The extreme case of a market economy, where the government has almost no economic role, is called a **laissez-faire economy**; in this case, the main purpose of government is to protect private property and to provide a legal system allowing free markets.

In a market economy, goods and services are produced and resources are supplied in competitive markets consisting of many sellers and buyers. This means that economic power is decentralized because it is widely distributed. A system of prices and markets, with profits and losses, determines *what, how,* and *for whom* to produce. Because suppliers are self-interested and attempt to maximize profits, they tend to combine resources in such a manner as to produce a good or service at the lowest cost. Suppliers also make production decisions according to the dollar expenditures of consumers who decide what goods to produce. Goods and services are distributed to consumers who have the income to purchase them. Households that have more income, due to their possessing more valuable resources, can afford more goods and services.

Although a market economy recognizes economic freedom and human initiative, it is not without problems. For example, the motivation to manufacture goods at least cost could lead to business firms making production decisions with little regard for the safety of workers or the quality of the environment. Firms might be able to cut costs by adopting unsafe working procedures for employees or by dumping hazardous wastes into the environment. Also, the ability of individual consumers to determine what goods and services should be produced is weakened if a small number of firms dominate a market. Furthermore, the operation of a market economy does not guarantee full employment for workers or the absence of poverty; it also does not ensure that firms will produce goods that are safe for use by consumers.

Command Economy

By contrast, a **command economy** (also termed a planned economy or communism) is one in which government makes all decisions concerning production and distribution. In a command economy, government owns virtually all means of production such as land and capital. Business firms are also government owned. Economic decisions regarding the organization of production, the level of resource use, and the prices of goods and services are made by government planners. Individual production units receive detailed plans and orders that carry the weight of law. The government also establishes the composition and distribution of output as well as wage levels for workers. In short, in a command economy, the government answers the fundamental questions of *what, how,* and *for whom* to produce through its control of resources and its power to enforce decisions.

Central planning was the primary method of organization in the former Soviet Union, other nations in Eastern Europe, and China prior to their movement toward market economies in the late 1980s. By the 1990s, command economies were disappearing rapidly. Cuba and North Korea, however, still make extensive use of central planning.

Advocates of a command economy contend that the system is superior to a market economy in achieving a fair distribution of income. Due to government ownership of the means of production, small groups of people are prevented from acquiring a disproportionate fraction of a nation's wealth. It is also argued that central planning can help decrease unemployment by channeling additional labor into production processes. For example, farming can be carried out by labor using hand tools or capital equipment such as tractors. If planners desire to keep agricultural workers employed, they will mandate that less equipment and more labor be used in farming. Finally, it is maintained that national goals can be easily formulated and pursued by a small number of central planners.

Central planning, however, can be criticized on the grounds that it is inconsistent with economic freedom and that it leads to an elite class of government bureaucrats. Central planning can also suffer from the problem of overproduction of some goods and underproduction of other goods. This is because the decisions of planners regarding the types and amounts of output produced may not coincide with the preferences of consumers. Moreover, the absence of a profit motive for innovation and entrepreneurship may lead to inferior product quality, production inefficiencies, and reduced economic growth. Finally, in an economy where central planners are distant from actual production operations, long-term environmental damage may occur. As witnessed in Eastern Europe, serious water and air pollution has been a consequence of the failure of central planners to include environmental quality in many of their decisions.

Mixed Economy

No modern economy exactly fits the description of the polar categories of a market economy and a command economy. Instead, all economies are **mixed economies,** with elements of both market and command.

In a mixed economy, the most important decision mechanism is the market that provides answers to *what, how,* and *for whom* to produce. However, the government plays an important role in modifying the operation of the market. Government establishes laws and rules that regulate economic behavior, provides public services such as education and national defense, regulates pollution and product safety, initiates policies to combat unemployment and inflation, modifies the distribution of income, and the like. In short,

international
ECONOMICS IN ACTION

Who's Free, Who's Not

Table 18.1 Index of Economic Freedom			
Free	Mostly Free	Mostly Unfree	Repressed
Hong Kong	Germany	Croatia	Tajikistan
Singapore	Austria	Uganda	Haiti
Luxembourg	Bahrain	Lebanon	Venezuela
Estonia	Cyprus	Moldova	Uzbekistan
Ireland	Lithuania	Swaziland	Iran
New Zealand	El Salvador	Guyana	Cuba
United Kingdom	Bahamas	Sri Lanka	Burma
United States	Italy	China	North Korea

Source: From The Heritage Foundation, *2005 Index of Economic Freedom*, at http://www.index.heritage.org.

Which nations of the world have the most economic freedom? Each year, The Heritage Foundation publishes its *Index of Economic Freedom*, which ranks the world's economies into 10 categories: banking and finance, investment flows, monetary policy, financial burden of government, trade policy, wages and prices, government intervention in the economy, property rights, regulation, and black markets. Table 18.1 gives examples from the 2005 *Index of Economic Freedom*. Hong Kong and Singapore had the highest degree of economic freedom, and economic freedom was strong throughout North America and Europe. Economic freedom was least in Burma and North Korea.

A good way to understand the implications of the table is to compare average per-capita incomes. The average person living in a mostly unfree or repressed economy in 2005 lived a life of poverty on only about $3,000 a year. Compare this with the prosperous residents of the world's free economies, where the average per-capita income was about $24,000, or nearly eight times greater. Simply put, economic freedom has a major impact on the difference between poverty and prosperity, according to The Heritage Foundation.

the objective of a mixed economy is to leave economic decisions to the market when it operates well, but to intervene in the economy when the market outcome is unacceptable.

Indeed, the blend of market and command varies among mixed economies. Today, most economic decisions in the United States are made in the marketplace, although government often modifies the operation of the market. However, governments are more heavily involved in the economy in Sweden and Denmark than in the United States. These nations embrace **socialism** as an economic system.

Socialists believe that a country's resources should be used according to an overall economic plan formulated by manufacturers, farmers, workers, and government officials working together. By such planning, socialists hope to adjust production to the needs of the people. Although the forces of supply and demand may influence production and prices under the socialist economic plan, many decisions regarding how much to produce and what to charge will be made by political authorities. Many socialists also call for redistribution of wealth through taxation. They favor laws to help the aged, the unemployed, the disabled, and other people in deed. Moreover, many socialists believe that the government should provide free education and medical services to everyone and should help all citizens obtain safe and sanitary housing at rents they can afford. Indeed, implementing socialist goals calls for a relatively large amount of government activity in a mixed economy.

CHECK POINT

1. Identify the fundamental economic questions that all economies must answer.

2. How do a market economy, a command economy, and a mixed economy answer the fundamental economic questions?

3. Why are all contemporary economies of the world best classified as mixed economies?

4. Why do nations such as Sweden and Denmark favor socialism rather than capitalism?

TRANSITION ECONOMIES

By the 1990s, the centrally planned economies in the former Soviet Union and Eastern Europe had collapsed and had begun switching to capitalism. Also, the Chinese economy started embracing capitalism. Let us consider some of the reforms that these countries have taken to introduce capitalism into their economic systems.

Eastern European Countries

In 1989, the world began to witness unprecedented developments in Eastern Europe, as many countries moved toward democracy and economic reform. Countries such as Hungary, Poland, Czechoslovakia, and the Soviet Union discarded their centrally controlled state economies and moved toward systems in which private ownership of property predominated and most resources were allocated through markets. These transitions reflected the failure of central planning systems to provide either political freedom or a decent standard of living.

In 1990, for example, per-capita real income in the Soviet Union was less than one-tenth of per-capita real income in the United States. Another example is the case of the two Germanys. Starting from the same point at the end of World War II and sharing a common culture, East Germany and West Germany followed two different paths. East Germany became an industrial wasteland with rundown, outmoded factories and a polluted environment, while West Germany achieved one of the highest living standards in the world.

The fundamental motivation for change in Eastern Europe was the failure of the economies there to generate a high standard of living for their people. The economic policies pursued in these countries failed because they were unable to provide adequate incentives for producers to supply efficiently the goods and services that consumers wanted to purchase. Widespread use of price controls, reliance on inefficient public enterprises, extensive barriers to competition with the rest of the world, and government regulation of production and investment all obstructed the normal operation of markets. The lack of enforceable property rights severely restricted incentives for entrepreneurs.

Over time, the weaknesses of the political and economic systems of Eastern Europe and the contrasting success of the market-oriented systems became obvious. This created pressure that led to the collapse of Eastern Europe's communist governments.

Economists generally agree that Eastern Europe's transition toward a healthy market economy requires major restructuring of their economies: Sound fiscal and monetary policies must be established, domestic price controls must be removed, economies must be opened to international market forces, private property rights must be established along with a legal system to protect these rights, domestic competition must be promoted, and government's involvement in the economy must be reduced.

China

For more than 2,000 years, China maintained a policy of self-reliance that caused its economy to lag far behind advanced countries. In 1978, China initiated a new policy of economic reforms, which are transforming one of the poorest economies in the world into one of the fastest growing. What underlies this transformation?

Modern China began in 1949, when a revolutionary communist movement captured control of the nation. Soon after the communist takeover, China instituted a Soviet model of central planning with emphasis on rapid economic growth, particularly industrial growth. The state took over urban manufacturing industry, collectivized agriculture, eliminated household farming, and established compulsory production quotas.

By the1970s, China could see its once-poor neighbors—Japan, Singapore, Taiwan, South Korea, and Hong Kong—enjoying extraordinary growth and prosperity. This led to China's "marketizing" its economy through small, step-by-step changes to minimize economic disruption and political opposition. In agriculture and industry, reforms were made to increase the role of the producing unit, to increase individual incentives, and to reduce the role of state planners. Most goods were sold for market-determined—not state-controlled—prices. Greater competition was allowed both between new firms and between new firms and state firms; by 2000, nonstate firms manufactured about 75 percent of China's industrial output. Moreover, China opened its economy to foreign investment and joint ventures. The Chinese government's monopoly over foreign trade was also disbanded; in its place, economic zones were established in which firms could keep foreign exchange earnings and hire and fire workers.

By the early 2000s, China had made all of the easy economic adjustments in its transition toward capitalism: letting farmers sell their own produce and opening its doors to foreign investors and salespeople. Other reforms still needed addressing: (1) a massive restructuring of state-owned industries, which were losing money; (2) a cleanup of bankrupt state banks; (3) the creation of a social security system in a society that once guaranteed a job for life; and (4) establishment of a monetary system with a central bank free of Communist Party or government control. If China were to shut down money-losing enterprises, millions of workers would be laid off with no benefits; their addition to the 100 million-plus workers already adrift in China could be volatile. In addition, banks that lent the state companies cash would require cash infusions if bankruptcies increased in the state sector. Such loans could render a central bank monetary policy ineffective and could fuel inflation.

Although China has dismantled much of its centrally planned economy and has permitted free enterprise to replace it, political freedoms have not increased. Recall the Chinese government's use of military force to end a pro-democracy demonstration in

Beijing's Tiananmen Square in 1989, which led to loss of life and demonstrated the Communist Party's determination to maintain its political power. China's evolution toward capitalism has thus consisted of expanded use of market forces under a communist political system. Today, China describes itself as a *socialist market economy*.

CHECK POINT

1. In the 1990s, why did the transition economies begin to move away from central planning and toward capitalism?

2. What changes did the transition economies make when they began marketizing their economies? Is marketizing an economy good for all people in Eastern Europe or China? Explain.

THE ECONOMICS OF DEVELOPING COUNTRIES

We have learned that no one economic system fulfills the objectives of all nations. As a result, nations embrace a variety of economic systems that embody elements of capitalism and central planning. Similarly, not all nations use the same strategy for promoting economic development. Thus, some nations, such as the United States, have advanced economies and high standards of living. Yet other developing nations, such as Bangladesh and Ethiopia, remain poor. What accounts for these differences?

It is a commonly accepted practice to array all nations according to real income and then to draw a dividing line between the advanced and the developing ones. Included in the category of **advanced nations** are those of North America and Western Europe, plus Australia, New Zealand, and Japan. Most nations of the world are classified as developing, or less developed, nations. The **developing nations** are most of those in Africa, Asia, Latin America, and the Middle East. Table 18.2 provides economic and social indicators for selected nations as of 2003. In general, advanced nations are characterized by relatively high levels of gross domestic product per capita, longer life expectancies, and higher levels of adult literacy. Today, the richest 20 percent of the world's population receives more than 80 percent of the world's income, suggesting that there is considerable income inequality among nations.

OBSTACLES TO ECONOMIC DEVELOPMENT

The economic development criteria are identical for developing countries and for the advanced economies. Both groups of countries must use their existing supplies of resources more efficiently and must also increase their available supplies of resources. Although all developing countries are aware of these criteria for economic development, why have some of them experienced economic growth while others have lagged far behind? The economic, institutional, and cultural conditions in these nations are the reasons why they experience different rates of economic growth. Consider the following obstacles to economic development:

Table 18.2	Basic Economic and Social Indicators for Selected Nations, 2003

	Gross National Income per Capita*	Life Expectancy (years)	Adult Illiteracy (percent)
United States	$37,500	78	Under 5%
Switzerland	32,030	70	"
Japan	28,620	80	"
Mexico	8,950	72	10
India	2,880	65	21
Guinea	2,100	46	76
Chad	1,100	48	52
Mozambique	1,070	46	59

*At purchasing power parity.

Source: From The World Bank Group, *Country Data*, at http://www.worldbank.org/data. Click on *Quick Reference Tables.* Also click on *Data by Country* and *Country at a Glance.*

- Many developing countries possess inadequate natural resources such as mineral deposits, arable land, and sources of power.

- There are problems with human resources in developing countries. Developing countries tend to be overpopulated and have high rates of population growth. These growing populations decrease the developing countries' capacity to save, invest, and increase productivity. Developing countries often experience both high levels of unemployment and underemployment.

- Developing countries generally have shortages of capital goods such as public utilities, machinery, and factories. These shortages stem from a lack of saving and investment in developing countries that arises because the nations are too poor to save. Insufficient amounts of capital goods contribute to low levels of labor productivity. Moreover, technological advance is slow in developing countries, which retards economic development.

- The economies of many developing countries are nondiversified and emphasize the production of primary products such as bauxite, copper, and agricultural goods. Developing countries would generally prefer to diversify their economies by fostering manufacturing industries.

- Besides economic factors, institutional and cultural factors can hinder economic development. For example, political corruption and bribery are common in many developing countries. Also, economic growth depends in part on the desire to develop. Are people in developing countries willing to make the necessary changes in their ways of doing things that will promote growth?

Another problem of developing countries is limited access to foreign markets. If we examine the characteristics of developing-nation trade, we find that developing nations are highly dependent on advanced nations. A majority of developing-nation exports go to advanced nations, and most developing-nation imports originate in advanced nations. Trade among developing nations is relatively minor.

Although developing countries as a whole have improved their penetration of world markets during the past two decades, global protectionism has been a hindrance to their market access. This is especially true for agriculture and labor-intensive manufactured

economics
IN ACTION

Does the Fair-Trade Movement Help Poor Coffee Farmers?

Nicaraguan coffee farmer Santiago Rivera has traveled far beyond his mountain home to publicize what is known as the "fair trade" coffee movement. Have you heard of fair-trade coffee? You soon may. Started in Europe in the early 1990s and just making its way across the United States, the objective of the fair-trade coffee movement is to increase the incomes of poor farmers in developing countries by implementing a system where the farmers can sell their beans directly to roasters and retailers, bypassing the traditional practice of selling to middlemen in their own countries.

This arrangement permits farmers, who farm mainly in the mountainous regions of Latin America and other tropical regions where high-flavor, high-priced beans sold to gourmet stores are grown, to earn as much as $1.26 per pound for their beans, compared with the $0.40 per pound they were getting from middlemen.

Under the fair-trade system, farmers organize in cooperatives of as many as 2,500 members, which set prices and arrange for export directly to brokerage firms and other distributors. Middlemen—known as "coyotes" in Nicaragua—previously handled this role. So far, 500,000 of the developing world's 4 million coffee farmers have joined the fair-trade movement. However, the movement has led to incidents of violence in some places in Latin America, mostly involving middlemen who are being bypassed.

The fair-trade coffee movement is the latest example of how social activists are using free-market economics to foster social change. Organizers of the movement say they have signed up eight gourmet roasters and about 120 stores, including big chains like Safeway, Inc. Fair-trade coffee carries a logo identifying it as such.

Fair trade achieved much success in Europe, where fair-trade coffee sells in 35,000 stores and has sales of $250 million a year. In some countries like The Netherlands and Switzerland, fair-trade coffee accounts for as much as 5 percent of total coffee sales. Based on those achievements, organizers in Europe are expanding their fair-trade efforts to include other commodity items, including sugar, tea, chocolate, and bananas. But fair-trade activists admit that selling Americans on the idea of buying coffee with a social theme will be more challenging than it was in Europe. Americans, they note, tend to be less aware of social problems in the developing world than Europeans.

The fair-trade movement has yet to get the support of major U.S. coffee houses such as Maxwell and Folgers. Nevertheless, organizers are trying to nudge Seattle's two coffee giants, Starbucks and Seattle Coffee Co., into agreeing to purchase some of the fair-trade coffee. In Oakland, Mayor Jerry Brown is persuading his colleagues to give more thought to how they purchase coffee. "I would hope that the people sipping their cappuccinos would take a moment to reflect on the sweat and labor of those who provided it."

However, critics question the extent to which "fair-traded" coffee actually helps. They note that the biggest winners are not the farmers, but rather the retailers that sometimes charge huge markups on fair-traded coffee while promoting themselves as corporate citizens. They can get away with it because consumers generally are given little or no information about how much of a product's price goes to farmers.

Source: "A Global Effort for Poor Coffee Farmers," *The Wall Street Journal*, November 23, 1999, pp. A-2 and A-4. See also "At Some Retailers, Fair Trade Carries a Very High Cost," The Wall Street Journal, June 8, 2004, pp. A-1 and A-10.

products such as clothing and textiles, as seen in Figure 18.1. These products are important to the world's poor because they represent more than half of low-income countries' exports and about 70 percent of least-developed countries' export revenues.

Developing countries themselves contribute to the problem. Although trade among developing countries is a relatively small share of total trade, average tariffs in manufactured goods are three times higher for trade among developing countries than for exports to industrial countries. Taken together and because of high protection for labor-intensive

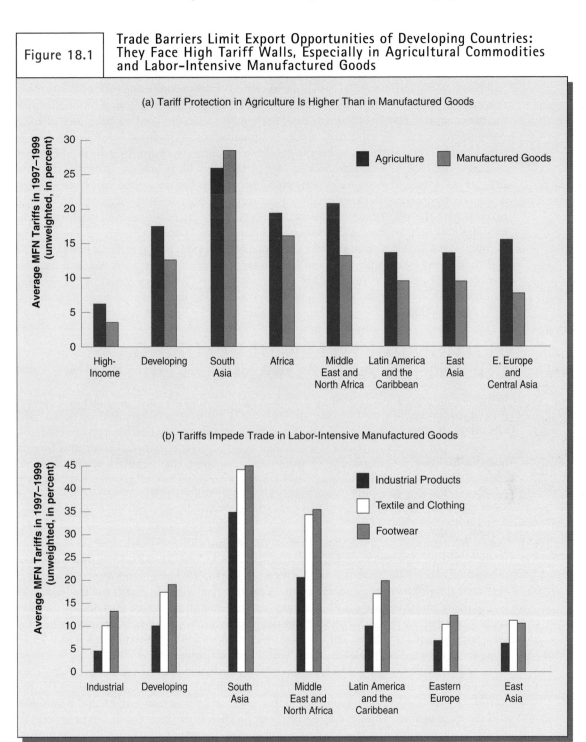

Figure 18.1

Trade Barriers Limit Export Opportunities of Developing Countries: They Face High Tariff Walls, Especially in Agricultural Commodities and Labor-Intensive Manufactured Goods

(a) Tariff Protection in Agriculture Is Higher Than in Manufactured Goods

(b) Tariffs Impede Trade in Labor-Intensive Manufactured Goods

Source: The World Bank, *Global Economic Prospects and Developing Countries*, 2002, p. 45.

products around the world, the world's poor face tariffs that are, on average, roughly twice as high as those imposed on the nonpoor.

Global protectionism in agriculture is another problem for developing countries. In addition to using tariffs to protect their farmers from import-competing products, advanced countries support their farmers with sizable subsidies. Subsidies are often rationalized on the noneconomic benefits of agriculture, such as food security and maintenance of rural communities. By encouraging production of agricultural commodities, subsidies discourage agricultural imports, thus displacing developing-country exports in advanced-country markets. The case of U.S. subsidies to sugar producers illustrates the adverse effects of support on developing countries' exporters. Moreover, the unwanted surpluses of agricultural commodities that result from government support are often dumped into world markets with the aid of export subsidies. This depresses prices for many agricultural commodities and reduces the export revenues of developing countries.

Simply put, developing countries experience a **vicious circle of poverty**. They save little and thus invest little in physical and human capital because they are poor, and because they do not invest, their outputs per capita remain low and they remain poor. Even if the vicious circle were to be broken, a rapid increase in population would leave the standard of living unchanged.

TENSIONS BETWEEN DEVELOPING COUNTRIES AND ADVANCED COUNTRIES

In spite of the economic frustrations of developing countries, most scholars and policymakers today agree that the best strategy for a poor country to develop is to take advantage of international trade. In the past two decades, many developing countries saw the wisdom of this strategy and opened their markets to international trade and foreign investment. And yet, ironically, in spite of the support that scholars from advanced countries have given to this change, the advanced world has sometimes increased its own barriers to imports from these developing countries. Why is this so?

Think of the world economy as a ladder. On the bottom rungs are developing countries that produce mainly textiles and other low-tech goods. Toward the top are the United States, Japan, and other industrial countries that manufacture sophisticated software, electronics, and pharmaceuticals. Up and down the middle rungs are all the other nations, producing everything from memory chips, to autos, to steel. From this perspective, economic development is simple: Everyone attempts to climb to the next rung. This works well if the topmost countries can create new industries and products, thus adding another rung to the ladder. Such invention permits older industries to move overseas while new jobs are generated at home. But if innovation stalls at the highest rung, then that's bad news for Americans who must compete with lower-wage workers in developing countries.

A predicament faced by developing countries is that in order to make progress, they must displace producers of the least advanced goods that are still being produced in the advanced countries. For example, if Zambia is going to produce textiles and apparel, it will compete against American and European producers of these goods. As producers in advanced countries suffer from import competition, they tend to seek trade protection in order to avoid it. However, this protection denies critical market access to developing countries, thwarting their attempts to grow. Thus, there is a bias against their catching up to the advanced countries.

Those who are protected in advanced countries from the competition with developing countries tend to include those who are already near the bottom of the advanced countries' income distributions. Many of these people work in labor-intensive industries and have limited skills and low wages. These are the people that income redistribution programs ought to aid, not hinder. To some extent, advanced countries face a trade-off between helping their own poor and helping the world's poor. But critics note that the world as a whole needs to treat all poor as its own and that a purpose of international institutions is to ensure that this occurs. For example, it is the responsibility of the World Trade Organization (WTO) to prevent advanced countries' trade policies from tilting too far in favor of their own people and against the rest of the world. This is why recent meetings of the WTO have been filled with tensions between poor and rich countries.

However, providing developing countries greater access to the markets of advanced countries will not solve all the developing countries' problems. They face structural weaknesses in their economies, which are compounded by nonexistent or inadequate institutions and policies in the fields of law and order, sustainable macroeconomic management, and public services.

ECONOMIC GROWTH STRATEGIES

In attempting to achieve economic development, poor countries have pursued two competing strategies. Let us examine these strategies.

During the 1950s and 1960s, the growth strategy of **import substitution** became popular in many developing nations such as Argentina, Brazil, and Mexico; some countries still use it today. Import substitution involves extensive use of trade barriers to protect domestic industries from import competition. For example, if fertilizer imports occur, import substitution calls for establishment of a domestic fertilizer industry to produce replacements for fertilizer imports. In the extreme, import-substitution policies could lead to complete self-sufficiency.

The rationale for import substitution arises from the developing countries' perspective on trade. Many developing countries feel that they cannot export manufactured goods because they cannot compete with established firms of the industrial countries, especially in view of the high trade barriers maintained by industrial countries. Given the need for economic growth and development, developing countries have no choice but to manufacture for themselves some of the goods they now import. The use of tariffs and quotas restricts imports, and the domestic market is reserved for domestic manufacturers. This rationale is often combined with the infant industry argument: Protecting start-up industries will allow them to grow to a size where they can compete with the industries of developed countries.

Another development strategy is **export-led growth.** The strategy is outward oriented because it links the domestic economy to the world economy. Instead of pursuing growth through the protection of domestic industries suffering comparative disadvantage, this strategy involves promoting growth through the export of manufactured goods. Trade controls are either nonexistent or very low, in the sense that any disincentives to export resulting from import barriers are counterbalanced by export subsidies. Industrialization is viewed as a natural outcome of development instead of being an objective pursued at the expense of the economy's efficiency. By the 1970s, many developing countries were abandoning their import-substitution strategies and shifting emphasis to export-led growth. Among the countries that have benefited from export-led growth are South Korea, Malaysia, and China.

What is the evidence concerning these growth strategies? Researchers generally have found that the economic performance of nations implementing export-led growth policies has been superior to that of nations using import-substitution policies.[1] This is because export-led growth policies introduce international competition to domestic

---

[1] David Dollar and Art Kraay, *Trade, Growth, and Poverty*, World Bank Development Research Group, Washington, D.C., 2001.

markets, which encourages efficient firms and discourages inefficient ones. By creating a more competitive environment, they also promote higher productivity and hence faster economic growth. Conversely, import-substitution policies relying on trade protection switch demand to products produced domestically. Exporting is then discouraged by both the increased cost of imported inputs and the increased cost of domestic inputs relative to the price received by exporters.

AIDING THE DEVELOPING COUNTRIES

Dissatisfied with their economic performance and convinced that many of their problems are due to shortcomings of the existing international trading system, developing nations have pressed collective demands on the advanced nations for institutions and policies that improve the climate for economic development in the international trading system. Among the institutions and policies that have been created to support developing countries are the World Bank, the International Monetary Fund, and the generalized system of preferences.

World Bank

During the 1940s, two international institutions were established to ease the transition from a wartime to a peacetime environment and to help prevent a recurrence of the turbulent economic conditions of the Great Depression era. The World Bank and the International Monetary Fund were established at the United Nations Monetary and Financial Conference held at Bretton Woods, New Hampshire, in July 1944. Developing nations view these institutions as sources of funds to promote economic development and financial stability.

The **World Bank** is an international organization that provides loans to developing countries aimed toward poverty reduction and economic development. Headquartered in Washington, D.C., it lends money to member governments and their agencies and to private firms in the member nations. The World Bank is not a "bank" in the common sense. It is one of the United Nations' specialized agencies, made up of 184 member countries. These countries are jointly responsible for how the institution is financed and how its money is spent.

The World Bank makes loans to developing members that cannot obtain money from other sources at reasonable terms. These loans are for specific development projects such as hospitals, schools, highways, and dams. The World Bank is involved in projects as diverse as raising AIDS awareness in Guinea, supporting education of girls in Bangladesh, improving health-care delivery in Mexico, and helping India rebuild after a devastating earthquake. The World Bank provides low-interest rate loans, and in some cases interest-free loans, to developing countries that have little or no capacity to borrow on market terms.

In recent years, the World Bank has financed debt-refinancing activities of some of the heavily indebted developing nations. The bank encourages private investment in member countries. In 2003, the World Bank lent about $18.5 billion to developing countries. The World Bank receives its funds from contributions of wealthy developed countries.

Some 10,000 development professionals from nearly every country in the world work in the World Bank's Washington, D.C., headquarters or in its 109 country offices. They provide many technical assistance services for members.

International Monetary Fund

Another source of aid to developing countries (as well as advanced countries) is the **International Monetary Fund (IMF)**, which is also headquartered in Washington D.C. Consisting of 184 nations, the IMF can be thought of as a bank for the central banks of member nations. Over a given time period, some nations will face balance-of-payments surpluses, and others will face deficits. A nation with a deficit initially draws on its stock of foreign currencies, such as the dollar, that are accepted in payment by other nations. However, the deficit nation will sometimes have insufficient amounts of currency. That is when other nations, via the IMF, can provide assistance. By making available currencies to the IMF, the surplus nations channel funds to nations with temporary deficits. Over the long run, deficits must be corrected, and the IMF attempts to ensure that this adjustment will be as prompt and orderly as possible.

The funds of the IMF come from two major sources: quotas and loans. Subscriptions, which are pooled funds of member nations, generate most of the IMF's funds. The size of a member's subscription depends on its economic and financial importance in the world; nations with larger economic importance have larger subscriptions. The subscriptions are increased periodically as a means of boosting the IMF's resources. The IMF also obtains funds through loans from member nations. The IMF has lines of credit with major industrial nations as well as with Saudi Arabia.

All IMF loans are subject to some degree of *conditionality*. This means that to obtain a loan, a deficit nation must agree to implement economic and financial policies as stipulated by the IMF. These policies are intended to correct the member's balance-of-payments deficit and promote noninflationary economic growth. However, the conditionality attachment to IMF lending has often met strong resistance among deficit nations. The IMF has sometimes demanded that deficit nations undergo austerity programs including severe reductions in public spending, private consumption, and imports in order to live within their means.

Critics of the IMF note that its bailouts may contribute to the so-called *moral-hazard* problem, whereby nations realize the benefits of their decisions when things go well but are protected when things go poorly. If nations do not suffer the costs of bad decisions, won't they be encouraged to make other bad decisions in the future? A second area of concern is the contractionary effect of the IMF's restrictive monetary and fiscal policy conditions. Won't such conditions cause business and bank failures, induce a deeper recession, and limit government spending to help the poor? Many analysts feel the answer is yes.

Generalized System of Preferences

Given inadequate access to markets of industrial countries, developing countries have pressed industrial countries to reduce their tariff walls. To help developing nations strengthen their international competitiveness and expand their industrial base, many industrialized nations have extended nonreciprocal tariff preferences to exports of developing nations. Under this **generalized system of preferences (GSP)**, major industrial nations temporarily reduce tariffs on designated manufactured imports from developing nations below the levels applied to imports from other industrial nations. The GSP is not a uniform system, however, because it consists of many individual schemes that differ in the types of products covered and extent of tariff reduction. Simply put, the GSP attempts to promote economic development in developing countries through increased trade, rather than foreign aid.

Trade preferences granted by industrial countries are voluntary. They are not WTO obligations. Donor countries determine eligibility criteria, product coverage, the size of preference margins, and the duration of the preference. In practice, industrial-country governments rarely grant deep preferences in sectors where developing countries have a large export potential. Thus, developing countries often obtain only limited preferences in sectors where they have a comparative advantage. The main reason for limited preferences is that in some sectors there is strong domestic opposition to liberalization in industrial countries.

CHECK POINT

1. Identify the obstacles to development encountered by poor countries.

2. Describe the "ladder of economic development."

3. Concerning economic growth strategies, what is meant by import substitution and export-led growth?

4. What policies and institutions have been created to aid developing countries?

Chapter Summary

1. Every society must make certain decisions regarding the production and distribution of goods and services: (1) *What* goods will be produced and in what quantities? (2) *How* shall these goods be produced? (3) *For whom* shall the goods be produced? These questions are known as the fundamental economic questions.

2. The manner in which the fundamental economic questions are answered depends on a society's economic system. The three broad types of economies are the market economy, the command economy, and the mixed economy. The United States has a mixed economy.

3. By the 1990s, the centrally planned economies in the former Soviet Union and Eastern Europe had collapsed and begun switching to capitalism. Also, the Chinese economy started embracing capitalism. These nations are known as the "transition economies."

4. The "advanced" nations are those of North America and Western Europe, plus Australia, New Zealand, and Japan. Most nations of the world are classified as "developing" nations. These nations are those in Africa, Asia, Latin America, and the Middle East. Compared to advanced countries, developing countries generally have low levels of real GDP per capita, shorter life expectancies, and lower levels of adult literacy.

5. For developing nations, obstacles to economic growth include inadequate natural resources, low rates of saving and investment, shortages of capital goods, low productivity levels, modest technological advances, and access to markets of advanced countries. Many developing nations experience a vicious circle of poverty: They save little and thus invest little in physical and human capital because they are poor, and because they do not invest, their outputs per capita remain low and they remain poor.

6. In attempting to achieve economic development, poor countries have pursued two competing strategies: import substitution and export-led growth. Researchers have generally found that developing countries have benefited the most from an export-led growth strategy.

7. Among the institutions and policies that have been created to support developing countries are the World Bank, International Monetary Fund, and the generalized system of preferences.

Key Terms and Concepts

fundamental economic questions (424)

market economy (425)

capitalism (425)

laissez-faire economy (425)

command economy (426)

mixed economies (426)

socialism (427)

advanced nations (430)

developing nations (430)

vicious circle of poverty (434)

import substitution (435)

export-led growth (435)

World Bank (436)

International Monetary Fund (IMF) (436)

generalized system of preferences (GSP) (437)

Self-Test: Multiple-Choice Questions

1. Before China and the Soviet Union began switching to a market economy, the institution that was most prevalent in their economies was

   a. central planning by the government.
   b. private ownership of property.
   c. goods rationed according to the ability to pay.
   d. flexible prices and wages.

2. For most developing countries, _____ constitute the largest share of domestic output.

   a. steel and automobiles
   b. banking and financial services
   c. oil and natural gas
   d. agricultural goods and raw materials

3. In a capitalistic economy, the role of government is best described as

   a. limited.
   b. unlimited.
   c. nonexistent.
   d. significant.

4. Economic growth in developing countries is hindered by all of the following *except*

   a. a low supply of capital goods.
   b. a low birth rate.
   c. the development of strong labor unions.
   d. high productivity of workers.

5. Which institution's main purpose is to provide low interest loans to developing countries to help them build hospitals, schools, roads, and bridges?

   a. The World Bank
   b. The Organization of Petroleum Exporting Countries
   c. The Bank of America
   d. The European Union

6. For most developing countries,

   a. productivity is high among domestic workers.
   b. adult literacy rates are high.
   c. saving and investment rates are low.
   d. technological advances are widespread.

7. Advanced countries include all of the following *except*

 a. Japan.
 b. Sweden.
 c. United States.
 d. Mozambique.

8. Capitalism includes all of the following *except*

 a. a pricing system based on supply and demand.
 b. a system of private property.
 c. self-interest among households and entrepreneurs.
 d. separation of the economy from the business sector.

9. The economic system that best describes the U.S. economy is a

 a. command economy.
 b. socialistic economy.
 c. capitalistic economy.
 d. mixed market economy.

10. The sources of aid to developing countries include all of the following *except*

 a. the generalized system of preferences.
 b. import tariffs of advanced countries.
 c. the World Bank.
 d. the International Monetary Fund.

Answers to Multiple-Choice Questions

1. a   **2.** d   **3.** a   **4.** d   **5.** a   **6.** c   **7.** d   **8.** d   **9.** d   **10.** b

Study Questions and Problems

1. Why do incentive and coordination problems arise in economies that embrace central planning? How are those problems dealt with in a market economy?

2. Why do nations such as Sweden and Norway prefer socialism to capitalism?

3. Evaluate the prospects for the transformation of the Chinese and Eastern European economies into market economies.

4. Why are some nations rich and other nations poor?

5. What are the ways that the advanced nations use to help developing nations?

6. Suppose you are the manager of an automobile assembly plant. Explain how you might attain production goals under a system of communism and under a system of capitalism.

7. Describe the merits of import substitution versus export-led growth as strategies for economic development.

Glossary

a

ability-to-pay principle Principle of taxation stating that people with greater income and wealth should be taxed at a higher rate because their ability to pay is presumably greater. *(Chapter 9)*

accounting profit Total revenue minus explicit costs; costs that are payable to others. *(Chapter 4)*

actual reserves The amount of vault cash and Federal Reserve deposits that a bank is holding; the sum of a bank's required and excess reserves. *(Chapter 14)*

administrative lag Inability to get quick action on fiscal policy because of the way Congress operates. *(Chapter 13)*

advanced nations Nations having relatively high per-capita income and standards of living. *(Chapter 18)*

advertising Attempt at product differentiation for imperfectly competitive firms, the goal of which is either to make buyers aware of unique features of products, to convince buyers that their product is better from their competitors, or both. *(Chapter 6)*

aggregate demand curve Graphic representation of the total demand of all people for all final goods and services produced in an economy. *(Chapter 12)*

aggregate quantity demanded The quantity of final output that buyers will purchase at a given price level. *(Chapter 12)*

aggregate quantity supplied The quantity of final output that will be supplied by producers at a particular price level. *(Chapter 12)*

aggregate supply curve Graphic representation of the total supply of all final goods and services in an economy. *(Chapter 12)*

antitrust policy The attempt to foster a market structure that will lead to increased competition and curb anticompetitive behavior that harms consumers; a law designed to prevent unfair business practices. *(Chapter 8)*

appreciation Strengthening of currency; fewer units of a nation's currency are needed to purchase a unit of some foreign currency. *(Chapter 17)*

arbitration Process whereby a person called an arbitrator listens to both sides of a labor dispute and makes a decision that is binding on both sides. *(Chapter 7)*

automatic stabilizers Changes in government spending and tax revenues that occur automatically as the economy fluctuates; prevent aggregate demand from decreasing so much in bad times and rising so much in good times, thus stabilizing the economy. *(Chapter 13)*

average fixed cost The total fixed cost per unit of output; average fixed cost equals total fixed cost divided by output. *(Chapter 4)*

average tax rate Tax rate equal to total taxes due divided by total income. *(Chapter 9)*

average total cost Total cost per unit of output; average total cost equals total cost divided by output. *(Chapter 4)*

average variable cost Total variable cost per unit of output; average variable cost equals total variable cost divided by output. *(Chapter 4)*

b

balance of payments A record of a country's international trading, borrowing, and lending. *(Chapter 17)*

balance of trade (trade balance) Component of the current account; balance that includes all of the goods (merchandise) that the United States exports or imports. *(Chapter 17)*

balance sheet A two-column list that shows at a specific date the financial position of a bank. *(Chapter 14)*

barriers to entry Impediments created by the government or the firm or firms already in the market that protect an established firm from potential competition. *(Chapter 5)*

benefits-received principle Principle of taxation stating that taxes should be paid in proportion to the benefits that taxpayers derive from public expenditures. *(Chapter 9)*

Board of Governors Seven-member board appointed by the president and confirmed by the Senate to serve 14-year terms of office; administers the Fed. *(Chapter 15)*

business cycle Recurrent ups and downs in the level of economic activity extending over several years. *(Chapter 11)*

c

capacity utilization rate The ratio of an industry's production to its capacity. *(Chapter 1)*

capital and financial account Component of the balance of payments; transactions that include all international purchases or sales of assets such as real estate or government securities. *(Chapter 17)*

capital and financial account balance Amount of capital and financial inflows minus capital and financial outflows. *(Chapter 17)*

capital goods Goods such as factories and machines, which are used for producing other goods and services in the future; a source of an economy's economic growth potential. *(Chapter 1)*

capitalism Free-enterprise system rooted in private property and markets; also called market economy. *(Chapter 18)*

cartel Formal organization of firms that attempts to act as if there were only one firm in the industry (monopoly); the purpose of a cartel is to reduce output and increase the price in order to increase the joint profits of members. *(Chapter 6)*

cashier's check Check purchased by someone who does not necessarily have a checking account; issued by a bank for a fee plus the amount of the check. *(Chapter 14)*

certified check Checks used when called for by a legal contract, such as a real estate or automobile sale agreement; considered less risky than personal checks because the bank on which they are drawn has certified that the funds are available. *(Chapter 14)*

change in demand A shift in a demand curve caused by a demand shifter. *(Chapter 2)*

change in quantity demanded A movement along a demand curve caused by a change in the price of the good under consideration. *(Chapter 2)*

change in supply Shift in a supply curve induced by a supply shifter. *(Chapter 2)*

classical economists Group of economists who dominated economic thinking prior to the Great Depression; believed that the market economy automatically adjusted to ensure the full employment of its resources; economic downturns are temporary so government should not interfere in economic affairs. *(Chapter 12)*

Clayton Act of 1914 Federal legislation enacted to make explicit the intent of the Sherman Act of 1890; broadened federal antitrust powers to outlaw price discrimination, some mergers, tying contracts between supplier and buyer, and interlocking directorates that exist when the same persons serves on the boards of competing firms. *(Chapter 8)*

collective bargaining A process whereby unions act on behalf of workers to bargain with employers on matters relating to employment; one negotiator acts as the workers' agent rather than having each worker negotiate his or her own labor contract. *(Chapter 7)*

command economy An economy in which the government makes all decisions concerning production and distribution; also called planned economy or communism. *(Chapter 18)*

command-and-control regulations Government-imposed restrictions or mandates on spillover costs of production. *(Chapter 8)*

comparative advantage Principle that states that individuals and countries specialize in producing those goods in which they are relatively, not absolutely, more efficient. *(Chapter 16)*

complementary good Goods that are used in conjunction with each other. A decrease in the price of one good will increase the demand for the other good; an increase in the price of one good will decrease the demand for the other good. *(Chapter 2)*

compound interest The increase in the value of your savings that is the result of earning interest on interest. *(Chapter 14)*

concentration ratios Percent of an industry's sales accounted for by the four largest firms in an industry; a low-concentration ratio suggests a high degree of competition; a high-concentration ratio implies an absence of competition. *(Chapter 6)*

conglomerate merger One firm combines with another firm, with both firms producing in different industries. *(Chapter 6)*

constant returns to scale Situation occurring when a firm's output changes by the same percentage as the change in all inputs. *(Chapter 4)*

consumer goods Goods such as food, electricity, and clothing that are available for immediate use by households and do not contribute to future production in the economy. *(Chapter 1)*

consumer price index (CPI) An indicator of inflation, calculated by the Bureau of Labor Statistics through a sampling of households and businesses; a monitoring of consumer expenditures on specified goods and services. *(Chapter 11)*

corporate average fuel economy standards (CAFÉ) Originally enacted in 1975, represents a foundation of U.S. energy conservation policy. *(Chapter 8)*

corporation Business organization that is a "legal person," conducting business just as an individual does; owned by stockholders who receive profits of the firm through dividend checks. *(Chapter 9)*

cost-of-living adjustment (COLA) Annual adjustment of Social Security benefits to reflect inflation. *(Chapter 9)*

cost-push inflation Inflation caused by upward pressure on the sellers' side of the market. *(Chapter 11)*

creative destruction In a dynamic economy, the drive to temporarily capture monopoly profits results in old goods and livelihoods being replaced by new ones; ideas and creativity are prime sources of growth in a capitalistic economy and profits are the fuel. *(Chapter 10)*

crowding-out effect Private spending (consumption or investment) falls as a result of increased government expenditures and the subsequent budget deficits. *(Chapter 13)*

currency The money in use in a country. *(Chapter 14)*

current account Component of the balance of payments; the dollar value of U.S. transactions in currently produced goods and services, income flows, and unilateral transfers. *(Chapter 17)*

current account balance The sum of the trade balance, the services balance, net income, and net unilateral transfers. *(Chapter 17)*

cyclical unemployment Fluctuating unemployment that coincides with the business cycle and is a repeating short-run problem. *(Chapter 11)*

d

deflation A continuing fall in the average price level; when price reductions on some goods and services outweigh price rises on all others. *(Chapter 11)*

demand Schedule that shows various amounts of a good or service a buyer is willing and able to purchase at each possible price during a particular period. *(Chapter 2)*

demand curve Graphical portrayal of the data comprised by a market demand schedule. *(Chapter 2)*

demand curve for labor The value of the marginal product of labor curve; the result of plotting on a graph the wage rates and the amounts of labor the firm is willing to hire at each of those rates. *(Chapter 7)*

demand deposit account A regular checking account that does not pay interest; money in the account is available to the account holder "on demand" by writing a check, making a withdrawal, or transferring funds. *(Chapter 14)*

demand shifter A change in a variable that can cause a shift in the demand curve. *(Chapter 2)*

demand-pull inflation Inflation originating from upward pressure on the buyers' side of the market; a situation where "too much money chases too few goods." *(Chapter 11)*

dependent variable A variable that is functionally dependent on another variable. *(Chapter 1)*

depreciation Weakening of currency; more units of a nation's currency are needed to purchase a unit of some foreign currency. *(Chapter 17)*

depression A very deep and prolonged recession. *(Chapter 11)*

deregulation Federal dismantling of regulations in industries (such as the airlines, trucking, and railroads) where the existing regulations have outlived their usefulness; an attempt by the government to increase price competition and provide incentives for companies to introduce new products and services. *(Chapter 8)*

derived demand The demand for an input that arises from, and varies with, the demand for the product it helps to produce. *(Chapter 7)*

developing nations Nations with relatively low levels of industrialization and low standards of living. *(Chapter 18)*

diminishing marginal returns Situation a firm realizes when adding additional workers causes output to increase by successfully smaller increments. *(Chapter 4)*

diminishing marginal utility As a person consumes additional units of a particular good, each additional unit provides less and less additional utility (satisfaction). *(Chapter 2)*

direct relationship When two variables show a positive relationship to each other. *(Chapter 1)*

discount rate The rate the Federal Reserve Banks charge for loans to banks. *(Chapter 15)*

discount window An expression for Fed loans that are repaid with interest at maturity, arranged by telephone, and recorded along with pledged collateral such as U.S. government securities. *(Chapter 15)*

discouraged worker A person who is out of work, would like to work, and is available for work, but who has stopped looking for work because of lack of success in finding a job. *(Chapter 11)*

discretionary fiscal policy The deliberate use of changes in government expenditures and taxation to affect aggregate demand and influence the economy's performance in the short run. *(Chapter 13)*

diseconomies of scale Situation realized by a firm when unit costs increase and the long-run average total cost curve turns upward. *(Chapter 4)*

distribution of income The way income is divided among members of society; reflects the manner in which people share in the rewards from the production of goods and services. *(Chapter 9)*

division of labor The process of allowing production processes to be divided so that workers can practice and perfect a particular skill. *(Chapter 16)*

dollarization The governments of some developing nations have replaced their currencies with the U.S. dollar as the official medium of exchange; by replacing their less stable currencies with the dollar, developing countries hope that they will experience a lower and more stable inflation rate. *(Chapter 17)*

e

economic growth Situation where increased productive capabilities of an economy are made possible by either an increasing resource base or technological advance. *(Chapter 1 and Chapter 10)*

economic profit Total revenue minus the sum of explicit and implicit costs. *(Chapter 4)*

economic regulation Federal legislation enacted to control the prices, wages, conditions of entry, standards of service, or other important economic characteristics of particular industries. *(Chapter 8)*

economic sanctions Government-imposed limitations, or complete bans, placed on customary trade or financial relations among nations. *(Chapter 1)*

economics The study of choice under conditions of scarcity. *(Chapter 1)*

economies of scale Situation realized by a firm when the long-run average total cost curve slopes downward, showing an increase in scale and production resulting in a fall in cost per unit. *(Chapter 4)*

efficiency Point reached when an economy operates along the production possibilities curve and realizes its output potential. *(Chapter 1)*

elastic demand When the percentage change in quantity demanded is greater than the percentage change in price. *(Chapter 3)*

equilibrium exchange rate Rate determined by the market forces of supply and demand; central bankers do not attempt to influence the exchange rate. *(Chapter 17)*

equilibrium price Price that sets the buyers' intentions equal to the sellers' intentions. *(Chapter 2)*

euro The single currency that was introduced by the European Monetary Union in 2002. *(Chapter 17)*

European Central Bank Created by the European Monetary Union to take control of monetary policy and exchange rate policy for member countries; this bank will control the supply of euros, set the euro interest rate, and maintain permanently fixed exchange rates for member countries. *(Chapter 17)*

European Monetary Union (EMU) European countries united to replace their individual currencies with a single currency. *(Chapter 17)*

European Union (EU) A regional economic bloc consisting of 15 European nations, the objective of which has been to create an economic bloc in which trade and other transactions take place freely among member nations. *(Chapter 17)*

excess capacity Difference between the output corresponding to minimum average total cost and the output produced by a monopolistically competitive firm in the long run. *(Chapter 6)*

excess reserves Extra reserves that a bank is holding; can be used to make loans or purchase government securities. *(Chapter 14)*

exchange rate The rate at which one currency trades for another. *(Chapter 17)*

expenditure approach Method of calculating GDP by totaling the expenditures on goods and services produced during the current year. *(Chapter 10)*

explicit cost Payments made to others as a cost of running a business. *(Chapter 4)*

export-led growth Growth based on exporting in foreign markets. *(Chapter 18)*

externality Cost or benefit imposed on people other than the producers and consumers of a good or service; also called spillover. *(Chapter 8)*

f

factors of production Inputs used in the production of goods and services. *(Chapter 1)*

fair-return price Price a regulated firm can charge that is only high enough to cover average total cost. *(Chapter 8)*

federal debt Debt representing the cumulative amount of outstanding borrowing from the public over the nation's history. *(Chapter 13)*

federal deficit The difference between total federal spending and revenue in a given year; the annual amount of government borrowing. *(Chapter 13)*

Federal Deposit Insurance Corporation (FDIC) Organization that has been insuring deposits and promoting safe and sound banking practices since 1933; FDIC conducts examinations and audits, insures deposits up to $100,000 in U.S. banks, and arranges for the disposition of assets and deposit liabilities of insured banks that fail. *(Chapter 14)*

federal funds market Trading market for reserves held at the Federal Reserve; those banks with surplus balances in their accounts transfer reserves to those in need of boosting their balances. *(Chapter 15)*

federal funds rate Benchmark rate of interest charged for short-term use of federal funds; a market-determined rate. *(Chapter 15)*

Federal Open Market Committee (FOMC) Policy-making body of the Fed that oversees the purchases and sales of U.S. government securities. *(Chapter 15)*

Federal Reserve System (Fed) The central bank of the United States; legislated by Congress and signed into law by President Wilson in 1913 to provide the nation with a safe, flexible, and stable monetary and financial system. *(Chapter 15)*

fiscal policy The use of government expenditures and taxes to promote particular macroeconomic goals such as full employment, stable prices, and economic growth. *(Chapter 13)*

fixed exchange rates Rates that are used primarily by small, developing nations to maintain pegs to a key currency such as the U.S. dollar. *(Chapter 17)*

fixed input Any resource for which the quantity cannot be varied during the period under consideration. *(Chapter 4)*

flat-rate income tax Proposed as a substitute for current federal taxes; tax system that would do away with the existing different tax rates on personal income and replace them with a single tax rate; exemptions, deductions, and credits would be abolished. *(Chapter 9)*

floating exchange rate system A system in which governments and central banks do not participate in the foreign exchange market; an equilibrium exchange rate equates the demand for and supply of the home currency. *(Chapter 17)*

foreign exchange market Market in which the buying and selling of currencies takes place. *(Chapter 17)*

free-rider problem Situation existing when it is impossible to exclude a consumer from consumption of a public good, whether the consumer pays for it or not; others pay for a consumer's use of a good. *(Chapter 8)*

frictional unemployment Unemployment that arises from normal labor turnover. *(Chapter 11)*

full employment To an economist, the natural rate of unemployment; something less than 100-percent employment of the labor force. *(Chapter 11)*

functional distribution of income Distribution showing the shares of a nation's income accruing to the factors of production as rent, wages, interest, and profits. *(Chapter 9)*

fundamental economic questions All societies must answer the following questions: What to produce? How to produce? How will income be distributed? *(Chapter 18)*

g

game theory Method of studying oligopolistic behavior by analyzing a series of strategies and payoffs among rival firms. *(Chapter 6)*

generalized system of preferences (GSP) Under this system, major industrial nations temporarily reduce tariffs on designated manufactured imports from developing nations below the levels applied to imports from other industrial nations. *(Chapter 18)*

GDP deflator Broadest index to calculate real GDP; equals the ratio of the cost of buying all final goods and services in the current year to the cost of buying the identical goods at base-year prices. *(Chapter 10)*

government expenditures Federal, state, and local government outlays of funds. *(Chapter 9)*

government purchases Expenditures by federal, state, and local governments on goods and services such as street lighting, sewage systems, national parks, fire trucks, engineers, teachers, and the like. *(Chapter 9)*

government purchases of goods and services Spending on final output by federal, state, and local government, including the entire payroll of governments. *(Chapter 10)*

gross domestic product (GDP) The market value of all final goods and services produced within a country in a given year. *(Chapter 10)*

gross private domestic investment All private sector spending for investment; also known as gross investment. *(Chapter 10)*

h

health-maintenance organizations (HMOs) An association of health care providers that has its own facilities such as clinics and hospitals. *(Chapter 3)*

horizontal merger One firm combines with another firm that sells similar products in the same market. *(Chapter 6)*

human capital The skills and training of the labor force. *(Chapter 9 and Chapter 10)*

hyperinflation A rapid and uncontrolled inflation capable of destroying an economy. *(Chapter 11)*

i

imperfect competition More than one seller competes for sales with other sellers, each of which has some price-making ability. *(Chapter 6)*

implicit cost A cost that represents the value of resources used in production for which no monetary payment is made. *(Chapter 4)*

import substitution Countries protect their import-competing industries by imposing tariffs on imported goods. *(Chapter 18)*

incentive-based regulations Government attempts to control spillover costs of production; regulations are flexible because they allow producers to find ways to fulfill objectives. *(Chapter 8)*

income Consists of earnings on U.S. investments abroad less payments on foreign investments in the United States. Also includes the net compensation of employees. *(Chapter 17)*

income effect A decrease in the price of a good creates an increase in the purchasing power of the consumers' money incomes. *(Chapter 2)*

increasing marginal returns The marginal product of an added worker increases the marginal product of the first worker and, thus, increases returns to the firm. *(Chapter 4)*

independent variable Initiates changes in other variables. *(Chapter 1)*

inefficiency When an economy fails to realize the output potential of its production possibilities curve. *(Chapter 1)*

inelastic demand When the percentage change in quantity demanded is less than the percentage change in price. *(Chapter 3)*

infant industry argument Argument for tariff protection that contends that for free trade to be meaningful, trading nations should temporarily shield their newly developing industries from foreign competition. *(Chapter 16)*

inferior good Good (such as secondhand appliances or inexpensive cuts of meat) for which demand falls as consumer income rises. *(Chapter 2)*

inflation A sustained or continuous rise in the general price level. *(Chapter 11)*

infrastructure Public capital, including roads, bridges, airports, and utilities. *(Chapter 10)*

International Monetary Fund (IMF) Another source of aid to developing countries. Consisting of 184 nations, can be thought of as a bank for the central banks of member nations. *(Chapter 18)*

inverse relationship Two variables show a negative relationship to each other. *(Chapter 1)*

k

Keynes, John Maynard British economist who theorized that a market economy is inherently unstable; the level of economic activity depends on the total spending of consumers, businesses, and government; the government must intervene to protect jobs and income. *(Chapter 12)*

l

Laffer curve Named after Arthur Laffer; shows the relationship between the income tax rate that a government imposes and the total tax revenue that the government collects. *(Chapter 13)*

laissez-faire economy An extreme case of a market economy where the government has almost no economic role except to protect private property and provide a legal system allowing free markets. *(Chapter 18)*

law of demand Price and quantity demanded are inversely or negatively related, assuming that other factors affecting the quantity demanded remain the same. *(Chapter 2)*

law of diminishing marginal returns Law explaining the falling portion of the marginal product curve; after some point, the marginal product diminishes as additional units of a variable resource are added to a fixed resource. *(Chapter 4)*

law of increasing opportunity cost The relationship occurring when the opportunity costs represent what occurs in the real world for most goods; opportunity costs increase as more of a good is produced. *(Chapter 1)*

law of supply Law stating that, in general, sellers are willing and able to make available more of their product at a higher price than a lower price, other determinants of supply being constant. *(Chapter 2)*

legal tender All U.S. currency, including paper money and coins; the federal government mandates its acceptance in transactions and requires that dollars be used in payment of taxes. *(Chapter 14)*

level playing field The contention of domestic producers that import restrictions should be enacted to offset foreign

advantages; all producers should compete on equal terms. *(Chapter 16)*

long run Period in which all inputs are considered as variable in amounts; there are no fixed inputs. *(Chapter 4)*

long-run average total cost curve Shows the minimum cost per unit of producing each output level when any desired size of factory can be constructed. *(Chapter 4)*

losses Situation realized when costs are greater than revenues; negative profit. *(Chapter 4)*

m

M_1 money supply Money supply consisting of currency in the hands of the public, demand deposits, other checkable deposits, and traveler's checks; the narrowest definition of the U.S. money supply. *(Chapter 14)*

macroeconomics The branch of economics that is concerned with the overall performance of the economy. *(Chapter 1)*

managed floating exchange rates The attempt to combine market-determined exchange rates with central bank intervention; central banks try to stabilize exchange rates in the short run to provide financial security. *(Chapter 17)*

marginal cost The change in total cost when one more unit of output is produced. *(Chapter 4)*

marginal product The change in output resulting from changing labor by one unit, holding all other inputs fixed. *(Chapter 4)*

marginal product of labor The extra output produced by hiring one additional unit of labor. *(Chapter 7)*

marginal propensity to consume (MPC) The fraction of additional income people spend. *(Chapter 12)*

marginal propensity to save (MPS) The fraction of additional income that is saved. *(Chapter 12)*

marginal revenue Ratio showing the total revenue divided by the change in quantity between any two points on the total revenue schedule; the increase in total revenue resulting from the sale of another unit of output. *(Chapter 5)*

marginal revenue = marginal cost rule Total profit is maximized where marginal revenue is equal to marginal cost. *(Chapter 5)*

marginal tax rate Tax rate that is the fraction of additional income paid in taxes (change in taxes due divided by change in income). *(Chapter 9)*

market Mechanism through which buyers (demanders) and sellers (suppliers) communicate to trade goods and services. *(Chapter 2)*

market economy Free-enterprise system rooted in private property and markets; also called capitalism. *(Chapter 18)*

market equilibrium Situation occurring when the price of a product adjusts so that the quantity that consumers will purchase at that price is identical to the quantity that suppliers will sell; point where the forces of demand and supply balance. *(Chapter 2)*

market failure Situation occurring when a market fails to allocate resources efficiently. *(Chapter 8)*

mediation Process involving outside help for a labor negotiation; a party is called in to assist in labor/management disagreements. *(Chapter 7)*

Medicare Government health insurance program; objective is to reduce the financial burden of illness on the elderly. *(Chapter 9)*

medium of exchange A function of money; something that people are willing to accept in payment for goods and services. *(Chapter 14)*

merger Practice where firms combine under a single ownership or control, become larger, possibly realize economies of scale as output expands, and usually have an increased ability to control the market price of a product. *(Chapter 6)*

microeconomics The branch of economics that focuses on the choices made by households and firms and the effects those choices have on particular markets. *(Chapter 1)*

minimum wage The smallest amount of money per hour that an employer can legally pay a worker. *(Chapter 7)*

mixed economies Economies having elements of both market and command economies. *(Chapter 9 and Chapter 18)*

models Simplified representations of the real world that we use to help us understand, explain, and predict economic phenomena in the real world; also called theories. *(Chapter 1)*

monetary policy Changing the economy's money supply to assist the economy in achieving maximum output and employment and stable prices; carried out by the Fed. *(Chapter 15)*

money The set of assets in the economy that people regularly use to purchase goods and services from other people; functions as a medium of exchange, a unit of account, and a store of value. *(Chapter 14)*

money multiplier Maximum amount of money the banking system generates with each dollar of reserves; the reciprocal of the required reserve ratio. *(Chapter 14)*

money order Serves the same function as a personal check for people who do not maintain a checking account or who prefer not to make payments with cash; can be issued by businesses other than banks; usually issued in smaller amounts and are cheaper than cashier's checks. *(Chapter 14)*

monopolistic competition Market structure closest to perfect competition; structure based on a large number of firms, each firm having a relatively small share of the total market. *(Chapter 6)*

monopoly Market structure characterized by a single supplier of a good or service for which there is no close substitute. *(Chapter 5)*

multiplier The ratio of the change in output to changes in aggregate demand; indicates the extent to which changes in aggregate demand are "multiplied" into changes in larger output and income. *(Chapter 12)*

multiplier effect The result of changes in aggregate demand caused by the multiplier. *(Chapter 12)*

n

national sales tax Another alternative to the current federal income tax, this system would entail a federal consumption tax collected at the retail level by businesses. *(Chapter 9)*

natural monopoly Market structure where one firm can supply the entire market at a lower cost per unit than would be achieved by two or more firms each supplying only some of it. *(Chapter 5)*

natural rate of unemployment The level of unemployment at which there is no cyclical unemployment; the sum of frictional unemployment and structural unemployment. *(Chapter 11)*

negotiable order of withdrawal (NOW) account Type of checking account that does pay interest but typically requires a larger minimum balance. *(Chapter 14)*

net exports Sales of a country's goods and services to foreigners during a particular time period. *(Chapter 10)*

nominal GDP Gross domestic product figured in terms of the prices existing in the year in which the goods and services were produced; also known as current-dollar GDP. *(Chapter 10)*

nominal income The actual number of dollars of income received during a year. *(Chapter 11)*

nominal interest rate Interest that a bank pays. *(Chapter 11)*

normal good Good (such as a ski trip or new car) that is purchased more often as consumer income rises. *(Chapter 2)*

normal profit The minimum profit necessary to keep a firm in operation; a situation realized when total revenue just covers the sum of explicit and implicit costs; zero economic profit. *(Chapter 4)*

normative economics Term used to describe economic value judgments that cannot be empirically tested. *(Chapter 1)*

North American Free Trade Agreement (NAFTA) Approved in 1993 by the governments of the United States, Canada, and Mexico; a pact removing trade restrictions among the member nations. *(Chapter 16)*

o

oligopoly Form of imperfect competition where a small number of firms compete with each other, and each firm has significant price-making ability. *(Chapter 6)*

open market operations Refer to the purchase or sale of securities by the Fed; a transaction made with a bank or some other business or individual but not directly with the federal government; the most useful and important Fed policy tool. *(Chapter 15)*

operational lag The time it takes a fiscal policy, once enacted, to be put into operation. *(Chapter 13)*

opportunity cost The value of the best alternative sacrificed; the cost of any particular economic choice. *(Chapter 1)*

Organization of Petroleum Exporting Countries (OPEC) A group of nations that sells oil on the world market; the best known cartel. *(Chapter 6)*

outsourcing Contracting out functions that had been done in-house. *(Chapter 7)*

p

partnership Form of business organization where two or more owners pool their financial resources and business skills. *(Chapter 9)*

peak Portion of a business cycle where real GDP is at a temporary high and employment and profits are strong. *(Chapter 11)*

peak-load pricing With peak-load pricing, a consumer pays more for electricity used during periods of peak energy demand and less during the offpeak periods. *(Chapter 8)*

perfect competition Market characterized by insignificant barriers to entry or exit, many sellers and buyers, a standardized product produced by firms in the industry, and perfect information; the most competitive market structure. *(Chapter 5)*

personal consumption expenditures Purchases of final goods and services by households and individuals. *(Chapter 10)*

personal distribution of income Distribution showing how the nation's income is shared by households; indicates the share of before-tax annual money income received. *(Chapter 9)*

positive economics Term describing the facts of the economy, dealing with what is believed about the way the economy works. *(Chapter 1)*

preferred provider organizations (PPOs) An organization that contracts with numerous doctors and hospitals to provide health care to their subscribers. *(Chapter 3)*

price ceiling Government-imposed maximum legal price a seller may charge for that produce. *(Chapter 3)*

price discrimination The practice of charging some customers a lower price than others for an identical good even though there is no difference in the cost to the firm. *(Chapter 6)*

price elasticity of demand Formula measuring how responsive, or sensitive, buyers are to a change in price. *(Chapter 3)*

price floor Government-imposed price to prevent prices from falling below the legally mandated level. *(Chapter 3)*

price index Used to adjust GDP figures so that the figures only show changes in actual output. *(Chapter 10)*

price taker A firm that has to "take," or accept, the price established by the market; a perfectly competitive firm. *(Chapter 5)*

private goods Goods produced through the market system; goods that are divisible, are subject to the exclusion principle, and the principle of rival consumption applies to the goods. *(Chapter 8)*

privatization The process of turning public firms or enterprises into private ones. *(Chapter 5)*

product differentiation Fundamental characteristic of monopolistic competition; assumption that the product of each firm is not a perfect substitute for the product of competing firms. *(Chapter 6)*

production Refers to the use of resources to make outputs of goods and services available for human wants. *(Chapter 4)*

production function Relationship between physical output and the quantity of resources used in the production process. *(Chapter 4)*

production possibilities curve A graphical illustration of the maximum combinations of two goods that an economy can produce, given its available resources and technology. *(Chapter 1)*

productivity A ratio that measures the quantity of output produced relative to the amount of work required to produce it. *(Chapter 10)*

profit The difference between the amount of revenues a firm takes in (total revenue) and the amount it spends for wages, materials, electricity, and so on (total cost). *(Chapter 4)*

public goods Goods such as the national defense, highways, lighthouses, and air-traffic control; goods that are indivisible and the exclusion principle does not apply. *(Chapter 8)*

q

quantity supplied Amount of a good available at any given time or price, assuming that other determinants of supply are unchanged; refers to a single point on the supply schedule. (Chapter 2)

quota A physical restriction on the quantity of goods traded each year. *(Chapter 16)*

r

rate of economic growth The percentage change in the level of economic activity from one year to the next. *(Chapter 10)*

real GDP Nominal GDP adjusted to eliminate changes in prices and measures actual (real) production, shows how actual production, rather than the prices of what is produced, has changed; also known as constant-dollar GDP. *(Chapter 10)*

real income The actual number of dollars received (nominal income) adjusted for any change in price; measures real purchasing power, the amount of goods and services that can be purchased with nominal income. *(Chapter 11)*

real interest rate Interest rate that is adjusted for inflation; the nominal interest rate minus the inflation rate. *(Chapter 11)*

recession Portion of a business cycle when real GDP decreases for at least two consecutive quarters; recession begins at a peak and ends at a trough. *(Chapter 11)*

recognition lag The time between the beginning of inflation or recession and the recognition that it is actually occurring. *(Chapter 13)*

recovery Portion of a business cycle where real GDP rises, industrial output expands, profits increase, and employment moves toward full employment; also called expansion. *(Chapter 11)*

rent controls Method to protect low-income households from escalating rents caused by perceived housing shortages and to make housing more affordable to the poor. *(Chapter 3)*

required reserve ratio A specific percentage of checking deposits that must be kept as vault cash or deposits at the Federal Reserve and directly limits the ability of banks to grant new loans; established by the Federal Reserve System. *(Chapter 14)*

required reserves The minimum amount of vault cash and deposits at the Federal Reserve that must be maintained by a bank. *(Chapter 14)*

reserves Deposits that banks have received but have not lent out; can be kept either in vault cash or deposits at a Federal Reserve Bank. *(Chapter 14)*

rule of 70 Indicator of the power of growth rates, determined by dividing 70 by the percentage growth rate. *(Chapter 10)*

s

Say's Law Law attributed to 19th century economist Jean Baptiste Say, stating that supply creates its own demand; whatever was produced (supplied) would create the income necessary to purchase the product; overproduction is therefore not possible. *(Chapter 12)*

scarcity There are not enough, nor can there ever be enough, goods and services to satisfy the wants and needs of everyone. *(Chapter 1)*

services Work done by doctors, dentists, lawyers, engineers, accountants, and the like for consumers. *(Chapter 17)*

share draft account A checking account at a credit union. *(Chapter 14)*

Sherman Act of 1890 Cornerstone of federal antitrust law; result of federal intervention into the private sector to prevent the acquisition and exercise of monopoly power and to encourage competition in the marketplace. *(Chapter 8)*

shock effect Assumption that the minimum wage could lead to the demand for labor increasing, thus moderating some unemployment. *(Chapter 7)*

short run Period in which the quantity of at least one input is fixed and the quantities of the other inputs can be varied. *(Chapter 4)*

shortage Amount by which quantity demanded exceeds quantity supplied; excess demand. *(Chapter 2)*

shut-down rule In the short run, the firm should continue to produce if total revenue exceeds total variable costs; otherwise, it should shut down. *(Chapter 5)*

slope The "rise" divided by the "run." *(Chapter 1)*

social regulation Government regulation to correct a variety of undesirable side effects in a market economy that relate to health, safety, and the environment; examples include regulations imposed by the Environmental Protection Agency, the Food and Drug Administration, and the Occupational Safety and Health Administration. *(Chapter 8)*

Social Security The largest retirement and disability program in the United States, created as a means of providing income security upon retirement to people who would not otherwise have that form of security; also known as OASDI. *(Chapter 9)*

socialism Where government is actively involved in the economy. *(Chapter 18)*

sole proprietorship A firm owned and operated by one individual. *(Chapter 9)*

spillover Cost or benefit imposed on people other than the producers and consumers of a good or service; also called externality. *(Chapter 8)*

spillover benefit A desirable spillover or externality; a benefit imposed on people other than the producers and consumers of a good. *(Chapter 8)*

spillover cost An undesirable spillover or externality; a cost imposed on people other than the producers and consumers of a good. *(Chapter 8)*

stagflation A decline in aggregate supply that results in falling output, increased unemployment, and rising prices; recession (stagnation) with inflation. *(Chapter 12)*

statistical discrepancy An adjustment for measurement errors that is reported in the capital account component of the balance of payments. *(Chapter 17)*

store of value A function of money; ability to save money and then use it to make future purchases. *(Chapter 14)*

strikes Work stoppages called by a majority of the voting members of a union when workers feel that doing so is the best way to pressure their employer into granting their demands. *(Chapter 7)*

structural unemployment Unemployment caused by skills that do not match what employers require or from being geographically separated from job opportunities. *(Chapter 11)*

substitute good Goods for which the reduction in the price of one good will decrease the demand for the other good; conversely, an increase in the price of one good will increase the demand for the other good. *(Chapter 2)*

substitution effect When the price of a good falls, other determinants of demand remaining the same, the price of the good falls relative to the prices of all other like goods. *(Chapter 2)*

supply Schedule showing the amounts of a good or service that a firm or household is willing and able to sell at each possible price during a specified period. *(Chapter 2)*

supply curve A graphical depiction of a supply schedule; a line showing the quantity of a good or service supplied at various prices. *(Chapter 2)*

supply shifter A change in a variable that can shift the supply curve. *(Chapter 2)*

surplus An excess quantity supplied over quantity demanded at a given price. *(Chapter 2)*

t

tariff A tax imposed on imports. *(Chapter 16)*

taxable income Gross income minus exemptions, deductions, and credits. *(Chapter 9)*

theories Simplified representations of the real world that we use to help us understand, explain, and predict economic phenomena in the real world; also called models. *(Chapter 1)*

total cost The sum of the value of all resources used over a given period to manufacture a good; the sum of total fixed and total variable costs. *(Chapter 4)*

total fixed cost A cost that does not vary with output; also called overhead cost. *(Chapter 4)*

total product Maximum quantity of output that can be produced from a given amount of inputs. *(Chapter 4)*

total revenue Dollars earned by sellers of a product, calculated by multiplying the quantity sold over a period by the price. *(Chapter 3 and Chapter 5)*

total variable cost A cost that changes as the rate of output is changed; cost dependent on weekly or monthly output. *(Chapter 4)*

transfer payments Payments of income (such as unemployment compensation or Medicaid) from taxpayers to individuals who make no contribution to current output for these payments. *(Chapter 9)*

traveler's check Checks usually issued in $20, $50, $100, and $500 denominations; are used by travelers to protect against loss or theft and are widely accepted both in the United States and abroad. *(Chapter 14)*

trough Portion of a business cycle where real GDP is at a low point, just before it begins to turn up; unemployment and idle productive capacity are at their highest level. *(Chapter 11)*

u

underground economy Unreported barter and cash transactions that take place outside recorded market channels. *(Chapter 10)*

unemployed Those individuals who do not have jobs but who are actively seeking work. *(Chapter 11)*

unemployment insurance System that helps support consumer spending during periods of job loss and provides economic security to workers through income maintenance; established as part of the Social Security Act of 1935. *(Chapter 11)*

unemployment rate The number of people unemployed divided by the labor force—the number of people holding or seeking jobs. *(Chapter 11)*

unilateral transfers Component of the current account; gifts that include transfers of goods and services or money between the United States and the rest of the world for which nothing is given in exchange. *(Chapter 17)*

union shop Employment situation where employees are required to join the recognized union within a specified length of time after their employment with the firm begins; each state may accept or reject union shops. *(Chapter 7)*

unions Organizations that allow their members to sell their services collectively, thus giving the members more bargaining power than they would have if they acted individually. *(Chapter 7)*

unit elastic demand When the percentage change in quantity demanded equals the percentage change in price. *(Chapter 3)*

unit of account A function of money; allows consumers to compare the relative values of goods due to the stated prices of those goods; a measure that specifies price. *(Chapter 14)*

V

value of the marginal product of a worker The increase in revenue to a firm resulting from hiring an additional worker; the dollar value of a worker's contribution to production. *(Chapter 7)*

value-added tax (VAT) A proposal as a substitute for current federal taxes; a tax that would be collected at the various stages of production of goods and services. *(Chapter 9)*

variable input Resources (such as labor and materials) whose quantities can be altered in the short run. *(Chapter 4)*

vertical merger One firm combines with another firm in the same industry, but that firm is at a different stage in the production process. *(Chapter 6)*

vicious circle of poverty Where developing nations cannot break out of low standards of living. *(Chapter 18)*

W

World Bank An international organization that provides loans to developing countries aimed toward poverty reduction and economic development. *(Chapter 18)*

World Trade Organization (WTO) An organization whose members acknowledge that tariff reductions agreed on by any two nations will be extended to all other members; encourages a gradual relaxation of tariffs throughout the world. *(Chapter 16)*

Index

Notes

Notes

Notes

Notes

Notes

Notes